Handbook of Clinical Sexuality for Mental Health Professionals

2nd Edition

Stephen B. Levine
Editor

Candace B. Risen, Stanley E. Althof
Associate Editors

Routledge
Taylor & Francis Group
New York   London

Routledge
Taylor & Francis Group
270 Madison Avenue
New York, NY 10016

Routledge
Taylor & Francis Group
27 Church Road
Hove, East Sussex BN3 2FA

© 2010 by Taylor and Francis Group, LLC
Routledge is an imprint of Taylor & Francis Group, an Informa business

Printed in the United States of America on acid-free paper
10 9 8 7 6 5 4 3 2 1

International Standard Book Number: 978-0-415-80075-4 (Hardback) 978-0-415-80076-1 (Paperback)

Library of Congress Cataloging-in-Publication Data

Handbook of clinical sexuality for mental health professionals / Stephen B. Levine, editor ; Candace B. Risen, Stanley E. Althof, associate editors.
     p. cm.
    Rev. ed. of: Handbook of clinical sexuality for mental health professionals. 2003.
    Includes bibliographical references and index.
    ISBN 978-0-415-80075-4 (hbk. : alk. paper) -- ISBN 978-0-415-80076-1 (pbk. : alk. paper)
    1. Sexual disorders--Handbooks, manuals, etc. I. Levine, Stephen B., 1942- II. Risen, Candace B. III. Althof, Stanley E., 1948-

RC556.H353 2010
616.6'9--dc22
          2009023510

Visit the Taylor & Francis Web site at
http://www.taylorandfrancis.com

and the Routledge Web site at
http://www.routledgementalhealth.com

Contents

SECTION I   Being a Therapist

SECTION II   Sexual Intimacy: Hopes and Disappointments

SECTION III Sexual Dysfunction: Women's Sexual Issues

SECTION IV Sexual Dysfunction: Men's Sexual Issues

SECTION V Additional Vital Topics

SECTION VI   Sexual Identity Struggles

SECTION VII   The Forgotten

About the Editors

Stanley E. Althof, PhD (associate editor), is voluntary professor in the Department of Psychiatry, University of Miami Miller School of Medicine, Miami, Florida.

Stephen B. Levine, MD (editor), is clinical professor of psychiatry at Case Western Reserve University School of Medicine, Cleveland, Ohio.

Candace B. Risen, LISW (associate editor), is assistant clinical professor of social work in the Department of Psychiatry at Case Western Reserve University School of Medicine, Cleveland, Ohio.

Contributors

Richard Balon, MD, is professor of psychiatry in the Department of Psychiatry and Behavioral Neurosciences, Wayne State University School of Medicine, Detroit, Michigan.

Rosemary Basson, MD, is a clinical professor in the Departments of Psychiatry and Obstetrics and Gynecology at the University of British Columbia and the British Columbia Centre for Sexual Medicine in Vancouver, Canada.

Sophie Bergeron, PhD, is associate professor in the Department of Psychology at Université de Montréal and clinical psychologist at the Sex and Couple Therapy Service of the McGill University Health Centre, Royal Victoria Hospital in Montréal, Canada.

Yitzchak M. Binik, PhD, is a professor of psychology at McGill University and director of the Sex and Couple Therapy Service of the McGill University Health Centre, Royal Victoria Hospital in Montréal, Canada.

Alisa Breetz, MA, is a PhD graduate student in the Department of Psychology at American University in Washington, DC.

Lori A. Brotto, PhD, is assistant professor at the Department of Obstetrics and Gynecology at the University of British Columbia (UBC) and is director of the UBC Sexual Health Laboratory, Vancouver, Canada.

Lorraine Dennerstein, AO, MBBS, PhD, DPM, FRANZCP, is professor in the Department of Psychiatry at the University of Melbourne, Australia, and is the foundation director of the Office for Gender and Health.

Karen M. Donahey, PhD, is an associate professor in the Feinberg School of Medicine at Northwestern University in Chicago, Illinois and the former director of the Sex and Marital Therapy Program in the Department of Psychiatry and Behavioral Sciences. She is currently in private practice.

Jennifer I. Downey, MD, is clinical professor of psychiatry at Columbia University's College of Physicians and Surgeons in New York.

J. Paul Fedoroff, MD, is director of the forensic research unit of the University of Ottawa IMHR and director of the Sexual Behaviors Clinic at the Royal Ottawa Mental Health Centre. He is also associate professor of psychiatry at the University of Ottawa, Canada.

Richard C. Friedman, MD, is clinical professor of psychiatry at Weill Medical College (Cornell) and lecturer in psychiatry at Columbia University in New York City.

Samir Khalifé, MD, is an obstetrician/gynecologist associated with the McGill University Health Center and Jewish General Hospital in Montréal, Canada.

Sheryl A. Kingsberg, PhD, is a clinical psychologist and associate professor in the Department of Reproductive Biology and the Department of Psychiatry at Case Western Reserve University School of Medicine in Cleveland, Ohio.

Peggy J. Kleinplatz, PhD, is associate professor in the faculty of medicine and clinical professor, School of Psychology, University of Ottawa, Canada.

I. David Marcus, PhD, is a codirector of the Silicon Valley Psychotherapy Center in San Jose, California.

William L. Maurice, MD, FRCPC, is associate professor emeritus in the Department of Psychiatry, University of British Columbia in Vancouver, Canada and former director of the Sexual Medicine Team at the Vancouver Community Mental Health Service.

Barry McCarthy, PhD, is a professor of psychology at American University in Washington, DC, and a partner and therapist at the Washington Psychological Center.

Marta Meana, PhD, is professor of psychology at the University of Nevada, Las Vegas, Nevada.

Lin S. Myers, PhD, is professor of psychology at California State University, Stanislaus, California.

Sharon G. Nathan, PhD, MPH, is a licensed psychologist in New York State and is in private practice in New York City.

Friedemann Pfäfflin, MD, is professor of psychotherapy and head of the Forensic Psychotherapy Unit at Ulm University, Germany.

S. Michael Plaut, PhD, is the former editor of the *Journal of Sex Education and Therapy.* He has recently retired as associate professor of psychiatry and assistant dean for student affairs at the University of Maryland School of Medicine. He now practices psychology in Hampstead, North Carolina, and teaches at the University of North Carolina Wilmington.

Derek C. Polonsky, MD, is a psychiatrist in private practice in Brookline, Massachusetts, and is an assistant professor of psychiatry at Tufts Medical School and an instructor in psychiatry at Harvard Medical School.

Deborah A. Richards, BA, CHMH, is manager of specialized services at Community Living Welland Pelham and a professor in the Developmental Disabilities Programme at Niagara College in Welland, Ontario, Canada.

Raymond C. Rosen, PhD, is chief scientist at New England Research Institute (NERI) and adjunct professor of psychiatry, Robert Wood Johnson Medical School, New Brunswick, New Jersey.

David E. Scharff, MD, is director of the International Psychotherapy Institute in Washington, DC, and clinical professor of psychiatry at Georgetown and the Uniformed Services Medical Schools.

David L. Scott, MD, is a staff psychiatrist at the Center for Marital and Sexual Health in Beachwood, Ohio, and clinical instructor in psychiatry at Case Western Reserve University in Cleveland, Ohio.

R. Taylor Segraves, MD, PhD, is professor of psychiatry at Case Western Reserve University School of Medicine, at the Department of Psychiatry at MetroHealth Center in Cleveland, Ohio.

Marcel D. Waldinger, MD, PhD, is a neuropsychiatrist in the Department of Psychiatry and Neurosexology at HagaHospital Leyenburg in The Hague, the Netherlands, and professor of sexual psychopharmacology in the Department of Psychopharmacology at the Faculty of BetaSciences at the University of Utrecht, Utrecht, in the Netherlands.

Morag Yule, BSc, BA, is a graduate student in clinical psychology at the University of British Columbia in Vancouver, BC, Canada.

Preface to the First Edition

Each mental health professional's life offers a personal opportunity to diminish the sense of bafflement about how health, suffering, and recovery processes work. Over decades of work in a mental health field, many of us develop the sense that we better understand some aspects of psychology and psychopathology. Those who devote themselves to one subject in a scholarly research fashion seem to have a slightly greater potential to remove some of the mystery for themselves and others in a particular subject area. But when it comes to the rest of our vast areas of responsibility, we are far from expert; we remain only relatively informed.

The authors of this handbook devoted their careers to unraveling human sexuality's knots. Their inclusion in this book is a testimony to their previous successes in helping others to understand sexual suffering and its treatment. Because one of the responsibilities of scholars is to pass on their knowledge to the next generation, in the largest sense, passing the torch is the overarching purpose of this book.

We humans are emotionally, cognitively, behaviorally, and sexually changeable creatures. We react, adapt, and evolve. When our personal evolution occurs along expected lines, others label us mature or normal. When it does not, our unique developmental pathways are described as evidence of our immaturity or psychopathology. Sometimes we are more colloquially described as "having problems."

Sexual life, being an integral part of nonsexual life processes, is dynamic and evolutionary. I think about it as having three broad categories of potential difficulties: disorders, problems, and worries. The *disorders* are those difficulties that are officially recognized by the *DSM-IV-TR*—for example, hypoactive sexual desire disorder, gender identity disorder, and sexual pain disorder. Many common forms of suffering that afflict groups of people, however, are not found in our official nosology and attract little research. I call these *problems*. Here are just two examples: continuing uncertainty about one's orientation and recurrent paralyzing resentment over having to accommodate a partner's sexual needs. *Problems* are frequent sources of suffering in large definable groups of the population—for example, bisexual youth and not-so-happily married menopausal women. Then there are sexual *worries*. Sexual *worries* detract from the pleasure of living. They abound among people of all ages. Here are five examples: Will I be adequate during my first intercourse? Will my new partner like my not-so-perfect body? Does my diminishing interest in sex mean that I no longer love my partner? How long will I be able to maintain potency with my young wife? Will I be able to sustain love for my partner? *Worries* are the concerns that are inherent in the experience of being human.

Sexual disorders, sexual problems, and sexual worries insinuate themselves into the therapy sessions even when therapists do not directly inquire about the patient's sexuality. This is simply because sexuality is integral to personal psychology and because the prevalence of difficulties involving sexual identity and sexual function is so high.

Unlike the frequency of sexual problems and worries, the prevalence of sexual *disorders* has been carefully studied. Their prevalence is so high, however, that most professionals are shocked when confronted with the evidence. The 1994 National Health and Social Life Survey, which obtained the most representative sample of 18- to 59-year-old Americans ever interviewed, confirmed the findings of many less methodologically sophisticated works. In this study, younger women and older men bore the highest prevalence. Overall, however, 35% of the entire sample acknowledged being sexually problematic in the previous 12 months.[1] There are compelling reasons to think that the prevalence is even higher among those who seek help for mental[2] or physical conditions.[3] Although people in some countries have unique sexual difficulties,[4] numerous studies have demonstrated that the population in the United States is not uniquely sexually problematic.[5,6]

To make this point about prevalence and, therefore, the relevance of this book even stronger, I'd like you to consider with me a retrospective study from Brazil. The authors compared the frequencies of sexual dysfunction among untreated patients with social phobia to those with panic disorder.[7] The mean age of both groups was mid-30s. The major discovery was that sexual aversion, a severe *DSM-IV* diagnosis previously thought to be relatively rare, was extremely common in men (36%) and women (50%) with panic disorder but absent in those with social phobia (0%). The sexual lives of those with social phobia were limited in other ways.

I find this information ironic in several ways. This finding probably would not have shocked therapists who were trained a generation or two ago because it was then widely assumed that an important relationship existed between problematic sexual development and anxiety symptoms.[8] Modern therapists, however, tend to be disinterested in sexuality and so are likely not to respond to these patients' sexual problems. Adding insult to injury, the modern treatment of anxiety disorders routinely employs medications with a high likelihood of dampening sexual drive, arousability, and orgasmic expression.

For most of the 20th century, sexuality was seen as a vital component of personality development, mental health, and mental distress. During the last 25 years, the extent of sexual problems has been even better defined, and their negative consequences have been better appreciated. Mental health professionals' interest in these matters has been thwarted by new biological paradigms for understanding the causes and treatments of mental conditions, the emphasis on short-term psychotherapy, the constriction of insurance support for nonpharmacological interventions, the political conservatism of government funding sources, and the policy to consider sexual problems inconsequential.

As a result of these five forces, the average well-trained mental health professional has had limited educational exposure to clinical sexuality. This professional is not comfortable dealing with sexual problems, skillful in asking the relevant questions, or able to efficiently provide a relevant focused treatment. It does not matter much if the professional's training has been in psychiatric residencies, psychology internships, counseling internships, marriage and family therapy training programs, or social work agency placements. Knowledgeable teachers are in short supply. The same paucity of supervised experiences focusing on sexual disorders, problems, and worries applies to all groups.

In my community, Cleveland, Ohio, there happens to be a relatively large number of highly qualified sexuality specialists. Most moderate-to-large urban communities, however, have no specialists who deal with the entire spectrum of male and female dysfunctions, sexual compulsivities, paraphilias, gender identity disorders, and marital relationship problems. Although many communities have therapists who deal with one part of this spectrum, the entire range of problems exists in every community.

A remarkable bit of progress occurred in the treatment of erectile dysfunction in 1998. Since then, primary care physicians, cardiologists, and urologists have been effectively prescribing a phosphodiesterase-5 inhibitor for millions of men. But despite the evidence of the drug's safety and efficacy, at least half of the men do not refill their prescriptions. There is good reason to believe that this dropout rate is due to psychological/interpersonal factors rather than to the lack of the drug's ability to generate erections. This fact alone has created another reason for mental health professionals to become interested in clinical sexuality. Most physicians who prescribe sildenafil are not equipped to deal with the psychological issues that are embedded in the apparent failures. The nonresponders to initial treatment need access to us. But mental health professionals need to be better educated in sexual subjects. So there are three reasons for developing this handbook: (1) to pass the torch of knowledge to another generation; (2) to better equip mental health professionals to respond to sexual disorders, problems, and worries as they appear in their current practice settings; and (3) to help patients take advantage of emerging advances in medication treatment by helping them to master their psychological obstacles to sexual expression.

Stephen B. Levine, MD

YOU CAN DO THIS!

We use this exhortative heading for a reason. "You can do this!" is our way of saying that the handbook provides coaching, encouragement, and optimism and aims to inspire others to turn their interests to clinical sexuality. Mental health professionals can learn to competently address their patients' sexual worries, problems, and disorders.

How We Created the Handbook

Once the editors decided to say yes to the publisher's invitation to develop a handbook, we set our sights on creating a unique book. We imagined it as a trustworthy, informative, informal, supportive, and highly valued volume that would encourage and enable mental health professionals to work effectively with patients who have sexual concerns. To attain this lofty goal, we knew that the book would have to be a departure from the usual excellent book on clinical sexuality.

We created the handbook through seven steps.

The first step we took was to define the intended audience. We quickly realized, having valued teaching so highly during our careers, that this audience was mental health professionals with little formal clinical training in sexuality. Although we thought some readers might be trainees in various educational programs, we envisioned that most of the readers would be fully trained, competent professionals. We thought that experienced clinicians would have already had many clients who alluded to their sexual concerns and might have already perceived how their sexual problems may have contributed to their presenting depression, substance abuse, or anxiety states. We wanted to help general mental health professionals think about sex in a way that diminished their personal discomfort, increased their clinical confidence, piqued their interest in understanding sexual life better, and increased their effectiveness. We wanted professionals to stop avoiding their clients' sexual problems. We also clarified that we were not trying to create a book that would update sexual experts. We were writing for those who knew that they needed to learn both basic background materials and basic practical interventions.

The second step was to realize that because we were writing an educational text, our authors would have to be excellent teachers. Excellence as a researcher or a clinician would not be a compelling reason to put a person on the author list.

The third step was to define our strategy for making the handbook unique. We decided it would be through our instructions to the authors about how to compose their chapters. We gave them 10 instructions:

1. Use the first-person voice—use "I" as the subject of some sentences.
2. Imagine when writing that you are talking privately to the reader in a supervisory session.
3. Reveal something personal about your relationship to your subject— how you became interested in the subject, how it changed your life, how your understanding of the subject evolved over the years.
4. Imagine that you are guiding your readers through their first cases with the disorder you are discussing. Do not share everything that you know about the subject. Try not to exceed your imagined readers' interest in the topic.
5. Keep your tone encouraging about not abandoning the therapeutic inquiry, even if readers are uncertain what to do next.
6. Discuss your personal reactions to patient care as a model for the appearance of countertransference. Illustrate how a therapist might use his or her private responses to better understand the patient.
7. Either tell numerous short stories about patients or provide one case in depth. Do not write a conceptual paper without clinical illustrations.
8. Annotate at least half of your bibliography. Your reference list is not there primarily to demonstrate your scholarship; it is there to guide the interested supervisee.
9. Be realistic about the reality of life processes and the limitations of professional interventions. Although we want the readers to be encouraged to learn more, we do not want to mislead them into thinking that experts in the field can completely solve people's sexual difficulties.
10. Be cognizant when writing that you are trying to prepare your reader to skillfully and comfortably approach the patient, to gain confidence in his or her capacity to help, and to rediscover the inherent fascination of sexual life.

The fourth step was the definition of relevant sexual topics. We did not want to deal with uncommon problems—for example, there was not going to be a chapter devoted to females who want to live as men, to female impersonators, or to serial sex murderers. This book was to help with common problems, ordinary ones, the ones that are often lurking behind other psychiatric complaints. This task was relatively easy.

The fifth task was slightly more difficult: to decide what basic information was necessary as background preparation for dealing with the common sexual problems. After this, we set about matching authors to the intended topics.

The sixth step was really fun. We had been told that it was often difficult to get people to write for edited texts and that it might take 6 months or more to complete the author list. The vast majority of our esteemed colleagues who were asked said yes immediately and thought that the idea for the book was terrific. A few needed several weeks to agree. Four pled exhaustion and wished us luck.

The final step—the seventh—involved the review of the manuscripts. It was during this 5-month process that we, the editors, more fully realized what modern clinical sexology is. While reading these 25 chapters, we realized that as a group we vary considerably in our emphasis on evidence-based, clinically based, or theory-based ideas. All of us authors, however, speak of having been enriched as we struggled to better understand and assist people with various sexual difficulties. All of us have seen considerable progress in our professional lifetimes with our specialty issues. Some of the chapters are stories of triumphs (treatment of rapid ejaculation, erectile dysfunction, female orgasmic difficulties), others of disorders still awaiting the significant breakthrough (female genital pain, sexual compulsivity, sexual side effects of selective serotonin reuptake inhibitors). A number of authors address essential human processes that are part of life (boundaries and their violations, menopausal changes, love), whereas others coach their readers about how to think of their roles and attitudes (sexual history taking, diagnosis of women's dysfunction, transgenderism). Some chapters focus on grave difficulties (aversion, sexual avoidance, sexual victimization) and yet others on hidden private struggles that tend to remain unseen by those around them (homoeroticism in heterosexuals, paraphilias, unhappy marriages). All in all, we find the field of clinical sexuality fascinating and hope that our readers will rediscover what they used to know: Sex is very interesting.

We designed this handbook with the idea that the vast majority of readers will look at only the few chapters that are relevant to their current clinical needs at one sitting. Those who are taking a course in clinical sexuality and reading the entire handbook, however, will quickly discover some redundancy. In editing, we objected to any redundancy within a chapter; we were reassured by it in the book as a whole. This was because it meant to us that teachers of various backgrounds focusing on different subjects shared certain convictions about the importance of careful assessment, how to conduct therapy, the limitations of medications, the possibility of being helpful despite not being expert, and so forth.

We are deeply indebted to the authors of the handbook for their years of devotion to their subjects that enabled them to write such stellar educational pieces. As editors, we considered it a privilege to have been immersed in their thinking. We hope that our readers feel the same way.

Stephen B. Levine, MD
Candace B. Risen, LISW
Stanley E. Althof, PhD

NOTES

1. Laumann, E. O., & Michael, R. T. (Eds.). (2001). *Sex, love, and health in America: Private choices, and public policies.* Chicago: University of Chicago Press.
2. Kockott, G., & Pfeiffer, W. (1996). Sexual disorders in nonacute psychiatric patients. *Comprehensive Psychiatry, 37*(1), 56–61.
3. Dunn, K. M., Croft, P. R., & Hackett, G. I. (1999). Association of sexual problems with social, psychological, and physical problems in men and women: A cross sectional population survey. *Journal of Epidemiology and Community Health, 53,* 144–148. Another demonstration that the chronically mentally ill have a high prevalence of sexual dysfunction, some of which is medication induced, some of which is illness induced, and some of which is simply part of the difficulties of living.
4. El-Defrawi, L. G., Dandash, K. F., Refaat, A. H., & Eyada, M. (2001). Female genital mutilation and its psychosocial impact. *Journal of Sex and Marital Therapy, 27,* 465–473.
5. Dennerstein, L. (2000). Menopause and sexuality. In J. M. Ussher (Ed.), *Women's health: Contemporary international perspectives* (pp. 190–196). Leicester, UK: British Psychological Society Books.
6. Madu, S. N., & Peltzer, K. (2001). Prevalence and patterns of child sexual abuse and victim-perpetrator relationship among secondary school students in the northern province (South Africa). *Archives of Sexual Behavior, 30*(3), 311–321. Childhood sexual abuse is a major concern everywhere. Although in the United States its prevalence varies widely from one economic group to another, this variation is not likely to be unique to the United States.
7. Figueira, I., Possidente, E., Marques, C., & Hayes, K. (2001). Sexual dysfunction: A neglected complication of panic disorder and social phobia. *Archives of Sexual Behavior, 30*(4), 369–378. Although this is only a retrospective study that awaits confirmation, those highly interested in anxiety disorders will profit from the implications of their data.
8. Freud, S. (1905). *Three essays on the theory of sexuality in the complete psychological works of Sigmund Freud, Volume VII* (p. 149). London: Hogarth. This is an interesting read even today, almost a century after it was written. Freud organized information about sexual life in a new language, which reflected a wonderful grasp of the range of sexualities in the population and what might account for the numerous variations that he categorized.

Preface to the Second Edition

The field of clinical sexuality evolves in response to changing general cultural trends, scientific advances, shifting professional ideologies, and the personal maturation of its practitioners. In less than a decade, much seems to have changed in how we think about and offer care for sexual problems. These usually slight, occasionally dramatic shifts are the main reason for bringing out a second edition of this handbook.

The purposes of this edition are both obvious and subtle. Writers were asked to imagine that they were directly addressing clinicians who are inexperienced in dealing with people with sexual problems. Their task was to try to replace their readers' natural anxiety with a quiet, confident eagerness to begin the work. Each of these 26 presentations has been designed to provide therapists new to these problems with what they need to know to be credible with their patients. This is the handbook's primary goal.

A more subtle purpose focuses on experienced therapists and teachers. The editors presume that these readers have sufficient immersion in clinical sexuality to anticipate that our distinguished assembly of authors would display no uniformity of ideology, agreement about etiology, or consensus about how to think about therapy. When they attentively plunge into a chapter, they are likely to differ with something being conveyed and to emerge with a novel concept that will refine their thinking or their teaching. Experienced clinicians already know that they learn from exposure to the richness of thought of their gifted colleagues. We hope that these readers will appreciate that the handbook reflects the state of the art of clinical sexuality in 2010.

Another vital, although understated, goal of the handbook is to set a tone of respect for the unique challenges that every clinician faces. With almost each patient that they see, inexperienced and veteran therapists confront a separate new reality that is complex beyond any author's capacity to capture. While we clinicians aspire to base some of our decisions on well-established scientific evidence, it is apparent that most decisions require us to integrate a set of unique factors that no single study has yet addressed. This integration creates the challenge, the joy, and sometimes the disappointment of clinical work.

Authors discuss the scientific work that justifies some of their decisions. They recognize that there are limitations inherent in these studies as well as in their preferred theories and ideologies. As readers move from chapter to chapter, they will notice a differing emphasis on clinical processes and on scientific findings. This is also reflected in the lengths and annotations of the reference sections. While all authors are trying to integrate their clinical approach with seminal work in the literature, they combine science, theory, and clinical experience in individual ways.

After using the handbook a number of times, we hope our readers will feel that numerous authors have facilitated their understanding that sexuality is an integral part of the ordinary processes of life, and that sexual concerns spring directly from these same processes. If our readers are able to approach patient care with a heightened awareness of patients' hopes for their therapy, of the limitations of modern interventions, and of their professional obligations, we will deem ourselves to have been successful.

Welcome to the second edition.

Stephen B. Levine, MD
Candace B. Risen, LISW
Stanley E. Althof, PhD

I

BEING A THERAPIST

One

Listening to Sexual Stories

CANDACE B. RISEN, LISW

INTRODUCTION

When I began listening to sexual stories, I was 27 years old, married, and returning to clinical practice after a 10-month maternity hiatus. I had been a social worker for 4 years, most of which were spent on an inpatient psychiatric unit. I heard that a psychiatrist, wishing to launch a new sexuality subspecialty clinic, was looking for an intake coordinator. It was not exactly what I had in mind, but I needed a job. In that new role I had to screen referrals, ascertain the nature of the sexual complaint, present the intake to the clinic staff for assignment, and see some of the cases myself. I had to talk about sex. I had to know about sex. How was I going to do that? My frame of reference was limited to my own personal life experiences. I had strongly internalized the cultural expectation that I was a good girl—that is, I could not be *that* worldly! My mother echoed my concerns when, on learning of my new position, she asked, "How do you know so much about sex that you can help people? ... No, no, don't answer that question. ... I don't want to know!"

Thus began the next 34 years, a journey of personal growth and discovery and ever-increasing confidence and competence in helping people tell their sexual stories. Over time, I learned to listen without anxiety, to ask pointed questions without fear of reprisal, and to articulate sexual issues in a manner that was extraordinarily helpful to many of my patients. Book knowledge certainly helped me along the way, but I learned far more from the patients themselves. I have spent thousands of hours hearing about a wider range of sexual experiences, feelings, thoughts, and struggles than I could have ever imagined. I am indebted to those countless patients who taught me through their sexual stories. In this chapter, I share what I believe are the key obstacles to overcome and the necessary skills to acquire to develop professional sexual comfort and expertise.

WHY DO I NEED TO LEARN THIS?

Everyone has sexual thoughts, feelings, and experiences that are integral to their sense of who they are and how they relate to the world. Sexual problems often manifest and mask themselves in the major symptoms that bring patients to treatment: depression, anxiety, failure to achieve, low self-esteem, and the inability to engage in intimate relationships. Yet, patients are shy about revealing their sexual concerns. These feel so private, so awkward, so potentially embarrassing that many are reduced to paralyzing inarticulateness. They dread being asked; they long to be asked. They know for sure that they need to be asked if their sexual concerns are to come out. Too often, therapists find themselves reluctant to initiate an inquiry. They rationalize, "If my patient doesn't bring sex up, it must not be an issue, and I should not be asking about it." At best, this can lead to a missed opportunity to be helpful; at worst, it can lead to the wrong therapy plan.

WHY DON'T I WANT TO?

The question "Why don't I want to?" is often the fundamental question behind "Why do I need to?" The reasons for not wanting to are many.

1. I'm not used to talking about sex. My discomfort and awkwardness will be obvious.
2. I don't exactly know why I am asking or what I want to know.
3. I won't know how to respond to what I hear back.
4. I may be unfamiliar with or not understand something my patient tells me.
5. I may offend or embarrass my patient.
6. I may be perceived as nosey or provocative.
7. I won't know how to treat any problem I hear.
8. I'll be too embarrassed to consult with my colleagues.

The anxiety and discomfort underlying these reasons can be overcome with the courage to try something new. Most of us can recall having some of these concerns about a wide range of issues when we first began our clinical careers. Questions about what to ask, how, when, and why were the ongoing central focus of our early learning. Patience, persistence, and a sense of humor helped to get us through the processes of gaining experience. Over time, increasing comfort and expanding knowledge made the job that much easier.

The concerns about being perceived as nosey or intrusive or about offending or embarrassing our patients may be more specific to sexual topics. While patients may initially react as though you have intruded into territory too personal to be shared, they are usually settled by a simple explanation regarding the relevance of the question.

Therapist: You've told me a lot about your ambivalence about marrying Joe ... your concerns about his lack of ambition and his relationship to his family. You haven't mentioned anything about your sexual life together. Can you tell me about that?

Jill: Well, uh ... it's OK, I guess (squirms in her seat). What do you want to know?

Therapist: Sexual intimacy is often a vital part of a relationship. ... It can really enhance it or can be problematic. How have you felt about your sexual relationship with Joe?

Jill: Well, sometimes it feels like he lacks ambition in bed, too. ... He doesn't seem to be interested that often. ... We are so busy during the week, I can understand, ... but it seems he would rather spend Sunday afternoon visiting his family than being, you know, intimate with me.

Therapist: How do you feel about that?

Jill: Well, I haven't told anyone. ... It's embarrassing to admit that we're not even married yet and already Joe seems disinterested. ... Isn't it supposed to take several years before that happens? It makes me feel like he isn't attracted to me, like I'm too fat or not sexy enough.

Jill is a little taken aback by the initial question. She doesn't know how to respond because she is not used to articulating aspects of her sexual life. A simple statement by her therapist about sexual intimacy helps Jill to get started.

Sometimes, however, it is the therapist, not the patient, who feels weird or embarrassed by the exploration of sexual material. This is particularly true when the topic is something the therapist has never experienced ("My ignorance will show"), cannot imagine experiencing ("That's disgusting!"), or has experienced with ambivalence and conflict ("I don't think I want to go there!"). The therapist may unwisely avoid the subject if it threatens to bring up painful memories.

Alan: I can't believe I slept with my roommate's girlfriend! I mean, I've had sort of a crush on her, but I wasn't thinking about that when he asked me to look out for her over the weekend while he was away. We were just talking, drinking some beer, and having a good time. One thing led to another. Now, she won't speak to me, and my roommate will be back tomorrow. What can I do?

Therapist: [This is making me very anxious. ... I don't want to remember what I did to Jim in college. ... It was the end of our friendship. ... To this day, I feel like a worm about it.] I'm sure everything will be OK. These things happen.

Alan is clearly upset by his behavior and wants to talk about it. The situation, however, reminds his therapist of a similar college experience. In an effort to ward off personal feelings of guilt, the therapist cuts off the discussion and falsely reassures Alan that everything will work out.

When the age, gender, and orientation of the client fits what the therapist finds sexually appealing, sexual issues may be more difficult to bring into the discussion. For example, if I am a heterosexual male in my 30s, I may have some trouble discussing any sexual matter with a heterosexual female in her 20s or 30s and even more trouble if I also find her sexually appealing. Likewise, if I am a lesbian, speaking with a lesbian client in my age range may initially create discomfort for me. How it plays out in my mind may also differ with gender. If I am male, I am more likely to worry about feeling excited if I pursue sexual issues with my client. If female, I am likely to worry more about being seen as provocative or inviting of my client's sexual interest.

WHO SHOULD I BE ASKING?

Everyone

Unless the chief complaint is so specific and narrow in focus or the time spent together so short or crisis oriented, *every* patient should at least be offered the opportunity to address sexual concerns. How will we know whether sexuality is of concern unless we inquire? Because sexuality is a topic that is difficult for patients to bring to the fore, the therapist must assume responsibility for introducing it as an area of possible relevance. If nothing else, the inquiry tells the patient, "This is OK to talk about. I'm interested in hearing about it if you want to tell me. I'll even help you talk about it by taking the lead."

Include the Elderly

Therapists are often reluctant to inquire about the sexual feelings and activities of the elderly (often defined as anyone as old or older than one's parents). Our culture emphasizes youth and beauty, and there is a tendency to see aging people as asexual or, even worse, to make fun of their displays of sexual interest. Older adults in turn may be embarrassed to admit that they still have needs for physical affection, closeness, intimacy, and sexual gratification. They may be told by their physicians that they are lucky to be alive and should not fret over sexual concerns.

Even If Your Patient Is the Couple

It is hard to imagine a marital relationship in which sexuality does not play a role. Yet, often marriage counselors refer patients to sex specialists and tell us, "Mr. and Mrs. X have done terrific work with me in the past year on their marriage. We were winding down, and they brought up a sexual issue. I'm sending them to you to deal with their sex life." This process is neither clinically nor financially efficient. It is a result of either the counselor's discomfort with the topic of sex or the assumption that sex is not within the range of marital counseling.

WHEN SHOULD I ASK?

Inquiring about sex when someone shows up in a crisis about his or her dying mother is not particularly relevant. Early and abrupt questions about sexuality will be off-putting unless the chief complaint is of a sexual nature. On the other hand, putting it off indefinitely or waiting until the patient brings it up reinforces the idea that sex is a taboo subject in your office. The situation that offers the most natural segue into the topic is the gathering of psychosocial and developmental information early in the assessment phase. Sexual matters can be incorporated into your inquiry regarding childhood and family of origin events, issues, and problems.

Therapist: You were telling me about your male friendships growing up. ... Do you remember when you first became aware of sexual feelings?

Jack: Do you mean liking girls? I didn't think much about girls until middle school. ... I had a crush on a girl in seventh grade. Her name was Judy. She was very popular and hung out with eighth-grade boys. She never knew how I felt. I was geeky. She wouldn't have given me the time of day.

Therapist: How did you handle that at the time?

Jack: Not well. I was very self-conscious, and it didn't go away in high school. I didn't date although I wanted to. That's when I found my brother's magazines under his bed, and I started masturbating. I guess most guys do, and it's not a problem, but I got hooked on it, and I think I still am. I don't know if that is related to why I'm here but it might be.

Jack's therapist made a smooth transition from the focus on growing up and friendships to a question about the emerging awareness of sexual feelings. The transition made sense to Jack, and he easily picked up on the question. In this case, Jack thinks that the issue of sexuality may be relevant to his seeking therapy. That is not always so. The advantage of inquiring about sex in the assessment phase, whether or not a sexual problem exists, is that it gives permission to speak of sexual issues in the future. If you, however, have forgotten to do this, it will not hurt to introduce it as a topic at a later date.

HOW DO I DO THIS WELL?

The Right Words

Even when clinicians are convinced of the worthiness of inquiring about sexual matters and are ready to do so, they often stumble over the vocabulary. The task of finding the right words and pronouncing them correctly can intimidate the best of us; we realize that we are far more comfortable reading such words as penis, vagina, clitoris, and orgasm than saying them out loud.

Nevertheless, it is up to the clinician to go first—that is, to say the words out loud so that the patient can follow suit. Sometimes, we may use a word that is confusing or foreign to our patient; sometimes, the patient will use words we do not understand. Shortly after I began this work, a patient told me, "I've lost my nature." I did not know what a nature was, never mind how one could lose one. I was too embarrassed to ask. I copped out by replying: "Tell me more about losing your nature." Eventually, I figured out that he was using the word to describe his erection. It would have been a lot easier if I had just inquired, "Tell me what a nature is. I haven't heard that expression." Over time, you can build up knowledge of a large repertoire of expressions, some clinical and formal, others slang and street talk. You will gain a working familiarity with both kinds.

Allow the Story to Be Told

While it helps to have an organized approach to the questioning, you should not become an interrogator who is wedded to a predetermined agenda or outline. I have found that the most useful conceptualization for my talking about sexuality is that of helping people tell their sexual story. Sexual stories, as with any story, have a pattern of flow and a combination of plots and subplots, characters, and meaning. Some stories unfold chronologically from beginning to end; others begin at the end and flash backward to illustrate and highlight the significant determinants to the ending. Either way, the events, characters, and meanings are eventually interwoven into one or two major themes that constitute the story. Whether one begins by asking about current sexual feelings and behaviors and then gathers history or begins by taking a developmental history depends on two factors: (1) the absence or presence of a current sexual issue that requires direct attention; and (2) the client's comfort with addressing current sexual functioning as opposed to historical narrative.

Be Flexible

Open-ended questions that encourage clients to tell their sexual story using their own language are ideal, but many clients are too inhibited or unsure of what to say. They require more direction. When your open-ended questions are met with blank stares, squirming, blushing, or other signs of discomfort, it is enough to make you regret ever having broached the topic. But, do not give up. Patience and calm encouragement along with the guidance of more specific questions will usually get the ball rolling. Looking for an aspect of the client's sexuality that is the least threatening—easiest to talk about first—may provide the direction.

Therapist: What is your sexual life like these days?

Joyce: I don't know what you mean ... like, am I seeing anyone?

Therapist: Sure ... we can start there.

Joyce: Well I've been dating this guy, Steven, for 3 months. We have been sexual ... [long silence].

Therapist: How has that been for you? Are you enjoying the sexual relationship?

Joyce: It's OK [silence].

Therapist: Is Steven your first sexual partner?

Joyce: No [silence].

Therapist: Tell me about the first one.

Joyce: I was 14, and he was a year ahead of me in high school. My parents didn't approve of him because he smoked and hung out with a crowd they didn't like. But I wasn't having a good year, and he was an escape for me. He had a car, and we would go driving around after school ... I told my mother I had to stay after school for one thing or another.

Therapist: What were the circumstances that led up to your being sexual with him?

Joyce: I didn't really want to, but he did, and I didn't want to lose him. The first time was in his car. ... I didn't really get anything out of it. We went together until he graduated and went to work. We were sexual the whole time, but I never really felt good about it. I didn't trust him. Later, after he broke up with me, I heard he had been with others, and I really felt used and angry with myself. ... I think it warped me or something. Sex has never been all that good. I don't get much out of it. I think I just do it to stay in a relationship.

In this case, the therapist helped Joyce by being willing to start with whatever Joyce brought up, "Like am I seeing anyone?" Even so, Joyce was reticent; so, rather than push her beyond a question or two, the therapist switched gears and inquired about her earlier experiences. Joyce had an easier time responding to this question and was then able to relax enough to go back to talking about Steven. Had she not seemed more comfortable, her therapist might have chosen to keep the focus on past experiences and inquire about Steven at another time.

TALKING WITH COUPLES

Talking to a couple about sexuality requires a sensitivity to three unique issues:

1. The absence of communication about sexuality in most couples
2. The distortion of facts that may occur when one or both partners fear correcting the other when telling their sexual story
3. The presence of private sexual thoughts, experiences, and secrets

Many couples, even those who enjoy an active and rich sexual life together, do not necessarily feel comfortable talking about their sexual desires, needs, fantasies, or fears. Youth and good health enable them to *be* sexual without having to talk about it. Inviting them to describe their sexual life together may produce an embarrassment and inhibition that might not be present if either was talking to you alone. Couples will usually giggle, look at each other helplessly, or in some other way convey an amused discomfort as they acknowledge, "We never talk about this!"

Talking to a couple about their sexuality requires a respect for each partner's private feelings, wishes, and behaviors. These should be addressed only in an individual session. Many therapists prefer to begin with a conjoint interview rather than with each person separately to get a sense of the quality of the relationship between the two people and to establish the therapist's role as responsible for both parties and therefore aligned with neither. However, it is wise to schedule at least one individual session with each partner early in the assessment so that each knows from the beginning that they will have some private time in which to discuss those feelings or life experiences that have never been shared with their partner or that cannot be discussed with as much candor in front of their partner. Presenting this format routinely at the first session reassures each partner that this is not being suggested because the therapist has gotten the indication that there are big secrets being withheld.

The difference between private and secret sexual feelings and behaviors is an important but sometimes confusing one. Private sexual thoughts include the myriad of images, fantasies, and attractions that do not have an impact on one's real sexual relationship but that one might not want to share with one's partner because to do so would be unnecessarily hurtful and serve no useful purpose (e.g., "I think my neighbor is cute," "I had a dream last night about an old boyfriend," or "I found myself flirting a little with that woman at the sales meeting last week"). It is not as if our partners do not know that we have private sexual feelings, fantasies, or thoughts. They just do not know the specifics, and most do not care to know. Secret sexual thoughts or behaviors are those that are having a negative impact on the relationship or would if discovered or those that represent a betrayal of a vow, agreement, or seemingly shared value system (e.g., having an extramarital affair or avoiding sex with a partner because of a persistent sexual fantasy that interferes with lovemaking). Our partners do not know that these thoughts or behaviors exist, although they often sense that there is something pulling our attention away from them. Some behaviors fall somewhere in the middle. Masturbation, for example, in some couples is a shared and openly accepted behavior; in others, it is a private behavior in which one or both partners engage but do not discuss. When it is experienced by one of the couple as a secret, it is usually because it is a breach of a shared value system that prohibits it or because it is accompanied by a persistent and compelling socially unacceptable fantasy that has potential or real consequences for the couple.

Amy: I walked in on my husband and found him masturbating with my panties on. I was at first shocked and then furious. I don't know why it
feels like such a betrayal of our marriage. I'm not sure how I feel
about his masturbating but wearing my panties is sick! He has kept
this from me, and I don't know if I can ever trust him again!

This distinction between private and secret sometimes poses a dilemma for
the therapist who hears personal and undisclosed sexual information from one
or both partners that may be having a negative impact on their sexual relationship. Making the correct determination whether that information can
harmlessly remain private or whether its privacy will undermine a successful
outcome if not shared with the partner is never a certainty. Open and frank discussion with the holder of the information regarding the power of the material
being withheld is the proper first step in making the difficult determination.

Therapist: You've told me about seeing another woman right now and your
inability to make a decision about whether or not you want to remain
in the marriage. Yet you want me to see you and your wife in marital
counseling and concentrate on your sexual relationship.
Sam: I'm hoping that if our sex life improves, it will be easier to give up seeing
Janet. Part of the reason I continue to see Janet is because sex with
my wife has never been good. She has never expressed any interest
in being sexual with me.
Therapist: Marriages usually have little to no chance of improving while there
is an affair going on. Your emotional energy is elsewhere. And it
would not be right for me to counsel the two of you, withholding this
information from your wife. Neither of you can successfully work on
your marital sexual relationship if she isn't aware of one of the major
issues that is now pulling you away.
Sam: I'll take your word for it, but I can't tell her. I know she will leave me, and
I'm not ready to end my marriage. What do I do now?

What was Sam's secret from Janet becomes something private between Sam
and the therapist. By respecting Sam's right to confidentiality, the therapist
must join in the secret, which becomes, in essence, a betrayal of Janet. To be
true to Janet, the therapist must break confidentiality with Sam.

I have always been amazed when a spouse presents me with this dilemma
and seems not to realize what a bind he or she has put us both in. Perhaps I
should not be. The spouse's ongoing denial of secrecy's potential for destruc-
tion merely extends to the therapeutic setting. It is up to the therapist to set
the course right. When I have reached this impasse with the holder of the
secret, I explore the options: Tell your partner; stop the affair without telling
your spouse; leave your marriage; or take a time-out and get some individual
therapy to sort out ending one relationship or the other before you work on the
one remaining. None of those options is without cost.

THE COMPONENTS OF SEXUAL EXPRESSION

Demonstrating interest, asking friendly questions, and being relatively accepting of what clients have to say will go a long way toward helping them tell

their sexual story, but they are not enough. Sexual stories are comprised of three components of sexual identity and three components of sexual function that cannot be readily expressed unless facilitated by the educated listener. Just as physical distress is more accurately described only after the physician has guided the patient through a series of questions that reflect the physician's knowledge about what might be wrong, so it is with sexual distress. Obtaining the complete sexual story requires that the therapist have a two-prong concept of the components of sexual identity and sexual functioning.

Sexual Identity

Sexual identity consists of three elements: gender identity, orientation, and intention. The *gender component* refers to both biologic sex (i.e., male or female) and the more subjective sense of self as either masculine or feminine. A relatively small number of people are distressed about their biologic gender and are confused by their strong persistent wishes to be the opposite sex. They may express this directly in their search for a therapist who will help them get hormones or surgery to correct the gender mistake, or they may present with a host of symptoms, such as cross-dressing, body dysmorphia, mutilation of breasts or genitals, and efforts to prevent, delay, hide, or reverse aspects of sexual development (e.g., binding or hiding the male genitals or female breasts). Often, there is an accompanying depression and failure to fit in with peers.

More frequently, however, gender issues involve a subjective sense of inadequacy and failure to live up to some yardstick of femininity or masculinity. Males express this in a number of ways: dissatisfaction with their body ("I'm too short," "thin," "fat," "soft"); athletic ability or lack thereof ("I am slow," "uncoordinated," "clumsy," "weak"); personality ("I'm too sensitive," "passive," "shy," "easily intimidated"); interests ("I am not interested in sports," "cars," "tools"); and sexual prowess ("I don't know how to make the move," "won't be able to perform," "won't satisfy my partner"; "My penis is too small"). Females will also express this in terms of their body ("I'm too tall," "big," "flat chested") and concerns about sexual desirability and performance, but culture allows for a much wider range of behaviors that, while not strictly feminine, will not damage a feminine self-image. Thus, females are more likely to enjoy pursuits such as athletics, interest in sports, a career in business, and so on without compromising their sense of femininity.

A negative gender identity sense can lead to low self-esteem, avoidance of partner-related sex and intimacy, and social and emotional isolation. Gentle inquiry about a client's gender identity is illustrated in the following questions:

- How did you feel about the changes in your body that took place during adolescence?
- How do you feel about your body now?
- Do your interests fit in with the interests of your peers?
- Do you feel more comfortable with males or females?
- Do you share interests more with males or females?

Such questions focus on body image, gender preferences, and gender role and will reveal areas of gender conflict.

The *orientation component* refers to the linkage of sexual feelings with a bias or predilection to prefer one gender over another for sexual and romantic purposes. Knowledge of one's orientation does not require sexual behavior (i.e., one often knows that one is homosexually or heterosexually inclined long before one is ready to participate in partner-related sexual activity). However, the terms *heterosexual* and *homosexual* are often used to indicate subjective interest, actual behavior, or both. This is not a problem if both the subjective and objective aspects of orientation are congruent, but it can be confusing and misleading if the two are not. For example, if a married man has sexual fantasies exclusively about males even when he is making love to his wife, is he a heterosexual because he is engaged in sex with a female, or is he homosexual because the objects of his sexual attractions are exclusively male? The following use of language may help differentiate the objective and subjective components of orientation:

Objective	Subjective
Contact with opposite-sex partner (heterosexual)	Fantasy about opposite sex (heteroerotic)
Contact with same-sex partner (homosexual)	Fantasy about same sex (homoerotic)
Contact with partners of both sexes (bisexual)	Fantasy about both sexes (bierotic)
Contact with neither sex (asexual)	Fantasy about neither sex (anerotic)

Therapists need to be clear that the subjective and objective aspects of orientation are distinct from each other and cannot be assumed from one another. When talking about orientation, you must always inquire about fantasies and behaviors with both opposite- and same-sex partners. It is best not to assume a heterosexual orientation by asking questions that steer in that direction, such as asking a male, "Who was your first girlfriend?" It is better to say, "Tell me about your first sexual experience." After a client has described his or her opposite-sex experiences or feelings, it is appropriate and wise to inquire, "How about same sex experiences? Have you ever had any or thought that you might like to?" While there is a slight risk that your client may be offended, that reaction can be managed by a matter-of-fact reply, "Well, many people do, and it's always better to ask." The goal is to give permission to *everyone* to speak about sexual feelings or behaviors that they may fear revealing.

The *intention component* refers to the idea that sexual behaviors are motivated by a certain intention. The decision to behave sexually, whether made after 1 night or 20 years, almost always conveys something about how the person feels about the other one and the role sexual behavior will play in conveying that feeling. The meaning of the behavior can range from, "I'm horny, and you are available. Let's have fun" to "I like you and want to be closer" or even "I love you" in one direction or "I will exert dominance and control over you" or "I'm angry and want to hurt you" in another.

When the intention is based on a wish to have fun or show affection and a genuine desire to be with the other person, it is hoped that the meaning of the sexual exchange will lend itself to emotional satisfaction, increased intimacy, and a sense of connection. Consider these intentions:

1. "I want to have sex with you because it will be pleasurable for both of us."
2. "I want to have sex with you to get closer to you."

3. "I want to have sex with you to see if I love you."
4. "I want to have sex with you because I love you."

When the intention is based on a need to avoid intimacy, to prove some-thing, or to dominate, control, or hurt the other person, the meaning of the sexual exchange may be experienced by the partner as empty, uncomfortable, or frightening, even if there is no actual coercion. Consider these intentions:

1. "I want to have sex with you to prove that I can."
2. "I want to have sex with you so that you will belong to me."
3. "I want to have sex with you to avoid getting closer to you."
4. "I want to have sex with you to dominate [or hurt] you."

Elaine: Arthur never wants to have sex with me except when I get home late and he accuses me of being with other men. He badgers me for hours about where I've been, and he persists in wanting sex even though I tell him I am tired and need to sleep. Eventually, I give in because I know he is upset, and I feel bad.

You can gain access to your client's intentions to be sexual with a partner by inquiring directly *and* by asking about the sexual fantasies that the client relies on during self-stimulation or with the partner. However, fantasies and the intentions embedded in them are intensely personal, private aspects of a sexual history and must be approached in the most gentle, nonjudgmental manner. Here are some questions about intention:

What determines when you feel ready to be sexual with a partner?
What are you feeling when you wish to be sexual with your partner?
When in the course of a relationship, do you usually become sexual with
    a partner?
How do you feel about being sexual with your partner?
Why do you not feel like being sexual with your partner?

Here are some questions about sexual fantasies:

What do you usually fantasize about when you masturbate?
Do you ever find yourself fantasizing about something else while engaged
    in sex?
What imagery in pornography most draws you?
Do you ever fantasize about sexual behaviors you would be reluctant to
    do?

The more conventional the imagery, the easier it will be to reveal it. It is a lot easier to relate a fantasy about walking on the beach holding hands with a partner at sunset than it is to speak of a wish to be sexual with a minor or a desire to force someone to do something unwanted. In those situations, the therapist should not expect that even the gentlest approach will neces-sarily elicit an honest, accurate response. With time and patience, the trust level may build up enough for the client to feel increasingly willing to reveal more. Periodically revisiting questions about the more personal and private aspects of sexual fantasy and behavior will often yield new and valuable information.

Stephen Levine has coined the phrase *sexual identity mosaicism* to express the idea that everyone has some elements (mosaic tiles) of both genders, orientations, and positive and negative intentions to be sexual. These elements unfold as people mature and participate in sexual behaviors and intimate relationships. Our unique mosaic patterns are the sum total of "a little bit of this and a little bit of that." These elements may or may not fit a preconceived idea of what the overall pattern should look like as measured by either personal or societal standards. When they do not, it can be confusing, even disturbing, and there is a temptation on the part of the client and the therapist to try to "force a fit" rather than allow for their uniqueness. Acknowledging that everyone's sexual identity is a mosaic and that there is an endless supply of patterns may be a very freeing and helpful approach to take, especially when a client is struggling with atypical elements.

Disorders of Intention

When the meaning or purpose of engaging in sexual behavior is unusual, hostile, dehumanizing, or coercive, therapists invoke the term *paraphilia*. The paraphilias are characterized by recurrent, intense sexually arousing fantasies, sexual urges, or behaviors generally involving (1) nonhuman objects, (2) the suffering or humiliation of oneself or one's partner, or (3) children or other nonconsenting persons; these occur over a period of at least 6 months. Exhibitionism, voyeurism, fetishism, pedophilia, and sadomasochism are some of the most common.

Many of the paraphilic themes are experienced as part of more conventional sexual behavior. For example, an interest in and arousal to silky lingerie is hardly noteworthy unless it is so narrow in focus and intense that there is no real interest in the person wearing the lingerie. Who has not experienced some voyeuristic interest in other people's sexual behavior? If no one did, then there would be no audience for romantic or erotic movies. That interest, however, is quite different from the compulsive, intense need of a "peeping Tom" to spy on others who are unaware of being viewed. Likewise, a mutual enjoyment of sexual role plays of dominance and submission or the use of props such as blindfolds, wrist restraints, and the like is quite different from the coercive infliction of pain or humiliation.

Many therapists recoil in disgust or anxiety when they are initially confronted with paraphilic disorders, particularly those that are hurtful to others. They are quick to say, "I don't treat that!" and refer the individual to a specialist. While seeking out an expert in paraphilic disorders may be appropriate, especially if the behavior involves legal consequences, the ideal first step is to discuss the topic in a helpful manner. The development of this skill increases the likelihood that the client will accept the referral to an expert. To attain this, we must suspend the anxiety and negative judgments that we have acquired over the years about these matters and put forth our intellectual curiosity. It helps to realize that many clients with these disorders are deeply troubled and ashamed of their behavior. Your willingness to discuss the subject will provide them with an opportunity to come out from hiding and get help.

Patients may voluntarily disclose a paraphilic disorder, but more typically such disorders are not revealed unless the person is "outed" by the law, a spouse, or an employer. When the disorder is revealed by a spouse in a conjoint session, the therapist should offer additional individual time with the patient to explore the issue further.

Amy: Ken and I haven't made love in a long time. Yesterday I went into his study to look for a bill, and I noticed the computer was on. Ken was upstairs with one of the kids. I looked to see what was on the screen, and I was horrified to see pornography. It was a woman tied up and a man standing over her. I looked further, and there were dozens of photos of bondage. Our kids could have seen this!

Ken: I forgot to turn it off when I left. It's no big deal. I just look occasionally.

Amy: It is a big deal! You've been spending hours on the computer lately. Last weekend you stayed up until 3 a.m. both nights, and you overslept Monday morning and missed a meeting. You used to ask me if I would let you tie me up during sex, but it turned me off. You said it was no big deal then, but sex has been practically nonexistent between us for a long time!

This interchange is typical in that Amy reveals Ken's secret, which he then minimizes or denies. The therapist's initial understanding of the problem will come from Amy's observations, but the establishment of a therapeutic alliance with Ken will come only if Ken is given the opportunity to explore his sexuality with the therapist privately. If this interferes with the therapist's role as a marriage counselor, a referral to an individual therapist for Ken is in order.

Sexual Functioning

Sexual functioning refers to the actual process of engaging in sexual behavior and the myriad of little and big things that can go wrong. Clients often present with complaints about some aspect of their or their partner's ability to function sexually. We break sexual functioning into three separate but interwoven phenomena: desire, arousal, and orgasm. Desire and arousal can precede or follow each other (Figure 1.1). An increase in one usually augments an increase in the other; that is, the better it feels, the more I want it, and the more I want it, the better it feels.

*These may be drive, fantasy, interpersonal, touching, or anything else that leads to sexual excitement.

Figure 1.1   The interplay of desire and arousal.

Sexual desire is in turn composed of the interaction of three elements (see Chapter 2):

- A biologic urge referred to as drive. This is experienced as a bodily tension or "horniness" that may or may not be associated with an anticipated partner.
- A cognitive wish to engage in sexual behavior. Cognitive wishes are reflections of internalized cultural values about the role of sexual behavior in our lives.
- A psychological willingness to allow one's body to respond to a sexual experience. Psychological willingness requires a degree of comfort with one's own body and sexual identity as well as trust and comfort with one's partner.

While men's desire, especially that of young men, is often most determined by drive, women's desire is often more defined by the psychological receptivity to an external sexual overture. Desire is complex, and ascertaining the nature of a patient's desire will take more than the question, How often do you desire sex? Asking several of the following questions will be necessary:

How often does your body need a sexual release?

How often do you masturbate?

Do you think about making love with your partner when he [or she] is not around?

How do you feel when your partner initiates sexual contact?

How often would you have sex if you could?

Currently, ever-increasing numbers of males with the chief complaint of "too much drive," alternatively labeled as sexual compulsivity or sexual addiction (see Chapter 22), are turning to clinicians for help. While the determination of what constitutes "too much" is often a source of contention (who gets to determine this—the man himself, his wife or partner, the therapist?), the label rests heavily on a history of (1) increasing and excessive amounts of time, money, and energy pursuing and engaging in sexual behaviors and (2) repeated efforts to stop or decrease the behaviors.

When the compelling high drive is directed toward activities that are unusual, hostile, dehumanizing, or coercive, it becomes a disorder of intention or paraphilia as defined in this chapter. While by criterion A all paraphilias have a compulsive quality to them and thus qualify as a sexual addiction, not all sexual addictions are paraphilic. For example, although the man who masturbates five times a day or engages in hours of sexual chatting online or multiple affairs may clinically qualify or self-identify as a sexual addict, there may be nothing about the content of his behavior that meets criteria for the unusual, hostile, dehumanizing, or coercive nature of a paraphilia.

Sexual arousal is a bodily experience, a subjective horniness or excitement that may be described as a warm, tingling, and increasingly pleasurable sensation, often, but not always, accompanied by increased blood flow to the pelvic area, resulting in an erection and vulvar swelling and lubrication. Arousal, or the lack thereof, is usually easier to describe than desire. Questions might include the following:

How does it feel when your partner stimulates you?
Do you experience a pleasurable sensation when your breasts or genitals are touched?
Do you get an erection when exposed to sexual stimulation?
Are you aware of lubricating when your partner stimulates you?
Does sensation build up as the stimulation continues?

Orgasm, the rhythmic contractions and accompanying pleasurable sensations, is the culmination of sexual excitement. The word *climax* is often used instead, as is the more colloquial expression "to come." It is rare to encounter a male who has never experienced an orgasm through self- or partner stimulation. Male complaints about orgasm usually center on their inability to control the timing of it. Either they climax too quickly to suit their or their partner's needs or they find it very difficult to accomplish. The former is a common complaint of young and relatively inexperienced males, the latter of males who may be taking medications that interfere with or delay orgasm. It is not rare, however, to encounter females who have never experienced orgasm. This is most likely due to a number of factors, including females' greater susceptibility to cultural taboos about self-exploration, less biologic urge, and greater internal conflict about expressing sexual longings. Female complaints typically center on their inability to build up enough arousal to reach orgasm or a sense of being left hanging at a peak of arousal with no prospect of orgasmic relief.

Amy: It feels good, but it doesn't go anywhere. ... Ken keeps touching me, but after a while I lose the feelings, and it actually gets unpleasant. I get frustrated and push his hand away.

Concerns about absent, low, or high sexual desire; difficulties in achieving or maintaining arousal; and problems with the timing or achievement of orgasm are highly prevalent in the general population and are referred to as *sexual dysfunctions*. When they have always been present, we describe them as *lifelong* or *primary*; when they reflect a distinct change in sexual functioning, we describe them as *acquired* or *secondary*. When they occur in all situations (i.e., with all partners and self-stimulation), we call them *global*, and when they occur only in some situations (i.e., with one partner but not another or with a partner but not with self-stimulation), we describe them as *situational*.

Rosemary is a 25-year-old single woman who has never been orgasmic with a partner. She is able to bring herself to orgasm through masturbation but shuts down when any partner attempts to stimulate her to orgasm (lifelong, situational anorgasmia).

John is a 60-year-old married man who has not been able to achieve a satisfactory erection for 5 years. Morning erections are nonexistent, erections via masturbation are floppy, and he is no longer able to achieve penetration during lovemaking (acquired, global erectile dysfunction).

Lifelong dysfunctions reflect some impediment in the development of a comfortable sexual self. Rosemary's ability to stimulate herself to orgasm suggests a mastery of her own sexual sensations, but her inability to be orgasmic with a partner probably represents her inhibition about letting go, a fear of being perceived as too sexual if she demonstrates what kind of stimulation she needs, or her unrecognized link between sexual arousal and being "bad." Because this has taken place with all sexual partners, it will not be fruitful to spend too much time exploring the dynamics with a particular partner; it makes more sense to explore childhood and familial sexual experiences, attitudes, messages, and beliefs that may have negatively impacted her comfort level with a partner.

We understand acquired sexual dysfunctions to mean that the person successfully navigated the development of a comfortable sexual self before something undermined their success. The destructive force may be a physical change such as illness, injury, medication, radiation, or surgery or an emotional change as a result of personal, partner, or familial discord. Some acquired sexual dysfunctions can be traced to both physical and emotional changes. The emotions that most commonly interfere with sexual functioning are anxiety, guilt, fear, anger, and sadness. John's erectile failure may reflect a change in his physical health, a deterioration in his marriage, personal depression, guilt over an affair, or other stressors. Therefore, the right approach would be to focus on what was going on 5 years ago, not on John's early childhood and sexual development.

> John reports that 5 years ago he was passed over for a promotion that he was certain he was going to receive. At the same time, his physician encouraged him to lose some weight after a glucose tolerance test suggested borderline diabetes. He lost some of the weight, but it has been a constant struggle.

John's failure to be promoted may have created depression, anxiety about his vocational future, anger at his employer, or guilt over his perceived less-than-stellar work performance. These feelings could negatively impact his ability to relax and receive sexual stimulation. The borderline diabetes presents two concerns; not only is diabetes highly correlated with erectile difficulties, it may well have been a blow to his view of himself as healthy and vital. His ongoing battle to lose weight may be accompanied by feelings of deprivation, the sense of inadequate discipline, and a negative body image. All of these may have contributed to John's acquired erectile problems.

When clients report multiple sexual difficulties, we must obtain an accurate picture of each of them. Ultimately, we want to understand how they relate to each other.

> John now reports a lack of desire for sexual relations. Five years ago, he kept trying to have sex and occasionally climaxed with a partial erection. He has not attempted to masturbate or initiate sex with his wife for several years. He avoids spending evenings with his wife and waits until she is asleep before retiring. He reports low self-esteem and a preoccupation with his mortality: "I am an old man."

The Sexual Equilibrium

Understanding the sexual functioning of a couple begins with the realization that the sexual function of one partner always has an impact on the other. Each partner's component characteristics—desire, arousal, orgasm patterns—has an impact on the other whether these components are positive or problematic. His premature ejaculation may bring about her lack of orgasm; her loss of sexual motivation may induce his loss of desire or, conversely, his hyperdesire as he attempts to woo her back. We refer to the balancing act that occurs within every couple's life as the *sexual equilibrium*. It continually occurs and accounts for the different outcomes from partner to partner and from episode to episode with the same partner.

IT IS NOT SO HARD ANY MORE

So, here I am, 34 years later, still interested in the complexity of sexual expression and the infinite number of ways people conduct their sexual lives. It is definitely easier now to do this work. For one thing, all of the experiences in my own life have contributed to my ever-expanding frame of reference. No one questions me any more about how I acquired my knowledge about sexuality. I have earned the badge (and the gray hairs) of maturity.

You do not have to wait until middle age, however, to be good at this work. The careful delineation of identity and functioning as they evolve and influence each other over a lifetime will yield a sexual story, each one rich and unique. You may feel at times that the book has been opened for you at Chapter 10. Just as you settle into the story line, the pages flip to the beginning—or the ending—or just about anywhere. Relax. With your interest and guidance, the story line will come together. Your willingness to help clients tell their sexual story for even a few months will catapult you far ahead of the majority of your colleagues who refer clients to a sex therapist at the mention of the word *sex* or avoid the subject altogether. You will be rewarded with grateful and appreciative clients, opportunities to help people sort through intensely private and personal issues to gain understanding, and if you are anything like me, a deeper appreciation of your own sexual expression. Return to this chapter after you have familiarized yourself with the contents of the other chapters. The combination of your expanding knowledge about sexuality along with the guidelines I have discussed will place you in an excellent position to do good work.

BIBLIOGRAPHY

Carnes, P. (1992). *Don't call it love: Recovery from sexual addiction.* New York: Bantam Books. This book is the most widely read in the sexual addiction community. It offers a basic introduction to the nature of sexual addiction, its impact on partners and children, and the 12-step process of recovery. It captures sexual addiction in males, but the perspective does not easily translate to the experience of females with this problem.

Kasl, C. (1990). *Women, sex, and addiction.* New York: Harper & Row. This volume addresses sexual addiction among females. My female clients have found this book extremely helpful, and it certainly provides material for therapeutic discussion.

Levine, S. (2007). *Demystifying love: Plain talk for the mental health profes-sional*. New York: Taylor & Francis. This is a thoughtful, easy-to-read book that speaks to the ambition to love, the interplay of love and sexual desire, and infidelity as both a reflection of and contribution to the failure of love's ambition.

Lyga, B. (2007). *Boy toy*. New York: Houghton Mifflin. This volume is the sexual story of a teenage boy who has a sexual relationship with a female teacher. The boy's account of how this relationship developed and the impact it had on his life is riveting.

Maurice, W. (1999). *Sexual medicine in primary care*. St. Louis, MO: Mosby. This book addresses the lack of education and training in medical schools that leaves physicians unprepared to tackle the topic of sexuality with the thoroughness and sensitivity that it requires. It takes on a "how-to" approach with the use of sample dialogues that cover a wide range of sex-ual issues.

Two

Understanding and Managing Professional–Client Boundaries

S. MICHAEL PLAUT, PHD

INTRODUCTION

In the normal course of doing our work, we are likely to meet colleagues, students, or clients to whom we develop feelings of closeness. This is not only normal, but if we are honest with ourselves, our caring for and about people probably has a lot to do with why we do what we do for a living. We are given the rare privilege of sharing in the intimacies of strangers. The vulnerability inherent in a client sharing private stories and feelings with us may have powerful meanings to us and may evoke feelings in us. Sometimes, these feelings may be particularly intense. How we handle these feelings is one of the great challenges for the health care professional. If these feelings are unrecognized, denied, or mishandled, we risk crossing appropriate provider–client boundaries. Boundary crossings may range from social contact outside the practice setting, to excessive personal disclosure, to sexual activity with a client.

Why are boundaries important? What are appropriate provider–client boundaries? Do these differ in various situations? What can we do to help ensure that appropriate boundaries are maintained?

In this chapter, I share with you what I have learned about these questions during more than two decades of reading, teaching, and consultation. For simplicity, I typically use the word *client* to refer to anyone over whom we may have professional responsibility—patient, student, supervisee, or employee. Occasionally, I use more specific terminology.

How I Got Involved in This Area

Like many other aspects of my career, my involvement in this area was, to some extent, an accident. From 1982 to 1985, I served on and chaired the Maryland State Board of Examiners of Psychologists. One of my predecessors on the board had correctly warned me that my experience would put me in touch with the "soft underbelly of psychology." During my tenure on the board, I saw no less than 12 disciplinary cases involving alleged sexual involvement with clients.

I was especially intrigued by two aspects of these cases. First, we were very awkward in addressing them. It was an era when licensing boards were seeing an increasing number of sex-related allegations and realized that they had to take them seriously. Previously, licensing boards did not always have a good track record of responsiveness to such allegations. During the 1980s, a vocal body of consumers was calling for criminalization of sexual boundary violations, in part because they felt that the professions were not adequately protecting the public.

Second, I initially found it hard to understand the ambivalence of the victims in pursuing their cases. I learned that much of their reluctance was more related to the real or anticipated pain of pursuing the case itself than any real concern about its validity. I saw that the betrayal of trust represented by a sexual boundary violation often led to severe consequences for the client, including estrangement from loved ones, depression, and occasionally suicide (Plaut, 1995). In working on the rehabilitation of professional offenders since that time, I have seen that the consequences for them are often severe as well.

Why I Have Continued My Involvement

My early experiences with such cases taught me that we were not doing nearly enough to prepare our students to competently manage psychological intimacy in the professional setting. I learned that the mental health professions were not alone in having to address boundary considerations; boundary issues were a concern in all helping professions (Peterson, 1992). I became committed to teaching about this important, potentially career-ending, issue to my students. After leaving the board, I continued to consult on cases brought to health profession boards in Maryland and other states, working with both victims and offenders. From 1994 to 1996, I had the honor of chairing a governor's task force on this issue in the State of Maryland. This role enabled me to become even better acquainted with how the issue was being addressed in various segments of our society (Plaut & Nugent, 1999).

This area is a difficult and often painful one in which to work. As time has gone on, it has found me more than I have sought it out. I continue to learn more about this critical and complex subject as I confront new situations in myself or in others. I am pleased to have this opportunity to share with you some of the things I have learned. As you read this, keep in mind that mental health professionals may play any of a number of roles in addressing boundary issues—as teachers, therapists, consultants, confidants, administrators, or licensing board members, for example. We are not simply all potential offenders.

Areas to Be Addressed

I discuss four major considerations: (1) the nature of and basis for our obligation to our clients; (2) risk factors for client and professional; (3) how we conceptualize provider–client boundaries; and (4) how and why boundary standards are determined. The chapter ends with a brief list of coping strategies.

I first briefly outline each of these considerations. Then, I discuss them in greater detail. I do not focus only on what may be considered right or wrong; rather, I emphasize behaviors that promote either an optimal or inappropriate professional–client relationship. In particular, I stress the process of deciding where boundaries ought to be for a given situation.

Our Obligation to Our Clients

While a part of our relationship to our clients may involve caring, empathy, or touch, there is a level of separateness and objectivity that is critical to an effective clinical, teaching, or supervisory relationship. Part of the need for that separateness is inherent in the power given to us by clients because of our knowledge, skill, and judgment. Excessive intimacy is thus likely to be considered a breach of trust on the part of the professional, regardless of who initiates a boundary crossing.

Risk Factors for Client and Professional

There may be personal characteristics or situations that either we or our clients are experiencing that make us more vulnerable to crossing boundaries and putting our professional relationships at risk. It is helpful to know what these risks are and to think about how we can effectively address them.

Conceptualization of Professional–Client Boundaries

The level of intimacy between professional and client exists on a continuum. The location of appropriate boundaries along that spectrum differs for different professional–client situations. Appropriate boundaries may be defined differently for a patient versus a student, for a psychologist versus a dentist, or even for a patient with a particular problem versus one with another type of problem. We are constantly challenged to decide where boundaries ought to be. Our decision is guided by knowledge of laws, ethical standards, local practices, and consultation with colleagues. Ultimately, however, it is based on our own good judgment.

Boundary limits apply to both sexual and nonsexual matters. Sexual matters get most of the immediate attention, but it is vital to all of us to realize that sexual boundary violations always are preceded by nonsexual boundary crossings (Strasburger, Jorgenson, & Sutherland, 1992). In addition, nonsexual boundary crossings are often harmful in their own right.

Historically, our concern with professional–client boundaries has focused on the one-on-one psychotherapy relationship between provider and patient and to a lesser extent between teacher and student. However, several recent trends highlight the need for us to address the complexity of professional–client boundaries in a broader sense: (1) an enhanced concern with behaviors and boundaries in faculty–student relationships; (2) the impact of public disclosure via the Internet and social networking Web sites, such as Facebook; and (3) greater focus on what is disclosed to patients by providers.

How and Why Professional Standards Are Determined: The Focus on Sexual Involvement

Despite the existence of a spectrum of intimacy, there has been a strong focus on sexual intimacy between professional and client. This emphasis is related to the symbolic nature of sexual intimacy in our lives and the level of harm that so often results from sexual contact in the professional setting. *Sexual misconduct* is defined as including a broad range of sex-related behaviors; it is not just intercourse.

Summary: Coping Strategies

Our ability to set and maintain appropriate boundaries depends to a great extent on our ability to be aware of our own needs, vulnerabilities, and how our behavior may be perceived in our work setting. We must guard against the tendency to rationalize behaviors that serve our personal interests rather than the client's welfare. We need to be aware of our inner messages, the red flags that signal progressive boundary crossings—the proverbial "slippery slope." Finally, we need to nurture our own personal relationships and support systems.

OUR OBLIGATION TO OUR CLIENTS: THE IMPORTANCE OF BOUNDARIES

We may all have different reasons for having entered a helping profession. Whatever those reasons, our clear professional obligation is to put our clients' needs above our own. We need to find a balance between caring, closeness, availability, and intimacy on one hand and distance and objectivity on the other.

Boundaries are important in all relationships, including committed partners in an intimate relationship. In her book, *Grown-Up Marriage*, Viorst (2003) encourages readers to "figure out how intimate you can be without suffocation and how separate you can be without alienation." Relationships can become so enmeshed that each member of the couple loses his or her individuality and privacy.

When we talk about the relationships of professionals to their patients, students, or employees, however, we are not talking about "peer" relationships. We are talking about people who are involved in a trust-based relationship with a person to whom they are providing a service.

A central and often-misunderstood concept about boundaries has to do with the power that we have as helping professionals. The relationships we have to our clients are often referred to as trust-based relationships. Our clients come to us because they trust our knowledge, skill, and judgment. The power we have is the power they give to us; it is not necessarily power that we assume on our own. We are very likely to have influences on our clients far beyond our intentions or awareness.

I once worked on a rehabilitation assignment with a chiropractor, who had become sexually involved with one of his patients. He told me that when he entered the profession, he expected that he would one day "adjust his future wife." Clearly, this expectation of intimacy with a patient had contributed to his current problems with his licensing board. Functioning in a professional setting with such an expectation in mind cannot help but compromise one's clinical priorities. How would any of us feel as clients if we had to be concerned about whether our provider was sizing us up as a potential friend or partner rather than focusing on the service he or she was supposed to provide for us?

The provider is expected to maintain appropriate boundaries (Feldman-Summers, 1989). The fact that a client may have given consent or even initiated a boundary crossing is typically considered irrelevant by licensing boards and courts (Bisbing, Jorgensen, & Sutherland, 1995; Plaut, 1995; Wertheimer, 2003).

RISK FACTORS FOR CLIENT AND PROFESSIONAL

The Vulnerability of the Client

Our clients are vulnerable just by virtue of their seeking our help. They may bring other vulnerabilities to the clinical setting as well, such as inadequate social supports; a history of physical, psychological, or sexual abuse; or the absence of genuine caring in their relationships. As a result, they may ask for more closeness from us, personal information, a longer period of assistance, or contact outside the professional setting.

Even in a medical setting, it is easy to see why a patient might develop feelings toward a health professional. The clinical setting is isolating, patients feel frightened, and a health professional may have provided a greater level of empathy and caring than anyone in the patient's personal life. Therefore, a patient's reaching out is more likely a symbolic gesture than one based on any real knowledge of the professional as a person. It is important that the provider acknowledge these feelings, maintain a balance between caring and professional objectivity, and confront such feelings only if they persist and if they obstruct one's ability to provide appropriate care. If we find that patients or students appear to be making advances toward us on a frequent basis, we may need to make an honest appraisal of our dress, the scents we wear, and verbal or nonverbal signals we may be giving our clients. It is often helpful to ask for feedback from colleagues.

Erotic feelings toward a psychotherapist are not only likely to be more intense, but these feelings may provide some of the basis for a successful therapeutic outcome. As Levine (1992, p. 216) put it, "Why should a patient not love a therapist who consistently provides a high quality affective connection, calm clear thinking, and a reliable interest in the patient's happiness?" We are, in fact, "paid for our ability to deal with our temptations, fantasies, and arousal with apparent calm" (p. 220). "When patients let their therapist know about their love, they expect to be helped to benefit from it. Sexually offending therapists often rationalize their sexual behavior with the patient as being for the patient's benefit. In the regression of therapy, patients may request and accede to the therapist's sexual advance. Even as it is occurring, most patients know that it is improper" (p. 222).

Managing such erotic feelings requires a careful balance of closeness and separateness on the part of the therapist. Levine (1992, pp. 226–229) described his patient Bea, who had repeatedly expressed intense and persistent erotic feelings toward him in therapy. She once presented him with a necktie at Christmas, which he accepted "after much conflict." Two months later, after dishonestly delaying her normal appointment so that her next session occurred on Valentine's Day, she presented him with a box of chocolates and an expensive pen. Despite her acknowledging the love and desire for a sexual relationship that were embedded in these gifts, Dr. Levine refused them. She was mortified and upset for weeks over her humiliation. By holding the line and allowing the patient to express her love in a safe environment, this recently divorced woman, who could not feel sexual interest in her husband, eventually came to feel safe with a man. "And this," she said as her therapy terminated, "has been worth everything to me."

Vulnerability of the Professional

We may experience a need for intimacy in our own personal lives, especially when we have experienced a loss or when we are having difficulties in our own primary relationships.

Our role as helper, whether as clinician, teacher, or parent, is to help our charges get to the point that they do not need us any more rather than to provide excessively for their needs. The trainees of a child psychiatrist colleague would sometimes express a desire to continue to care for a child or adolescent beyond what was pragmatic in a given clinical setting. He would ask them, "How big is your basement?" Our own need to be needed can lead us to do things for our clients that do more to serve our own needs than theirs and may exceed what is either practical or what is in the client's best interest in the long term.

There is a tendency to rationalize our behavior when it comes to sexual boundary violations. Offenders often hide behind the reproductive definition of sex as vaginal intercourse. Thus, one may claim that one has not had sex unless one ejaculates. A psychiatrist I interviewed for the Maryland Board of Physician Quality Assurance insisted that he had not had sex with his patient and in fact could not as he was hypertensive and could not maintain an erection. I asked him if there had been genital contact between him and his patient, and he went on to describe their activity in that regard. A minister convinced his female parishioner that he would not be betraying his wife if they limited their activity to oral sex.

Another trait that we often see in professionals who violate professional boundaries is the sense of entitlement that comes with the privilege of being a recognized, licensed professional. This may lead one to feel that he or she is above the need to observe certain rules, standards, and courtesies. Often in these cases, professional power and status inflame preexisting personality patterns. At its extreme, such people are serial offenders who may never appreciate the consequences of their actions. However, the assumption that "rank has its privileges" can never be said to apply to an ethical obligation.

Senior professionals must be role models for those coming behind them. Thus, our obligation to maintain appropriate boundaries with clients in the clinical setting also extends to our students and clinical supervisees (Plaut, 1993). Like many other aspects of professionalism and ethics, the issue of professional–client boundaries has often been ignored in professional education. Our teaching needs to go beyond the simple admonition, "Don't have sex with your clients." Abstract discussions of transference and countertransference will not alone help students to understand the realities of everyday boundary challenges. Students need to struggle with some of the more subtle boundary challenges that we face every day (Bridges, 1995; Norris, Gutheil, & Strasburger, 2003; Plaut, 2008). We, as teachers and supervisors, need to be able to discuss openly the dilemmas we so often face ourselves. Finally, we need to model appropriate boundaries in our own behavior. This means not only that we maintain boundaries with our own clients in the clinical setting, but that we do so with our students and trainees as well (Plaut, 1993).

White (1997) emphasized that professionals need to find nurturance in their personal lives through relationships, hobbies, vacations, and so on. We need to find a balance between the professional and personal aspects of our lives. We cannot perform well as professionals if we do not also care for ourselves (Brancu & Page, 2008). To the extent that boundaries between our personal and professional lives become less permeable, our professional, social, and sexual energy may tend to become increasingly focused within the "organizational boundary" (Figure 2.1). White referred to this as "organizational incest." The "organization" can be a therapist–client dyad or an entire hospital or clinic. By seeing to our personal needs and relationships and keeping personal and

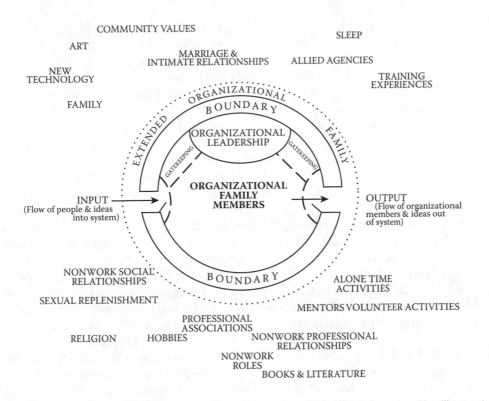

Figure 2.1 Our ability to easily cross boundaries between our professional and personal worlds will prevent excessive professional, social, and sexual energy from being expended within the "organizational boundary," as often happens in a closed system. (Adapted from *The Incestuous Workplace: Stress and Distress in the Organizational Family* by William L. White. Originally copyrighted 1997 by Hazelden Foundation. Adapted here by permission of the author.)

professional priorities in balance, we maintain sufficient boundary permeability and are thus less likely to exercise our personal needs within the professional realm.

In her autobiographical book, *A Year by the Sea* (1999), Anderson describes having dinner at her cottage on Cape Cod with an unnamed middle-aged psychotherapist from the Boston area who was working on the topic of professional–client boundaries. She quotes him as saying:

> I might be attracted to a 21-year-old client, not an unusual occurrence for a man of my age, and yet if I acted on my lustful fantasies there might be all hell to pay. But simply denying these thoughts is sheer repression. I might have had to turn off such thoughts when I was newly married and we were raising our children, but now I have more freedom and will gain nothing from denying my fantasies. Rather, it behooves me to bring them to the surface, look at what I might be missing, and then move ahead to incorporate, say, more passion in my life, within the bounds of my marriage. (p. 115)

THE SPECTRUM OF PROVIDER–CLIENT BOUNDARIES

It is typical to discuss professional–client boundaries as being of two types: sexual and nonsexual. Virtually all health professions prohibit the crossing of sexual boundaries, although definitions of sexual misconduct differ somewhat (Bisbing et al., 1995; Plaut & Nugent, 1999). Nonsexual crossings are referred to by both the American Psychological Association (2002) and the National Association of Social Workers (1993) as *dual* or *multiple relationships*. These are situations in which a professional has two or more simultaneous professional relationships (e.g., both therapist and teacher) or both a professional and a personal relationship with a client at the same time. Examples of professional–personal dual relationships might include such things as treating a family member, employing a client in one's practice, giving or accepting gifts, hugging clients, or socializing with clients. Ethical standards about such relationships are rather flexible and are influenced by contextual factors.

Are dual relationships wrong? A few authors have expressed the opinion that they are always wrong. To be sure, it is well known that certain kinds of nonsexual boundary crossings have a tendency to precede or accompany sexual boundary violations. These may include, for example, disclosure of personal problems by a therapist, exchanges of greeting cards or expensive gifts, or planned contact outside the therapeutic setting. However, a realistic consideration of dual relationships makes it quickly apparent that avoiding all dual relationships is neither possible nor necessarily advisable. Gutheil and Gabbard (1993) distinguish between boundary crossings and boundary violations. For example, casual exchange of gifts may fit a social norm, whether in a given culture or a given clinical setting, such as homemade cookies brought in for the clinical staff or even for a given professional at a holiday time. However, an expensive or very personal gift may be presented with a very different intent or expectation. Speaking from a purely clinical and ethical point of view, one might say that a boundary crossing constitutes a violation if it involves a substantial risk of compromising professional effectiveness. This might occur by confusing the client about the role of the professional, reducing the professional's ability to make decisions that reflect the client's welfare rather than his or her own, or reinforcing a client's expectation of a personal component to the relationship.

There are certain differences in such practices among the various professions, depending in large degree on what is expected in that profession (Peterson, 1992). For example, dentists often treat members of their immediate families (Plaut & Wilson, 2008). Physicians are not supposed to do so (Council on Ethical and Judicial Affairs, 1998). Certain physicians may socialize to some degree with their patients, but mental health professionals typically do not. However, there may be differences even within professions or within specialties regarding what may be considered appropriate behavior. One might not consider boundary issues to be very important for, say anesthesiologists, who tend not to develop close, enduring relationships with their patients. However, this may be quite different for the anesthesiologist who runs a chronic pain clinic, where regular contact may occur over a period of time and where clients may be especially grateful for the relief that the physician has given them.

Finally, whereas certain isolated boundary crossings that are considered problematic may be seen initially as naïve, unintentional, or ill-considered in a given situation, patterns of such behaviors may be cause for greater concern.

Closed Systems

Dual relationships are often unavoidable in what are called "closed systems" (White, 1997). For example, those of us who work in hospitals may often treat patients who are also employees of that hospital. In a small town, one's client may be encountered in a supermarket, at a party, or at a religious institution more frequently than in larger urban areas. In such situations, the professional may sometimes have to make a special effort to keep professional and personal aspects of a relationship separate and to realize when objective decision making may be compromised.

Another aspect of the closed-system phenomenon is the fact that many of the things we do are observed by others in the professional environment. Therefore, we need to be concerned not only with what we do but how it may be perceived by others in our professional environment. For example, a heterosexual faculty member may invite his male graduate students or residents to go fly fishing with him, knowing well that if he had invited his female trainees that eyebrows might be raised. What he may not realize, however, is that the women may then feel not only that they are being discriminated against as women, but also that the male trainees enjoy special access to their mentor and have become "favorite children."

Socializing with students or trainees can be an important aspect of the mentoring process. A group activity, such as a barbecue at the home of a faculty member, perhaps including partners and even children, might a more inclusive way to achieve this objective.

Our need to address faculty–student relationships more directly has been reflected in recent concerns in the medical education community about student mistreatment. Medical schools accredited by the Liaison Committee on Medical Education are now expected to have in place policies on faculty–student relationships, including mechanisms for reporting violations, such as abuse or harassment, without fear of retaliation (Liaison Committee on Medical Education, 2008). As with patients who feel they have been victimized by their therapists, students are often reluctant to express concerns about mistreatment or coercion because they are concerned about effects that such complaints may have on grades or evaluations. Hopefully, these new guidelines and policies will engender more discussion among students and faculty about how these relationships can be improved and how faculty can more effectively model appropriate professional behavior.

Dual relationships are sometimes unavoidable and even necessary. The late Jerri Nielsen, the physician who recounted her experiences at the South Pole in the book, *Ice Bound* (2001), provides a poignant example. During her year in isolation with about 40 other workers, she served as the only trained health care provider, with her responsibilities ranging from planning social events to maintaining psychological well-being and morale to doing root canals. The very survival of this small, isolated group of people required a high level of interaction and interdependence. Excessive aloofness on Nielsen's part might actually have compromised trust, and the consequent isolation of the physician might have reduced her own morale and thus her clinical effectiveness.

Yet, the dilemma presented by this situation was not an easy one. She writes, "The terror of a doctor in Antarctica is that one of your friends (and that includes everyone) will be seriously sick or injured and there won't be much you can do about it" (Nielsen, 2001, p. 149). Nielsen later tells about learning of her own diagnosis of breast cancer in a rather impersonal e-mail message from a pathologist in the United States. "The next thing I remember from that morning was seeing one of the carpenters lying on the cart in Biomed. While examining him, I realized from the expression on his face that he could tell something wasn't right with me. For once I couldn't summon up the impassive mask that I always wore when I saw my patients. There was no way I could hide my feelings from him, or any friend at the Pole. We were too connected by now, like cells in a simple organism. He deserved to know what was wrong. 'I just found out that I have cancer.' The patient got up from the bed and held the doctor" (p. 258). While one might try to prevent such a role reversal in the "real world," it was virtually unavoidable in this setting.

Disclosure to Clients

The Internet has added a new dimension to the question of appropriate boundaries (Behnke, 2007). Our patients are increasingly likely to "google" us and learn things about us outside our clinical lives that were heretofore less apparent, such as our letter to the editor of the local newspaper.

Social networking sites such as Facebook may provide a more personal and sometimes embarrassing look into our lives, and students or patients may even ask to become our "friend" on such a site. Here is a slightly edited example of a patient's dilemma:

> I started seeing my therapist about 3 months ago. At that time I googled her— I'm naturally curious and frequently google people. I saw that she has a facebook account and that kind of concerned me. I didn't at all expect her to be [on] facebook with a picture of herself. Her profile is private, but I think she probably doesn't realize that anyone can still see her list of friends, and then look at any of her friends' pages if they have public profiles. Well, I did just that. I've seen a bunch of comments that she's posted on her friends' facebook profiles and I feel horribly guilty for it. I know she has a child and is married, but that's only because it has been mentioned in some of her comments. Now I'm nervous that I'm going to accidentally reveal some information about her that I shouldn't [k]now. I feel like I want to tell her that I've looked, but I'm very afraid that she'll be angry or think I'm stalking her. On the other hand, I also think she may appreciate knowing that her information is easily accessible on facebook. I'm wondering if I've already ruined the relationship because I know too much about her. She's very careful in our sessions to not answer personal questions, so I think that this may cause her to terminate therapy. Anyone else encountered this situation? (Trident, 2008)

Obviously, the patient has no obligation to raise this issue in therapy. However, the patient's discovery has brought the proverbial elephant into the treatment room. It is hoped that a perceptive therapist may pick up a hint of some uneasiness, if not inadvertent disclosure, and address it in therapy. In any case, this is an issue that deserves more discussion over the next few years.

The issue of disclosure and of the possible value of relaxing boundaries in that regard has been discussed in some settings. For example, the Psychotherapy Committee of the Group for the Advancement of Psychiatry (2001) has recommended that the psychotherapy community explore ways in which personal disclosure may serve the therapeutic relationship, while realizing that in some circumstances it may represent an excessive level of intimacy. With the exception of unique situations such as the one in which Nielsen found herself, I feel that one should draw the line at least at disclosing one's personal problems to a client. Such disclosures tend to result in a reversal of roles as the client begins taking care of the provider.

In discussions of treatment methods for substance abuse and major mental illness, the more hands-on approach of the so-called recovery model is sometimes pitted against the authoritarian, aloof image of the medical model. For example, Ragins (2002) writes, "Although professionals are excluded from 12-step programs, most spiritual recovery programs, and even most psychosocial rehabilitation and consumer-run mental health programs, the model does not require this exclusion. What does need to be excluded, instead, are the heavily ingrained medical model traits of professional: professional distance, emotional detachment, absolute authority, strict hierarchies and guilds, invulnerability, etc." Whatever the merits of this approach, it sometimes engenders boundary dilemmas in community treatment programs, especially when some of the counselors themselves have a history of mental illness or substance abuse. The tendency to relate outside the treatment setting, lend money, give and accept gifts, and disclose personal experiences becomes more of a challenge in such environments. A few of the vignettes at the end of this chapter provide specific examples and issues for further discussion.

Addressing Boundary Dilemmas

When we are not sure how to handle a given dilemma, there are three ways we can get help. First, there may be policies or informal guidelines about dual relationships where you work—about accepting gifts, for example. Second, consult with one or more trusted colleagues about your uneasiness. Do not be embarrassed; we all face ethical dilemmas. Third, be honest with yourself. What is my motivation for crossing this boundary or not doing so? It is finding that balance between overinvolvement and an insensitive aloofness that is one of the central challenges of a professional–client relationship. We are paid and recognized for our good judgment as much as we are for our knowledge and skill.

The Importance of Self-Awareness

Probably the most effective signal that a boundary crossing is potentially problematic is the responses that a situation arouses within us. We need to be in touch with these feelings and address them honestly (Rutter, 1989).

For example, when I am with a female colleague who I find attractive, how willing am I to bring my wife into our conversation when it might be natural to do so? When I walk down a corridor and see a group of medical students coming toward me, does my eye contact focus equally on male and female students in the group? To the extent that it does not, what is the real significance of that difference? When I encounter any woman in the professional setting, to what extent do I see her as a colleague, student, or patient worthy of my respect and to what extent do I see her as a potential intimate partner, even if only in fantasy?

Bridges (1995) uses case vignettes in discussing countertransference issues with psychiatry residents. In my own teaching, I use one- or two-line open-ended descriptions of nonsexual boundary issues to stimulate thought and discussion (Plaut, 2008). For example, "Your client has just lost her job, and you are in need of a receptionist." Would you hire a client—or even a former client—as a receptionist under any circumstances? Why or why not? As you consider how you would address this situation, to what extent do age, gender, or level of attractiveness of the client enter into your considerations? If you did hire this person, what might be the possible consequences? What if she performed inadequately as an employee? How would you handle it? Considering such hypothetical situations openly and honestly can only encourage us to look at ourselves more closely and to be better prepared for issues that may actually arise in practice. I provide a number of such vignettes at the end of this chapter.

Whenever we consider actually crossing a boundary with a client, be that patient, student, or secretary, we might go through a similar thought process that I call "progressive boundary analysis." What would be the impact of this boundary crossing on the client? On our relationship? On the environment in which we work? Is it likely to lead to further boundary crossings? If so, how would I handle it? Stephen Behnke (2007), director of the Office on Ethics of the American Psychological Association, also emphasizes the value of reflection in making ethical decisions. "Central to our ethics," he says, "is considering how our actions are going to affect others."

HOW AND WHY PROFESSIONAL STANDARDS ARE DETERMINED: THE FOCUS ON SEXUAL INVOLVEMENT

Where boundaries need to be set depends on the nature of the professional–client relationship and the risk of harm when they are crossed. Just as governments set speed limits because of the risk of danger when they are exceeded on a given type of road, so each profession needs to assess for itself the risk to clients of certain kinds of professional behavior. When the State of Maryland decided in 1998 to require that all health occupation boards define sexual misconduct in their regulations, each profession was permitted to define it in its own way, following guidelines that had been recommended by a governor's task force 2 years earlier (Plaut & Nugent, 1999). The task force defined *sexual misconduct* in three ways:

1. Sexual activity in the context of a professional evaluation or procedure or other service to the client. This kind of behavior is typically seen in the medical rather than in the psychotherapeutic setting and might include such things as excessive genital stimulation during a pelvic or genital exam, draping techniques that leave the patient unnecessarily exposed, or genital exams that are not clinically justifiable.
2. Sexual activity on the pretense of therapeutic intent or benefit. Such behaviors might include asking a client to disrobe or masturbate during a psychotherapy session in the interest of "getting in touch with one's body or sexual feelings" or sponsoring nude hot tub sessions for groups of clients. A provider may sexualize the clinical setting by using humor inappropriately, often with good intent. A chiropractor whose patient could not raise his leg in a range of motion test, quipped, "Can't get it up, eh?" Such a comment might not sit well with a patient who happened to be experiencing erectile dysfunction. An acupuncturist

required all of his female patients to disrobe to their panties regardless of the procedure he was planning to do. He "justified" this behavior by embedding this practice in a consent form that all patients signed before their first appointment.

3. Sexually exploitative relationship. This comprises an ongoing intimate relationship between provider and client, perhaps of the type that would be referred to as an "affair" between truly consenting partners. However, because of the power differential and the irrelevance of consent, such relationships are typically considered exploitative by their very nature.

Those of us in the mental health professions are certainly aware of the vulnerability of many of our clients to exploitation and the tendency of sexual abusers to rationalize their behavior. Our professions have decided that the frequency of violations and risk of harm are great enough that these behaviors need to be formally proscribed. This is not a recent occurrence, although the problem had been largely ignored until the last 25 years or so. The original version of the Hippocratic oath prohibited sexual intimacies between physician and patient, "man or women, free or slave."

Some may feel that for a profession to set boundary standards denies a constitutional right to freedom of association. However, as an assistant attorney general I once worked with put it, when we accept a license to practice, we trade certain personal freedoms for the standards of our profession. In this case, those standards are based on what is likely to be either beneficial or harmful to our clients.

Because of the lasting effects of the transferential aspects of the professional relationship and the fact that a client who has terminated therapy might need to return at a later time, the mental health professions also proscribe sexual contact with clients for at least 2 years after a professional relationship has been terminated. In most cases, it is probably best to follow the standard of the psychiatry profession: "Once a patient, always a patient."

A FEW SUGGESTIONS

The most effective approach to boundary issues is not simply following "the rules." Rather, it is based on a consistent consideration of what is best for the relationship with a client and for the client's ultimate welfare. Although there generally are no specific rules except with regard to the most flagrant boundary violations, sexual intimacy in particular, much of the time boundary decisions are based on good judgment.

Given that commitment, how do we address boundary challenges on a day-to-day basis? First, we need to realize that we face boundary challenges each day of our professional lives. Most of these are subtle, such as whether to accept the gift of homemade cookies, but many are not. I offer seven suggestions for effectively addressing these challenges:

1. Make the importance of professional boundaries an open issue in your own thinking, in your relationships with colleagues, and in your teaching. Model good boundaries for your students; expect good modeling from your teachers and supervisors.

2. Know the laws, ethical standards, and local policies and practices related to professional boundaries.
3. Enter and always remain in the professional world with the mind-set that patients, students, and supervisees are not to be seen as intimate partners any more than one's own child would be seen as an intimate partner.
4. Know the personal and situational risk factors for both professionals and clients that can facilitate boundary crossings.
5. Nurture your own personal life and relationships.
6. Be aware of your inner experience. Be aware of how you perceive others in the professional environment and consider the possible consequences of boundary crossings that you may be considering.
7. Consult a colleague when ethical dilemmas arise; do not remain isolated.

CONCLUSION

Boundary violations reflect a failure of our professional responsibility, and they can cause severe consequences to the client, to us, to others in our lives, and to public trust in our professions. We better serve our public and our clients by understanding what our professional obligations are, by depending on peer or professional support when we need it, by nurturing our personal needs in our personal world, and by taking seriously the spectrum of risk factors that can lead to boundary violations. We must remember that we are trusted to operate on the precarious balance between an uncaring aloofness and a level of intimacy that can sometimes harm more than it helps.

In 1983, the commencement address at the University of Maryland, Baltimore, was given by the noted Washington attorney and then owner of the Baltimore Orioles, the late Edward Bennett Williams. After receiving his honorary degree, he gave an address about professionalism, inviting his "classmates" to join him on a crusade to preserve what he considered to be an endangered species—the CI or caring incorruptible. In two words, Williams touched on the core of professionalism: client-centered service in an atmosphere of inviolable trust. I believe that this is a worthy objective for all of us as we pursue our clinical and teaching careers.

APPENDIX: CASE VIGNETTES

These vignettes provide examples of boundary considerations that may be relevant to education and training, community treatment, and psychotherapeutic settings. You may want to supplement these with other examples that may be more relevant to your experience and current situation.

Church. A case manager at a psychosocial day program invites a member of the program (a client) to her personal church to attend a support group for people who are recently divorced. The member starts to attend the church regularly and wants to sit with the case manager and her family at the Sunday service.

Conference. A faculty member shares a hotel room with a student at a conference that the student could not otherwise afford to attend.

Disclosure. An attending physician tells one of his female fellows about the hormonal shifts of his wife in the first trimester of pregnancy, saying that she is not behaving normally or rationally.

Dress Code. A student on a clinical service wears skirts that when she sits rise to midthigh or higher or wears spaghetti strap tank tops.

Dog Sitting. A clerkship faculty instructor asks a student to babysit her dogs for the weekend while she is away at a conference.

Dying. You are a grief counselor sitting at the bedside of a dying patient, and you feel an urge to hold the patient's hand.

Facebook. A student invites a faculty member to be a friend on her Facebook page.

Gift. A patient who has been in treatment with you for 3 years brings you a piece of art for your office.

Golfing. A clerkship director invites a couple of male med students on his current rotation to play golf with him on the weekend.

Hugging. You are working with a young woman who was sexually abused. You want to hug her after each session to comfort her.

Invitation. A 17-year-old patient with whom you have worked for the past 5 years is graduating from high school. She invites you to her graduation ceremonies and to her house for a party afterward.

Parent. The mother of a child on the child psychiatry service is a single parent. A psychology intern assigned to the service asks the mother out on a date.

Perceptions. A patient on a psychiatric inpatient unit thinks that you, a psychiatric resident, spend more time with a certain other patient because you like the other patient better.

Receptionist. Your patient needs a job, and you have just lost your receptionist.

Referral. You are a faculty member in a graduate social work program. A student has been referred to you as a patient. Although you have never met this student, you are aware that this student will be taking a required course with you next year.

Ride. A faculty member consistently gives a certain student a ride to a community clinic where their weekly joint preceptorship occurs.

Sharing. You are an alcoholic in recovery, and one of your patients not only has depression but is also alcoholic. You wonder whether it would be helpful for you to tell your patient about your experience with alcohol.

ACKNOWLEDGMENT

I am indebted to Mira Brancu, Catherine D. Nugent, Judith M. Plaut, and Daniel Watter for their comments on the manuscript.

REFERENCES

American Psychological Association. (2002). *Ethical principles of psychologists and code of conduct.* Washington, DC: Author. Retrieved 8/12/09 from http://www.apa.org/ethics/code2002.pdf

Anderson, J. (1999). *A year by the sea: Thoughts of an unfinished woman.* New York: Random House.

Behnke, S. (2007). Posting on the Internet: An opportunity for self (and other) reflection. *Monitor on Psychology, 38,* 60–61. Retrieved 8/12/09 from http://www.apa.org/monitor/jan07/ethics /html

Bisbing, S. B., Jorgenson, L. M., & Sutherland, P. K. (1995). *Sexual abuse by professionals: A legal guide.* Charlottesville, VA: Michie. This is the "legal bible" of the field, covering criminal, civil, and administrative (licensing board) laws and practices. Well written by three of the leading attorneys in the field, one of whom is also a psychologist, supplements have been published periodically to update the material.

Brancu, M., & Page, L. (2008). Recognizing boundary violations as an issue of self care: A graduate student perspective. *The North Carolina Psychologist, 60*(4), 5, 12.

Bridges, N. A. (1995). Managing erotic and loving feelings in therapeutic relationships: A model course. *Journal of Psychotherapy and Practice Research, 4,* 329–339. Nancy Bridges teaches at the Harvard Medical School and the Smith School for Social Work and has developed an interactive model of teaching about professional–client boundaries that encourages students to grapple intensively with issues of countertransference. She has written a number of thoughtful, insightful articles, replete with excellent case examples.

Council on Ethical and Judicial Affairs, American Medical Association. (1998). *Code of medical ethics: Current opinions.* Chicago: Author.

Feldman-Summers, S. (1989). Sexual contact in fiduciary relationships. In G. O. Gabbard (Ed.), *Sexual exploitation in professional relationships* (pp. 193–209). Washington, DC: American Psychiatric Press. This is one of a number of chapters in the Gabbard volume, which is one of the key resources in this field. The author provides an excellent discussion of the issues of power and vulnerability in professional relationships.

Gutheil, T. G., & Gabbard, G. O. (1993). The concept of boundaries in clinical practice: Theoretical and risk management dimensions. *American Journal of Psychiatry, 150,* 188–196.

Levine, S. B. (1992). *Sexual life: A clinician's guide.* New York: Plenum Press. In his own inimitable style, Dr. Levine has given the health professions his perspectives on love, intimacy, and sexuality. He has suggested ways in which we can facilitate those critical aspects of human life in our own patients and perhaps in ourselves as well.

Liaison Committee on Medical Education. (2008, June). *Accreditation standards, MS-32.* Retrieved 8/12/09 from http://www.lcme.org/functionslist. htm#learning%20environment

National Association of Social Workers. (1993). *NASW code of ethics.* Washington, DC: Author.

Nielsen, J., with Vollers, M. (2001). *Ice bound: A doctor's incredible battle for survival at the South Pole.* New York: Hyperion.

Norris, D. M., Gutheil, T. G., & Strasburger, L. H. (2003). This couldn't happen to me: Boundary problems and sexual misconduct in the psychotherapy relationship. *Psychiatric Services, 54,* 517–522.

Peterson, M. R. (1992). *At personal risk: Boundary violations in professional relationships.* New York: Norton. While the bulk of the literature in this area focuses on psychotherapeutic relationships, this book is a comprehensive treatment of professional–client relationships that includes various kinds of professional relationships in various gender combinations. This book is still my first choice as recommended reading on professional–client boundaries.

Plaut, S. M. (1993). Boundary issues in teacher-student relationships. *Journal of Sex and Marital Therapy, 19,* 210–219. Retrieved 8/12/09 from http://www.advocateweb.org/home.php?page_id=79

Plaut, S. M. (1995). Informed consent for sex between health professional and patient or client. *Journal of Sex Education and Therapy, 21,* 129–131. Retrieved 8/12/09 from http://www.advocateweb.org/home.php_id=55. This short article was written as a tongue-in-cheek effort to capture the impact on the patient of sexual involvement with a therapist. It has probably had the greatest impact of any article written by the author in this area. The Web site from which it can be obtained is an excellent resource for articles, support groups, chat rooms, and other information about sexual exploitation by professionals.

Plaut, S. M. (2008). Sexual and nonsexual boundaries in professional relationships: Principles and teaching guidelines. *Sexual and Relationship Therapy, 23,* 85–94.

Plaut, S. M., & Nugent, C.D. (1999). The Maryland Task Force to Study Health Professional–Client Sexual Exploitation: Building understanding and facilitating change through collaboration. *Journal of Sex Education and Therapy, 24,* 236–243.

Plaut, S. M., & Wilson, M. B. (2008). How intimate can I be with my patients? *AGD Impact, 36,* 40–42. Retrieved 8/12/09 from http://www.agd.org/publications/articles/?ArtID=2699

Psychotherapy Committee of the Group for the Advancement of Psychiatry. (2001). Reexamination of therapist self-disclosure. *Psychiatric Services, 52,* 1489–1493.

Ragins, M. (2002). *Recovery with severe mental illness: Changing from a medical model to a psychosocial rehabilitation model.* Retrieved 8/12/09 from http://www.village-isa.org/Ragin's%20Papers/recov.%20with%20severe%20MI.htm

Rutter, P. (1989). *Sex in the forbidden zone.* New York: Fawcett Crest. Peter Rutter has given us two excellent books on professional–client boundaries—one focusing on sexual exploitation, the other on sexual harassment. While his Jungian approach leads him to focus almost exclusively on male as offender and female as victim (which, in fact, is the case the great majority of the time), his impassioned and well-informed discussion is compelling.

Strasburger, L. H., Jorgenson, L., & Sutherland, P. (1992). The prevention of psychotherapist sexual misconduct: Avoiding the slippery slope. *American Journal of Psychotherapy, 46,* 544–555. The authors are psychiatrists and attorneys, and their article focuses on the nonsexual aspects of professional–client relationships that tend to precede or accompany more intimate relationships between provider and client.

Trident. (2008, November 10). Therapist on facebook. Retrieved 8/16/09 from http://www.dr-bob.org/babble/psycho/20081104/msgs/862028.html

Viorst, J. (2003). *Grown-up marriage: What we know, wish we had known, and still need to know about being married.* New York: Free Press, p. 258. A lot of experience and wisdom are offered by an author who has spent much of her life and writing reflecting on the experiences of adult development. I often recommend this book to my patients who are grappling with relationship issues—and who isn't at some level?

Wertheimer A. (2003). *Consent to sexual relations.* Cambridge: Cambridge University Press.

White, W. L. (1997). *The incestuous workplace: Stress and distress in the organizational family.* Center City, MN: Hazelden Foundation. White's book, originally published in 1986, highlights the tendency for institutional systems to close themselves to outside influences, a phenomenon that is characteristic of therapists who become overinvolved with clients.

II

SEXUAL INTIMACY: HOPES AND DISAPPOINTMENTS

Three

What Patients Mean by Love, Intimacy, and Sexual Desire

STEPHEN B. LEVINE, MD

INTRODUCTION

A family is a collection of people of different genders and ages who are related by birth, marriage, adoption, or affiliation. Ordinarily family members glibly say that they love each other and plan to relate to one another throughout life. The meanings and the intensities of their love differ greatly at any given time and throughout the inevitable evolution of their relationships. Sexual love is expected in families only between the couples in each generation. Couples generally keep their sexual lives private from the rest of the family, but indirectly they remain relevant to everyone. When sexual lives become so unsatisfying that they seem to be a major factor in couples' breakups, entire families change. I want you to keep these obvious patterns in mind as you and I explore the underpinnings of sexual love: Sexual love is only part of a larger system of loves within the family. If a couple, of any orientation, spends many years together, they move through several major stages of adult sexual development. Significant relationship problems within or outside the bedroom threaten to create a premature loss of regular or satisfying sexual expression. At times, sexual love seems to us and our patients to be the most important form of love; at other times, it does not seem that significant. We are always looking for the proper perspective.

WHAT IS LOVE?

Love is not one thing. I refer to the interlocking aspects of the adult sexual love as the nine nouns of love:

1. Love is a grand, idealized, culturally reinforced *ambition*. Here are three ways of stating the ambition:
   a. To attain a lasting state of interpersonal harmony that will ensure enough contentment that the person will be able to focus on other important matters such as raising healthy children, having a good job or successful career, or enjoying life.
   b. To live a life characterized by mutual respect, behavioral reliability, enjoyment of one another, sexual pleasure and fidelity,

psychological intimacy, and a comfortable balance of individuality and couplehood.

c. To secure a partner who will accompany, assist, emotionally stabilize, and enrich us as we evolve, mature, and cope with life's demands.

The ambition of love has two faces: to be loved and to be able to love another. The strength of these ambitions should not be underestimated. They can persist for a very long time after a partner continues to disappoint. Optimism that tomorrow will be a better day sustains the ambition. Even when the love relationship has been declared a failure, the twin faces of the ambition often continue to operate. The ambition to love and to be loved is not readily exchanged for a lesser set of expectations—although sometimes the partner is exchanged.

2. Love is the label for the *arrangement* that people make with each other. Courtship is the most obvious process of making this arrangement. During it, individuals privately weigh various aspects of the other person to determine whether the relationship will prove to be a good deal over time. When it is judged to be a good one, each person begins to pledge themselves to the lofty ambitions of love. Love is then said to exist.

3. This love gives birth to a tenacious *bond*. Clinicians use the term *attachment* for this bond. Most people prefer either term to the economic or legal term *contract*. Love is nonetheless an agreed-on contract to be a couple. The terms of the contract are rarely fully spelled out. They tend to be discovered over time as two people happen on their disagreements and find that they have differing expectations for their relationship.

4. Love is a *moral commitment.* Society is deeply involved with love. Society pressures heterosexuals to ritualize the new unit through religious or secular ceremonies so that the relationship can become imbued with sacred, moral, and legal implications. The ceremonies declare the couple's mutual obligations to work hard to realize love's lofty ideals. The ceremonies, however, give few clues regarding how this work is to be accomplished or about the disappointments with which the individuals will need to cope.

5. Love is a *self-management process.* It is commonly said that love is work. The work is the private intrapsychic conscious and unconscious processes required to live up to the contractual and moral implications.

6. Love is a *force in nature* that has its way with us throughout the life cycle. It is something far larger than what is happening in individual lives. Love challenges us to abide in a supportive manner even as we grow older and care for each other in diminished states. Both the charm of new love and the caregiving of love's end processes are part of nature. This instinctual life force has always proven difficult to capture in words.

7. Love is an *ever-changing pattern of emotions* experienced with and about another person. Love is most commonly thought of publicly in terms of its extensive emotional potentials—intense suffering,

comforting stabilities, and joyful highs. The emotional aspects of love are frequently oversimplified by representing love as a unique feeling state. Love is *not* a simple feeling. Rather, at any particular moment, love is a kaleidoscopic array of feelings, including pleasure, interest, optimism, sexual desire, and devotion. Sexual love is not a universal homogeneous affective experience.

8. Love is a socially perpetuated *illusion.* The functions and processes of love are too important to us to ever be totally free of illusions. Illusions are necessary to fall in love, to be in love, and to stay in love. Denial of the illusory aspects of love prevents understanding love's richness. Love is not entirely an illusion but it also is not what we and the culture at times make it out to be. Clinicians who try to learn about a person's love relationship quickly may encounter the ninth meaning of love in the form of "don't go there!" Some details of personal love may be concealed, even though other details may be readily discussed.

9. Love is a *stop sign.* We clinicians often inquire about a person's relationship when we are baffled about why certain behaviors are tolerated. We then may discover that although our questions are reasonable and relevant to the suffering at hand, the only answer is "because I love him (her)." This phrase is a euphemism either for the unwillingness to explain the answer to the therapist or for the disinclination to personally consider the topic. This well-disguised command to stop reminds us that what we think, feel, and do in relationship to our lover or spouse are simply very private matters. Even a psychoanalyst who conducts 5-days-a-week therapy with a patient cannot expect to learn about all of the motives and considerations that have gone into creating and maintaining the patient's social circumstances.

These nine interlocking nouns of love, however illuminating, are ultimately an insufficient explanation of love. They serve to clarify that love is a continuous process of sharing some aspects of the self with another. In other words, love is a process of connection. The nine nouns of love are merely snapshots of an ever-moving process. Many key moments in this process are highly affectively stimulating. Love sometimes brings joy, sexual desire, contentment, disappointment, competitiveness, frustration, jealousy, rage, grief, helplessness, confusion, and hopelessness. While the transient positive emotions are the most celebrated aspects of love, therapists cannot afford to confuse these emotions with love itself. Fromm wrote that love was only an abstraction. He argued that only acts of love existed—that is, activities of caring for, knowing, responding, affirming, and enjoying the person.

I find these interlocking ideas to be extremely helpful in understanding temporary and chronic unhappiness that occurs in love relationships. Patients bring their relationships to us when they have evidence that they are not experiencing anything close to love's ideals. Their partners are not accompanying, assisting, emotionally stabilizing, or sufficiently enriching their lives. They have not felt much pleasure, interest, optimism, devotion, or sexual desire for their partners lately. The deal that they originally made is now perceived to have evolved into a distinctly bad one. The partner is unfair, refuses to see the world in a compatible way, and too frequently provokes profound disappointment. Cynicism about the partner and love in general is gathering because the partner is perceived as having reneged on the contract. So many negative experiences with the partner have occurred by the time they seek our assistance that they can no longer maintain the internal idealized image of their partner. Regardless of what they tell us, they may be seriously considering ending the arrangement.

Even in the face of their bitterness and disappointment, those who seek our services often clearly state that they still have love for their partner. They mean that they still feel a moral commitment to them. The bond still is there because of their promise to make it last, because they have shared these years of their lives, because they maintain hope that the partner can eventually overcome his or her deficiencies, and because, aside from the problem being brought to us, other aspects of the marriage and family functioning may be good enough. They seek help because they fear that they may one day grow to be indifferent toward their partners.

"I love him, doctor, but I am not in love with him" often means that I am still committed to him, but I have no pleasure or interest in him any longer. I view him far more realistically now. Such relationships often are described as empty. When such a couple arrives for conjoint work, the therapist is fortunate if their statement of moral commitment is sincere and they are genuinely willing to invest in an affectively powerful process that may lead to better behaviors, greater genuineness, and a change in attitude toward the partner. The therapeutic goal is to facilitate the recurrence of psychological and sexual intimacies within the union.

BECOMING A COUPLE

Falling in Love: One Person

Falling in love is a one-person intrapsychic process stimulated by some, even slight, experience with a would-be partner. These experiences generate a positive assessment of the person's social merits—attractive, employed, similar values, similar life experience, available, comparably intelligent, and so on. They stimulate a crucial act of imagination. When the person is designated as "the one," three processes appear: a sense of excitement, motivation to be with this person, and worry about being "crazy." Often, such romantic excursions are followed by disappointment, embarrassment, and self-castigation about one's foolishness. Please do not think that this process is rare or confined to adolescence.

Falling in Love: Requited Love: Being in Love

People who fall in love are often keenly aware of the need for something different in their lives. This need for psychological or social change is likely to be the predisposing factor to "falling." Others, watching them, comment on their defenses. Lovers are often privately accused of having exaggerated the capacities and minimized the limitations of their newly beloved. They are either thought to be unrealistically idealizing each other or naively not appreciating the implications of what they do see.

It is difficult to think clearly while falling because we expect love to transform us into a better person and an improved life. This hope is intoxicating. Despite the exhilaration, falling in love is accompanied by anxieties about being damaged from disappointment.

As social experiences reinforce each person's private positive assessment of the other, intimate touching begins to appear. In the uncertain, often-turbulent processes of two people ascertaining whether they are simultaneously falling in love, their willingness to behave sexually often approaches a pinnacle. Whether sexual behavior consists of slow, gradual tentative explorations of each other's bodies or quickly attained genital union, sex is wanted, rehearsed mentally, and experienced with a deliciousness that is long recalled. These early sexual pleasures enhance the sense of rightness of the union, and the couple's attachment deepens. This state is referred to as *passionate love*. Therapists need to recognize that while "passionate" conveys the sexual desire inherent in early love, what is passionately desired is to be happy, to be understood, to be in agreement about important things, and to live an exalted extraordinary life.

When lovers tell one another that they "love" each other, they are saying "I have imagined a fine life with you." The couple cannot then be together too much. The world of others tends to disappear as they privately relish the idea that they have become their newly beloved's beloved. The recognition that each has idealized the other creates the sense of *being in love*. Exhilaration predominates. They may be at their sexual pinnacle in terms of sexual motivation, frequency, and subjective pleasure. Once this has occurred, the attainment of their imagined life becomes the organizing force for much of their subsequent behavior. Their emotional intensity begins to diminish. As they begin to deal with practical matters, they more acutely notice their new partner's coping style. Many couples soon destruct over what they learn about each other in this process. When couples do not run into major dissatisfactions with what seems to be the character of the lover, the issue of commitment begins to loom. "Do we move in together? Marry?" For many people the matter of commitment introduces an anxiety that may ruin the relationship even though the pleasures of the relationship are great. The reasons for not making the commitment are often carefully guarded from the new partner.

Staying in Love

Staying in love is the product of two ongoing hidden mental activities: the assessment of the partner's character (appraisal) and the granting of cooperation (bestowal). People often erroneously assume that their partners simply and constantly love them. But, a partner notices the other's behavior, interprets it, and decides whether to behave lovingly. When "love" can be genuinely bestowed, it is typically immediately reflected in cooperation, affection, and enjoyment of the partner. The vital unseen consequence of positive appraisal and mutual bestowal is the shoring up of the idealized internal image of the beloved.

Although we do not love our partners constantly, we allow them to think that we do. They make these erroneous assumptions because we sometimes genuinely feel pleasure in their company. And when we do not, our commitment to behave in a kind, helpful fashion may carry the moment. Our idealized image of our partner enables us to act loving because we do feel loving toward the partner's image—if not to the actual partner sulking upstairs. Continuing negative appraisals, however, interfere with sensations we called love, the commitment to love, and the internal image of the partner as worthy of our affection and cooperation.

Love Exists in Privacy

Falling, being, and staying in love are phases of our internal relationship with our partners. Of course, these phases are based on transactions with them, but the transactions are mediated through the meanings that we attribute to their behaviors. Meaning making is a profoundly individual process that continually remakes our internal image of our partner.

Falling in Love Again

During an affair, after a heterosexual, gay, or lesbian breakup, after divorce or the death of a partner or spouse, a person can fall in love another time. But since time, maturation, and many life experiences have passed at this point, the previously employed illusions of falling in love may have faded away, leaving the person with a far more practical assessment of the social assets of the new partner. Unlike the first time in youth, there is little defense against thinking clearly about the question, "What will this person bring to my life—socially, economically, aesthetically, recreationally, sexually, medically, time to death, and so on?" When a patient is considering a new partner and says to you, "I'm not sure I'm in love with him [her]," this often means that I think I'm too old for the romanticism of my youth, yet I think the relationship might work out well.

MORE TERMINOLOGY

Sternberg has described six typologies of love based on how three essential characteristics are arranged:

1. *Infatuation* = passion (sexual desire) without commitment or intimacy (friendship). This corresponds to the one person falling in love.
2. *Romantic love* = passion and intimacy. This corresponds to being in love.
3. *Consummate love* = passion, intimacy, and commitment. This is culture's ideal beginning for marriage.
4. *Companionate love* = intimacy and commitment. This is the ideal picture of long-lasting love.
5. *Fatuous love* = the combination of passion and commitment without intimacy that others find perplexing, foolish, or silly.
6. *Empty love* = commitment without intimacy or passion.

The first four categories represent the usual ideal evolution of love. Companionate love eventually emerges from long-lasting consummate love, despite much hard work by couples and prosexual drugs. The timing varies from couple to couple. The fifth and sixth categories are often encountered in our patients when regular sexual behavior is expected.

A Glimpse of a Fatuous Sexual Phase

In the 6 months since I told Sharon I might be leaving, she could not talk about it. Dammit! She never could talk about her inner experience of anything. She began to want to have more sex. At first I went along with it, but because I felt so alienated from her, this became increasingly difficult. Sharon's frequent initiations began to feel pathetic to me. I soon refused, and we both knew it was over.

A Glimpse of an Empty Love

Bill: Yes, I love him, I guess, but how can I know it, how can I feel it when he is so consistently aggravating? And he expects me to have sex with him!

Jason: I know Bill loves me. So why can't he have sex with me more often? I said I was sorry!

Bill: You say you are sorry all the time, but your behavior does not change.

UNDERSTANDING SEXUAL DESIRE

Spectrum of Sexual Desire

Even during periods of stable happy relationships, sexual desire is remarkably changeable, fluctuating from intensely positive through neutral to intensely negative. In the positive range, people feel their desire in their bodies, such as when they utter sentences like "I'm so horny!" In the neutral range people grant sexual behavior primarily because of the other person's expressed desire. This is referred to as *receptivity*. Negative desires range from the prospect of sex being unappealing to the more intense, "I can't stand the thought of sex with you tonight!"

The ordinary spectrum of sexual desire looks like this:

Aversion—Indifference—Interest—Need—Passion

The ill-defined word *passion* is sometimes referred to with the poorly defined term *lust*. Whereas passion connotes the emotionally rich aspiration to restructure life through love and continued psychological intimacy, lust connotes the intensity of desire generated by high levels of sexual arousal. While both sexes experience passion and lust, women more often invoke passion, and men more often invoke lust. Either term might be used to anchor the right side of the spectrum. Ultimately, they both convey intensity.

When patients complain of a desire problem—absent, low, incompatible, or high—they tend to focus on only one location of the spectrum. Careful questioning over time usually reveals, nonetheless, that their desire moves along a spectrum. Curing their difficulty only returns them to a freer movement along the desire spectrum.

Sexual Temperament

Clinicians need a word for the strength of desire over long periods of time. We have not agreed what the word should be, but it needs to convey desire's capacity to organize a person's life. It has to communicate that desire can behave like a ferocious tiger or a secretive house cat. Here are some sentences that evoke sexual temperament:

"All 20-year-old lesbians' ids are not alike."
"After his wife became psychiatrically ill when she discovered his 5-year sexual addiction, his seemingly relentless libido all but disappeared."

"She never had much sexual energy."

"My third wife was the most sexual woman I have ever known."

The Evolution of Sexual Desire

Sexual desire evolves through the life cycle. Older people often report that they more or less reside to the left of the middle of the spectrum. Their felt episodes of desire for their long-standing partner occur less frequently and are less intense. While clinicians teach that humans are sexual beings from birth to death, we also convey that sex has different qualities among youth and older age. Youthful sex is intense, impatient, and a bit clumsy; older age sex is quieter, more skillful, perhaps more emotionally satisfying and is often biologically limited. In middle age, many people explain their decrement in desire by invoking partner familiarity or boredom. Repetition with the same partner is a factor but so is the weakening of the biology of desire. Many, but not all, men in their 50s report an increased comfort in *not* having sex as often. Many, but not all, women experience a decrement in desire within 1 to 2 years of their natural menopause. From a population perspective, the trend toward quieting of sexual desire as we move through the life cycle is biologic in origin. In any individual person's life, however, the cause may be far more interpersonal or psychological, as can be seen when a middle-aged person falls in love again and experiences a recrudescence of sexual desire.

Evolving Social Contexts

Clinicians understand sexual desire by first recognizing the relevant social context. As patients move from being unattached to becoming engaged, happily married, parents, unhappily married, having an affair, divorcing, divorced, widowed, remarried, and so on, their sexual desire often dramatically changes. When young and single, we often feel an intense desperate need to connect intimately with others as we search for an ideal life partner. As that connection is established, we celebrate it with exuberant sexual behaviors. Soon, however, despite the expectation to continue regular and frequent sexual behavior, the sexual desire of one or both members lessens. When a woman wants to get pregnant, her intense sexual motivation returns. When we want to reaffirm our love or commitment or want to convey our remorse for our past bad behavior, sexual desire may intensely reappear. When we grieve for a partner and later if no replacement is available, desire may quietly slip away.

Partner loss can also induce more motivation for sex. In the midst of bitter divorce processes, numerous men angry at their wives seek sexual behavior at a great rate with a large variety of partners, keeping secret from those partners and from themselves how much private anger at "women" they are discharging through sex. After divorce, some women worry that they have become "oversexed" because they think about sex far more than they have in many years. They have been genitally reawakened to sexual possibilities that they long felt were dead with their husbands. Some people after a relationship breakup are so devastated that they tell themselves that they never want to have sex again. Their desire for any partner fades. These phenomena are seen among heterosexual and homosexual persons.

Because sexual behavior is a means of expression that does not require words, many an embarrassing sentiment—such as, "I'm sorry," "I missed you," "I'm angry," "I want to feel like a woman"—is carried on its wings. Most of these sentiments are private from the partner, but some may not be fully known by the person. Clinicians tend to assume sexual desire may shift without the person being aware of the inciting source, but it simply may be that it shifts without the patient being willing to initially share its source with us. Either way, when we try to unravel the mystery of a desire problem, we get curious about subtle evolutionary processes from happily to unhappily married, from admiration to loss of respect, and from optimism to pessimism about love.

Gender Differences, Desire, and Politics

Sexual desire is different for men and women. Every account of sexual desire reflects the differences in patterns of males and females at any given era of the life cycle. This often-mentioned subject is not well studied. I assume there are two basic differences. The first is that males generally have more sexual desire beginning with puberty. Male desire lasts longer in the life cycle and is far more reliable. Female sexual desire, being weaker, is more easily ignored and eradicated by cultural and interpersonal forces. Sexual desire distorts women's sensibilities far less than it skews men's thinking. If androgenic compounds are the hormone system of desire, female desire is less strongly biologically supported. Normal young women have 10–15% of normal young men's testosterone levels. Women's desire fluctuates in response to the menstrual cycle, pregnancy, lactation, menopause, and fatigue. Women's desire is highly sensitive to subtle positive and negative interpersonal contexts. Each woman defines this context within her subjectivity. The second is the differences in how men and women use psychological intimacy. Women aspire to psychological intimacy as a gateway to sex. Men aspire to sex as a gateway to the sense of closeness.

Refining Desire Into Its Three Elements

Desire can be refined into its three elements: drive, motive, and values.

Drive

I think of these sex differences as primarily reflecting the biological aspects of desire. I use the term *drive* to describe the subjectively recognized moments of genitally felt, sex-motivating behavior. Sexual drive manifests itself in genital tingling, vaginal wetness, clitoral or penile tumescence, erotic fantasy, focus on physically appealing aspects of people's bodies, plotting for orgasm with a partner or through masturbation, and dreams of sexual activity. Drive generates patterns of sexual initiation and receptivity. The ease with which a person can forgo sexual expression is a manifestation of drive. Almost all biologically intact people have moments of sexual drive. Biological sexual drive occurs within a personality and a culture; these other sources can suppress the awareness of sexual drive.

Motive

While sexual desire has biological underpinnings that involve the cerebral cortex, the limbic system, and the endocrine system, all individuals must manage their drives. In doing so, they discover they have choices, emotions, aspirations, and stated and ulterior motives for bringing their bodies to the sexual experience with a particular person. Sexual motivation derives from individual psychology and interpersonal connection. We clinicians spend most of our time with patients with desire disorders trying to grasp their motivations to have and not to have sex—that is, to discern the conditions under which they would be willing to bring their body to their partner for sexual behavior.

Values

Sexual motivation is also subtly programmed by culture because culture provides guidelines for how to be a good person. These are internalized in the conscience before or during adolescence and contribute to a style of being a sexual person. How culture, subculture, school, religion, and family shape a person's willingness to know about his or her sexual self and willingness to express it to another is largely uncharted. Nonetheless, culture programs the sexual mind and becomes an important part of sexual motivation. Although sexual desire always contains biological, psychological, and cultural elements, the last two elements often arrange themselves into dilemmas or paradoxes. Chief among these are clashes between conventional pro-marriage values and impulses toward infidelity. Values also evolve over time. Adult sexual values are quite different from adolescent values. As values change, sexual behaviors can and do change. They are reflected, however, through the second component of desire—motivation.

Sexual Temperament Creates Politics

The drive endowments of the individuals within a couple are different from one another. This forces every couple to negotiate for sex. What begins as sexual temperament in individual life becomes a private political matter for every couple. The subjects of the negotiations are the management of each partner's drives and psychological intimacy needs. Many of our patients expect to negotiate with few, if any, words. We therapists need to conceptualize the possibility that inadequate negotiations play a role in generating a couple's sexual withdrawal from one another. We get to see people labeled sexually "hypoactive" or "hyperactive" whose disorder ameliorates when we help them to define and create the necessary conditions for them to conduct a regular sexual life together. The therapist has to be a politically sensitive mediator and educator.

My Definition of Sexual Desire

Sexual desire is the sum of the forces that incline us toward and away from sexual behavior.

PSYCHOLOGICAL INTIMACY

Because psychological intimacy is the key to maintenance of sexual motivation in new and established relationships, clinicians need to know what psychological intimacy is and how intimacy is generated. We actually employ our psychological intimacy skills when we quickly establish rapport with patients to assess, diagnose, and begin to offer our patients relief from their difficulties. And, since psychological intimacy enables easy negotiation with a partner for sex, we need to be able to teach others how to attain it.

The First Step
Psychological intimacy begins with one person's ability to share her or his inner experiences with another. This deceptively simple-sounding capacity actually rests on three separate abilities:

1. The capacity to know what one feels and thinks
2. The willingness to say it to another
3. The language skill to express the feelings and the ideas with words

The crucial first step is the sharing by one person of something from within the inner self. What is shared need not be elegantly said, lofty in its content, or unusual in any way; it just needs to be from the inner experience of the self—from the continual monologue of our self-consciousness, from our subjectivity.

The Second Step
The listener has to respond to the speaker in a manner that conveys the following:

1. A noncritical acceptance of what is being said
2. An awareness of the importance of the moment to the speaker
3. A grasp of what is being said
4. The interest in hearing what the speaker has to say

Clinicians need to be excellent listeners. We have our subtle variations from one professional to another, but when a professional and a patient are in conversation, it is the patient's lack of self-awareness, unwillingness to share, or inability to express what is felt that should be the only obstacles to professional intimacy. In social interactions, when a listener negatively judges what is being said by saying, "You shouldn't feel that way!" or doesn't acknowledge the significance of what is being said by impatiently remarking, "Can't this wait? Don't you see how busy I am?" or listens but misses the point of the speaker's words, intimacy will not occur.

Definition of Psychological Intimacy
Psychological intimacy is transient rarefied pleasure of emotional connection. The pleasure has at least several components. The speaker's pleasure is in large part solace—a form of peace or contentment that results from sharing the inner self, being listened to with interest, and being comprehended. Solace is the response to being seen, known, understood, and accepted. With the solace soon comes a sense of excitement and energy and an uplifting of mood. If the listener is a therapist, this combination may be stunning for the speaker because it offers hope for relief. If the listener is a social equal, it offers the hope for friendship. If the social context is dating, it offers the hope of love and sex.

The listener's pleasure results from hearing about the speaker's inner experiences. The listener is trusted enough to be told, competent enough to have enabled the telling, perceptive enough to understand the speaker's story, and wise enough to respond without censure.

If the conversation continues with the speaker speaking and the listener listening, it is one-sided, but if they switch roles, the intimacy is two-sided. One-sided psychological intimacies are common between children and their parents, patients and health care professionals, clients and lawyers or accountants, and advice seekers and clergy. Two-sided intimacies are the basis of friendships and love relationships and are the best day-in-day-out aphrodisiacs ever discovered. Within these two basic forms, there are countless degrees of self-disclosure and nuances of attention and understanding. No two intimacies are quite alike; each relationship is uniquely rich or poor in its possibilities.

The Consequences of Psychological Intimacy

The Bond, Visible and Invisible

On the way to the solace of being understood, and on the way to the pleasure and privilege of hearing another person's inner self, internal processes are stimulated. Intimate conversation creates a bond between the speaker and listener. Thereafter, each regards the other differently. The two people are together in a new way: They glance at each differently; touch each other differently; laugh together differently; and can continue to readily discuss other aspects of their private selves.

Yet more occurs. In two-sided intimacies, a mutual attachment occurs. Social indifference toward one another is lost as each is designated as special. Each listener becomes internalized within the other. Internalization weaves the listener into our psyches. This results in

1. Imagining the person when she or he is not present
2. Inventing conversations with the person
3. Preoccupation with the person's physical attributes
4. Anticipation of the next opportunity to be together—that is, missing the person
5. Dreaming about the person
6. Thoughts about that person as a sex partner

Transference Is Stimulated

Our new intimate partner is not only reacted to as a unique individual, he or she stimulates thoughts, feelings, and worries that we previously experienced in relationship to others. In one-sided psychotherapeutic intimacies, we designate this as *transference* and try to use it to help patients to understand the source of their overreactions to their partner. But, such weaving of the current and past partners is also the ordinary intrapsychic response to two-sided psychological intimacy.

The amount of time required to imagine the person as a sex partner—that is, the speed of the eroticization provoked by intimacy, is modified by age; sex; sexual orientation; social status; purpose in talking together; the nature of other emotional commitments; and the person's attitudes toward private sexual phenomena. If the pair consists of a comparably aged, socially eligible heterosexual or homosexual pair, the eroticization triggered by sharing of some aspects of their inner selves can occur with lightning speed—in both of them. The stimulation of the erotic imagination may never occur, may take a long time to occur, or may occur only in a fleeting disguised way depending on how these factors line up.

Friendships are valued because they afford an opportunity to share the self without the intrapsychic burden of eroticization. But, clinicians need to be quietly alert about friendships. The specific emotional experiences that occur as a result of intimate conversations are usually guarded with extreme care. They can be exceedingly exciting both generally and erotically. Some individuals who are new to intimate conversations may have fear about their intense responses to their new friend. They feel so excited that they wonder if they are losing their minds. The processes of a new psychological intimacy with a friend are strikingly similar to falling in love.

When people recognize that they are falling in love with a potential sexual partner, they at least have the culture's teaching to understand their general and erotic excitement. Some friendships, however, end abruptly without satisfying explanation because one person cannot tolerate the excitement it creates. In response to the private eroticization of the mutually revealing conversations, the individual may worry that the relationship is "homosexual" or could lead to sexual behavior.

Some individuals are so unnerved by their responses to psychological intimacy that they extol emotional closeness but subvert it when it is near. The again-disappointed partner hears, "I don't know why I do that." We clinicians need to act as though we know why.

Long-Term Effects

Without repetition of the solace/pleasure experience, the positive consequences of intimacy are short-lived. For two-sided psychological intimacy to fully blossom, periodic sharing of aspects of the inner self is required. There are good reasons to continue to share over time. Reattaining psychological intimacy provides a sense of security about the relationship. It calms the individuals. Intimacy allows people to be seen, known, accepted, understood, and treated with uniqueness. This is the stuff of friendship, good parenting, and of course, being and staying in love. While most friendships are not bothered by eroticization of each other, most sexual partners expect to be dear friends. Dear friendships and good lovers do some of the same things for us: They stabilize us—make us feel secure, happy, and good; they create greater stability, self-cohesion, self-esteem, and improved ego function. When psychological intimacies disappear from previously important relationships—no matter whether they involve spouses, lovers, friends, or a parent–child unit—various anxiety, depressive, or somatic symptoms may appear.

Gender and Psychological Intimacy

Women typically require more frequent psychologically intimate experiences—with each other, with children, with lovers, with husbands—than do men. They complain more often about the lack of psychological intimacy in their relationships to men. Men are more typically patterned to more autonomous operational patterns. They have trouble understanding why women complain about their lack of communicating, why they say their marriages do not contain enough intimacy. Psychologically healthy women organize their lives to a far greater degree around relationships—to friends, family, lovers, children, and spouses—than do healthy men. Women expect themselves to be relational, to gravitate to connection, and to personally evaluate their successes in terms of psychologically intimate relationships and responsiveness to other person's lives. Men tend to think of themselves as successful more often in terms of the creation of a unique self-sufficient wage-earning self. When we generalize about gender differences, we must leave room for the fact that no psychological trait is the exclusive province of either gender. Men also prosper in intimate relationships.

Relationship Between Psychological Intimacy and Sexual Intimacy

Psychological intimacy lays the groundwork for select people to become lovers. It is often the trigger to falling in love. Once a couple becomes lovers, the sexual behavior creates a further sense of knowing each other. But, it is the reattainment of psychological intimacy that enables them to make love again and again over time, to shed their inhibitions during lovemaking, and eventually to discover the limits of their sexual potential with one another.

Over time, most people find that it becomes increasingly difficult to behave sexually together without psychological intimacy. Lovers may quickly discover that sharing how one thinks and feels about a matter increases their willingness to behave sexually. Psychological intimacy, however, requires partners to set aside time to reestablish it when the sense of distance is felt by either of them. This can be a formidable problem for those who do not intuitively understand these ideas, cannot provide the requirements for speaking or listening, are chronically overwhelmed by other external demands, or who originally could manage only a meager intimacy. The sexual potential of psychological intimacy then does not get realized.

CONCLUSIONS

Specializing in sexual life has been a wonderful developmental journey for me. I began with an interest in sexual dysfunction. After a few years, I realized that without even trying I had become a relationship therapist. My clinical identity gradually shifted to an enabler of intimacy skills and teacher who helped people find the words to articulate their private dilemmas. When I began to write about love, I quickly realized that no one's contributions could be more than a modest description of this profound subject because it is the ultimate multidisciplinary topic. It needs to be reconsidered by every field in every era even though the tools of every field are insufficient for its richness.

I hope that you have found this chapter useful in organizing aspects of your personal and clinical experiences. If you immerse yourself further in this subject, I think you are likely to discover both how commonly these problems exist in your patients and how much they appreciate your interest in helping them to think about their sexual lives.

BIBLIOGRAPHY

Alberoni, F. (1983). *Falling in love: A revolutionary way of thinking about a universal experience* (L. Venuti, Trans.). New York: Random House. A charming, brief philosophical treatise about this aspired-to process (original in Italian).

Bergner, R. M. (2005). Lovemaking as a ceremony of accreditation. *Journal of Sex and Marital Therapy, 31*(5), 425–432. A clear exposition of the relationship of lovemaking to internal remaking of the self, this article explains why people love to make love in the beginning of their relationship and subsequently.

de Botton, A. (1993). *On love.* New York: Grove Press. A bibliography on love must include novels, but the sheer number of relevant works is overwhelming, so I include this short one because it is a story of the rich interpersonal and intrapsychic processes of a new relationship. Few mental health professionals can capture love in the way that some novelists can.

Fromm, E. (1954). *The art of loving: An inquiry into the nature of love.* New York: Harper and Row. Admittedly, a very old reference, but when one feels like thinking about love as an abstraction versus a pattern of behaviors, when one wants to escape the jargon de jour of science, Fromm is worth spending some time with—still.

Gottlieb, L. (2006, March). How do I love thee? *Atlantic Monthly, 297,* 58–71. Using modern neuroscience technology, the popular press in recent years has been eager to describe love as a neurochemical process that lights up the brain. *Time* magazine also covered the science of love in early February 2008.

Hatfield, E., & Rapson, R. L. (1993). *Love, sex, and intimacy: Their psychology, biology, and history.* New York: HarperCollins College. This is an erudite, award-winning book that reviews the academic understanding of these topics based on publications up to the early 1990s.

Jankowiak, W. R., & Fisher, E. F. (1992). A cross-cultural perspective on romantic love. *Ethnology, 31,* 149–155. Almost every field has studied love, but a common question about love is how its expressions and subjective experiences vary from culture to culture.

Kernberg, O. (1995). *Love relations: Normal and pathological.* New Haven, CT: Yale University Press. A classic psychoanalytic take on love that is difficult to read for most therapists early in their careers.

Levine, S. B. (2005). A reintroduction to clinical sexuality. *Focus: A journal of lifelong learning in psychiatry, 3*(4), 526–531. In this article, I describe the six phases of sexual development.

Levine, S. B. (2006). *Demystifying love: Plain talk for the mental health professional.* New York: Routledge. This book contains an elaboration of each of the three major concepts—love, desire, and intimacy—described in this chapter.

McCarthy, B. W., & McCarthy, E. (2003). *Rekindling desire: A step-by-step program to help low-sex and no-sex marriages.* New York: Brunner/Routledge. The authors provide a practical alternative discussion of sexual desire emphasizing its behavioral treatment.

Regan, P. C. (2000). Love relationships. In L. T. Szuchman & F. Muscarella (Eds.), *Psychological perspectives on human sexuality* (pp. 232–282). New York: Wiley. This is a research-oriented update based on the literature until the late 1990s.

Regan, P. C., & Atkins, L. (2006). Sex differences and similarities in frequency and intensity of sexual desire. *Social Behavior and Personality: An International Journal, 34*(1), 95–101.

Savin-Williams, R. C., & Cohen, K. M. (2004). Homoerotic development during childhood and adolescence. *Child and Adolescent Psychiatric Clinics of North America, 13*(3), 529–549. Sexual desire is a teacher. Teenagers come to form their identity from their experiences of desire.

Singer, I. (1984). *The nature of love: 2 Courtly and romantic.* Chicago: University of Chicago Press. This is one of three books by this philosopher exploring love over the ages. My ideas about appraisal and bestowal derive from Dr. Singer's perspectives.

Sternberg, R. J. (1988). Triangulating love. In R. J. Sternberg and M. L. Barnes (Eds.), *The psychology of love* (pp. 119–138). New Haven, CT: Yale University Press. Dr. Sternberg's concepts have been empirically supported. The reason they are widely quoted, however, is that they make a great deal of sense and are helpful to therapists and patients.

Sternberg, R. J., & Weis, K. (2006). *The new psychology of love.* New Haven, CT: Yale University Press. The most up-to-date compilation of diverse academic discourses on the nature of love from researchers in diverse fields and countries.

Viorst, J. (1986). Love and hate in the married state. In J. Viorst (Ed.), *Necessary losses* (pp. 185–204). New York: Free Press. I rarely find a book for laypersons that is as sophisticated and profoundly clarifying as this one.

Four

Lessons From Great Lovers

PEGGY J. KLEINPLATZ, PHD

INTRODUCTION

Over the last 25 years, I have been fascinated by the many individuals referred to me for treatment of problems of low desire. Many of them describe a gradual deterioration in frequency of sex and, on inquiry, in the quality of their sexual relations. Among the innumerable variations, one seems to worry that "it takes too long" for her to reach orgasm, another complains that maintaining erections is hit and miss, yet another finds that intercourse hurts after a while. They say that they are best friends, enjoy each other's company, and communicate well, except around sex. Many find a way of saying that sex used to seem "natural and spontaneous" but now is laborious, routine, and limited to intercourse, or that initiating sex feels like stepping onto a minefield.

Individuals and couples are typically referred to me because of some sexual disorder. Even after I complete an initial evaluation, I may still be uncertain which individual needs treatment for what pathology. While clearly there is quite a problem between these two people, there may not be any "pathology" per se. As I try to figure out what the problem is and where it lies, it often becomes obvious that the nature of their "sex" together leaves much to be desired.

I often wonder what it is that couples actually want when they complain about the sorry state of their sex lives. Two of their phrases recur: "The mystery is gone," and "There's no more passion." They share fond, wistful recollections of their early "honeymoon phase" when sex seemed effortless. Now, they are bored, disgruntled, and disappointed.

Twenty-five years ago, I began asking all clients referred for treatment of desire disorders to describe the best sexual experiences of their lives. Their answers shaped my clinical and research investigations ever since. Twenty years ago, I saw three new clients in the same week for treatment of low desire. I asked them to identify the best sex of their lives. These three individuals vividly recalled being filled with desire and extremely aroused during their high school years while they were virgins. Their tremendous excitement occurred during mutual exploration at a time before sex culminated in orgasm. Their memories made me delve more deeply into what people *do* want when they report they do not want "sex." I began to question what sex per se meant to clients. Now, I recognize that this question is profoundly relevant to mental health professionals who are asked by clients to help them get more of what they hope for in bed.

I began to focus my research on those who report having wonderful sex lives. Among others, I turned to old married people—the group most neglected by sex researchers as fonts of data—because I hoped their views might help others learn how to make sexual passion last a lifetime.

This chapter is about what I have learned about "great sex" from extraordinary, older lovers. I believe that their opinions are relevant to the readers of the *Handbook of Clinical Sexuality for Mental Health Professionals* because clients with sexual concerns are not simply seeking to reverse their sexual complaints; they often aspire to have the kind of memorable and delightful sex that really is worth wanting.

OPTIMAL SEXUALITY AND THE ELDERLY

The operating paradigm concerning sexuality in elderly populations seems to be that sexual desire decreases with age as a result of lower hormone levels, illness, medication, injury, or access to sexual partners (e.g., Nicolosi et al., 2006). The impression is that sex becomes dismal with age. The image is that long-term partnerships and optimal sexuality just do not go together; there has been little research to suggest otherwise. Some writers suggest another view. Shaw (2001) claims that there is much to be gained from studying older men and women—people who have a richness of life and sexual experiences. Zilbergeld (2004) proposed that sex can be "better than ever" as we age.

It is quite uncommon for the fields of psychology and sexology to study what is "optimal," that is, what is beyond healthy and functional, beyond positive and satisfactory, beyond good (Mahrer, 2008a, 2008b). This lack of attention to the optimal end of the continuum of sexuality is striking given the wishes of our clientele to improve their sex lives rather than only to ameliorate dysfunctions. When empirical research is absent, speculation and unrealistic expectations are likely, often with detrimental effects. Popular commercial culture is only too happy to profit from the fears of sexual inadequacy and desires for sexual thrills. Many people wonder aloud why sex seems so much more complicated than in the movies—why sex is not simple and easy. I hope our research might challenge conventional assumptions, may ultimately be used to prevent sexual problems, and of course, to help our clients move past mediocre sex toward discovering their own greater capacities for erotic intimacy (Kleinplatz, 1992, 1996a, 1996b, 2001, 2006; Ogden, 1999, 2006; Schnarch, 1991, 1997).

THE RESEARCH EFFORT

My research team set out to study those who were apt to be able to teach us about the kinds of sex so many people seem to yearn for—the stuff of our dreams. We were not interested in random or representative sampling or concerns about generalizablity; on the contrary, our goal was to discover from very special people whatever lessons they uniquely could offer. We studied a variety of experts or "key informants" (Polkinghorne, 1994), including people over 60 years of age who have been partnered (gay or straight) for at least 25 years and who self-identify as having "great sex." We recruited our samples of older individuals who self-reported having experienced great sex through announcements posted in community groups. Semistructured interviews were conducted over the telephone and were recorded with informed consent.

Sixty-seven participants were interviewed for 45 minutes to 2 hours, including 25 participants recruited on the basis of their age and experience in long-term relationships (14 men, 11 women). The average age of this smaller group was 66.6 years, with a range from 60 to 82 years (Kleinplatz, et al., 2009). Fifteen of them described themselves as able-bodied; 10 were currently experiencing physical disabilities or illness. We asked them many questions, such as those concerning what makes their sex great, how they came to experience optimal sexuality, whether they believed that one can develop the capacity to experience optimal sexual intimacy, how it changes over time, and more.

In previous research, we identified eight major components of optimal sexuality. These components were *described universally* by study participants, regardless of sex/gender, sexual orientation, lifestyle, and educational background (Kleinplatz & Ménard, 2007). We found that:

1. It was important to be completely present, focused, embodied, and utterly immersed in the experience.
2. Optimal sexuality involved a sense of connection, alignment, being in synch, merger, and loss of self with the partner.
3. Deep sexual and erotic intimacy was characterized by mutual respect, caring, genuine acceptance, and admiration.
4. Great sex involved extraordinary communication, heightened empathy, sensitivity, and a complete and total sharing of themselves verbally and nonverbally before, during, and after sexual encounters.
5. Interpersonal risk taking through exploration was viewed as fun. Sex was seen as an adventure, an ongoing exploration, a journey that required a continual push to expand sexual boundaries in a context of humor and laughter.
6. It provided a chance to be authentic, genuine, uninhibited, un-self-conscious, transparent, and totally free to be themselves with their partners.
7. Part of what made sex great was letting go, letting themselves be vulnerable, getting "swept away," reveling in the sensation, and surrendering to their partners.
8. These experiences were often characterized by a sense of transcendence, bliss, peace, awe, and the feeling of utter timelessness (and were often reminiscent of what Maslow [1971] referred to as "peak experiences"). Many found that these encounters had been transformative, growth enhancing, and healing.

LESSONS FROM THE "EXPERTS" ABOUT OPTIMAL SEXUALITY

In examining the interview transcripts of the 25 older participants, six lessons emerged and are discussed in this section.

Great Lovers Are Made—Not Born

None of the participants in this study felt that his or her facility for optimal sexuality was a natural talent that had sprung fully formed in youth. They believed that the quality of their sex lives and their perceptions of what sex could become had blossomed over time. In youth, simply having satisfying sex could seem wonderful, and perhaps later, in early to mid-adulthood, with busy careers and children at home, just finding the time to have sex together was great. However, for individuals so inclined, the heights of sexual relations could grow given time, experience, and the commitment to making sex extraordinary. Furthermore, the pinnacle—thus far—of their sexual experiences far exceeded their hopes and expectations.

Here are some of their comments:

Instead of rushing by the windows in a train, one watches the scenery.

As sex became "greater" it became slower, less goal directed and orgasm focused.

It's like, there's not a goal, and I think before one of the differences was ... it was like reaching a peak and ejaculating or something, and that was the end product, and I don't think of it that way, I think of it more as riding a wave and trying to stay on the crest as long as you can. It seems now silly to focus on the end, on an end state, on *any* end state as if that's what you've got to do. It just seems silly and counterproductive and just inconsequential [laughing] to the experience. But that's been a big change for me.

Whereas most of the participants had enjoyed sex prior to it having become "great," the difference in their minds between "good" and "great" sex and their ability to demarcate the beginnings of great sex indicated a clear and distinct improvement in their sex lives as they reached midlife.

Ironically, most stated that a prerequisite for developing the capacity to experience great sex was *unlearning* everything they had learned about sex while growing up. For example, one older man noted, "I think that we start out simply because we're conditioned, we're looking out for the answers to anything that the culture gives us, to assume that, umm ... 'Well if that gal is beautiful, uh, it's going to be great sex' and, certainly that has changed." An older woman stated, "For the first few times, I just assumed I had to lie there, and the guy would do all the work, and, and somehow I was supposed to be in ecstasy, and I learned that no, I had to be an active participant. ... And that improved things." Specifically, they emphasized the necessity of jettisoning conventional sex scripts and especially overcoming the shame with which they had been raised. Some examples included concerns about body image, performance expectations, and the idea in their youth that sex should be "natural and spontaneous," which had to be dealt with and overcome to come into their own as sexual beings. That is, to become great lovers, they had to develop new, personalized visions of sexuality and get rid of the old one-size-fits-all norms that had never actually fit at all.

With maturity came self-knowledge, a remarkable level of comfort with themselves and the willingness to confront themselves on their own values and expectations and reconsider their fears, anxieties, expectations, and other manifestations of standing in their own way. This required developing courage, daring, boldness, creativity, openness, and the freedom to take chances without worrying about making mistakes. These sexual journeys are risky precisely because they are not scripted or postured; they are real and raw. Their genuineness may be related to the focus on the present moment (see Csikszentmihalyi, 1990). There is nothing but authentic expression and emerging.

They described becoming clearer regarding what they wanted, better able to articulate and ask for it, and more skillful at negotiating. These individuals were "black belt" communicators—an acquired skill—but also made the *choice* to reveal themselves daringly and listen with rapt attention. They appeared to be comfortable seeing themselves as they truly are while in the presence of another. Sex is optimal when, as one participant stated, there is a mutual inclination to "face one another and ourselves."

Optimal Sexuality Flourishes in the Context of a Relationship Deepening With Time

In addition to the changes in the individual with maturity, optimal sexuality is always contextual and seems to thrive in ever-deepening relationships characterized by an invested sexual interest in oneself or another. Optimal sexuality flourishes during privileged, intimate moments between equal partners. The profound connection growing over time was a key to its development. The qualities of optimal sexual relations identified previously, such as being present, mutually transparent, vulnerable, safe, and respectful (Kleinplatz & Ménard, 2007), seem to blossom with commitment to one another and to sexual intimacy. "Great sex" occurred most frequently in relationships characterized by trust, consideration, respect, and most especially, open, expressive, responsive, and empathically attuned communication. As one participant noted, "I think that communication and honesty—because communication isn't always honest—but communication and honesty, uh, to me are, are the most cherished, um, incendiary ingredients to great sex." And, as an older woman noted, "I think it requires generosity and go back to the old things that I keep saying again and again, communication, openness, truthfulness, an atmosphere of trust in the relationship. I have my best sex, always, with my partner that I've been with for 40 plus years, and the fact that we have been through so much and through so many changes and have so much history makes a relationship that is just rich beyond measure." These qualities in turn invite a mutual sense of union/merging and transcendence. As one woman stated:

> It's not a technique to be a good lover. It's an involvement. It's an acceptance of ourselves and of our partners, uh, open-mindedness, ability to communicate what we really need and want and trust that the other person is willing to hang in there and understand and do it. [pause] So it's a whole relationship evolution rather than a sexual technique. And I could explain to 10 other men what my husband does that turns me on and if they did it, I don't know that I'd be turned on; I think I wouldn't.

Less Willing to Settle

With experience, many found that they were less willing to settle for anything less than what they really wanted. As one older man stated, "The older I've gotten, the more *particular* I have been in my choice of partners. … And I'm willing to make fewer compromises about what I want sexually as I get older." Another older man spoke of now insisting on sex between equals, which entailed discarding conventional gender role norms and seeking women who would be full partners with equal input in sexual relations:

In my travels, I have so often encountered *beautiful* women. I've encountered prostitutes … who are just there, and I look at these, and I say, "By God! You've got a nice-looking body … but, you know, I would *never, ever* go to bed with you!" Why? Because I could not see myself communicating with that person's mind. And if it's just a matter of release, I'm a man. I can go back to my hotel room. I can masturbate … and my urge to have sex is gone for a while. So, really great sex is between equals.

These individuals stand in marked contrast to the clients described at the outset. Many people are expecting to have high desire for whatever forms of sex are available. There is little questioning of which kinds of sex one is expected to desire. It has been a quantity-framed discourse. The reality is that those who refuse to settle are creating the foundations for only having sex worth wanting.

Great Sex Takes *a Lot* of Time, Devotion, and Intentionality

The fourth major theme was that sex of this calibre does not simply "happen" but must be welcomed and invited into one's life. In fact, it often requires considerable planning, prioritizing, being deliberate, and acting intentionally. All the participants emphasized devoting a lot of time to sex. Although with age the frequency of sex may decrease, the total amount of time dedicated to sex may actually increase. For example, an older man stated, "We'll play for 6 hours until maybe 11 at night or 12 at night." Participants would set the scene and engage the senses creatively. Another couple described building anticipation and readiness for sex by creating the optimal conditions in advance: They would spend Thursdays preparing 3 days worth of finger foods, comprised of a carefully considered grouping of carbohydrates and proteins. They liked neither the feeling of having sex on a full stomach nor getting out of bed to cook and clean dishes. Therefore, they would organize the fuel for sex in advance and have it arranged in the refrigerator by Thursday evening. This planning (their "foreplay") enabled them to play together from Friday morning, uninterrupted even by hunger except momentarily, until Sunday night. Sex therapists often speak about planning a "date night," but the level of planning and anticipation exemplified by this couple goes well beyond that. Or as another woman stated, "We choose to be together in particular ways but devote a certain amount of time without interruption to nothing but each other."

Similarly, many described the importance of creating an environment suited to the couple's sexual inclinations. The details of such an environment might vary, but the intent was invariant: "The most important thing is that it not interfere with whatever kind of sex you wanted to have that day. So, it could be quiet and private and comfortable with no interruptions for about 4 days, or it could be that the participants lose themselves in a room with other people in it or nearby. It depends what you want" (as described by an older woman). Another participant, an older man, captured not only the necessary time and space but also the intense focus on one another that calls for such planning: "She and I … almost insisted on being with one another rather than with a bunch of other people. So we would not go to parties, we would not go to restaurants, would not attend concerts, we just want to be together. That's all, just the two of us. Anywhere." Or as summarized by another older man,

"You set up your space intentionally, and you spend time within an intentional sexual arena. So, I don't think that great sex happens spontaneously."

Exploration and Familiarity Both Have Advantages

The fifth theme that emerged was that in optimal sexual relationships, both exploration and familiarity are advantageous. While the media often trumpet the need for novelty, the participants in this study belie this notion. First, when magazine headlines blare out the importance of new positions, techniques, and sex toys to keep sex exciting, they miss the more subtle type of emotional risk valued by the participants in this study. These individuals treasure the opportunity for self-exploration afforded in truly intimate relationships; this is not about trying out new activities so much as revealing one another anew and in ever-deeper ways. An older man described it as "always a dance ... with different steps," while an older woman mentioned "a frisson of newness." Trial and error and the role of continual learning are important for optimal sexual development.

Second, the role of familiarity is overlooked in all the emphasis on novelty. Together, exploration and familiarity create an atmosphere rich with "anticipated surprise." For these participants, a balance was required between discovery and trust. "It's the thing that makes me feel freest ... when I feel safe" (as stated by an older man). As described by another older man, "You've been through so many ups and downs that you know you're going to come out of it OK." Many participants noted that the lifetime of experience they shared together had created the bond and provided the trust that enabled them to "dive in" and sometimes "make mistakes" without being afraid or closing down emotionally. Or, as another participant said, "I think that exploration is one thing ... it may be with some suddenly finding a new thing, not a new thing to do with, but a new, sudden surprising moment of newness with my wife. ... 'Oh this is odd, this is unusual, this is interesting.'"

Improving one's sex life is not about novelty for its own sake and trying new positions and toys and techniques; it is about continuing to explore one another at deeper and deeper levels. The challenge is not to keep sex fresh and exciting so much as it is to penetrate more fully and to see one another anew. Or, as one participant described it, "The better we are, the more I am dazzling and dazzled by you." Love, intimacy, and the development of trust are not to be taken for granted. They are the foundation for the safety required to become increasingly naked during sex. That in turn is the raw material for erotic intimacy.

Aging, Chronic Illness, and Disability Are Not
Necessarily Obstacles to Optimal Sexuality

Among the encouraging findings here is that aging, chronic illness, and disability are not necessarily impediments to and may be assets toward optimal sexual development. Many of the participants in this investigation reported that they did not experience great sex until at least midlife or beyond. Almost all of the participants believed that sex improved with increasing age, personal growth, and maturity: "Young people are more performance oriented, and ... they're just too anxious. Older people have more understanding for what it takes. ... Sex comes with maturity. Sex becomes better and better with time" as described by an older man. If anything, the participants' conceptions of "great sex" had become increasingly demanding over time. A 67-year-old man commented, "Well, I was not as good a lover as I was 19 to 40 as I was thereafter, and I probably am a better lover today than when I was 40."

Although many of the older participants might be assessed as in poor health and had serious physical impairments, their subjective perceptions were of being able-bodied. This intriguing finding alone is worthy of further investigation. Similarly, in a society that equates youth with beauty and physical perfection, it is remarkable to hear older women who have undergone mastectomies saying that they have never felt more sexy and desirable. In any event, for those who fear aging will entail the inevitable loss of sexuality, it is heartening to discover that personal and relationship development over the course of a lifetime can help open the door to optimal sexuality.

At the outset of each interview, all participants were asked about their ability or disability status. Almost everyone self-defined as able-bodied initially. We generally did not find out until almost by happenstance in the course of the interviews that many participants were disabled, chronically ill, or had cared for and outlived partners who had been sick. Their casual comments (e.g., "Could you hold on for a moment please? I can't breathe. I'll be right back ...") first brought their medical problems to our attention. Such offhand remarks were fascinating not only because they were unexpected but also because the participants did not perceive any incongruity between their health status and the quality of their sex lives. Their medical conditions included heart disease, strokes, multiple sclerosis, epilepsy, spinal stenosis, arthritis, hearing loss, incontinence, chronic obstructive pulmonary disease, HIV/AIDS, and cancer (and treatments for them, including antihypertensive medications, anti-inflammatory medication, hysterectomies, prostatectomies, etc.).

I was struck by the contrast between the physical impediments to sexual functioning that most of us—including many sex therapists—would see on encountering such individuals and the fact that their ill health did not interfere with their capacity for optimal sexuality. Their ways of resolving this nondilemma involved their relationships, their notions about sexuality, their self-concepts, and the relationships among them: As one older man said, "With the right partner, I don't need Viagra or Cialis. Without the right partner, drugs won't help!" An older woman noted, "You can always have sex in a new form." An older man in the advanced stages of a terminal illness moved us deeply as he explained:

> Someone who looks on themselves as being somehow broken ... need not map to any kind of externally defined disability. ... It never struck me as being a defining issue in terms of sexual engagement, sexual passion. ... If there *were* a disability that restricts one's access to sexual fulfillment, I would say it was a disability of the energy or the imagination.

An older woman who had survived breast cancer spoke of never having enjoyed sexuality or her body and body image more than since her mastectomy, which had freed her to move beyond conventional ideas of sexiness. Similarly, a male participant stated, "Great sex increased my level of desire and gives me energy for all sorts of things. ... My life is better than it's ever been, even though I've never been more disabled." These kinds of comments were not the exception but rather common among these participants. Such remarks, however, may illuminate precisely the nature of the kinds of individuals who are inclined to experience optimal sexuality and to be in our study. Or, as another participant reflected, "A lot of barriers to great sex [exist] for *able-bodied people* as they hold themselves to standards that get in the way of open-mindedness and experimentation."

CLINICAL IMPLICATIONS

Disappointing Sex Lives Can Change

We can help clients to explore any feelings that might be contributing to shame as well as expectations and inhibitions that stand in the way of desire and expression of it. It is not merely a matter of discarding sex guilt but of jettisoning the entire aspirational package of paint-by-numbers sex (Kleinplatz, 1996b). Each individual's sexual desires are unique. Attempts to play out some scripted amalgam can never do justice to those who simply want to *be* more themselves, genuine, authentic, and intimately so with a trusted partner. That capacity can grow with time and experience and can make a huge difference in the quality of one's sex life.

Help Patients Redefine and Reconceptualize "Sex"

For many couples, when their sex lives begin to falter, if only out of a desire to maintain the vestiges of their sexual relationship, they attempt to go through the motions of sex without really being engaged; that is, they push themselves (and sometimes each other) to participate in whatever "foreplay" activities are absolutely necessary—or none at all—to demarcate that they have just had "sex." (This is quite noticeable in therapy when couples with sexual desire discrepancy argue about how often they have "sex" or when the last time was that they had "sex.") In heterosexual couples, the conventional sex script ensures that the ultimate end of sex is intercourse. However, it is precisely the notion that whether or not the couple has managed to complete having "sex" X number of times per month that prevents them from discussing and exploring what they might actually find more appealing and fulfilling. Sometimes, it means that you as the therapist must instruct them very specifically to reenvision sex—to spend time paying attention to what makes them feel alive and connected within and with one another during mutual caressing rather than attempting to continue some "sex act" without delight. If it does not feel great, stop. If it does feel arousing, continue, attend to and tell your partner what makes it feel so good whether or not it involves genital contact. Many couples rediscover the delights of mutual sexual exploration and a whole set of "dormant" erogenous zones only once they discard the goal of having "sex." Or to put it another way, there are disadvantages to choosing the most expedient route to tension release, orgasm, and intercourse: It may leave each individual with the sense of being in the hands of an expert at producing a predictable orgasm while being left with the feeling of being untouched (Kleinplatz, 1996b). Or, as one of our participants put it, she had finally given up on having sex with a man who knew how to play her "like a pinball machine" in favor of a partner with whom she could savor erotic delight.

Encourage Clients to Say "No" to Sex Unless They Are Full of Desire

When couples try just to slog their way through sex because they ought to, or they are aware that too much time has elapsed since the last time, or the partner is sure to get grouchy if they do not have some sex soon, the quality of the sex will likely be miserable. They might be able to get away with doing the other "a favor" every once in a while in a sexual relationship that is otherwise of very high calibre. However, sooner or later, if merely pleasing the partner—or even worse, trying to avoid upsetting the partner—becomes the predominant motive, the body will not lie. Healthy individuals who engage in sex without desire on a regular basis will encounter difficulties with arousal that are normal in that context and to be expected. So, when his erection begins to falter in the middle of intercourse or her vagina is sore afterward, it may be that they were just (barely) aroused enough to begin intercourse but not aroused enough to really enjoy it (Kleinplatz, 2006). More important, somewhere inside they knew it, and because they did not articulate either the reluctance or the desire to be more turned on before proceeding further, their bodies spoke for them.

Let patients know that such "symptoms" are not necessarily indicative of dysfunctions requiring treatment so much as signposts saying, "Be careful. Pay attention. What is it that you really want? What changes do you need to make so that sex between you is worth wanting?" Clients will need to articulate explicitly just what sorts of stimulation—physical, intellectual, emotional, or erotic—they are silently hoping for from their partners. If patients can tolerate waiting for sex until the conditions are met to be filled with desire, their bodies will often take care of themselves, and when they do not, couples are often having too much fun to notice or care.

Let Patients Know That Attention to Emotional Intimacy Is Essential for High-Quality Sex

Sometimes, it seems so obvious that we forget to emphasize it, but passion will not continue to blossom outside the context of individuals who continue to value each other and put energy into intimacy. Trust, most especially, needs to be cultivated in an atmosphere of emotional accessibility and goodwill. It is not as though the couples in this study did not struggle; the point is that they chose to remain emotionally available even when that was somewhat scary in the hope that the resulting vulnerability would be cherished as a gift. It is not that they did not argue, whether about sex or otherwise, but that they trusted each other enough to stay present even when that required them to expand their comfort zones. They chose to communicate about their desires, even when they differed, with a precision and a transparency that we would all do well to emulate. This meant going beyond the ordinary communication skills of paraphrasing and validating to awareness of subtleties in meaning and nuances of nonverbal communication, especially in touch, that far exceeds the skills of most therapists (Mahrer, Boulet, & Fairweather, 1994). Or, as an older woman noted, "People I think who are great in bed seem to have an almost uncanny ability not only to hear what's said but what isn't said." We will have much to learn by studying such expert communicators (Kleinplatz & Ménard, 2007). Ultimately, the goal of working with sexual problems in therapy is not to manage the problem but to make the space—and the relationship—just safe enough for the couple to take interpersonal and erotic risks together.

Do Not Downplay Disappointment: Help Patients Aim for Sex Worth Wanting

Clients who have sexual problems often enter our offices feeling defective and in need of repair; the irony is that their lack of arousal and lack of desire are indicators of psychosexual health. That is, their low desire is for lousy sex. As therapists, we could attempt to normalize the decreasing frequency of their sexual activities in a long-term relationship. In fact, this is what too many therapists already do. The alternative entails learning from extraordinary lovers and acknowledging that the quality of their sexual encounters is, at best, lackluster. According to McCarthy and McCarthy (2003), disappointment with sex is among the most common causes of low desire. Do not advise clients to adapt by lowering their expectations. Acknowledge aloud, "If I had the kind of sex you've been having, I wouldn't want it either." This should be among the first steps of therapy. The reason clients are so miserable is because they have an inkling from somewhere deep within or—for the lucky ones—some memories of what they really want.

You can help them to tune in to these vague and unspoken wishes by asking them to recall their three favorite sexual memories. If the partner is present in the room, you can preface this request by saying that you will not be asking the clients to spell out the content of their recollections but merely to note aloud when they have located them. (After all, the memories may not involve the current partner.) Sometimes, clients will have difficulty identifying memories, in which case you can ask them to locate instead their three favorite sexual fantasies. Once both partners have identified three fantasies or memories and have jotted down separately three markers for them, ask them to think about what these three images have in common and what they might reveal. What is distinctive about the sex of their dreams? What would it take to make these dreams a reality? What obstacles stand in the way of living their dreams, and how could these be overcome? The tone of this part of the session should be fanciful, playful, and wistful rather than in problem-solving mode. The spirit should be of enthusiastic discovery rather than searching for "correct" answers. Let your clients dare to dream so that they never feel tempted to settle again.

Forget "Natural and Spontaneous": Teach Clients That Sex Worth Wanting Is Worth the Effort

Although couples often reminisce about the stage at which every time they saw each other, they quickly fell into each other's arms and into bed with no forethought, the reality was probably a bit more complex. When two people live apart and are dating, they discount—and later forget—the extra time they took after work or school and before meeting to prepare for the night ahead and make sure that everything was just so. That meant taking off their grungy work clothes and the graying underwear with loose elastics, then showering, shaving, brushing their teeth, choosing something appealing to wear, dabbing on some cologne or perfume, straightening up the apartment, having some music or candles or wine ready, and so on. By the time the date "began," there had actually been considerable preparation mentally, physically, and in whatever way would be conducive to engaging the senses for the possibility of sex play. Then, once the two would meet, it would *seem* as if the sex that ensued was magically effortless.

If couples want to recapture or go beyond the calibre of sex they recall from courtship days, they will need to expend at least as much energy as they did once to making their wishes a reality. It should not feel like work, but it surely will require devotion.

On the basis of this study, it is not clear if all people are capable of optimal sexuality or would even wish to experience it; however, it is clear that among those who now live it, the capacity for optimal sexuality was acquired and developed rather deliberately, thus allowing for the prospect that others who might value optimal sexuality could also cultivate the ability.

To experience optimal sexuality, at least on a semiregular basis rather than merely once or twice, by happenstance, it was helpful to engage in a series of steps to increase the likelihood that it would occur as follows:

Desire → Intention → Practice → Develop ability

First, one must want to attain this experience. It is the desire to make it happen, the feeling that it really matters, that leads to the next subtle step, which is the intention to make it a reality (Mahrer, 2008a). Wonderful sex might occur by stroke of luck on some rare and extraordinary occasions, but for it to become a regular feature of one's life, one had to want it or want more of it. Some people are exquisite chefs, and the minute you see, smell and taste their cooking, you know you are in for a treat. It is the serious aspiration that first distinguishes the hobby gardener from the creative, Japanese gardener. One can sense it in the precision they bring to bear on their chosen focus. Similarly, there are those who will focus all their attention on just how to meet fully in the flesh in the moment.

Second, those who intended to make memorable sex a reality made sex a priority. They devoted time and energy to creating the right circumstances, making themselves physically and emotionally available, seeking out the right partners, choosing to make their wishes known, and so on. Third, they practiced the required skills even though this entailed making mistakes within view of their partners. They taught themselves to become more open, attuned, and sensitive so that they could be absorbed with the partner in the moment. There is no guarantee that this sequence will necessarily lead to optimal sexuality—as we were reminded occasionally and poignantly by widows and widowers—but that it is unlikely that optimal sexuality will become a reality without notable efforts.

The objective here is in no way to suggest that all people *ought* to strive for extraordinary sexuality but only to acknowledge that those who have attained it had set out to do so and devoted substantial resources and development of skills to make it happen. They did not start out as "erotic geniuses" but chose to commit their energies in this particular direction.

Sexual Functioning and Optimal Sexuality Are Very Different Phenomena

Participants seemed quite dumbfounded when we asked about the role of sexual acts and activities in optimal sexuality, as if they were incredulous at the irrelevance of the question. This suggested to us that although sexual functioning is expected for ordinary sexual activity, it is neither necessary nor sufficient for extraordinary sex. That is at least, in part, because it is not sexual "acts" that make for optimal sexuality. I now encourage some patients to explore new ways of experiencing sexuality unconstrained by traditional definitions of sex itself. Their new, broadened range of meanings will surely be to their advantage in sexual expression as they grow older in the face of diminishing physical capacities (Kaufman, Silverberg, & Odette, 2007).

Clients will need to let go of the idea that having healthy, functioning genitals are the be-all and end-all of sex. The key to fulfilling sex is in being present so fully that the body will take care of itself. Masters and Johnson's (1970) initial insight about the role of spectatoring (i.e., watching one's body perform as if from a distance, from the bleachers) was on point. To the extent that clients are worrying about the mechanics of their genitals, sex will not be worth wanting. Masters and Johnson's sensate focus exercises were designed to take the pressure off of the poor genitals. However, we can go even further. We can help clients to be so fully engaged with one another not only at the level of physical stimulation but by encouraging them to continue exploring one another emotionally and erotically that sex cannot help but be exciting.

Some couples end up revising their sexuality when they are forced into it; however, for those who choose to rewrite their sex scripts freely, being true to themselves and authentic with one another, embodied within and engaged with one another, the benefits may well be unlimited.

CONCLUSIONS

We have good news for the physically limited and sexually dysfunctional: Full sexual functionality is not *necessary* for optimal sexuality. There is bad news for the physically healthy: Full sexual functionality is not *sufficient* for wonderful sex.

People of any age who aspire to high levels of sexual fulfillment should guard against falling into the trap of making love as the world seems to dictate. They must let go of conventional sex scripts by expanding their conceptions of sex to what they really want. Clinicians need to understand this idea to guide their clients.

We want to help clients to pay much more attention to the *quality* than the frequency of sexual encounters. We need to convey that optimal sexuality requires both intentionality and abandon—that is, one needs to plan for it, make time for it, and make oneself emotionally available for it. In this way, the person becomes free to be swept away by it.

I hope these ideas have tempted you to think about the *possibilities* for you and your patients. Please consider your clients' sexual difficulties to be an invitation to explore these possibilities. The epitome of sexual intimacy entails being free, brave, and trusting enough to venture into the unknown with a partner. It is an ongoing journey of mutual exploration, of being naked physically and emotionally together. We therapists can support clients to expand their sexual boundaries and facilitate these adventures in trust.

ACKNOWLEDGMENT

I would like to acknowledge and thank the following members of the Optimal Sexuality Research Team of the University of Ottawa, A. Dana Ménard, Nicolas Paradis, Meghan Campbell, and Tracy Dalgleish, for their invaluable contributions to the research underlying this chapter, collecting, analyzing, and making sense of the interview data, and for their reviews of previous drafts of this chapter.

REFERENCES

Csikszentmihalyi, M. (1990). *Flow: The psychology of optimal experience.* New York: HarperPerennial. This book is a comprehensive introduction to the author's concept of "flow," a form of optimal experience in which an individual is so absorbed in an activity that nothing else seems to matter. The eight major components of flow are enumerated and described in detail. The ability to find flow within a variety of activities (from work to sports) is described from the perspectives of interview participants who have experienced it.

Kaufman, M., Silverberg, C., & Odette, F. (2007). *The ultimate guide to sex and disability.* San Francisco: Cleis Press. A valuable resource for individuals or clinicians seeking an introduction to the field of sexuality and disability. The authors address a wide range of disabilities (from spinal cord injuries to ileostomies) and sex acts of all kinds. It is refreshing to see authors in this area take such a sex-positive stance toward disability and emphasize pleasure and possibilities.

Kleinplatz, P. J. (1992). The erotic experience and the intent to arouse. *Canadian Journal of Human Sexuality, 1*(3), 133–139.

Kleinplatz, P. J. (1996a). The erotic encounter. *Journal of Humanistic Psychology, 36*(3), 105–123. I outline my theory that eroticism is the missing component in unsatisfying sexual encounters, the factor that makes "sex sexy." I define eroticism as the intent between partners to contact and arouse one another, deliberately heightening pleasure and arousal for its own sake. This reference would be of particular interest to clinicians seeing clients presenting with low desire.

Kleinplatz, P. J. (1996b). Transforming sex therapy: Integrating erotic potential. *The Humanistic Psychologist, 24*(2), 190–202.

Kleinplatz, P. J. (2001). A critique of the goals of sex therapy or the hazards of safer sex. In P. J. Kleinplatz (Ed.), *New directions in sex therapy: Innovations and alternatives* (pp. 109–131). Philadelphia: Brunner-Routledge.

Kleinplatz, P. J. (2006). Learning from extraordinary lovers: Lessons from the edge. *Journal of Homosexuality, 50*(3/4), 325–348. I outline 10 lessons gleaned from SM practitioners who attained extraordinary sexual relations through their activities, even though in many cases their relationships would be pathologized. This reference would be of special value to sex therapists given that these lessons advocate going far beyond the conventional approach of ameliorating dysfunction to reach deeper levels of erotic intimacy.

Kleinplatz, P. J., & Ménard, A. D. (2007). Building blocks towards optimal sexuality: Constructing a conceptual model. *The Family Journal: Counseling and Therapy for Couples and Families, 15*(1), 72–78. We outline the first six components of optimal sexuality based on analysis of interviews with key informants. These components include being present, intense connection, deep intimacy, communication, authenticity, and transcendence. Clinical implications of the findings are discussed.

Kleinplatz, P. J., Ménard, A. D., Paradis, N., Campbell, M., Dalgliesh, T., Segovia, A., et al. (2009). From closet to reality: Optimal sexuality among the elderly. *The Irish Psychiatrist, 10*(11), 15–18.

Mahrer, A. R. (2008a). *The manual of optimal behaviors.* Montreal: Gontovnick.

Mahrer, A. R. (2008b). *The optimal person.* Montreal: Gontovnick. Mahrer describes his model of optimal personality and behaviors. He explains how optimal ways of being are beyond "positive" or "healthy" but yet are attainable for those so inclined. He details how individuals can become more optimal and more of what they are capable of being and becoming. This is a companion book to *The Manual of Optimal Behaviors* (Mahrer, 2008a).

Mahrer, A. R., Boulet, D., & Fairweather, D. (1994). Beyond empathy: Advances in the clinical theory and methods of empathy. *Clinical Psychology Review, 14*(3), 183–198.

Maslow, A. H. (1971). *On the farther reaches of human nature.* New York: Viking Press.

Masters, W. H., & Johnson, V. E. (1970). *Human sexual inadequacy.* Boston: Little/Brown.

McCarthy, B., & McCarthy, E. (2003). *Rekindling desire: A step-by-step program to help low-sex and no-sex marriages.* New York: Brunner-Routledge.

Nicolosi, A., Laumann, E. O., Glasser, D. B., Brock, G., King, R., & Gingell, C. (2006). Sexual activity, sexual disorders and associated help-seeking behavior among mature adults in five Anglophone countries from the Global Survey of Sexual Attitudes and Behaviors (GSSAB). *Journal of Sex and Marital Therapy, 32*(4), 331–342.

Ogden, G. (1999). *Women who love sex: An inquiry into the expanding spirit of women's erotic experience.* Cambridge, MA: Womanspirit.

Ogden, G. (2006). *The heart and soul of sex: Making the ISIS connection.* Boston: Trumpeter.

Polkinghorne, D. E. (1994). Research methodology in humanistic psychology. In F. Wertz (Ed.), *The humanistic movement: Recovering the person in psychology* (pp. 105–128). Lake Forth, FL: Gardner.

Schnarch, D. (1991). *Constructing the sexual crucible: An integration of sexual and marital therapy.* New York: Norton. This book describes sexual intimacy as a developmental task of adulthood. Schnarch approaches sex and marital therapy from a family systems (specifically Bowenian) perspective. The author regards sexual problems as opening the window for therapists to see the underlying and systemic problems for the individual and couple to use if they wish to grow in relationship.

Schnarch, D. (1997). *Passionate marriage: Love, sex, and intimacy in emotionally committed relationships.* New York: Wiley.

Shaw, J. (2001). Approaching sexual potential in relationship: A reward of age and maturity. In P. J. Kleinplatz (Ed.), *New directions in sex therapy: Innovations and alternatives* (pp. 185–209). Philadelphia: Brunner-Routledge. The author describes what she has learned from interviews conducted with 65 older couples. She advocates the importance of personal differentiation and maturity as the gateway to sexual actualization. Recommendations are made for therapists regarding the characteristics of sexual potential.

Zilbergeld, B. (2004). *Better than ever: Love and sex at midlife*. Norwalk, CT: Crown House. This book is based on interviews Zilbergeld conducted with older couples and on his clinical work. In the first section, myths about sex and aging are outlined and refuted; the suggestion is made instead that one of the rewards of old age might be wonderful sex. In the second section, "lovers" (those who have great relationships and sex) and "nonlovers" are compared and contrasted with regard to individual and relational characteristics to illustrate the elements necessary for sex that is better than ever.

Five

How Development Structures Relationships

DAVID E. SCHARFF, MD

INTRODUCTION

I first came to see the importance of the crises and transitions that restructure each life when, thrown into a particular life crisis of my own, I read "Death and the Mid-Life Crisis" by Elliott Jacques (1965). He documented the changes that occurred in the organization of the middle of life of many creative figures. Jacques revealed the major shifts in their art. Shakespeare moved from comedy to tragedy. Some stopped writing or painting. Some, like Gauguin, only began painting then; some ended their lives, as did van Gogh. Jacques broadened my understanding of development. Before Jacques, I had been accustomed to only thinking of the development of children. This is not surprising because I trained as a child psychiatrist. I now saw that development did not stop after adolescence, getting married, or even until death.

These periods of transition are the ordinary stuff of life, shifts that mark life's inconspicuous continual growth. These periods also reflect the fact that we all have a reservoir of creativity that enables us to take what we are up to at a certain point and reinvent ourselves. We retain this creative developmental potential to change how we live all of our lives (Scarf, 1987; Viorst, 1986). These occurrences of discontinuous development offer fascinating stories. Studying how they work has enhanced my understanding of patients of all ages—from birth to old age—whether I was doing psychotherapy, psychoanalysis, or family, couple, or sex therapy. People's overt difficulties always intertwine with their development. More recently, as I am aging, my attention has been drawn to the idea of a late-life crisis. Older people need to find new organizations that fit with their new capacities, incapacities, relationships, and opportunities.

The idea I would most like you to learn in this chapter is the relevance of developmental processes throughout the life cycle for each of your patients. If I am successful as your teacher, I will have helped you to find what is most important to a patient at a particular stage of life. Patients seek our help at vulnerable points in their lives; these are typically at transition points. Even though your patients who present with sexual difficulties may act as though sex is unrelated to other aspects of their lives and their current development, please remain skeptical.

MATURATIONAL REORGANIZATION

Freud and his followers thought the oedipal reorganization, not only of sexual aims but more importantly of the mind, began about age 3 and lasted until about 6 years of age. For Freud, this was the first time that awareness of relationships moved to the center of consciousness for children. He believed that this oedipal period formed the foundation for the structuring organization of mind, setting the stage for all that followed. Freud did not emphasize the continual reorganizations of mental and emotional process throughout life; he and his early followers were preoccupied with the ones that relatively rapidly occurred through the end of adolescence.

At whatever age they occur, periods of maturational reorganization are periods of discontinuity. They show great variance and are not precisely predictable ahead of time because they are determined by both individual differences and the crucial influence of external events. Nevertheless, they form a rough map of development that serves to orient assessment and treatment planning for individuals and couples with sexual difficulty. I discuss sexual development within the life cycle in this chapter. I highlight life events that influence and structure relationships within the family. Developmental discontinuities present vulnerabilities that are expressed in sexual symptoms at various stages. Such developmental shifts have been ignored by many specialists in sexual health. But, when we therapists create a map of each patient's or couple's life course, we often can locate the meaning of a difficulty or symptom within the narrative of their life course. Seeing the sexual symptom as the product of development and personal narrative helps patients to get better.

Early Life Parental Attachment

Recent work on development has helped us to understand with more precision how the earliest relationships between children and parents form a developmental foundation for all that follows (Bowlby, 1969, 1973, 1980; Fairbairn, 1952; Scharff & Scharff, 2006). Fonagy, Gergely, Jurist, and Target (2002) argued that, from the standpoint of psychological health, the earliest attachment to parents promotes children's mental development, especially their capacity to understand the workings of other people's minds. Our minds are formed in the crucible of relationships, and minds free from excessive anxiety and fear develop to create healthier relationships. Trauma and marked neglect, on the other hand, constrict both brain growth and the richness of interpersonal understanding. It is not hard to see that someone who grew up in unreliable or abusive parental relationships will later interpret sexual signals as dangerous rather than as safe and inviting. So, the quality of the early attachment relationship has direct relevance both to general emotional maturity and to the sense of safety in relating that is needed for full intimate and sexual expression (Clulow, 2001).

Each of us carries a template for attachments throughout life. Recent work has shown that an adult's attachment style can be classified in ways comparable to those of children. It has also been established that an adult's attachment style and security are predictive of the attachment bond they will establish with their children. On the other hand, despite the lasting quality of early parental attachment, having new healthy relationships as might occur in a good marriage or psychotherapy can help people achieve an "earned secure attachment" to replace their previously insecure or disorganized styles.

Sexuality

These issues from children's early development are relevant to the sexually active adolescent or adult because sexual interaction and vulnerability are embedded in relationships. Even solo masturbation is centered on internal aspects of relating. The template for attachment patterns formed in the early years is the model each person carries when forming primary emotional relationships in later years. If a woman is capable of secure relating, she is off to a good start, even if she has some specific difficulty with sexual functioning. Ideally, she enjoys relationships, picks partners who are securely attached, and enjoys sex without feeling that she is unreasonably obligated to provide it to her partner. On the other hand, if a woman has an anxious or wary attachment pattern going into a sexual relationship, that long-standing pattern tends to undermine her capacity for sexual relating. She may feel that she cannot rely on the relationship, so she had better be sexually available to hang on to a partner. This way of using sex may leave her feeling exploited, resentful that she has to be sexual with her partners in violation of her own wishes. People with a severely dismissive attachment style may only be able to have sex with a partner to whom they have no emotional attachment. Those who carry the template of a disorganized, fearful attachment need to check constantly on the other person for safety. They may feel particularly vulnerable during sex with a partner, and their behavior may be quite unpredictable to themselves. Their partners may experience them as suspicious, frightened, untrusting, and unpredictably rejecting, never suspecting how much they fear for their own existence.

Adolescents often develop sexual interest slowly, at first using masturbation to try out their sexual feelings and later talking with same-sex peers with less sense of threat than when confronting possible sexual partners. They often move with peers in groups of several teens, protected against premature intimacy. But some young adolescents, or even preteens, rush headlong into sexual relationships and then feel trapped by the resulting intense intimacy and heightened feeling. If they feel that sex is the only intense feeling of which they are capable, they may substitute sex for intimacy.

Susan, 15 years old, was interested in boys but also frightened. Coming from a disorganized family, she looked to peers for a stability she lacked. She recklessly threw herself at boys without thinking. When two boys used her roughly sexually and then spurned her, she turned to an older girl for comfort. When Susan was 17, this motherly girl persuaded Susan that boys were all like that, and that Susan would be safer as a lesbian. Susan surrendered to an active homosexual pattern. Only later did she question the basis for her decision to become lesbian and began to notice that not all boys were exploitative.

When Does Sexual Symptomatology Develop?

Sexual symptoms are signs that a person has internalized relationships in a way that presents sexual behaviors as a solution to problems in relating. A number of factors predispose children, adolescents, and adults to develop sexual symptoms (Scharff, 1982/1998).

1. Disruptions to safety or health during periods in which sex is a major way of handling things: the period of infantile masturbation, the

oedipal period, or the normal period of adolescent sexualization of development.

2. Families who sexualize too many processes. For some families, everything is sexual, beginning with the first identification of the genitals at birth. These parents talk about sex and flaunt sexual life. These families predispose to later sexual symptomatic patterns.

3. Families who strongly suppress sexuality. In these families, nothing is recognized as sexual: Oedipal sexualization is unrecognized and denied, for instance. Families who suppress sexuality tend to produce young adult children for whom sex is denied, feared, and avoided.

4. In some love-starved families, parents look to their children for love. A parent may say openly that the child gives what the spouse denies. The ensuing excitement can sexualize children's growth and, at the extreme, lead to incest, but even without incest, it may contribute to premature sexualization of adolescent relationships.

5. Sexual abuse carries this tendency to a disastrous extreme. The invasion of children's body by a parent is fundamentally a sexual invasion of the mind. The result skews development to varying degrees, depending on how closely related the abuser is and the amount of support the child gets in dealing with the abuse. The sequelae vary, from serious disruptions of total personality like multiple personality, to sexualization of all development, or to phobic avoidance of genital sex or all personal intimacy (Scharff & Scharff, 1994/2008).

6. Trauma to a child's parent, even when not directly communicated to the child, can still influence development through unconscious communication. *Projective identification* refers to the way a part of a parent's mind is unconsciously communicated to the child when a parent cannot tolerate or contain personal anxieties. This is done through overt and covert expressions of anxiety and fear and overprotectiveness (Scharff & Scharff, 1991; 1994/2008; 2006). When parents have suffered physical or emotional trauma, such as the overwhelming trauma of a parent's own sexual abuse or the horrors of the Holocaust, they often communicate the anxieties of their horror to their children, who then build their minds around the expectation of trauma.

Freda came to see me because of persistent pelvic pain. Her gynecologist could find no organic cause. She knew that her parents had been negligent, but only in therapy did she discover that she had been invited into their bed from the age of 3 to watch intercourse. Later, she remembered her father had forced fellatio and intercourse on her at least as early as the age of 8. At 14, he stopped when she threatened to kill herself. When she married, she "wasn't there" during sex with her husband, just as she had psychologically removed herself from her body through dissociation when her father forced himself on her. Her childhood dissociation led to her adult dissociative mechanism and her sexual symptom.

Freda's children grew up avoiding their maternal grandfather, whom they thought was "a lecher." They were without symptoms themselves until Freda's 15-year-old son, Tom, hooked up with a disturbed, traumatized girl, who began to threaten him with suicide unless he agreed to have a baby with her. The whole family got involved in caring for this desperate girl until a family session uncovered the way that Tom was unconsciously trying to repair the damage done to Freda through taking care of his girlfriend.

That realization set the family free of the spell cast by the girl, whom they persuaded instead to get personal individual psychotherapy.

Freda had communicated her anxiety about sexuality as a traumatic factor to her children through her inability to discuss her father's seductiveness despite her obvious distress whenever he was around. Her wordless state of tension communicated her heightened anxiety (that is, it got into them through unconscious projective identification) that put them on guard but without the words that would have enabled them to understand why she was constantly on guard against her father. Then, Tom undertook to guard another female against sexual trauma but in a roundabout way that would have exposed him to another trauma. Verbalizing the trauma to Freda freed the family for appropriate action.

Adult Developmental Transitions

Development continues into adulthood and includes decisions about marriage, having children, marital separation, marital affairs, and divorce. The ticking of the clock is always a part of these developments. Either marriage or pairing with a mate of the opposite or same sex happens, or life is channeled to a significant degree by the fact that it does not happen. So an individual either chooses to live outside a committed partnership or does so by the default of being unable or unwilling to marry. Having or not having children introduces the same dilemma: Either you do it or your life is partly defined by the fact that you did not.

Mate Selection

The choice to get married (or partnered) shapes each person's life in significant ways, although the patterns of married and partnered life are now widely varied. Each of us carries within our psyche a composite image of an "internal couple," of what couples are like: loving couples, warring couples, the couple as parents, sexual couples, divorced couples. The internal couple plays a significant role in orienting each person during mate selection and the trying-out period of courtship or living together that tests compatibility for relationships.

Michelle and Lenny came to see a cotherapist and me with a strange complaint. Michelle said, "He wants to get married, and I want to break up. So, we should do something about that. Can you give us something? A pill maybe?"

"Would it be to break up or to stay together?" my cotherapist asked.
"To break up," said Michelle. "I don't want to stay with him, even though he did ask me to marry him and gave me a diamond ring. I had to try it on. It was so beautiful! But I had to give it back."

Michelle and Lenny had a teasing, emotionally perverse relationship in which he clung to her like an infant with a cruel mother, while she taunted him mercilessly. They did offer something positive to each other.

Lenny said, "I'm the rock in the river for Michelle, there for her while she runs up and down stream."
Michelle said, "He's immovable. I have to light a fire under his tush, or he won't move."

For Lenny, being the rock meant providing the stability and durability Michelle did not have, while she provided the liveliness and vitality he feared that he lacked. Although Michelle hated Lenny's immovability, she secretly leaned on him for the stability that shored up her shaky self-esteem.

People unconsciously seek mates to make up for deficiencies in their selves and to repair bad things that have happened to them. When their lives have been good, they seek a mate with whom to continue what has been good and loving. In seeking partners, we all generally want someone to support us, and we want someone through whom we can find meaning by giving. At the same time we want someone to give to us, we also need someone to help us find goodness in ourselves by accepting what we offer. At another level, we look partly for someone like ourselves, who shares our values and interests as well as our unconscious issues, and we look for someone to provide aspects of ourselves that have been lost to us or about which we feel deficient. Then through projective identification, we hope to find in our mates and partners help for the parts of ourselves that feel bad or weak. Michelle could not bring herself to break up with Lenny because he was a convenient receptacle for the badness she unconsciously felt in herself and because when he offered to suffer her recriminations and insults, he somehow knew that he was doing her a service. He said, "I grew up learning that men could be terrible to women, and I vowed that I would make up for that." When he offered to be "the rock in the river," he felt good about the way he made her feel better, and while he found a vitality in her that he felt he lacked, he also felt an increase in his self-esteem by standing by her.

Commitment and Marriage

Sexuality plays a central role in adult partnering, carrying the physical aspect of emotional intimacy and playing a continuing role in renewal of that intimacy over the long haul (Scharff, 1982/1998). But, I have found that among couples that seek our help, a funny thing has often happened at the altar or at the moment of commitment, which is no longer necessarily simultaneous with the wedding in Western culture. During courtship, as the couple woos each other into long-term relationships, the forces of romance, yearning, and mutual idealization cover over each partner's darker side of fears and anxiety, anger and distrust. If this were not so, many people could never get married. Indeed, some couples now choose to live together for seemingly endless periods, shunning actual marriage for fear of what will be brought on by the formal seal of commitment.

Sex is often caught up in this reordering of personality. Under the exciting, come-hither organization of courtship, sex often goes well, only to fall victim to the emergence of disappointment and aggression following marriage or commitment. This may parallel a general deterioration in the relationship, but it may happen for other reasons. Often, one partner unconsciously locates the frightening or frightened feelings in the genitals and breasts. That is, the person acts as though these parts of the body contain a threat to the self and the partner. We call this a *conversion reaction,* when a bodily problem comes to stand for an emotional problem. A couple may appear to have a generally loving relationship, but closer examination reveals that sexual incapacity contains a mutual sense of dread. When this happens, an ongoing loving relationship may help them move past the difficulty, but often couples are unable to overcome the sexual dread without psychotherapy or sex therapy.

> Gabbi is 29. His mother died when he was 15. His father, who had immigrated from Israel, never felt fully at home in the United States and had always been self-absorbed, spending long periods back in Israel and leaving Gabbi and his sister alone. Their parents had married when Gabbi's father was 41 and his mother 25. His mother died after a year-long painful illness when Gabbi's sister was 4. Gabbi had a series of girlfriends he felt passionately about and had good sex with at first, only to pull away from them sexually after several months. Now, he was in my office because he had found Indira, a beautiful, loving Indian American woman. He was also pulling away from her, but this time he felt that the relationship was too good to sacrifice to this pattern. The threat of having to make a commitment to a woman he loved had repeatedly attacked Gabbi's sexual desire. In our exploration, we were able to understand that the loss of his mother together with the repeated abandonments by his father formed an important part of his anger and distrust of women. The model of his father as someone who had only made a marital commitment late in life also factored in to Gabbi's unconscious distrust of women at the same time that he longed for a mother to care for his lonely and needy self. The fact that his mother's protracted death came when he was a newly sexual but still needy adolescent had folded the sense of combined need and distrust into his sexual interest. The idea of making a commitment to a woman then aroused his deep but unconscious anger and distrust, and in the ensuing unconscious battle, he lost sexual interest.

In ordinary courtship, excitement about the other person and sexual excitement support the couple's path toward each other. But at the moment of commitment, each person cries out to be fully known by the partner, and this is often a time of trouble. So, I often ask if anything changed at the moment they first felt really committed, decided to get married, or on the actual wedding day. In primary relationships, the unlikable parts of each person also cry out for recognition—the parts we are afraid others will not tolerate, much less love. Some partnerships are able to tolerate and soothe these aspects of partners, but many are torn by previously repressed forces that now come out from hiding. A man who felt neglected as a child wants his wife to understand and compensate for the deprivation he suffered. A woman who was victim to her father's rage carries unconscious resentment that now, for the first time, is loosed on her lesbian partner as though that partner were the angry father.

Often, the spouse is surprised by this previously hidden part of the partner, although there may have been hints overlooked before marriage or commitment. But, it also often seems that the partner was unconsciously chosen precisely because of the traits that were consciously ignored. For instance, I recently saw a man who had chosen a woman with low self-esteem and who was constantly self-defeating. Picking a needy partner like this provided him with endless opportunity to heal her, and this filled an unconscious fantasy that he could repair his depressed mother.

Infertility

For most couples, pregnancy and the birth of children are joyful despite the troubles children inevitably bring their parents. For many couples now, fertility has been a concern as the average age of marriage and conception rise for middle-class couples. Infertility and struggles to conceive often become formidable obstacles to ordinary and satisfying sex. Feelings of inadequacy, pressures to perform on a limited and precise schedule impinge on spontaneity and a sense of sexual adequacy. Many couples who have had good sex for years experience a decline in satisfaction, frequency, and pleasure as they try to comply with the rules of fertility treatment or deal with disappointment at their inability to conceive. The drugs used to promote pregnancy take a physical and emotional toll on women, expose them to risk, and create a climate of anxiety. While most couples survive these hazards, they also report that the going has not been easy and often, afterward, that there is a toll on their ongoing sexual life. One couple I saw was on the verge of divorce after many failures to conceive, when a pregnancy they no longer expected almost miraculously revived their relationship, which later succumbed to the forces of hostility that had dogged the relationship before the surprise pregnancy.

The following is a story with a different wrinkle on infertility:

Dr. and Mrs. T came because sex had always been infrequent, but more or less satisfying to them. Their individual stories made sense of the rather low levels of sexual desire they each had before meeting. Mrs. T was a runner who lost her periods during adolescence as she tried to keep up with her four brothers. She remained unsure of her femininity. Dr. T's divorced parents had sent him to boarding school, where he had occasional homosexual experiences with teachers that became mixed with a distrust of his self-absorbed mother, leading to worries about himself and distrust of women. This couple loved each other, but sex was infrequent, and when they did not conceive, they adopted a baby boy. But, when they went to the adoption agency again, the vigilant caseworker realized that their infertility might reflect their sexual inactivity rather than a medical problem. With sex therapy, this couple discovered these dynamic issues rather quickly, began a more active sexual life, and was able to have three children over the next few years.

Pregnancy

Pregnancy brings bodily and hormonal changes to the mother, but it also brings psychological change to the father, who experiences his partner's changes physically and emotionally. A woman's preoccupation with her body and her own well-being or concern whether continued sex will harm the pregnancy may constitute real barriers to sex. When pregnancy goes well for a couple, both partners relate to the pregnancy as the culmination of their love and hopes. The fantasies of the baby present a future that expresses each of them in creative ways. Hope triumphs over anxiety. But, there are many unavoidable anxieties that may overpower the hopes for couples with a shaky start.

Tammy came to see me because she thought her husband of 2 years was having an affair. She was 6 months pregnant with their first child, and he had been getting suspicious cell phone calls that she had traced to a work colleague. In a joint session, Don quickly but shamefully admitted to the affair, the first he had had, and said he loved Tammy. He did not know why he had begun an affair with a woman he did not respect. We were able to trace the panic that led to his affair to his intense neediness for Tammy. He grew up with an anxious, needy mother. As Tammy's anxiety about her pregnancy increased, Don's unconscious fear of losing Tammy increased. Work on their shared neediness enabled this couple to pull together and slowly put the affair behind them.

Parenthood

Children are a significant challenge to the intimacy and sexual life of couples. All couples experience a challenge to their intimacy and sexual expression at one or more phases of their children's growth, but for some it is worse than usual. One couple, pregnant immediately after marriage, suffered during and immediately after the pregnancy. Each felt that their spouse no longer had eyes for them. The husband was feeling threatened at work, the wife increasingly depressed as she had gone off antidepressant medication during pregnancy. While they each loved the baby, she came between them as a barrier rather than a bridge. They came to therapy after the husband began to scream at and threaten his wife, echoing for the first time the volatile reactions of his own parents.

As a child grows older, a mother may be angered by her 4-year-old daughter's oedipal love affair with her husband that shuts her out. For some parents, having a boy may be threatening because it triggers memories of some painful event in the past, while for others, a girl baby symbolizes something painful. Or, the accumulation of several children may overwhelm parents who did well with a smaller family. Perhaps a child's burgeoning sexuality in adolescence may challenge one or both parents, who have not mourned the passing of their own youth.

For any given couple, it is not that any one event will automatically introduce strain, but that the meaning of any event may be toxic when it would not have been in different circumstances. It is the specific meaning of the event to the couple that matters. Almost any couple, even in the heartiest and most loving marriages, can be strained to the breaking point by the serious chronic illness or death of a child.

Illness

The same considerations that apply to developmental strains in early or middle adulthood continue to exert influence throughout the life cycle. Middle-aged couples continue to experience developmental crises—menopause or the early sexual aging processes in men—cause physical wear and tear, erectile difficulty, or loss of ease in vaginal functioning as a woman loses hormonal support and lubrication is diminished. All these events introduce changes in an individual that affect the couple's relationship. Some couples handle these better than others, but as they grow older, all couples have to face challenges. Illness does the same thing to couples. Whether the illness is acute or chronic, the challenge to a couple to continue their intimacy and maintain support for each other can be severe. The more severe the threat and the longer it goes on, the more difficult the challenge. All the kinds of issues we have been discussing are up for grabs as a couple struggles to maintain their equilibrium. Losses, guilt, anger, or the resurgence of previous marital strain may come into play. It is important for the clinician to know the obstacles of particular illnesses—cancer, heart disease, rheumatoid arthritis, gynecological difficulty—but it is also incumbent on us to look for the psychological causes that result in anxiety and fear in couples who did well together but now pull away sexually and emotionally. Of course, aging and increasing illness and disability go together, so we have to look at the complexity of reaction to both of these factors when both exist. Illness can have profound impact on sexual and emotional life whenever it occurs within the life cycle. Here is an example of gynecological difficulty in a relatively young couple:

> Robert and Irene, in their mid-30s, grew up in physically abusive families and vowed not to express anger or raise their hands against each other or their children. "If it came to that," Robert said to me, "I'd leave first." So, Irene's complete hysterectomy, done to stop hemorrhagic periods from uterine fibroids, came as a challenge to them. Having difficulty mourning the loss of her fertility, she became depressed and developed pain on intercourse for the first time. No physical cause could be found, but with vaginal pain she became reluctant to have intercourse and moody, irritable, and depressed. Robert felt her withdrawal, exacerbated by her moodiness and her new angry irritability. He also became resentful, but motivated by his determination not to express the anger, he withdrew. Now, Irene felt depressed and abandoned. She told me, "I knew that Robert missed sex, but I got to resenting him for wanting it, even though he never insisted." Over time, their distant and resentful relationship came to bear little resemblance to the loving and cooperative one they had for the first several years of their marriage.

Infidelity

I have found that therapists are often too anxious to allow themselves to ask about extramarital affairs. Most do not know what to think if a patient or couple has had affairs. If you ask, you often do not get a straight answer, but it puts you on record as wanting to know and thinking that this kind of information is important. With familiarity, a therapist can learn to think about affairs with the same clarity as about other marital issues. For most marriages, affairs express disappointment and deprivation that has developed in the years leading up to the affair. One or both partners seek out—or are susceptible to—invitations from someone who offers what the partner does not. These affairs are a living extension of the fantasies I mentioned, but when affairs actually happen, they dramatically restructure a couple's relationship. Now, the partner reacts to the secrecy that almost inevitably accompanies affairs, to the exporting of love and interest that goes with it, and to the sense of violation that comes with discovery. The discovery of an affair can catalyze a new opportunity for growth and rediscovery, or it can deliver a deathblow to a marriage.

> Zachary, a successful money manager, idealized his wife, Sarah, and felt emptiness about his own life and career. He saw Sarah as a beautiful, successful doctor, himself as underachieved and worthless. He could not explain the affair he began a year ago with his office manager, whom he felt had seduced him and then flaunted the affair in front of his friends. Sarah hired a detective, who got the goods on him, but still he denied the affair until one day the light dawned. He broke off the affair and begged Sarah's forgiveness. He could see the origins of his actions in his own depression and in a critical mother he carried within, but he felt his wife had done nothing to deserve what he had done to her. When I saw them, I felt that Zachary's affair had come in reaction to Sarah's aggressive control. He had no awareness of her domineering style, but underneath the surface, I thought, he was reacting to it. She demanded complete submission and repentance, and that he "submit to therapy." Zachary accepted her terms and admitted to all the blame, and because I agreed that he did need therapy, I referred him to a colleague. Sarah, having no insight into her own role in the marital tension, soon ended the couple therapy, continuing the pattern of placing blame on Zachary and, I thought, dramatically limiting the chances for growth in the marriage.

Divorce and Other Losses

Divorce is the end point for a marriage that failed, regardless of the reason for the failure. But, there is the rest of life to be lived. Frequently, people have difficulty investing in what is next. But being single again, or being a single parent, forces a new perspective on life, brings on new challenges, and calls on new resources. A man who makes a positive decision to leave an unhappy marriage may nevertheless founder at the prospect of being on his own, or a woman who is bereft when her husband of 25 years leaves or dies may find that the new structure of her life holds opportunities that were never in her dreams. The key to successfully negotiating these adult restructurings is the capacity to mourn, to give up on lost loved ones, and to go through a variable sequence of angry protest, sadness or despair, and the generation of new hope.

> Thomas came to see me because his second wife complained about his lack of sexual interest in her. He had married her after having an affair with her during his first marriage. Unable to give her up although more interested in his first wife, he had driven that first wife to distraction until she finally demanded a divorce. Now, 8 years later, he was still preoccupied with the first wife and unable to invest in the second marriage. The divorce should have led to a reconfiguration of his life and, through mourning, to a capacity to invest in someone new. His inability to commit to either woman and his incessant dwelling on his lost first wife despite the fact that she was happily remarried were now costing him a second chance.

The incapacity to mourn a lost marriage, regardless of whose fault the divorce (usually both significantly contribute) can make it impossible to move forward. But when the lost marriage can be mourned, sadness gives way to openness for reconnection to the next phase of life, whether single or partnered.

Old Age and Death

Losing a mate through death or living with a mate with a chronically debilitating illness, as so often happens, impinges on the phases of late adult development. These conditions restructure life, and their successful negotiation requires active restructuring in turn. In elderly couples, one spouse often lives for several years with a debilitating physical illness or dementia from Alzheimer's or stroke. Then, the relatively healthy spouse has to decide whether to limit her own life to care for and stay with the debilitated one or whether to carve out time and space for herself.

> A woman in her 70s, married to a man a few years her junior, was able to care for him as he grew weaker from diffuse vascular disease that affected his mobility and strength, although not his mind. For 10 years, she was restricted by his disability, punctuated by medical crises requiring hospitalization. In the last 2 years of his life, she could not leave the city to see her children and grandchildren because each time she did, he went into a life-threatening crisis. He died when she was over 80. She mourned him deeply, saying she had lost her best friend. But, she also took the new freedom to travel and to visit children and friends. She said she felt she did not have much time with good health, and she was going to enjoy herself while she could.

Losing a partner through death is a challenge to everyone who survives a spouse, whether in a young marriage or at the end of a long partnership. Sometimes, the surviving spouse feels he or she does not have the energy to reshape life, but that feeling is not limited to the elderly. Depression is more frequent in old age but can immobilize those who suffer loss at any age.

A SUMMARY: WHEN THINGS DO NOT GO WELL

We all have unconscious fantasies that guide us through our lives at every stage. We maintain deep hopes to repair the damage of our childhoods as we imagine a better future for ourselves. These fantasies are embedded in us from past experience and former relationships. The conscious derivatives of these deep-structure fantasies include daydreams and night dreams, the hopes and fears present from the time a child dreams of becoming a hero or movie star through the fantasies of being a pop star or having a love affair with one to the fantasies about sexual partners that are fed by erotic magazines and movies. Some people fantasize a secret life of sexual passion or even of more mundane extramarital affairs from the beginning of their marriage, using these fantasies to live out wishes and to calm fears that they unconsciously feel will contaminate marriage. This may be a minor theme that can be contained by the marriage, but in people who later turn to therapists for help, it often happens that the vitality needed by the marriage has been funneled into this fantasy life.

Ian, a mild-mannered man in his 30s, loved his wife but had no sexual interest in her. He thought he never had, although he knew she was beautiful. His lack of interest seemed inexplicable. She grew increasingly angry that they had no sex and no children. He masturbated but felt upset when she suggested sex. In therapy, he told me about a secret fantasy life that excited him greatly. He was held in a sultan's prison. The sultan's beautiful wife would seek him out. They had passionate sex, but in the end, fearing betrayal, and with great regret, he felt he had no alternative but to kill the sultan's wife. The cycle of passion, regret, and violence excited him greatly as he masturbated.

The fantasy contained the split-off versions of his experience of his mother. An alluring and unavailable woman, she was also a frightening ball-breaker. His wife did not stand a chance. Out of fear and out of concern that she would become the victim of his unconscious fury at his mother, he had suppressed his sexual interest in her. Therapy helped him to become conscious of the paralyzing effects of his fantasies and move to an active sexual life with his wife.

FINAL THOUGHTS

The more a therapist has a developmental framework in mind, the easier it is to form a life map for his or her patients. We all draw from our life experience, so in a way the older we get, the bigger our personal map. Fortunately, we draw on more than our individual experience. All we have read, the movies we have seen, the study of development we have done, and everything our patients teach us goes into our databank. As our careers continue, the bank gets richer. I have found that is one of the elements of our profession that is most satisfying: Life, in its infinite complexity, gets more understandable as we go. It is a big help in the job we all want to do personally and for our patients: to keep growing and changing in response to the forces that restructure our lives.

REFERENCES

Bowlby, J. (1969, 1973, 1980). *Attachment and loss* (Vols. 1–3). New York: Basic Books. The basic and readable text on early attachment relationships.

Clulow, C. (Ed.). (2001). *Adult attachment and couple psychotherapy: The "secure base" in practice and research.* London: Brunner-Routledge. This useful volume relates attachment research to couples in health, in situations of trauma history, and in couple therapy.

Fairbairn, W. R. D. (1952). *Psychoanalytic studies of the personality.* London: Routledge. This volume is not easy going, but it is the foundation of all object relations theory and has reformed psychoanalysis by making it completely relevant to family and couple therapy and therefore to an understanding of sexuality in relationships.

Fonagy, P., Gergely, G., Jurist E., & Target, M. (2002). *Affect regulation, mentalization and the development of the self.* New York: Other Press.

Jacques, E. (1965). Death and the mid-life crisis. *International Journal of Psychoanalysis, 46*, 502–514.

Scarf, M. (1987). *Intimate partners: Patterns in love and marriage.* New York: Random House. This book was written for the general public but is well researched and grounded in solid theory. It gives all the basic references available until the time of its publication. It is the best book on couple life development and difficulties for the general public or the beginning therapist.

Scharff, D. E. (1998). *The sexual relationship: An object relations view of sex and the family* [paperback edition with a new introduction]. Northvale, NJ: Aronson. In this book, I described development from infancy through adulthood and applied the developmental way of thinking to sexual growth and pathology through the life cycle. (Original work published 1982)

Scharff, D. E., & Scharff, J. S. (1991). *Object relations couple therapy.* Northvale, NJ: Aronson. This book covers the issues of development in couples. It is the place to read about the definition and illustration of projective identification, and about how to apply a developmental framework to treating couples.

Scharff, J. S., & Scharff, D. E. (2006). *New paradigms for treating relationships.* Lanham, MD: Aronson. This book has the up-to-date models of the relational and developmental issues, including neuroscience, attachment theory, and chaos theory, that have come to inform my developmental thinking.

Scharff, J. S., & Scharff, D. E. (2008; originally published 1994). *Object relations therapy of physical and sexual trauma* [paperback edition with a new introduction]. Lanham, MD: Aronson. In this volume, we deal with the developmental problems introduced by childhood physical and sexual abuse and the varieties of pictures that show up in adulthood, from multiple personality to sexual inhibition.

Schore, A. N. (2001). The right brain as the neurobiological substratum of Freud's dynamic unconscious. In D. E. Scharff (Ed.), *The psychoanalytic century: Freud's legacy for the future* (pp. 61–88). New York: Other Press. This chapter is a readable version of the way the right brain leads in early affective development, in the description of the way that mothers and babies have minds that are entrained in early development, and on the importance of chaos theory in understanding both neurological and psychological development.

Viorst, J. (1986). *Necessary losses.* New York: Simon and Schuster. A well-researched and well-written popular book on developmental life crises and transitions.

Six

Infidelity

STEPHEN B. LEVINE, MD

INTRODUCTION

I paid little attention to the topic of infidelity during my psychiatric residency. Infidelity rarely came to my clinical attention. I began to see the emotional, familial, social, and economic changes it could unleash when I entered private practice. I watched some individuals' infidelity rearrange the lives of the couples, their children, and extended families. Now, 36 years later, I feel that I have a more balanced view of the subject. It may seem shocking, but I spend a part of most work weeks talking about the subject with individuals of all ages who are having an affair, thinking about having one, trying to end one, trying to repair its effects, coping with an unfaithful partner, or lamenting a close friend's or relative's unfaithful behavior.

Infidelity can evocate strong countertransferences that impair our capacity to think clearly. In this chapter, I encourage you to

1. Recognize the power of your values and life experiences in organizing your clinical perceptions in this arena.
2. Remain empathic without certainty regarding what the individual or couple should do.
3. Regard your role as clarifying the private struggles in people's lives.
4. Restrain yourself from being authoritative.

IS INFIDELITY SICK?

I used to answer, "Yes," to the question of whether infidelity is sick, but now I see that this ambiguous question involves the intersection of public, professional, and personal values. American public values about infidelity are rather homogeneous. Infidelity is viewed as a violation of the standard for how people in committed relationships ought to behave. The public holds that infidelity is a moral sickness—a sin and a reflection of poor character. Privately, however, individuals occupy one of four value positions.

1. An absolute moral prohibition against it
2. A contextual position that states that fidelity is an ideal that should be understood in a nuanced and flexible manner because of the reality of people's lives

3. A skeptical posture that assumes that long-term fidelity is stifling to pleasure, against biological tendencies, and the source of boredom and numerous marital woes
4. A shoulder-shrugging mixture of these

Whatever the therapist's personal values may be on the topic, the rules governing our professional behavior ask us to keep our personal value position private. We have also been taught not to make moral judgments or discuss behavior in terms of sin so that we may serve people with a wide diversity of values.

The inherent conflicts among public, private, and professional values make it difficult for us to think of an elegant reply to, "Isn't infidelity sick, doctor?" We may perceive the question as rhetorical and not answer it, or we may sense it as a request to join the patient in condemnation of the partner, which we should avoid. We may hear it as an opportunity to educate the patient about the psychiatric conditions that lower sexual constraint, which is often not what the patient is interested in at that moment.

As a frontline clinician, I feel the tensions among public, personal, and professional values. I tell myself that values organize meanings, and meanings generate our emotional responses. My work usually begins with learning about patients' emotions. I try to help them articulate the meanings behind their emotions, and eventually we discern the values that they hold about this important topic. This focus on the patient's or couple's emotions and meanings constitutes the powerful beginning of our relationship and the therapy process that will eventuate in the patient calming down and feeling slightly less tumultuous. Before I elaborate on the clinical intervention, however, let us try to understand infidelity further.

FLIRTING

Infidelity is far more diverse, complicated, and widespread than I had initially imagined when I entered into practice. Once I realized that it is very difficult to remain faithful for a lifetime to whatever values one has—political, religious, professional, or sexual—the high prevalence of infidelity ceased to surprise me. Let us take a look at flirting—the common behavior that illustrates that we do not always behave based on our stated values.

Flirtation is early courtship behavior, a means of getting the erotic attention of another. Its observable mechanisms involve prolonged eye contact, apparent interest or enjoyment in the person's conversation, standing or sitting close to the person, and a slight excess of innocuous touching. No verbal expressions of personal interest are necessary to create the excitement that comes from the realization that this person is "interested in me."

For the flirting person, the behavior creates a tantalizing, promising, exciting *un*certainty. The motivation to create such uncertainty is not necessarily to initiate an affair. It can be to make social occasions less boring; to affirm one's attractiveness, social worth, or power to provoke the interest of others; to pretend that one has more relationship possibilities than one knows exists; to celebrate the overcoming of one's former social shyness and sense of social inadequacy; to provoke sexual desire in the self or another person; to present a false impression to others as a comfortable sexual person. These motivations explain why some think flirtation is a harmless social game that is not in conflict with their values.

Flirtation becomes dangerous when its signal is received with serious interest. Intimate talk, arranging for the next intimate talk, and escalation of intrapsychic arousal and erotic imagery can then quickly occur. Soon, both individuals know exactly what is transpiring. Men and women who have decided that these liaisons are part of their pleasure of living—their personal value system—can perfect the process of spotting, alerting, and negotiating with another to an impressive degree. For them, flirtation is a means of initiating partner sexual behavior.

THE CONNOTATION OF TERMS FOR INFIDELITY

Most of the terms for infidelity convey moral disapproval, bad character, or sickness (cheating, betraying, deceiving); sexual adventuring (swinging, partner swapping, philanderer, womanizer, slut, tart); whoring, affair, affair of the heart, love affair; adultery, dalliance, indiscretion, just sex, fling, one-night stand, casual sex, sex buddy, and sexual addict.

The expectation for fidelity arises from the evolving process of commitment to one another in most modern Western cultures. As dating becomes exclusive to one person, the identity of each person begins to change as each begins to experience being part of a couple. These identity shifts do not occur at the same rate in each person. Fidelity is widely understood to be inherent in both the process of falling in love and the commitment to be a couple. We typically expect it of each other without any formal discussion.

Sex with another partner during courtship may be a marker for "I'm not ready yet." It also may be a reflection of the belief that fidelity rules do not personally apply. This vital distinction can be a difficult discernment for each person. Once a couple is going steady, "cheating" is commonly used to describe current undisclosed extra-relationship sex. "Cheaters" may prefer to think of their sexual behaviors as an entitled adventure—"sowing my wild oats," "having enough fun now so I won't regret missed opportunities later," "a last hurrah," or "I'm not ready yet."

Youthful cheating may give way to thinking that fidelity is not an expectation that applies personally. This value judgment is kept secret from partners. When a man is thought to have been repeatedly unfaithful, he may be called a philanderer or womanizer. Women are referred to with terms like "loose" or "slut." Name-calling notwithstanding, individual men and women may not believe that they should be faithful.

Not all extra-relationship sex is secret. Some partners agree to have sex outside their relationship. Here are some examples: a married couple participates in a swingers club, best friends "swap" partners for an evening, a couple agrees to take on a third person for fun, or two people marry strongly believing that fidelity is neither possible nor desirable. Crossing the fidelity boundary leaves most people at least a little uneasy, but such open sexual adventurers remind us that all people do not have the same value systems when it comes to fidelity.

Frank and I are thinking about bringing a woman into our bed as an experiment. The woman, a graduate student in my department, approached me about it. She told me that she was an adventurous bisexual who was sexually attracted to me. Frank has long had a fantasy of being with two women. We have talked about it: We agree it is both weird and intriguing. I have never been with a woman sexually—other than when my older sister introduced me to sex when I was a first grader. I don't know if I will do it. I don't think I like her. Nonetheless, the idea seems exciting.

Some infidelity involves an evolving personal attachment between two clandestine lovers. The actual affair usually begins at some moment of psychological intimacy that stimulates each other's erotic imagination. This is sometimes referred to as *emotional infidelity*. One or both partners may think that they have fallen in love. When their sexual behavior begins, it usually deepens the bond and begins the processes of more talking, being together, sexual interaction, and a large degree of intimate psychological knowledge of the other. Other surreptitious unions are quickly sexual but carry no emotional, social, or sexual obligation beyond the original physical acts. These are "just sex." Liaisons with prostitutes, pickups at bars or parties, convention flings, or other one-night stands are typical heterosexual examples. Arrangements made at parks, bars, parties, bookstores, or bathhouses are male homosexual counterparts. These secret sexual adventures are of interest to us when the adventurer is in a committed relationship. These adulterous experiences involve little to no intimate psychological knowledge of the sexual partner. Nonetheless, they can be quite influential because of their meaning for the person.

I went to Vegas, spent $500 to be with a beautiful young woman. We talked, had lovely unrushed sex, and talked some more. I think I'll remember this for a long time. It reminded me that there are possibilities for me beyond the resentful sex that Sherrie doles out monthly.

Some sexual processes seem to be neither affairs nor just sex. They may begin as sexual adventuring and become an affair or begin as an affair and not engage the person's heart. These in-between states are sometimes called *casual* or *convenient sex*. These terms convey a relaxation that does not jibe with the anxiety, deception, and guilt that cause their fits and starts, confusions, advantage taking, and wavering. After a while, sometimes quite a while, both partners realize that they are ashamed of how they behaved within the relationship and would simply like it to end. Some people, however, come to realize eventually that they are friends who have sex. They may or may not think of themselves as "lovers"; they both accept what can and what cannot be in the relationship. This is quite an accomplishment because each person's understanding of the arrangement keeps evolving.

I thought both of us were unhappily situated with our husbands, and that we had happened upon a very nice arrangement. We had very intense sex for 4 months. Then she seemed to change the rules. She wanted me to leave Jim because she had decided to leave her guy. It ruined everything.

You will undoubtedly meet patients in committed relationships who have a masturbatory life excited by external sources. Such heterosexual men typically use explicit still pictures, videotapes, chat rooms, or strip shows for this purpose, while homosexual men may use explicit male-on-male videos and opportunities for voyeuristic excitement at movies, bathhouses, and parks for the same reason. Until the Internet appeared, large numbers of women were not known to be interested in such outlets. The Internet now can provide 24-hour, 7-day-a-week sexual stimulation for everyone. This medium allows the imagination to be stimulated by conversations with strangers and looking at images of men and women engaged in a wide variety of sexual behavioral patterns. Until these people meet for sex, as occasionally happens, this constitutes quasi-imaginary, quasi-extramarital sex. Many people feel uncertain whether cybersex represents a moral lapse, whereas others interpret it as just another form of cheating.

We mental health professionals have our own vocabulary; we call extra-relationship sex *acting out*. We use the term in six ways. To discern which meanings are being invoked, we must pay attention to context clues:

1. The behavior is disapproved of in a conventional sense. A Catholic priest is thought to be acting out regardless of his sexual partner because of his religion's expectation of celibacy.
2. The behavior expresses a fantasy. A faithful married couple having sex on a beach with the tide washing over their feet may be acting out a fantasy that one of them has long had.
3. The behavior carries a high risk of negative consequences.
4. The behavior is created by the psychopathology of major psychiatric disorders, such as, psychopathic personality disorder and narcissistic personality disorder, paraphilia, bipolar disorders, schizophrenia, and substance abuse. These are commonly thought to reduce a patient's capacity to remain faithful to a partner. Both the dangerousness and its frequency among people with severe psychiatric disorders support the professional judgment that acting out is a symptom of "sickness."
5. Unconscious forces motivate the behavior. "She seemed to have no idea that her promiscuity was related to her incestuous experiences with her stepfather; she was acting out for years because of this."
6. The person does not have the capacity to put into words what he or she is experiencing. Children and adolescents routinely act out their feelings rather than explain them. It takes many people years longer to recognize and describe their sexual feelings than other emotions.

We need to be careful about using acting out because all six of these connotations tend to run together in the minds of those who listen to us and by those who invoke it. Our aim is to think clearly about infidelity. The multiple meanings of acting out inevitably create confusion. When colleagues invoke the term, try to discern which of these six meanings they are pointing to so you do not unwittingly collude to find agreement that the infidelity offends our personal values. We need to aspire to precise meanings.

THREE VITAL CLINICAL QUESTIONS

Rather than quickly answering whether your patient's infidelity is sick, try to discern the answers to these three questions:

1. What are the motivations for this person's extra-relationship sex?
2. Is there evidence for a major psychiatric diagnosis as a significant cause for the infidelity?
3. What have been the consequences of this infidelity?

Here are two extreme examples to see how the answers to these questions help you:

Joy, a faithful, unhappily, tensely married 29-year-old mother of two, worked as a pharmaceutical rep. She has regretted her marriage for at least 3 years and occasionally has fantasies of running away with a kinder man. Joy developed a mania when treated with an SSRI (selective serotonin reuptake inhibitor). Before being hospitalized because of grandiosity and boundless energy and irritability, she had physical intimacies with three men within 1 week. When she recovered from her mania, she became horrified over her public flirtatious behaviors and was paralyzed by her husband's cold, hostile name-calling: "You slut!" She resigned her job, lost her self-respect, and doubted even her minor decision making. She was more depressed after her mania than before she began taking the SSRI.

Joy's infidelity was a product of her SSRI-induced mania. Her motivations were to find a man to take her away from her critical husband. Her restraint mechanisms, which previously were intact, failed. The consequences were profound—deeper depression, more marital tensions, and grave personal doubt. While others may think of her as immoral, mental health professionals would think that her decision to have sex with others was a symptom of impaired judgment due to a toxic brain. Her therapist, when addressing her husband, may choose to speak of her sickness to soften his narcissistic injury and to interest him in considering the more important issue of their long-standing marital tensions.

Beverly, a highly religious, extremely bright, accomplished mother, and now grandmother, and high-level administrator, is long married to a highly accomplished man she has continuously loved since college. After 35 years together, they still emanate warmth, respect, and mutual affection. Beverly, a person with high sex drive, discovered before marriage that her fiancé was nervous sexually and could rarely ejaculate. He improved somewhat over time and even more so in response to therapy, but he continues to have less sexual drive, be less comfortable, and not able to be sensuous enough to regularly attain orgasm. When I met them 20 years ago, they had long ago worked out an arrangement. She has lovers who are her friends. Her husband knows some of them personally but prefers not to interact with them. Beverly keeps him informed about them. He knows when they are together. Although I initially had a difficult time believing this arrangement was acceptable to Beverly's husband, now, having seen them periodically for two decades, I conclude that it is. "Beverly is a very sexual woman," her husband explains. "I satisfy her in every other way but not sexually. We love each other very much."

I have never been able to see Beverly as mentally ill. She speaks openly and knowledgably about her motivations and her ability to be in love with her husband but have sex friends she never loves in that way. She and her husband manage their reactions to her extramarital sex sensitively. Her husband has had no interest in other partners. Beverly did not consider herself "sick," and she did not meet my professional criteria for illness.

MEANING MAKING

It is in the realms of values and meanings that we can find the differences between those who are deeply disturbed by infidelity and those who are not. In the typical previously clandestine affair of the heart that comes to psychiatric attention, there is a cast of characters. These include the person having the affair; the person with whom the affair is conducted; the committed partner; the adolescent and adult children; the family of origin; and you.

You, the therapist, are apt to repeatedly hear such sentences from couples in front of you as, "I can't understand how you could do that!" or "Yes, we had a fling, but it was nothing really." Distressed spouses may not be able to pay attention when the partner tries to explain the meanings and motives of the affair. They may argue over whose meanings are correct. Your patient may not feel you are an ally when you explain that the meanings of events are ultimately private, and one person's meanings cannot be superimposed on the other. Even if a spouse has egregiously violated marital norms, his outraged wife does not actually dictate the meaning of the infidelity to him. That is a separate matter. The same is true for an outraged husband.

> John may tell his wife in front of you that her affair was despicable, that she is a moral reprobate who is not worthy of being in his children's presence. John may indignantly announce this with the conviction that anyone—man or woman—in a similar situation would feel the same way. When his wife tries to speak, John may interrupt her to tell her the meaning of her affair to him. "You are just talking bullshit rationalizations for your immoral behavior!" What John cannot conceptualize during this session is that come tomorrow he may think differently about her affair—that is, have a different set of meanings at his disposal just as others today interpret her affair differently.

Over time, perspective on everything changes. Our feelings change, our meanings change, and whether we like to admit it, our values change. In helping people with their current anguish, we try to prevent them from destroying their possibilities for relating in the future. May I suggest that you should tell the couple that together you are trying to work through the meanings of this event so that they can make decisions *in the future* about how they want to relate to one another.

THE PREAFFAIR MENTAL PROCESS IN
AN UNHAPPY RELATIONSHIP

From the 50% American divorce rate, it is safe to assume that many individuals are not satisfied in their marriage. They may be disappointed about what does or does not happen within the home, bedroom, or social activities. They may be frustrated over what they have learned over time about the nature or character of their spouse. Or, they may reach their conclusion simply from the frequency and strength of their sexual or romantic fantasies or behaviors with others. However they arrive at their judgment, they may find themselves preoccupied with their perception that their love for their partner is diminishing.

What they know with certainty is that they desire something fresher, more pleasing, or exciting. They want something less encumbered by their appraisal of their partner, less burdened by their partner's appraisal of them.

They imagine beginning anew, but of course the reality of their commitment immovably stands there like a fortress. They flirt a little—that is, they pretend that they are not seriously entrapped within a marriage and family or within a culturally sanctioned commitment.

A friend may have recently decided to divorce or take a lover, but still, such a drastic serious step may not feel like a realistic personal possibility. A search for safer interests may begin—in work, recreation, children, or the community. An otherwise-unexplained period of depression, however, may appear. Because the person may not be willing to acknowledge this state of feeling unhappily married, a clinician may think the patient has a mood disorder. The depression may be induced by the dawning perception that there is no hope for marital happiness.

Some feel rebellious against what fate has brought to them. The possibility of beginning anew, of revitalizing the self in a new relationship, of behaving differently with someone else keeps appearing in consciousness. Pleasures are deliciously imagined; dangers are minimized.

"But what will happen to my partner and children if the affair is discovered?" "Can the honest me tolerate the tantalizing dishonesty?" "Didn't I always want to be faithful?" Other thoughts may be at war with these. "Oh, stop being so self-depriving! Others do it; it is not the end of the world! It is just a little dalliance. What if my partner has been doing it, and I don't have any awareness of it? Just make the ground rules clear from the beginning. I'll look for somebody who is looking for something that fits with what I am looking for."

The unhappily married person is experiencing the paradox between the self as socially committed and mentally uncommitted, between honesty and deception, between the wish to have a new life and the need to keep this wish a secret. One needs a sense of humor to bear such paradoxes. Private subjective life is not always logical. Rather than simply feeling, knowing, and smiling about one's paradoxical self, some people decide to have extra-relationship sex. They may come to explain their infidelity as due to some irresistible force, having been overwhelmed by sexual attraction, or by being seduced by an evil person. Such melodramatic concepts lose their appeal as we age—as we come to realize that we have to choose to have an affair. Temptations to be unfaithful are widespread internal mental dramas that typically go nowhere. They are part of many committed relationships. Something precipitates an affair.

UNRAVELING

Spouses usually become suspicious because of their perceptions that the partner is talking less, away more, increasingly irritable, has less sexual interest, and suddenly is daydreaming. The concerned spouse asks, "What is happening?" The answer is an artless dodge, such as "I'm just working too hard" or "Nothing." The spouse may gradually develop a new anxiety, jealousy, suspicion, increased alcohol consumption, or depression. The spousal consequence of the affair may begin *before* it is discovered. When the evidence of the affair is finally in, the aggrieved spouse often passionately says, "Not only did you deceive me with *that* person, but when I was suffering, when I felt like a crazy person and did not understand why, you willfully allowed my pain to continue! You sacrificed me to your comfort! I don't know which is worse!"

Once an affair becomes known, life really changes. You are called when life feels like it is unraveling.

THE CRISIS OF THE BETRAYED

When you are consulted by a person who has recently discovered the affair of a spouse, you will have the opportunity to observe the thoughts, feelings, defenses, modifying circumstances, and coping strategies of the betrayed. The betrayed feel confused by the intensity of their emotions and the fact that a large number of questions appear at the same time.

Regardless of their sex or orientation, the minds of the betrayed swirl with questions. While they can take many individual forms, they are initially variations on these four:

1. What is the personal meaning of the infidelity to me?
2. What is the best way I can respond to it?
3. Will I be abandoned?
4. Why did this happen?

After a while, another set appears:

Will I, does anyone, ever get over this?
Will I ever be able to forgive my partner?
Will I ever be able to forget this?
Will I be able to trust my partner again?
Will I be able to trust any partner again?
Shall I take this opportunity to end this relationship?
Does it now matter what I have done wrong in the past?

Many feel uncertain whether they want their partner back. If they clearly do, however, they worry whether they are being disgracefully weak for wanting to preserve the union.

Therapists can helpfully distinguish those feelings that are likely to last a long time and those that are more transient. The emotional swirl the patient is experiencing is, of course, tied to the questions. Whether you pay attention to the emotion or the question, you help with both because, of course, they are two sides of the same coin. Please realize that although the questions are good ones, you do not actually know the answers to most of them. As long as you listen well with interest and appreciation of the pain and uncertainty, the betrayed will find some relief with you.

The patient may be tempted to do something—create a separation, tell the children or in-laws, file for divorce, and so on. You may be similarly inclined—be wary. Such suggestions may increase the social and coping demands on the patient, who is already overwhelmed. It is enough to listen well to the patient and try to help the patient consider the pros and cons of each option. You must also listen well to your own inner reactions. Your goal is not to add to the tumult. Try to slow the pace of the unfolding drama by being calm and supportive of using time as an aid to decision making. You need to know that some patients survive the crisis of a discovered affair quite well after a while.

In the meantime, pay attention to the patient's insomnia and consider the temporary use of a minor tranquilizer during the early rough days.

Countertransference

You should expect that your early experiences with the betrayed will be quite emotionally evocative and difficult for you. This may be true even if this is your first personal experience with the subject. But, just think of your burden if your parent's marriage broke up over an affair in your adolescence or if your affair devastated your partner. The patient's tumult will likely restimulate your angst for a while—distress that you thought you had worked through. Several errors tend to recur in dealing with the betrayed before we gain better self-control and reestablish better boundaries. If our personal values do not endorse extramarital sex, we may privately begin to feel very negatively toward the spouse who is not in the room. We are immersed in the distress that he (or she) has caused. We may find ourselves authoritatively declaring, "He's a scumbag; get rid of him!" Or, "Your partner is sick!" Or, if infidelity has been in our life experience, we may be inclined to say something like, "Believe me, I know what you are going through; my partner did the same thing to me." Or, if we have been unfaithful to our partner and feel uncomfortably guilty again, we may be too coolly intellectual and try to quickly bypass the patient's pain with encouraging comments like, "You will get over this."

I still vividly recall the shock I felt 20 years ago when a sheepish, frightened husband brought his disturbed wife to me in mid-July. Their presentation led me to assume for 30 minutes that she had discovered his affair "over Memorial Day weekend." When I finally realized that it was Memorial Day weekend 7 years ago, I was stunned. My distress continued for days as I considered the apparent facts the couple reported: (1) She was mentally well before the discovery of the affair; (2) since that time, she has been continuously depressed, obsessed with the affair, and too anxious to function for herself or the family.

Sometimes, the emotional burden in dealing with the betrayed exhausts me. I work to be there with the patient's questions and emotions, to provide clarification when I can, and to allow hope to grow through my constancy, interest, and calmness. It has also helped me considerably to spend equal time with those who have done the betraying.

THE MIND OF THE PERSON HAVING THE AFFAIR

It may not be easy for the patients having the affair to talk about what they have done. They are often ashamed or uncertain about what your response may be. Some may never tell you. Even generally honest people find that they cannot be honest about this. Even when people speak at their first session about having an affair, people rarely tell you *all* about it. In particular, they find it onerous to share details of their preaffair processes and motives; the direct and indirect promises they made; and the lies they told to the new partner.

When you begin asking questions, you may frequently hear, "I did not think about that." Or "I don't think I had any idea of what this could have brought." On the other hand, you will also encounter those who do not regret their affairs; some, in fact, cherish them and feel that the benefits were worth the conundrums that ensued. Nonetheless, they want to discuss them because so much is cognitively and affectively swirling within them.

Eventually, the person confronts his or her motives for the affair. "Am I doing this because my partner is so unsatisfying?" "Because I have lost respect for my partner?" "Because I am angry, deeply resentful, of my partner?" "Because I want to have this, I deserve to have this, I need this?" "Did it serendipitously begin, and I decided to take the opportunity?" "Do I continue simply because it would be too ugly to directly stop it?" Other questions soon occur. "How am I to think of myself now?" "I have become such a liar, yet I am generally an honest person." "Do I really want to stop?" "Whom shall I hurt—my lover or my spouse?" "I am going to hurt somebody." "Should I stay married just for my children?" "Who might be of help to me?" "Was I crazy to begin with, or am I just crazy now?"

Such questions can last a very long time, cause considerable suffering, and make you think the basic problem is obsessive–compulsive disorder. It is not.

> Bill, a 43-year-old politician, originally sought help with his wife because of his indecision about whether to leave the family for his never-married lover of 3 years. Everyone, his wife, three teenage daughters, lover, and he had become highly symptomatic. For the last year, he had left each woman twice with the announcement of having made a final decision. Each time, however, he missed the other too much. He was living on the cell phone, secretly calling the other one. Although "not serious," he was beginning to think of suicide. At his 10th visit, I told him:
>
>> I call what you have a dilemma. Some problems have elegant solutions, but a dilemma is a problem without a painless solution. Make no mistake—your dilemma is an unenviable, terrible one: Whatever you decide, it will be quite difficult for a long time. But it is time for a real decision. Please remember that whatever you decide, you will have to work every day to make it a good decision. You may not end up with either women or with a family. Go decide.
>
> Bill took my suggestion to go away, contacting no one; to read *Solitude* (Storr, 1988); and to weigh his desires against the costs to himself and his family and friends. When he returned, he had decided on his lover because he considered that with her he would have a greater chance of emotional and physical love. (Six years later, he reported that he made the right decision.)

Many men and women in these indecisive situations never are able to make a decision; they waver for years, waiting for the partner to give up on them.

The Therapist

Eventually, most patients ask you for some explanation of why it occurred. I think the best answer is, "I'm happy to try to figure it out with you." I am wary of single explanations that stem from developmental and remote explanations such as a repetition compulsion stemming from an early trauma. The trauma may be a parent's infidelity, oedipal excitement, the unconscious oedipal implications of marriage, childhood sexual abuse, family traditions of separations and interpersonal chaos, preoedipal attachment anxiety and distrust, replacement for a mother who died when the individual was young, or replacement for the emotionally distant father. It is not that these ideas have no clinical validity, at least as one of many forces that enter into the mix. When we offer such explanations for extra-marital behaviors, we have lost sight of the fact that the patient knows—is aware—of some of the personal considerations that went into the decision to begin the extramarital relationship. By invoking an unconscious motiva-tion, we imply that the patient did not have control or responsibility.

We can also hear ourselves offering system formulations for the back-ground of the affair:

1. The couple was always unable to discuss anything disagreeable. The affair arose to end their locked-in pattern of conflict avoidance.
2. The couple cannot overcome their fear of deep psychological intimacy. The affair helps them to avoid being close.
3. The person having the affair is an addict trying to fill up personal emptiness in a search to soothe their abused child within.
4. The couple's children are gone, and they exist in a loveless devitalized marriage. The affair was designed to provoke the spouse to end the marriage, something that the unfaithful one does not have the courage to do.

Each of these published explanations may apply to some couple sitting in front of you. But, by providing the explanation in these terms, you become the meaning maker. Your role is to understand the patient's meanings first. Temptations to various forms of sexual acting out, after all, are very common, if not nearly universal. Stay with the spouses' meanings and try to keep such elegant sophisticated summaries to yourself for a while. Eventually, you and your patients will be working together, exchanging concepts of motivations, and moving to deeper explanations than were offered by either of you at the beginning of your relationship.

Countertransference

There are dangers in listening to the sexual experiences of others. It may stim-ulate your own yearnings for a new partner. You may spend too much time asking for details, encouraging the person to tell of other experiences, and find yourself admiring the courage and risk taking of the patient. Or, you may feel disgusted by the patient's "immorality" and find no reason to see him or her further. Just imagine if your father's affair, in your view, broke up your home, and you could not talk with him for years. In comes this patient in his 40s who is having an affair. He is not conspicuously ill or character disordered. You learn of his views of his marriage, his failed attempts to emotionally con-nect through the various stages of his marital development, and of how his friendship evolved into sexual behavior with a person he highly regards and understands. Not only do you have to think about his patterns, choices, conse-quences, and possibilities, but also you have to rethink your own life experi-ences. This can be hard work during and after the session with the patient.

It is easier, less personally burdensome, to deal with men and women who are having affairs when their behavior seems clearly related to long-stand-ing psychopathology and when your own life experiences are quite removed from their behavior. Some patterns of extramarital involvement indicate the presence of chronic difficulties. These include compulsive sexual behavior syndromes (i.e., addictions); inability to have sex with a valued partner although readily attracted to others; paraphilia; repeated infidelity from early in marriage; attractions that are limited to married or socially unavailable men or women.

> Rocco, a semiliterate tradesman who has been a binge drinker for over 40 years, had failed 12 treatment attempts to gain sobriety. He was referred from an inpatient service where he finally acknowledged his other problem: compulsive exhibitionism. Immediately after he was given naltrexone as a new treatment for his alcoholism, he noticed a "miraculous absence of craving for a drink." Rocco had exhibited himself to 13- to 14-year-old girls three times a week since his early 20s. In early adolescence, he only sporadically exhibited himself, but his other behaviors would have qualified him for a diagnosis of a psychopathic personality. When Rocco was arrested in his 30s, his lawyer plea-bargained so he could pay a fine, and his wife did not learn about the matter. A father of three girls who was rarely home, he had not had sex with his wife for 3 years. I placed him on 60 mg medroxyprogesterone acetate daily. Within a few days, he experienced a marked decrease in his urge to exhibit and an increase in his confidence about his ability to control his urges. He was pleased to take it, but he has kept his contacts with me and his medication secret from his wife. Sex with adults he met in bars, prostitutes, and women his buddies arranged for him punctuated his adult married life.
>
> We spent our sessions discussing our views about tactics for self-control. I asked many questions about his work, his childhood, his hoodlum days, and his courtship. He was pleased to share his history, but without being asked, he never knew what to say. He liked to see me. He taught me what passed as normal in his family: violence, alcoholism, neglect, and no educational encouragement.
>
> When his sexual relationship with his wife restarted, she teased him that his affair must be over now. They both felt a lot better about his newly found time to be with his family at home. At year 3, he went on a bender, started to exhibit his penis but stopped. He claims to be free of drinking and exhibitionistic behavior since that time. The impulses to exhibit persist but are not acted on any longer.
>
> Four years later, having ceased to regularly visit me and having stopped some of his medications, Rocco was rearrested and jailed briefly for exhibitionism.

EXTRAMARITAL SEX EXPERIENCES THREATEN THE STRUCTURE OF OUR LIVES

Infidelity has the potential to rearrange our individual psyches, our relationships, our children's psyche's, and the developmental trajectory of our future. They threaten our partners with abandonment. They assault our identities. They show us that we cannot control our destiny, let alone our partner. They unleash a firestorm of judgment against us. They confront us with the fact that our future is not certain. They humble us by quickly demonstrating to us that our planned sequence for our life is not going to occur. They assault us much like death does, but death is public, inevitable, and generally carries little shame with it. Affairs convey, however erroneously, personal failure as if the betrayed one caused the partner to decide and implement the new relationship.

Even if affairs are rarely mentioned, they are not forgotten. They are part of our history as a couple. When other issues are discussed heatedly years later, the again-aggrieved person may bring it into the discussion. But more importantly, when affairs are ended for the sake of the marriage, a period of private grief occurs. If it is the man, for instance, who has been having the affair, his wife is not likely to have a large capacity to remain sympathetic to him as he recalls the sweet experiences of the past and feels sad for his loss. Of course, it is exactly the same if it is the woman who has been having the affair.

Affairs are often the prelude to divorce because the feelings, attitudes, and concerns that they generate are beyond both partners' capacities to work through and master—even with our help. Divorce puts all parties on a new developmental trajectory, filled with uncertainties that cause almost all persons, however inherently mentally well, considerable anxiety, guilt, and regret.

I try to help my patients to separate the effect of affairs per se from the effects of the decision to divorce. This is often initially difficult because swirling within the emotional upheaval induced by the knowledge of a spousal affair are the reactions to a potential divorce.

Even though people restructure their lives, beginning with an affair, in the hopes of finding an improved social, sexual, emotional, and interpersonal life, it is not always clear that they have accomplished these goals. A particular heavy burden is the ex-spouse who does not do well after all the dust settles. And, of course, the person who decided to divorce to find happiness is far from guaranteed that happiness will be secured.

Not So Unique Examples

A Gay Husband's Affair Is Discovered

When a wife has to deal with her husband's affair with a man as he rediscovers his homoerotic nature, she often feels that she is in an extremely awkward circumstance. Her questions and thoughts could also include: How do I compete with a man? Is he going to leave me, stay with me and be unfaithful, or stay with me forever longing for his private desire in a way with which I can never compete? Did he ever really love me? Do I have AIDS? Will I get the disease if I stay with him? After all these good years together, is his right to pursue his desire to love and be loved by a man more important than my desire not to enter into the realm of the divorced? Do I have the right to tell my friends, family, or children about why he has left, or does his wish for not being known as a homosexual person supersede my needs? I love him. I know he loves me in his relatively asexual way. What am I to do?

The Cuckold

Men and women both may become highly symptomatic from their spouses' affairs. The emotional issues are essentially the same. Men, however, may think that they have been particularly humiliated by the affair. Men who are cuckolds think that others are laughing at them. Their idea that there is something unique about their intense embarrassment reflects how little they appreciate what any betrayed person experiences.

What are often different are the coping opportunities. Men do not often have friends who can listen to them or help them process what has occurred to them. They usually do not associate with other men in the same position. Men are not used to relating in this way. They tend to turn inward, drink or abuse substances, overwork, and pretend that they feel better and are functioning better than they are. The alienation that they had from their inner experiences earlier in their lives reaches a crisis point: They either return to it, hiding their emotional realities from themselves or others, or they surrender to the profound sadness, anxiety, and anger and allow this painful experience to assist their maturation. While some try to replace their wives, many others begin making-do relationships that tide them over until they can regain their internal sense of themselves.

FINAL THOUGHTS

I do not think one's learning about this subject is ever complete. During my lectures about the subject, I discovered the enormous interest in the topic from diverse mental health professionals. While I am loathe to joke about the subject during my teaching, I would be remiss not to mention how commonly infidelity is dealt with humorously—that is, how in jokes, cartoons, plays, short stories, and novels these art forms provide more private views that get at the secret preoccupations and activities of many people.

My aspiration in this chapter was to comfort your initial fears about dealing with infidelity. I did not tell you what to do to manage them in detail because I am still uncertain myself. I have tried to interest you in the role of trying to find the opportunities for growth from the dangers in which the patients are immersed. Some of the references and suggested reading may be useful to you now or in the future.

SUGGESTED FURTHER READING

Anton, R. F. (2008). Naltrexone for the management of alcohol dependence. *New England Journal of Medicinc, 359*(7), 715 721.

Brown, E. (1992). *Patterns of infidelity and their treatment*. New York: Brunner/ Mazel.

Fisher, H. E. (1992). Why adultery? In *Anatomy of Love: The Natural History of Monogamy, Adultery, and Divorce* (pp. 75–97). New York: Norton. Fisher provides a nice cross-cultural and anthropological view of the widespread mental interest in extra-relationship sex.

Kipnis, L. (2003). *Against love: A polemic*. New York: Pantheon.

Levine, S. B. (1998). *Sexuality in mid-life*. New York: Plenum. Chapter 7 provides an incomplete registry of myriad forms of sexual infidelities.

Levine, S. B. (2006). *Demystifying love: Plain talk for the mental health professional*. New York: Routledge. Chapters 6 and 7 (pp. 97–142) deal with the topic in more clinical detail. The book has been useful reading for some patients in the midst of some aspects of the infidelity dilemma.

Perel, E. (2006). *Mating in captivity: Reconciling the erotic and the domestic*. New York: Harper Collins. The author helpfully discusses the possibility of infidelity as the shadow of the third, meaning the extramarital partner.

Person, E. S. (1998). *Dreams of love and fateful encounters: The power of romantic passion*. New York: Norton.

Shanahan, D. (2007). *Bad sex*. New York: Abrams Image. This is a book of sex cartoons, many of which lightly deal with infidelity.

Scheinkman, M. (2005). Beyond the trauma of betrayal: Reconsidering affairs in couples therapy. *Family Process, 44*(2), 227–244.

Storr, A. (1988). *Solitude: A return to the self.* New York: Free Press. This is a wonderful book extolling the virtues of being by oneself at important life transitions. This psychiatrist writes of the lives of many musical greats and figures from Greek and Roman history to illustrate his points.

Synder, D. K., Baucom, D. H., & Gordon, K. C. (2007). *Getting past the affair: A program to help you cope, heal, and move on—together or apart.* New York: Guilford Press. This self-help book contains many useful suggestions for getting through the arduous process of realizing, coping, and deciding what to do about a partner's or one's own infidelity.

Weiderman, M. W. (1997). Extramarital sex: Prevalence and correlates in a national survey. *The Journal of Sex Research, 34*(2), 167–174.

Seven

When Love and Sex Go Wrong
Helping Couples in Distress

MARTA MEANA, PHD

INTRODUCTION

The first couple I ever treated for sexual problems is etched in my memory with the force that only sheer panic can produce. With no access to the notes I took those 15 years ago as a graduate student, I can still remember exact phrases they used in that first session, the way they looked at me and at each other; I could even tell you what each was wearing. I was terrified. Individual therapy was complex enough, with every person an intricate universe unto themselves. Establishing a corrective presence in that private world was one of the most difficult, though engrossing, things I had ever done. My fledgling confidence was starting to stabilize when suddenly I was expected to do the same with two people simultaneously. It felt awfully crowded in that room. Within minutes, it became apparent to me that there would be at least six entities with which to contend in the course of treatment; the individual personalities of the three of us, the couples' relationship, and the relationship of each of them with me—all with their own narratives. How would I manage it all?

Well, I did manage it, and I continue to do so with varying degrees of success in what has personally been the most fulfilling of psychotherapy modalities—couple therapy. I have seen couples struggle bravely with many different types of relationship problems, and, in line with the research on couple therapy efficacy (Christensen & Heavey, 1999; Shadish & Baldwin, 2003), I think I have helped a significant number of them. Sex was implicated in most cases as cause, consequence, or something in between. All of these struggles were emotionally moving manifestations of the human need for connection and the deep pain felt when this connection is damaged or altogether severed. In this chapter, I plan to tell you a small part of what I have learned to help you develop a sense of calm, competence, and confidence in your attempts to help couples in distress.

ARE SEXUAL AND RELATIONSHIP PROBLEMS RELATED?

The treatment for any one couple with sexual concerns will be shaped by an ongoing assessment of both the sexual problem and relationship dynamics. This assessment continues long after the intake. The nature of the association (if one exists) between the sexual difficulties and nonsexual aspects of the relationship will unfold as the therapy progresses. Treatment plans can then be adjusted to address emerging facts about the sexual problem and related relationship dynamics.

Not all couples with sexual problems have a deep-rooted relationship conflict. Some do, and some don't. Bad sex can happen to happy couples. Even if you discover latent resentment or anger, do not assume that these are necessarily related to the sexual problem. There is no sustained empirical support for a specific psychosocial etiology underlying any one sexual problem or dysfunction. Moreover, it is often difficult to tease apart the maladjusted patterns of relating that gave rise to the sexual problem from those that developed as a consequence of it. To further complicate the picture, a minority of couples who have conflicted, unhealthy relationships also have what they describe as great sex. These couples seek consultation for the "other stuff." Good sex can happen to unhappy couples. So, do not fall into the trap of thinking that sexual problems automatically signal relationship conflict, or that relationship problems necessarily result in unsatisfying sex. The strategy that has worked best for me has been to work simultaneously on both the sexual and relationship problems without obsessing too much about the connections that may or may not exist between these two dimensions of couples' lives. It is a win–win strategy. If the connection exists, great. Progress in one area is likely to induce progress in the other. If there is no connection, then you are working on two possibly independent areas of difficulty, both of which may improve through this bi-targeted approach.

WHEN BAD OR NO SEX HAPPENS TO GOOD COUPLES

After a torrid love affair in graduate school (sneaking sex between the low-traffic book stacks of the library), Sandra and Nick had married and moved on to high-status positions in banking. They enjoyed each other's company, stayed up late at night talking about their work, socialized frequently, and made love three or four times per week. After a few years, they decided to start a family while attempting to maintain their career lives as unchanged as possible. When they showed up at my office, they were in their 40s, had been married 15 years, and had three children between the ages of 3 and 8; both worked full time. They were wealthy and appeared to have a respectful and close relationship but complained that they had lost their sexual connection. They rarely had sex. Sandra recalled four times in the previous 6 months. Nick insisted it was even less than that. Worse yet, both agreed it was boring when it happened. They described themselves as "cooperative roommates" and good parents, but they missed their sex life and did not know how to get "that loving feeling" back. They wondered if they had lost their attraction and were afraid about what this meant and where it might lead.

I have seen many couples in some version of this situation. Long-term relationships can be hard on sex and passion. The type of sexual desire that is usually referred to as passion is typically highest at the start of a relationship and suffers a decrease in the lives of most couples over time (Levine, 2003). When we add the stress and time crunch of professional careers and child rearing to that natural waning, it is hardly surprising when couples find themselves drifting toward sexual stagnation. It is not a far leap to

outright sexual dysfunction and relationship conflict. The positive association between relationship quality and sexual satisfaction has been empirically validated in many studies (Sprecher & Cate, 2004). It is thus important
for us to understand how couples lose their sexual connection and how to
get them back on track.

In an attempt to further our understanding, my lab recently conducted a
study of 20 married women complaining of distressing decreases in sexual
desire (Meana & Sims, 2008). We inquired about their personal theories of
how they had lost their desire. Three major themes emerged as particularly
damaging forces in these committed women, who reported that they loved
their husbands.

The first of these was the institutionalization of the relationship. Many
blamed the formalization of their union for having robbed sex of that sense of
transgression they had found sexy when they were dating. Sex had become
an obligation rather than a suspension of the mundane. It was overaccessible,
leaving little room for desire to build to a crescendo. The responsibilities that
were part and parcel of the institution of marriage had also had a dampening
effect on desire and arousal. Marriage came with budgets, mortgages, juggling
work and kids' schedules, and much anxiety about future security. Little room
was left for the carefree, present-focused abandon that they associated with
exciting sex.

The second theme, overfamiliarity, was related to the gradual loss of individuality in both wives and husbands. The seemingly inevitable enmeshment
of married life was blamed for the dissipation of romance and the devolu-
tion of sex into a mechanical, rigidly scripted, orgasm-centered exercise. They
missed those clumsy first encounters in which excitement trumped precision
and skill.

Finally, women complained of the desexualizing roles associated with most
of their daily activities. Enacting their roles as mothers, housewives, and working women felt largely incompatible with the sexual role they felt expected to
adopt in the bedroom. They had stopped seeing themselves as sexual or as
sexually desirable despite their husbands' compliments and assurances.

Although we have not yet conducted a parallel study with men, I imagine
they are struggling similarly with the challenge of keeping sex vibrant and
functional in the context of long-term relationships.

These findings align well with the clinically inspired writing of Perel (2006),
who focuses on the identification and correction of the deeroticizing elements
of intimacy. Curiously, intimacy was the very principle that generations of
therapists had been told was requisite for a satisfying sex life. What nobody
seemed to be saying was that most of us had had two very common types of
cases: (1) couples with solid, loving relationships whose sex was nonexistent
or unarousing and (2) couples whose relationships had improved significantly
through therapy without any improvement in sexual relating or function.

Maybe we are finally starting to integrate the paradoxical necessity of a
healthy distance to experience true closeness. Over 30 years ago, Bowen (1972),
a family systems theorist, emphasized the importance of the differentiation
of self to the success of family relationships. Schnarch (1991, 2003) popular-
ized its direct application to the relationship and sexual problems of couples.
In the latter formulation, both real intimacy and satisfying sex require that
individuals maintain a sense of self such that they

1. Not expect their partner to allay all of their anxieties (they can self-soothe)
2. Tolerate discomfort in the service of personal and relationship growth (it does not necessarily signal abandonment or narcissistic injury)
3. Not get swept up in each other's reactivity

In other words, real intimacy and good sex are contingent on the ability to relate to a partner as an individual who exists separate from you or your needs and vice versa.

Baumeister and Bratslavsky (1999) proposed the intriguing idea that passion may be a function of changes in intimacy rather than of any specific level of intimacy. They argued that the literature suggested that passion might be highest during periods when intimacy jumped from one level to a higher one. This clearly is most evident at the beginning of a relationship when one revs from 0 to 60, as a stranger quickly becomes a lover and a friend. However, as soon as that level of intimacy stabilizes, the passion subsides until the next leap occurs. In other words, passion is energized by discovery rather than by familiarity. These intriguing ideas have useful implications for the treatment of couples whose commitment and love is not seriously in question, but whose sex lives have become impoverished. Brainstorming the creation of opportunities for increasing this type of intimacy and reenergizing of passion can be fruitful. You might be wondering whether a couple can forever continue to find new levels of intimacy or whether there is a natural end to this journey of mutual discovery. Considering the complexity of the human spirit, I would bet on the former. As a therapist, I bank on it.

HELPING HAPPY COUPLES HAVE GOOD SEX

I have found two strategies particularly effective in improving the sex life of couples who otherwise relate well: fixing structural problems and calibrating the balance between intimacy and distance.

Structural problems relate to issues of context, timing, and prioritizing. These are increasingly being investigated in a growing literature about the challenges of balancing work and family (e.g., Zimmerman, Haddock, Current, & Ziemba, 2003).

> Sandra and Nick were making some common structural mistakes. Filling their weekdays with foot-long to-do lists, there was literally no time left in their schedules for quality time alone. Their only private "free" time was at approximately 11 p.m., when they were both dragging themselves into bed, exhausted and already stressing about tomorrow's list. Was this when great sex or any sex was supposed to happen? Weekends were no different. Running from piano lessons to soccer games to kids' birthday parties, they occasionally reserved evenings for dinner parties, which they typically left early because they were either sleepy or anticipating a 7 a.m. soccer game on Sunday morning. Occasionally, one of them would panic about how long it had been since they last made love. Awkward initiation attempts were inevitably inopportune and mostly met with a lukewarm reception. The initiator would often skulk away, thinking "this is never going to happen." Sometimes that was Sandra, and sometimes that was Nick.

The first necessary intervention was to ensure that sex and the relationship were not lost in the shuffle of responsibilities. Both needed attention and nurturing. Many couples function as if their relationship is background music that can only be turned up after all the more urgent tasks have been addressed (which of course never seems to happen). This is not so. A sexual connection is quite fragile and does not generally survive delays half as well as do house renovations or that golf game. Sandra and Nick would have to stop taking the relationship for granted. They would have to make real time for it, rather than feed it the crumbs of an overscheduled life. This involved a concerted effort concerning a series of choices that privileged their emotional and sexual connection over a number of other concerns. After all, if the relationship came crumbling down, so would everything else. The reprioritizing had to be seen as essential rather than as a luxury.

The second reconfiguration involved increasing the right type of intimacy and distance in Sandra and Nick's relationship. They thought they were very close because they believed they could read each other's minds and finish each other's sentences. Reassuring as that was, that type of intimacy was not helping them relate well sexually. Most people do not want to have sex with a mirror image of themselves. The excitement of sex lies, at least in part, in the union of two separate beings who will never be completely knowable to each other.

> We learned in therapy that Sandra was not really that accurate at reading Nick's mind, and that when Nick finished Sandra's sentences, she often did not have the heart to tell him he was wrong. The discovery of these lacunas in their "closeness" was unsettling but exciting for them.

Recalling Baumeister and Bratslavsky's (1999) concept of passion as a function of jumps in intimacy, I figured that their discovery of difference could lead to an increase in intimacy. I think I was correct because passion for each other ensued. Sandra and Nick came to see that they had to commit themselves to being creative to promote these wonderful opportunities.

Distance also had to be protected. I encouraged Sandra and Nick to regularly make plans separate from each other—to go out with friends, to open themselves to the gaze of others. Perhaps most important, I wanted them to recapture the gaze they had for each other prior to getting married. When making a date for dinner, I encouraged them to meet at the restaurant instead of driving there together. I wanted Sandra to walk into a bistro and look at Nick sitting there for that brief moment before he noticed her, much as she would look at a handsome man unconnected to her. I wanted Nick to attend one of Sandra's conference presentations so he could look at this competent, beautiful woman enact a performance that had nothing to do with him. I wanted him to look at her the way the other men in the audience were likely doing.

Now that a few years have passed, I wonder whether Sandra and Nick have maintained their gains by continuing to employ the strategies that helped them. The literature suggests that they had half a chance or maybe less. Assessment at 2 years or more after termination indicates significant deterioration in 30–60% of treated couples (Jacobson, Schmaling, & Holtzworth-Monroe, 1987; Snyder, Wills, & Grady-Fletcher, 1991). I imagine they go through periods when they falter and lose the thread of their romantic and sexual connection yet again. I hope one or both initiates a call to action when he or she senses the diminution of passion. That would mean that I successfully taught them to carefully tend to their sexual lives on an ongoing basis.

WHEN BAD OR NO SEX HAPPENS TO UNHAPPY COUPLES

> Gerry and Norma were pushing 60 and had been married for 35 years. The marriage had been difficult from the start for these two high-achieving music industry professionals. They both had very strong personalities, but each manifested their need for dominance differently. She was emotionally reactive and expressive, and he was the quiet, unyielding type; both seemed intent on winning every disagreement, no matter how trivial. She had always had a high sex drive, while he had never seemed that interested, even when they were young. They had stopped having sex altogether shortly after the birth of their fourth son, who was 17 when I met them. They came to therapy when she discovered that he had repeatedly paid for sex with prostitutes procured online over the past 5 years. Although she was very hurt by the discovery and his confession, she was also heartened by the fact that he actually wanted sex at all. She wanted to work on the relationship and reignite their sexual connection. Grateful though he was for her forgiving attitude, he was decidedly less enthusiastic about the sex part than the relationship part.

While healthy couples can occasionally fall into patterns that make for boring sex, unhappy couples usually do not maintain a good sex life in the long run. Unhappy couples also have a tendency to experience sexual difficulties much more detrimentally. If sex is a sensitive issue for most couples, it can be positively explosive for couples who are not relating well otherwise. For Gerry and Norma, it had become so radioactive that forgoing sex altogether had become the easiest option. Perhaps more astonishingly, their union had survived 16 years of no sexual contact whatsoever.

There are many types of unhappy couples with many different types of problems. The challenges of long-term relationships can also shift as the relationship moves from one developmental stage into another (Kurdek, 1999). I could fill more than one book (and many folks have; e.g., Gottman, 1994) on the dynamics of unhappy couples. Variations notwithstanding, my experience has been that there are a number of relationship characteristics commonly found in unhappy couples. Their sexual activities often become infected with the same unhealthy dynamics that plague the rest of their interactions. I have found it helpful to target four common central problems:

1. Their battleground mentality
2. Their attachment to failing strategies
3. Their narcissistic fragility
4. Their systemic secondary gain

These themes appear widely throughout the couple therapy literature under different monikers and with varying degrees of emphasis placed on them (Gurman, 2008).

Battleground Mentality

The unhappy couple is often engaged in a daily duel. Rather than considering themselves a team whose collaboration will be mutually beneficial, the unhappy couple is often involved in a zero-sum game that includes every-thing from who takes out the garbage to whose friends are more interesting. Their lives together are a battleground, and only one person can win any given melee. Within this dynamic, sex is just another opportunity for victory. Sex becomes a contingency to be granted or withdrawn—a power play.

> When Gerry was angry with Norma, he would discourage her sexual advances, claim-ing fatigue or even criticizing her way of initiating sex as being "crude." When Norma had been angry with Gerry, she would stop herself from having an orgasm or, in a reversal of the more common story, fake not having had one. She called these her "quiet orgasms," silent weapons aimed straight at the sexual competence of her part-ner. Even her discovery of his infidelity, hurtful though it had been, gave her a certain sense of power. He was the one on the ropes now. Trying to one-up each other, Gerry and Norma had eventually destroyed their sex and hurt themselves and each other terribly in the process.

What the unhappy couple does not realize is that there are no victors in this type of scorched earth relationship policy.

Attachment to Failing Strategies

One of the most striking characteristics of many unhappy couples is their persistence in continuing to behave in ways that do not get them what they want or need. Ironically, they become attached to failing strategies. They fall into a vicious cycle of relating that repeats itself endlessly, with a negative outcome pretty much guaranteed every time. Gottman (1999) identified four particularly pernicious ways of relating that lead to relationship distress and failure: criticism, defensiveness, contempt, and stonewalling. The most empirically validated of these types of patterns is the demand–withdrawal pattern (Heavey, Christensen, & Malamuth, 1995), in which one partner insists on openly pushing their agenda while the other reacts to this insistence by withdrawing. It is also by far the most common pattern that I have experi-enced in my work with couples. The more one withdraws, the more the other demands, and the more one demands, the more the other withdraws.

> Norma would plead for emotional expression or sexual interaction, while Gerry with-drew. The more Gerry withdrew, the louder Norma's protestations became. He hated her vociferous pleas, and she hated his stonewalling. The irony was that they were each engaged in a behavior that got them more of exactly what they so claimed to dislike.

Narcissistic Fragility

A third common manifestation of unhappy couples is a lack of differentiation rooted in narcissistic fragility or insecurity. Although the couple's lack of a well-functioning connection makes them appear distant, a closer look reveals that they are actually enmeshed. Often, the problem is that neither of them is sufficiently securely attached to be able to truly listen and empathize with their partner's experiences without worrying about how these negatively reflect on them. Every partner doubt or anxiety or personality trait is potentially threat-ening when viewed through the solitary lens of self-defense.

In his 20s, Gerry had thought it was great to have a girlfriend who wanted a lot of sex. It was not long, though, before her sexual desire became threatening. Could he possibly ever satisfy her? Did it mean that she had been promiscuous? Would she seek satisfaction elsewhere? He started admonishing her libido, making her feel that there was something wrong with her. Norma interpreted his rejection to mean that he was not attracted to her. This made her try harder. She had breast augmentation surgery. She bought expensive lingerie and had tummy tucks after the birth of two of her children.

None of these tactics worked because both Gerry and Norma had been working under false assumptions produced by their own insecurities. Gerry was very attracted to Norma, and Norma simply loved sex, especially with Gerry. Unfortunately, a lifetime of getting that wrong had seriously damaged both Gerry's attraction to Norma and Norma's enjoyment of sex with Gerry.

Systemic Secondary Gain

Understanding the sexual problems of unhappy couples also requires a close examination of the extent to which the sexual difficulty may be serving a purpose that keeps the system of the couple stable: the secondary gain. Happiness and stability do not always go hand in hand. One could say that Gerry and Norma had a stable marriage—it had lasted 35 years through many professional and personal ups and downs, the raising of four children, and most recently, a confession of repeated infidelity. For all of their mutual torture, divorce only surfaced as a routinely empty threat that neither of them had pursued with any vigor. Theirs was the archetypal miserable but stable marriage.

How was that stability maintained? I suggest that it was in part maintained by their problems in and outside the bedroom. Norma had always been drop-dead gorgeous and sexually desirous to boot. What better way to control Norma than to make her feel unattractive and constantly striving to please sexually? Gerry had always exuded stoic confidence and competence and been attractive to women more because of these qualities than because of his looks. What better way to control Gerry than to make him feel sexually incompetent and insecure? Note that when Gerry finally strayed, it was with sex workers. When I asked him, "Why prostitutes?" he said, "Because there was no pressure; they did not care how good I was or how I felt about them."

My experience has been that the core conflicts in the sexual lives of unhappy couples are pretty similar to the core conflicts they experience outside the bedroom. Sexual dynamics are often, although not always, an extension of relationship dynamics. Some therapists may think that there is no way to work on the sexual lives of couples who are that severely damaged without first fixing everything else. Once the relationship is on track, then good sex has a chance. I have preferred to work on both the sex and the relationship simultaneously because they often seem indelibly intertwined. In some cases, addressing the nonsexual problems in the relationship has been the route to improving sex. In other cases, addressing problems in their sex led to an improvement in their overall relating.

Three Principles to Help the Unhappy Couple

It is difficult to improve relationships that have been malfunctioning for years. As a therapist, the blueprint you draw up for this improvement needs to be customized to each couple and their specific dilemmas. There are currently as many as a dozen self-identified types of couple therapy filling the chapters of handbooks and texts on theory and practice (Gurman, 2008). Among these, you will find cognitive behavioral, emotionally focused, structural, narrative, and integrative couple therapy. There are also shelves on shelves of self-help books offering tips based on these theoretical approaches to help our patients with their sex and relationships. They all likely make useful contributions, although research has found little evidence of differential effectiveness across theoretical orientations (Shadish & Baldwin, 2003). I urge you to review the major contributors as you start to develop your own style and approach to treating couples. Gottman's body of work is particularly helpful as it is empirically grounded and organized in a clinically useful manner. For the purposes of your getting started seeing couples in your career, I am going to focus on three basic guiding principles that are likely to apply to all couples regardless of their age, the developmental stage of their relationship, or their sexual orientation: acceptance, responsibility, and agency.

Principle 1. Accepting That Some Things Are Outside Our Control or Simply Not Our Business to Change

As Jacobson and Christensen (1996) point out in their introduction to integrative couple therapy, the idea that long-term relationships depend largely on a certain degree of acceptance is probably as old as the hills. However, for such a supposedly popular and accepted notion, it has hardly been in great supply among the distressed couples that have sought my services. Many bitterly complain about characteristics in their partners that have been there since they met. Often, the personality trait in question is the very thing that had attracted them to their partner in the first place.

When Jacob met Mike, he was drawn to his outgoing nature, his openness, and the ease with which he expressed himself. Although Jacob had already come out, he remained self-conscious and reticent to public gestures that might announce his orientation. Mike was a breath of fresh air, and Jacob openly credited him with increasing his confidence and his self-acceptance. Mike found Jacob's shyness endearing, and he loved his "big, quiet man." Twenty years later, Jacob found Mike obnoxious, embarrassing, and emotionally insatiable. Mike claimed to be "bored to death." They had not had sex for a year. Although they had both long agreed to have a nonmonogamous relationship, they claimed to want a sexual presence in each other's life, and they were alarmed at this year of nothing.

Jacob and Mike were not unlike Gerry and Norma. Two introverts had hooked up with two extroverts, and the supposed complementarity of their personalities had turned on them. They had spent a good part of their time together bucking the personality and behavioral styles of the other while becoming more and more entrenched in their own. What to do?

A useful first task is to get both members of the couple to agree on what the core conflict in the relationship actually is. Jacobson and Christensen (1996) called this the "formulation," and they offered a number of common conflict themes, such as closeness–distance; control and responsibility; you don't love me—yes, I do, it is *you* who doesn't love me; conventionality–unconventionality. These conflict themes are by no means exhaustive, and you should feel free to formulate your own, one perhaps customized more specifically to your couple's dilemma. Getting agreement on the identification of the problem, however, is a crucial first intervention. It communicates powerfully to the couple that, contrary to the polarization to which they have become so attached, they both have the same problem. This can be a transformational insight. It builds empathy and is the first step in potentially turning two opponents into a team.

Another acceptance-based strategy consists of reacquainting each member of the couple with the positive aspects of the partner's disposition that have now become annoying. Most couples will still be able to access this, but they have had much more practice focusing on the negative consequences, so it will require some retraining. When I met Norma, she was terribly bothered by Gerry's emotional unflappability, but when she started a weekly tracking of its benefits as manifested in specific incidents, she started evaluating his emotional steadiness more favorably. There were still moments when it drove her to distraction, but there were times when it calmed her. At yet others, Gerry's reticence to pronounce judgment on some event or person even felt generous. Mike's exuberance at times made Jacob want to scream, but at others it made him lighten up and laugh. Most cognitive or emotional styles or tendencies have their pros and cons. We do not get to control the dosage in another person, just as nobody else gets to control it in us.

This reemphasis on the positive does not deny that certain behaviors are annoying or hurtful; it simply balances the evaluation. Part of that balancing act also has to incorporate a decatastrophization of the negative behaviors. It is likely that partners will forever engage in behaviors that are disliked. The question becomes one of degree. Are these behaviors intolerable? Clearly, some are, and acceptance strategies in couple therapy are not intended to give a pass to these. The couple gets to decide which ones are deal breakers. Gerry frequenting prostitutes was one such example. No one, including Gerry, expected Norma to accept that. The problem is that unhappy couples often act as if everything is a deal breaker, without ever actually breaking the deal. They are stuck in perpetual crisis mode. This is an important pattern to undo, and acceptance is a big part of the solution.

Principle 2. Taking Responsibility for Our Role, Good and Bad, in Life and Relationships

Many couples enter therapy after years of trying and failing to change each other. They each think the therapist will see it their way, and that the partner transformation that has eluded them will finally occur. Each is trying to double up on their efforts by hiring you. This will be the one way you will want to disappoint both of them. Whatever shape the relationship, both members of the couple had a hand in making it so. Fixing it will require an even greater joint effort.

Stella was engaged to be married when she met Michelle at a party. They became fast friends. Michelle was a lesbian but unattached at the time, and although she was very attracted to Stella, she gave Stella no indication. After all, Stella was straight and 6 months away from getting married; there seemed little point. Their friendship continued to intensify, and one day it was Stella who "jumped" Michelle. Their very passionate affair became solidified when Stella, who had never before "felt sexual" about a woman, broke off her engagement and quickly moved in with Michelle. Five years later, they sought therapy because they fought continuously, and their sex life alternated between "whole weekends spent in bed" and weeks of no sexual contact. Stella complained that she felt "swallowed up" by Michelle's neediness and high sex drive, and Michelle doubted Stella's commitment and attraction to her. Every day, she half expected Stella to say she had fallen in love with a man and was leaving. Both had come to experience the other as selfish.

Stella wanted me to help her make Michelle less needy, and Michelle wanted me to help her make Stella more present. After getting them to agree about their common core conflict (neither felt loved), I needed to instate a paradigm shift. The emphasis had to shift from blaming the other to self-evaluation. Each one had to take responsibility for having created and maintained the problem, and each had to take responsibility for changing it. Rather than focus on the complaints one had about the other, I asked them to focus on what they thought they could do better or maybe not do at all. I could tell that this was rather disappointing to them at the start. Both had been looking forward to cathartically spewing complaints about each other for weeks in the supposedly safer environment of the therapy room. Stella seemed certain I would find Michelle overbearing (who wouldn't?) and ask her to tone it down. Michelle's tearful extended stares at me were begging for confirmation that her partner was cold and uncaring (wasn't it obvious?).

I first initiated the responsibility shift with the formulation of the common problem. They shared the dilemma. There were no victims. Michelle and Stella were both stuck in the "you don't love me as much as I love you" conflict. Stella experienced Michelle's neediness as a type of cannibalization that felt anything but loving. Michelle experienced Stella's supposed independence as a form of rejection and impending abandonment. The bad news was that they both felt unloved. The good news was that they could relate to each other's pain given their shared dilemma. I then furthered the responsibility shift with a second reconceptualization of their relationship as one in which competition made no sense. Even when Michelle or Stella had forcefully and irrefutably made her point, the resentment and alienation the other felt from that type of battle mentality left both of them feeling like they had lost. The crucial insight here was that this was not a battlefield. If Stella and Michelle really wanted this relationship, they would have to trade their battle-weary opponent garb for team uniforms. They had a common goal (the success of the relationship), and they had a common problem (feeling unloved). The attainment of their goal and the solution to their problem would inevitably entail a middle-ground solution that would not align perfectly with either of their idealizations but be far superior to what they had now. The necessity of this team mentality may seem as self-evident as the concept of acceptance, but it is just as difficult to integrate and enact. It is also just as powerful and transforming when it happens.

A third step in the responsibility shift is the couple's decision to disrupt their vicious cycle of negative relating to each other, a feedback loop that only results in each person becoming more and more ensconced in the mutually alienating style. The more Michelle demanded Stella's time and attention, the more Stella's schedule filled up with work obligations. The more Stella withdrew her attention, the more desperate and emotionally pitched Michelle's appeals became. To break this cycle, they would each have to try something new. What they had done to date had clearly not worked for them. It had actually gotten each of them more of what they did not want. The status quo had gotten Stella a more emotionally out of control Michelle and Michelle an increasingly unavailable Stella. What did they have to lose by trying something completely different? I urged Michelle to act against her impulses and communicate acceptance when Stella was unavailable for an evening together or when she was not interested in having sex. I urged Stella to act against her impulses and go out of her way to make evening plans for alone time with Michelle as well as to initiate sex. It is unlikely that either of them would ever enact this to the complete satisfaction of the other, but it almost necessarily had to be an improvement.

When couple therapy is successful, it is not that easily distinguishable from individual therapy, other than by the number of people in the room. That is because the emphasis on responsibility necessitates individual change. My experience has been that couples truly change only when the individuals within them do. Like most couple therapists, I have had about as many successful as unsuccessful outcomes (if by the latter we mean couples who either broke up or stayed together without any significant improvement in their relationship). Reviews of couple therapy outcome studies indicate that in only half of treated couples do both partners show significant improvement in couple satisfaction at termination (Snyder, Castellani, & Whisman, 2006). What is interesting is that some of my couple failures were actually individual successes. Occasionally, the focus on responsibility, differentiation, and self-improvement was fully integrated by one member of the couple, while the other remained unchanged. In these cases, at least we can take heart in the fact that, although the relationship did not survive, the member of the couple who changed is likely to have a better chance at success the next time.

Principle 3. Deciding to Become an Agent of Positive Change

Among the most common things I hear in the first stages of both individual and couple therapy is "I can't help feeling this way," "This is just the way I am," "He/she has always been that way." I tell my clients that if I actually believed in the inevitability of any of those statements, I would not be a therapist. What would be the point if people cannot help thinking or feeling what they do, or if people have a way of being that is so cemented that change is impossible? My promotion of accepting what we cannot change is surpassed by my promotion of being active in changing what we can. The crux is in our determination of which is which. I like to err on the side of agency as long it pertains to ourselves and not to others. I tell my clients that making a project out of yourself is usually a good thing, even if you do not completely succeed in reaching your goals. Just as important, I also remind them that making a project out of someone else, however, is not. It rarely works, and when it does, it often backfires.

Changing the couple's mind-set from one of inevitability to one of decision making is an important way to build agency. Most of my clients are at first perplexed when I talk about their thoughts and feelings as decisions they are constantly making. I explain to them that, although they may not make a decision about a thought that enters their head, they can make a decision about the weight they will give that thought and the extent to which they will allow it to influence their emotions and actions. Cognitive–behavioral couple therapy emphasizes the reconsideration of these automatic thoughts (Baucom, Epstein, LaTaillade, & Kirby, 2008). In regard to emotions, many clients start therapy with the adage, "If I feel it, it must be true." We privilege emotions even more than we do thoughts, as if they have a straight connection to the truth. This is generally not helpful. Again, we may not decide to suddenly feel sad, angry, or joyful, but we can decide the influence the emotion will have on us, how long we hold on to it, whether or not to express it, and perhaps most important, whether or not the emotion is actually commensurate or even related to the event that triggered it. If it is not, then it is important to investigate the origin of that emotion. One of the foci of emotionally focused couple therapy is the restructuring of maladaptive emotion (Johnson, 2008).

If the couple has decided that they will work to become agents of change in their relationship, you will have to help them build their relationship self-efficacy. You can do this by instilling hope and enhancing their skill sets (e.g., skills related to communication, problem solving, conflict resolution, cognitive restructuring, emotional regulation). However, it is important that you accurately assess and monitor the couple's commitment to relationship-building agency at different stages in therapy. If the motivation to change or to improve the relationship is lacking in one or both members of the couple, no skill-building effort is likely to help them. It is simply too difficult a task for half-hearted attempts. The fact that the couple initiated therapy is insufficient evidence of their commitment. I have witnessed the following scenarios: Both members of the couple actually want out of the relationship but feel guilty about dissolving it without appearing to try; one wants out but is playing along for a while to ease the partner into the breakup; one or both want confirmation that the relationship just does not work; one is looking for a safe place in which to eventually disclose that the relationship is over; one is punishing the other by making them go to therapy, although they have already checked out of the relationship.

Assessing the commitment level in both members of the couple usually takes more than the question, "How committed are you, really, to working on this relationship?" The more informative assessment of commitment usually occurs by confronting the couple about behavior that seems to be communicating "I want out." When I have doubted the commitment of one partner, I have generally found it useful to assess this further in an individual session with that person. In this individual session, the uncommitted person is likely to feel freer to express the truth. This truth can then be brought back into the joint session in as productive a way as possible. There is no point in continuing a charade. On the other hand, you want to remain open to the possibility that the commitment weary or even half-dead can and sometimes do develop the will to forge ahead through the process of therapy.

MANAGING THE THERAPIST–COUPLE RELATIONSHIP

For a therapist new to treating couples, the most immediate and obvious challenge is the management of the relationship with the couple. As I mentioned, many individuals walk into therapy hoping for a personal alliance with the therapist so that, together, you will talk some sense into their remiss partner. The pressure for the therapist to form an alliance usually emanates from both partners at different times, especially early in therapy. They will each turn to you with that "See, what I mean?" look after their partner has, in their eyes, confirmed their complaint. It will be harder than you think not to comply in some form with that implicit request, but it is essential that you not do so.

You will often like one person more than you do the other. You will sometimes find that one is the more difficult personality, is not trying hard enough, or seems to have an agenda at odds with the supposedly agreed-on goal. You will experience countertransference in couple therapy much as you experience it in individual therapy. You may have a particularly strong reaction to a couple's dilemma because it harkens back to another important relationship in your life, maybe even your current one. This may lead you to minimize a problem that is important to the couple or focus on one that they do not much care about. Self-reflection, awareness, and conference or individual consultation for particularly thorny countertransference issues remain good ways to combat these potential complications. The integrity of the therapy depends on your enactment of impartiality and on your successful private management of countertransference, whether the couple successfully works through their problems or not (Broderick, 1983). Even the couple whose relationship is ultimately not helped by therapy should feel that the therapeutic process honored both individuals equally and treated their struggle with respect.

Another formidable challenge and opportunity in couple therapy is the tendency to idealize the therapist. When the couple problem is sexual, that idealization often includes eroticization. You are sitting in your chair appearing to be all understanding, eminently reasonable, warm, empathic, and an apparent promoter of sexual connection and creative sexual interactions—the perfect partner. This idealization/eroticization may at first act as a spark that helps the couple on the road to relating well, but it has its pitfalls. First, the idealization is rarely experienced in the same measure by both partners. This can lead to a perceived or real alliance that threatens progress. Second, the eroticization is typically sexual-orientation dependent. In the case of a heterosexual couple, only one of them is likely to be eroticizing you. This might engender jealousy on the part of the nonsmitten partner, which can obfuscate the real problem in their relationship. Third, and most important, it is false. Please be careful not to be believe in their idealization. You are no more the perfect partner than either of them is. The idea that the solution lies in finding the perfect partner works directly against the promotion of acceptance, responsibility, and agency. So, when idealization/eroticization occurs, it is important for you to notice and address it with your clients. It represents an excellent opportunity to examine relationship fantasies that may be obstacles to the enjoyment and appreciation of relationship realities.

Finally, there is one question that you will have to answer for yourself in every case: "Should I always see the couple together, or might it be advisable to occasionally break them up for individual sessions?" Different therapists have different approaches to this issue. There are pros and cons to both; ultimately, each therapist and each couple need to decide what is best for them. Joint sessions can reduce perceived or real triangulation; no one will try to tell you a secret, no one will fantasize that you are separately conspiring or bonding with the other partner, and you will always be dealing with the shared reality of the couple rather than with their private struggles. The major disadvantage, therefore, is that you may be missing out on important information that will not be disclosed in as honest a way with the partner in the room. That information may be crucial. It may contain the very reason that progress is eluding the couple, despite what looks like their best effort. You may also be forgoing the opportunity to coach each member of the couple on relationship or sexual skills. This is sometimes best done privately so that the individual's initiatives are not dismissed by the partner as mere aping of what you had recommended.

When I started doing couple therapy, I only conducted joint sessions. Individual sessions felt a little dangerous, and I was not sufficiently confident in my ability to manage the potential complications. Over time, however, I started feeling that I needed to do some individual work to get clarity on the couples' problem and possibly to accelerate their progress. Currently, my approach to the first session is to tell the couple that I sometimes find it useful to speak to them individually. I ask them if they would be willing to do this as needed, under one condition. The condition is as follows: I do not guarantee the confidentiality of the individual sessions in relation to the partner, and the disclosure of individual session information during a joint session is at my discretion. If they agree, I have them sign an informed consent that stipulates the conditions. If they do not agree, then we proceed with joint sessions only. In the last 10 years, I can remember only three couples not agreeing to this, and two of them changed their minds and requested individual sessions a few weeks into the therapy. Although this method has worked for me, every therapist has to choose what will be comfortable for them. There is no one right way. The important thing is for everyone to be clear about the ground rules.

POSTSCRIPT

Norma's trust in Gerry improved significantly, with only the rare outburst when he came home later than usual. After a brief period of minimizing his infidelity, Gerry became more understanding of Norma's bouts of insecurity and revealed his own vis-à-vis her love for him. They still occasionally lock horns, but the combativeness is down and the affection up. Recovery time after still too frequent arguments has reduced dramatically. Sex has become a once-a-week event that neither seems too thrilled about, but both adhere to religiously.

Mike fearfully admitted that he was no longer sexually attracted to Jacob. Having suspected this and knowing Mike's love of sex, Jacob was sure this would spell the end of the relationship of his life. Well acquainted with Jacob's sensitivity, Mike also thought this disclosure would surely spell disaster. As it happens, Jacob was not much interested in sex with Mike or anyone else for that matter. They reconfigured their relationship as a companionate rather than a sexual one and reaffirmed their love for each other. Their annoyance for each other's personalities decreased substantially, and a new, good-natured sense of humor about each other's quirks appeared to take its place.

Michelle made enormous strides in identifying her insecurities and correcting her reliance on Stella to compensate for them. She stopped demanding. She stopped acting needy. She regained a sense of her self, her dignity, and her ability to soothe her own anxieties about her desirability and her sexual orientation. Stella seemed impatient with therapy, and none of the changes in Michelle prompted Stella to work on herself or to reconnect. Michelle left her.

Of the couples in the cases I selected for this chapter, one did not make it, and the two that did would hardly be described as ideal outcomes by many readers. As a reality check, Gerry and Norma were delighted because "we got our relationship back!" Mike and Jacob credit the work they did during couple therapy with saving the most important relationship in both of their lives. Michelle was sad that hers was not made of the right stuff, but she was transformed by the realization that it was not she who was not made of the right stuff. Stella was never in the game, surprised and maybe a little narcissistically injured by Michelle's departure, but hardly devastated.

I could have chosen any number of cases to present, but I chose ones that I thought represented the range of what generally transpires in couple therapy. There are many breakups and very few fantasy endings. In my experience, the largest group falls into that middle range of significant but not mind-blowing improvement. Our clients get to decide what relationship is worth keeping and what kind of sex is good enough. They come to us because their relationships and sexual lives are falling short of what they need, not of what we want for them. Ideals are mostly unattainable, and they are rarely universal. Even the concepts of acceptance, responsibility, and agency that I have proposed as safe guidelines to our intervention efforts are surely calibrated differently across ethnic and sexual minority cultures, especially in regard to sexuality (McGoldrick, Loonan, & Wohlsifer, 2007). We must remain vigilant that our applications of even general guiding principles remain sensitive to individual, cultural, and sexual minority needs and wishes.

In conclusion, we need to be able to do the very same thing we are asking of our clients: get over ourselves to connect to others. Whenever I start thinking that I know what people should want, I remind myself of an early experience during graduate training. For 1 week, I conducted intake assessments of couples seeking therapy. Among of these was a wealthy retired couple in their 50s who had reached an impasse because she desperately wanted to move to Las Vegas, and he was dead set against it. I maintained my impartial demeanor, but secretly I was dismayed. I clearly remember thinking, "Who in the world would want to live in Las Vegas?!"

Guess where I have lived for the last 12 years … very happily?

REFERENCES

Baucom, D. H., Epstein, N. B., LaTaillade, J. J., & Kirby, J. S. (2008). Cognitive–behavioral couple therapy. In A. S. Gurman (Ed.), *Clinical handbook of couple therapy* (pp. 31–72). New York: Guildford Press.

Baumeister, R. F., & Bratslavsky, E. (1999). Passion, intimacy, and time: Passionate love as a function of change in intimacy. *Personality and Social Psychology Review, 3*, 49–67.

Bowen, M. (1972). On the differentiation of self. In J. Framo (Ed.), *Family interaction: A dialogue between family researchers and family therapists* (pp. 111–173). New York: Springer.

Broderick, C. (1983). *The therapeutic triangle*. London: Sage. Although now almost 30 years old, this is still a gem and provides very practical advice about the management of the triangular relationships inherent to couple therapy.

Christensen, A., & Heavey, C. L. (1999). Interventions with couples. *Annual Review of Psychology, 50,* 165–190.

Gottman, J. M. (1994). *What predicts divorce? The relationship between marital processes and marital outcomes*. Hillsdale, NJ: Erlbaum. In this classic text, this foremost marital researcher presents his findings on behavioral predictors of marital dissolution.

Gottman, J. M. (1999). *The marriage clinic*. New York: Norton.

Gurman, A. S. (Ed.). (2008). *Clinical handbook of couple therapy*. New York: Guildford Press. This is the definitive reference guide to current couple therapy theories and approaches.

Heavey, C., Christensen, A., & Malamuth, N. (1995). The longitudinal impact of demand and withdrawal during marital conflict. *Journal of Consulting and Clinical Psychology, 63,* 797–801. This is an excellent empirical investigation of perhaps the most common interactional pattern found in couples seeking therapy.

Jacobson, N. S., & Christensen, A. (1996). *Acceptance and change in couple therapy: A therapist's guide to transforming relationships*. New York: Norton. This well-organized and informative book is essential for those wanting to know more about the practice of integrative couple therapy than that found in chapters on the topic.

Jacobson, N. S., Schmaling, K. B., & Holtzworth-Monroe, A. (1987). Component analysis of behavioral marital therapy: 2-year follow-up and prediction of relapse. *Journal of Marital and Family Therapy, 13,* 187–195.

Johnson, S. M. (2008). Emotionally-focused couple therapy. In A. S. Gurman (Ed.), *Clinical handbook of couple therapy* (pp. 107–137). New York: Guildford Press.

Kurdek, L. A. (1999). The nature and predictors of the trajectory of change in marital quality for husbands and wives over the first 10 years of marriage. *Developmental Psychology, 35,* 1283–96.

Levine, S. B. (2003). The nature of sexual desire: A clinician's perspective. *Archives of Sexual Behavior, 32,* 279–285.

McGoldrick, M., Loonan, R., & Wohlsifer, D. (2007). Sexuality and culture. In S. R. Leiblum (Ed.), *Principles and practice of sex therapy* (4th ed., pp. 416–441). New York: Guilford Press. This chapter is a succinct delineation of issues that might be of importance in sex therapy with cultural and sexual minorities.

Meana, M., & Sims, K. (2008, November). *Between lust and love: A model of sexual desire in married women*. Paper presented at the annual meeting of the Society for the Scientific Study of Sex, San Juan, Puerto Rico.

Perel, E. (2006). *Mating in captivity: Reconciling the erotic and the domestic*. New York: Harper Collins. This is an innovative approach to the treatment of couples whose sexual connection has been damaged by the familiarity, routine, and multiple demands of domesticity and long-term relationships. It is useful for both clinicians and their clients.

Schnarch, D. M. (1991). *Constructing the sexual crucible: An integration of sexual and marital therapy.* New York: Norton.

Schnarch, D. M. (2003). *Resurrecting sex: Solving sexual problems and revolutionizing your relationship.* New York: Harper Paperbacks. This is an excellent clinical application of the concept of differentiation and real intimacy to the reenergizing of couples' sexual lives and is useful for both clinicians and their clients.

Shadish, W. R., & Baldwin, S. A. (2003). Meta-analysis of MFT interventions. *Journal of Marital and Family Therapy, 29,* 547–470.

Snyder, D. K., Castellani, A. M., & Whisman, M. A. (2006). Current status and future directions in couple therapy. *Annual Review of Psychology, 57,* 317–344. This comprehensive review of the most recent empirical data on the efficacy of couple therapy has good suggestions for research and clinical training.

Snyder, D. K., Wills, R. M., & Grady-Fletcher, A. (1991). Long-term effectiveness of behavioral versus insight-oriented marital therapy: A 4-year follow-up study. *Journal of Consulting and Clinical Psychology, 59,* 138–141.

Sprecher, S., & Cate, R. M. (2004). Sexual satisfaction and sexual expression as predictors of relationship satisfaction and stability. In J. Harvey, A. Wenzel, & S. Sprecher (Eds.), *Handbook of sexuality in close relationships* (pp. 235–256). Mahwah, NJ: Erlbaum.

Zimmerman, T. S., Haddock, S. A., Current, L. R., & Ziemba, S. (2003). Intimate partnership: Foundation to the successful balance of family and work. *The American Journal of Family Therapy, 31,* 107–124. This interesting qualitative study of dual-earner couples with children who perceive themselves as successful in balancing family and work has good pointers for couples who struggle with the balance.

Eight

Single Again

LIN S. MYERS, PHD

INTRODUCTION

I became aware that some drastic changes had occurred in how young people viewed the dating world when an 11-year-old client told me she was going out with a boy in her class. A little alarmed that an 11-year-old would be dating, I asked her what they did when they went out. She looked at me like I was a stupid adult and stated that they did not go anywhere; her parents would not let her go alone with him—they were just dating. A teen client, with a tragic face and voice, told me her relationship was over. I asked how long they had been together—her reply, a week. I was confronted with the way the meaning of phrases I thought I understood had changed; dating, going out, and relationship had all taken on very different meanings than when I was younger.

I also was personally confronted with new issues in the dating world when, as a 44-year-old first-time mother, I was confronted with my older adopted children's negative reaction to my dating. Somehow, I saw my private life as separate from my new role of being their mother. We had many struggles as we all adjusted to our new family and life, and it made me consider how other parents might have to handle their personal intimate life. In addition, I have been teaching a relationship and sexuality counseling class to marriage and family therapy students for many years and felt that the issues involved with being single again are not currently represented in books I have used. Thus, the idea for this chapter was born out of my professional and personal experiences. I hope to give you a flavor for the many issues that may face those who are single again. Let us begin by looking at some demographic realities of the single life in the early twenty-first century.

A DEMOGRAPHIC VIEW

We all are aware that teens and young adults have to navigate the often-treacherous waters of dating, the rite of passage from single to coupled life. We see that many young people become ensconced in a committed relationship or marriage and get on with the business of life, believing that their relationship will last. Yet, the separation and divorce rates belie the romantic and traditional view of "until death do us part." I think all of us have seen the aftermath of separation, divorce, and loss of a partner from death in our families, clients, or ourselves but perhaps have not considered how common a feature of life having multiple relationships has become.

While marriage and divorce rates are down in recent years, figures from the 2000 U.S. census show that there were approximately 18.3 million divorced people in the United States (U.S. Department of Commerce Census, 2000). People aged 45 to 55 reported being divorced at the highest rate (15% for men and 18% for women). Divorce rates go up a bit for men as they age, but the difference is not very striking. However, the picture for men and women is very different when looking at the statistics for those widowed. Once they are both in their mid-to-late 40s, the widowed rate is significantly higher for women and sharply increases as the women get older (45–54, 3.7%; 55–64, 11.9%; 65–74, 64.6%) compared to men (45–54, 1.0%; 55–64, 2.8%; 65–74, 8.3%). We can see that women and men will have sharply different experiences in the potential dating world.

Racial/ethnic differences are also found in marriage and divorce rates, with Asians having the highest current marriage and lowest separation or divorce rates, and African-American men and women having the lowest percentages of those currently married. White and Hispanic women have comparable rates of being single, cohabiting, or being married, but black women are about twice as likely to be single throughout all age ranges. The groups with the highest overall percentage divorced were American Indians and Alaska Natives. Clearly, age and racial/ethnic background are factors that will influence aspects of dating, as will geographical variables such as living in certain parts of the United States or residing in urban, suburban, or rural communities.

Being single in middle adulthood and later life are topics that have received some attention in research (e.g., Bulcroft & Bulcroft, 1991), but much has changed since; more people are divorcing, and more who have never married are ending long-term relationships. There is little known about the rates of separation or breakup for those who cohabit, but there has been a sevenfold increase in unmarried couple households since 1970.

MY FOCUS

In this chapter, I hope you will become more familiar with the many issues that will be faced by people from their 30s through old age who are considering dating again. Clearly, there are different developmental factors to consider in these different age groups; however, getting back into the dating scene and becoming emotionally and sexually intimate carry benefits and risks that transcend age. I hope to assist you, the mental health clinician reader, in broadening your understanding of the emotional issues involved in dating again. I focus primarily on heterosexual individuals because issues pertaining to lesbians and gays are discussed elsewhere in this handbook.

WHO IS SINGLE?

Being *single* used to refer to those who had never been married and less commonly those who were divorced or had lost a spouse through death. Because of changing patterns of relationship commitment, the meaning of being single now encompasses those in any age group who have never been married, may or may not have cohabited with an intimate partner, have been divorced, have ended a long-term relationship, or have lost a partner or spouse to death. We may also be surprised to find that our clients have varying definitions of single.

One person may think he or she is not single until the divorce papers are signed, while another will behave as single as soon as they feel their romantic relationship is not working for them. I think it is important to ask our clients for their meaning first so that we do not impose ours on them and second so that we can be more present in their lived experience.

FIVE ISSUES THAT MAKE DATING AGAIN COMPLEX

In preparing this chapter, five major factors emerged that can affect a person dating again. I discuss them throughout this chapter as we consider developmental, interpersonal, societal, multicultural, and medical aspects of being single again.

1. Quality of the previous relationship
2. Minor or adult children and their attitudes and responses
3. The quality of the relationship with the ex-partner
4. New ways of connecting
5. How therapists' values shape perceptions and interventions

DEVELOPMENTAL ASPECTS OF DATING

Dating or courtship serves a socialization purpose that allows us to develop and practice communication and interpersonal skills, to negotiate and compromise, and to learn the rewards and risks of revealing oneself through emotional and sexual intimacy (Furman & Shaffer, 2003). The crux of much of our work with clients will be how they practice the vulnerability inherent in this realm.

Yet, despite the great implications of dating for future pair bonding and the course of life, there is surprisingly little in the way of specific educational programs to help young people understand the process. Sex education in the United States is most frequently taught in middle or high schools as something supposedly value-free (a "just the facts, ma'am" approach) that is neither intimacy nor sexuality positive. It is highly likely that our single-again clients, regardless of age, will have a variety of ineffective dating scripts and skills.

Chorney and Morris (2008) published work about the emotional impact of early dating experiences and what they define as "dating anxiety." An important distinction they make for us clinicians is the separation of the concept of dating anxiety from the anxiety one may feel in response to other social settings. A person may feel competent to meet and interact with others in a variety of settings, but when it comes to dating, a type of performance anxiety may happen that can become debilitating and even cause panic attacks. Do we consider that our clients, with otherwise healthy social interactions, may not feel confident about dating? Movies about adolescents and sexually naïve people often portray a person's embarrassment, fear, panic, or discomfort as comedic (e.g., *The 40-Year-Old Virgin*), usually resulting in the person being rescued by the kindness and power of another's understanding. This is not a particularly good model for action on the part of the person entering the single world again or one with dating anxiety. Chorney and Morris's work can offer new insights for mental health professionals. Grover (2008) provided an important commentary on their research that stressed why clinicians should consider understanding this area. For example, early work on dating was too narrowly focused with little or no consideration of age, culture, and sexual orientation. There is a definite need for more valid and reliable measures to assist us in understanding dating and the phenomenon of dating anxiety throughout the life span.

We clinicians are well aware that our clients' lives are shaped by many factors. Other factors such as racial or cultural expectations around dating across the life span and spiritual or religious beliefs have also received scant research focus. The impact of these aspects of a person's life will also expand and contract throughout the life span, and we need to be prepared to help clients consider them. Since there is little empirical work in this specific area to guide us, I rely on my general approach to multicultural issues by asking the client to educate me about his or her religious beliefs or cultural experiences and by monitoring myself for assumptions I might have. This is especially true with respect to age.

DATING THROUGH THE DECADES

Twenties

Daters in their teens and 20s are more likely to focus on finding a spouse or long-term partner and put more emphasis on specific characteristics, such as attraction, love (especially romantic love), and sexuality. Being in training or school or in various entry-level jobs will bring young people into contact with a variety of others to date. In this age group, there may be more freedom to experiment or escape family expectations, especially if living away from home for the first time. Yet, many expect to find a mate and to start a family.

Thirties–Forties

The focus of dating in one's 30s and 40s may still be on finding a partner for childrearing as the ticking of the biological clock gets louder. Men and women who have an established career can be looking to take another developmental step, or those who are divorced may want someone to help raise their children. Divorce or separation is a common reason for singlehood for people in these first two age groups, while the death of a spouse is less common. Various factors may contribute to a narrowing of opportunities to meet new partners, such as an established job or parental responsibilities.

Fifties–Sixties

For older adults in their 50s and beyond, companionship, friendship, sexual connection beyond fertility, caretaking, prestige, self-esteem, and life changes such as retirement can motivate one to date. In comparison to younger people, dating in later life may not be done with an aim to marry. However, family expectations can be different, and adult children may not be enthusiastic about their parents' dating, and many people hide it from their children, especially anything to do with their sexuality. Our clinical and research interpretations can be impacted if we do not consider what might affect dating and sexual patterns of older adults. For example, in some of my previous research in sexuality and menopause I was looking over the daily logs of one of our women participants and noticed that all sexual behavior had disappeared for a short period of time. When I asked her what had happened, she said it was because her adult children had come to visit, and her boyfriend did not stay over at her place during that time. While the children knew she was dating, they would not have approved of her sexual behavior outside marriage, and she felt it was easier to hide that part of her relationship than deal with their disapproval. If an older adult is living with adult children, their choices will be impacted.

Other external factors can differentially impact dating for men and women in this age group and should be kept in mind as suggestions we have for clients may not be helpful. Bulcroft and Bulcroft (1991) found that involvement in social roles derived from organizational participation, having been divorced (vs. widowed), and length of time being single predicted men's dating patterns, and that men in their study remarried faster and at greater rates than women. Two major factors that predicted older women's dating patterns were mobility and health. While organizational participation played a lesser role, working or religious activities did not predict dating, and a negative factor for women was living in their own single-family home. It is interesting to consider that while owning one's own home may offer a sense of financial security, it may also be an impediment for women. Perhaps there is an isolation factor that makes it more difficult to meet others on a day-to-day basis, or perhaps the memories of the previous partner associated with their house somehow interferes for the woman or any potential partners. Those who live alone may also have substance abuse problems that are easier to hide.

Sixties Plus

Some more recent research has found that older people in their 60s to 80s will also have different reasons for wanting to date—companionship, sharing hobbies, travel—again, many do not want a permanent relationship that resembles a marriage (Davidson, 2001). We need to remember that sexual intimacy, broadly defined, can still be very important for people as long as they live.

THE NEED TO RECOGNIZE GRIEF

While motivations may vary across the life span, an essential focus of our work will be how a person experiences and handles the loss of an intimate relationship. Our attention to clients' grief processes over the loss of a partner at any age is important, but particularly so in those over age 45. As discussed, rates of divorce are higher after 45 years of age, and the rates of widowhood climb quickly, especially for women. The widowed are better recognized as going through a prolonged grief process, but anger toward an ex-spouse or partner often masks the underlying shock, grief, and sadness over their loss. We must consider the meaning of and feelings about a divorce or separation. And, while the loss of a known intimate and sexual partner can result in grief, anger, and fear, for some it is a relief.

In trying to ascertain the meanings of the loss of their previous relationship, I also learn about the role the previous sexual relationship played for them. Not all clients have had a traditional, monogamous relationship. They might have had an emotional commitment without sex, important changes could have happened over the course of the relationship, or they may have even been committed to multiple people (polyamorous). Newly dating people will bring quite different backgrounds to this social process and will have differing responses or unresolved issues from their previous situations.

OTHER OBSTACLES TO DATING

Being mindful of what brings a person back into the dating scene has implications for our work with clients. As we have seen, there are a variety of responses to being "single" again, depending on the circumstances. Here is a partial list of other obstacles to starting again with another partner: loyalty to the previous partner or spouse, financial obligations, health limitations, children or grandchildren, or what others think (Davidson, 2001). Consider influences of religious/spiritual or multicultural expectations, geographical realities, and the pool of potential partners. Many middle-aged people are responsible for taking care of aging parents or relatives. Physical changes associated with aging may make body image as salient an issue as it was in younger years. Having or contracting a sexually transmitted disease or infection, which I also discuss in this chapter, will impact dating behavior.

The advent of erection-enhancing drugs, considered a boon for men, has created a disadvantage for many older women I have known. They report that even men 10–15 years their senior, believing that what matters is sexual performance, have bypassed them to try to snag much younger women. This has fueled fears of rejection from a decreasing pool of available men. The acceptance of goal-directed or performance-based sexual intimacy does not help men or women in any age group.

GENDER ROLE CONSIDERATIONS

More current work in the area of masculinity establishes a continued adherence to masculine norms (Smiler, 2006), especially the belief that the measure of a man is based on performance in all areas of life (e.g., school, sports, work, and sexuality). This sex-role strain has clear implications for how men negotiate and experience sexual and intimate relationships. As men get into their 40s and beyond, normal changes in erectile and ejaculatory functioning can seriously impact a man's sense of masculinity. We need to be aware of this and not dismiss these concerns. I directly ask my male clients how dating and sexual intimacy are tied to their definition of masculinity. (An excellent resource is the DVD *Effective Psychotherapy with Men* by Levant [2006]). Exploring the meaning of masculinity in later years and in relation to interpersonal relationships is an important aspect of a redefinition of self. Many men are relieved to have the topic raised.

Interestingly, a positive factor for women as they age is feeling less tied to gender roles, especially as the caretaker. Along with societal changes in gender role expectations, as they get older many women feel more freedom to initiate dating and sexual intimacy. Others, however, do not want to date or remarry because they want their freedom, are not in love with the person they are dating, or are in poor health. As one 64-year-old woman of my acquaintance put it, "The last thing I ever want to do again is have to wipe some old man's ass!"

Let us see how some of these issues may present themselves in therapy.

Jeremy, a successful business administrator, had married in his mid-20s and had divorced his wife after 25 years of marriage. His three grown children resided elsewhere. At 52, he lived alone, had financial security, and was in excellent health. He had been dating a bit and enjoying the social aspects, but he was frustrated at not feeling he knew what to do to move from kissing to more intimate sexuality. He and his wife had dated briefly and gotten married quickly. He had been sexually faithful to his wife throughout their relationship. In the last 6 years of his marriage, there had been no physical intimacy, and this in part had contributed to the breakup of the marriage. Being a highly educated and successful businessman, he exuded confidence and found asking women out to be an enjoyable experience. There was no sexual dysfunction or problem per se, but he was not able to get to physical intimacy with women, even after several months, unless they made the first move. He felt he had been rejected by some women because he was not forceful enough. He told me that when he was younger he had waited until there was a signal from his dating partner. He was not really able to articulate what the signal was, simply that sexual intercourse, when it did happen, was because his partner had allowed it to happen. Because he had married young and was relatively inexperienced with woman in an emotional and intimate way, Jeremy lacked the language and confidence with which to become closer to the women he dated. Not only did he not know how to talk to a partner about sexually transmitted diseases, he had thought that birth control was still a woman's responsibility. Further, he was not always attracted to his dating partners but felt it was necessary to be sexually intimate if a woman initiated it.

First, we explored what sexual intimacy meant to Jeremy. In his marriage, he realized that he had gotten emotional intimacy through sexual intimacy with his wife. When their sexual life disappeared, he felt loneliness and loss. Like many men, he did not have a well-developed emotional vocabulary, and we worked on his becoming aware of and labeling his feelings while on a date and in his day-to-day life. We also explored his feelings of vulnerability around getting to know another person, and he felt that maybe he had wanted to move to sexual intimacy not only because he might have felt some attraction, but also because this was how he knew how to be emotionally close. We found that not feeling safe for emotional intimacy was not only tied to early socialization and few relationship experiences but also to continued financial dealings with his ex-wife that made him angry and, by extension, distrustful of women he was dating. His realization of his underlying feelings and how they may be interfering with his behavior in dating was a surprise for him. Confronting resentments toward his ex-wife was an important step. I utilized a solution-focused approach, and we identified areas in his life in which he was aware of his feelings and able to negotiate comfortably. As Jeremy was a very goal-directed person in other areas of his life, I asked him to envision approaching his dating as he did his business, with confidence and a vision of where he wanted to go. We were able to identify his skills in that area to apply to dating. Our sessions also focused on exploring his dating script, which he began to see was outdated. Effective ways to communicate emotional and physical needs were practiced in session, as were ways to combat anxiety in the moment on a date. We practiced specific dating skills and various ways he could bring up topics at safer times for him in the dating process. I think it is especially important to remember that men may feel shame for not feeling confident in emotional and sexual aspects of their lives, and that we clinicians should also recognize the demands that our society (and sometimes ourselves) place on men to "do" masculinity well.

DATING SKILLS TIPS FOR CLINICIANS

I have compiled 10 dating skills tips for clinicians to use with their clients; these tips are listed next. They are based on the PLISSIT (permission, limited information, specific suggestions, intensive therapy) approach in sex therapy and focus on the first three. I also delve into more information about intensive therapy needs elsewhere in this chapter. These tips are not meant to be exhaustive, but in teaching I have often found I have recommended skills training of various sorts without giving specific examples. Remember to check with your clients' about how these suggestions align with their moral and spiritual values. I hope you find these helpful.

1. Support clients' decision making about dating by helping them to decide when it is right for them, while challenging their assumptions about dating. Support clients in their need to put away both positive and negative events from the past to move forward.

2. Give your clients permission to take their time to get to know other people. Loneliness, loss, and need may push people into seeking intimacy to feel better and put them at risk emotionally, physically, and financially.

3. Dating again often requires new skills. Let them know that finding a person that they really like and who likes them is not easy. Perfectionism and performance demands can kill confidence and create negative experiences, so help them see where they may be applying these killers.

4. Explore possibilities of where to start. Brainstorm old and new places to meet others and remember that relatives, friends, and even ex-partners may make finding someone in their new area more difficult. Mention these means of meeting others: speed and Internet dating, personal ads, social organizations, volunteer opportunities, religious/spiritual communities.

5. Advise the client when asking a person out to have ideas of several things to do. For the first few dates, it is better to do more casual and spontaneous activities as this means far less pressure and anxiety for everyone.

6. Stress the need to be honest in ads, on dating sites, and before meeting others as lies eventually come out. Sensitive topics such as education, job/career, finances, religious/spiritual beliefs, living situation, children, and marital status eventually need to be discussed. Ask clients if they have secrets that will sabotage their dating.

7. Practice interpersonal skills, such as
   a. Opening remarks that are not shopworn pickup lines.
   b. Making eye contact and smiling to show interest.
   c. How to flirt a little to start a conversation.
   d. Developing phone skills, such as clearly identifying himself or herself, describing how they know the person or how they have connected in the past (at an event, through friends, etc.).
   e. Enhancing conversational skills: Teach them to ask open-ended questions since asking too many direct questions can feel intrusive. Practice listening completely.

8. Reading nonverbal cues and managing rejection: Is your client aware of body language cues that signal interest or dislike? When clients are not attuned to tone of voice or other physical cues, practice identifying them. Be aware that you will have to help clients manage rejection. Here are some suggestions:
   a. Reduce clients' expectations: A date is a date—a time to get to know the person, not the immediate start of a marvelous relationship.

  b. Consider what makes a person say yes or no to a date: "No" some-
      times means the person is busy, is tired, has other obligations, or
      just does not like the activity that was offered for the date. It may,
      of course, also mean that the person did not care for him or her on
      first impression.
  c. Brainstorm alternatives for handling rejection: They can follow
      up on a negative response by asking if there is a time soon when
      it would be possible to get together. Being graceful when rejected
      leaves the door open for further interactions.
  9. Does a no mean no? What constitutes respectful behavior needs to
      be discussed, especially in this world of instant communication.
      Repeatedly calling, e-mailing, or texting may be seen as desperate or
      even stalking, just as much as hanging out waiting for the person.
      This is a reason why meeting someone at their local hangout might not
      always be a good idea.
  10. Developing good boundaries. Our society has become one in which
      revealing everything about oneself is commonplace. Such emotional
      flashing or telling a person too much information too quickly signals
      a lack of boundaries and will likely lead to rejection. I advise clients
      that it is not a good idea to speak about their past relationships too
      much. Those who have lost a partner or spouse, especially if the rela-
      tionship was positive, are more likely to talk about how great their
      partner was. Those who have been deeply hurt by others are more
      likely to talk about how they are looking for someone without those
      traits. Neither of these two groups will be aware of the effect on the
      others. Intensive therapy may be called for here.

SINGLE, DIVORCED, AND BLENDED FAMILY DATING ISSUES

Single-parent numbers have grown considerably, with 18.6 million children
under the age of 18 living with one parent, a 12% increase in such households
between 1970 and 1994 (Saluter, 1994). This is particularly salient for women,
as 92% of children under the age of 18 live with their mothers (Ellwood &
Jencks, 2002). Thus, child care and financial issues may impact a person's dating life.
    Here is a set of questions that newly dating parents face.

How do I handle returning to the dating scene when I have minor
    children?
How do I introduce a new partner to my children?
How do I handle my new sexual intimacy with my children around?
What impact will my dating or having a new relationship have on my
    children?
Will my ex be jealous or cause problems?
What do I do now that one of my adult children objects to my dating?

Some parents consider that their children should not be aware of their parents' emotional or sexual lives, while others feel that such awareness provides a healthy model for their children. Strategies that have been suggested
move from no disclosure or downplaying a dating relationship, especially if

children show any distress at their parent seeing another, to gradual exposure, especially with regard to sleepovers. Yet, Anderson et al. (2004) found that where there was at least one child at home, dating happened rather quickly and in some cases before divorce papers were filed. By 1 year after divorce, 53% were in a serious relationship. Letting children know about the parent's dating was split equally between disclosing from the first date to only letting children know once the relationship became serious. Clearly, there is variety in how parent clients approach informing their children of their return to dating. Parents will probably feel conflicted between their needs and the needs of their children.

We clinicians need to work within the value systems of our clients even when we do not fully agree with their choices, and this may be more difficult when working with their children. I had a single mother bring in her two daughters, 8 and 11 years old, because of what she called out-of-control behavior. They apparently were making comments about sexual matters that disturbed her. She had not given them any sex (or intimacy) education directly, and she emphatically did not want to do it. When inquiring about her dating life, she reported that since she could not afford child care, she usually had men she met come to her house when the children were already asleep. They would always drink together and then go to her bedroom for sex. She firmly believed her children were not aware of her sexual activity and could not understand their interest and discussion of sex at such an early age. Her description of her dating life was a challenge for me with respect to her beliefs and behavior toward her children, but since she was not my client, I had to focus on what I could do for the children (and by extension, I hoped, her). With her permission, I gave the girls age-appropriate "talks"—that is, information about basic anatomy, menstruation, and babies. I also focused on healthy boundaries and the right to say no. I also suggested various books appropriate for children of their age and offered the mother collateral services that were available since I suspected she might have a drinking problem. She declined, and I only saw the girls for four sessions, but I had to hope that their education would wear off on her.

Other Obstacles for Parents

For parents with shared custody arrangements, private time for dating and intimacy is easier to arrange. For others, the cost of child care or a desire to keep their new relationships from their children until what they feel is an appropriate time for disclosure may interfere with dating. Those who are separated or divorced may not have worked through issues with their ex-spouse or partner and so want to keep the other from learning of new relationships for fear of retaliation.

When a new partner is introduced, shifts in the relationship between the children and parents should be expected, and parents will need our help to manage their own and their children's responses. Children *of any age* may feel jealous of the time their parent is spending with the new person and feel a sense of loss. They can also feel sad and angry because the new person represents the finality of their parent's separation or divorce. Sabotage, retaliation, and acting out are common, and children who have already experienced loss from their parents' previous dating relationships that have ended often fight new ones (Sumner, 1997). Parents, who push their children to accept the new partner or ignore the child's feeling to keep the new relationship going, cause harm to those parental relationships (Koerner, Rankin, Kenyon, & Korn, 2004). While adult children may reasonably be worried about their parent being taken advantage of, they may also be protecting their other parent's "place" or their own potential financial loss if a partnership ensues. Family disapproval can be stressful and persistent enough to keep some clients from dating at all.

Obviously, there will be many times when minor and adult children are happy to see their parent move on with his or her life. Unfortunately, there is not much research about the dynamics of adult children's adjustment to their parents' dating or about aspects such as divorced fathers' dating. For now, clinicians will have to rely on general family therapy approaches to the problems a parent's dating might bring to the family system.

THE NEW DATING SCENES

Meeting someone to date, for some of our older or more traditional clients, happened through an introduction through family or friends, social organizations such as religious or hobby-oriented settings, or workplace settings. Now, singles groups abound in a variety of communities (e.g., singles groups organized by religion, Parents Without Partners, 55-plus communities), and there are new ways of meeting others, such as personal ads or speed dating. To many, these no longer seem novel. Within the last two decades, the Internet has arisen as a powerful medium for social and sexual networking that is used by almost all adult age groups. Given that our clients may live in large or small communities, may be wishing only to date someone with specific characteristics, may be part of a sexual minority, or may want to practice getting back in the dating scene with a sense of anonymity and adventure, our understanding of the advantages and disadvantages of these outlets is important.

Speed Dating

Speed dating was first developed as a place to meet others face to face who were interested in a new romantic relationship. The beauty of these social events is that, unlike sitting in a bar and hoping to catch the eye or interest of another or having to initiate conversation with a stranger where others might see you, there is an organized direction of social interaction with a specified time frame. The time frames are usually 3–8 minutes, with the opportunity to list those one would want to see again. If the other person has also indicated interest, the organizers give each person limited contact information and leave real first-date details to them. Some of the advantages for people are meeting a wide range of individuals in a short period of time, being able to go to speed dating events with friends of a similar religion or interest, meeting others safely, and having a companion to buffer disappointing results.

Speed dating allows the therapist and client to work together to process the experience and modify expectations. Our clients can practice self-presentation and social interaction skills and can learn to handle rejection or disappointment. Clients can have unrealistic expectations of early dating experiences or can be strongly attracted to characteristics in others that are not predictive of healthy, lasting relationships. If a client goes with a friend, the friend may be able to provide feedback that the therapist cannot. If clients secure dates after the event, we can help them in considering their initial perceptions compared to their experiences later, as shown in my dating tips for clinicians. For those who reside in smaller cities, these types of events are being held online, which may be the only option. However, online-only interactions have their own set of advantages and disadvantages.

Internet Connections

Online communities such as Facebook and Second Life as well as dating sites like Match.com or eHarmony.com, provide a means to anonymously and safely meet others for romance or sexual interaction. The disembodiment inherent in the medium, even with the use of a webcam or Skype, may make Internet connections more freeing or more disconnected. I suggest becoming familiar with the positive and negative aspects of this medium. One major advantage is the control over self-presentation. A good assignment for a client is developing a profile to tell who she or he is (or wants to become). Some clients are very computer savvy, while others need assistance to understand the caveats of the medium. Interestingly, this is not just for younger people. Adams, Oye, and Parker (2003) report that older adults are increasingly using the Internet for information as well as to enhance their sexual selves. In fact, they assert that baby boomers and older adults are probably enjoying the Internet because they can form connections that might otherwise be sidetracked by stereotypes about them as older people. Sites such as ThirdAge.com, Zelgo.com, and SassySeniors.com are some examples. As there are many sites that might have explicit erotic or pornographic images, blogs, and chat rooms, clinicians may want to screen some of the possibilities, depending on the sensibilities of the client. Since clients also use the Internet for sexual information, we may need to help our clients make sense of the vast amount of information out there, and we should consider that older adults probably still need psychoeducation when it comes to sexuality.

Some dating sites are free; others charge a membership fee. For example, eHarmony offers a free personality assessment, which might be interesting for some, but charges a fee to link up with "compatible" matches. I generally suggest that a client set up a new e-mail address to use for any of these sites for control and privacy. An advantage is anonymity, and this may be particularly freeing for some clients.

I use Internet opportunities to facilitate work on self-esteem and sense of the new self without the previous partner as interacting with others online becomes a means of negotiating one's identity (Couch & Liamputtong, 2008). Since many sites ask people to list their characteristics, issues around body image, aging, or sexual problems can be great clinical areas to explore. Working on social and dating skills is also possible with online interaction. Another advantage for the shyer client is the opportunity to screen potential partners at a distance. Rejection in this format may not sting as much but does provide experiences to process with the client, especially for those who let fears inhibit them from meeting others in public.

I stress being truthful in one's profile because clients often hope to meet someone in person. Photographs that a client might consider can also be an interesting way for a clinician to discuss self-presentation and new directions in self-concept. Some clients who have been in a relationship of long duration may not have many recent photographs, and getting a new photo can be a good assignment. Inaccurate or fake profiles and out-of-date or otherwise misleading pictures are reported to be one of the most annoying things about online dating (Couch & Liamputtong, 2008; Lawson & Leck, 2006).

When to trust another on the Internet is difficult to determine. Loneliness can lead to vulnerability or gullibility at any age. Online dating may lead to a false sense of intimacy, and people will sometimes act recklessly. Women may be more likely to engage in unprotected sex because of this instant intimacy (Padgett, 2007). The issue of safety when going to meet others for the first time is also a crucial factor. I advise my clients to meet in a public place, to let others know where they are going, and initially to meet for something nonromantic, like a cup of coffee. This way escape is possible, and others are there if needed. I think it is also important for clients to be realistic about what their expectations are and to review their dating scripts. Some clients have been upset when their new date tried to become sexually intimate too soon. For example, on a second date, a man told one of my friends, who is in her late 70s, that they both were not getting any younger, so they should get together sexually now.

AN OLD DATING ISSUE: SEXUAL HEALTH

Two crucial topics to cover with our clients are pregnancy and sexually transmitted diseases (STDs). Older adults may not have been using any types of birth control or protection with their previous partners or shifted to other, less-familiar methods as they began dating. Later-life pregnancy can occur due to use of less-effective means of birth control, and it carries greater risks of morbidity for women (Sherman, Harvey, & Noell, 2005).

While overall infection rates for STDs are lower in older adults, about 10–15% of new AIDS cases in the United States are diagnosed in those 50 years and older. Women have a greater percentage of HIV infections than men. Black men and women have the highest rates, while Latino and White men and women have about equal in risk (for more information, see Levy, Ory, & Crystal, 2003; Mack & Ory, 2003). Heterosexual intercourse, men having sex with men, and intravenous drug use are the main sources of new infections. Singles in their 30s, 40s, and even into the 50s may have a better idea of their risk, but those in the older age groups are frequently unaware of or in denial about their risk. Unfortunately, those diagnosed with AIDS at older ages are frequently at a later stage of the disease, may not be able to take medications that could slow the effects of AIDS, and typically die quicker. Older adults may also be at greater risk because they only associate condoms with pregnancy protection, are vulnerable due to illness or disability or dependence on alcohol or drugs, or have no skills for talking about their sexual history.

Men with erectile changes may not want to use a condom for fear of losing an erection, and postmenopausal women may have thinner vaginal mucosa and less lubrication, which may increase risk of infections. Some people may not want to lose the chance for potential intimate contact by insisting on use of protection.

As with people of any age, when an STD is contracted, there can be significant anger, grief, and a sense of violation. We must help clients practice safer sex talks and how to reveal their sexual history to a potential partner in a safe and truthful way.

COUNTERTRANSFERENCE ISSUES ABOUT STDs

As clinicians, we may feel uncomfortable bringing up safer sex issues with our clients, perhaps thinking they already know all they need to know by their age or worry about offending them. Health care workers, caretakers, and mental health professionals who believe that sexual interactions are not as frequent or desirable in older adults are less likely to talk about the risk of contracting a sexually transmitted infection with those in their 50s and beyond. This stereotype of adults becoming increasingly uninterested in sexual interaction with aging is not supported by empirical research (see Gott & Hinchliff, 2003; Hillman, 2008). Reports of diminished importance of sex later in life are usually associated with impaired health or sexual dysfunction in the individual or his or her partner.

We clinicians have to challenge our beliefs about sexuality and aging (countertransference) to help older clients who are dating again. We need to become knowledgeable about general aging and health changes that may affect sexuality, such as menopause and prostate diseases, as well as understand effects of various chronic illnesses and medication. I think it is crucial to include sexual health as a component of holistic health for our clients. We are responsible for broaching the topic and helping our clients become informed about the pleasures and dangers of sexual interactions at any age.

WHAT YOU WILL BE DOING WITH CLIENTS

It should go without saying that a comprehensive assessment is an important tool for addressing the complexities of a client being single again. As glimpsed from the literature I have cited, a psychological, biological, and social approach is critical to understanding what each client may be facing. I have 11 specific suggestions for your consideration of how to work with single-again clients:

1. Set goals
2. Clarify values
3. Do grief work
4. Review experiences from previous relationships
5. Explore the role of honesty in dating and relationships
6. Explore the new self
7. Discuss the physical body
8. Emphasize the role of social support
9. Discuss trauma and serious mental health interventions
10. Examine child issues
11. Provide sex ed 101, especially about STDs

Set Goals

Clarify the person's ultimate goals, reasons, or expectations of dating and intimacy again, such as fertility, parenting, companionship, economic stability, religious/spiritual connection, or simply sexual connection. The development and strength of intimacy goals have been associated with facilitating entering into a dating relationship (see Sanderson, Keiter, Miles, & Yopyk, 2007, for examples).

Clarify Values

Help your client explore what he or she means by love, intimacy, sex and sexuality, and so on. Implicit assumptions can sabotage dating experiences. See Levine's work (2007) for more description of what he so eloquently calls "demystifying love." The most important values to a person will fluctuate with life experiences and life stage.

Do Grief Work

Consider using stages of grief (denial, anger, bargaining, depression, and acceptance) as a starting point for discussing loss of an adult relationship and losses within their family of origin. For those who have been satisfactorily married a long time and lose their spouse, letting go may be quite a protracted process. Clients can idealize a lost partner or believe that loving another again dishonors their past relationship. Conversely, grief about loss may be masked or avoided with feelings and behaviors such as anger or perfectionism.

Review Experiences From Previous Relationships

Review previous relationships with an eye for dysfunctional patterns that can doom new relationships. I find many clients are not aware of anger and resentment they have toward others, from parents to past intimate relationships. Many clients may not be aware that these emotions are being projected onto the people they meet. Positive experiences may also be an impediment, especially if no one can ever measure up.

Explore the Role of Honesty in Dating and Relationships

One specific area I think is very important to explore is an understanding of honesty. Not telling the truth about our needs and experiences can really lead to problems in relationships, but clients may be sabotaging themselves by too (honestly) strongly stating their expectations of the future (I'm only looking for a marriage partner; I'll never go dancing; My mother was a bitch). If later the other person declines future interaction, our client may complain that being honest does not work. Helping clients see how their behavior might be driving the interaction is crucial; see Bader, Pearson, and Schwartz (2001) for specific examples and interventions.

Explore the New Self

Explore dating anxiety and encourage development of positive perceptions of self, especially as these may have an impact on the client's ability to be emotionally or sexually intimate with new partners. Point out that dating can also be a boost to one's self-esteem.

Discuss the Physical Body

Emphasize general health, hygiene, and body image. Improving body image, taking care of health issues if possible, and the importance of hygiene cannot be overemphasized. For older women who have not been sexually active for some time, atrophic vaginal changes need to be addressed. Be prepared to discuss effects of chronic illness and medications on sexuality, become conversant on the advantages and disadvantages of drugs like Viagra, use of lubricants, and improving self-awareness through self-pleasuring. For men, understanding how drugs such as Viagra, Cialis, or Levitra (phosphodiesterase—PDE-5 inhibitors) work, the limits of these erectile medications, and the importance for consulting with their partners before use are crucial.

Emphasize the Role of Social Support

Explore their social networks, but be aware that having an extended family may or may not be helpful to a client's reentry into the dating world. Clients can also seek support online, and we can help brainstorm ways of expanding old contacts or making new ones. You might consider developing a postrelationship adjustment group (e.g., Lee & Hett, 1990).

Discuss Trauma and Serious Mental Health Interventions

Even our best assessments will miss issues clients choose to keep hidden at first. Be prepared for the possibility of post-traumatic stress disorder (PTSD), sexual assault, substance abuse, and any serious mental health problem that emerges during therapy and may be made worse by dating or impair the person's ability to be safe with others.

Examine Child Issues

Explore how to balance parental need for dating with children's needs. We can help our clients determine how they want to approach letting their younger or adult children know about their dating and how they will handle sleepovers. Some older adults also need to consider the reactions of their grandchildren whom they are raising. Older adults who live with their grown children may not be given much privacy or support for their dating lives.

Provide Sex Ed 101, Especially About STDs

General knowledge of and attitudes toward physical intimacy can be explored with the idea of developing realistic and flexible sexual scenarios and expectations. This may be easier for women than for men in terms of changing performance demand-oriented scripts, but other sexual outlets, such as masturbation, may require dealing with guilt or shame. See the work of Williams and Donnelly (2002) and McCarthy and Metz (2008) for specific suggestions.

Jeanie is a 33-year-old mother of an 8-year-old daughter from a previous relationship. She came to therapy because she was separated from her husband of 3 years after revealing that she had had an affair with another man. Jeanie worked as a radiology technician at a local hospital and enjoyed her job. She had a joint custody arrangement with the father of her child, which left her some time to herself. Jeanie described being raised as a strict Christian and had confessed to her family about her affair. She was struggling with the response of her family and her own shame regarding her affair. She described it as being a sexual relationship that had filled some needs for her, but she was no longer seeing the man and had no desire to continue any relationship with him. Her relationship history revealed that she had rarely felt very connected to the men she was involved with, and that she did not understand why she could not get close to others. Her biological parents had divorced when she was young, and they shared custody of her and her younger brother. While currently close with her mother and stepfather, Jeanie had not seen her father in some time and felt that he had not been a good father to her. With further questioning and discussion over a number of sessions, Jeanie was able to begin to reveal that starting around age 14 her father had sexually fondled her when she stayed at his house. She had been unable to tell her mother, so the molestation continued over many years. Her defense was to shut herself off from her emotions, and she began to understand that she could have an affair because the physical aspects of sexual connection had not really ever been well connected with safe vulnerability, reciprocal caring, or voluntary intimacy.

Our sessions focused first on her exploration of her feelings about the sexual abuse. Over the next 6 months, we worked on the development of her sense of self and personal values, her relationship with her family, how she wanted to parent her daughter, as well as clarifying what she wanted in an intimate relationship with another. Vulnerability, trust, and boundaries were topics we explored. Emotional and sexual needs were discussed, with an aim to give her permission to explore these needs more slowly in her dating relationships.

FINAL THOUGHTS: COUNTERTRANSFERENCES WILL OCCUR

We clinicians can count on having some countertransference issues appear as we work with clients who are dating again. Despite setting clear boundaries at the beginning of therapy, we will still find ourselves feeling uncomfortable about role-playing dating scenarios with our clients when we have had similar experiences. This need not be a problem. The therapist must simply be aware of what is occurring within her or himself. By this continuing monitoring of our feelings and memories, we generally can keep separate from our clients. But if this seems stressful, please seek supervision. It helps me considerably to always document the goals and interventions that I work on with clients. I clearly note discussions about sexuality as appropriate to those goals as a way to protect my clients and myself. This attention to boundaries, goals, and documentation has protected me ethically as I help clients with this important area of their lives.

I hope this introduction to being single has broadened your horizons about what your clients are experiencing as they transition to single life and about what you can do to assist them. All lives are historically complicated, layered with individual nuances, and accompanied by intense feelings. By appreciating this, we mental health professionals become qualified to be helpful.

What it means to be single has changed profoundly in the last 20 years, and we must be prepared to understand the many factors that can affect our clients. In this chapter, I have covered a variety of them, but I know that you will find others. I have offered some specific dating skills to work on with clients as well as reminders about other crucial issues, such as processing grief, trauma, and anxiety. I have described new ways people can connect and some obstacles to dating. I hope my role here as your supervisor has encouraged you to courageously breach through the barriers to competently deal with these issues.

REFERENCES

Adams, M. S., Oye, J., & Parker, T. S. (2003). Sexuality of older adults and the Internet: From sex education to cyber sex. *Sexuality and Relationship Therapy, 18,* 405–415.

Anderson, E. R., Greene, S. M., Walker, L., Malerba, C. A., Forgatch, M. S., & DeGarmo, D. S. (2004). Ready to take a chance again: Transitions into dating among divorced parents. *Journal of Divorce and Remarriage, 40,* 61–75.

Bader, E., Pearson, P. T., & Schwartz, J. (2001). *Tell me no lies.* New York: Macmillan. The authors offer a developmental view of relationships and give excellent examples of how people use lies to protect themselves in relationships. I think this book is especially important for helping clients consider what they may have been doing in their previous relationships that lead to disappointment and dissolution. Ellen Bader and Pete Pearson run the Couples Institute and offer many resources to couples and clinicians at www.couplesinstitute.com/

Bulcroft, R. A., & Bulcroft, K. A. (1991). The nature and functions of dating in later life. *Research on Aging, 13*, 244–260.

Chorney, D. B., & Morris, T. L. (2008). The changing face of dating anxiety: Issues in assessment with special populations. *Clinical Psychology and Scientific Practice, 15*, 224–238. This article will be very valuable to anyone interested in understanding the concept of dating anxiety. Those interested in expanding the research to special populations will find suggestions.

Couch, D., & Liamputtong, P. (2008). Online dating and mating: The use of the Internet to meet sexual partners. *Quantitative Health Research, 18*, 268–279.

Davidson, K. (2001). Late life widowhood, selfishness and new partnership choices: A gendered perspective. *Ageing and Society, 21*, 297–317.

Ellwood, D. T., & Jencks, C. (2002). *The spread of single-parent families in the United States since 1960.* Unpublished manuscript, Harvard University, Cambridge, MA.

Furman, W., & Shaffer, L. (2003). The role of romantic relationships in adolescent development. In P. Florsheim (Ed.), *Adolescent romantic relations and sexual behavior* (pp. 3–22). Mahwah, NJ: Erlbaum. This book provides a thorough reference on adolescent romantic and sexual behavior that will help clinicians and clients understand developmental aspects that affect future relationships.

Gott, M., & Hinchliff, S. (2003). How important is sex in later life? The views of older people. *Social Science and Medicine, 56*, 1617–1628.

Grover, R. L. (2008). Riding the second wave of research on dating anxiety: Commentary on Chorney and Morris (2008). *Clinical Psychology: Science and Practice, 15*, 239–242.

Hillman, J. (2008). Sexual issues and aging within the context of work with older adults patients. *Professional Psychology: Research and Practice, 39*, 290–297.

Koerner, S. S., Rankin, L. A., Kenyon, D. B., & Korn, M. (2004). Mothers repartnering after divorce: Diverging perceptions of mothers and adolescents. *Journal of Divorce and Remarriage, 41*, 25–38.

Lawson, H. M., & Leck, K. (2006). Dynamics of internet dating. *Social Science Computer Review, 24*, 189–208. This study provides some interesting material from qualitative interviews and participant observation that is unique in its methodology.

Lee, J. M., & Hett, G. G. (1990). Post-divorce adjustment: An assessment of a group intervention. *Canadian Journal of Counseling, 24*, 199–209. While an older article, there is nice detail of exactly what went into their group intervention. I think it provides a framework for developing a group and incorporating suggestions from this chapter.

Levant, R. (2006). *Effective psychotherapy with men.* Available at http://www. psychotherapy.net. This DVD has an excellent explanation and demonstration of how to approach men in psychotherapy when they are avoidant about expressing feelings and emotions. There is a training manual and examples of an emotional response log available with purchase.

Levine, S. B. (2007) *Demystifying love: Plain talk for the mental health professional.* New York: Routledge.

Levy, J. A., Ory, M. G., & Crystal, S. (2003). HIV /AIDS interventions for midlife and older adults: Current status and challenges. *Journal of Acquired Immune Deficiency Syndrome, 33*, S59.

Mack, K. A., & Ory, M. G. (2003). AIDS and older Americans at the end of the twentieth century. *Journal of Acquired Immune Deficiency Syndrome, 33*, S68.

McCarthy, B. W., & Metz, M. E. (2008). *Men's sexual health: Fitness for satisfying sex.* New York: Routledge. This excellent self-help book clearly presents the authors' positive approach to a lifetime of realistic and pleasurable male and couple sexuality. The good-enough sex model is described and can help men and women abandon fantasy-driven expectations of sexual intimacy that are sex negative.

Padgett, P. M. (2007). Personal safety and sexual safety for women using personal ads. *Sexuality Research and Social Policy: Journal of NSRC, 4*, 27–37. There is quantitative data from women participants that are directly relevant to understanding safety in online dating. I could only touch on a small portion of what they found, and I like being able to use more personal examples with my students and clients.

Saluter, A. (1994). *Marital status and living arrangements.* Census Bureau Reports. Retrieved December 3, 2008, from http://www.census.gov/ population/www/pop-profile/msla.html

Sanderson, C. A., Keiter, E. J., Miles, M. G., & Yopyk, D. J. A. (2007). The association between intimacy goals and plans for initiating dating relationships. *Personal Relationships, 14*, 225–243.

Sherman, C. A., Harvey, S. M., & Noell, J. (2005). Are they still having sex? STIs and undecided pregnancy among mid-life women. *Journal of Women and Aging, 17*, 41–55.

Smiler, A. P. (2006). Conforming to masculine norms: Evidence for validity among adult men and women. *Sex Roles, 54*, 767–775.

Sumner, W. C. (1997). The effects of parental dating on latency children living with one custodial parent. *Journal of Divorce and Remarriage, 27*, 137–157.

U.S. Department of Commerce Census 2000. Retrieved December 8, 2008, from http://www.census.gov/population/socdemo/marital-hist/p70–80/tab01. pdf

Williams, E., & Donnelly, J. (2002). Older Americans and AIDS: Some guidelines for prevention. *Social Work, 47*, 105–111.

III

SEXUAL DYSFUNCTION: WOMEN'S SEXUAL ISSUES

Nine

When Do We Say a Woman's Sexuality Is Dysfunctional?

SHARON G. NATHAN, PHD, MPH

INTRODUCTION

The question, "When do we say a woman's sexuality is dysfunctional?" has intrigued—and confused—me ever since the late 1970s. I encountered it for the first time when I disquietingly undertook simultaneous postdoctoral fellowships in psychiatric epidemiology and in sex therapy. In the epidemiology program, I reviewed previously published sex surveys to learn about the distribution of dysfunction in the population. Conducting that research, I became convinced that we needed highly explicit criteria to define dysfunction (e.g., has orgasms all of the time, most of the time, some of the time; better still: has orgasms 95–100% of the time, 75–94% of the time, etc.). Only with this degree of specificity could we use surveys to establish base rates of functioning in the population, a step I believed crucial for defining sexual dysfunction scientifically (Nathan, 1986).

In my clinical work in the sex therapy program, however, I found that these highly refined criteria were less useful, telling me both more and less than I needed to know. They told me more than I wanted to know because distinctions between, say, "has orgasms occasionally" and "has orgasms frequently" were usually clinically unimportant. A woman who had orgasms only occasionally, I learned, might be content, while a woman who had orgasms frequently might not be. And, they told me less than I wanted to know because to treat a patient I needed to understand when, how, and why she had orgasms even more than I needed to know how often she did.

I did not know 32 years ago that my dilemma was actually one of choosing between two classic approaches to defining sexual dysfunction. The *objective approach* compares the woman's behavior with established standards of sexual functioning, demarking a point at which good functioning ceases and dysfunction begins. The *functional approach*, on the other hand, is not concerned with how this woman's sexuality compares with that of others but with how it promotes satisfaction, or causes problems, for her or her partner.

In this chapter, I show what an objective approach can tell us. I discuss the source of our norms and describe their limitations in clinical practice. Then, I examine the functional approach to assessing dysfunction. I suggest that, despite the softness of its criteria, it is a far better standard for you to employ and the one on which sexual specialists actually rely in practice. The conversation continues with the idea that even the functional approach does not adequately get at the larger context of the patient's life. Something more is needed by the therapist.

THE SEARCH FOR OBJECTIVE STANDARDS OF DYSFUNCTION

When we use the objective approach to say a woman's sexuality is dysfunctional, we are implicitly or explicitly measuring it against some standard, compared to which her performance is found to be deficient or lacking. But, what is the source of our standards? In deciding what level of functioning is normal, we can consult five sources: the *Diagnostic and Statistical Manual of Mental Disorders, Fourth Edition* (*DSM-IV*; American Psychiatric Association [APA], 1994); clinical judgment; population data; laboratory studies; and common knowledge.

Diagnostic and Statistical Manual of Mental Disorders, Fourth Edition

In theory, assessing female sexual dysfunction using *DSM-IV* (APA, 1994) seems straightforward. A woman presents a sexual complaint (e.g., "I don't have orgasms," "I have no sexual desire") that approximates one of the *DSM-IV* disorders, and the clinician, considering the woman's problem in light of the diagnostic criteria provided by the *DSM*, formalizes the diagnosis—"female orgasmic disorder," "hypoactive sexual desire disorder"—or fails to find a diagnosis warranted. In practice, it is almost never that simple.

Problems arise because the *DSM-IV* (APA, 1994) criteria for sexual dysfunctions are not operationally defined in the way the criteria for, say, major depressive episode are. For major depressive episode, the clinician is directed to determine whether the patient has experienced five or more of nine listed symptoms over a period of 2 weeks consecutively; furthermore, many of the symptoms themselves are defined, or at least exemplified, rather specifically. In contrast, the diagnostic criteria for the sexual dysfunctions are vague to the point of being tautological. Thus, hypoactive sexual desire is defined as "deficient (or absent) fantasies or desire for sexual activity" (p. 496), a criterion that really does not go much beyond saying that hypoactive sexual desire is desire for sex that is hypoactive. It is certainly not much help in deciding whether a particular woman qualifies for the designation.

Clinical Judgment

Recognizing the vagueness of the criteria it provides, *DSM-IV* (APA, 1994) turns the matter of operationalizing them over to "clinical judgment." Thus, for *Hypoactive Sexual Desire Disorder*, the "*judgment of* [italics added] deficiency or absence is made by *the clinician* [italics added], taking into account factors that affect sexual functioning such as age and the context of the person's life" (p. 498). And, for female orgasmic dysfunction: "The diagnosis of Female Orgasmic Disorder should be based on *the clinician's judgment* [italics added] that the woman's orgasmic capacity is less than would be reasonable for her age, sexual experience, and the adequacy of the sexual stimulation she receives" (p. 506). But, clinical judgment cannot do all it is called on to accomplish.

Clinical judgment, whatever else it may be useful for, cannot be utilized to establish norms. And yet, that is explicitly what *DSM-IV* (APA, 1994) is calling on it to do: "Because of a lack of normative age- or gender-related data on frequency or degree of sexual desire, the diagnosis must rely on clinical judgment based on the individual's characteristics, the interpersonal determinants, the life context, and the cultural setting" (p. 496). In other words, the clinician must decide, for example, whether a particular level of sexual desire is appropriate for a 51-year old, happily married, lower-middle-class, Greek American woman—when, and *because*, nothing is known about what level of sexual desire is normal for a woman with any one of these characteristics, let alone for all four in combination. What knowledge or experience would equip the clinician to make such a judgment, even if the clinician were a seasoned woman practitioner over aged 50 and not, as might also be the case, a first-year resident? Lest you think that making such an assessment might in some way be easier than I am suggesting, let me present you with some actual clinical examples requiring correlating sexual desire with the variables *DSM-IV* says are relevant to it:

Individual Characteristics

David insisted that his fiancée Emily's level of sexual desire was not only low in an absolute sense but also lower than she was capable of because she was someone with a highly refined appreciation of other sensual pleasures, such as food, wine, and art. (This sounds logical, but do we really have any evidence supporting the notion that sensuality is a dimension of personality such that if someone appreciates some sensual pleasures, she can appreciate all?)

Interpersonal Determinants

Sally had always been puzzled why her mother had stayed with her father, a man who had been physically and verbally abusive to her throughout the marriage. After her father's death, Sally asked her mother about it and was stunned to hear in reply, "Ah, yes, but the sex was perfect." (When we read in *DSM-IV* [APA, 1994] that sexual desire should be assessed in light of "interpersonal determinants," the chances are that our first thought is that sexual desire should be higher in good relationships than in bad ones. So, why do we see so many couples—like Sally and her husband, for that matter—for whom the relationship is great and the sex is minimal? And certainly Sally's parents' marriage does not stand alone as a bad relationship with good sex. What, if any, are the interpersonal determinants with which sexual desire actually correlates?)

Life Context

I relied on my clinical judgment to confidently reassure a couple that they should not worry about having sex only on the weekends because "couples with two careers and two kids just don't have sex during the week." (I believed it—or rather, I believed a less-emphatic version of it—when I said it, and, truth to tell, I believe it now, but I cannot say on the basis of any evidence that it is true.)

Cultural Setting

By coincidence, a few years ago I was seeing two couples with sexual desire problems, each of which comprised a Jewish man and an Italian American woman. In one case, it was the Jewish man who had the desire problem, and in the other case it was the Italian American woman. What was fascinating was that the nondysfunctional partner in each couple explained the couple's problem in cultural terms. Couple A: "What do you expect? He comes from a scholarly, cerebral Jewish tradition, and I'm a passionate Mediterranean type." Couple B: "What do you expect? I'm from a liberal Jewish background, and she's grown up as a typically repressed Italian Catholic." And you know what? They were both right as far as their own individual situations were concerned. (The lesson here is that a cultural setting is not one-dimensional; therefore, assessing sexual desire in light of it is likely to rest on stereotype and prove to be arbitrary.)

Population Data

What if we did have good epidemiological data about how sexual functioning variables, like sexual desire and frequency of orgasm, were distributed in the population? What if we actually could consult a table and find out what the average level of sexual desire is for a 51-year-old, happily married, lower-middle-class, Greek American woman? How far would that go toward solving our problem of determining if a woman's sexuality is dysfunctional? It certainly would be of some help, I think, but it would not solve all the problems by a long shot.

Most sexual functioning variables are probably arrayed in the population the way other population characteristics, like height and intelligence, are, that is, in a bell-shaped or normal distribution, with most people clustered around the mean and fewer and fewer people the further out from the mean you go.

This is probably not the correct model for the distribution of dyspareunia, vaginismus, and sexual aversion. We might better conceptualize the distribution of these variables as bimodal: Either you have dyspareunia or you do not. Of course, some women with dyspareunia may have more pain than others, but the most important distinction for determining dysfunction is between those who have any pain at all and those who have none.

So, here is the first problem: It is simply an unalterable statistical fact that for any characteristic we select, *half the population is going to be below average.* Half the women are going to have fewer than average orgasms, less than average sexual desire. Surely, we are not willing to call half the female population dysfunctional—not on the basis of statistical prevalence alone, at any rate. But, an individual woman might see herself as dysfunctional for just this reason. We live in a culture in which average equals mediocre and below average equals deficient. Everyone wants to be at least above average (indeed, surveys of motorists show that most do rate themselves as above average drivers) and outstanding, if possible. Being statistically outstanding has become the goal, and even the expectation, of some contemporary women, particularly those who have been exceptionally high achievers in other areas of their lives. We need to make it clear that the failure to be above average is not the definition of dysfunctional.

So, where do we draw the line? Perhaps more important, *on what basis* do we draw the line? With a characteristic like intelligence, we draw a dysfunction-indicating line where we expect a person will actually have difficulty functioning; with an IQ of, say, 70 or lower, a person will not be able to function independently in society. The IQ score of 70 is two standard deviations below the mean, but it is not its statistical placement but the actual consequences of having an IQ that low that makes it a dysfunctional score. A woman who is 4 feet 11 inches tall, a height that is also a good two standard deviations below the population mean, would not logically be labeled dysfunctional because this height does not seriously handicap her functioning; she is statistically deviant but not dysfunctional.

There is also the consideration of how someone got to where she is in the distribution. A woman can be 4 feet 11 inches because that is her genetic destiny or because something stunted her growth. Similarly, a woman can have little sexual desire because of putative inborn factors (we do not know what these might be) or because her expected level of desire was inhibited by negative experiences. Does it matter in determining dysfunction how a woman got to be where she is in the distribution, or is it only her absolute placement that counts? Thus, dysfunctionality can only be defined *in terms of something*. We must then ask how her persistent or recurrent delay in, or absence of, orgasm handicaps her. After all, female orgasm is not needed for conception, and from our clinical experience we also know that women who do not have orgasms can desire and enjoy sex (and that some women who do have orgasms may dislike and avoid it). Statistical norms do not take us very far.

Masters and Johnson's Laboratory Studies

Masters and Johnson's (1966) laboratory studies provide us with very important information about female sexual functioning. By showing how similar men and women are in what they identified as the four stages of the human sexual response cycle—arousal, plateau, orgasm, and resolution—they showed women to have the same capacity for sexual response that men have. This was very definitely news when they published *Human Sexual Response*. Because it was outside the scope of a laboratory study of sexual physiology, they could not address whether the meaning and import of sexual functioning was the same for men and women. Just because women are at least as capable as men of arousal and orgasm does not mean that men and women value them and seek them out to the same extent. To what extent should our norms for sexual desire, sexual arousal, and orgasm be based at all on women's capacity (except, of course, to make sure they are not higher than what is possible)? There is a fine line between what Masters and Johnson did—give women the opportunity to fulfill their sexual potential—and a standard that turns that opportunity into an obligation and then into a dysfunction if they fail to achieve it.

Common Knowledge

At the beginning of my first social science course in graduate school, the professor extolled the value of studying human behavior scientifically. Why, within the last decade alone, he proclaimed, social science had made some remarkable discoveries, and he went on to enumerate half a dozen significant findings. Someone's hand shot up impatiently from the back of the classroom. Called on, the student said what many of us had been thinking: "With all due respect, sir, I think all that research was a waste of time. It only showed what everybody already knows." Having gotten the response he hoped, the professor smiled and responded, "Actually, it is the exact opposite of all of those statements that has been proven in the past 10 years." I instantly became a whole lot more skeptical about common knowledge.

Subsequent experience as a sex therapist has further reinforced the notion that it is wise to question what everybody knows. When I graduated from college, it was common knowledge that women had two kinds of orgasms, clitoral and vaginal, and that vaginal orgasms were better. They were better in the sense of being the orgasms that more mature women, those who had overcome masculine striving, experienced. Soon afterward came Masters and Johnson and their tiny cameras to prove that all orgasms were not only equal but actually the same physiologically; whether occurring during direct clitoral manipulation or intercourse, orgasms were produced by stimulation of the clitoris. It became common knowledge that all orgasms were clitoral, and that vaginal orgasms were a myth. Subsequently, within the last two decades common knowledge has expanded the concept in a way that allows for some variety of experience. Women are now allowed to have vaginal and "blended" orgasms as long as they do not proclaim these orgasms to be superior to the other kind. Had I used common knowledge to assess female orgasm dysfunction in 1965, 1975, and 1995, I would have come up with quite different answers. We have no choice but to be limited by the state of knowledge at the time we make our assessment; we should never assume that our current notions represent eternal truths.

A Note on Stimulation

Although *DSM-IV* (APA, 1994) requires the clinician to assess the adequacy of stimulation only when making a determination of female orgasmic disorder, in fact adequacy of stimulation is a critical variable in evaluating each of the female sexual dysfunctions. I think stimulation is mentioned only for female orgasmic disorder because stimulation is meant to be understood narrowly as physical stimulation. But, psychological and situational stimulation are critical for a woman's feeling sexual desire and arousal, and they may also play a role in some cases of sexual aversion, dyspareunia, and vaginismus. By psychological and situational stimulation, I mean that the woman is motivated to be sexual because of ideas about who she and her partner are to one another and about the meaning of their sexual encounter.

> Matt and Kitty had been husband and wife for 34 years, business partners for 32 years, and parents for 28 years. They also had had a barely detectable sex life for 27 years. Over that time period, due to Kitty's lack of sexual desire, the couple had had sex an average of twice a year—and even this was with Kitty's only nominal participation. In sex therapy, Kitty was able to design a scenario that engendered in her a genuine desire for sex: a quiet dinner with Matt in a lovely restaurant that served good food and wine. Kitty thought this scenario worked for her because it enacted courtship, a feature that was otherwise little in evidence in their lifestyle of constant partnership and togetherness.

Frequently, the woman's sexual desire is triggered by psychological intimacy with her partner—the exchange of confidences, the sharing of hopes and dreams and fears (see Chapter 3). Men are often baffled that factors like courtship behavior and psychological intimacy trigger sexual interest in their partners because their own desire is elicited through sexual drive mechanisms and visual stimulation, but many women cannot be said to have received adequate stimulation unless these features are present.

The differences between men and women highlight the problem of using introspection to decide what is functional or dysfunctional in another, particularly when the other is of the opposite sex. In a recent therapy session in which the couple was dealing with their greatly discrepant levels of desire, the husband fumed at the wife, "I don't think you have any desire at all. Do you ever see a handsome man on the street, and undress him with your eyes, and want to go to bed with him?" This was exactly the analogue of his desire experience, but it is not a pattern frequently found in women. Clinicians also do this sort of thing. I recall at a professional meeting a decade ago that a presenter expressed puzzlement about one of his research findings: Most of the women in his study with low sexual desire had orgasms when they did have sex. So, why wouldn't they want to have sex more often to experience this pleasure? The women in the audience exchanged meaningful looks with one another, looks that said, "Doesn't he know that female sexual desire is about how the woman feels about herself that day, about how she feels about her partner (not just in the long run but at that very moment), about half a dozen factors more immediate and important than the prospect of orgasm?"

Overall, when we assess how little normative data about female sexual functioning we have from *DSM-IV* (APA, 1994), clinical judgment, laboratory studies, common knowledge, and introspection—and how difficult it is to draw a dysfunction-defining line even when we do—it becomes apparent that we need some other standard to guide us in making diagnoses, either as a supplement to the objective approach or as a replacement for it. It is hoped, when *DSM-V* appears in 2012, new concepts about female dysfunction and new criteria for diagnoses will make my discussion outdated. But, I confess, I have my doubts because women's sexuality is often a matter of potential thwarted by various contexts and competing interests. Drawing a line between the dysfunction and the functional seems inherently problematic.

ASSESSING THE SYSTEM'S FUNCTIONING: A PROBLEM IS A PROBLEM IF IT IS A PROBLEM

A second criterion is included in *DSM-IV* (APA, 1994) that points toward a functional approach to diagnosing dysfunction. For each of the *DSM-IV* sexual disorders, a diagnosis is not to be made unless "the disturbance causes marked distress or interpersonal difficulty," a criterion that requires the clinician to look at what, if any, effect the disturbance is having on the system.

For a long time, this criterion annoyed me, first because it seemed motivated by political correctness ("No, no, if you're not bothered by your vaginismus, who am I to say it's a dysfunction?"), and second because it would be such an obviously absurd requirement were we talking about a medical condition ("No, no, if you're not troubled by your serum cholesterol of 383, who am I to say it's a dysfunction?"). Even most of the other *DSM-IV* diagnoses, let alone medical diagnoses, allow for objective impairment to be a criterion for diagnosis even if the condition does not cause marked distress or interpersonal difficulty. Actually, for some psychiatric conditions, the lack of concern about the condition is part of the pathology; that is one of the things we can mean when we talk about poor judgment, lack of insight, or inappropriate affect. If "marked distress or interpersonal difficulty" was to be considered at all, I thought it should be a way of defining subtypes—the way "lifelong type" and "acquired type" are—rather than part of the main diagnosis itself.

Table 9.1   Hypoactive Sexual Desire: Criterion
A "Disorder" (Deficient or Absent Desire)

+	−
A	B
C	D

It seemed especially inappropriate to have this criterion be a part of the diagnoses if we were thinking about doing epidemiological studies of the general population. Surely we would be interested in knowing what percentage of the population suffered from "recurrent or persistent genital pain associated with sexual intercourse" whether or not the pain caused distress or difficulty. Knowing what percentage of the affected experienced marked distress or interpersonal difficulty on account of it would be an interesting additional fact—an interesting *additional* fact. But, I no longer object to distress or interpersonal difficulty being part of the very definition of a disorder because I have come to realize that from a clinical perspective the reaction to a sexual situation is actually more important than the objective situation itself in determining the sexual system's functionality and in determining when someone will seek treatment.

Let us take a look at the ways the objective and subjective criteria can covary. For this purpose, just as a way of having terms to refer to these two aspects of an overall situation, let us refer to the objective sexual pattern of the woman (e.g., delayed orgasm) as the putative "disorder" and the distress or interpersonal difficulty as the "problem." By separating these two aspects of the overall situation (just as *DSM-IV* [APA, 1994] does in labeling them criterion A and criterion B), we can construct a fourfold table based on whether one, both, or neither is present. Table 9.1 represents the four possible situations; in this case, the dysfunction in question is hypoactive sexual desire.

The situations represented by cells A and D is straightforward. In A, the woman has little interest in sex, and she or her partner are troubled by it; this couple, other things being favorable (belief in seeking professional help for problems, ability to pay for therapy, etc.), are likely to present for treatment. In D, the woman's level of sexual desire is satisfactory, and she and her partner are content with it; this is a satisfied couple we are unlikely to see in clinic. Situations B and C are more interesting because they represent discordant conditions: sexual problems that are not caused by disorders (B) and disorders that do not cause sexual problems (C).

DSM-IV (APA, 1994) anticipates situation B, a problem without a disorder, and suggests that in some cases it can be caused by "two people in the normal range at different ends of the continuum" (p. 497). A sophisticated presentation of this problem is the couple who comes into treatment saying "we are sexually incompatible," but not all couples exhibit this much self-awareness and generosity toward the partner:

John and Sarah had levels of desire that were normal but incompatible. John would have enjoyed having sex with Sarah almost every day, but Sarah was interested in sex perhaps once a month. The designation of this as a normal level of desire was Sarah's own, but John did not contest it. Sarah used the fact of her desire's presumed normality to dismiss out of hand John's wishes for more frequent sex. It had never occurred to

John that he could likewise assert his normality and demand that Sarah meet his level; this was in part because John was less certain that he was normal and in part because he would have never sought a solution that required his wife to do all the compromising. Interestingly, I did not see John and Sarah as a couple. I saw John individually when he presented with concern about his increasing preoccupation with Internet sex chat rooms. It was only in the course of discussing John's problem that I became aware of this desire disparity as a contributing factor.

DSM-IV (APA, 1994) also warns that a couple can present for treatment of a woman's hypoactive sexual desire when the real cause is "excessive need for sexual expression by the other partner" (p. 497).

Although the presenting problem was his wife's lack of sexual desire, Mike came to see me alone for the first session. He told me that he was on the verge of divorcing his wife of 17 years because she was not interested in sex. Mike had an intense craving to feel wanted by his partner, something he had experienced in an affair he had the previous year. The contrast with his marriage was so striking it was almost unbearable. With Mike's description of the situation, I was totally unprepared for meeting his wife, Millie, the next week. She was stunning, warm, and sensual. She said that the couple usually made love twice a week, and that she enjoyed sex and almost always had at least one orgasm. The problem was, she said, that it was never good enough for Mike. If she enjoyed an hour's lovemaking and felt satisfied, Mike was furious that she did not want to have intercourse again. If they were having an intimate dinner as a prelude to sex, the whole evening could be ruined if she mentioned something about one of the children, a sign to Mike that she was not really "into it."

We also get to see women with marked distress about their sexual life even though they have no dysfunction. These are cases of the "worried well," often with unrealistic expectations.

When 30-year old Maria, a fellow in a surgical subspecialty, sought treatment for her purported orgasmic dysfunction, she had had intercourse exactly seven times. Brought up by conservative European Catholic parents, Maria had decided early on to save her virginity for her husband. When she became engaged about 3 weeks before I saw her, she decided the circumstances were finally right for to have intercourse. Maria had enjoyed intercourse, just as she had enjoyed the foreplay the couple had experimented with previously, but she was terrified that she would never have an orgasm. I tried allaying her fears by saying that it often took a bit more practice and experimentation before orgasms occurred during intercourse. For once, I even had objective data to back me up: I cited Kinsey's 1953 data showing how the percentage of women having orgasms increased month by month throughout the first year of marriage (back in the days when the start of marriage and the start of sexual activity were more likely to coincide than they do today) (Kinsey, Pomeroy, Martin, & Gebhard, 1953). But Maria, who had never failed to be precocious at anything she did, was too anxious to let things happen naturally—she was already developing performance anxiety and "spectatoring"—and so I felt I had to treat her for female orgasmic disorder even though I did not think she had it.

The situation of a sex therapist treating a dysfunction that does not meet the *DSM-IV* (APA, 1994) criteria for it is actually common with female orgasmic disorder. That is because a woman cannot be said to have female orgasmic disorder if her deficient orgasmic response can be attributed to inadequate sexual stimulation. And yet, many of the anorgasmic women we see are anorgasmic precisely because they are receiving inadequate stimulation. Indeed, increasing the adequacy of the stimulation is usually the first thing we focus on in treating the problem.

The last cell in fourfold Table 9.1, C, is the case of deficient or absent desire on the woman's part that does not create a problem for either her or her partner. Since these are women we do not see in treatment, I cannot present any illustrative case material from my own experience. I can speculate that these may be women whose partners also have low desire. (The only cases I have seen of a couple seeking treatment because both partners have low sexual desire have been lesbian couples. In these instances, even though neither woman wants sex, both want to want it.) Or, they may be mistresses. These may be relationships in which the woman's lack of sexual desire is considered normal and expected, and the partner does not mind—as long as she does not use her lack of sexual desire as an excuse not to have sex. As sex therapists, we may feel sad for these women, who do not know or care what they are missing, but as the good liberals *DSM-IV* (APA, 1994) requires us to be, we have to acknowledge their right to choose their own goals, their right *not* to fulfill their sexual potential. (It is certainly the case that many of us do not fulfill our potential in other areas, and we may leave, say, the fitness gurus and personal trainers of the world similarly shaking their heads at our value systems.) Actually, we do see women who do not know or care what they are missing. They have ego-syntonic hypoactive sexual desire, and we see them when their lack of interest presents "interpersonal difficulties" for their partners rather than "marked distress" for them. Their disgruntled partners usually drag them into treatment. The hallmark of their presentation is the statement, "If I never had sex again for the rest of my life, I wouldn't miss it."

HOW AND WHY IS A SEXUAL PROBLEM A PROBLEM? OR, WHAT ARE THE CAUSES OF "MARKED DISTRESS" OR "INTERPERSONAL DIFFICULTIES"?

Why Is This Complaint a Cause of Marked Distress for the Dysfunctional Woman?

The question, Why is this complaint a cause of marked distress for the dysfunctional woman? seems silly, doesn't it? The reason is obvious: A sexual complaint is a problem because it diminishes the woman's sexual pleasure. But, the obvious answer is the correct answer only a fraction of the time. There are many other ways in which a sexual complaint can constitute a problem. Some are discussed next.

Sexual dysfunction can make a woman feel flawed and abnormal.

Luz avoided getting close to people, male and female, because she believed that to do so was to chance revealing how peculiar she was. While most of the ways in which Luz felt odd were being explored in excellent psychotherapy, her psychotherapist referred Luz for sex therapy because she believed that Luz's unusual way of having orgasms—they would happen spontaneously while watching someone enact a repetitive motion, such as tapping a pencil—was adding to her sense of being abnormal.

By the time we see some of these women, their sense of being abnormal has often been exacerbated by previous psychotherapies, which unlike Luz's, posit serious psychopathology as the cause of their sexual problems—thus, their vaginismus has been interpreted as a rejection of the female role and their anorgasmia as derivative of abandonment fears and an inability to trust.

Some women believe that not enjoying sex will be a handicap in the race for a relationship, in which being eager for sex and performing it ably are advantages. Better sexual functioning in these cases is sought out in the same way that cooking lessons or breast implants might be, not because they provide pleasure in and of themselves but because they are seen as instrumental in achieving something else—marriage—that is desirable.

A sexual complaint can also be a problem because the woman's sexual functioning is in conflict with her other goals. Occasionally, a woman enters sex therapy after years of unconsummated marriage to achieve pregnancy rather than pleasure.

> Tricia was in the third year of her second unconsummated marriage. According to Tricia, the absence of intercourse was not the reason her first marriage ended, and her second, happier marriage seemed quite stable. Although her current husband wanted to have intercourse, he had known about Tricia's difficulty before he married her and accepted it because he loved her and because the couple did enjoy other types of sexual activity. Tricia had never been motivated to seek treatment for her vaginismus (the problem preventing consummation) for her own pleasure or for that of her husband; what motivated her at age 34 was her wish to have a baby.

A woman's distress about her sexual functioning can stem even from a cause that is quite remote from sexuality itself.

> Grace and Paul had not had sex since they conceived their now 8-year-old daughter, Sasha. Paul was bothered by the situation, but Grace was not—until she realized that soon Sasha would learn the facts of life and would ask her parents if they "did it." Grace could not bear either lying to her daughter or admitting to such a humiliatingly abnormal sex life. To develop a sex life that would allow her to say yes truthfully to Sasha's anticipated question was the entire reason Grace sought sex therapy for her sexual aversion disorder.

An even more extreme case of someone seeking sex therapy for a goal other than increased sexual pleasure is that of Linda, who had no problems falling into any category of dysfunction but who nonetheless had a serious problem with her sex life.

> After 20 years of "vanilla sex" in an unhappy marriage, Linda felt freed by her divorce to seek out partners who were enthusiasts, as she was, of domination and submission sex. This kind of sex was highly exciting and gratifying for Linda, but it was so largely because for her it enacted a fantasy of being so precious to a man that he had to subordinate and control her to keep her his. Linda was shocked to find that this was not the fantasy her partners were entertaining—for them the fantasy was of degrading a woman. To make matters worse, Linda's goal was not only *sex* that focused on her preciousness but also a *relationship* with the same premise. Her sex partners, who were turned on by demeaning her, were poor candidates for such a partnership.

Why Is the Complaint a Cause of "Interpersonal Difficulty"?

Regarding why the complaint is a cause of interpersonal difficulty, often the complaint about the woman's sexuality is voiced not by her but by her partner. The partner's distress is perfectly understandable in the many cases when the woman's sexual functioning prevents her partner from having an enjoyable sex life or, in some cases, a sex life at all.

> Elizabeth and Frank had lived together in a virtually sexless relationship for 10 years. From the outset, Elizabeth, who had had no previous sexual experience, was both uninterested in, and phobic about, sex. She did not become aroused with foreplay and had such severe dyspareunia that intercourse was not even attempted after the first few tries. At Frank's angry insistence, she had made desultory attempts at having the possible medical causes of her dyspareunia investigated, but she seemed unconcerned that his sexual needs were thwarted, and she was unaware that she herself might be missing anything at all.

This lack of concern about a nonexistent sex life is not unique to Elizabeth. Some women who have no sexual desire of their own seem unable to understand how important sex might be to their partners. I have seen marriages in which the woman acted as if her partner's not putting his dishes in the dishwasher constituted a greater threat to the relationship than did their lack of a sex life. Sometimes, the first few sessions of sex therapy are devoted just to getting the woman to take her partner's wishes seriously. As one exasperated husband fulminated, "Try to understand that this is as important to me as shoe shopping is to you."

While we refer to men like Frank as "invested partners," and feel sympathy for them, "overinvested partners" evoke different responses. These men require the women to function at a particular level for their self-esteem or self-image rather than for their sexual satisfaction. This is commonly the situation when a man seeks treatment and insists that his partner must have orgasms or orgasms during intercourse. He seems to want this for his partner's pleasure even though the woman is satisfied with the status quo. His anger at his partner's "dysfunction" usually betrays a more complex motivation.

> Newlyweds William and Courtney presented for sex therapy because William was enraged that Courtney did not have orgasms during intercourse. Every partner that he had been with before marrying Courtney was orgasmic in this way, he said, and he was quite insistent that there was something wrong with his wife that needed to be fixed. In an individual session, Courtney told me what she was afraid to say in front of her husband: She had always had orgasms during intercourse before, but William ejaculated prematurely, within 1–2 minutes of intromission (an estimate that William did not dispute), too little time for her to reach climax (or for most women to reach climax, she added with a note of suspicion regarding the accuracy of William's previous partners' reports).

Sometimes, there can be a Catch 22 flavor to the partner's demand:

> Marla's level of sexual interest was admittedly lower than Peter's, but she was glad to engage in sex with him even when she was not feeling particularly interested herself. Peter would not accept this. He had grown up in a home where a tyrannical

father terrorized the family into constantly seeking to placate him by doing whatever he wanted, and he saw Marla's having sex with him when she was not interested as her trying to placate him as if he were a tyrant like his father. He was slower to realize why his angry insistence that Marla develop a higher intrinsic level of sexual desire so he would not feel he was forcing her to have sex to placate him was in itself perceived by her as a need to do something to placate him.

This concludes my thoughts on the functional approach to diagnosis. Perhaps I should summarize them with advice to listen carefully to what each person is saying, do not expect the partners to agree entirely, and expect your understanding of their motivation to evolve quickly from session to session. This clinical awareness of the layers of motivation underlying sexual behavior has led me eventually to the concepts that I now want to share with you.

SEXUAL DYSFUNCTION AND DYSFUNCTIONAL SEXUALITY

As a sex therapist, I find that more and more I am confronting not just sexual dysfunction—disruption in the sexual response cycle—but "dysfunctional sexuality"—sexuality that causes turmoil in a woman's life.

There is no way this was supposed to happen. The sexual revolution of the 1960s and 1970s was expected to liberate sexuality, to bring an era of joyful, guilt-free, anxiety-free sex. (All forms of sexual expression between consenting adults are permitted. Women are as capable of sexual pleasure as men are. If it feels good, do it.) Early sex therapy was part of that revolution, charged with sweeping away the functional glitches that could interfere with a utopian sexual world. And, it has been quite successful in doing so. But, in the 1980s came a counterrevolution in which we were forced to confront the dark side of sexuality: sexual abuse, sexual harassment, sex addiction, and serious sexually transmitted diseases, including AIDS. Sex was suddenly seen as capable of causing distress, trauma, and disease.

Being a sex therapist today requires finding a way to respect both the sexual revolution and the sexual counterrevolution because we are presented with problems stemming from both, sometimes in the same patient:

Patricia was an attractive, conservatively dressed, 54-year-old university research librarian, referred by her gynecologist. Patricia said that she had no sexual desire, and as I learned in taking a brief sexual history, she also did not lubricate during arousal, had only weak orgasms, and experienced pain during intercourse—four sexual dysfunctions reported in the first 3 minutes of the interview. I was pleased because I saw a unifying diagnosis—postmenopausal changes—and a possible route to alleviating her symptoms—hormonal therapy. But, when I conveyed this understanding to Patricia, not only was she not enthusiastic about what I had to say, but also she actually seemed disgruntled. I knew this meant that I was missing something important, and in taking a fuller history I learned the following:

Patricia suspected her rigid fundamentalist Protestant minister father had sexually abused her. She had a recollection of sitting on her parents' bed, reading the Bible with her father, but she thought this could be a screen memory for the abuse.

When Patricia entered junior high school, her father began to call her a whore, claiming that she was dressing to tempt boys. (Although Patricia matured early, she dressed like the other girls in her class and had little interest in boys.)

Patricia won a full scholarship to a prestigious state university. Dating for the first time, she had no idea that she could say no to sexual advances and had many unpleasant sexual experiences. She was raped by an older man to whom she had said no.

Patricia had several boyfriends but always lost interest in having sex with them after a few months.

In her 20s she married an abusive man from a rich and powerful family, who soon divorced her, leaving her quite literally homeless and with almost no money.

She developed an erotomania for a kindly professor, and her shame when forced to confront reality led her to withdraw from graduate school.

Patricia was quite sexually forward when she met her second husband, but her sexual interest plummeted when she acknowledged her alcoholism and stopped drinking.

Patricia was currently married to her second husband, a nice but somewhat ineffectual workaholic. He liked to have Patricia dress up in a garter belt, stockings, and high heels when they had sex. Patricia considered this perverted on her husband's part and felt humiliated when complying.

Patricia had orgasms only when she masturbated while entertaining fantasies of abuse and humiliation. She had never shared these fantasies with any of her partners and was adamant that she would never do so.

Patricia came the closest of any woman I have ever worked with of "lying back and thinking of England" during intercourse. She experienced intercourse with her husband as rape and thought about nothing except when it would be over.

Given this woeful sexual history, it is not surprising that what Patricia wanted when she initially told me of her current sexual dysfunctions was not sex therapy but the equivalent of a doctor's note excusing her from any further participation in sex. There was a kind of precedent in her family. Patricia's father told her that when her mother had a hysterectomy, the doctor had sewed her up so that she could no longer have intercourse. Therapy with Patricia and women like her is a long-term reconstructive endeavor. Respecting her experience and dealing with the multiple sexual traumas are prerequisite to introducing the idea that she could find something in sex for herself.

Some other examples of what I am calling dysfunctional sexuality are the following:

- Sex addiction. Although female sex addicts seem to live lives that revolve around sex—serial affairs, one-night stands, pornography, hours spent in sexually oriented Internet chat rooms—their problem is not an excess of sexual desire. It is the misuse of sexuality, calling on compulsive sexual activity to dispel painful feelings and to promote in fantasy a pumped-up self-image that evaporates in the light of day.
- Women seeking treatment with the aim of getting more comfortable with, or even excited by, the abusive sexual treatment demanded by their partners, whom they fear otherwise losing. The abuse to which they hope to more enthusiastically submit can be physical (e.g., aggressive anal sex that results in pain, tissue rupture, and bleeding) or psychological (e.g., having sex with strangers while the partner looks on).

WHAT'S A CLINICIAN TO DO?

Despite all the complexities discussed, a few considerations can take the clinician a long way toward deciding if a woman's sexuality is dysfunctional:

1. *Get a rough idea of what area of sexuality is the patient's concern*, but do not assume that just because you are a sex therapist, the patient is necessarily complaining of a sexual dysfunction or complaining of only a sexual dysfunction.
2. *Before focusing on any objective assessment of dysfunction, examine the "marked distress" and "interpersonal difficulty."* It is highly unlikely that the patient is consulting you on account of mere intellectual curiosity about her sexual functioning. Start with what is really bothering her or her partner, always keeping in mind that the patient and her partner may be bothered by different things.
3. *Evaluate dysfunction objectively.* No orgasms, painful sex, absent desire, inability to "get into" sex mentally or physically, problems achieving penetration—these are complaints that would seem to make a prima facie case for dysfunction. With subtler manifestations, the dysfunction-determining line is a matter of debate, a debate that is probably not worth engaging in the consulting room. Even when presenting feedback to the patient, the clinician does not have to dwell on whether she has a sexual dysfunction. "I think you can enjoy sex more than you do now" not only fudges the dysfunction issue but also tells the patient what she probably really wants to know.
4. *Determine the adequacy of stimulation.* Inadequate stimulation, broadly understood to include psychological and situational as well as physical stimulation, is the major cause of female dysfunction as well as the most obvious place to begin intervention and treatment. Dysfunction cannot be understood apart from it.
5. *The relationship of dysfunction and distress is not always obvious.* Even if a dysfunction is present, its connection to the individual's or couple's distress needs to be determined. A dysfunction is a nice concrete problem to present to a clinician, but it is the presumed effect of the dysfunction that has actually led the patient to seek help.
6. *Expect complexity.* The easy cases have already been cured by girlfriends, self-help books, and increasingly sophisticated nonspecialist psychotherapists and physicians. Today's sex therapist more often functions as a "tertiary-care facility" for the sexual problems that cannot be fixed simply by sex education, permission giving, sensate focus exercises, or a good vibrator.

I hope I have not discouraged you in illuminating the complexities and limitations of sexual diagnoses for women. I think of it as an intellectually stimulating process, so rich that it has sustained my interest throughout my career. I know many of my colleagues feel the same way. I hope this chapter will keep you from making some of the same wrong assumptions that I made when I was getting started. I believe that I have helped many women understand their sexuality better and improved their lives. I am sure you can as well.

REFERENCES

American Psychiatric Association. (1994). *Diagnostic and statistical manual of mental disorders* (4th ed.). Washington, DC: Author.

Basson, R. (2008). Women's sexual function and dysfunction: Current uncertainties, future directions. *International Journal of Impotence Research, 20,* 466–478.

Kaschak, E., & Tiefer, L. (Eds.). (2001). *A new view of women's sexual problems.* Binghamton, NY: Haworth.

Kinsey, A. C., Pomeroy, W. B., Martin, C. E., & Gebhard, P. H. (1953). *Sexual behavior in the human female.* Philadelphia: Saunders.

Masters, W. H., & Johnson, V. E. (1966). *Human sexual response.* Boston: Little, Brown.

Nathan, S. G. (1986). The epidemiology of the *DSM-III* psychosexual dysfunctions. *Journal of Sex and Marital Therapy, 12,* 267–281.

Ten

Women's Difficulties With Low Sexual Desire, Sexual Avoidance, and Sexual Aversion

ROSEMARY BASSON, MD

INTRODUCTION

On beginning my career in sexual medicine after 15 years in internal medicine and family practice, I was honored to be asked to be involved in the teaching of human sexuality and its problems to medical students—teaching I had never had. Medical students were to be taught how to respectfully and diligently inquire about their patients' sexual function and dysfunction. They were to learn how to manage erectile dysfunction, orgasm problems, and dyspareunia, but little mention was made of problematic low sexual desire, especially in women. Some advised me that this is basically untreatable. Laumann's published data (Lauman, Paik, & Rosen, 1999) were still some 8 years away, but I knew that in Vancouver at least, many referrals to our university-associated sexual medicine clinic requested assessment and treatment of women's low sexual desire or "low libido." I had two very basic questions: Did so many women really have a sexual disorder or dysfunction? If at least some of them did, was it really "untreatable"?

As I spoke with women who did and did not have desire concerns, some themes were readily apparent.

1. A minority spoke of their sexual desire in terms of a physical urging, but the overriding wanting was to be emotionally closer to the partner. It followed that poor emotional intimacy was often associated with loss of desire, but women largely found this logical and not a sign that they had any "dysfunction."
2. Sexual stimuli and sexual context were vital. Thus, nothing sensual or erotic in the immediate environment or happening through the day and lack of attractive behavior by their sexual partners all had the expected negative effect on sexual desire. Conversely, a new partner was typically a powerful sexual stimulus, sometimes causing women who had self-diagnosed as having low libido, and unable to be aroused, to become problem free.
3. Not to be able to focus on the moment, on the sexual stimulation, on the emotions associated with being so close to another person was

commonly a component of the difficulties of women labeling their dysfunction as low sexual desire.

4. With little desire, some women would be avoidant, some even aversive of sexual activity by declining or deliberately being busy, needing to go to bed earlier than the partner, even allowing interpersonal disagreements to foster or lessen the partner's sexual motivation. Others would be less avoidant but would limit activity mostly to intercourse—"I want him just to get on with it"—and remain unaroused. Some women "tried to get into it" but had difficulty in responding such that they also did not become aroused or trigger desire during the sexual encounter. Yet others were able to slow the pace, explain the caresses and physical stimulation they needed and thereby trigger arousal along with very definite desire for more sexual tension and possible release.

I learned the traditional human sexual response of Masters and Johnson and Kaplan and was soon requested to teach it, but to me, it did not contain the vital elements. So, after some 10 years of listening and checking, moving on to presenting these themes to colleagues at conferences, to hear their feedback, I started to do what my patients had repeatedly encouraged—to write it down. So began the so-called Basson cycle.

Even before the media blitz on safe and effective medication for men's erectile dysfunction, women frequently couched their most common sexual concerns—those of low sexual desire—in medical terms: "I know I have some kind of hormone imbalance," or "I have had no desire since my tubal ligation, second pregnancy, hysterectomy, or menopause." Ready access to the Internet further aided these various self-proposed etiologies, but these beliefs had been conveyed to me from the early 1970s onward in clinics of internal medicine, family practice, and sexual medicine. Women usually acknowledge that an unhappy relationship, emotional or physical abuse, drug or alcohol addiction, and depression would logically interfere with their sexual desire. However, when they examine their own relationships and feel none of this is relevant for them, they conclude their lack of desire must be something other than a psychological or interpersonal issue, that is, presumably something "medical" (even if previous health professionals have not been able to identify it). Promotion in the North American media of "previously ignored biological causes of women's sexual dysfunction" further fueled these beliefs. Subsequent studies have clearly identified robust correlation of women's sexual desire and satisfaction with their mental health and with the quality of the interpersonal relationship. To date, there is no comparable clarity concerning intrinsic biological/medical factors; rather, even in the context of chronic disease such as renal failure, multiple sclerosis, diabetes, or breast cancer, it has been shown that mental and relationship health remain the major factors determining women's sexual desire.

THE CHANGING NATURE OF DESIRE THROUGH ONE RELATIONSHIP

Women often recall desire early on in relationships when they were caught up in the excitement of the "chase," likely idealizing their (potential) partners, and having many motivations to be sexual in addition to fulfilling any innate sexual hunger. For any one woman, these may have included the enjoyment of feeling attractive and attracted; perhaps playing a role; fulfilling an expectation; feeling better about herself; wanting to cement the relationship; wanting the relationship in order to feel loved, to feel "normal," not to feel lonely, to leave the family of origin, even to further a career or to distance herself from a culture, church, or extended family. Perhaps she was oblivious of these various motivations—it seemed easy for the woman to accept or instigate sexual activity, often to enjoy it—because typically the novelty and presence of many sexual triggers and settings conducive to sexual awareness made this desire for sex appear easy and even "spontaneous." Provided the sexual outcome was rewarding, the wanting of shared sexual sensations and the mutual vulnerability increased. Within the context of desirable erotic stimuli, she was consciously aware of a desire for sex and all that it fulfilled. In some relationships, the secrecy of the liaison, its uncertainty, even its lack of societal approval may have enhanced the potency of the stimuli. The experiences resulted in increased emotional intimacy such that some women, even in the very early stages of their relationships, state that their main reason for agreeing to or instigating sex is to feel closer to the partner.

When women speak of why they agree to or initiate sex with their long-term partners, they emphasize nurturing of the emotional intimacy with that partner as very important (Basson, 2000; Regan & Berscheid, 1996; Tiefer 1991; Tiefer, Hall, & Tavris, 2002). To show that the partner is wanted, loved, missed, appreciated; to give something to the partner; to show that an argument is over; to increase the sense of bonding, commitment, trust, and confidence in the relationship—these aspirations become cemented by sexual experiences with the partner, assuming those experiences are satisfying. Accessing sexual arousal becomes more clearly a deliberate choice (Basson, 2000). Recent empirical data showed 235 discreet reasons younger women (and men) identified as motivating them to sexual activities (Meston & Buss, 2007). The researchers divided these reasons into four domains: love and intimacy, physical pleasure and stress relief, goal attainment, and protection of the relationship ("mate guarding"). During a qualitative study of 34 women, when asked to define their goal or object of desire, 80% identified sharing emotional contact, whereas the goal of intercourse was far less frequent as was the goal of orgasm (Brotto, Heiman, & Tolman, 2009). Triggers of desire/arousal included physical stimuli as well as visual images or triggers from the partner's behavior or from their own memories. These studies confirmed the clinical impression that initially, during any one sexual engagement, a woman may be sexually neutral but motivated by multiple reasons. The presence of appropriate sexual stimuli in a context that is conducive to physical intimacy plus the ability to attend to those stimuli appear to be crucial to the human sexual response. Any initial, apparently spontaneous desire/drive adds to this response at any or all points, as shown in Figure 10.1, but it is not an essential component.

ALTERNATIVE SEXUAL RESPONSE CYCLE FOR WOMEN

The following diagram is a model of a composite, flexible, and alternative sexual response cycle that is frequently confirmed by women as reflective of their experiences. Unlike the traditional model of human sexual response

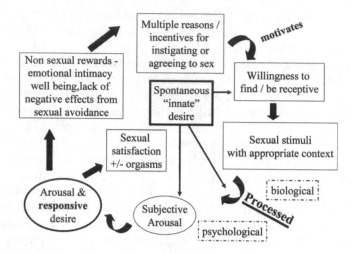

Figure 10.1   Model of female sexual response cycle.

stemming from the writings of Masters and Johnson and Kaplan (of a linear sequence of discreet events with a predominantly genital focus), this alternative model is circular, and within it, arousal can precede and then accompany an accessed or "developed" form of desire (Basson, 2001a). This echoes Kaplan's (1979) concept of both intrinsic and extrinsic (responsive) desire. Intrinsic/spontaneous desire can reinforce the cycle as shown in Figure 10.1, but it is not essential.

The circular response shown in Figure 10.1 may be cycled many times during one sexual encounter. While positive experiences provide further motivation for sex in the future, negative outcomes will efficiently do the opposite.

EMOTIONAL INTIMACY AS A MAJOR MOTIVATING FORCE BEHIND THE CYCLE AND THE INTEGRAL ROLE OF SEXUAL STIMULI

As Levine clarified in Chapter 3, growing psychological intimacy can breed wanting for sexual intimacy. However, for very many women, the psychological intimacy—although vital—I would suggest, is by itself insufficient. Although emotional intimacy can fuel a willingness to move on from sexual neutrality to a state of sexual arousal, useful sexual stimuli and appropriate context are vital. Entities external to the woman are, in fact, integral components of her sexual response cycle, moving her from sexual neutrality to sexual arousal. The needed stimuli are both mental and physical, and the context may be more important than the actual stimuli themselves; for instance, visually explicit sexual stimuli out of context, although possibly causing a fairly prompt genital vasocongestive response of which the woman is relatively unaware, are typically not considered subjectively arousing. Women speak frequently of the need for caring, attractive behavior from their partner throughout the day, which will determine the effectiveness of the specific sexual stimuli when the time comes to interact sexually. An empirical study has confirmed the importance of partner compatibility in determining sexual dysfunction and sexual distress (Witting et al., 2008).

When sexual stimuli and an appropriate context are missing, despite psychological intimacy, the woman's feelings for her partner are typically those of affection, love, and caring. A woman often discusses her likely contentment if she and her partner could be just "soul mates," but adds any contentment would be marred by guilt: "I know this sounds awful—but I wouldn't care if we never have sex again." There is sadness that this is not what society expects, and there is fear that the relationship will suffer. These feelings tend to counterbalance any positive thoughts of "no more sex."

RESPONSIVE DESIRE IS PROBABLY MORE IMPORTANT THAN SPONTANEOUS DESIRE

What then is the role of "spontaneous" or "intrinsic" sexual desire? We know that sexual function is a highly complex blending of mind and body, and that certain neurotransmitters and hormones permit sexual stimuli to register unconsciously and thereby alter autonomic nervous responses. This leads to a number of physiological changes, including increased genital blood flow. The stimuli are also appraised as mentally sexually arousing/attractive, triggering a responsive desire. The neurotransmitters and hormones permit this process, but there is no evidence that in normal physiological amounts these neurochemical agents actually generate a feeling of sexual desire. It could be argued that all of sexual desire is responsive to something—whether a thought or a memory. The term *spontaneous desire* is usually meant to describe a seemingly innate neediness of the experience of building sexual tension and its release, preferably with someone else, and which appears not to be triggered by anything in the current environment or by deliberate focusing of the mind on sexual matters.

This brings us to the difficulties with the traditional markers of women's spontaneous sexual desire as reflected in the definition of hypoactive sexual desire disorder (HSDD) in *DSM-IV* (APA, 1994). Sexual fantasies, self-stimulation, and spontaneous thinking about sex have been considered correlates of healthy sexual desire. However, women tell of the use of fantasy to become aroused or to stop distraction during the sexual experience (Lunde, Larson, Fog, & Gard, 1991). For them, the presence of fantasies is hardly a reflection of a high innate spontaneous desire. The previously mentioned qualitative study of 34 women illustrates the lack of importance of fantasies for the participants: Fantasies were recorded as present on the validated questionnaire (the Female Sexual Function Index, FSFI), but as the women spoke about desire, fantasies were not featured (Brotto et al., 2009).

Older, smaller studies such as that by Galyer, Conaglen, Hare, and Conaglen (1999) focused on women who had undergone hysterectomy from 18 months previously versus those with nongynecological surgery to show that the majority of both groups reported engaging in sexual activity without awareness of sexual desire. Larger studies are now available, such as those from the Study of Women Across the Nation (SWAN), which showed that the majority of 3,250 multiethnic, middle-aged women in North America confirmed moderate or extreme satisfaction with their physical sexual pleasure but documented that they never or infrequently sensed desire (Cain et al., 2003).

Using self-stimulation as a marker of spontaneous desire is also problematic. Women will give many reasons other than to release sexual tension for their self-stimulation; to soothe, to get to sleep, to relax, and even "to prove it still works" are reasons frequently offered to me. Laumann, Paik, and Rosen's (1999) study showed not only far fewer autoerotic practices in women compared to men but also a much wider spectrum of frequency.

Another difficulty with the current definition of HSDD is the necessity to document personal or interpersonal distress about the lack of desire and fantasy. Given the woman's personal distress may well stem from her partner's reaction, it becomes apparent that, most unfortunately, women may or may not receive a diagnosis of a mental disorder based on the personality and sexuality of their partner. It is important to note the huge discrepancy between complaints about low desire and distress about that situation and to use nationally representative studies rather than those obtained from convenience samples such as medical insurance companies' or other commercial databases. A national North American study showed that, of 2,200 women, 52% of those who were naturally menopausal had concerns of low desire, but only 6.6% confirmed distress such that a diagnosis of HSDD might be considered (West et al., 2008). Of women younger than 45 years who were surgically menopausal, 36% had desire complaints (similar to aged-matched women with intact ovaries), but importantly 20% of the surgically menopausal women had significant distress. Looking at the surgically menopausal women who were older than 45 years and had remote ovariectomy, 36% had concerns about desire—interestingly, less than the 52% of aged-matched women with intact ovaries—and 8.5% were distressed. Women older than 45 years who had bilateral ovariectomy after the age of 45 showed similar numbers of complaints about desire as their aged-matched naturally menopausal counterparts, but again in these women with recent surgical intervention there was an increase in distress: 52% of them showed significant distress. This all illustrates the contextuality of women's sexuality: Partners' reactions or surgical intervention appear to modulate distress about reduced desire, but the latter may not be different from other aged-matched women.

I would suggest that more useful criteria for low sexual desire might include both the following:

1. A marked absence of sexual thinking, fantasizing, self-stimulation, or conscious yearning for the physical experience that is over and beyond a normative lessening with relationship duration and with age
2. Inability to trigger desire by becoming sexually aroused

Studies have confirmed the previously documented comorbidity between arousal and desire disorders (Dennerstein, Koochaki, Barton, & Graziottin, 2006; Leiblum, Koochaki, Rodenberg, Barton, & Rosen, 2006).

CAN WOMEN DISTINGUISH BETWEEN SEXUAL DESIRE AND SEXUAL AROUSAL?

Qualitative studies have proven enlightening. Of 80 women aged 18 to 84 engaged in small focus groups, the majority did not clearly differentiate between desire and arousal and confirmed that interest or desire sometimes followed and sometimes preceded arousal (Graham, Sanders, Milhausen, & McBride, 2004). Moreover, there were wide-ranging signals of arousal, including physical ones (e.g., "butterflies in the stomach"), increased heart rate, increased skin sensitivity, flushing, muscle tightness, erect nipples, genital tingling and fullness, and increased vaginal lubrication. These women clearly identified the emotional components (e.g., feeling nervous and excited), cognitive aspects (including anticipation and a heightened sense of awareness), as well as behavioral components (including sighing or moaning). In the previously mentioned qualitative study of 34 women, the majority confirmed desire was both cognitive and emotional (Brotto et al., 2009). As well, 80% confirmed desire as physical (nongenital) and somewhat fewer (75% in younger and 50% in older) as genital. Nearly all women found it difficult to differentiate between desire and arousal.

AROUSABILITY

Given the premise that arousal often precedes desire, what alters the ease or difficulty with which the woman becomes subjectively aroused? What governs this "information processing," to use recent terminology (Janssen, Everaerd, Spiering, & Janssen, 2000)? Biological and psychological factors are involved. Clinical experience suggests that negative cognitions include nonsexual distractions; concerns of being sexually substandard, taking too long to reach orgasm; appearing sexually naïve, inexperienced, infertile; fear of dyspareunia; and concerns for emotional safety or for physical safety or safety from sexually transmitted disease and unwanted pregnancy. Research has pointed to "arousal contingency" factors, meaning the need for circumstances to be "just right" (Sanders, Graham, & Milhausen, 2008). This preliminary research suggests that distractions or arousal contingency factors commonly inhibit arousal. Negative emotions, including guilt or shame, can also modulate and possibly preclude any subjective arousal. Concern about her sexual response (or its lack) may also distract. Functional magnetic resonance imaging (fMRI) suggests that women with low desire focus more on their own physical response than do controls (Arnow et al., 2009). Management of low desire in our clinic has mostly involved cognitive–behavioral techniques with some sex therapy. An important more recent addition is the instruction and encouragement of mindfulness practice (Brotto, Basson, & Luria, 2008). This meditative technique is defined as "relaxed wakefulness" or "nonjudgmental, present moment awareness." Regular practice in nonsexual ways allows the woman to "stay in the moment" when she is sexual. She learns to observe but not to follow distracting thoughts. She recognizes the thoughts underlying any guilt or shame and so learns not to follow them. Her physical sexual sensations become more intense, arousal is easier, and desire to continue the experience is triggered. Empirical research confirms that the degree of attention given to sexual stimuli correlates with a person's reported level of desire (Prause, Janssen, & Hetrick, 2008).

Researchers using brain imaging with positron emission tomography (PET) scans, have shown areas of reduced brain activity with sexual arousal as well as areas of increased activity (Redouté et al., 2000; Karama et al., 2002). Clearly, any inhibition can be partly programmed by life's experiences, but the postulate is that some of it must be inherently "set" (i.e., "biological"). Knowledge of neurotransmitters and neuropeptides and hormonal central control of sexual arousal is rudimentary. Medications with partly or completely known mechanisms of action may have pro or antisexual effects. Broadly speaking, prosexual neurotransmitters and hormones include dopamine, oxytocin, centrally acting noradrenalin, serotonin acting via 5HT1A and perhaps 5HT2C receptors, luteinizing hormone-releasing hormone (LHRH), melanocortins, and androgens (Herbert, 1997). On the other hand, serotonin acting via some 5HT2 and 5HT3 receptors, β-endorphin, prolactin, and GABA (γ-aminobutyric acid), are sexually negative, with opioids potentially increasing sexual wanting but lessening the ability to be physiologically aroused. Since depression alters the balance of these neurotransmitters, it is clear why it is commonly associated with reduced arousability and complaints of low desire. Even when clinical depression is excluded, women seen consecutively for complaints of low desire report more mood lability, poorer self-image, and more depressed and anxious thoughts than control women (Hartmann, Philippsohn, Heiser, & Rüffer-Hesse, 2004). Moreover, the SWAN data showed that a history of depression predisposes to current complaints of low sexual desire despite controlling for current mood and antidepressant medications (Cyranowski et al., 2004).

The question of the role of androgens is frequently raised. Sudden complete loss of all ovarian androgen can lead to a typical picture in which mental and physical stimuli become minimally effective; then, arousal can only be very slowly reached with deliberate focusing on the stimuli, and no intense arousal is experienced. Sometimes, a brief low-intensity orgasm may occur, shutting off further arousal, a concept totally foreign to the woman who previously likely had the potential for continued arousal after orgasm with or without further orgasmic release. Although clinicians see the syndrome, it has proven remarkably difficult to identify any "androgen-deficiency syndrome." Serum levels of testosterone (however measured) have not correlated with women's sexual desire or sexual function in any of the larger studies. An enormous problem in the past was the lack of an available sensitive accurate assay of serum testosterone; the available assays were designed to be accurate in the male range. Mass spectrometry is now available in research centers and may be clinically availably reasonably soon. Another important issue is that sex hormone-binding globulin (SHBG) usually decreases with age. This protein attaches itself to testosterone (and estrogen), rendering these sex hormones largely unavailable to the tissues; only the free portion is currently thought to be useful. So, with SHBG decreasing, a bigger fraction (albeit of a smaller total amount) of testosterone is available to the tissues, such that free testosterone may actually rise. To complicate matters further, if oral estrogen therapy is given, SHBG rises, so free testosterone falls.

A possible further major confound is the intracellular production of testosterone from adrenal and ovarian precursor hormones. This is testosterone that is produced in peripheral cells and not picked up by testing serum levels. Measuring testosterone metabolites is currently considered a better means of measuring total testosterone activity (Labrie et al., 2006). To date, testosterone metabolites have not been found to correlate with women's sexual desire. Adrenal precursors, including androstenedione (A_4), dehydroepiandrosterone (DHEA), and DHEA sulfate (DHEAS) reduce by some 70% beginning in the late 20s. Ovarian production of DHEA and A_4 also declines with age, while ovarian testosterone production is ongoing but variable. Yet another potential major confound is the fact that the brain produces sex hormones de novo starting from cholesterol. There is early evidence that this production may increase when the serum level of sex hormones decreases with age and with menopause.

Despite the clinical syndrome mentioned, for other women the loss of both ovaries results in no sexual changes; presumably, their adrenal production of testosterone precursors (which does not "pick up the slack" when the ovaries are removed or destroyed by chemotherapy) is nevertheless sufficient. Three prospective studies of perimenopausal women whose elective hysterectomy required for benign pathology included bilateral oophorectomy showed no subsequent sexual dysfunction over the next 3 years. In one study the surgeon chose whether to remove the ovaries (Farquar, Harvey, Yu, Sadler, & Stewart, 2006), and in one the women chose (Aziz, Brannstrom, Bergquist, & Silfverstolpe, 2005); the third involved women who chose the oophorectomy plus women who proved to have pathology such that oophorectomy was needed (Teplin et al., 2007).

Another biological factor is fatigue, which commonly affects arousability. This may be from poor sleep due to small children, chronic pain, or debility from any cause or sleep disturbance from chronic stressors. The most common medications associated with reduced arousability that I encounter include serotonergic antidepressants, tranquilizers, β-blockers, and those analgesics that include codeine.

WOMEN'S CONTEXTUAL AND RELATIONAL SEXUALITY: "THE NEW VIEW"

The circular model reflects flexibility and variability among women and within any given relationship. By focusing on context, it echoes themes from "the new view of women's sexual function." (Tiefer et al., 2002). This view maintains that there is no one "normal" sexual response or experience; rather, there are four major aspects of women's sexual lives that potentially cause sexual difficulty: sociocultural/political/economic, relationship, medical, and psychological aspects. This view reflects many themes in this chapter. Frequently for women labeled with "sexual disorder," there is no evidence of innate dysfunction of sexual response; rather, a paucity of reasons to begin or problematic stimuli or context explain the reported "dysfunctional" sexual encounters.

THE CIRCULAR MODEL AS COMPOSITE AND COMPATIBLE WITH OTHER CONCEPTUALIZATIONS

The circular "Basson model" reflects the work of many others. Masters and Johnson described a linear sequence of arousal, a plateau of excitement, followed by orgasm and resolution. Although after the publication of *The Human Sex Response Cycle* by Masters and Johnson the arousal phase in women often became synonymous with genital events (lubrication and swelling), the original description included both genital and subjective arousal. Kaplan noted desire could be triggered during the sexual experience, or it could be present at the outset. She called the former "extrinsic/responsive" and the latter "intrinsic/biological." No simple drawing was used to emphasize the extrinsic/responsive component; thus, the accepted model of human sex response for three decades was linear: desire, arousal, orgasm, and resolution. Clinicians involved with patients with disabilities and chronic illness emphasized the importance of a positive outcome that would allow "reflection" that would subsequently fuel "a seduction phase" that encompassed desire (Whipple & Brash-McGreer, 1997). Thus, a more circular response was envisioned. Levine, in his tripartite model of sexual desire, identified drive, motivation, and wish components (2003). Authors, including Regan and Berscheid (1996), Singer and Toates (1997), and Whalen (1966) identified many motives or reasons for men and women to be sexual in addition to any awareness of an intrinsic urge for sexual activity. These "nondesire" motivations awaited incorporation into a composite model. Janssen and Everaerd's information processing model of sexual arousal emphasizes the importance of the mind's processing of sexual stimuli: unconscious processing leading to an automatic genital response and conscious appraisal of the sexual content of the stimulus to allow subjective arousal are involved (Janssen et al., 2000). Also noted is that the genital activation and the awareness of excitement can then become further sexual stimuli, i.e., additional to the original sexual stimulus. I have suggested the former is more effective in men (Basson, 2001a). Divergence between automatic genital response and the more slowly developed conscious appraisal of arousal underlies dysfunctional arousal in men and women. Recent work by Sanders and Graham has begun to identify themes that underlie women's propensity to become aroused from sexual stimulation and factors that tend to preclude or inhibit (Sanders et al., 2008). None of these models were meant to represent the sexual response cycle of only one gender. However, one difference between the sexual experiences of a majority of women compared to a majority of men is that the initial desire leading up to a sexual experience is less frequent in women (Baumeister, Catanese, & Vohs, 2001).

COMPLEXITIES OF SEXUAL AROUSAL FOR WOMEN

Women's subjective arousal appears to be largely reflective of how sexually exciting they find the stimulus and context (Everaerd, Laan, Both, & van der Velde, 2000; Laan E, van Driel EM, & van Lunsen, 2008). This correlates to an extremely variable degree with objective genital engorgement; that is, there is high variability between different sexually healthy women. This is in marked contrast to sexually healthy men whose subjective sexual arousal correlates closely with their degree of genital congestion (erection). Objective measurement of female genital congestion resulting from an erotic (usually visual) stimulus has, to date, mainly stemmed from the use of the vaginal photoplethysmograph. This is a tampon-like probe placed in the vagina; it contains a light source and a phototransistor, that is, a light detector. Light is backscattered by the blood in the vaginal vascular plexus, and changes in vaginal congestion cause changes in the output from the light detector. Short-term changes in vaginal engorgement are reflected by changes in the vaginal pulse amplitude (VPA); in other words, with each heartbeat there is a phasic change in blood content of the vaginal tissues.

The results of studying women with arousal disorders are interesting. When watching an erotic video, they will typically report no subjective arousal or minimal arousal accompanied by negative emotions but are found to have plethysmograph studies identical to women who are acting as controls and who are subjectively aroused by the video (Everaerd et al., 2000; Laan et al., 2008; van Lunsen & Laan, 2004). The same increase in VPA is shown by both groups of women. Note that it is the accessing of *subjective* arousal that I am suggesting will allow a developed form of desire (see Figure 10.1). The degree of awareness of genital tingling, throbbing, swelling, and lubrication is also highly variable among sexually healthy women, correlates rather poorly with objective measurement of that congestion, and is not the main influence determining their subjective state (Chivers & Bailey, 2005; Heiman, 1998).

It has also become clear that genital congestion can follow a stimulus that is sexual but in no way erotic. Women (but not men) viewing primates mating associate the video as biologically sexual but not erotic and yet have prompt genital responses that were measured as comparable to their response to an erotic sexual video (Chivers & Bailey, 2005). The important point is that the genital response is an involuntary unconscious reflex—a rapid autonomic nervous system response. The response confirms that the woman's mind has recognized the sexual nature of the stimulus but does not itself confirm that appraisal of the stimulus and context is subjectively arousing (Basson, 2002; Chivers & Bailey, 2005; Everaerd et al., 2000).

This is not to say that genital engorgement is unimportant. For many women, it is vital:

1. To allow a genital stimulus to move them from neutral to sexually aroused (Basson, 2000). Physical massage of engorging vulval erectile tissue can be increasingly pleasurable, leading to intense sexual sensations with or without orgasms, whereas physically massaging nonengorged vulval erectile tissue can be unpleasant, irritating, or painful.
2. In the absence of vulval and vaginal engorgement, vaginal entry by penis, finger, or vibrator is not associated with pleasure and frequently is associated with pain or discomfort. From the model of sexual response, it is clear that the negative outcome from dyspareunia can cause a woman to complain of low desire. Indeed, a study of 1,400 sexually active North American postmenopausal women confirmed a strong association between symptoms of vulvovaginal atrophy that can cause pain or bleeding with intercourse and overall sexual function (Levine, Williams, & Hartmann, 2008).

Vulvar and vaginal engorgement are dependent on a minimum amount of estrogen activity. For some women when postpartum, postmenopause, or receiving a gonadotrophin releasing hormone (GnRH) agonist for endometriosis, for instance, estrogen is insufficient to permit the increased vasocongestion needed to allow genital caressing to be pleasurable and vaginal lubrication to be adequate for painless intercourse.

After menopause, women are dependent on intracellular production of estrogen from adrenal and ovarian precursor hormones; this may or may not be sufficient for sexual function. The debate about postmenopausal estrogen therapy continues, and those in the field of sexual medicine need to be able to explain the current as opposed to the 2002 understanding of who may benefit and who may be harmed. Although benefit on the basis of vasomotor symptoms, bone density, and dyspareunia has been repeatedly confirmed, there has been much debate over long-term estrogen therapy with a view to cardiovascular protection versus increased cardiovascular, breast cancer, and deep venous thrombosis (DVT) risk. With accumulating data from some 40 observational and 5 prospective randomized studies, reviews clarified overall benefit for estrogen therapy initiated at or within 6 years of menopause with yet more cardiovascular benefit accruing with longer use (Hodis & Mack, 2008).

As clinicians, many of us have seen the negative sexual effects of the dramatic cessation of estrogen therapy in North America subsequent to just one randomized controlled trial (RCT), the 2002 Women's Health Initiative (WHI) study, which recruited older, heavier, postmenopausal women (more than 90% were older than 55 years at recruitment) who were generally asymptomatic (Writing Group for the Women's Health Initiative Investigators, 2002). This is clearly not the clinical population of younger symptomatic women who would usually be given estrogen therapy. Clinicians remain hesitant to prescribe estrogen therapy and confused regarding the current understanding of accumulated data. I therefore summarize recent reviews.

Reanalysis of that WHI study confirmed that younger women (i.e., those recruited within 10 years after menopause) had 12% reduction in coronary heart disease (CHD) from the use of combined conjugated equine estrogen (CEE) and medroxyprogesterone acetate (MPA), whereas women randomized between 10 and 20 years after menopause had a 23% increase risk of CHD, and those randomized more than 20 years after menopause had a 66% increase risk of CHD (Grodstein, Manson, & Stampfer, 2006). When the CEE plus MPA and the CEE alone trials are combined, the trend in CHD reduction according to time of initiation of hormone therapy (HT) is even stronger (because of a greater sample size). Women randomized to HT within 10 years of menopause had a 24% reduction in CHD (Rossouw et al., 2007). Observational studies indicated that beneficial effects of HT and CHD risks depend on time of initiation (Grodstein et al., 2006). A large meta-analysis has been done using 23 RCTs; the effects of estrogen therapy on CHD over all ages were null, but a 32% reduction in CHD was then found for women less than 60 years old or within 10 years since menopause when randomized (Salpeter, Walsh, Grebyer, & Salpeter, 2006). It is important to note that the effect of estrogen therapy on total mortality is also related to the age of initiation, with a 31% reduction in total mortality in the women who were randomized between the ages of 50 and 59 (Rossouw et al., 2007). Women randomized between the ages of 60 and 69 had a 9% increase in total mortality, and women over 70 years old had a 6% increase. This beneficial effect on total mortality has also been confirmed in the large meta-analysis.

Risks of estrogen therapy in recently menopausal women are rare (less than 1 event per 1,000 women per year) (Hodis & Mack, 2008). Again, recently postmenopausal women and younger postmenopausal women have a lower absolute risk for adverse outcomes than older and remotely menopausal women.

Many women fear increased risk of breast cancer from estrogen therapy, not realizing first that the increase is very small and second that it is comparable to the increased risk from statin therapy. Meta-analysis of breast cancer and statin therapy suggests the latter may cause 7 more cases of breast cancer per 10,000 women per year, similar to the 9 extra cases per 10,000 women per year found in the WHI study of estrogen plus progestin and in comparison with the

8 fewer cases in women in the WHI study who received only estrogen (Dale, Coleman, Henyan, Kluger, & White, 2006).

Another confound is the increasing use of transdermal as opposed to oral estrogen and the use of progesterone as opposed to synthetic progestin. An observational study has shown cardiovascular protection from transdermal estrogen formulations (Clarkson & Karas, 2007).

Future research may increase our knowledge of differences between recently menopausal women such that for some, but only some, estrogen is protective (Carim, Hodis, Stanczyk, Lobo, & Mack, 2008).

Unfortunately, sexual function was not adequately assessed in these various trials of hormonal therapy. By modulating mood and vasomotor symptoms estrogen has indirect effects on desire. Many women I see date their low desire and subjective arousability to the WHI study induced stopping of their estrogen therapy. Focusing only on the genital sexual symptoms, these can be relieved by local use of estrogen in the form of sialastic ring, cream containing CEE, or a vaginal suppository of estradiol. Systemic absorption can be minimized this way perhaps most effectively by the use of the ring or smaller dose suppository or limiting the cream to 0.5 grams twice weekly. Lost desire on the basis of negative outcome from dyspareunia can be thereby restored. Very recent research shows local vaginal DHEA to improve all aspects of sexual response in postmenopausal women, without systemic absorption of DHEA, nor increase in either serum estrogen or testosterone (Labrie et al., 2009).

IMPORTANCE OF A REWARDING EMOTIONAL AND PHYSICAL OUTCOME

Despite accessing arousal and desire and enjoying both, if the ultimate outcome is negative, neither the original goal (e.g., to be emotionally close to the partner) nor the accessed goal (to enjoy more intense sexual sensations with ultimate sexual satisfaction), is reached. Instead, emotional distancing, feelings of being used, even of being abused can surface. Common causes of negative outcome include chronic dyspareunia, partner sexual dysfunction, lack of sexual skills or inability to communicate the type of sexual stimulation required (Basson, 2000, 2001b; Binik, Bergeron, & Khalifé, 2000). Clearly, one break in the cycle usually leads to others—an unrewarding outcome can weaken the "motor," the emotional intimacy with the partner. The woman no longer finds or focuses on sexual cues and stimuli—she is distracted when they are present such that arousal is not experienced (Basson, 2002). When does this become aversion? Clinical experience suggests that a past history of sexual abuse predisposes to aversion as opposed to dislike, reluctance, or simply avoidance. However, aversion and lack of desire may be on a continuum: Many women will state their experiences are "almost aversive." Another clinical finding is that women who feel unable to control the situation (i.e., to say "no" or to set the pace or frequency of sexual contact) are more likely to speak in terms of aversion.

WHEN IS LACK OF "SPONTANEOUS DESIRE" A DISORDER?

Marked or sudden loss of this innate spontaneous desire, rather than a gradual lessening with relationship duration and with age, needs assessment. Depression is the most frequent cause, but other causes include medication effects, hyperprolactinemia, and physical or emotional stress (e.g., recently recalled childhood abuse, loss of a loved one, absorption in studies or work).

This apparently spontaneous sexual neediness, as mentioned, often gradually lessens as the years and decades go by even in healthy, rewarding relationships, sometimes to be rekindled should a new relationship follow. This lessening is mostly not seen to be problematic simply because of the woman's ready sexual arousal and her ongoing responsivity. It is worth recalling which women complain about low desire; repeatedly, it is those with mood disorders currently or in the past, those with marked low self-esteem and mood lability, as well as those reporting rather minimal emotional closeness with a partner. In our clinic, we have very strong confirmation of this link between depression and complaints of low desire; attempting to recruit 120 women complaining of low desire but who are not depressed and not currently taking antidepressants has proven difficult. Our records show that close to 80% of such referrals were for women already on antidepressants; a further 6% scored in the depressive range on the screening questionnaire.

Case of Sandra and Gerald

Sandra, 44, has been married to 52-year-old Gerald for 20 years. The complaint is low sexual desire for Sandra since Shelly's birth, which necessitated a cesarean section for failure to progress. Sandra feels somehow this surgical intervention altered her sexual function.

The couple has two children, Ken (13) and Shelly (8). With a background in practical nursing, Sandra is currently working for a nonprofit society providing resources for teens at risk. Gerald is a chartered accountant and has had well-controlled type 1 diabetes since age 20. Physically, Sandra is healthy with regular menses. Although not diagnosed, history suggests a postpartum depression after Shelly's birth. There are also ongoing anxious thoughts, particularly about the care of her invalid mother; the concerns of the children she cares for at work; worries about Ken, who has learning disabilities and now some behavioral problems; and long-term worries about Gerald's diabetes and its control. Aside from the diabetes, Gerald is well. His physicians tell him that he has no complications of the diabetes. Although he can manage his glucose control himself, Sandra is also very involved with his medical care.

The current sexual situation is that Gerald rarely instigates, suggesting that he does not want to pressure his wife, although when seen alone, he admits that also he does not like being rejected. There is a more or less mutual understanding between the partners that they would be sexual on waking on weekend mornings—if the children get up before them, they look after themselves. Also, when Shelly and Ken stay with Gerald's parents, usually during the school holidays, the couple has more frequent sexual activity, but often this is late at night. Mostly, Sandra is not aroused or orgasmic. Of note, though, she limits the nongenital touching and genital touching. When seen alone, she speaks of "just wanting to get it over with." In the more distant past, Sandra was more orgasmic with intercourse; this has lessened in recent years—intercourse is briefer as Gerald ejaculates quickly. Also, sometimes Gerald's erection is not firm, even to the point of discontinuing the attempt of intercourse occasionally. When sexually engaged, Sandra's mind is usually elsewhere; distractions include worrying about the children in her care, and her son. In the past, she was worried about what was wrong with her sexually; she now worries about Gerald's diabetes. Sometimes, Sandra is able to focus and will prolong the nonpenetrative sexual touching; she has pleasure and arousal, and then she moves Gerald to enter her, but intercourse remains brief, and usually she is not orgasmic. These are times when Sandra is feeling emotionally closer to Gerald, less stressed in general; often, the children are away at the grandparents. Inquiring into the effectiveness of other kinds of sexual stimuli, such as books, movies, or music, it seems that there are very few in Sandra's life.

The couple's sexual life before the pregnancy with Shelly was rewarding for both partners. There was more nonpenetrative sex. Sandra would be regularly orgasmic with intercourse. However, she has never self-stimulated, and she did not allow clitoral touching to continue to the point of orgasm but would feel a need to move on to intercourse as those sensations increased in intensity. Nevertheless, despite a limited menu, both partners were satisfied with their sexual experiences.

Inquiry into Sandra's developmental history identified a rather unhappy upbringing with a very critical father and a recurrently medically unwell mother such that Sandra often felt like the parent. Sandra was the only child. School was also not particularly happy, with Sandra finding some subjects challenging but always wanting to please the teachers. Church, a fairly fundamentalist Christian church, was a big part of her life; themes about sexuality were that it was definitely to be reserved for marriage. Sandra tells of accepting this and of remorse at being sexually active, including intercourse, for a few months with a boyfriend when she was 18. More distressing was the fact that she told Gerald about this, and he had told her that he was "deeply disappointed." This was during their engagement; it would seem that this is still a source of sadness for Sandra, and it is not a subject the couple ever discusses. Sandra's parents are still in her life; her mother needs increasing care, causing Sandra considerable stress. Her father is less critical now, but there is little warmth between the father and daughter. As we traced her developmental history, Sandra was very willing to admit that her source of happiness and contentment has always been in caring for and pleasing others. However, she was quite aware that currently there was some resentment about this, and this spilled over into the sexual scene in that, again, she was feeling a need to "give," this time to her husband, namely, sex when she was not in the mood.

When Gerald was seen alone, he told how his father had died from complications of diabetes when Gerald was 12, and he had become the man of the house. He was very responsible, looking after younger siblings and (rather like Sandra) taking care of his mother, who was emotionally quite fragile. Understandably, there was no recall of acting out or being a typical teenager; that simply was not possible with his responsibilities. His background was also Christian, with the encouragement not to be sexual until marriage. Gerald had girlfriends but no intercourse until marrying Sandra.

DIAGNOSES

Diagnoses for Sandra were as follows: *DSM-IV* (APA, 1994) hypoactive sexual desire disorder; situational desire/interest disorder according to the American Urological Association Foundation; and situational combined arousal disorder.

FORMULATION

Multiple factors are involved, including the paucity of sexual triggers and the fact that the context is not particularly conducive to erotic thoughts and feelings. The actual physical stimulation is quite limited; in addition, Gerald rarely flirts or instigates anything sexual for fear of undue pressure on his wife. The lack of being able to be assertive or rebellious as a teen may have suppressed both his assertiveness and sexuality. Another major factor is that Sandra finds it very difficult to stay in the moment but reports multiple distractions. Although in the past she felt better about herself by caring for others, she is now at the point of feeling somewhat resentful about this; being resentful and angry is not conducive to feeling sexual. Importantly, she has a low self-image and sexual self-image; in fact, she feels "sexually broken." With the background of her father's constant criticism, she has been highly self-critical, in particular feeling a failure sexually (by having intercourse before marriage), a failure sexually currently (by having no desire), and a failure as a mother (needing to have the cesarean section).

Compounding factors include Gerald's current premature ejaculation and occasional erectile dysfunction. Theoretically, at this time there is also less androgen support of Sandra's sexual response, which may or may not be relevant—androgen precursors are already reduced by some 50% in the mid-40s.

TREATMENT

Before embarking on any treatment for the couple, Sandra attended four 2-hour sessions for group psychoeducational therapy. These consist of a combination of cognitive–behavioral therapy (CBT), mindfulness practice, sex therapy themes, and information about women's sexuality. Projects/homework to be done between the sessions included keeping thought records, creating the woman's own sexual response cycle with various breaks and areas of vulnerability, as well as practicing mindfulness.

When seen together, the couple was again given information regarding men's and women's sexual responses and the essential role of stimuli and context. We also addressed the degree of emotional intimacy; this was judged to be fair, but it seemed that Sandra wished Gerald would be more communicative and open up more about his feelings, especially when she noticed that his mood was low. A brief, modified, structured sensate focus approach helped the couple create more useful sexual context and stimuli, and this along with the mindfulness practice allowed Sandra to be very present and feel more intensely. As well, she was encouraged to stay with nonpenetrative sexual stimulation and reported orgasms from direct clitoral manual stimulation. Gerald's variable erectile dysfunction was treated with a phosphodiesterase inhibitor, and the more reliable erection also took care of the fast ejaculation. When last seen, he reported firm erections without the drug: "Sandra's arousal was contagious."

CONCLUSION

You will see many women with complaints of low desire and many looking for a medical solution (even if there is no identified medical etiology). Sharing with them this model of their sexual response that reflects their many reasons to be sexual over and beyond any innate sexual hunger provides logic to their situation, which in itself is therapeutic. The importance of the degree of emotional intimacy becomes obvious. When this is lacking, the willingness and ability of both partners to address this lack clearly governs the effectiveness of addressing any problematic context or paucity of sexual stimuli and any psychological and interpersonal (and sometimes biological) issues affecting the woman's arousability. Moreover, addressing any cause of negative outcome such as partner sexual dysfunction or chronic dyspareunia requires true motivation from both partners, which will also be dependent on a certain degree of emotional closeness.

Thus, improving the emotional intimacy per se, although often necessary, may well be insufficient. Deliberately giving some priority to sexual times and finding suitable contexts and types of mental and physical stimulation are also often needed. Some couples will need information about women's sexuality in longer-term relationships, including the need for the partners to guide each other as physical responding changes with age and hormonal milieu. The frequent need for more nongenital and genital nonintercourse pleasuring can be emphasized. Less-healthy habits of perfunctory intercourse associated with previous fertility testing or attempting sex when she is exhausted with young children may need to be addressed. The key element to the woman's sex response cycle is that it is a response, and the context of the stimuli eliciting that response is crucial. Essential also is her ability to stay in the moment: The increasing use of mindfulness appears promising. Thus, a woman's sexual response can be nurtured and can potentially increase rather than decrease with the relationship's duration.

REFERENCES

Arnow, B. A., Millheiser, L., Garret, A., Lake Polan, M., Glover, G. H., Hill, K. R., et al. (2009). Women with hypoactive sexual desire disorder compared to normal females: A functional magnetic resonance imaging study. *Neuroscience, 158,* 484–502.

Aziz, A., Brannstrom, M., Bergquist, C., & Silfverstolpe, G. (2005). Perimenopausal androgen decline after oophorectomy does not influence sexuality or psychological well-being. *Fertility and Sterility, 83,* 1021–1028.

Basson, R. (2000). The female sexual response of different model. *Journal of Sex and Marital Therapy, 26,* 51–65. I outlined the need for a model of women's sexual responding that can reflect issues important to women's sexuality, including trust, the ability to be vulnerable, respect, communication, affection, and pleasure from sexual touching. A woman's sexual cycle can begin without innate desire. Rather, she is willing to make a deliberate choice to become sexually aroused to access some sexual desire "en route." The major underlying motivation to do this is to increase emotional intimacy with her partner. However, she does also enjoy and come to hunger for more sexual sensations with or without orgasmic release as the whole experience continues. Factors external to her are in fact integral to her sexual cycle, including suitable sexual stimuli and context.

Basson, R. (2001a). Human sex response cycles. *Journal of Sex and Marital Therapy, 27,* 33–43. The alternative model of sexual responding, by which initially there is an intimacy-based motivation rather than an innate "biological" sexual hunger or sense of sexual deprivation, is applied to the sexual experiences of men and women. The model is further developed to allow cycles within the basic simple cycle presented in Basson (2000). The concept of feedback cycles is introduced, commenting on the feedback from emotions, cognitions, and genital events in both men and women.

Basson, R. (2001b). Rethinking low sexual desire in women. *British Journal of Obstetrics and Gynecology, 109,* 357–363. Here, the alternative models are described; then, their use is illustrated in the management of low sexual desire in the context of chronic dyspareunia, chronic infertility, potential gradual reduction of ovarian androgen from midlife onward, and sudden complete loss of ovarian androgen with premature surgical or medical menopause.

Basson, R. (2002). A model of women's sexual arousal. *Journal of Sex and Marital Therapy 28,* 1–10. I attempt to construct a simple model capable of reflecting the modulation of the woman's subjective sexual arousal by her cognitions, emotions, and highly variable genital feedback, the last being potentially direct (throbbing, tingling) and indirect (sexual pleasure from massaging physically engorged genital structures, breasts, and other body areas). I also offer subtyping of female sexual arousal disorder to promote further understanding and improve therapy of the same.

Baumeister, R. F., Catanese, K. R., & Vohs, K. D. (2001). Is there a gender difference in strength of sex drive? Theoretical views, conceptual distinctions and a review of relevant evidence. *Personality and Social Psychology
Review 5*, 242–273.

Binik, Y. M., Bergeron, S., & Khalifé, S. (2000). Dyspareunia. In S. Leiblum &
R. Rosen 3rd (Eds.), *Principles and practices of sex therapy* (pp. 154–180).
New York: Guilford Press.

Brotto, L. A., Basson, R., & Luria, M. (2008). A mindfulness-based group psychoeducational intervention targeting sexual arousal disorder in women.
Journal of Sexual Medicine, 5, 1646–1659.

Brotto, L. A., Heiman, J. R., & Tolman, D. (2009). Narratives of desire in mid-
age women with and without arousal difficulties. *Journal of Sex Research,*
Mar 16 e pub ahead of publication.

Cain, V. S., Johannes, C. B., Avis, N. E., Mohr, B., Schocken, M., Skurnick, J.,
et al. (2003). Sexual functioning and practices in a multi-ethnic study of
midlife women: Baseline results from SWAN. *Journal of Sex Research, 40*,
266–276.

Carim, R., Hodis, H. N., Stanczyk, F. Z., Lobo, R. A., & Mack, W. J. (2008).
Relationship between serum levels of sex hormones and progression of
sub-clinical atherosclerosis in post-menopausal women. *Journal of Clinical
Endocrinology and Metabolism, 93*, 131–138.

Chivers, M. L., & Bailey, J. M. (2005). A sex difference in features that elicit
genital response. *Biological Psychology, 70*, 115–120.

Clarkson, T. B., & Karas, R. H. (2007). Do the cardiovascular disease risks and
benefits of oral versus transdermal estrogen therapy differ between perimenopausal and post menopausal women? *Menopause 14*, 963–967.

Cyranowski, J. M., Bromberge, J., Youk, A., Matthews, K., Kravitz, H. M., &
Powell, L. H. (2004). Lifetime depression history and sexual function in
women at midlife. *Archives of Sexual Behavior, 33*, 539–548.

Dale, K. M., Coleman, C. I., Henyan, N. N., Kluger, J., & White, C. M. (2006).
Statins and cancer risk: A meta-analysis. *Journal of the American Medical
Association, 295*, 74–80.

Dennerstein, L., Koochaki, P., Barton, I., & Graziottin, A. (2006). Hypoactive sexual desire disorder in menopausal women: A survey of western European
women. *Journal of Sexual Medicine 3*, 212–222.

Everaerd, W., Laan, E., Both, S., & van der Velde, J. (2000). Female sexuality.
In L. T. Szuchman & F. Muscarella (Eds.), *Psychological perspectives of
human sexuality* (pp. 101–146). New York: Wiley. This is a comprehensive
review of the literature on women's sexual arousal. It is clear and detailed
in its descriptions plus its theoretical explanation for the observed desyn-
chrony between objective genital physiological congestion in women and
their total experience of sexual arousal. This is followed by discussion of
the definitions of female sexual dysfunction plus a brief review of assessment methods.

Farquar, C. M., Harvey, S. A., Yu, Y., Sadler, L., & Stewart, E. W. (2006). A
prospective study of three years of outcomes after hysterectomy with and
without oophorectomy. *Obstetrics and Gynecology, 194*, 714–717.

Galyer, K. T., Conaglen, H. M., Hare, A., & Conaglen, J. V. (1999). The effect
of gynecological surgery on sexual desire. *Journal of Sex and Marital
Therapy, 25*, 81–88.

Graham, C. A., Sanders, S. A., Milhausen, R. R., & McBride, K. R. (2004). Turning on and turning off: A focus group study of the factors that affect women's sexual arousal. *Archives of Sexual Behavior, 33,* 527–538.

Grodstein, F., Manson, J. E., & Stampfer, M. J. (2006). Hormone therapy and coronary heart disease: The role of time since menopause and age at hormone initiation. *Journal of Womens Health, 15,* 35–44.

Hartmann, U., Philippsohn, S., Heiser, K., & Rüffer-Hesse, C. (2004). Low desire in midlife and older women: Personality factors, psychosocial development, present sexuality. *Menopause, 11,* 726–740.

Heiman, J. R. (1998). Psychophysiological models of female sexual response. *International Journal of Impotence Research, 10,* S94–S97.

Herbert, J. (1997). Sexuality, stress, and the chemical architecture of the brain. *Annual Review of Sex Research, 7,* 1–43.

Hodis, H. N., & Mack, W. J. (2008). Post menopausal hormone therapy and cardiovascular disease in perspective. *Clinical Obstetrics and Gynecology, 51,* 564–580.

Janssen, E., Everaerd, W., Spiering, M., & Janssen, J. (2000). Automatic processes and the appraisal of sexual stimuli: Toward an information processing model of sexual arousal. *Journal of Sex Research, 37,* 8–23.

Kaplan, H. S. (1979). *Disorders of sexual desire.* New York: Brunner-Mazel.

Karama, S., Lecours, A. R., & Leroux, J. M. (2002). Areas of brain activation in males and females during viewing of erotic film excerpts. *Human Brain Mapping, 16,* 1–13.

Laan, E., van Driel, E. M., & van Lunsen, R. H. W. (2008). Genital responsiveness in healthy women with and without sexual arousal disorder. *Journal of Sexual Medicine 5,* 1424–1435.

Labrie, F., Bélanger, A., Bélanger, P., Bérubé, R., Martel, C., Cusan, L., et al. (2006). Androgen glucuronides, instead of testosterone, as the new markers of androgenic activity in women. *Journal of Steroid Biochemistry, 99,* 182–188.

Labrie, F., Archer, D., Bouchard, C., Fortier, M., Cusan, L., Gomez, J. L., et al. (2009). Effect of intravaginal prasterone (DHEA) on libido and sexual dysfunction in postmenopausal women. *Menopause,* Aug 5 e pub ahead of publication.

Laumann, E. O., Paik, A., & Rosen, R. C. (1999). Sexual dysfunction in the United States: Prevalence and predictors. *Journal of the American Medical Association, 10,* 537–545.

Leiblum, S. R., Koochaki, P. E., Rodenberg, C. A., Barton, I. P., & Rosen, R. C. (2006). Hypoactive sexual desire disorder in postmenopausal women: U.S. results from the Women's International Study of Health and Sexuality (WISHeS). *Menopause, 13,* 46–56.

Levine, K. B., Williams, R. E., & Hartmann, K. E. (2008). Vulvovaginalatrophy is strongly associated with female sexual dysfunction among sexually active postmenopausal women. *Menopause, 15*(4, Pt. 1), 661–666.

Levine, S. B. (2003). The nature of sexual desire: A clinician's perspective. *Archives of Sexual Behavior, 32,* 279–285.

Lunde, I., Larson, G. K., Fog, E., & Garde, K. (1991). Sexual desire, orgasm, and sexual fantasies: A study of 625 Danish women born in 1910, 1936 and 1958. *Journal of Sex Educcation and Therapy, 17,* 111–115.

Meston, C. M., & Buss, D. M. (2007). Why humans have sex. *Archives of Sexual Behavior, 36,* 477–507. This research gives empirical confirmation of the multiple reasons women and men choose to have sex. Interestingly, the subjects were young when one might have intuitively thought drive/urge would be more dominant, especially in the men. Emotional reasons were common to both genders, although more common in the women.

Prause, N., Janssen, E., & Hetrick, W. P. (2008). Attention and emotional responses to sexual stimuli and their relationship to sexual desire. *Archives of Sexual Behavior, 37,* 934–949.

Redouté, J., Stoléru, S., Gréoire, M. C., Costes, N., Cinotti, L., et al. (2000). Brain processing of visual processing of visual sexual stimuli in human males. *Human Brain Mapping, 11,* 162–177.

Regan, P., & Berscheid, E. (1996). Belief about the states, goals and objects of sexual desire. *Journal of Sex and Marital Therapy, 22,* 110–120.

Rossouw, J. E., Prentice, R. L., Manson, J. A., Wu, L., Barad, D., Barnabei, V. M., et al. (2007). Postmenopausal hormone therapy and risk of cardiovascular disease by age and years since menopause. *Journal of the American Medical Association, 297,* 1465–1477.

Salpeter, S. R., Walsh, J. M. E., Grebyer, E., & Salpeter, E. E. (2006). Coronary heart disease events associated with hormone therapy in younger and older women: A meta-analysis. *Journal of General Internal Medicine, 21,* 363–366.

Sanders, S. A., Graham, C. A., & Milhausen, R. R. (2008). Predicting sexual problems in women: The relevance of sexual excitation and sexual inhibition. *Archives of Sexual Behavior, 37,* 241–251.

Singer, B., & Toates, F. M. (1997). Sexual motivation. *Journal of Sex Research, 23,* 481–501.

Teplin, V., Vittinghoff, E., Lin, F., Learman, L. A., Richter, H. E., & Kuppermann, M. (2007). Oophorectomy in premenopausal women: Health-related quality of life and sexual functioning. *Obstetrics and Gynecology, 109,* 347–354.

Tiefer, L. (1991). Historical, scientific, clinical and feminist criticisms of "the human sexual response cycle." *Annual Review of Sex Research, 2,* 1–23. This is a very readable critique of the human sex response cycle and its historical background, emphasizing the narrow genital focus that has developed since the model of Masters and Johnson was first published. The subjects selected to study and Masters and Johnson's definitions of "normal human sexual responding" are discussed in detail. The author questions why some sexual difficulties but not others are taken seriously and given title of "disorder."

Tiefer, L., Hall, M., & Tavris, C. (2002). Beyond dysfunction: A new view of women's sexual problems. *Journal of Sex and Marital Therapy, 28,* S1225–S1232.

van Lunsen, R. H. W., & Laan, E. (2004). Genital vascular responsiveness and sexual feelings in midlife women: Psychophysiologic, brain and genital imaging studies. *Menopause, 11,* 741–748.

West, S. L., D'Aloisio, A. A., Agans, R. P., Kalsbeek, W. D., Borisov, N. N., & Thorp, J. M. (2008). The prevalence of low sexual desire and hypoactive sexual desire disorder in a nationally representative sample of U.S. women. *Archives of Internal Medicine, 168,* 1441–1449.

Whalen, R. E. (1966). Sexual motivation. *Psychology Review, 73,* 151–163.

Whipple, B., & Brash-McGreer, K. (1997). Management of female dysfunction. In M. L. Sipski & C. J. Alexander (Eds.), *Sexual function in people with disability and chronic illness: A health professional's guide* (pp. 509–534). Gaithersburg, MD: Aspen.

Witting, K., Santtila, P., Varjonen, M., Jern, P., Johansson, A., von der Pahlen, B., et al. (2008). Female sexual dysfunction, sexual distress, and compatibility with partner. *Journal of Sexual Medicine, 5*, 2587–2599.

Writing Group for the Women's Health Initiative Investigators. (2002). Risks and benefits of estrogen plus progestin in healthy menopausal women: Principal results from the Women's Health Initiative randomized controlled trial. *Journal of the American Medical Association, 288*, 321–323.

Eleven

Female Orgasmic Disorder

KAREN M. DONAHEY, PHD

INTRODUCTION

I began my career more than 20 years ago as a clinical social worker specializing in children and adolescents. In the course of working with this population for the next 6 years, I found myself working increasingly with their parents in marital therapy. We rarely discussed the couple's sexual relationship or any sexual problems that might exist. If they did not bring sex up, I did not either. I either did not think to bring it up or did not know how. When sex was brought up, I was keenly aware that I was not sure what I could say or do that would be helpful. When I made the decision to return to graduate school for a doctoral degree in psychology, I decided to focus my clinical training on working with couples. I did my internship at the University of Chicago in the Department of Behavioral Medicine, and my primary rotation was in the sex and marital therapy program. For that year, I met with numerous couples, some presenting with sexual problems and some who did not. All of them were asked about their sexual relationship as part of the diagnostic evaluation. In addition, I spent two afternoons each week in the urology clinic asking men of all ages about erectile functioning, orgasm, and sexual desire. I ended up staying 2 years more, one as a postdoctoral fellow and the other as a faculty member.

During these years, I became more comfortable and skilled in asking people about their sexual functioning and concerns. I came to believe that I could finally be of some help to them. I then joined the faculty at Northwestern University, where I later became the director of the sex and marital therapy program. Little did I realize that in my initial effort to get more skilled in working with couples and addressing sexual problems I would be spending my career as a sex therapist. I currently am in private practice and remain on faculty at Northwestern University. I continue to see individuals and couples for sex therapy and teach students about sexual dysfunction. And, these days, any person or couple I see for therapy can usually expect to be asked about their sexual functioning and relationship, even if it is not the presenting problem.

I have been asked to write about how to work with females who are experiencing problems with orgasm. For teaching purposes, I have selected three cases that are illustrative of the different types of orgasm disorders more commonly seen in sex therapy. I begin by briefly summarizing these cases. I return to them throughout the chapter to highlight relevant aspects of evaluation and treatment.

Case 11.1: Laura

Laura, age 42, has recently married for the first time. This is her first sexual relationship. She states that she loves her husband, describes him as "the kindest and most wonderful man I've ever known," and worries that she is letting him down because she is unable to orgasm. She states that they are sexual usually once a week and would probably be more so if she could "enjoy herself more." She reports that she loves to kiss and touch her husband, loves to be kissed and touched by him, but does not feel very aroused when they have intercourse, and after a few minutes, when "nothing happens," she tells him to go ahead and orgasm, which he does. She reports that she feels disappointed that sex "does not seem to be as great as I'd heard." She wonders what is "wrong" with her and hopes that I can help her.

Case 11.2: Barbara

Barbara, age 36, has been dating a man for the past 2 years and has been unable to orgasm with him. She was previously married for 5 years. In her marriage, she had been able to orgasm with her husband until she learned he had cheated on her with her best friend. Her marriage ended. Two years ago, she met her current boyfriend. She describes having a passionate relationship with him and in the initial 4 months was usually orgasmic with him. It was around that time that her boyfriend revealed his first marriage ended in divorce because he had cheated on his wife and left her for the other woman. The relationship with the other woman ended 3 months before he met Barbara. Since his disclosure, Barbara has been unable to orgasm with him. She is able to orgasm with masturbation. She wonders if the similarities between this relationship and her previous marriage are affecting her ability to orgasm with him. He has assured her repeatedly that he has been sexually faithful to her.

Case 11.3: Ellen

Ellen, age 40, has been divorced for 10 years. In her first marriage, when she was in her 20s, she remembered sex as infrequent, somewhat boring, and occasionally painful. She did not experience orgasm with her husband or with her two previous college boyfriends. For several years after her divorce, she focused on her career. She had a handful of brief sexual encounters that were only somewhat sexually satisfying and never resulted in orgasm. One year ago, she met a man over the Internet. In the past month, he has moved in with her, and they are contemplating marriage. She reports that sex with him is different from what it was in her marriage and previous sexual encounters. They have sex once or twice a week, and she is very aroused when she is with him. However, she has been unable to orgasm with any type of sexual stimulation. She is able to orgasm when she masturbates. She wants to know how she can have an orgasm with her partner.

DEFINITION AND DIAGNOSTIC FEATURES

Julia Heiman, the coauthor of *Becoming Orgasmic: A Sexual and Personal Growth Program for Women* (Heiman & LoPiccolo, 1988) stated that orgasms are usually defined as a combination of both subjective experiences and physiological changes in the vagina and pelvic area. While many descriptions of orgasm exist, a common description is feeling a sense of building tension and then a release, usually accompanied by genital contractions. Women often report a sense of well-being and physical satisfaction following an orgasm.

When we consult the *DMS-IV* (*Diagnostic and Statistical Manual of Mental Disorders, Fourth Edition;* American Psychiatric Association [APA], 1994) for the definition of *female orgasmic disorder*, it is defined as follows: "a persistent or recurrent delay in, or absence of, orgasm following a normal sexual excitement phase" (p. 505). The *DSM-IV* further goes on to say that women exhibit wide variability in the type or intensity of stimulation that triggers orgasm, and that the diagnosis of female orgasmic disorder should be based on the clinician's judgment that the woman's orgasmic capacity is less than would be reasonable for her age, sexual experience, and the adequacy of sexual stimulation she receives. In addition, the disturbance must cause marked distress or interpersonal difficulty and cannot be accounted for by another axis I disorder (except another sexual dysfunction) and is not due exclusively to the direct physiological effects of a substance (including medications) or a general medical condition. Finally, the *DSM-IV* concludes by stating that once a female learns how to reach orgasm, it is uncommon for her to lose that capacity unless poor sexual communication, relationship, a traumatic experience (e.g., rape), a mood disorder, or a general medical condition intervenes. Many females increase their orgasmic capacity as they experience a wider variety of stimulation and acquire more knowledge about their own bodies (p. 505).

ASSESSING ORGASMIC DYSFUNCTION

Chief Complaint

With any patient coming in for help with a sexual concern, the therapist must obtain a description of the chief complaint (e.g., presenting problem). When a woman (or a couple) comes to my office with the chief complaint of female anorgasmia, I want to know what she means by this as I have learned over the years that I should assume nothing. In many cases, the woman, or her partner, will report that she is unable to orgasm. However, when I question her further, I may learn that she does orgasm with masturbation or with manual or oral stimulation. What she, or she and her partner, are talking about is that she cannot orgasm during intercourse. There have also been times when I have spoken to women who believe that they are not having orgasms or are not sure if they are, but their descriptions of what happens when they are sexual sound like orgasms. In these cases, these women have been comparing themselves to what they see in movies, read in magazines, or hear from friends or their partner and conclude that they are not having orgasms because their experience is less dramatic. An example of this is illustrated next:

> Jill, age 25, was a student who had heard me give a lecture on female sexuality to her medical school class. She came in stating she was not sure if she was having orgasms. I asked her what made her think she may not be having them, and she reported that in comparison to what she had seen in movies and read in magazines, she was more "low key"; for example, she said, "I don't yell or lose all sense of control." She also reported how her best friend told her that when she had an orgasm she "felt outside herself," would say things she normally would not say, and would get very loud. Jill laughed when telling me this and said she felt "boring" in comparison. She reported that she always felt aroused during sex and would after a period of time reach what she would consider a peak; this would culminate in a very intense physical sensation accompanied by contractions. This was true when she masturbated as well. Until she had this talk with her

friend, she had not really questioned her sexual functioning. Why was she now? This became the focus of further discussion since it appeared to me that anorgasmia was not Jill's problem.

After obtaining a description of the problem, it is important to learn if the problem is global (happens all the time under all circumstances) or situational (happens under specific circumstances). You also need to ask if it has always been a problem, which would be defined as *primary*, or if the problem occurred after a time of normal functioning which would be defined as *acquired*. For example, in the first case example, Laura's anorgasmia is global and primary. She has seldom masturbated in her life. She has always lived with her mother and still does, even after her marriage. She reports she never had much privacy as a child. When she masturbated, she always "kept one ear open for mother to walk in without knocking." Consequently, masturbation was associated with anxiety about being caught rather than feeling pleasure, and Laura does not think she ever had an orgasm. In Laura's sexual relationship with her husband, she is unable to have an orgasm with manual or oral stimulation or intercourse. While she no longer worries about her mother walking in on her, she now worries about her mother, as well as her mother's live-in caretaker, hearing her have sex with her husband. In Barbara's case, her anorgasmia is situational and is acquired. She can have orgasms when she masturbates and has been orgasmic with partners during intercourse. She was orgasmic with her current partner until he told her of his infidelity. After this, she has been unable to orgasm with any type of sexual stimulation from him. In the third case example, Ellen's anorgasmia is situational. She is able to have orgasms with masturbation, but not with her partner. This was true in her previous sexual relationship as well. Unlike Barbara, Ellen has not encountered the violations of trust in her sexual relationships and views her anorgasmia with her partner as a set of skills she wants to learn.

Sexual Status Examination

As part of assessing orgasm disorder, I ask the patient or the couple to describe a typical sexual scenario or what Kaplan (1983) referred to as the *sexual status examination*. Many people are understandably a bit embarrassed or uncomfortable doing this, and I acknowledge that I appreciate how difficult it is to be telling someone they do not know something so private. I explain that it allows me to understand more fully their particular problem as well as what might be contributing to it. During the account, I usually stop the patient or couple to ask more detailed questions (i.e., What were you thinking when this happened? How long do you think you spent kissing before you began having oral sex or intercourse? How do you let your partner know what you want him or her to do? etc.). For example, here is an account of Laura's sexual status examination from the first interview.

Laura: I usually like to have a martini before we begin. It relaxes me. We'll take our drinks and go into the bedroom. Mother is usually in her bedroom watching TV or already asleep. Victor and I will start kissing and begin to undress each other. We'll lay on the bed and keep kissing and touching. He gets aroused very quickly.

KMD: What do you mean?

Laura: He'll get an erection in about 5 minutes.

KMD: Are you aroused?

Laura: Yes, but not as much as him. We'll touch some more; Victor mostly touching me.

KMD: Where?

Laura: All over my body.

KMD: Are there any parts of your body you particularly like to be touched?

Laura: Yes, my back, neck, breasts.

KMD: Does he touch your genitals? Is this something you like?

Laura: Yes. He'll do this until I'm lubricated, and then we start having intercourse. We have intercourse a long time usually, about 10 minutes, so that I can try to have an orgasm, but it never happens. I get tired, and a little sore, and so I tell him to go ahead and have an orgasm. He does, but feels bad that I didn't have one.

KMD: What happens after he has had an orgasm?

Laura: We hold each other, usually fall asleep.

KMD: How are you feeling?

Laura: I feel frustrated that I didn't have an orgasm. I wonder what's wrong with me. I don't want Victor to think he's done something wrong.

By asking Laura to recount a typical sexual scenario, I get some ideas of other questions to ask and where I may be able to intervene when developing the treatment plan. For example, I wonder if her husband ever stimulates her manually until she has an orgasm rather than doing it until she is lubricated enough for intercourse. I wonder if they have engaged in oral stimulation, and if so, for how long and under what circumstances. Does she masturbate? Does she fantasize, and if so, what are her fantasies? Given that her mother and the caretaker live in the same house, does she worry about being heard? What is she thinking about when she is sexual with Victor? Does she ever experience any discomfort or pain, and if so, how frequently does that occur and under what circumstances? I also want to know from Victor what he is thinking. What are his ideas about why Laura is not able to have an orgasm? How does he feel about that? What does he think needs to happen?

I use the sexual status exam throughout the therapy process with the patient as a way of assessing what changes the couple is making and what changes continue to be necessary. It helps me to customize the treatment plan to each individual or couple.

Sexual History

In addition to discussing what is happening currently, I also am interested in getting a sexual history from the patient and her partner. This refers not only to the sexual experiences she has had with masturbation and with partners but also to the messages and meanings she has received since childhood about sex and sexuality from her family, religion, and culture. Was sex discussed in her home? If so, how was it discussed? What was discussed? Were there different standards for females and males in the home? How old was she when she had her first sexual experience with a partner? How did she feel about this? How would she describe that experience?

A sexual history also includes asking about unwanted sexual experiences (e.g., molestation, incest, sexual abuse, date rape, stranger rape) and how this was or was not addressed by the patient or by her family. Does the patient believe this has affected her sexual behavior or functioning? If yes, in what way? Many women, based on their sexual histories, end up feeling guilty when they are sexual. Cass (2007), in her book *The Elusive Orgasm,* describes how children, when first discovering their bodies, do not have the language to call what they are feeling sexual. They just know that what they are doing feels good. It is the parent's attitude or reaction that can set the groundwork for adult guilt. If the parent reacts negatively, the child learns that her feelings of pleasure are wrong or bad. They are something to stop or control. This can greatly impact a woman's attitude toward her own sexual arousal. As sexual arousal gets greater, sexual feelings grow, the woman feels guilty, and consequently these sexual feelings are turned off as a way of avoiding punishment. If she is unsuccessful in doing this, she experiences guilt for being "bad."

The sexual histories of Laura and Barbara could not be any more different. Laura is the younger of two children and the only daughter of eastern European parents who immigrated to the United States when she was 9 years old. Barbara is the youngest child of three girls who grew up on the East Coast and whose parents are both college educated. Laura reports having an experience when she was about 6 years old of being in a room with several of her cousins, and the eldest, a boy of about 12, suggesting they all take off their clothes. She remembers doing so, rather reluctantly. Her aunt discovered the children moments later, and everyone was told to put their clothes on immediately. Laura's mother punished her by giving her a beating (when asked for more details, she explained she was spanked with a belt). Laura remembers a few times when she would be masturbating in her room, and her mother would come in unexpectedly. She thinks her mother suspected that she was masturbating but never actually caught her. Her mother then made a rule that both Laura and her brother had to keep their bedroom doors open. Laura also recalls her mother telling her when Laura was a teenager that sex was something you had to do with your husband when you were married. She does not remember ever seeing her parents kiss or show affection. Her father was a quiet man who worked long hours in a manufacturing company and interacted more with her brother than he did with her. She was not allowed to date in high school and was only allowed to attend college if she lived at home (despite having been awarded a scholarship to a 4-year university). During college, her father died in an automobile accident. Laura was expected to remain at home with her mother and help with the finances. Her brother was already married and the father of two children.

In contrast to Laura's sexual history, Barbara remembers her mother telling her about menstruation and "the basics" about intercourse. She does not recall any other talks, either positive or negative, about sex. Her parents were affectionate with one another, and she believes they had a good marriage (her father died of cancer rather suddenly 4 years prior to the interview). She was allowed to date in high school and did so. She had a boyfriend in her senior year, and they had sexual contact, although not intercourse. She met her husband-to-be at college, and they began a sexual relationship that she described as positive and satisfying. Her mother once made a comment to Barbara about hoping she was using birth control, but that was the extent of their conversation. She and her boyfriend married while they were in graduate school. She recalls the first few years as very good sexually. She then learned her husband was having an affair with her best friend. Barbara and her husband remained together for almost a year following the husband's promise to end the relationship with the other woman. This is when Barbara first had difficulties with orgasm. However, her husband continued to be unfaithful and eventually left her for this other woman.

Medical/Psychiatric History and Medications

In assessing any sexual disorder, it is important to ask about any medical conditions, surgeries, illnesses, and medications that could affect sexual functioning. In addition, you need to inquire about smoking, alcohol consumption, and recreational drug use. With regard to specifically assessing orgasm disorders, it is most important to learn what medications the patient is taking. Antidepressants, especially the selective serotonin reuptake inhibitors (SSRIs) and the selective noradrenergic serotonin reuptake inhibitors (SNRIs), are widely prescribed to women today. While they can be quite helpful in treating depression and anxiety problems, they can also adversely affect orgasm responsiveness. I have spoken to many women over the years who report they were not made aware of this by the prescribing physician, or if they had, hoped this side effect would not happen to them. In these cases, lowering the dose or switching to another antidepressant may be indicated. Plus, the use of bupropion, either as an antidote to the SSRI or SNRI or as the sole antidepressant medication, can be done. Women who have tried several different types of antidepressants and finally found one that worked in treating their depression or anxiety may not want to change their medication, even if it means not having an orgasm. For some of them, having an orgasm is not essential for their sexual satisfaction, and they will focus on other aspects of the sexual interaction they find pleasurable. For others, if they are open to this, I suggest that they try using a vibrator to see if this will assist them in achieving orgasm. In some cases, this has worked for them.

TREATMENT

Sex therapy often involves the combined use of a number of therapeutic techniques, customized to the needs of particular patients (Plaut & Donahey, 2003). To date, there are no pharmacological treatments proven to be successful beyond placebo in treating women with diagnosed female orgasmic disorder (Meston, Hull, Levin, & Sipski, 2004). The therapeutic techniques would include directed masturbation, sensate focus, sex education and bibliotherapy, communication skills training, use of fantasy and visualization, and Kegel exercises. Some of these treatments are illustrated in the cases introduced in the beginning of this chapter.

Case 11.1: Treatment: Laura

Although Laura is 42 years old, she reminds me more of my female patients who are in their 20s who come in with complaints of low sexual arousal and anorgasmia. If you will recall, Laura has been married for a little over a year. This is not only her first marriage but also her first sexual partner. She has lived with her mother all of her life. After the death of her father, she finished college and obtained a job with a large accounting firm, where she still works today. She met her husband 10 years ago, when he came to work at the same firm. They had been friendly with one another from the beginning, but it was not until 3 years ago that he asked her out on a date. Laura reports that she had only been on a few dates in her life before Victor asked her out. She acknowledges that she had not put much effort into meeting or dating men, even though she had always imagined herself married one day. Her mother was diagnosed with multiple sclerosis when Laura was 27, and it has progressively gotten worse, so that now she is confined to a wheelchair. Laura reports that when she told her mother that Victor had proposed, her mother's first question was where would she (the mother) live. Victor and Laura decided to have a home built that would accommodate her mother's disability, allow for a live-in caretaker, and have their bedroom on the second floor.

Laura reports that when she and Victor were dating, it took several months before they had any sexual contact. They would kiss passionately, and she enjoyed this immensely. She told Victor she had never had a sexual relationship and was nervous about moving too fast. He was accommodating to her wishes and stated he had not been surprised to learn this. His own dating and sexual history is not extensive, and his first sexual experience was not until he was 25 years old. Laura and Victor moved on to sexual touching, and she reports she was aroused and enjoyed this. Of note is that, while dating Victor, her mother would comment on how late Laura was getting home and want to know of her whereabouts. Laura reports that it was not until after she and Victor were engaged that she stayed overnight at his apartment. She reports that she informed her mother that she would not be coming home one particular night, and her mother said, "But you're not married yet." She endured her mother's disapproval the next day and from then on would stay periodically at Victor's place. Victor was willing to wait until marriage to have intercourse, thinking she would feel more comfortable with this. However, Laura stated that she did not want to wait any longer. They had intercourse about 4 months before they married. She was disappointed that it was not as pleasurable as she expected it to be. This has continued to be her experience.

Most of the literature recommends directed masturbation as the treatment modality for primary, generalized anorgasmia (Cass, 2007; Heiman & LoPiccolo, 1988; Maurice, 1999; Meston et al., 2004). It is believed that if women can learn how to stimulate themselves to orgasm, they may then be able to teach their partner how to stimulate them to orgasm. Laura was not opposed to doing this but stated she had already tried this, even purchasing a vibrator, and had had no success. We discussed in depth her experience with this, and the following observations were made:

- She was often distracted by the knowledge that other people were in the house (e.g., Victor, mother, caretaker) when she masturbated.
- If she waited until everyone was asleep, she was often too tired.
- The vibrator she purchased was too loud, and she worried someone in the house might hear it.
- She felt she had too little time for herself and Victor as it was and said she preferred to be sexual with him rather than masturbating.

In listening to her concerns, and remembering what Laura and Victor had told me in the sexual status exam, I decided to introduce sensate focus exercises. The sensate focus technique was developed by Masters and Johnson (1970) in an effort to help partners expand their approach to sexuality while reducing the focus on performance. The partners are asked to take turns touching one another, not specifically to sexually stimulate their partner, but to learn what the other likes and does not like, how they like touching their partner, and how they can communicate constructively with their partner about their likes and dislikes. They are instructed to refrain from intercourse. If you will recall from the sexual status examination, Laura described how Victor would manually stimulate her to get her lubricated, then they would try intercourse. From that description, it appeared to me that the manual stimulation was a means to an end (e.g., intercourse and hopefully orgasm) and less about simply pleasuring. Just because Laura was lubricated did not mean she was necessarily experiencing high arousal. Laura and Victor agreed to try the sensate focus exercise. They returned in 2 weeks, having done the exercise three times. Laura was extremely enthusiastic. She loved the touching and said that it reminded her of the "earlier days" when they were first dating. She reported that she felt very aroused by the touching and did not want it to stop. In fact, the third time she suggested to Victor that they have intercourse ("I know we broke the rule") and reports that this was the first time she really enjoyed herself. She said to me in the session, in a somewhat embarrassed tone, "I think I need more touching." As the session continued, it became clear to me that when Laura and Victor had added intercourse to their sexual relationship, they cut down on the amount of touching they had previously done because intercourse had become the main focus. This was true as well the few times they engaged in oral stimulation. I suggested they read *Sexual Awareness* by Barry and Emily McCarthy (1993) as a way of educating themselves about how to enhance their sexual pleasure. I also encouraged them to continue with the sensate focus. As the sessions continued, the sensate focus exercises allowed more genital contact, with the instruction not to engage in intercourse. They did not always follow this.

In the middle of the therapy, Laura had to go away for a few days to a business conference. She decided to use these three nights of privacy in a hotel room to experiment with masturbation. In addition to reading the McCarthy book (1993) she had also been reading Heiman and LoPiccolo's book (1988) *Becoming Orgasmic.* She returned to therapy very happy—she had had her first orgasm.

Laura and Victor continue to meet with me in therapy. While she has not yet been orgasmic with him, she feels confident she will eventually. Both agree that their sexual relationship has become more enjoyable and interactive. Laura has become less apologetic about asking for what she needs sexually while she grows more comfortable in seeing herself as a sexual person. This was vividly illustrated most recently when her mother told Laura that she "didn't want to embarrass" Laura, but she could hear Laura and Victor one morning having sex. Laura's response to her mother was, "Turn up the television".

Case 11.2: Treatment: Barbara

When working with someone whose orgasm disorder is situational and acquired, the obvious question is what has changed in this individual's life or circumstances. For Barbara, she first experienced orgasm difficulties after she learned of her husband's infidelity with her best friend (a double betrayal). When she began dating her boyfriend after her divorce, she had no difficulty experiencing orgasm in her sexual relationship with him. It was only after he confided in her, months after their relationship began, that he had been unfaithful in his previous marriage and left his wife for the other woman that Barbara was unable to orgasm with him. This was further exacerbated when he also told her that he had met with "the other woman" once for dinner for "closure" shortly after he began the relationship with Barbara (he had not told Barbara of this at the time it occurred). He swears he has been sexually faithful to her during their 2-year relationship, and Barbara states, "I have seen no evidence that tells me he's lying." She ruefully acknowledges this is not an endorsement of his honesty.

Barbara can see how her boyfriend's behavior in his marriage closely paralleled her ex-husband's behavior. He also left his wife for the other woman, as Barbara's exhusband had, and lived with her for a period of time. Second, he had not told Barbara about having dinner with her and only did so after Barbara specifically questioned him about whether he had seen the other woman since their relationship ended. While this was close to 2 years ago, and he swears this was the only time, Barbara finds herself periodically looking for evidence that he is cheating on her. She states that she wants to believe him and on some level does, but is having difficulty "letting my guard down." She is insightful enough to realize that this is a metaphor for her anorgasmia. In this case, teaching Barbara to have an orgasm with her partner is not what is indicated.

Addressing the breach of trust in the relationship is, as is Barbara's unaddressed feelings regarding her marriage. I recommended that she and her boyfriend get into couple therapy. I also told Barbara that she could benefit from individual therapy as well. In the initial evaluation, Barbara had been surprised to find herself weeping when telling me about her father's death and how much she still misses him. She also became very emotional when describing the day she learned that the woman her ex-husband was having the affair with was her best friend. Barbara agreed with my recommendations and decided that since she had already met with me and her boyfriend had not, she would meet with me in individual therapy and see another therapist for couple therapy with her boyfriend. I referred them to a colleague. Barbara's feelings of grief and abandonment by father, ex-husband, and former best friend have been the focus of her individual treatment. Her relationship with her boyfriend continues, and by her account, they are working hard in couple therapy. She feels hopeful about their future together and is less focused on her ability to have orgasms with him. While she experiences her anorgasmia as sometimes a nuisance, she knows why it exists and hopes that someday she will no longer "need to be on her guard."

Case 11.3: Treatment: Ellen

Ellen was referred to me by her gynecologist for help with her situational anorgasmia. She reported that she has always been able to be orgasmic with masturbation but never with a partner. Her sexual history revealed that she was the eldest of three children, was raised Catholic, and had her first sexual encounter with her boyfriend when she was a sophomore in college. Her mother told Ellen and her sister about menstruation, and she suspects her father talked to her brother. She heard about sex from girlfriends. She dated but was not sexually active until college. She has no history of unwanted sexual contact. She married when she was 26 years old. Sex had never been a big part of their relationship, even while dating. She thinks she got married because she felt "it was time." Many of her friends were marrying, and she had been dating this man for over 2 years. Neither she nor her husband talked much about their sexual relationship. She states that in hindsight they did not talk much about anything. Four years later, they divorced amicably.

She spent the next decade focusing on her career and is a very accomplished professional in her field. She reports she made little time to date and would have "the occasional one-night stand" if she was traveling on business. None of these times were particularly sexually satisfying to her. She masturbated a few times a month, occasionally with a vibrator, and was usually orgasmic. A friend of hers kept encouraging her to try a popular Internet dating site to meet men. She finally relented, and after meeting a few men who did not interest her, met her current boyfriend. Ellen admits she is surprised at how she feels when she is with him. For the first time in her life, she states she feels like a sexual person. She likes being sexual. Her boyfriend is very caring and is interested in her pleasure, something she had never experienced in her earlier relationships. She states she was surprised when he once asked her what she would like for him to do ("I didn't know what to say"). Sex had always been what she could do for the other person.

In the sexual status exam, what was most noticeable was Ellen's belief that she was "taking too long" and her worry that her boyfriend would eventually become bored. Consequently, she would tell her boyfriend to stop even when she really was enjoying herself because she was worried about him. It also became clear that she was conflicted about having the attention on her. She liked it yet felt selfish. Her boyfriend assured her that he was not bored, tired, or experiencing her as selfish. He just wanted them to have fun.

Therapy focused on challenging Ellen's thought processes during sex. She read *The Elusive Orgasm* by Cass (2007), which helped her to think about her sexual behavior in a new way. Sensate focus exercises were used to help her learn more about what she liked and how to communicate that to her boyfriend. She also had to learn to make time for sex. For the past 10 years, a good deal of her time had been focused on her career. It was not unusual for her to work 50 to 60 hours a week, often willingly. Making time just to be with her boyfriend, let alone making time for sex, was initially challenging for Ellen. However, she was very motivated to make changes. She and her boyfriend recently took their first vacation together, and not surprising to me, given how things were going in the therapy, Ellen was orgasmic several times on their trip. She returned happy and pleased. Her remark to me was, "Where were you when I was 20!" She went on to say that she wished she had known how "great sex can be" earlier in her life.

CONCLUSION

This chapter has focused on female anorgasmia and the different ways it may present. I selected these particular cases because I felt they were representative of the more common types of orgasm disorders seen frequently in sex therapy. I wanted to demonstrate how treatment, as for any sexual disorder, must take into account the unique characteristics of the person and situation and be tailored accordingly. By introducing you to Laura, Barbara, and Ellen, I hope that you have been able to appreciate the similarities and differences between these three cases. While all three of them presented with orgasm difficulties, you also saw that Laura and Ellen (at 42 and 40, respectively) were women just coming into their own sexually, despite the differences in their sexual histories. Barbara's orgasm disorder, while situational as was Ellen's, was directly related to the trust issues in her current relationship, which intersected with her traumatic experience in her previous marriage. In your own work with women presenting with anorgasmia, you also will see a variety of situations in young and middle-aged women. You will also see many more older women seeking help for new or acquired anorgasmia due to age or health-related changes. I hope that in writing this chapter I have given you some useful ideas about how to help your patients with this problem.

REFERENCES

American Psychiatric Association. (1994). *Diagnostic and statistical manual of mental disorders* (4th ed.). Washington, DC: Author.

Cass, V. (2007). *The elusive orgasm.* New York: Marlow. This is a very pragmatic, helpful book for women to read. It is filled with advice and suggestions on how to overcome the factors that may be preventing orgasm. I have been using this book with many of my patients as an adjunct to therapy.

Heiman, J., & LoPiccolo, J. (1988). *Becoming orgasmic: A sexual and personal growth program for women.* Paramus, NJ: Prentice Hall. This is a classic in the sex therapy field. I continue to use this book as an adjunct to therapy.

Kaplan, H. S. (1983). *The evaluation of sexual disorders.* New York: Brunner/ Mazel.

Masters, W., & Johnson, V. (1970). *Human sexual inadequacy.* Boston: Little, Brown.

Maurice, W. (1999). *Sexual medicine in primary care.* St. Louis, MO: Mosby. This is a very helpful, useful book that reviews all the sexual disorders and gives the reader step-by-step instructions regarding how to ask the patient about a sexual problem.

McCarthy, B., & McCarthy, E. (1993). *Sexual awareness: Enhancing sexual pleasure*. New York: Carroll & Graf. This book is filled with detailed suggestions and ways to enhance a couple's sexual relationship.

Meston, C., Hull, E., Levin, R., & Sipski, M. (2004). Disorders of orgasm in women. *The Journal of Sexual Medicine, 1*, 66–68.

Plaut, S. M., & Donahey, K. (2003). Evaluation and treatment of sexual dysfunction. In T. Sexton, G. Weeks, & M. Robbins (Eds.), *The handbook of family therapy* (pp. 351–363). New York: Brunner-Routledge.

ADDITIONAL READINGS AND RESOURCES

Barbach, L. (1975). *For yourself: The fulfillment of female sexuality*. New York: New American Library.

Dodson, B. (1987). *Sex for one. The joy of selfloving*. New York: Crown.

Ellison, C. R. (2003). Facilitating orgasmic responsiveness. In S. Levine, C. Risen, & S. Althof (Eds.), *Handbook of clinical sexuality for mental health professionals* (pp. 167–185), New York: Brunner-Routledge.

Friday, N. (1998). *My secret garden: Women's sexual fantasies*. New York: Pocket Books.

Komisaruk, B., Beyer-Flores, C., & Whipple, B. (2006). *The science of orgasm*. Baltimore: John Hopkins Press.

Leiblum, S., & Sachs, J. (2002). *Getting the sex you want*. New York: Crown.

Winks, C., & Semans, S. (1997). *The new good vibrations guide to having sex*. San Francisco: Cleis Press.

The following Web sites offer self-help videos, books, vibrators, and erotic films to assist women who are experiencing difficulties with orgasm:
www.bettersex.com
www.sinclairinstitute.com

Twelve

Painful Sex

SOPHIE BERGERON, PHD, MARTA MEANA, PHD,
YITZCHAK M. BINIK, PHD, AND SAMIR KHALIFÉ, MD

INTRODUCTION

The reason this chapter has four authors is that our treatment approach for this problem has evolved through a fruitful 15-year collaboration, which dates to when Marta Meana and Sophie Bergeron began their doctoral studies with Irv Binik and Samir Khalifé. Together, we have conducted research, shared clinical work, and presented at meetings. We are still learning from one another and valuing each other's input.

We hope that this chapter communicates our enthusiasm for working with women who experience painful sex and for using a multidisciplinary approach. We convey the challenges that we have encountered and provide guidelines that we wished had been available when we were starting out with this population. You do not need to be a pain specialist or a sex therapist to work with women who suffer from painful sex. All it takes is an eagerness to learn more about genital pain associated with sexual activity—its range of underlying physical pathologies and the recurrent therapeutic issues.

Laura

Following the use of antibiotics for a throat infection 3 years previous, Laura, a successful lawyer in her late 20s, began to suffer from repeated vaginal yeast infections. No prescription or over-the-counter cream alleviated her symptoms. Over time, she noticed intercourse had become increasingly painful. Her entire vagina felt on fire, and she became apprehensive about sexual activity. Laura used to enjoy sex with her husband very much but now hardly has any desire even for nonpenetrative activities. When she does have sex, it is prompted by the insistence of her frustrated husband and the terrible guilt she feels about not being the lively sexual partner she used to be. Under these conditions, she experiences very little sexual arousal, which further contributes to her pain. Laura wonders whether she will ever enjoy sex again and worries that she may never be able to have children. Her gynecologist—the fifth one she has consulted since the onset of her problem and the first to tell her that it was not "all in her head"—recently diagnosed her with provoked vestibulodynia. She recommended that Laura take part in a pain relief therapy program involving cognitive–behavioral group psychotherapy combined with individual physical therapy.

Fifteen years ago, when a woman complained to us of painful sex, we treated her with a "sex therapy" that focused on psychosexual and relationship issues and employed vaginal dilation. We seldom asked about the characteristics of the pain. However, as we accumulated more experience with these women, the limits of our approach became apparent. We started to question the theoretical bases and validity of standard treatments. Nobody had really studied painful sex in any systematic way, let alone attempt to treat its multiple dimensions. We embarked on a journey that has taken us from questions about sex to questions about pain; from sex therapy to pain management, physical therapy, and gynecologic surgery; and from unidimensional clinical interventions to a concurrent multidisciplinary and individually tailored treatment approach.

THE MANY FACES OF PAINFUL SEX

A couple consults their family doctor because they want to conceive a child but have been unable to have intercourse for the past 2 years. A young woman complains to her gynecologist of repeated yeast infections that consist mostly of a burning sensation. A couple seeks out a sex therapist because the woman has lost interest in sex and reports intense pain on penile penetration, during thrusting, and for days afterward. A depressed anxious woman in her 50s attributes her psychiatric symptoms to the development of chronic vulvar pain that interferes greatly with her daily activities. Most probably all of the above are among the 8 to 21% of American women who suffer from painful sex (Laumann, Paik, & Rosen, 1999), yet this problem often goes undiagnosed and, when diagnosed, may be left untreated. An epidemiological study showed that only 60% of women who reported suffering from chronic genital pain sought treatment for this symptom, and 40% of those never received a formal diagnosis (Harlow, Wise, & Stewart, 2001). This finding highlights the importance of making questions concerning painful sex a routine part of medical and mental health assessments. It also explains why the majority of women who end up in our offices are generally well educated and persistent: It is difficult to find a physician or a psychologist who can diagnose and treat the many conditions associated with painful sex.

Within the mental health professions, painful genital sexual activity has traditionally been diagnosed as either dyspareunia or vaginismus, two sexual disorders classified under the category of sexual pain in the *DSM-IV-TR* (*Diagnostic and Statistical Manual of Mental Disorders, Fourth Edition, Text Revision;* American Psychiatric Association, 2000). In addition to the fact that it is unclear why painful genital sexual activity is considered a sexual dysfunction any more than other pain syndromes interfering with sexual activity (e.g., low back pain) (Meana, Binik, Khalifé, & Cohen, 1997b), one of the main problems with this classification is that there is considerable overlap between dyspareunia and vaginismus. Two recent studies showed that the only factor differentiating women with dyspareunia from those with vaginismus was the avoidance of penetration by the latter (de Kruiff, ter Kuile, Weijenborg, & van Lankveld, 2000; Reissing, Binik, Khalifé, Cohen & Amsel, 2004). Dyspareunia and vaginismus can encompass a broad array of underlying physical pathologies, ranging from endometriosis and a retroverted uterus resulting in deep dyspareunia, to provoked vestibulodynia (formerly vulvar vestibulitis) causing entry dyspareunia (Meana, Binik, Khalifé, & Cohen, 1997a). Developmental events such as vaginal birth delivery and menopause can also be a source of painful sex (Kao, Binik, Kapuscinski, & Khalifé, 2008; Paterson, Davis, Khalifé, Amsel, & Binik, 2009). Finally, many vulvar diseases classified under the umbrella term of *vulvodynia*—a general condition characterized by chronic, unexplained vulvar pain and minimal physical findings—are a source of genital pain that can interfere with sexual activity (Moyal-Barracco & Lynch, 2004). The main vulvodynia subtype is provoked vestibulodynia, a syndrome characterized by a burning pain that is elicited via pressure to the vulvar vestibule or attempted vaginal penetration. There is no known physical cause for this condition, although recent research has identified sensory abnormalities and other peripheral and central alterations (for a review, see Pukall, Bergeron, & Goldfinger, 2008). Vulvodynia also includes generalized vulvodynia, a debilitating syndrome involving chronic burning of the vulva. Regardless of the often-elusive initial cause, pain during sexual activity diminishes overall quality of life (Arnold, Bachmann, Rosen, Kelly, & Rhoads, 2006). It has a negative impact on all phases of the sexual response cycle for the woman and sometimes for her partner; it puts a strain on otherwise stable relationships while rendering more difficult the establishment of new ones; and, after years of unresolved pain, it can also result in mood disturbances and their attendant negative functional impact.

WHAT'S WRONG WITH ME? ASSOCIATED DIFFICULTIES

The difficulties associated with genital pain, or any health problem affecting one's sex life, are inevitably linked to the sociocultural context within which the problem occurs. A young woman unable to take part in intercourse can experience devastating consequences, especially if the pain dates to the first attempt, as is the case for about half the women suffering from dyspareunia (Bazin et al., 1994). At some point during the course of this problem, most will question their worth as women, wonder what is wrong with them psychologically and sexually, and doubt their love and attraction for their partner (Ayling & Ussher, 2008).

We demonstrated in our studies that women with dyspareunia had more psychologic distress, negative attitudes toward sexuality, sexual dysfunction, and relationship problems than no-pain controls (Meana et al., 1997a). When we subtyped this sample based on physical pathology, women without physical findings had higher rates of psychologic symptomatology and relationship maladjustment despite their similar deficits in sexual functioning. When we compared women with provoked vestibulodynia with normal controls, we found that all aspects of these pain patients' sexual response cycle were negatively affected. They had lower intercourse frequencies, desire, and arousal and less orgasmic success (Meana et al., 1997a). These impairments have been replicated. However, it is still unclear whether women with dyspareunia show lower relationship adjustment than women without this condition as findings have been mixed (for a review, see Desrochers, Bergeron, Landry, & Jodoin, 2008).

Some clinicians have reported that a third to a half of their samples of women with dyspareunia had difficulties with penetration to the point of warranting a diagnosis of vaginismus (Schover, Youngs, & Cannata, 1992; van

Lankveld, Brewaeys, ter Kuile, & Weijenborg, 1995), a presumed spasm of the outer third of the vagina that makes intercourse impossible. Following these clinical accounts, we investigated the pelvic floor hypertonicity often reported as a correlate of painful sex (Reissing et al., 2004). Results of this study demonstrated that women with vaginismus showed higher average muscle tension than those with provoked vestibulodynia, who in turn showed higher muscle tension than no-pain controls. These findings have lead us to believe that hypertonicity is probably contributing to the pain experienced during intercourse and should be dealt with in the context of a multidisciplinary treatment approach.

We have attempted to identify some of the multiple mediating factors that exacerbate and maintain painful sex (Gatchel & Turk, 1999). Interestingly, women with dyspareunia who attribute their pain to psychosocial factors report higher levels of pain, more sexual dysfunction, as well as more psychological and marital distress than those who attribute their pain to physical factors, regardless of actual etiology (Meana, Binik, Khalifé, & Cohen, 1999). We learned that, as is the case for other chronic pain problems, anxiety related to pain and somatic symptoms is also associated with painful sex (Meana & Lykins, 2009). Pain catastrophizing, fear of pain, hypervigilance, and lower self-efficacy also appear to predict pain intensity and sexual impairment (Desrochers, Bergeron, Khalifé, Dupuis, & Jodoin, 2009; Meana, Binik, Khalifé, & Cohen, 1998). Further, the role of the partner has begun to receive some empirical attention in the last few years (e.g., Davis & Reissing, 2007). In one study, we found that hostile and solicitous partner responses were associated with increased pain intensity in women with vestibulodynia (Desrosiers et al., 2008). Thus, cognitive, affective, and relational factors are likely to have an impact on the experience of pain, even if neither completely accounts for the pain's initial onset.

HISTORICAL OVERVIEW

The history of approaches to understanding and treating pain during sexual intercourse is disjointed and confusing. There are at least three important potential reasons for this. First, gynecologists, the mental health professionals, dermatologists, and most recently, pain specialists have developed theories and treatments for the problem. Typically, there has been controversy within each discipline and little communication between them. Second, there is disagreement concerning whether painful sex is a syndrome, as proposed by the *DSM-IV-TR* (APA, 2000), a symptom of underlying pathology as proposed by many gynecologists, or a combination of both. Third, until recently, this problem did not appear to be a major concern for clinicians or researchers from any discipline. The only very clear historical point is that the problem of pain during intercourse and penetration has been known for many centuries (Binik, Bergeron, & Khalifé, 2007; Meana & Binik, 1994).

Gynecologists have traditionally been the frontline clinicians and researchers in this area. They have demonstrated a fairly straightforward dualistic approach by attempting either to equate the pain with some known physical pathology or, in its absence, by assuming a psychogenic origin. Many gynecology texts have long lists of possible physical causes for pain during intercourse (e.g., Baram, 1996). Their presumption has been that if you treat the physical cause, the pain will disappear. If this is not effective, patients are typically referred to mental health professionals. There has been very little controlled research that supports this view or method of treatment. A different "biopsychosocial" view is emerging among gynecologists interested in chronic pelvic pain (e.g., Steege, Metzger, & Levy, 1998). This view conceptualizes all forms of pelvic pain, including dyspareunia, as multidetermined and relies heavily on models from pain research and health psychology.

Mental health professionals shared the dualistic attitude and approach of gynecologists, although they were much more likely to assume psychogenic causation. The specific treatment approach depended primarily on the reigning theoretical model of the time. For at least half of the 20th century, pain during intercourse was likely to be considered a hysterical symptom. Later approaches saw the pain as the result of faulty couple interaction/communication, poor sexual technique, inadequate arousal, sexual abuse, or some combination of these. In practice, mental health professionals have only recently become involved in the treatment of dyspareunia. On the other hand, sex therapists are probably the primary practitioners for the treatment of vaginismus.

The terms *dyspareunia* and *vaginismus* entered the psychiatric nosology in *DSM-III* (*Diagnostic and Statistical Manual of Mental Disorders, Third Edition;* American Psychiatric Association, 1980). They became sexual disorders because of the enormous influence of Masters and Johnson, Kaplan, and early sex therapists. The *DSM-IV* (*Diagnostic and Statistical Manual of Mental Disorders, Fourth Edition;* American Psychiatric Association, 1994) places dyspareunia and vaginismus in a separate subcategory termed the *sexual pain disorders*. It assumed that dyspareunia and vaginismus are discrete syndromes. Recent consensus conferences concerning sexual problems have retained these terms (Basson et al., 2004). The concept of "sexual pain" as separate from other pain problems is confusing. It implies that sex is the originating problem rather than the context in which the pain is usually, although not always, provoked. It is unclear why dyspareunia is defined by the activity with which it interferes rather than by the location and characteristics of the pain. This is an unusual formulation of a pain problem further distinguished by the fact that "sexual pain" is the only pain left in the *DSM* outside the category of pain disorder.

In the last 15 years, painful sex has begun to interest the pain research and treatment community (e.g., Wesselmann, Burnett, & Heinberg, 1997). Vaginismus and dyspareunia have been included in the International Association for the Study of Pain (IASP) classification of chronic pain along with other forms of urogenital and pelvic pain (Merskey & Bogduk, 1994). This classification and approach relies heavily on models of pain suggested by gate control theory (Melzack & Wall, 1983) and its descendants, all of which suggest complex interactions of biopsychosocial determinants in the experience of pain.

We like the "pain" approach because it avoids the earlier pitfalls of dualism and single-cause pathway traps since it is multidisciplinary by nature, focuses on the pain, and provides a new multiaxial approach to classification. It has resulted in many new research avenues with clinical implications. The majority of these have emanated from the parallelism being discovered between vulvovaginal pain and other chronic pain syndromes. We have examined central nervous system involvement (Pukall et al., 2005), the role of pain catastrophizing and somatic hypervigilance (Payne, Binik, Amsel, & Khalifé,

2005), and the role of partner reactions (Desrosiers et al., 2008) to the pain—three categories of findings with important treatment implications. In another study we conducted (Reissing et al., 2004), we found that women suffering from vaginismus were indistinguishable from matched vestibulodynia controls on measures of pain. Together, these data have convinced us that pain is an essential part of the diagnosis of dyspareunia but may be insufficient to distinguish it from vaginismus.

These sets of findings have led Binik (2005) to formally argue that dyspareunia be classified as a pain syndrome in the *DSM V* rather than as a sexual dysfunction. This has generated controversy as some are concerned that losing the classification link to sexuality may have a limiting effect on treatment. Regardless, it is clear that the study and treatment of painful sex has come a long way in a very short time. Promising though the pain approach currently appears, whether it will pass the long-term scrutiny of empirical investigation and clinical outcomes remains to be seen.

CURRENT THERAPEUTIC OPTIONS

Current therapeutic options include medical, cognitive, behavioral, physical therapy, and surgical interventions. However, most efforts to date remain unidimensional as they aim to alleviate only one aspect of the complex array of symptoms that characterize painful sex. Moreover, empirically validated treatments are still the exception: There is only one published randomized clinical trial for vaginismus (van Lankveld et al., 2006) and only two involving psychotherapy for dyspareunia (Bergeron et al., 2001; Masheb, Kerns, Lozano, Minkin, & Richman, 2009). We have suggested that a concurrent multimodal treatment approach may be optimal for a set of conditions that have an impact on different areas of functioning (Bergeron et al., 1997).

Medical interventions are recommended during the first stage of treatment for entry dyspareunia. Initially, physicians typically suggest minimally invasive treatments such as the topical application of different types of antifungal, corticosteroid, or estrogen creams. In our experience, corticosteroid creams appear to be the most commonly prescribed first-line treatment for superficial dyspareunia, with or without vaginismus, while many women self-medicate with or are prescribed antifungal agents. There is no published evidence, however, that any of these creams are effective. Nightly applications of topical lidocaine have recently shown promising results (Zolnoun, Hartmann, & Steege, 2003). Barring symptomatic relief from the aforementioned measures, systemic treatments, including oral corticosteroids and antifungals, have been suggested as the next treatment stage. Only one controlled study examined the use of an oral medication for vestibulodynia (systemic antifungal), and results showed that it is no more effective than placebo (Bornstein, Livrat, Stolar, & Abramovici, 2000). There are typically no medical treatments for the single diagnosis of vaginismus.

Behavioral interventions include sex therapy, pelvic floor physical therapy, and cognitive-behavioral pain management. Sex therapy has been conducted based on the assumption that increases in desire and arousal, as well as a decrease in vaginismic muscle contraction, would impact some of the mechanisms that might mediate painful sex. Success with a combination of sex therapy and behavioral pain management has been reported in two studies focusing on dyspareunia, although these did not include control groups (ter Kuile & Weijenborg, 2006; Weijmar Schultz et al., 1996). A randomized clinical trial examining cognitive–behavioral sex therapy for vaginismus yielded a mere 15% success rate, highlighting the limits of this "talk therapy" approach (van Lankveld et al., 2006). However, a case series has shown that intensive exposure therapy in women with vaginismus can lead to 90% of patients being able to achieve vaginal intercourse (ter Kuile et al., 2009). Whether this type of treatment also results in significant pain reduction and improved sexual functioning is not yet clear.

In our recent randomized clinical trial comparing group cognitive-behavioral therapy (CBT) and a corticosteroid cream treatment, completers of both treatment groups reported reductions in pain and improvements in sexual functioning at posttreatment. However, global assessments of pain and sexual functioning were significantly better in the CBT group. Further, women having undergone CBT reported significantly less pain catastrophizing—the most robust psychosocial predictor of pain and disability—as well as greater treatment satisfaction (Bergeron, Khalifé, & Dupuis, 2008). Results support our view that mental health professionals have an important role to play in the treatment of painful intercourse.

Therapeutic effectiveness was reported in one retrospective study of pelvic floor biofeedback in a mixed group of women with vulvar pain. The presence of vaginismus was not formally assessed in this sample, but its frequency was probably high considering that an important proportion of participants were not engaging in intercourse at the beginning of the study (Glazer, Rodke, Swencionis, Hertz, & Young, 1995). At least two other prospective studies have confirmed the effectiveness of biofeedback in treating vestibulodynia (Danielsson, Torstensson, Brodda-Jansen, & Bohm-Starke, 2006; McKay et al., 2001). Further, the use of other physical therapy techniques focusing on pelvic floor rehabilitation is increasingly popular with patients and health professionals alike, as witnessed on Internet sites devoted to genital pain and in recent publications (e.g., Rosenbaum, 2005).

In our study evaluating the effectiveness of physical therapy, including biofeedback in the treatment of vestibulodynia, physical therapy was successful for 51.4% of women and unsuccessful for the rest. Prospective measures of pain during gynecological examination, as well as self-reported pain during intercourse, showed a significant decrease from pre- to posttreatment. In addition, there were significant increases in frequency of intercourse, sexual desire, and sexual arousal. Physical therapy can be a potentially successful noninvasive treatment option for painful sex. Our patients also tend to enjoy this intervention and feel satisfied with both the treatment delivery and resulting improvements (Bergeron, Brown, et al., 2002).

Vestibulectomy is the most commonly reported treatment for provoked vestibulodynia. Usually recommended following the failure of less-invasive treatment strategies, this minor surgical intervention is also consistently reported as achieving the best therapeutic outcome. It consists of an excision of the hymen and of all the sensitive areas of the vestibule to a depth of about 2 mm, most frequently located in the posterior fourchette. The vaginal mucosa is then sometimes mobilized and brought downward to cover the excised area (Friedrich, 1987). This intervention is done under general or epidural anesthesia (e.g., Goetsch, 1996). Women are instructed to gradually resume intercourse about 6 weeks postsurgery. Bornstein, Zarfati, Goldik, and Abramovici's (1999) and Landry, Bergeron, Dupuis, and Desrocher's (2008) critical reviews of the vestibulodynia surgery literature revealed vestibulectomy success rates ranging from 43 to 100%, with average success rates typically surpassing 65–70%. Patients often considered this procedure to be a "quick fix"; hence, you, as a mental health professional, should carefully assess their motivation and expectancies before giving them the green light to go ahead with the surgery.

Despite their reported success, surgical interventions for genital pain have been the source of much controversy and puzzlement regarding the basic mechanism by which surgery produces its effect. We conducted the first randomized treatment study of vestibulodynia comparing vestibulectomy, group CBT, and biofeedback (Bergeron et al., 2001). We found significant improvements at posttreatment and at 6-month follow-up for all treatments. Vestibulectomy resulted in approximately twice the pain reduction (47–70%) as compared with the two other treatments (19–38%). These findings need to be interpreted with caution since 7 women refused the surgery after randomization, and 2 of the 22 who had the surgery reported being worse at posttreatment. There were significant improvements in overall sexual functioning at the 6-month follow-up, with no treatment differences. However, there were no changes in frequency of intercourse, which remained well below national averages for this age group, with a mean frequency of four times per month in comparison to the average of eight times per month reported (Laumann, Gagnon, Michael, & Michaels, 1994). Our 2.5-year follow-up of these study participants indicated that all treatments had effected significant improvements in pain over time (Bergeron, Khalifé, Glazer, & Binik, 2008). Vestibulectomy remained superior in its impact on clinically assessed vestibular pain but was equal to CBT in terms of self-reported pain during intercourse. This has led us to conclude that the effects of CBT may be slower to appear, and that if one is patient, surgery can be avoided. There were no changes in frequency of intercourse or overall sexual functioning between the 6-month and 2.5- year follow-up.

How do we help a patient choose between the widely varied existing interventions? Despite the superior outcome results of the vestibulectomy condition in our randomized study (Bergeron et al., 2001), our overall clinical approach to the treatment of painful sex begins by recommending less-invasive behavioral options, considering the risks involved with the surgery. After careful evaluation and diagnosis, the gynecologists on our team typically recommend that the woman choose between cognitive-behavioral sex therapy/pain management (group, couple, or individual format) and physical therapy. If one or a combination of these treatments does not yield improvement that is satisfactory to the patient, the gynecologist will consider performing a vestibulectomy in the case of vestibulodynia only. The traditional medical approach postulates that we should always offer the more conservative treatment first. However, in many cases of genital pain, (1) conservative medical treatments such as corticosteroid creams typically do not help, and (2) many of our patients have already tried a number of creams without success.

HOW TO WORK WITH WOMEN WHO SUFFER FROM PAINFUL SEX

The following suggestions will help in working with women who suffer from painful sex:

Be prepared to work hard. The treatment of women who regularly experience painful sex is hard work. Well defined and specific though the problem may seem, pain with intercourse exists within a complex constellation of physical and psychological etiologic and mediating factors that will challenge even experienced therapists. Sex is a complicated union or disunion of physiology, psychology, relational dynamics, and social mores. Adding pain to the mix does not simplify it, neither does the frustration of multiple failed attempts at professional help. The end result is almost always a multilayered case that will demand all of your therapeutic talents.

Although painful intercourse has received an unprecedented amount of research and clinical attention in the last few years, it remains likely that many of your patients will be frustrated about the quality of care they have already received. Some will tell stories about being dismissed as either making too much of their "discomfort" or as using the pain, consciously or unconsciously, to mask a relational or intrapsychic conflict. Others will speak of well-meaning providers whose mounting frustration became increasingly evident when their interventions failed and who ultimately gave up trying.

Do not think of yourself as the patient's savior. Be ready for cynical patients and for extremely hopeful ones. In both cases, avoid the trap of setting yourself up as the savior. You can empathize with their frustration at treatment failures without creating the impression that you will be the one to resolve the problem completely. Previous health professionals often failed to provide true validation of the patient's pain and an honest appraisal of probable treatment outcomes. When you make these your starting point, you will be off to an excellent start.

Avoid attempts to attribute the pain to a single cause. This is not easy. In session, you may still find yourself trying to pin the pain down to a single cause. Or, you may find the patient trying to do just that. After all, both of you would dearly love a simple explanation that would indicate a straightforward treatment direction. Unless it really does jump out at you or them, and this is rarely the case, think in more complex terms. Coherent but inaccurate narratives about one factor cause satisfaction only temporarily.

Be humble. Adopting a multidisciplinary approach to the conceptualization, assessment, and treatment of a disorder requires it. This approach forces you to admit to yourself that you will have neither all the answers nor all the skills necessary to address the problem. Treatment requires a team effort. You should assume that treatment success is not entirely within your control. On the other hand, do not limit yourself to the psychological distress and comorbid sexual difficulties associated with the pain. Make the pain a significant target of your intervention efforts. Failure to do so will cause many clients to disengage from you. You can be very effective in reducing the pain with psychoeducation and pain management. You can be instrumental in coordinating access to and communication with the other disciplines. This is a growth-promoting opportunity for those of you who are unaccustomed to working collaboratively in a concurrent fashion with other professionals. Remember, however, that ultimately you can only control the dimensions of the problem you are treating.

Educate yourself about what the other disciplines do. The optimal situation requires that all team members have at least some basic knowledge everyone's area of work. As a therapist, you need to educate yourself about the gynecologic conditions that are implicated in genital pain, as well as physical therapy, medical, and surgical treatment options. There are two important reasons for this. First, you need to understand what your client is undergoing to provide accurate empathy and feedback. Second, you may have to intervene to help the client navigate the challenges of certain treatment components (e.g., her inhibition regarding pelvic floor manipulation).

Aim your treatment at multiple targets simultaneously. By the time you see them in your office, women will likely have been experiencing painful sex anywhere from months to several years. They are thus likely to have developed difficulties in a number of other areas, such as deficits in desire and arousal, depressive and anxious symptoms, a preoccupation with the consequences of pain and unpleasant somatic sensations, relationship stress, and diminished self-worth. This may seem shocking to you now, but target all problem areas simultaneously with reasonably modest goals. Do this because one area is not likely to improve without a commensurate improvement in the others. A small increase in desire, coupled with a small improvement in arousal, coupled with slightly enhanced partner communication and a somewhat reduced level of hopelessness are likely to have a surprising additive effect, despite the modest gains in any one single target area.

Do not be disheartened if patients are not immediately enthusiastic about significant improvement in the pain. A couple will arrive at a session reporting a much less painful or pain-free episode, and yet they do not seem sufficiently happy or relieved. In some cases, this reaction is simply a defensive, cautious strategy. The couple has been struggling with the pain for so long that they do not want to get their hopes up only to be disappointed. Most women's pain is variable, so they need evidence of sustained improvement before considering it more than temporary easing of the pain. In other cases, the less-than-joyful reaction to improvement signals a more complicated dynamic in which the pain is serving a systemic purpose. For example, a woman who is sex averse may feel that she has lost a truly "legitimate" reason (pain) for avoiding sexual interactions. Or, perhaps an insecure partner fears abandonment now that his partner's pain is resolved. In any case, the muted reaction to improvement is an excellent clinical opportunity to investigate psychological or relational factors that may be maintaining the pain and doing other damage to the couple's relationship.

Expect treatment gains to come in relatively small increments. What seem to us small improvements can mean a world of difference to the sexual lives of our patients. Although we have treated women who experienced complete resolution of their pain, the more common outcome is improvement. Even a seemingly small reduction of pain can radically improve the quality of sexual interactions because it allows the woman to concentrate on pleasurable aspects of the experience. It can be just enough for these other pleasurable experiences to overpower the discomfort and perhaps lead to orgasm. Every maintained increment in pain reduction is important. Both you and your clients should acknowledge small gains and patiently witness their additive effect.

Multidimensional Assessment

In keeping with our biopsychosocial model, we find that the assessment of organic, cognitive, affective, behavioral, and relationship factors as either causal or maintenance factors is crucial. We know that factors that initiated the onset of the pain may be different from those maintaining it. Thus, simplistic, dualistic etiological frameworks are of little utility. Unfortunately, the comprehensive evaluation of women with dyspareunia has traditionally been a neglected dimension of the overall health care delivery for this population. Despite recent advances, too many of these women are still not taken seriously, and too many physicians fail to perform the three medical tests required for a proper diagnosis: (1) a careful gynecologic history, (2) a cotton-swab palpation of the vestibular area with the woman rating her pain at various sites, and (3) vaginal and cervical cultures to exclude the possibility of infection-related pain.

You should first assess the quality, location, duration, onset, elicitors, and intensity of the pain. These variables are the best predictors of underlying physical pathology (Meana et al., 1997b). Further, by asking these questions, you will validate the patient's suffering and establish the therapeutic alliance. We use a 0-to-10 scale with 0 representing *no pain at all* and 10 representing *the worst pain ever* as a tool throughout the therapy. We also use a similar scale to evaluate accompanying emotional distress. Since many women also suffer from genital pain during nonsexual activities (e.g., urination, tampon insertion and removal, etc.), we recommend that you inquire about these as well. Such questions allow the patient to feel that she is with someone familiar with the problem.

After having obtained a good description of the pain, we move on to the cognitive, behavioral, and affective reactions that usually accompany the pain, in both the woman and her partner. The assessment of behavioral factors is particularly relevant in attempting to distinguish between dyspareunia and vaginismus since it has been shown that only avoidance of penetration differentiates between the two (de Kruiff et al., 2000; Reissing et al., 2004). Since these disorders often overlap and co-occur (van Lankveld et al., 1995), we have suggested that they might best be viewed along a continuum rather than as qualitatively distinct diagnostic entities (Meana & Binik, 1994). Nevertheless, the extent of penetration avoidance provides some important clues concerning the role of psychosocial factors in the sexual dysfunction resulting from painful intercourse.

A major part of the assessment should focus on the impact of pain on sexual functioning. We tend to ask fairly detailed questions about the couple's typical sexual scenario, past and current frequency of intercourse and masturbation, and who usually initiates sex, how, and for what reason. Women who experience painful sex rarely initiate sex, and when they do, it is out of guilt rather than desire. The frequency of intercourse for these couples has thus usually taken a downward slope. Other negative impacts on sexual functioning include diminished sexual arousal and reduced orgasmic capacity, which can in turn worsen the pain (Meana et al., 1997a).

We try to ask our patients about two groups of cognitive distortions that play a role in the maintenance of painful sex. One type has to do with thoughts concerning the overall pain condition, for example "I will be stuck with this problem for life" or "No man will ever want me because I cannot give him the sexual pleasure he desires." These causal attributions or personal meanings are powerful. We have found that women with dyspareunia who believe that their pain is affecting all aspects of their life report lower dyadic adjustment, more impaired sexual functioning, and increased psychological distress (Jodoin et al., in press). A second type of cognitive distortion observed in our patients involves the thoughts preceding, during, and following the pain experience. Examples include "I know I will be in terrible pain in a couple of minutes; it will be a horrible experience that will end badly for me and my partner," and "The pain I am feeling now is so intense, it's like a knife piercing through my vagina." We call such thinking "pain catastrophizing." Catastrophizing involves magnification, rumination, and helplessness and is related to higher pain intensity (Sullivan, Bishop, & Pivik, 1995). Changes in catastrophizing have been shown to correlate with better treatment outcome following CBT for dyspareunia (Desrochers, Bergeron, Khalifé, Dupuis, & Jodoin, in press). These thought patterns can be targeted with the pain management component of our program via cognitive restructuring.

Much like its cognitive counterpart, the affective component of the pain experience can take on a general form (e.g., an elevated degree of anxiety concerning the disorder in general) and a more situational one (e.g., fear of pain during a given sexual encounter). Fear of engaging in the activities that generate pain is a common response in chronic pain sufferers and can lead to an avoidance of such activities (Vlayen & Linton, 2000). We know from research conducted in our laboratory that women who report high levels of fear of pain, anxiety, and avoidance have worse topical treatment and psychotherapy outcomes (Desrochers et al., in press). By assessing the extent of pain-related fear and anxiety early in the therapy, you will have identified what is probably the biggest obstacle to improvement and hence given yourself some leverage to work with it rather than against it.

Last, we always carefully inquire about past treatments. We know that there is a wide array of interventions, a preponderance of ineffective ones, and numerous professional misconceptions about the condition. Our inquiry enables us to counter the patient's demoralization and to provide her with hope simply from our thoroughness and knowledge of what she has already been through.

Initial Phase of Therapy: Alliance Building, Education, and Goal Formulation

The main purpose of the initial phase of therapy is to help the patient reconceptualize her genital pain as a multidimensional problem influenced by a variety of factors, including her thoughts, emotions, behaviors, and couple interactions (Turk, Meichenbaum, & Genest, 1983).

One of our first treatment objectives is to get patients to think about how different cognitive, affective, behavioral, and relationship factors affect their pain experience, as well as to notice the variations in their current pain. For example, one woman may notice that when she engages in sexual activity to please her partner, she tends to feel more pain, or that when she has sex during the week following her period, the pain is less intense. A pain diary is useful in this process, and we have devised one that is specific to painful sex. The diary contains pain intensity ratings as well as questions about their menstrual cycle stage; thoughts and feelings before, during, and after the pain; how they tried to cope with the pain; and how aroused/relaxed they were before sex. This diary often becomes the basis for subsequent interventions since it richly informs us about the different dimensions of the patient's pain experience.

In terms of therapeutic objectives, we try to help our patients formulate two or three short-term, realistic goals that will engage and motivate them and guide our interventions. These typically consist of at least one pain reduction goal and one sexual functioning improvement goal. We avoid making the complete elimination of pain a goal as our treatment alone may not provide this. We emphasize that, even though some women do not always notice a reduction in their pain, they usually feel that it has a less-negative impact on their lives following therapy. In addition, we do not make the increase in frequency of sexual activities a goal as we do not want to further stigmatize and alienate the woman suffering from genital pain. In the case of couple therapy, helping the partners to see how they have each contributed to the current polarization of sexual roles and resulting lowered frequency of intercourse creates a more balanced alliance between the therapist and each member of the dyad (Schnarch, 2000). We also try to steer the focus away from intercourse and to help the couple find enjoyment and fulfillment in other, nonpenetrative sexual activities.

Treatment Strategies for Reducing Pain and Sexual Dysfunction

Once the patient recognizes that she has more control over her pain than previously thought, we suggest ways to use this newly acquired awareness to actually reduce the pain. A first exercise we propose is genital self-exploration. Common to many sex therapies, we give it a different twist by emphasizing the localization of the pain. The woman is not exploring for the sake of exploring but rather is attempting to delineate the painful area to know exactly where it hurts and to show it to her partner when relevant. Education about sexual anatomy is provided at this point, if necessary.

We also introduce breathing/relaxation exercises fairly early, providing the following rationale:

> As you have noticed in your diary entries and in our discussions, the anticipation of pain creates anxiety, which has two consequences: (1) it inhibits arousal, which in turn inhibits lubrication, which increases your pain on penetration; (2) it often contributes to an involuntary contraction of the vaginal muscles, which again makes penetration a lot more painful, and sometimes impossible. For these reasons, an important part of the treatment is to learn to reduce your anxiety. One major way in which you can learn to do this is via breathing/relaxation techniques.

If the woman already practices some form of relaxation, we simply focus on helping her see how it can be used to reduce her pain and encourage her to make it an integral part of her daily routine. We also suggest that she use this technique during her physical therapy sessions, gynecologic examinations, and when she experiences pain.

We have learned from our close collaboration with physical therapists that Kegel exercises prescribed by a sex therapist who can never know whether the woman is doing them correctly is practically useless. For example, she may be contracting her thighs and abdomen rather than the relevant pelvic floor muscles. For this reason, we always recommend that the woman see a physical therapist at least once or twice so that she can be coached regarding the proper way to perform these exercises. We then recommend that she practice them daily, particularly prior to vaginal penetration to relax the pelvic floor as much as possible. Similarly, vaginal dilation done in the context of a hypertonic pelvic floor is not very useful and can even be counterproductive since the chances of experiencing pain are very high. Coordinating a systematic desensitization program in collaboration with a physical therapist is generally more productive and will help break the association between pain and penetration.

Cognitive restructuring focusing on pain is probably one of the most successful components of psychotherapy for dyspareunia and vaginismus. We divide it into the three following steps: (1) preparing for the onset of pain (anticipation of pain), (2) confronting and handling the sensations (pain during and after intercourse), and (3) handling feelings after an episode of painful intercourse. The woman is encouraged to begin to identify her automatic thoughts, to jot them down in her pain diary, and to communicate them to her partner and to you, the therapist. In a group format, this strategy is particularly powerful and serves to break the isolation of individual suffering.

An issue that often needs to be discussed at length is the avoidance of penetration and other forms of sexual activities. We try to break the avoidance habit by helping patients (1) acknowledge that they have been avoiding sex, (2) raise their awareness regarding the fact that pain is probably only one of many reasons for their avoidance, and (3) identify unrealistic beliefs, inhibitions, or maladaptive attitudes about pain and sex. We eventually help them get reacquainted with painless sexual activities. Sensate focus exercises have sometimes been useful in this context. Again, the emphasis here is not on blaming the woman for her normal reaction of not wanting to engage in a painful activity, but rather for her and her partner to become cognizant of non-pain-related factors that might have contributed to the current reduction or absence of pleasure, creativity, and passion during sex.

A related and very important issue is that of the nearly universal decrease in sexual desire and arousal observed in this population. Since many of our patients are young women, we find that focusing on the identification of sexual needs is of paramount importance. What sexual activities, moods, scenarios, ambiances, or fantasies facilitate desire and arousal? Can she communicate these to her partner? Sometimes, we find that assertiveness skills have to be improved to enable the woman to communicate her sexual preferences to her partner. An extensive overview of how to deal with sexual desire problems is beyond the scope of this chapter. However, a systemic conceptualization is often helpful in dealing with desire issues and in working on the relationship difficulties of women with dyspareunia in general.

The last component of the therapy consists of a review and consolidation of learned strategies and progress with the goal of (1) facilitating internal attributions of improvement and (2) identifying what will require continued attention once therapy is terminated. This may include recommending readings or another treatment when the present one has failed to bring about the desired improvements. Some women will at this point opt for surgery or for an alternative treatment such as acupuncture. The treatment of painful sex is generally a lengthy process, with our psychosocial approach only one of many available options.

Five Common Therapeutic Issues

Most of the therapeutic issues that arise in the treatment of women suffering from painful sex are similar to those found in other pain and sexual problems. However, there are at least five frequently encountered issues that should be anticipated.

Resistance to psychological interventions for pain. The suggestion of psychotherapy for painful sex can easily be experienced by women as a way of implying that their problem is primarily mental or emotional. This can feel dismissive. In our research, the most well-adjusted women seem to be relatively convinced that there is a physical component to their pain despite repeated assertions from gynecologists that there is no obvious pathology (Meana et al., 1998). It is thus understandable that the first reaction to a mental health professional may be a defensive one. You need to be aware of this sensitivity and strongly validate the patient's experience of pain. Only then can you educate her about the ways in which psychosocial factors can have an impact on the pain experience and how the pain itself, even if originally caused by a physical change, can result in psychosocial disturbances. Working on the credibility of psychological treatments for pain is an important part of the initial phase. The patient has to believe that this treatment has the potential to have an impact on pain and is not merely supportive, important though the latter may be.

Compliance with monitoring and homework assignments. Some patients can initially be resistant to these assignments for a variety of reasons, ranging from a lack of belief in their effectiveness, to an inability to prioritize assignments in an otherwise overscheduled day, to an unwillingness to devote that much time to a disturbing topic. Regardless of the underlying reason, you need to explore treatment nonadherence with the patient and her partner as it often reflects a degree of ambivalence regarding change. Uncompleted homework can sometimes be as informative to the therapist's conceptualization of the pain problem as are diligently performed exercises. One strategy that often helps patients understand the importance of homework is to provide them with the rationale for how a given exercise may have a direct impact on their pain. We have also found that the timing in assigning homework is a key factor in its successful implementation; for example, a prescribed ban on intercourse may prevent a woman from asserting herself with her partner by refusing to continue intercourse when she is in too much pain. In this case, this intervention would interfere with an aspect of the woman's personal growth that might be meaningfully related to the pain problem. Finally, in some cases patients need to be confronted about their degree of commitment to making the resolution or improvement of pain a major priority during the course of treatment.

The exhilaration/disappointment roller coaster. Initial gains can produce a feeling of joy and unbounded optimism in some patients who finally envision the possibility of having pain-free intercourse. However, these initial gains are sometimes not maintained with every attempt at intercourse, or more commonly, patients quickly adapt to them, and expectations of further improvement rise exponentially. This can lead to disappointment and defeatism, which can constitute a significant therapeutic setback. It is important that you explain to patients that treatment for vulvar pain more resembles a marathon than a sprint. The speed of progress throughout treatment will vary from slow to fast to sometimes being at a standstill. It is best to maintain a guarded optimism and steady emotional stance to avoid the pitfalls of a damaging reactivity.

Partner resistance. Partners are often the big unknown. Although we believe the active involvement of partners enhances treatment outcome, we never know beforehand the extent to which the partner will be helpful. A supportive partner who actively participates in the treatment can be the most powerful component of the treatment plan. On the other hand, not all partners are willing to be active in the treatment. For example, in one case, a woman's unusually large improvements in sexual function and pain reduction were met with very lukewarm reinforcement from her husband. Before his resistance could be investigated (i.e., sexual dysfunction of his own? the threat of a sexually functional wife who might leave him? etc.), he insisted on both terminating treatment. Since relationship dynamics can play a major role in the outcome of therapy, we recommend that partners be involved as early as possible. When partners do not wish to participate despite attempts to include them, we must accept this limitation and do our best with the woman alone. We try to determine the basis of a partner's resistance when he is actively sabotaging our efforts. Fortunately, it is not usually the case.

Patients may not share our treatment philosophy. Patients sometimes credit one of the disciplines exclusively for their improvement. Looking for a quick cure and wanting to reduce their time devoted to treatment, patients may drop certain treatment ingredients as surplus. In a perfect world, all team members would share a similar conceptualization of the disorder. The patient gets a similar message about etiology and treatment from each team member, thereby reinforcing the interdependence of all aspects of treatment. In most health care environments, you have to work toward the model teaching both the clients and team members. Sometimes, it is the patient and sometimes it a colleague who undermines the multidisciplinary approach. Keep at it; the results make it worth it.

EXPECTED OUTCOMES IN CLINICAL SETTINGS

Susan, an investment banker in her early 30s who has been living with her partner for 1 year, has had pain during intercourse since her first sexual experience when she was a teenager. This pain often made penetration impossible for her. Since she also had pain during manual stimulation and almost no sexual desire, her partner did not know how to approach or touch her anymore; he was becoming increasingly frustrated. Fearing that he would leave her, she decided to seek treatment. She first took part in a pain management group at a local hospital where two cotherapists provided tools to help with pain coping and the improvement of sex and romantic relationships. Susan only saw a modest improvement and felt that her partner was not very supportive of her efforts. About 6 months later, she decided to seek help again, this time in individual therapy. She wanted to work on family issues that she thought might be related to her pain and sexual difficulties. Besides, her partner felt that this was her problem and was not interested in taking part in the therapy. After about a year of therapy focusing on her familial and individual issues, Susan again only evidenced a modest improvement in her pain. She finally convinced her partner to come to couple therapy with her, and the last we heard, their sex life had improved, but the pain was still present, albeit somewhat less intense.

Susan's experience reflects one of the many possible treatment outcomes. Other patients prefer surgery and are not interested in time-consuming and costly therapy; they come to us because their physician recommended a few consultations. Once they see the work that is involved, they drop out. Sometimes, surgery puts an end to patients' pain, but we are concerned by our finding that while their sexual functioning improved, the frequency of intercourse did not (Bergeron et al., 2001).

While we are committed to a combination of treatments because this approach results in the most pain relief, improved sexual functioning, reduced psychological distress, and satisfying relationships, we are beginning to study factors such as the length of treatment, patient degrees of self-efficacy, and other patient and therapist characteristics to better predict which patients benefit from which treatment combinations (Bergeron, Binik, & Khalifé, 2002).

WHAT WORKING WITH WOMEN WHO SUFFER FROM PAINFUL SEX HAS MEANT TO US

Our experience in treating this population has been both challenging and highly rewarding. We are challenged by the need to be humble and ambitious. We are rewarded by our capacity to help a group of women who had known nothing but previous failure. We have found the challenges to keep us interested. We appreciate the complexity of the clinical picture caused by the interrelation of multiple factors. It forces us to think multidimensionally and to integrate theoretical perspectives and health disciplines. We are not in the least bored after many years of efforts. We are also sustained by our belief that research in this area and in nongenital pain syndromes will continue to help us. We have abandoned the unidimensional model of single organic or psychological causal pathways. We hope we have encouraged your interest in accepting the ordinary complexity of women's experience of painful sex and increased your motivation to contribute to their treatment.

REFERENCES

American Psychiatric Association. (1980). *Diagnostic and statistical manual of mental disorders* (3rd ed.). Washington, DC: Author.

American Psychiatric Association. (2000). *Diagnostic and statistical manual of mental disorders* (4th ed., text rev.). Washington, DC: Author.

Arnold, L. D., Bachmann, G. A., Rosen, R. C., Kelly, S., & Rhoads, G. G. (2006). Vulvodynia: Characteristics and associations with comorbidity and quality of life. *Obstetrics and Gynecology, 107*, 617–624.

Ayling, K., & Ussher, J. M. (2008). If sex hurts, am I still a woman? The subjective experience of vulvodynia in hetero-sexual women. *Archives of Sexual Behavior, 37*, 294–304.

Baram, D. A. (1996). Sexuality and sexual function. In J. S. Berek, E. Y. Adashi, & P. A. Hillard (Eds.), *Novak's gynecology* (12th ed., pp. 279–298). Baltimore: Williams and Wilkins.

Basson, R., Weijmar Shultz, W. C., Binik, Y. M., Brotto, L. A., Eschenbach, D. A., Laan, E., et al. (2004). Women's sexual desire and arousal disorders and sexual pain. In T. F. Lue, R. Basson, R. Rosen, F. Giuliano, S. Khoury, & F. Montorsi (Eds.), *Sexual medicine: Sexual dysfunctions in men and women* (pp. 851–974). Paris: Editions 21.

Bazin, S., Bouchard, C., Brisson, J., Morin, C., Meisels, A., & Fortier, M. (1994). Vulvar vestibulitis syndrome: An exploratory case-control study. *Obstetrics and Gynecology, 83*, 47–50. One of the first rigorous etiological studies on vulvar vestibulitis syndrome.

Bergeron, S., Binik, Y. M., & Khalifé, S. (2002). In favour of an integrated pain relief treatment approach for vulvar vestibulitis syndrome. *Journal of Psychosomatic Obstetrics and Gynecology, 23*, 7–9.

Bergeron, S., Binik, Y. M., Khalifé, S., Meana, M., Berkley, K. J., & Pagidas, K. (1997). The treatment of vulvar vestibulitis syndrome: Toward a multimodal approach. *Sexual and Marital Therapy, 12*, 305–311.

Bergeron, S., Binik, Y. M., Khalifé, S., Pagidas, K., Glazer, H. I., Meana, M., et al. (2001). A randomized comparison of group cognitive-behavioral therapy, surface electromyographic biofeedback, and vestibulectomy in the treatment of dyspareunia resulting from vulvar vestibulitis. *Pain, 91*, 297–306. The first randomized treatment outcome study of dyspareunia, focusing on one of its main subtypes—vulvar vestibulitis.

Bergeron, S., Brown, C., Lord, M. J., Oala, M., Binik, Y. M., & Khalifé, S. (2002). Physical therapy for vulvar vestibulitis syndrome: A retrospective study. *Journal of Sex and Marital Therapy, 28*, 183–192.

Bergeron, S., Khalifé, S., & Dupuis, M.-J. (2008, March). *A randomized comparison of cognitive–behavioral therapy and medical management in the treatment of provoked vestibulodynia*. Paper presented as part of a symposium at the annual meeting of the Society for Sex Therapy and Research, Chicago.

Bergeron, S., Khalifé, S., Glazer, H. I., & Binik, Y. M. (2008). Surgical and behavioral treatments for vestibulodynia: 2.5-year follow-up and predictors of outcome. *Obstetrics and Gynecology, 111*, 159–166.

Binik, Y. M. (2005). Dyspareunia looks sexy at first but how much pain will it take for it to score? A reply to my critics concerning the *DSM* classification of dyspareunia as a sexual dysfunction. *Archives of Sexual Behavior, 34*, 63–67.

Binik, Y. M., Bergeron, S., & Khalifé, S. (2007). Dyspareunia and vaginismus: So called sexual pain. In S. R. Leiblum (Ed.), *Principles and practice of sex therapy* (4th ed., pp. 124–156). New York: Guilford Press. Another chapter on the treatment of dyspareunia, mainly geared toward practicing sex therapists. A good complement to the present chapter.

Bornstein, J., Livrat, G., Stolar, Z., & Abramovici, H. (2000). Pure versus complicated vulvar vestibulitis: A randomized trial of fluconazole treatment. *Gynecologic and Obstetric Investigation, 50*, 194–197.

Bornstein, J., Zarfati, D. Goldik, Z., & Abramovici, H. (1999). Vulvar vestibulitis: Physical or psychosexual problem? *Obstetrics and Gynecology, 93*, 876–880.

Danielsson, I., Torstensson, T., Brodda-Jansen, G., & Bohm-Starke, N. (2006). EMG biofeedback versus topical lidocaine gel: A randomized study for the treatment of women with vulvar vestibulitis. *Acta Obstetricia et Gynecologica Scandinavica, 85*, 1360–1367.

Davis, H. J., & Reissing, E. D. (2007). Relationship adjustment and dyadic interaction in couples with sexual pain disorders: A critical review of the literature. *Sexual and Relationship Therapy, 22*, 245–254.

de Kruiff, M. E., ter Kuile, M. M., Weijenborg, P. Th. M., & van Lankveld, J. J. D. M. (2000). Vaginismus and dyspareunia: Is there difference in clinical presentation? *Journal of Psychosomatic Obstetrics and Gynecology, 21*, 149–155.

Desrochers, G., Bergeron, S., Landry, T., & Jodoin, M. (2008). Do psychosexual factors play a role in the etiology of provoked vestibulodynia? A critical review. *Journal of Sex and Marital Therapy, 34*, 198–226.

Desrochers, G., Bergeron, S., Khalifé, S., Dupuis, M.-J., & Jodoin, M. (2009). Fear avoidance and self-efficacy in relation to pain and sexual impairment in women with provoked vestibulodynia. *The Clinical Journal of Pain, 25*(6): 520–527.

Desrochers, G., Bergeron, S., Khalifé, S., Dupuis, M.-J., & Jodoin, M. (in press). *Provoked vestibulodynia: Psychological predictors of topical and cognitive-behavioral treatment outcome. Behavior Research and Therapy.*

Desrosiers, M., Bergeron, S., Meana, M., Leclerc, B., Binik, Y. M., & Khalifé, S. (2008). Psychosexual characteristics of vestibulodynia couples: partner solicitousness and hostility are associated with pain. *Journal of Sexual Medicine, 5*, 418–427.

Friedrich, E. G. (1987). Vulvar vestibulitis syndrome. *Journal of Reproductive Medicine, 32*, 110–114.

Gatchel, R. J., & Turk, D. C. (1999). *Psychosocial factors in pain: Critical perspectives.* New York: Guilford Press.

Glazer, H. I., Rodke, G., Swencionis, C., Hertz, R., & Young, A. W. (1995). The treatment of vulvar vestibulitis syndrome by electromyographic biofeedback of pelvic floor musculature. *Journal of Reproductive Medicine, 40*, 283–290.

Goetsch, M. F. (1996). Simplified surgical revision of the vulvar vestibule for vulvar vestibulitis. *American Journal of Obstetrics and Gynecology, 174*, 1701–1707.

Harlow, B. L., Wise, L. A., & Stewart, E. G. (2001). Prevalence and predictors of chronic lower genital tract discomfort. *American Journal of Obstetrics and Gynecology, 185*, 545–550. The only epidemiological study to date on the prevalence of vulvar pain and its associated features, such as early menarche.

Jodoin, M., Bergeron, S., Khalifé, S., Dupuis, M.-J., Desrochers, G., & Leclerc, B. (in press). Attributions as predictors of psychosexual and dyadic adjustment in women with vestibulodynia. *Archives of Sexual Behavior.*

Kao, A., Binik, Y. M., Kapuscinski, A., & Khalifé, S. (2008). Dyspareunia in post-menopausal women: A critical review. *Pain Research and Management, 13*, 243–254.

Landry, T., Bergeron, S., Dupuis, M. J., & Desrochers, G. (2008). The treatment of provoked vestibulodynia: A critical review. *Clinical Journal of Pain, 24*, 155–171.

Laumann, E. O., Gagnon, J. H., Michael, R. T., & Michaels, S. (1994). *The social organization of sexuality*. Chicago: University of Chicago Press.

Laumann, E. O., Paik, A., & Rosen, R. C. (1999). Sexual dysfunction in the United States. Prevalence, predictors and outcomes. *Journal of the American Medical Association, 281*, 537–545.

Masheb, R. M., Kerns, R. D., Lozano, C., Minkin, M. J., & Richman, S. (2009). A randomized clinical trial for women with vulvodynia: Cognitive-behavioral therapy vs. supportive psychotherapy. *Pain, 141*(1–2): 31–40.

McKay, E., Kaufman, R. H., Doctor, U., Berkova, Z., Glazer, H., & Redko, V. (2001). Treating vulvar vestibulitis with electromyographic biofeedback of pelvic floor musculature. *Journal of Reproductive Medicine, 46*, 337–342.

Meana, M., & Binik, Y. M. (1994). Painful coitus: A review of female dyspareunia. *Journal of Nervous and Mental Disease. 182*, 264–272. A thorough review of the descriptive/diagnostic, etiologic, and treatment aspects of dyspareunia.

Meana, M., Binik, Y. M., Khalifé, S., & Cohen, D. (1997a). Biopsychosocial profile of women with dyspareunia. *Obstetrics and Gynecology, 90*, 583–589. The first controlled study of the biological, psychological, and relationship characteristics of women with dyspareunia.

Meana, M., Binik, Y. M., Khalifé, S., & Cohen, D. (1997b). Dyspareunia: Sexual dysfunction or pain syndrome? *Journal of Nervous and Mental Disease, 185*, 561–569.

Meana, M., Binik, Y. M., Khalifé, S., & Cohen, D. (1998). Affect and marital adjustment in women's rating of dyspareunic pain. *Canadian Journal of Psychiatry, 43*, 381–385.

Meana, M., Binik, Y. M., Khalifé, S., & Cohen, D. (1999). Psychosocial correlates of pain attributions in women with dyspareunia. *Psychosomatics, 40*, 497–502.

Meana, M., & Lykins, A. D. (2009). Negative affect and somatically focused anxiety in young women reporting pain with intercourse. *Journal of Sex Research, 46*, 1–9.

Melzack, R., & Wall, P. D. (1983). *The challenge of pain*. New York: Basic Books. This textbook was written by two of the world's foremost leaders in pain research. Accessible to the novice reader, it covers everything one needs to know about pain, from etiologic theories and purported basic mechanisms to the main treatments for acute and chronic pain.

Merskey, H., & Bogduk, N. (1994*). Classification of chronic pain* (2nd ed.). Seattle, WA: IASP Press.

Moyal-Barracco, M., & Lynch, P. J. (2004). 2003 ISSVD terminology and classification of vulvodynia: A historical perspective. *The Journal of Reproductive Medicine, 49*, 772–777.

Paterson, L., Davis, S., Khalifé, S., Amsel, R., & Binik, Y. (2009). Persistent genital and pelvic pain after childbirth. *Journal of Sexual Medicine, 6*, 215–221.

Payne, K. A., Binik, Y. M., Amsel, R., & Khalifé, S. (2005). When sex hurts, anxiety and fear orient attention towards pain. *European Journal of Pain, 9*, 427–436.

Pukall, C. F., Bergeron, S., & Goldfinger, C. (2008). Vulvodynia: A review of pathophysiological factors and treatment options. *Basic and Clinical Medicine, 28*, 421–436.

Pukall, C. F., Strigo, I. A., Binik, Y. M., Amsel, R., Khalifé, S., & Bushnell, M. C. (2005). Neural correlates of painful genital touch in women with vulvar vestibulitis syndrome. *Pain, 115*, 118–127.

Reissing, E. D., Binik, Y. M., Khalifé, S., Cohen, D., Amsel, R. (2004). Vaginal spasm, pain and behavior: An empirical investigation of the diagnosis of vaginismus. *Archives of Sexual Behavior, 33*, 5–17.

Rosenbaum, T. Y. (2005). Physiotherapy treatment of sexual pain disorders. *Journal of Sex and Marital Therapy, 31*, 329–340.

Schnarch, D. M. (2000). Desire problems: A systemic perspective. In S. R. Leiblum & R. C. Rosen (Eds.), *Principles and practice of sex therapy* (3rd ed., pp. 17–56). New York: Guilford Press. An invaluable resource for gaining a greater understanding of the systemic issues that may contribute to maintain desire problems in couples in which the woman suffers from painful genital sexual activity.

Schover, L. R., Youngs, D. D., & Cannata, R. (1992). Psychosexual aspects of the evaluation and management of vulvar vestibulitis. *American Journal of Obstetrics and Gynecology, 167*, 630–636.

Steege, J. F., Metzger, D. A., & Levy, B. L. (1998). *Chronic pelvic pain: An integrated approach.* Toronto: Saunders. A comprehensive book covering a wide range of dimensions of chronic pelvic pain, ranging from pelvic neuroanatomy to overcoming the mind–body split.

Sullivan, M. J. L., Bishop, S., & Pivik, J. (1995). The Pain Catastrophizing Scale: Development and validation. *Psychological Assessment, 7*, 524–532.

ter Kuile, M. M., Bulté, I., Weijenborg, P. T., Beekman, A., Melles, R., & Onghena, P. (2009). Therapist-aided exposure for women with lifelong vaginismus: A replicated single-case design. *Journal of Consulting and Clinical Psychology, 77*, 149–159.

ter Kuile, M. M., & Weijenborg, P. T. (2006). A cognitive–behavioral group program for women with vulvar vestibulitis syndrome (VVS): Factors associated with treatment success. *Journal of Sex and Marital Therapy. 32*, 199–213.

Turk, D. C., Meichenbaum, D., & Genest, M. (1983). *Pain and behavioral medicine: A cognitive–behavioral perspective.* New York: Guilford Press. A great book for learning more about the clinical management of chronic pain.

van Lankveld, J. J. D. M., Brewaeys, A. M. A., Ter Kuile, M. M., & Weijenborg, P. Th. M. (1995). Difficulties in the differential diagnosis of vaginismus, dyspareunia and mixed sexual pain disorder. *Journal of Psychosomatic Obstetrics and Gynecology, 16*, 201–209.

van Lankveld, J. J., ter Kuile, M. M., de Groot, H. E., Melles, R., Nefs, J., & Zandbergen, M. (2006). Cognitive–behavioral therapy for women with lifelong vaginismus: A randomized waiting-list controlled trial of efficacy. *Journal of Consulting and Clinical Psychology, 74*, 168–178.

Vlayen, J. W. S., & Linton, S. J. (2000). Fear-avoidance and its consequences in chronic musculoskeletal pain: A state of the art. *Pain, 85*, 317–332.

Wesselmann, U., Burnett, A. L., & Heinberg, L. J. (1997). The urogenital and rectal pain syndromes. *Pain, 73*, 269–94. An extensive review of the literature on the various types of urogenital and rectal pain in both women and men.

Weijmar Shultz, W. C. M., Gianotten, W. L., van der Meijden, W. I., van de Miel, H. B. M., Blindeman, B., Chadha, S., et al. (1996). Behavioural approach with or without surgical intervention for the vulvar vestibulitis syndrome: A prospective randomized and non-randomized study. *Journal of Psychosomatic Obstetrics and Gynecology, 17*, 143–148.

Zolnoun, D. A., Hartmann, K. E., & Steege, J. F. (2003). Overnight 5% lidocaine ointment for treatment of vulvar vestibulitis. *Obstetrics and Gynecology, 102*, 84–87.

Thirteen

The Sexual Impact of Menopause

LORRAINE DENNERSTEIN, AO, MBBS, PHD, DPM, FRANZCP

INTRODUCTION

My interest in the effect of the ovarian sex steroids on female sexual functioning was triggered by the women patients who consulted me when I was a young general practitioner in the early 1970s. A number of women asked me whether the oral contraceptive pill could have affected their mood and sexual functioning, which they perceived to have deteriorated with the use of the oral contraceptive pill. In trying to answer their questions, I embarked on a journey that has led to a career in academic research with clinical training in psychiatry and a doctoral degree in reproductive endocrinology. For the last 30 years, I have studied the effects of changes in endogenous or exogenous sex steroid hormones on sexuality. Thus, our studies have examined changes in mood or sexuality with the menstrual cycle (Dennerstein et al., 1994a); oral contraceptive pill use (Dennerstein, 1999); in the postpartum period (Dennerstein, Lehert, & Riphagen, 1989); after hysterectomy (Dennerstein, Wood, & Burrows, 1977, Ryan, Dennerstein, & Pepperell, 1989); with the natural menopausal transition (Dennerstein, Dudley, & Burger, 2001; Dennerstein, Guthrie, Hayes, DeRogatis, & Lehert, 2008; Dennerstein, Lehert, & Burger, 2005; Dennerstein, Randolph, Taffe, Dudley, & Burger, 2002; Dennerstein et al., 2007a); after surgical menopause (Dennerstein, Koochaki, Barton, & Graziottin, 2006); and with use of estrogen and progestin after bilateral oophorectomy (Dennerstein, Burrows, Hyman, & Sharpe, 1979; Dennerstein, Burrows, Hyman, & Sharpe, 1980). Our studies have involved double-blind, randomized clinical trials, observational studies, bioavailability studies, and critical literature reviews—the full gamut of research. These approaches are complimentary and are drawn on in this chapter, which focuses on the menopausal transition.

There is a high incidence of sexual problems reported by women attending menopause clinics (Sarrel & Whitehead, 1985). How representative is this of most women's experience of the menopausal transition? If there is a deterioration in sexual functioning experienced by mid-aged women, is this related to menopause or simply to aging? The menopausal transition is a time of psychosocial as well as biological change. If there are adverse changes in sexuality, do they reflect ill health, hormonal changes, or psychosocial factors, and what is the relative importance of these factors? Sorting out this issue is of concern to clinicians because if there is a decline in sexual functioning specifically related to the hormonal aspects of the menopausal transition, then hormone therapy could be expected to play a role in therapy of such sexual problems.

215

Of course, reports derived from clinic or convenience samples are known to be based on a small proportion of self-selecting, predominantly ill women and may not be representative (McKinlay, McKinlay, & Brambilla, 1987; Morse et al., 1994). We can learn more about possible links between menopause and sexuality from population-based surveys. Yet, relatively few of the population studies of the menopausal transition in mid-aged women have inquired about sexual functioning. Even fewer have used a validated questionnaire to assess the different aspects of sexual functioning. Cross-sectional studies are unable to establish a difference between cohort membership (effects of social change on different age groups) and aging. Aging and length of the relationship are both known to affect sexual functioning of both men and women. For example, James (1983) used cross-sectional and longitudinal data to show that coital rate halved over the first year of marriage and then took another 20 years to halve again. The role of aging per se has to be disentangled from that of menopause, with which it is often confounded. Longitudinal studies of samples derived from the general population are in the best position to sort out whether there is a change in sexual functioning, and if so whether this reflects aging, health status, hormonal, or psychosocial factors.

Other methodological issues include the need for an appropriate age band that covers the menopausal transition; use of standardized objective definitions of menopausal status; distinctions between those with natural menopause and those with an induced menopause; separation of women who are taking exogenous hormones from those who are in the natural menopausal transition; inclusion of physical measures of hormonal change rather than subsuming this by menstrual status; limitations imposed on women by questionnaire design; and need for appropriate data analysis techniques (Dennerstein, 1996).

With these limitations in mind, I utilize the results of population-based surveys to address the impact of the menopause on women's sexual functioning. In this chapter, I refer in particular to results from our longitudinal observational study of the menopausal transition, the Melbourne Women's Midlife Health Project. This study provides important data as the sample was derived by population sampling rather than using convenience samples, and we obtained, prospectively and concurrently, hormone measures and information from a validated sexuality questionnaire. In the following review, I first examine changes in sexual functioning with aging and any references to midlife effects, the concomitant effects of the menopausal transition, differential effects of hormones and psychosocial factors, determination of the roles of androgens versus estrogens, and then the implications for the clinician.

IS THERE A CHANGE IN FEMALE SEXUALITY WITH AGING?

A number of studies report a decline in aspects of sexual functioning with aging by midlife. The early work of Pfeiffer and Davis (1972), using cross-sectional data from the Duke University study, found a pattern of declining sexual activity in both men and women. These results relied on coital or orgasmic rates, which may reflect availability of a partner rather than the woman's own sexuality. When Pfeiffer, Verwoerdt, and Davis (1972) reported results on sexual interest, they found that 7% of women in the 46- to 50-year group reported no interest compared to 51% in the 61- to 65-year group, whereas the incidence of no sexual interest reported by men of the same age rose from 0 to

11%. The sharpest decline in interest for women occurred between the 45- to 50- and 51- to 55-year groups, which encapsulates the mean age of menopause in the United States. The Duke study sample of 502 married men and women initially aged 46–71 was followed at 2-year intervals for 4 years (George & Weiler, 1981). Analysis was restricted to those who attended all interviews and remained married (278). Only 57 individuals of the sample were women aged 46–55 at the beginning of the study. Despite the authors' conclusions that sexual activity remained more stable over time than was previously suggested, inspection of their data reveals that 20% of the total group reported a decrease in activity, while 5% reported an increase. A limitation of the Duke study was that it obtained the sample from people enrolled with an insurance company and so was biased to middle- and upper-class employed people with few health problems, and most of the sample were aged over 55 years.

These problems were overcome by the Swedish study of Hallstrom (1977), who used population sampling in Gothenburg to find 800 subjects aged 38, 46, 50, and 54. He found a dramatic decline in sexual interest, capacity for orgasm, and coital frequency with increasing age. Not all women reported a decrease, but the majority of the postmenopausal women did. The number reporting an increase in interest or orgasmic capacity was small and less likely with rising age.

Hallstrom and Samuelsson (1990) carried out a prospective study utilizing the women in the Hallstrom (1977) cross-sectional study. The women were surveyed about their sexual desire on two occasions, 6 years apart. Data from 497 women, married and cohabiting, on both occasions was analyzed. The study found significantly decreased sexual desire between ages 46 and 60. After the age of 50 years, no subject was aware of a strong sexual desire; 27% reported a decrease in desire between the interviews and 10% an increase.

The Oxford study of Hawton, Gath, and Day (1994), involving 436 women aged 35–59 who had sexual partners, was derived from general practice registers. Interviewer-administered questions found that frequency of sexual intercourse, orgasm, and enjoyment of sexual activity with partner were most closely associated with younger age.

In an international cross-sectional study of women aged 20 to 70, a significant decline in sexual desire was observed with aging, but women were also observed to become less bothered or distressed by this with aging. As criteria for sexual dysfunction requires that women have both low levels of sexual function and are distressed by this, the results of the interaction of aging on these two parameters are that the sexual dysfunction of hypoactive sexual desire disorder (HSDD) does not increase with age (Hayes, Bennett, Dennerstein, Gurrin, & Fairley, 2007).

Thus, there is a consensus for a decline in sexual functioning (if not dysfunction) in midlife.

DOES CHANGE IN FEMALE SEXUALITY RELATE TO MENOPAUSAL STATUS OR TO INCREASING AGE?

The Gothenburg study of Hallstrom (1977) was in a better position to disentangle the effect of age on women's sexuality as it was age stratified instead of having age groups. Within each age group were pre-, peri-, and postmenopausal women. When age was controlled, the relationship between menopausal status and decreased sexual functioning remained highly significant, but when menopausal phase was held constant, the relationship between age and sexual functioning was not significant. These findings indicate a contribution from menopause independent of the age factor alone.

A significant, but small, independent adverse effect of menopausal status on female sexual interest and frequency of intercourse was also reported by Pfeiffer and Davis (1972) using stepwise regression on their cross-sectional Duke University study.

A postal survey of 474 women attending an ovarian screening program in London (Hunter, Battersby, & Whitehead, 1986) reported that the sexual functioning factor (dissatisfaction with sexual relationship, loss of sexual interest, vaginal dryness) increased significantly from pre- to peri- to postmenopausal. Sexual interest significantly decreased in peri- and postmenopausal women. Age was associated with reduced interest, but menopausal status was more important. The stepwise reduction in sexual interest from pre- to peri- to postmenopausal status remained when the effects of age were controlled. Vaginal dryness was more frequently reported in the postmenopausal period. Sexual satisfaction did not change significantly with menopausal status. Multiple regression found that sexual functioning (like vasomotor symptoms) was significantly associated with menopausal status only, unlike other factors, which were also associated with social class or employment status.

Conflicting evidence was reported by Hawton et al. (1994). The lack of menopausal effect may have related to small sample sizes in the age-matched groups. Using the same community sample, Osborn, Hawton, and Gath (1988) reported that sexual dysfunction was not associated with menopausal symptoms of hot flushes, sweats, vaginal dryness, or cessation of menses of at least 3 months.

In a further analysis of the WISHeS cohort, we found that women who had undergone surgical menopause (hysterectomy and bilateral oophorectomy) were twice as likely to have HSDD, and that the risk of HSDD occurring was highest if the women were still aged less than 50 (or before the mean age of natural menopause) (Dennerstein et al., 2006).

The Melbourne Women's Midlife Health Project set out to overcome many of the methodological limitations of previous research by utilizing a population-derived sample of 2,001 women aged 45 to 55 years and following the menstruating women through the menopausal transition with annual assessments. We questioned women at baseline about changes in sexual interest in the past 12 months, reasons for any changes, occurrence of sexual intercourse, and unusual pain on intercourse (Dennerstein et al., 1994b). Logistic regression was used to identify explanatory variables for change in sexual interest. The majority of women (62%) reported no change in sexual interest; 31% reported a decrease. Decline in sexual interest was significantly and adversely associated with natural menopause ($p < 0.01$); decreased well-being ($p < 0.001$); decreasing employment ($p < 0.01$); and symptomatology (vasomotor, $p < 0.05$; cardiopulmonary, $p < 0.001$; and skeletal, $p < 0.01$). Eleven to 12 years of education was associated with a lowered risk of decreased sexual functioning ($p < 0.01$). Heterogeneous results were reported by users of hormone therapies. Only 7% of women reported increased sexual interest, which was usually attributed by them to having a new partner. The results of this randomly derived population study of Australian-born women are strongly suggestive that the sexual functioning of some women is adversely affected by the natural menopause transition. The baseline cross-sectional analysis did not use a detailed or validated sexuality questionnaire, and no hormonal measures were available. These measures were introduced into our prospective study of 438 women who were still menstruating at baseline (Dennerstein et al., 2001). The main outcome measure was the shortened version of the Personal Experiences Questionnaire. By the late menopausal transition, there was a significant decline in sexual responsivity and the total score of sexual functioning and an increase in partner's problems. By the postmenopausal phase, there was a further decline in sexual responsivity, frequency of sexual activities, libido, and the total score and a significant increase in vaginal dyspareunia and partner's problems. The relationship with the partner and his ability to perform sexually was also adversely affected by the menopausal transition. To me, this suggests, somewhat intriguingly, that passing through the menopausal transition may alter the way women feel toward their partner and about sex.

How do these findings relate to what women themselves say? The sexuality questionnaire used does have a place for further comments. All the comments provided by the women relating to changes in their sexual behavior during the longitudinal phase of the study were downloaded and subjected to a preliminary content analysis. There was a variety of responses listed, but these fell predominantly into four groups. Some comments typical of women in each of these groups are described (Dennerstein, Lehert, Burger, Garamszegi, & Dudley, 2000):

> No partner: "No current partner"; "I have been widowed for two years"; "Have been divorced for some time—no partner for the last 5 years."
> Husband's problems: "My partner is impotent, so I don't have sex with him"; "Some things have changed since my husband's operation for bowel cancer 1 year ago"; "Husband currently working overseas with infrequent visits home."
> Her decreased interest: "The last five years have been quieter in the sex department than were the previous years"; "We seldom have sex. Our relationship is good but not sexual these days"; "Sexual intercourse is less exciting now than earlier years, and I seem to find other things take time partner & I spend together e.g. children, friends, work. Put less effort into making it 'fun.'" "At 47 I don't feel like instigating sex."
> Increased interest: "I was separated 3 years ago. I have a new partner (9 months duration). My new partner has transformed my life and love life"; "I don't think I have changed. The difference between now and 5 years ago is that I have a different partner"; "My sex life with the same partner has improved greatly from being satisfactory before in the past 5 years because we have deliberately made time for each other, such as going away for weekends once or twice a year."

DOES CHANGE IN FEMALE SEXUALITY IN THE MENOPAUSAL TRANSITION REFLECT HORMONAL CHANGE OR PSYCHOSOCIAL FACTORS?

Clearly, sexual functioning is affected by a range of health status and psychosocial variables in addition to hormonal factors.

Pfeiffer and Davis (1972), using the Duke University data and stepwise multiple regression, found that the variables contributing to sexual enjoyment, sexual interest, and frequency for women (after eliminating previous sexual experience to see effect of other independent variables) were marital status, age, education, postmenopause status, employment status (being employed [positively]). For sexual enjoyment these were marital status, age, education (positively).

The Gothenburg study of Hallstrom (1977) found sex may be protected for those in higher social classes because of better educational standards, greater freedom to express individuality, and increased freedom from traditional stereotyped sex roles. Factors characterizing the group with low sexual interest included high age, advanced menopausal phase, low mental health status, high depression, frequent dyspareunia, insufficient emotional support from husband, negative marital relationship, poor health of husband, high number of stressors, unhappy with work outside home, and some personality factors: low extraversion, exhibition, and rational dominance factors. No relationship was found between impaired interest and total 24-hour estrogen output in 146 postmenopausal women. Hallstrom concluded that sexuality is affected not only by the advancement of the climacteric but also by other factors, particularly social class, mental health status, personality, and other psychosocial factors.

The Gothenburg follow-up study of Hallstrom and Samuelsson (1990) found decrease in desire was predicted by age, high desire at first interview, lack of a confiding relationship, insufficient support from spouse, alcoholism in spouse, and major depression. Correlates of decreased desire at second interview included degree of mental disorder, anxiety neurosis, psychopathology rating scale score, use of psychotropic medications, duration of mental disorder between visits and life event stress. This follow-up study did not appear to examine the role of menopause.

The Oxford study (Hawton et al., 1994) found significant effects on female sexual functioning of marital adjustment, partner's age, and the duration of relationships. Higher neuroticism scores were associated with lower frequency of sexual intercourse. These authors concluded that aging of both women and their partners, length of a relationship, and marital adjustment were the more important influences on female sexual behavior, response, and enjoyment. Sexual dysfunction (Osborn et al., 1988) was significantly associated with increasing age, psychiatric disorder, neuroticism, and marital disharmony.

The longitudinal Danish study of Koster and Garde (1993) found that infrequent sexual desire at age 51 was predicted by baseline (at age 40) variables of coital activity less than once weekly, marital status single, physical fitness worse than peers, lower social status, and anticipation of decreased desire as a consequence of menopause and by variables recorded at age 45 of coital activity less than once weekly, marital status single, poor self-rated health, and anticipation of symptoms during menopause. The 51-year-old women's experience of frequency and change in sexual desire was not related to menopausal status but only to anticipation of declining sexual desire as a consequence of menopause. Low frequency in sexual desire correlated with women who reported "weak nerves," were single, and belonged to social class V. No variables were significantly associated with change in desire in this study, which may have reflected the 11-year time frame of the question.

In the Melbourne Women's Midlife Health Project, we found a significant association at baseline between decline in sexual interest and advanced menopausal status, decreased well-being, hormone therapy use, less than full-time paid employment, and presence of bothersome symptoms. Increased years of education were associated with a lower risk of declining sexual interest (Dennerstein et al., 1994b).

WHICH HORMONES RELATE TO THE DECLINE IN SEXUAL FUNCTIONING DURING THE MENOPAUSAL TRANSITION?

There is much controversy about the relative contribution of androgens and estrogen to female sexual functioning. Low libido, lack of well-being, blunted motivation, and fatigue are listed as major features of the proposed syndrome of female androgen deficiency (Davis, 1999; Davis & Burger, 1996). There are several problems in relation to the syndrome; as described, symptoms are vague and difficult to operationalize, and all can occur in other syndromes, such as major depressive disorder. As well, there is currently no definition of what comprises low levels of testosterone, reflecting variation in assays and lack of sensitivity. We do know that there are pronounced age-related and phase-related changes in androgens. Testosterone reaches an apparent peak in the early reproductive years (third decade) and then declines with age so that women in their 40s have approximately half the level of circulating total testosterone as that of women in their 20s (Zumoff et al., 1995). The rate of age-related decline in total testosterone then seems to slow and is not specifically related to menopause (Burger et al., 2000). As described previously, the amount of bioavailable testosterone actually increases as women become postmenopausal because of the decrease in SHBG (sex hormone-binding globulin; Burger et al., 2000). Dehydroepiandrosterone sulfate (DHEAS) shows similar changes to those described for testosterone but has an even more pronounced age-related decline after the early reproductive years that continues through to later life (Carlstrom et al., 1988; Ravaglia et al., 1996). There are both diurnal- and menstrual cycle-linked changes in testosterone and androstenedione (Judd & Yen, 1973). Testosterone (and androstenedione) levels are highest in the morning before 10:00 a.m. (Ankarberg & Norjavaara, 1999) and in the middle third of the menstrual cycle (Sanders & Bancroft, 1982). The menopausal transition is associated with a marked decrease in estradiol and increase in gonadotrophic hormones (Burger et al., 1999).

While some small observational studies provided suggestions that there is a link between androgens and sexual functioning in women, there is no body of substantial evidence based on large samples and using validated questionnaires to confirm these findings.

The longitudinal phase of our Melbourne Women's Midlife Health Project included annual hormone determinations (Burger et al., 1995). I was stunned to find that from early-to-late menopausal transition the percentage of women with short Personal Experiences Questionnaire scores indicating sexual dysfunction rose from 42% to 88% (Dennerstein et al., 2002). There were no significant changes in mood scores. In the early menopausal transition, those women with low total scores on the Short Personal Experiences Questionnaire had lower estradiol ($p = 0.052$) but similar androgen levels to those with higher scores (Dennerstein et al., 2002). Decreasing scores on the Short Personal

Experiences Questionnaire correlated with decreasing estradiol but not with androgens. We did not find any direct relationships of hormone levels to mood scores (Dennerstein et al., 2002).

The Melbourne study has shown that with natural menopause the detrimental effect on female sexual function is the decline in estradiol levels. (Dennerstein et al., 2002, 2005). Statistical modeling using structural equations can demonstrate the relative importance on each domain of sexual function of changes in estradiol to that of other factors such as symptoms, mood, and relationship factors (Dennerstein et al., 2005, 2007a). The Melbourne data showed that while estradiol level did affect sexual response significantly, prior level of sexual response (reflecting developmental factors and life experiences) and current psychosocial factors such as change in partner status, feelings for partner, and mood have relatively greater effects on sexual response. In contrast, relationship factors had less effect on vaginal dryness /dyspareunia. For these aspects, the only significant determining factors were prior level of vaginal dryness/dyspareunia and estradiol.

Hormonal change will not occur at the same age and in the same way for each woman. These changes are not linear; the exact trajectory of that change can be modeled and the impact of initial level, final level, slope of decline, and age can be modeled for symptoms and each sexual domain of function (Dennerstein et al., 2007b). Thus, powerful statistical techniques can be utilized to help unravel the relative effects of hormonal change to other factors as we seek to uncover information on how to maintain health and quality of life as women age. Sexual response (sexual interest, arousal, enjoyment, orgasm) was significantly associated with the final estradiol value. Thus, this indicates that estradiol replacement therapy would be expected to help maintain sexual function in these naturally postmenopausal women (Dennerstein et al., 2007b).

At 11-year follow-up of the Melbourne women, we noted that women who were still using hormone therapy then had significantly greater sexual responsivity and higher frequency of sexual activities than nonusers, suggesting that hormone therapy use appeared to be helping these women maintain their sexual function into their sixth decades (Dennerstein et al., 2008).

The most reliable way of determining response to hormones is via the randomized, double-blind clinical trial. In a classic study I carried out nearly three decades ago (Dennerstein et al., 1980), 50 oophorectomized women were randomized to receive 3 months each of 0.05 mg ethinyl estradiol, 250 μg levonorgestrel, the combination of the ethinyl estradiol and levonorgestrel (Nordiol), and placebo in randomized order. No androgen comparison was included in the study design, which nevertheless demonstrated powerful effects of ethinyl estradiol on mood and sexuality. I found that ethinyl estradiol had a beneficial effect on female sexual desire, enjoyment, and vaginal lubrication (all measured by ordinal scales) and on orgasmic frequency (recorded daily). The combination pill was less beneficial than estrogen alone, but levonorgestrel was found to be more inhibitory. Thus, these results suggest that women on continuous combined preparations of hormone therapy may not have as beneficial a result as those on estrogen therapy only, and that the addition of a progestin has an inhibitory effect on sexuality.

Oophorectomized women have lost the important contribution of ovarian production to the total androgen pool. They have also lost ovarian production of estrogens and progesterone. The incremental improvement for oophorecto-mized women of adding androgen to estrogen replacement has been assessed (Davis et al., 1995; Sarrel, Dobay, & Wiita, 1998; Sherwin, Gelfand, & Brender, 1985). These studies have found testosterone to have significant positive incremental effects over that of estrogen alone on mood or on aspects of sexual functioning. It was not clear from these studies whether testosterone was acting physiologically or as a pharmacological agent with a pronounced psychotropic effect. Whereas earlier trials used doses that were often above physiologic levels, later trials used lower doses of hormones similar to the upper end of laboratory ranges (Shifren et al., 2000). Subsequent double-blind randomized trials have confirmed a significant beneficial effect of testoster-one patches on female sexual interest (Braunstein et al., 2005; Buster et al., 2005; Simon et al., 2005).

There have been relatively few negative trials, suggesting that whatever the role of testosterone physiologically on mood and female sexuality, testosterone administration can have a powerful pharmacological effect (Kotz, Alexander, & Dennerstein, 2006).

IMPLICATIONS FOR CLINICIANS

Population-based studies such as our Melbourne Women's Midlife Health Project have found a deterioration in several aspects of female sexual func-tioning associated with the midlife years. The analysis also demonstrates that hormonal change is only one aspect of the many factors that impact sexual functioning. These include the woman's premorbid level of sexual function-ing, presence of bothersome symptoms, well-being, stress, and the presence and quality of the sexual relationship with a partner.

When mid-aged women report sexual problems, I take a detailed history involving the woman and her partner, alone and together. Given the range of factors affecting sexual functioning and the significantly more powerful effect of partner factors over that of hormonal factors, I utilize a broadly based biopsychosocial approach. I specifically ask for bothersome symptoms that are known to be responsive to hormone therapy. These should be treated, as they impact aspects of sexual functioning as well as causing distress in their own right. I give consideration to supplementation with estrogen if the woman has other indicators of estrogen deficiency (hot flashes, genital atro-phic changes, oophorectomy) and the deterioration in sexual functioning is time related by the woman to the menopausal transition, natural or induced. Bilaterally oophorectomized women may benefit from the addition of testos-terone to estrogen. With each woman, I discuss contraindications (absolute and relative) to the use of either hormone and risks and side effects of hor-mone therapies. But, hormonal prescription alone is rarely enough. I give par-ticular attention to the assessment of the relationship with the partner and other stressors in the woman's life. Recall that we found from women's com-ments that the midlife transition allows the opportunity for positive change in sexual relationships if couples increase their intimacy at this time.

Finally, reflecting on my 35 years of research on this topic, I can conclude that sex steroids such as estrogen, progestins, and androgens have subtle but important effects on female sexual functioning. These effects can be over-ridden by powerful psychosocial factors, such as a new relationship or the effects of past learning, which affect premorbid functioning. In every patient presenting to my practice, an individual approach is needed to sort out the relative role of these factors so that appropriate therapy can be planned.

REFERENCES

Ankarberg, C., & Norjavaara, E. (1999). Diurnal rhythm of testosterone secretion before and throughout puberty in healthy girls: Correlation with 17betaestradiol and dehydroepiandrosterone sulfate. *Journal of Clinical Endocrinology and Metabolism, 84*, 975–984.

Braunstein, G., Sundwall, D., Katz, M., Shifren, J., Buster, J., Simon, J., et al. (2005). Safety and efficacy of a testosterone patch for the treatment of hypoactive sexual desire disorder in surgically menopausal women: A randomized, placebo-controlled trial. *Archives of Internal Medicine, 165*, 1582–1589.

Burger, H., Dudley, E., Cui, J., Dennerstein, L., & Hopper, J. (2000). A prospective longitudinal study of serum testosterone, dehydroepiandrosterone sulfate, and sex hormone-binding globulin levels through the menopause transition. *Journal of Clinical Endocrinology and Metabolism, 85*, 2832–2838. This article from the Melbourne Women's Midlife Health Project details androgen levels across the menopausal transition.

Burger, H., Dudley, E., Hopper, J., Groome, N., Guthrie, J. R., Green, A., et al. (1999). Prospectively measured levels of serum FSH, estradiol and the dimeric inhibins during the menopausal transition in a population-based cohort of women. *Journal of Clinical Endocrinology and Metabolism, 84*, 4025–4030. This article from the Melbourne Women's Midlife Health Project details changes in estradiol and the gonadotrophins across the menopausal transition.

Burger, H., Dudley, E., Hopper, J., Shelley, J., Greene, A., Smith, A., et al. (1995). The endocrinology of the menopausal transition: A cross-sectional study of a population-base sample. *Journal of Clinical Endocrinology and Metabolism, 80*, 3537–3545.

Buster, J., Kingsberg, S., Aguirre, O., Brown, C., Breaux, J., Buch, A., et al. (2005). Testosterone patch for low sexual desire in surgically menopausal women: A randomized trial. *Obstetrics and Gynecology, 105*, 944–952.

Carlstrom, K., Brody, S., Lunell, N. O., Lagrelius, G., Mollerstrom, A., Pousette, G., et al. (1988). Dehydroepiandrosterone sulphate and dehydroepiandrosterone in serum: Differences related to and sex. *Maturitas, 10*, 297–306.

Davis, S. R. (1999). Androgen treatment in women. *Medical Journal of Australia, 170*, 545–549.

Davis, S. R., & Burger, H. G. (1996). Androgens and the postmenopausal woman. *Journal of Clinical Endocrinology and Metabolism, 81*, 2759–2764.

Davis, S. R., McCloud, P., Strauss, B. J. G., & Burger, H. (1995). Testosterone enhances estradiol 's effects on postmenopausal bone density and sexuality. *Maturitas, 21*, 227–236.

Dennerstein, L. (1996). Well-being, symptoms and the menopausal transition. *Maturitas, 23*, 147–157. This is a review article prepared for the World Health Organization.

Dennerstein, L. (1999). Psychosexual effects of hormonal contraception. *Gynaecology Forum, 4*(3), 13–16.

Dennerstein, L. (2000). Menopause and sexuality. In J. M. Ussher (Ed.), *Women's health: Contemporary international perspectives* (pp. 190–196). Leicester, UK: British Psychological Society Books.

Dennerstein, L., Burrows, G. D., Hyman, G., & Sharpe, K. (1979). Hormone therapy and affect. *Maturitas, 1*, 247–259. This is a classic double-blind randomized clinical trial of the effects of the components of the oral contraceptive pill on mood.

Dennerstein, L., Burrows, G., Hyman, G., & Sharpe, K. (1980). Hormones and sexuality: Effects of estrogen and progesterone. *Obstetrics and Gynecology, 56*, 316–322. This is a classic double-blind randomized clinical trial of the effects of the components of the oral contraceptive pill on sexuality.

Dennerstein, L., Dudley, E., & Burger, H. (2001). Are changes in sexual functioning during midlife due to aging or menopause? *Fertility and Sterility, 76*, 456–460. This article from the Melbourne Women's Midlife Health Project details how female sexual functioning changes with aging and with menopausal stages.

Dennerstein, L., Gotts, G., Brown, J., Morse, C., Farley, T., & Pinol, A. (1994a). The relationship between the menstrual cycle and female sexual interest. *Psychoneuroendocrinology, 19*, 293–304. This article involves a prospective observational study using daily diaries and daily hormone levels.

Dennerstein, L., Guthrie, J., Hayes, R., DeRogatis, L., & Lehert, P. (2008). Sexual function, dysfunction and sexual distress in a prospective, population-based sample of mid-aged, Australian-born women. *Journal of Sexual Medicine*, 5, 2291–2299.

Dennerstein, L., Koochaki, P., Barton, I., & Graziottin, A. (2006). Hypoactive sexual desire disorder in menopausal women: A survey of western European women. *Journal of Sexual Medicine*, 3, 212–222.

Dennerstein, L., Lehert, P., & Burger, H. (2005). The relative effects of hormones and relationship factors on sexual function of women through the natural menopausal transition. *Fertility and Sterility, 84*, 174–180.

Dennerstein, L., Lehert, P., Burger, H., Garamszegi, G., & Dudley, E. (2000). Menopause and sexual functioning. In T. Aso, T. Yanaihara, & S. Fujimoto (Eds.), *The menopause at the millennium. Proceedings of the Ninth International Menopause Society World Congress on the Menopause* (pp. 46–53). New York: Parthenon. This chapter includes the qualitative data from the Melbourne Women's Midlife Health Project.

Dennerstein, L., Lehert, P., Burger, H., & Guthrie, J. (2007b). New findings from non-linear longitudinal modelling of menopausal hormone changes. *Human Reproductive Update, 13*, 551–557.

Dennerstein, L,. Lehert, P., Guthrie, J., & Burger, H. (2007a). Modelling women's health during the menopausal transition: A longitudinal analysis. *Menopause, 14*, 53–62.

Dennerstein, L., Lehert, P., Koochaki, P., Graziottin, A., Leiblum, S., & Alexander, J. (2007). A symptomatic approach to understanding women's health experiences: A cross-cultural comparison of women aged 20 to 70 years. *Menopause, 14*, 688–696.

Dennerstein, L., Lehert, P., & Riphagen, F. (1989). Post partum depression—risk factors. *Journal of Psychosomatic Obstetrics and Gynaecology, 10*, 53–67. This details a prospective study of changes in mood from pregnancy to postpartum.

Dennerstein, L., Randolph, J., Taffe, J., Dudley, E., & Burger, H. (2002). Hormones, mood, sexuality and the menopausal transition. *Fertility and Sterility*, *77*(Supplement 4), 42–48. This article from the Melbourne Women's Midlife Health Project details how changes in female sexual functioning are related to hormone levels.

Dennerstein, L., Smith, A., Morse, C., & Burger, H. (1994b). Sexuality and the menopause. *Journal of Psychosomatic Obstetrics and Gynecology*, *15*, 59–66. This article from the Melbourne Women's Midlife Health Project details the results from the baseline phase (cross sectional) on sexuality.

Dennerstein, L., Wood, C., & Burrows, G. (1977). Sexual response following hysterectomy and oophorectomy. *Obstetrics and Gynecology*, *49*, 92–96.

George, L., & Weiler, S. (1981). Sexuality in middle and later life; the effects of age, cohort, and gender. *Archives of General Psychiatry*, *38*, 919–923.

Hallstrom, T. (1977). Sexuality in the climacteric. *Clinics in Obstetrics and Gynaecology*, *4*, 227–239.

Hallstrom, T., & Samuelsson, S. (1990). Changes in women's sexual desire in middle life: The longitudinal study of women in Gothenburg. *Archives of Sexual Behavior*, *19*, 259–268.

Hawton, K., Gath, D., & Day A. (1994). Sexual function in a community sample of middle-aged women with partners: Effects of age, marital, socioeconomic, psychiatric, gynecological, and menopausal factors. *Archives of Sexual Behavior*, *23*, 375–395.

Hayes, R., Bennett, C., Dennerstein, L., Gurrin, L., & Fairley, C. (2007). Modeling response rates in surveys of female sexual difficulty and dysfunction. *Journal of Sexual Medicine, 4*, 286–295.

Hunter, M., Battersby, R., & Whitehead, M. (1986). Sexual dysjunction among middle-aged women in the community. *Maturitas*, *7*, 217–228.

James, W. (1983). Decline in coital rates with spouses' ages and duration of marriage. *Journal of Biosocial Science*, *15*, 83–87.

Judd, H., & Yen, S. (1973). Serum androstenedione and testosterone levels during the menstrual cycle. *Journal of Clinical Endocrinology and Metabolism*, *36*, 475–481.

Koster, A., & Garde, K. (1993). Sexual desire and menopausal development: A prospective study of Danish women born in 1936. *Maturitas*, *16*, 49–60.

Kotz, K., Alexander, J., & Dennerstein, L. (2006). Estrogen and androgen hormone therapy and quality of life in surgically postmenopausal women. *Journal of Women's Health, 15*, 898–908.

McKinlay, J., McKinlay, S., & Brambilla, D. J. (1987). Health status and utilization behavior associated with menopause. *American Journal of Epidemiology*, *125*, 110–121.

Morse, C. A., Smith, A., Dennerstein, L., Green, A., Hopper, J., & Burger, H. (1994). The treatment-seeking woman at menopause. *Maturitas*, *18*, 161–173.

Osborn, M., Hawton, K., & Gath, D. (1988). Sexual dysfunction among middle aged women in the community. *British Medical Journal*, *296*, 959–962.

Pfeiffer, E., & Davis, G. (1972). Determinants of sexual behavior in middle and old age. *Journal of the American Geriatric Society*, *20*, 151–158.

Pfeiffer, E., Verwoerdt, A., & Davis, G. (1972). Sexual behaviour in middle life. *American Journal of Psychiatry*, *128*, 1262–1267.

Ravaglia, G., Forti, P., Maioli, F., Bernardi, M., Pratelli, L., Pizzoferrato, A., et al. (1996). The relationship of dehydroepiandrosterine sulphate (DHEAS) to endocrine-metabolic parameters and functional status in the oldest-old: Results from an Italian study on healthy free-living over 90-year-olds. *Journal of Clinical Endocrinology and Metabolism, 81*, 1173–1178.

Ryan, M., Dennerstein, L., & Pepperell, R. (1989). Psychological aspects of hysterectomy—a prospective study. *British Journal of Psychiatry, 154*, 516–522.

Sanders, D., & Bancroft, J. (1982). Hormones and the sexuality of women—the menstrual cycle. *Journal of Clinical Endocrinology and Metabolism, 11*, 639–659.

Sarrel, P., Dobay, B., & Wiita, B. (1998). Estrogen and estrogen-androgen replacement in postmenopausal women dissatisfied with estrogen-only therapy. *Journal of Reproductive Medicine, 43*, 847–856.

Sarrel, P., & Whitehead, M. (1985). Sex and menopause: Defining the issues. *Maturitas, 7*, 217–224.

Sherwin, B., Gelfand, M., & Brender, W. (1985). Androgen enhances sexual motivation in females: A prospective, crossover study of sex steroid administration in the surgical menopause. *Psychosomatic Medicine, 47*, 339–351.

Shifren, J., Braunstein, G., Simon, J., Casson, R., Buster, J., Redmond, G., et al. (2000). Transdermal testosterone treatment in women with impaired sexual function after oophorectomy. *New England Journal of Medicine, 343*, 682–688.

Simon, J., Braunstein, G., Nachtigall, L., Utian, W., Katz, M., Miller, S., et al. (2005). Testosterone patch increases sexual activity and desire in surgically menopausal women with hypoactive sexual desire disorder. *Journal of Clinical Endocrinology and Metabolism, 90*, 5226–5233.

Zumoff, B., Strain, G. W., Miller, L. K., & Rosner, W. (1995). Twenty-four hour mean plasma testosterone concentration declines with age in normal premenopausal women. *Journal of Clinical Endocrinology and Metabolism, 80*, 1429–1430.

IV

SEXUAL DYSFUNCTION: MEN'S SEXUAL ISSUES

Fourteen

The Sexual Challenges and Dilemmas of Young Single Men

DEREK C. POLONSKY, MD

INTRODUCTION

Talk to most parents about adolescents and sex and their reactions range from denial ("Not my kid!") to confusion ("I don't know how to talk about it") to panic ("Where do I get total body condoms or stainless steel chastity belts?"). Therapists often mirror this discomfort by being hesitant to initiate direct discussions about sex with teens. There is a concern that it may be intrusive or inappropriate. When the gender of therapist and patient is different, therapists may believe that it should be left to the teen to bring up the topic. In addition, most physicians have little formal teaching in human sexuality at either medical school or residency training programs (Leiblum, 2001).

The reluctance to deal directly with sex is unfortunate. Most teens are hungry for reliable information. They are usually poorly served. Parents avoid talking about it; sex education programs in schools cover the dangers of sex (have sex, you'll die), the biology of sex, and a cursory comment that masturbation is normal if not overdone. Pleasure and sex are rarely mentioned in the same sentence (Brown & Brown, 2006). The mechanics of sex, what problems people encounter and how to manage them, and the emotions associated with partner sex are almost always avoided.

The frequency of sexual problems for adult men is high, often having origins in early sexual exploration (Laumann, Gagnon, Michael, & Michaels, 1994). Although treatment for individuals and couples who have had long-standing sexual difficulties is often helpful, many relationships have been defined, silently, by sex that is almost always disappointing. A sense of being "sexually incompetent" becomes internalized.

I believe that it is important and helpful to ask and talk about sex with adolescent patients because it provides an opportunity to positively influence their emotional and sexual development. I try to convince you of this in this chapter.

ADOLESCENT SEXUAL DEVELOPMENTAL TASKS

The developmental tasks for the late adolescent involve

1. Separation (emotionally and physically) from parents
2. Solidification of sexual identity through experience with masturbation and partners
3. Creation of new attachments to others in which understanding of the self and relationships becomes increasingly sophisticated

Think of a three-legged stool as a metaphor for these tasks: Without all three legs, sexual and emotional development may have an unstable base.

In recent years, much attention has been directed to the emotional development of boys (Zilbergeld, 1999). Until age 6 to 8, it is fine for boys to be vulnerable and dependent. Beyond that point, emotional expression is discouraged (big boys don't cry), and as Thompson and Kindlon (2000) point out, they do not receive much education in acquiring an emotional vocabulary. As they mature into young men, they are often berated for not being emotionally expressive. When it comes to sexual development, boys frequently have to fend for themselves; they get little useful guidance from adults about the range of sexual behaviors and the need to be prepared to encounter powerful feelings in themselves and their partners. Most adolescents get their sex education from television, magazines, and currently the Internet (Kunkel, Eyal, Finnerty, Biely, & Donnerstein, 2005). The portrayal of sex and relationships in media is often unrealistic and destructive. Sex is equated with being "cool" by exercising power. Rarely is there any expression of uncertainty or examples of reciprocal relationships.

Regrettably, medical education parallels the avoidance of discussion about sex. Physicians rarely approach the issue of sex directly, are uncomfortable with the topic, and often rationalize avoiding it. I want to encourage my readers to "jump in," ask about sex, and tolerate their initial discomfort. I recall struggling with my own awkwardness when talking with my adult patients about sex. It took me a while to develop a workable personal style. I was again in unfamiliar terrain when I worked with teens, late adolescents, and young adults. I sounded like a clumsy self-conscious parent. I was not prepared to manage the monosyllabic responses. I thought was perceived as old and out of touch. I helped myself by imagining what I would have found helpful. My friends and I did talk about masturbation and sex, agreed that it was fun, and generally embraced it as a positive pastime. I knew the engineering details of intercourse, although I had no idea of how to get there. What actually went on "down there" for girls? Where was "it"? How did you get in? That sex was an endeavor that involved two people escaped my imagination because I was so lost in the worry about how to do it.

My dermatologist gave me an idea of how to talk to adolescents. When I was in the midst of what to me was an outbreak of facial leprosy, he addressed me directly and respectfully. Acne, he said, is awful for teens; it is on your face, you feel self-conscious about it, and you are convinced no one would want to be near you. He explained, using drawings, the blockage of the sebaceous gland ducts, and told me that he would be able to help. Although it did not change my appearance, having someone speak about what I felt, say out loud what I could not, and having him not talk down to me was a great relief that I have always remembered. I strive to offer this kind of support, guidance, and encouragement to my teen and young adult patients.

Sexuality needs to be seen as an essential part of psychological development. For some adolescents with sexual concerns, information and guidance about sex is all that is needed. For others, the complexities of their emotional lives are paramount in the therapy.

The nature of sexual difficulties for adolescent boys includes:

1. *Lack of information, worry about performance, and nervousness about sex* with a partner are universal. Some adolescents master these tasks smoothly, while many struggle with conflicts that affect sexual functioning.
2. *Erectile difficulties* affect about 10% of young men and improve readily with guidance, support, and at times a PDE5 (phosphodiesterase type 5 inhibitor).
3. *Premature ejaculation* (PE) is extremely common (between 30 and 40% of men), and *retarded ejaculation* (RE) affects about less than 3% of men.
4. *Sexual abuse experience* is seen in approximately 15% of boys. The impact on relationships and on sexual development may be considerable.
5. *Internet pornography* is almost universal among young teens, with some surprising consequences.

Boys often suffer silently when sex does not go well. It is rare that they will admit it to friends for fear of ridicule, and most will not ask their parents for advice. The following case involves a high school senior who was developing well but reached a sexual block. His was a close family, connections were valued, and he had just emerged from a 2-year separation struggle with his parents. By dealing quickly and directly with his sexual problem, his emotional growth was not stifled.

Greg, a High School Senior: The Sexual Block

- "I can't keep it up!"
- Long-term girlfriend.
- Reassurance, coaching, plus Viagra.
- Information please:
  "Is my penis big enough?"
  "I don't know what I'm doing when I go down on her."
  "How do we argue, fight, and resolve differences?"
  "Why would a girl want to give me oral sex?"
- "I did it without Viagra!"

Greg was a senior in high school, was in a committed relationship, and was unable to maintain an erection to have intercourse. He and his girlfriend cuddled, kissed, fondled, and had orgasms together. When it came to getting his penis in her vagina, "limp dick" ruled. Greg was freaked out. It is a huge step for teens to admit to someone that they are having a difficult time with any feelings, let alone sex. My first step therefore was affirming his gutsiness in seeking help:

Greg, first, let me say that I am impressed with how you have handled this. Talking with your dad was gutsy, and coming to see me was brave. Many guys have a hard time sexually, although they will never say so. The fact that you are in a close relationship, that you have perfectly fine erections in all the activities you describe including masturbation is great. I am sure that you will get over this. "Limp dick" is a guy's worst nightmare. You feel like a real loser, humiliated with no clue what to do. Donna sounds like she is caring and supportive, which is a key in dealing with this.

I will not detail the richness of Greg's family history; it was solid, connected and supportive. Greg and Donna talked easily and openly together. Kissing and touching was fun. They were comfortable with genital play and oral sex.

Greg, sex can be really enjoyable when it is reciprocal. Do you go down on her?
Greg said that he did, but "I don't know what the hell I am doing!" Using illustrations from one of my books, I showed him the details of a woman's genitals, including techniques of oral sex. Talking with an adult about sex being fun and pleasurable is rare for most teens. It is invaluable.
I asked Greg what they did if he could not get it up and suggested that they go back to what had earlier been arousing, then try again.
Greg, sex does not have to go in a straight line: A to B to C to D to intercourse! You can go from A to C, C to B. And if going to D does not work the first time, it does not mean the failure is preordained.

VIAGRA, LEVITRA, CIALIS: PHOSPHODIESTERASE INHIBITORS

The PDE5s can be of enormous value with adolescents who have erectile difficulties for which inexperience and anxiety are the probable cause. Every sexual encounter is colored by the worry of failure, which in turn guarantees it. They have not experienced the pleasure of having a penis in a partner's vagina or anus. (Remember, erectile dysfunction [ED] also affects gay adolescents.) All they know is the dread and shame associated with trying to accomplish this. PDE5s are an adjunct to the therapy and make it possible for the teen to feel some success. Their own experience of pleasure is now available to lessen the impact of the familiar dread. I do not prescribe the PDE5 until I have a clear understanding of the problem and a picture of the teen's relationship with his partner and family. My aim is not to be the engineer of a "steel penis"; it is to help strengthen all three legs of the "development stool."

Greg was eager to try the medication. I described how the PDE5 worked and said I was certain that he would have a great erection that would not fade. I encouraged him to ask Donna to help guide his penis into her vagina. An e-mail a few days later was titled "We did it! Thanks!"

Within a few months, he no longer needed the PDE5. At our last meeting, he told me how he and three of his close friends got into a discussion about sex. One admitted that he had PE; another talked about ED, and when Greg joined in and told them about his experience, they were incredulous that a "shrink would talk so directly about sex." Three years later, Greg is grounded emotionally and is confident sexually. He has had a few long-term relationships with pleasurable, problem-free sex. My therapy with Greg was not complicated. I provided a safe place for him to share his worry; I saw the obvious strength in his family and built on what he had started with his girlfriend.

James's Story: Emotional Development Interrupted

- Erectile difficulties
- Urological problem; hypospadias
- Close relationships problematic
- Drinking problem
- Family of origin: early divorce; repeated losses
- The "corrective emotional experience"

James's treatment was far more complicated than that of Greg, lasting for 3 years. His initial presentation was sexual, although family relationships were troubled. We spent some time addressing the sexual problem before I was able to understand the protective nature of his ED. James was 20, a college sophomore who had difficulty getting or maintaining an erection with his partners, none of whom were long term. In addition, he used porn frequently to masturbate and was often drunk when he had sex. While he had a reputation as the comedian at high school, he avoided dating, often feeling that the girls were out of his reach. He had intercourse for the first time as a freshman in college but initially had a very difficult time getting an erection.

His parents were divorced when he was 2, and for several years his father was mostly absent from his life. He was born with a mild hypospadias (where the urethral opening is lower down on the shaft of the penis), which was corrected early. He had recurrent symptoms of pain and poor urine stream as a teenager, which required repeated surgical procedures.

I have condensed several of my comments to James as we discussed sex.

I think that when you try to have sex with people you don't know, or when you are drinking too much, you make it more difficult for yourself. When you are with someone you trust, you can let her know about your difficulties. If she is able to be supportive it is likely that your anxiety will diminish with improved functioning.

Try not to monitor the progress of your hard on; it takes you out of the connection with the other person. The more you do this, the more you will worry, and probably the less it will work. Instead, pay attention to the physical feelings in your penis. Let that pleasure be the engine that drives the erection.

Listen, I know this is hard, but the more you can talk with your partner about what you like, and learn what she likes, the better it is going to be for you both.

I don't have a moral position about most porn, James, but if you use that to get turned on, you will find it difficult to get turned on by your partner.

There were many interruptions in James's therapy, the meaning of which only became clearer several years later. I use e-mail and texting as adjuncts to my work with adolescents, believing that it should be part of therapy with this age group. Weekly meetings are insufficient given everything that happens in their lives; e-mail and texting adds a dimension to the therapy. The "voice" in the e-mail is often different from that in the office, with each enhancing the other. I e-mailed James periodically when he would disappear, although it took a while for me to realize how important this was to him.

In the third year of his therapy, the weakness in each of the three legs of his developmental stool became clear. James was devastated by his parents' divorce and the loss of a connection with his father. This was repeated several times with the subsequent men in his mother's life. Having hypospadias complicated a positive investment in his sexuality and penis. His penis, in fact, became the "emotional circuit breaker." The fact that it did not work unless he was drunk spared him the dread and anxiety associated with attachments and their anticipated inevitable loss. The transference, my being a reliable, constant figure in his life, always inviting him back and not giving up on him finally facilitated his reconnecting with his father in a mature way, his cutting down on his drinking, and his entering into a relationship with a girl he liked and with whom he could have good sex without alcohol.

James's treatment had many interruptions. I remember being told in training not to pursue the resistant patient. I have learned the value of rejecting that advice with adolescents who needed me to reach out actively. Separation and attachment were treacherous for him, and alcohol was the medication he used to limit his awareness of loss, disappointment, and vulnerability in relationships. Sexual dysfunction was the symptom that brought him to treatment. His vulnerability regarding attachment and loss was, however, the central theme.

A year after treatment ended, I received an e-mail:

> Things with Anne and me have been great. We never really have any sexual problems and always have fun. We are both understanding and open with sex so it's been really good for me. If I'm thinking too much or having a problem getting hard or want something, I just tell her and vice versa. It's great and always fulfilling.

It is tempting to think that all sexual difficulties for adolescents are psychological. A differential diagnosis needs to include consideration of vascular and hormonal pathology. I have seen several young men who had months of therapy to understand their "anxiety about sex," only to find that their levels of testosterone were extremely low. There will always be a secondary psychological overlay, but it is particularly burdensome to feel both psychologically and sexually impaired.

Bill (23): It Is Not Always in the Mind

- No good erection since age 15.
- Pushed himself to date and develop sexual skills.
- Detailed sexual history did not sound like primary performance anxiety.
- Urological consult with angiography.
- Intrapenile injections: "I am no longer a virgin!"
- Microvascular surgery.

Bill was a college senior referred by his internist for ED. He was distressed and anxious about not being able to get a good erection. At the time, he did not have morning erections, and masturbation only resulted in a semisoft penis. Because of this pattern of consistent poor erections, I suspected that the cause might be physiological and not psychological. Bill began masturbating when he was 12 and had positive feelings about it. Erections were frequent and reliable, and his orgasms were pleasurable. He had a warm, connected family and many friends. Around 14, he noticed it was difficult to get erect. He did not appear to have any conflict about sex, and I was impressed that he pushed himself to date in spite of the ED and became more knowledgeable in giving his partners pleasure.

Pelvic trauma has been identified as a cause of ED in which blood supply to the penis is damaged. I asked him if he had ever fallen on the bar of a bicycle, and that was the key to understanding the problem. This *had* occurred when he was about 14, and he subsequently noticed the erectile difficulty. I referred him to a urologist, who confirmed through blood vessel studies that he had only 50% of normal penile blood flow, and corrective microvascular surgery was suggested (Goldstein, Bastuba, Lurie, & Lubisch, 2008).

He was preoccupied with not wanting to graduate college a virgin and while awaiting the surgery began using the trimix intrapenile injections, a testament to his motivation. Once he gained confidence with the procedure, he tried it with his girlfriend, and at our next visit came in beaming: "I am no longer a virgin!" He did undergo the surgery, and initial results were positive.

The key with Bill related to his having a solid family; supportive, sex-positive parents; many friends; and several girlfriends. His persistence in the face of his ED seemed inconsistent with a primarily psychological cause.

Max and Panic Attacks: Unless You Ask, They Will Not Tell

Unless your patient's presenting problem is specifically sexual, do not assume that he will bring up anything sexual unless *you ask directly!*

- Panic attacks for several years, but now under better control.
- Asking about sex: Some guys come quickly, some have trouble getting it up, and some do not feel like it.
- "I'm 'quick on the trigger'; it is very embarrassing."
- Combined medication, support, and masturbation exercises.

Max was 23 and was referred to me because of his history of panic attacks. Public speaking was often the precipitant. In the course of my initial evaluation, I asked about sex, talking in the "third-person invisible."

> When it comes to sex, some guys have trouble getting or keeping it up, some guys come very quickly, and some guys don't much feel like it. Has any of this happened with you?

He immediately said that he was glad that I asked that. He had always come very quickly, and it had been a source of worry for him.

He came from a close, supportive family, and relationships were solid. He had many friends and was very successful academically. He had dated a number of women, and the emotional connections had been good.

My treatment plan included cognitive support for his panic and anxiety, as-needed antianxiety medication (clonazepam [Klonopin]), with the plan to address the PE at some later time. Max's panic became more manageable and less frequent, and the discussion returned to his sexual function. I explained to Max that PE affects between 30 and 40% of men, and that worry about coming quickly becomes preoccupying. The usual suggestions to try and distract oneself, use anesthetic jelly, or think of a baseball game never work. I have suggested a program (Polonsky, 2000) that involves masturbating regularly with some specific instructions:

- Masturbate until you feel that an orgasm is approaching. Then stop, and using the second hand of a watch, wait 1 minute. Resume masturbating and time how long it takes to get to the point just before orgasm. Stop again and wait 1 minute. Repeat this four or five times and then allow the sensations to build and come. (The purpose of the timing is twofold. Men often feel reassured when there is a defined task, and with frequent practice, they will notice that it takes longer, after first getting to the preorgasm place, to get there again. He is able to notice improvement and be encouraged.)

- Once you feel more control, masturbate until you feel you are getting closer to orgasm (7.5 on a 1 to 10 scale, where 10 is orgasm). Slow the masturbation, try to keep the level of arousal constant, and stay at that level for about 10 to 15 minutes. With increased practice, the threshold for orgasm begins to rise, and more stimulation is required to get there. The therapist often needs to provide encouragement to keep doing this, but often the changes noticed are motivating.

- The third phase is to use a lubricant (K-Y jelly, Astroglide, Lubriderm) because this more closely approximates the sensations of being inside a vagina. The same technique applies, with the idea of maintaining the high level of arousal for 15 minutes or longer. With this longer time, orgasm is usually more intense.

- When a partner enters the picture, talk with her (or him) about the concern with PE, and enlist the partner's help. The same kind of practice is required with penetrative sex as outlined. Although there is less spontaneity, this will aid in developing better control. Take turns in giving each other sexual pleasure.

At this time, although Max is not dating, he is doing his "orgasm control exercises" religiously. It should be noted that SSRIs (selective serotonin reuptake inhibitors), which in many instances delay ejaculation, have been used to treat PE. I am hesitant to use therapeutic doses of a medication for its side effect but have found that 25 to 50 mg of clomipramine (Anafranil) can be helpful when the behavioral approach is not effective.

Premature ejaculation is suffered silently. Boys simply will not talk about problems, emotional or sexual. They know that they are reaching orgasm quickly; their partner might ask what is wrong, sympathetically or critically, and they struggle with shame and embarrassment. The subjective importance to boys of having a "great penis" that does "great things" and is an "object to be admired" should not be minimized. PE is a real downer to sexual confidence. One "leg" of the development stool is missing and interferes significantly with confident attachments. I gradually realized that specific details of *how* boys masturbate were necessary to understand how to help them change; many boys race to orgasm, knowing that they can get another erection soon. Without knowing it, they are training themselves to come fast. When teachers or parents talk about the "M" word, it would be valuable if they acknowledged that masturbation felt really good and was fun. They might add that it is a way to learn about one's sexual feelings. I point out that the journey to orgasm is arousing, relaxing, and extremely pleasurable. I encourage my young patients to take their time and not rush to the big "O."

RETARDED EJACULATION

The frequency of RE (difficulty having an orgasm either with masturbation or with a partner) is thought to be less than 3% (Perelman & Rowland, 2006).

I have seen many college students with this serious problem. For some boys, reassurance and some instruction may help. For others, the problem may be related to variant techniques of masturbating, in which inordinate friction has been used to stimulate the penis. It is impossible to reproduce this degree of friction in a vagina. As always, a complete psychiatric history helps differentiate the people who require some simple guidance from those for whom there are also problematic relationships.

Brad: "I'm 19, and I Can't Come With Sex": Coach and Encourage

- "I can't come with my girlfriend!"
- Referred by father, who also had RE.
- Only two therapy sessions were possible.
- You have to talk to her (relationships 101) and ask for help.
- Three months later: problem gone.

When I received the call from Brad, a 19-year-old college sophomore, I was intrigued. He had been directed by his parents to call me after tearfully telling them that he has a serious sexual problem; he had never been able to have an orgasm with any of the women he had dated and was fearful of entering another relationship. I had been seeing his parents, who had been married for nearly 25 years, for the same problem: His father was rarely able to have an orgasm with his wife. I wondered if his RE might be genetic. Brad was handsome and had an outgoing personality that I could imagine made people feel at ease. He talked about how he had many friends and developed relationships with both men and women easily. However, whenever the relationship became sexual and he had intercourse, he was unable to have an orgasm, and this was "driving him crazy." Nothing in his history stood out as problematic. Brad was soon returning to college and could meet only twice. I did not know what to do. This is when the "flying by the seat of your pants" approach comes in.

> Brad, I suspect that many of your friends are probably bragging about how much they are getting laid, and understandably this is hard to hear. Most are probably exaggerating, but given that guys never talk about problems, you would not know. Sex on the first or second date is not for you. In fact, you need to get to know the person before the relationship gets sexual. I'm going to suggest something you may think is nuts: When you are with a woman you have gotten to know and like and are planning sex, you will need to say to her, "I have a sexual problem; when it comes to having intercourse, I get anxious, and it is difficult for me to come."

> Brad did not roll his eyes and leave, so I continued:

> Look, if you don't say anything, you and I know that you are faking it; you will be pretending to be Mr. Cool, and we know that you are not. It will be a huge burden to shoulder, and in the end, you will again not have an orgasm. If you know her better and trust her, it is likely that she will be supportive and ask if there is any way she might be helpful. If she freaks out and says that you must be weird, you are better off ending the relationship right there.

I saw Brad again the next week and I repeated some of what I had said. I talked more about sexual responses and physiology, encouraging him to let me know how things were going for him. A few months later, he e-mailed me that he had a new girlfriend and had talked with her openly about the "problem," which quickly resolved.

I was moved by the impact of these two meetings. I had seen the pain and struggle his parents had experienced throughout their marriage. Rather than seeing the retarded ejaculation as a familial, genetically based problem, I realized that Brad's father, in the absence of an encouraging sexual coach when young, got stuck and incorporated the idea of being sexually incompetent into his view of himself. With Brad, the "sexual leg" of the three-legged stool needed a little shoring up, and the rest he did on his own.

On the other hand, Robert, a 23-year-old graduate student, presented a more complicated picture. He had used pornography from an early age to become aroused, masturbated using the "death grip" (a very tight fist) with no lubrication and furious stroking. Therapy involved guidance in gentler masturbation techniques and suggestions to decrease his reliance on pornography. Over time, he was able to focus more on the sensations in his penis with light touch and began experimenting with a Fleshlight® (a silicone vagina). Sensation in his penis increased, there was more pleasure, and he reached orgasm easily. (The Fleshlight has also been helpful for men who have PE. They can practice developing more control on their own, with a more realistic experience of being in a partner's vagina.)

Once his RE had been addressed, our focus shifted to difficulties he had with close relationships, his lack of confidence, and his career uncertainty. It was the RE that brought him to therapy, but it was deeper psychological concerns that kept him returning.

GAY TEENS: NOT AS DIFFERENT AS YOU MIGHT THINK

The sexual problems of young men, it must not be forgotten, include those of gay young men. When talking to patients about sex, do not make the error of assuming that everyone is heterosexual. Therapists should ask the patient if he is attracted to women, men, or both. For the gay teen, there are additional sexual developmental challenges. He first comes to realize that he is different from many of his friends. This becomes more pronounced around puberty, when he notices an attraction to boys and none to girls. Although one might think that the meaning of these attractions would be obvious, many boys feel confused and disoriented, not understanding what this is about. Giving it a name, "I am gay," is complicated. Many boys I have seen have felt embarrassed, ashamed, guilty, and disappointed, thinking, for example, that they would have gotten married and had a family like everyone else.

Coming out is a real challenge; it means going public and dealing with unpredictable responses. Parental reactions are all over the map, and it is clear that families who are supportive and loving ("you are the same person today as yesterday") make this transition easier. Too often, the reactions are negative and rejecting, with great emotional cost to the adolescent, who has to deal with his family's disgust and rejection, which often may mirror his own.

David, Age 19

- "I'm gay, and it is harder than I thought."
- "My father died when I was 14."
- "How do I date?"
- "How do I get physical?"

- "I want a relationship, not a one-night stand."
- The relationship and developing sexual competence.

David was a 19-year-old college freshman who had come out in the 10th grade. He felt confused about his sexual attraction to boys and the total absence of sexual interest in girls. He searched the Internet and found a number of gay teen sites and shared his concerns with one of his teachers. She responded in a thoughtful and caring way, confirming that she had thought that he was gay. In her quiet acceptance, she facilitated his coming out to his mother and then to his class. He was comfortable telling people that he was gay but was anxious about how he was going to date. It is ironic that some straight teenagers have more same-sex experimentation during their initial explorations of their sexual feelings and masturbation than gay teenagers. For gay teenagers, the idea of revealing these interests is filled with shame, fear, and possible negative repercussions.

When I initially saw David, he was quite depressed and talked about the dilemma posed by being gay. He did not want to lead a segregated existence and wanted to go to the same clubs as his straight friends. However, he was painfully aware that for the straight kids, "hitting on people" was fair game and was part of the evening's activity. For him, if he saw a guy he found sexy and attractive, he had to be vigilant in reading the signals correctly, knowing that if he was mistaken the consequences could be dire.

The therapy involved addressing three main issues. One related to his father's illness and death; the second related to his feelings about being gay and the third to his fear about engaging in sexual activity with other guys. All concerns were the focus in our initial meetings.

With regard to his dating, I noticed that he repeatedly rationalized not going on more than one date. He would talk about the guys being boring, stupid, and unattractive, refusing to see them again. He could not admit that he felt frightened and incompetent about getting physical and sexual with another person. I was struck that his worries were similar to those of many of the straight young adults I counsel. He felt vulnerable about not knowing what to do sexually and was immobilized by possible partner rejection. About another date, he again said, "I'm not attracted to him!" I pushed David with "Did you kiss him?" He turned bright red and playfully told me I was embarrassing him with my directness. I went on, "Well, if you don't actually try and see what it might feel like for you to kiss him, how would you know?" My matter-of-fact response was intended to be encouraging as well as to reinforce how normal this was.

The next week he told me that he had been uncomfortable with my confrontations, but "don't stop!" We talked more about his fear of being rejected and rehearsed some possibilities of how he might handle himself when meeting another guy. A few weeks later, he was invited to go on a date with someone he liked (Peter). I asked him to imagine what the date might be like and then raised the possibility of their beginning to touch and kiss each other. At the end of our meeting, he seemed less anxious and more upbeat.

On his next date he went to Peter's apartment but again became anxious. Peter suggested they lie on the bed and began to hold David, who nearly jumped out of his skin. Peter tried to reassure David, but he was unable to settle himself; David tried kissing Peter, but decided that he needed to leave. Much like many of my straight young adults, as soon as he left Peter's place he was self-critical about being so tentative. I reassured him that there would be another opportunity. He set up another date, which turned out more positively. They kissed, held each other, and engaged in some genital play that David enjoyed.

Over time, David became more self-accepting and confident and began to seek out relationships more easily (i.e., getting to know the person, deciding whether he liked him, and then engaging in more sexual experimentation).

My role as an accepting, encouraging "parental" figure was the unspoken validation that helped strengthen the sexual and self-accepting leg of his development stool.

Therapy continued for several years. Our talks dealt with many topics: his
school work, his relationship with his family, the people he dated, and many
times sex. His first long-term relationship lasted about 18 months. He developed
a deep attachment to his boyfriend, and when conflicts arose, he worked hard to
resolve them. At some point, it became clear to David that he had outgrown his
boyfriend. With considerable pain, he finally ended the relationship.

SEXUAL ABUSE: THE GHOST IN THE BEDROOM

Sexual abuse is always a breach of trust and boundaries, with consequences
for attachments, trust, and sexuality. Kluft (1990) described the defensive
dissociation that children employ to deal with it. The problem is that the
dissociation may persist in relationships when it is no longer necessary. For
both boys and girls, sexual pleasure may be associated with the abuse, which
results in anxiety and panic if arousal occurs with a partner.

Sam, Age 17

Fifteen percent of boys are sexually abused. The long-term effects depend on the age,
the circumstance and the identity of the abuser, the length of time of the abuse, and the
parental response. For teens, the presenting symptoms may vary, although talking directly
about the sexual impact should be an essential part of treatment. Sam was referred to me
by his therapist for an evaluation for medications to treat his chronic anxiety. The school
psychologist was limited in the number of kids he could see and consequently suggested
that I continue as Sam's therapist. Sam, 17, was bright and articulate. He experienced
anxiety and dread almost constantly even as he continued to keep his grades up.

As he became more comfortable with me, he told me that he had been abused sexually by a coach in a previous school. The abuse consisted of fondling his penis. He was
frightened to tell any other teachers or his mother, managing it alone.

I tried to put into words what I thought he might have experienced:

You had to struggle with this all on your own. It was confusing and pretty awful.
I wish there had been someone whom you might have told who would have taken
action to fire the coach and protect you.

I wanted to gauge whether this had an impact on his current sexual development
and asked Sam about his sexual experiences. He did have a girlfriend, and the extent
of their activities comprised kissing and holding. When I asked about masturbation, he
said that it had changed from being enjoyable to having his penis feel numb. Over time,
we were able to connect this with his coach's abuse. I explained that often in situations
like this, kids feel that they are somehow responsible for the sexual activity, and this
was reinforced by his not having anyone with whom to discuss what happened. I suggested that this may have been the cause of the numbness. It is crucial to help victims
of sexual abuse reclaim their sexuality, and I share with you what I said. I approached
this mindful of the possibility that my suggestions might be experienced by my patient
as disturbing, not unlike the feelings when he was with the coach.

Masturbation is special for all of us. It is a way to derive a special kind of pleasure
from your body, and you deserve to have this. Here's what I suggest. I want you

> to take some time alone doing the following exercise. Put on some of your favorite
> music and lie on your bed. Do some deep breathing as a way of relaxing and then
> begin to rub your hand lightly over different parts of your body. Close your eyes
> and focus your attention simply on how this feels. After a while, I want you to
> begin to touch your penis very lightly, again paying attention to the sensations.

This exercise was enormously helpful for Sam, and he described having experienced some good feeling when touching his penis.

> I think that the numbness in your penis was connected to this abuse. Often, kids
> who are abused notice that they did feel aroused sexually, about which they feel
> very guilty. I think that the way your mind handled that was to "numb" your
> penis, which deprived you of enjoyment and pleasure.

Sam noticed that the numbness was beginning to subside, and he began to feel a return of pleasure associated with masturbation. He and his girl-friend were spending more time with each other, with more touching and fondling. Sam wanted information about sex. What should he do? What could he do? How do you have intercourse for the first time? I encouraged him to talk directly with his girlfriend to ask her what she would like and to tell her what felt good for him. Sam wanted to make sure that she was comfortable and that they were both in agreement regarding what they did. After a few months, his girlfriend suggested that they have intercourse. Sam had been rehearsing this with me but was quite apprehensive. He told his girlfriend that he was nervous, and that it probably would not be that great the first time they tried. I had shown him drawings of the vulva, illustrating the clitoris, labia, and vaginal opening, as a way of providing guidance and support.

They did have intercourse, but as Sam had predicted, it was not that great—*for him*. His girlfriend, on the other hand, had a wonderful experience. She was relaxed with him and enjoyed the physical closeness. Sam became a little dissociated, with a return of the numbness of his penis.

> Sam, this is terrific. What you did by saying that "it may not be that great" was
> wonderful. Few guys will ever say that out loud. It was realistic, and I am sure
> reassuring for your girlfriend. Don't worry about the numbness. I'm pretty sure
> that this was a visit from the past, that is, your mind telling you that you are bad
> and dirty and should not feel any pleasure. It will change.

And it did! With each time, he described getting more out of his head and into his body.

He had not discussed his numb penis with the previous therapist, who had never asked about sex. Once he understood the causes, his sexual development began to flourish. The dramatic shift for Sam could not have taken place without integrating the understanding of the abuse with direct guidance and encouragement related to his sexual activities in the present.

His development until the time of the abuse had seemed uneventful. He minimized the impact of his parents' divorce and did well in school as a resourceful and creative student. He had emerged from puberty and enjoyed masturbating. The coach's abuse was like an emotional sledge hammer. He was dazed, removed from sexual feelings, and confused about trust. It was to his credit that he formed the attachment to his girlfriend, and his seeking therapy helped him integrate this event.

By contrast, many adults I have seen who have been abused sexually as children and have not received this kind of reparative therapy have suffered with many years of troubled relationships and impaired sexual adjustments. Sam was able to repair the damaged legs of his stool.

PORNOGRAPHY: INFINITE SEX ON THE INTERNET

Pornography is a thriving, multibillion dollar industry that has to be considered when treating men. I routinely ask, "Any Internet sex sites that interest you?" It is truly a new phenomenon with serious implications for preteen and adolescent boys, who usually have a techno expertise that is way beyond their parents. As a way of informing yourself, try a Google search using the following words: teen sex, vaginas, penis, gay sex, big breasts, oral sex, BDSM. Many boys may now begin their masturbation using Internet porn. This can be problematic for a number of reasons. The porn is filled with images that bear no relation to mutual sexuality in the context of a relationship; it is compelling as there is always a new site to visit, and this may create problems with partner sex. I have seen several teens and young men who have difficulty getting aroused in partner sex without first using pornography. One graduate student said to me, "If it has a screen, you can get porn," and proceeded to demonstrate his collection on his cell phone. It used to be that boys would find their father's *Playboy* magazines and would masturbate using their imagination. They learned to generate their own fantasies, and there was perhaps an unconscious connection with their dads, who were also interested in these images. Internet pornography is totally different. Many believe that television has a negative impact on children's imaginations because they read less and rely more on the visual images. I think that the porn may hamper the development of self-generated sexual fantasy.

I encourage the teens to change their pattern of masturbation. It is a process of redirecting their attention from the Internet images to sensations in their bodies. It is similar to the "sensate focus" described by Masters and Johnson (1970). Initially, they can use the porn to get aroused, but then I instruct them to close their eyes and focus attention on the sexual feelings in their genitals. It is a slow process, but they usually enjoy the changes.

THE ART OF OUR WORK IS BASED ON OUR ASSUMPTIONS

Thus far, I have stressed the importance of discussing sex with teens and young adults, but now I want to consider another aspect of therapy. The art of our work rests on our ability to helpfully identify and integrate unconscious themes in the young man's life. The adolescent is like an inexperienced juggler to whom an increasing number of balls is being thrown. He has not had enough life experiences to have noticed patterns and repetitions in his relationships, so he focuses on current events in his life. We therapists pay attention to family dynamics and notice their characteristic patterns, hesitancies to trust and to reveal themselves to partners, depression, and reliance on substances of abuse to regulate their affects.

The way teens separate from parents is determined by the nature of attachments in the family. It is in this area that the therapist tries to develop a road map to understand where the teen has come from and to anticipate the path forward. James's parents' divorce and its aftermath, for example, set the stage for him to be wary of close attachments. He had disavowed and repressed his negative feelings for the father, choosing, instead, to idealize him. His limited awareness of these feelings resulted in his avoiding the disappointments of investing emotionally in relationships with girls.

As parents and therapists, we want the choices in a relationship outside family of origin to be sound. We realize, however, that the teen's level of emotional development makes that difficult. His first extrafamilial attachment may be idealized and seem at odds with the parents' view of who is appropriate. Tension around this choice may be useful to him in this way: "You disapprove of my choice; it makes us both angry; this leads to distance, which helps us separate." When given leeway with this new attachment, the young person will eventually notice and confront his own concerns and dislikes about the girlfriend. If parents make known their strongly negative feelings about the girlfriend, although the teen may share them, he may gallantly come to her defense. The negatives will be assigned to the parents, who may intensify his dependence on the new partner. There is much emotional learning in store for the teen when his first sexual relationship ends. The struggles are no longer with parents. The teen faces the fact that the relationship was either insufficiently positive or excessively negative to be sustainable—that is, on its own insufficient merits. Separation from her sets the stage for a more mature future choice.

Even though the chief complaint is sexual, I routinely deal with parental and school issues. I challenge my patient to think of alternative ways of behaving. I help him develop a reciprocal emotional vocabulary (Thompson & Kindlon, 2000). "What did you say to her about ___ [add the appropriate term]?" "How do you listen to what she says?" "How do you respond to conflict?" "What are you angry about?" "Have you let her know?" "Can you own your part and apologize?" I point out ways in which this new relationship repeats experiences with parents. "Your parents were so often critical; sounds like something similar goes on with your girlfriend. You do things that get her angry, and then she sounds to you like your parents did."

Recall the case of Greg. Greg had much going for him. He had good models for relationships and had already gone through a painful rebellion with his parents. His ED related to inexperience and worry. His first relationship lasted 9 months; both felt close, open, and trusting. Sex was enjoyable, and Greg was able to move past his worry. Over time, however, they began to have more "issues," and the difference in their levels of emotional development became clearer. Greg used our meetings to understand his decreasing enjoyment of this relationship, and although painful for both, he did break up with her.

James's therapy was far more nuanced. His ED was more entrenched, and he was limited in his ability to form an intense relationship. His joviality masked his loneliness and his aversion to attachments. James was living emotionally in a world eloquently described years ago by Dicks (1964)—one filled with repetitions, collusions, and projections from his family of origin. His fear with women paralleled his skittishness in therapy. Although he disappeared from me repeatedly, I kept inviting him to return and spoke of his distrust of me.

Ultimately, he came to understand the impact on him of his parents' divorce, his father's inconsistent connection, and his mother's serial boyfriends. He was not hopeful that any relationship could last, and we revisited these themes many times.

Brad's RE was cured with a speed that surprised me. He was then able to engage in longer meaningful relationships with women and no longer felt sexually defective (as did his father, unbeknownst to Brad). I encouraged him to return to therapy the following summer, but he did not. When his mother returned to therapy a few years later, she sadly described Brad's relationship with his wife as discordant in a manner that reminded both of us of his parents.

Sam also made some dramatic changes in a short amount of time. He graduated from high school, but I have only heard from him intermittently. He is now struggling with issues relating to his parents' divorce and has had a hard time maintaining long-term relationships. Sex waxes and wanes; it is good in the early part of a relationship, but waning desire is a recurrent problem, which usually precedes the breakup with the woman he is dating.

David was bright and insightful and had a supportive family; relationships held much promise for him. David wanted to have a long-term relationship. He was also anxious sexually. Please recall the guidance I gave him. Once in a relationship, I began helping David to understand what felt good and what did not. In the course of an 18-month relationship with his young male lover, David grew enormously—he learned to disagree, to argue, to get angry, and to define his limits. When the relationship ended, David emerged confident and clear about what he needed in a partner. When I first met David, he was a sad teenager—he was now a mature young adult.

Parents and patients themselves often ask me to predict outcomes and the likely duration of therapy; I am generally reluctant to do this. While I am fundamentally optimistic about helping young people, I know that many factors shape outcome. Chief among them is the connection or fit with the therapist. When parents have been consistently available and caring, I anticipate that my work will be relatively brief. I am reinforcing all the strengths already there. With patients from less emotionally rich backgrounds, I anticipate longer therapies. The goal becomes to model a quality of relationship that they may not yet have experienced. However, I cannot always bring this about. I have seen young men with sexual difficulties who could not trust me, could not be vulnerable with me, and could not benefit from what I had to offer. Their symptoms—ED, PE, low desire, quick and badly ending serial relationships—did not matter as much as their inability to trust me. Although their first meetings with me went reasonably well, their transference quickly became infused with the earlier disappointments. I am always saddened by this but have come to accept that it is an inevitable possibility in the work we do.

SUMMARY

- In raising sons, parents are often unaware of the need for providing an "emotional vocabulary." The statement "boys will be boys" is a poor response to dealing with behavior that is seen as problematic. It discourages boys from developing an empathic awareness of the effects of their actions on others.

- There is rarely useful guidance and instruction as boys develop sexually; many rely on friends and the media for sexual information.
- Boys often experience anxiety as they develop closeness with a boy- or girlfriend, with concern about their sexual function and competence.
- Both straight and gay teens have sexual concerns regarding erectile and orgasmic functioning, what they would like to receive physically, and what they do with a partner's body.
- The therapist is in a unique position to help with emotional separation and conflict with parents and provide more awareness regarding repetitions of early family patterns in current relationships.
- By providing sexual information, suggestions, and coaching, the therapist gives the teen a unique experience with a respectful, knowledgeable adult who encourages sexual competence and pleasure.
- Guidance in relational dynamics is central. The therapist offers an emotional vocabulary and a model for reciprocity in a relationship.
- Internet pornography is frequently a part of a young boy's early sexual exposure, and unless this can be discussed in a caring, nonpunitive way, he will share little about what he sees, and this can have negative impacts on his sexual development.
- By addressing the emotional *and* sexual challenges in therapy, our patients come to experience relationships in a more integrated, satisfying way.

REFERENCES

Brown, R. T., & Brown, J. D. (2006). Adolescent sexuality. *Primary Care: Clinics in Office Practice, 33.*

Dicks, H. V. (1964). Concepts of marital diagnosis of therapy as developed at the Tavistock Family Psychiatric Clinic, London. In E. M. Nash, L. Jessner, & D. W. W. Abse (Eds.), *Marriage counseling in medical practice.* Chapel Hill: University of North Carolina Press. Dicks provides an elegant framework for understanding couple dynamics. He was a contemporary of Fairbairn, Guntrip, Klein, and Winnicott. It has added enormously to my perspective of the complexity of relationships—useful in individual, couple, and family therapy.

Goldstein, I., Bastuba, M., Lurie, A., & Lubisch, J. (2008). Penile revascularization. *The Journal of Sexual Medicine, 5,* 2018–2021.

Kluft, R. P. (1990). *Incest related syndromes of adult psychopathology.* Washington, DC: American Psychiatric Press.

Kunkel, D., Eyal, K., Finnerty, K., Biely, E., & Donnerstein, E. (2005). *Sex on TV 2005.* Menlo Park, CA: Kaiser Family Foundation.

Laumann, E. O., Gagnon, J. H., Michael, R. T., & Michaels, S. (1994). *The social organization of sexuality: Sexual practices in the United States.* Chicago: University of Chicago Press.

Leiblum, S. R. (2001). An established medical school human sexuality curriculum: Description and evaluation. *Sexual and Relationship Therapy, 16,* 59–70.

Perelman, M. A., & Rowland, D. L. (2006). Retarded ejaculation. *World Journal of Urology, 24,* 645–652.

Polonsky, D. C. (2000). Premature ejaculation. In S. Leiblum & R. Rosen (Eds.), *Principles of sex therapy* (3rd ed.). New York: Guilford.

Richardson, J., & Schuster, M. (2003). *Everything you never wanted your kids to know about sex, and were afraid they would ask.* New York: Crown. For parents and therapist, it is as the title suggests, a well-written book about surviving your children's sexuality; therapists can learn much in terms of treatment approaches.

Thompson, M., & Kindlon, D. (2000). *Raising Cain—protecting the emotional life of boys.* New York: Ballantine Books. This is a well-written and moving book about the psychological needs for boys. Using much case material, the authors deal with a range of problems boys confront, providing a social and cultural context in which to understand them.

Zilbergeld, B. (1999). *The new male sexuality.* New York: Bantam. This is another classic book. Although written before the Viagra/Levitra/Cialis era, it is written with a wonderful sense of humor. It is not simply a book about sex; Zilbergeld tackles the complexity of emotional development for men, their loss at not having close relationships with their father, and the pitfalls for them in couple relationships.

SUGGESTED READING

Calderone, M. S., & Johnson, E. (1981). *The family book about sexuality.* New York: Harper and Row. Although published nearly 30 years ago, this is a remarkable book that can guide parents in dealing with their teens' sexuality.

Cornog, M. (2004). *The big book of masturbation.* San Francisco: Down There Press. Just when you wondered what more could be written about masturbation, Cornog reviews the topic from an historical, ethnic, and cultural perspective. This book is excellent, covering not only masturbation but also beliefs and customs held by different cultures regarding sexuality.

Filiberti Moglia, R., & Knowles, J. (Eds.). (1997). *All about sex: A family resource on sex and sexuality.* New York: Three Rivers Press.

Fonseca, H., & Greydanus, D. (2007). Sexuality in the child, teen and young adult. Concepts for the clinician. *Primary Care: Clinics in Office Practice, 34.* The authors review with clarity the developmental issues, both emotionally and sexually, for children, teens, and young adults. They have excellent summary charts of development and behavior and comprehensive references.

Framo, J. L. (1982). *Explorations in marital and family therapy.* New York: Springer. This is a classic. Framo writes clearly, and his warmth comes through. His discussions of partners in a relationship having similar levels of emotional development are compelling and useful.

Joannides, P. (2008). *The guide to getting it on.* Oregon: Goofy Foot Press. This is a book I often recommend for many of my patients, students, and friends. It is written with a sense of humor and no moral judgments, is gender neutral, and describes about every sexual activity you can imagine in a direct way. The author lists the positives and negatives of different activities, with advice regarding safety and well-being.

Lamb, S. (2006). *Sex, therapy, and kids.* New York: Norton.

McGee, M. Advocate for youth. Retrieved from www.youth.org/parents/experts/ mcgee.htm May 27, 2006.

Mosher, W. D., Anjani, C., & Jones. J. (2005, September 25). *CDC Sexual Behavior and selected Health Measures: Men and Women 15–44 Years of Age, United States, 2005*. Division of Vital Statistics. Number 362.

Semans, J. H. (1955). Premature ejaculation: A new approach. *Southern Medical Journal, 49*. 353–358. Although this is a very old reference, I include it for its historical importance. The "squeeze technique" is often referred to for premature ejaculation. Semans, a urologist, was the first to promote this. His article is remarkable for its time and for its involvement of the spouse.

SIECUS (Sex Information and Education Council of the U.S.). (1996). *Guidelines for comprehensive sexuality education: Kindergarten through 12th grade* (2nd ed.).

Fifteen

Combining Medical and Psychological Interventions for the Treatment of Erectile Dysfunction

STANLEY E. ALTHOF, PHD, AND RAYMOND C. ROSEN, PHD

Stanley E. Althof: I am a clinical psychologist whom my colleagues refer to as a sex therapist or sexologist. My preferred identity as psychologist anchors me in two complementary worlds, that of the clinician who treats men, women, and couples and that of the scientist who studies the effects of pharmacological treatments on sexual function, psychological well-being, and interpersonal relationship quality. I serve as a consultant to several pharmaceutical companies to help design outcome measures that assess sexual and psychosocial variables. I also work in two clinical settings: a private practice that specializes in marital and sexual problems and an outpatient urology practice. In my private practice, I see men and women in individual, couple, and group therapy, some briefly and some for several years. In the urology setting, I see men for a consultation session prior to their visit with the urologist. I try to identify obstacles that may limit their response to the likely prescription of a PDE5 (phosphodiesterase type 5 inhibitor), I make suggestions for restarting their dormant sexual lives, and I make referrals for those who require more extended psychological interventions.

Raymond C. Rosen: I have long been involved with sexuality research, sexual health education, and sex therapy. I am presently chief scientist at the New England Research Institutes in Watertown, Massachusetts, where I design and conduct large-scale studies in sexual epidemiology, design clinical trials for prosexual drugs, develop outcome measures for these trials, and devise disease registries to observe the impact of sexual problems on men and women over time. I have had the privilege to participate in the design and the conduct of clinical trials of sildenafil (Viagra™), tadalafil (Cialis™), and vardenafil (Levitra™). These studies have demonstrated how couples manage living with erection problems, the impact of the man's dysfunction on the woman's sexual function, how depression impacts erectile function, and the importance of establishing sexual confidence. I have spent more than two decades treating couples and individuals with sexual dysfunctions.

Our goal in this chapter is to teach you how to think about individuals and couples with erectile dysfunction (ED). We emphasize the integration of pharmacological treatments with psychotherapy. To a lesser extent, we discuss integrating different ideological orientations (e.g., psychodynamic approaches with behavioral techniques) and multiple modalities of psychotherapy (e.g., individual and marital therapy).

The four vignettes in this chapter involve heterosexual couples. Obviously, single and partnered gay men are also susceptible to ED. We believe that the ideas discussed in the chapter apply to men of all orientations.

INTRODUCTION TO ERECTILE DYSFUNCTION

Multiple Possible Etiologies

From an epidemiologic or population-based vantage point, ED results from a complex amalgam of interrelated biological, psychological, and contextual factors (contextual factors are those issues in the individual's or couple's lives that cause distress, e.g., financial worries, infidelity, health issues, concerns with children and parents, etc.). Several large-scale studies in the United States and abroad have shown that, on average, 22% of men aged 40 and above suffer from moderate or severe ED (Laumann et al., 2007). In addition to increasing age, these studies have also shown that physical and mental health factors (e.g., diabetes, depression) are highly predictive of ED across geographic and racial/ethnic samples.

Erectile dysfunction may be a symptom of or an early warning for cardiovascular disease, a complication of diabetes or hypertension, a consequence of treatment for prostate cancer, or an adverse side effect of medications like β-blockers or cancer chemotherapy agents (Lewis et al., 2005; Thompson et al., 2005). Psychologically, interpersonally, and contextually ED may stem from performance anxiety or distractibility during sexual behavior, depression, a deteriorating interpersonal relationship, substance abuse, or stress from life events that overwhelm the man's psychological coping capacity or resiliency (Althof et al., 2005).

Based on this information, you can see why it is important for you to gather information about medical, psychological, interpersonal, and contextual factors that exist in the ED patient's life.

The Biopsychosocial Perspective

The National Institute of Health's Consensus Conference report stated that in the majority of cases, ED results from the additive and interactive nature of various neurologic, vascular, pharmacologic, hormonal, affective, cognitive, behavioral, lifestyle, and social influences (NIH Consensus Conference, 1993).

The biopsychosocial model encompasses the psychological life of the man, the impact the dysfunction has on the partner's and couple's sexual life, the fluctuating influences of medication, substances of abuse, lifestyle, surgery, and disease. The biopsychosocial model, which has been used broadly in medicine and psychiatry for decades, captures the ever-changing influences of biology and psychological life (Althof & Seftel, 1999). It is a dynamic and additive model rather than a fixed image of the man or couple at only one point in time. Regardless of the precipitating causes of ED, biological and psychosocial changes will occur over time that will impact this sexual symptom.

Examples of these changes in physical health may include the man beginning to take a medication that negatively affects his erectile function; the slow, gradual process of recovery of erectile function that is sometimes apparent 18 months after bilateral nerve-sparing radical prostatectomy; or the positive impact of weight loss on erectile function. Examples from his psychosocial life may include a slow deterioration in his relationship, a loss of attraction to his partner, recognition of his unwise financial decisions, or an increase in his substance abuse.

While ED is the focus of this chapter, you need to know that men presenting for treatment of ED can also have problems with sexual desire or ejaculation. Many patients with ED report a concomitant decrease in sexual interest. There are others who develop premature ejaculation because they fear losing their erection. Thus, they hurry lovemaking, reinforcing rapid ejaculation. Your careful history taking will clarify the true character of the sexual problems and how they are interrelated.

What you will also find useful is how to think about the pathogenesis of ED. We categorize etiological variables into predisposing, precipitating, maintaining, and contextual factors. Predisposing factors create the susceptibility for ED. Precipitating factors trigger its onset. Maintaining factors reinforce its persistence, while contextual factors interfere with arousal (Althof et al., 2005; Hawton & Catalan, 1986).

Combination treatment, sometimes referred to as integrated treatment, is a logical extension of the biopsychosocial model. Combination treatments aspire to address all the relevant medical and psychosocial issues that predispose, precipitate, and maintain ED. Treatments based on a simple medical model fail to address the salient psychosocial issues. Psychological interventions alone can also be stiflingly narrow when they fail to consider relevant medical factors.

THE EVOLVING ROLE OF MENTAL HEALTH CLINICIANS IN THE TREATMENT OF ERECTILE DYSFUNCTION

When we began working in the field 35 years ago, we readily perceived men with psychogenic ED. This was based on our careful sexual histories. Variability in erectile function is the hallmark of psychogenic ED. These men would report moderate-to-good erections in the morning, with fantasy, and with masturbation but poor-quality erections with foreplay and intercourse.

We sent those diagnosed with organic ED to the urologist or endocrinologist, who offered penile prosthesis surgery or androgen replacement. Over time, academic support for the perception of a psychogenic/organic duality waned. The field began to recognize the contributions of both organic and psychogenic factors to the onset and maintenance of ED.

In the 1980s, we witnessed the introduction of two innovative medical therapies for ED: intracavernosal injection and vacuum pump therapy. By contemporary standards, these treatments now seem primitive. Each of these methods kept some men from undergoing surgery. Because neither severely damaged penile tissues, they were offered to men with psychogenic ED who failed to benefit from psychotherapy and to men with mixed and organic ED.

We were fascinated to observe men whose psychological issues minimized or negated the erectogenic effects of these two therapy modalities. We began to provide individual or couple psychotherapy to help them better utilize the treatments. Having men simultaneously use injection or vacuum pump therapy and participate in psychotherapy proved to be the beginnings of combined medical and psychological treatment for ED.

The treatment landscape forever changed in 1998 after sildenafil (Viagra) was approved by the Food and Drug Administration (FDA) as the first PDE5 for the treatment of ED. Five years later, two other PDE5s, tadalafil (Cialis) and vardenafil (Levitra), received FDA approval. Currently, over 90% of men with ED are treated with PDE5s. The remaining 10% of ED patients use one or more of these options: intraurethral suppositories (MUSE™), intracavernosal injection (EDEX™, Caverjet™, trimix [a compounded formulation of papaverine, phentolamine, and regitine]), vacuum tumescence therapy, and penile prosthesis surgery.

All of us who treat men with ED need to understand how the PDE5s function to create an improved erection. Normal penile erection depends on the relaxation of smooth muscles in the penile corpora (Burnett, 1995; Rajfer, Aronson, Bush, Dorey, & Ignarro, 1992). In response to sexual stimulation, cavernous nerves and endothelial cells release nitric oxide, which stimulates the formation of cyclic guanosine monophosphate (cGMP), which in turn causes vasodilation and relaxation of the corporal smooth muscle tissue. PDE5s are a selective inhibitor of cGMP-specific phosphodiesterase type 5. By selectively inhibiting cGMP catabolism in cavernosal smooth muscle cells, PDE5s restore the natural erectile response to sexual stimulation but do not cause erection in the absence of sexual stimulation.

Cardiac safety does not appear to be a major concern, based on current evidence, except for patients receiving nitrates in any form or who have other cardiac risk factors associated with sexual activity itself (Rosen, Jackson, & Kostis, 2006). PDE5s are contraindicated for men receiving nitrate therapy, including short- or long-acting agents delivered by oral, sublingual, transnasal, or topical administration. The side effects of PDE5 therapy include headaches, flushing, dyspepsia, and nasal congestion. A small percentage of men (2–3%) may also experience mild alterations in color vision (blue hue), visual brightness or sensitivity, or blurred vision.

Men experiencing ED are far more likely to first seek medical evaluation and treatment with a family physician or urologist rather than a mental health professional. By the time we see them in treatment, they have typically already been prescribed, used at least once, and often failed PDE5 therapy. Over 50% of men who begin PDE5 therapy discontinue use of the medication within the first 3 months (Althof, 2002). The high discontinuation rate with PDE5 drugs demonstrates the limitations of medical treatment alone and strongly suggests that we need to change the manner in which men/couples with ED are dealt with by primary care doctors, urologists, and mental health professionals.

COMBINATION THERAPY

Combination or integrated therapy is an important concept that has the potential to significantly advance the manner in which men, women, and couples receive treatment for sexual dysfunctions (Althof, 2006; McCarthy & Fucito, 2005; Perelman, 2005; Rosen & Leiblum, 1995). Combining medical and psychological interventions harnesses the power of both treatments to enhance efficacy, increase treatment and relational satisfaction, and decrease patient discontinuation (Althof, 2006). Combination therapy also provides patients with rapid symptom amelioration, thereby "jump-starting" the treatment process. Combination therapy, sometimes called *coaching*, is not a novel concept. It has been successfully employed in the treatment of depression, childhood anxiety disorders, schizophrenia, and posttraumatic stress disorder (Keller et al., 2000; Walkup et al., 2008). It is an important treatment approach for chronic illnesses like diabetes and breast cancer whenever psychosocial support is a crucial component of caregiving. Combination therapy is also the usual outcome of professional maturation among psychotherapists who gain comfort and confidence with multiple modes of treatment interventions.

Unanswered Questions

There are, however, four questions about combination therapy that require further clarification:

1. What is the best theoretical model for combination therapy?
2. Who is to deliver the care (nurse, mental health clinician, physician)?
3. Where is the intervention performed (medical clinic vs. mental health office)?
4. Should the treatment components be applied concomitantly or in a stepwise fashion?

In this chapter, we address the mental health clinician who treats patients at the site of the health care provider or in a private office.

Research Findings

An evolving body of literature is emerging strongly in support of the use of combination medical and psychological therapy (Abdo, Afif-Abdo, Otani, & Machado, 2008; Bach, Barlow, & Wincze, 2004; Banner & Anderson, 2007; Melnick, Soares, & Nasello, 2008; Phelps, Jain, & Monga, 2004). These studies compare men with ED taking a PDE5 with a comparable group of men who receive both a PDE5 and some form of psychological intervention. The population of men with ED includes those with psychogenic ED only, mixed ED, and one study of men who underwent radical prostatectomy. Support for combination therapies have been found in studies of intracavernosal injection and vacuum pump therapy (Hartmann & Langer, 1993; Titta, Tavolini, Moro, Cisternino, & Bassi, 2006; Wylie, Jones, & Walters, 2003).

A range of psychological interventions has been used in these studies, including a 90-minute psychoeducational group, weekly group treatment, weekly individual counseling, and the use of a manual instructing men how to treat themselves with optional telephone assistance from a therapist. These studies demonstrate that combined medical and psychological treatment results in improved efficacy of the medical interventions, decreased discontinuation rates, and enhanced treatment and sexual satisfaction compared to medical therapy alone. Their consistency challenges us to move beyond traditional pill giving alone. Applying these findings to the ordinary world of medical care delivery is quite a challenge.

From experience, we know the traditional referral of patients from a primary care, urological, or gynecological specialist to a sex therapist is fraught with difficulties. For a variety of reasons (stigma, cost, insurance issues, lack of motivation, etc.), only about 10% of patients follow through. In addition, sex therapists are a rare commodity. Many patients are not willing to pay for our services or cannot commit to treatment over a period of several months. Our challenge then is to develop innovative strategies that decrease the current barriers to patients with ED and their partners accessing mental health care.

More therapists need to consider providing services at the site of the medical practitioner. Doing so minimizes patient burden and the resistance to going to a mental health practitioner's office and also provides potential cost savings. From a practice-building perspective, this option offers therapists the opportunity to shift the ongoing care, if necessary, to their private offices. Most important, it provides patients with what they need.

Levels of Intervention

Jack Annon (1976) conceived the PLISSIT (permission, limited information, specific suggestions, intensive therapy) model in the mid-70s, recognizing that patients with sexual problems require different levels of psychological intervention. This paradigm is relevant today for conceptualizing levels of treatment intervention. Annon was ahead of his time in understanding that the needs of men with ED differ due to variable degrees of psychosocial complexity or obstacles to recovery.

We have developed a three-level hierarchy based on the men's/couple's level of psychosocial complexity. Each level leads to an alternative treatment plan.

> Level 1: No or insignificant barriers preventing the couple from making use of the medical intervention
> Level 2: Mild-to-moderate barriers
> Level 3: Severe psychological or interpersonal difficulties that are likely to render any treatment ineffective (Althof, 2003)

In level 1, we encounter a couple with a high-quality relationship. Although the partners may be struggling with a sexual dysfunction, they are affectionate and maintain noncoital sexual play. One or both have realistic expectations about treatment. They value their return to a satisfying sexual life. In these circumstances, pharmacotherapy will likely reverse the ED. Nothing more than a prescription and advice about how to use the drug is necessary. Alternatively, in a level 1 man who suffers from primarily psychogenic ED, a brief coaching session to restore sexual confidence may be all that is necessary.

In level 2, which represents the majority of patients presenting with ED, we clinicians encounter mild-to-moderate barriers. We meet a couple who has been sexually abstinent for an extended period of time. The partners' expressions of affection have dwindled. At least one person is mildly depressed and uncertain how to reinitiate lovemaking. Brief, directed coaching is often helpful in improving this couple's sexual life. We provide them with guidance about talking calmly about their wish to resume sex and for ensuring that they are prepared emotionally. We acknowledge the depression that exists, speak about performance anxiety, and inquire about other physical obstacles to lovemaking, such as vaginal dryness. We should speak realistically about treatment and provide guidance about how best to use the pharmacological treatment. With sildenafil, for instance, this means instructing patients to avoid eating fatty meals before taking the drug and to wait 45 minutes before beginning lovemaking. Please do not forget to schedule a follow-up appointment.

In level 3, we encounter complicated situations in which profound psychological or interpersonal difficulties exist. We intuitively recognize that the obstacles are too great to be surmounted with medication and our coaching. Their psychological and interpersonal lives are not adequately prepared to make use of effective medical treatments, even if the partners emphasize that their goal is to resume lovemaking. You may notice one or more of these obstacles in a level 3 situation: poorly managed or unresolved anger, struggles over power and control over nonsexual matters, abandonment concerns, infidelity, substance abuse, serious depression, contempt, and disappointment. These psychological states complicated by prolonged sexual abstinence have to be addressed prior to or during the pharmacological treatment intervention for the couple to achieve emotional satisfaction from sex. New therapists should be wary when couples voice unrealistic expectations, such as, "When I'm potent again, we will make love far more frequently," "I will feel more lovable/successful in life," or "This will cure my marital woes."

When these expectations are inevitably not realized, the patient announces, "It didn't work." They rarely say, "My expectations were unrealistic." Hiding behind such unrealistic expectations often is a story that the patient has not yet told you involving his sexual arousal patterns. Examples include the man whose wife is intensely attracted only to women, the man who has no sexual desire for his wife, or the man who is hiding his sexual arousal to young children, to sadomasochistic behaviors, or to some other paraphilic pattern. Any of these arousal patterns is very likely to interfere with therapeutic success. Each requires your tactful questioning.

IDENTIFYING SPECIFIC PSYCHOSOCIAL OBSTACLES

Broadly speaking, five categories of psychosocial obstacles recur (Althof, 2002):

1. Patient variables: performance anxiety, depression, unrealistic expectations, and unconventional sexual arousal patterns
2. Partner variables: her disinterest in having sex because of sexual dysfunction, active illness, depression, or other serious mental health concerns; consequences of medication, surgery, or radiation; or physical changes due to menopause
3. Interpersonal variables: quality of the relationship, recent separations, tendencies to argue over "everything"
4. Sexual variables: duration of sexual abstinence or incompatible sexual interests
5. Contextual variables: stress over finances, children's problematic behaviors, parent's health, or occupation worries

Within these categories, you will find the source of the patients' resistance to beginning to use a medical intervention, quickly dropping out of treatment, or refusing to talk more with the mental health professional. When we invoke the concept of resistance, we mean that something unsaid—occasionally unconscious, but usually simply not articulated with the clinician—is more powerful than the wish to resume sexual activity with the partner. The "something" is almost always in one of these five areas. These factors explain a large percentage of the dropouts from PDE5 therapy.

TWO CLINICAL PRESENTATIONS

The Man Who Seeks Treatment at the Behest of His Wife

Sam is a 54-year-old hypertensive diabetic husband who waited 2 years before seeking evaluation. One of his four medications is likely to interfere with his erectile function. His ED worsened while he avoided seeking help. Sam developed feelings of inadequacy, lost his sexual confidence, felt intense performance anxiety, developed mild depression, and blamed his wife, Gina, for the problem. While Sam repeatedly tells Gina that he is too tired or too busy to make love, he is quite aware that he is only trying to avoid embarrassment or failure. Sam's affectionate touching decreased and so did his verbal and nonverbal signals of sexual interest. Eventually, lovemaking disappeared.

During this process, Gina wondered, "Does Sam still love me?" "Is he having an affair?" "Is Sam still attracted to me since I've gained weight over the years?" "Is sex over in our relationship?" She may have initially colluded with him by avoiding sex play to lessen her pain of feeling rejected and because she did not wish to embarrass him. Their relationship now feels emptier without lovemaking and affection. She perceives Sam as somewhat down, irritable, preoccupied, and defensive. She is hurt and angry that he blames her for the problem. Unlike wives who are content that their sexual life is over, Gina misses sex and is frustrated by Sam's refusal to address the problem.

The Man Who Does Not Inform His Partner of His Treatment

A large minority of men receive a PDE5 from a physician without telling their partners. Typically, these men have not attempted lovemaking in several months or years. When they return from the physician, they suddenly attempt lovemaking. This unexpected event is unsettling to the partner, who experiences an amalgam of amazement, anger, dismay, and anxiety: "Can I get ready for this again?" "Will his erection last?" "I was hoping we were past this." He, of course, also is anxious about his performance on the drug but comes to realize that he has put himself in a new dilemma. If she discovers that he has taken a PDE5 without telling her, she may feel betrayed and believe that his arousal was due to the medication and not to her. If he informs her about using the drug, she may be angry that she was left out of the decision loop. She may find that menopausal-induced lubrication and arousal difficulties cause intercourse to be uncomfortable and did not have time to psychologically and physically prepare herself. The sexual experience for each of them is disappointing. His recent brief sexual enthusiasm quickly wanes.

When either of such men announces at a follow-up visit that the medication "did not work," you and I would hope that he knows that the emotional barriers that maintained his ED were too difficult for him to overcome. This rarely happens. The physician will likely increase the dose, change medications, and counsel the patient regarding food interaction and need for sexual stimulation. The doctor will rarely discuss psychological or couple's concerns. The patient now needs the assistance of the mental health professional to enable the PDE5 to "work." We have to assist the couple to recognize and overcome their resistance.

Both cases illustrate the five categories of psychological resistance that can converge to defeat ED treatment: (1) the length of time the couple has been asexual before seeking treatment, (2) the man's nonverbal approach to resuming a sexual life with his partner, (3) the female partner's physical and emotional unreadiness to resume lovemaking, (4) the meaning to each partner of using a medical intervention to enable intercourse, and (5) the negative quality of the nonsexual aspects of the relationship (Althof, 2002).

Illness, medication, and surgery can have a severe impact on erectile function. Too often, men do not receive any psychological intervention for sexual difficulties stemming from these sources. The following vignette describes one such therapy:

Robert, a 49-year-old divorced man, underwent a bilateral nerve-sparing radical prostatectomy 2 years ago. Prior to surgery, he never had any problems with erectile function; postsurgery he had no erections. His surgeon counseled him that sometimes erectile function returns after 18 months. At the time of Robert's surgery, the concept of penile rehabilitation (daily PDE5 or intracavernosal therapy) was in its infancy, and he did not participate in any rehabilitation program. He was given a prescription for a PDE5 and asked at follow-up whether they helped him to achieve erections.

I first saw Robert 1 year after surgery. His wife left him 3 years ago after having an affair. Robert was significantly depressed and felt betrayed and abandoned by her. Although having opportunities to date, Robert refused because he perceived himself as "damaged goods." I told Robert that getting his penis to be erect again would be much easier than getting him to use it with a partner.

I referred Robert for psychiatric consultation, and he was placed on an antidepressant. It seemed to relieve the severity of his depression, but he remained hopeless about ever being in a relationship again. Much of his self-deprecation and self-criticism was an outgrowth of his relationship to his parents and became a major focus in therapy, as did his feelings regarding his wife's affair and abandonment. I reassured Robert that when he was ready to date that we would help him to develop strategies to deal with the sexual problem.

One year later, Robert met someone through his social network who asked him out. He did not know what to do. He felt attracted to this woman and liked her but was certain that ultimately no woman would accept him given his sexual limitations. We discussed when and how he might talk to her about his sexual concerns. They began to date; however, Robert avoided sexual activity and mentioning it for a month. When he mustered the courage to talk about his erection difficulties, he was surprised at the woman's accepting attitude and interest in helping him overcome his problem. PDE5s proved to be unreliable; at best, he achieved a 75% erection. He reconsidered injection therapy and had an excellent response to trimix. We were both surprised by the observation that as his confidence improved and his depression lessened, his response to PDE5s improved!

Three other issues are important to consider when treating with PDE5 inhibitors:

1. Some men, generally older men, present for evaluation not because they intend to use a PDE5 with a partner but simply to reassure themselves that if they wanted to make love again, they could. Sometimes, these men are widowers or men who have been asexual for a significant period of time. It is comforting for these men to know that a sexual life is possible, that the potential still exists. These men often are grateful for the evaluation and tend not to fill their prescription. We call these cases men seeking to fulfill their "male potential."

2. Use of PDE5s requires that the man experience arousal with his partner. If he finds his partner unattractive or he cannot generate any personal arousal while touching her, these compounds will not induce a genital response. This is because his absence of arousal means he is not secreting nitric oxide (NO) in his corpora cavernosa, so the PDE5 has no utility.

3. If his sexual preference is for something other than conventional lovemaking (e.g., a sadomasochistic encounter), he is not likely to generate an erection with his partner under conventional circumstances.

John is a 35-year-old accountant who sought marital treatment because he and his wife of 8 years were having difficulty conceiving a child. Actually, this was not medically accurate because they were simply not having intercourse. John would find excuse after excuse to avoid being sexual. When Megan insisted, he could not achieve or sustain his erection. Their physician had prescribed sildenafil, to no avail.

In my first individual meeting with John, he spoke of his Internet addiction. He admitted to spending several hours every day engaging in "cybersex" with women. Without sildenafil, he achieves firm erections and orgasms easily as long as the women follow his sadomasochistic script. Megan has no interest in sadomasochism and refuses to participate in even the mildest behaviors suggested by John.

During their courtship, John had been interested in Megan as a sexual partner and was able to perform reliably. Over time, his interest in conventional sexual encounters waned. Megan grew increasingly frustrated, especially in response to other family members becoming pregnant.

During psychotherapy John developed gradual insight into the cost of his Internet addiction. Megan, who initially perceived John's time on the computer as excessive but "as a harmless activity that most guys engage in," became aware of the psychological and relational consequences of his behavior. John is still struggling to control his Internet behavior but now he is trying to develop more interest in conventional lovemaking. Megan alternates between being supportive and feeling betrayed and cheated.

Do you see that sildenafil could not have provided the sexual arousal necessary for John to make love to Megan? He was not aroused because he required domination activities refused by Megan. The short-term goal of my combined treatment was to help John understand the origins of his unconventional wishes. I hoped that this would diminish somewhat the power of fantasies and would help Megan not to personalize the rejection she experienced. John was relieved to no longer hold his secret; Megan is still struggling to come to terms with what she now knows about John. The absence of sex continues.

This is not an easy case, and decisions regarding how to best treat them are challenging. Ultimately, I continued to see them in couple therapy but referred them both for individual therapy. Individual therapy proved to be supportive and helpful in processing the thorny issues raised in marital therapy as well as helping each partner with their individual psychological issues.

PSYCHOTHERAPY FOR ERECTILE DYSFUNCTION

We want to conclude this chapter with a discussion of traditional psychotherapy conducted without a medical intervention. The focus of psychotherapy for ED is to identify and work through the obstacles to lovemaking. Generally, we "work through" these resistances by conducting a brief symptom-focused therapy with an emphasis on the "here and now." Our psychotherapies, whether conducted with a PDE5, without such a drug, with the man alone, or with the couple attempt to help the man or the couple to

1. Express and accept difficult feelings regarding onerous life circumstances
2. Find new solutions for old problems
3. Understand the emotions experienced by the man and his partner during lovemaking
4. Surmount barriers to psychological intimacy
5. Increase communication
6. Gain sexual confidence
7. Lessen performance anxiety
8. Transform destructive attitudes that interfere with lovemaking
9. Modify rigid sexual scripts or repertoires

By dealing with the relevant items from this list in psychotherapy, patients come to understand how the dysfunction serves as their "friend" by protecting them from confronting unpleasant personal and interpersonal dilemmas (Althof & Wieder, 2004).

Many otherwise well-educated men and women believe in the mechanistic theory of arousal (Zilbergeld, 1999), namely, that the penis should become erect with anyone, anytime, and under any circumstance. We therapists need to be clear that this is not the case. What impacts arousal is how partners feel about each other, the circumstances of their lives, and the conditions under which they make love. This seems simple and obvious to us, but many couples fail to appreciate this straightforward truth.

James, a healthy 54-year-old businessman has been divorced from his wife of 25 years for 1 year. Initially, James enjoyed his new-found bachelorhood and had no problems with sexual function. He recently discovered an old girlfriend, Barbara, through Facebook, and they began dating. However, as the relationship became more serious, James began to experience ED episodically. His physician performed a comprehensive assessment and could find no physical cause for his ED. The physician gave him a prescription for a PDE5; however, James did not wish to use it. He wanted to solve the problem on his own and therefore sought psychological consultation.

After listening to James describe the episodic pattern of his ED and the relationship to Barbara, I confirmed that his ED was, as James suspected, psychological in nature. I also told him that the ED was his friend, and that his penis was "smarter" than he was. This initially seemed shocking to James, but I gently explained what I had understood from James about the relationship, namely, that he was becoming increasingly aware of aspects he did not like about Barbara, her mood swings, difficulties with her children, and tendency toward substance abuse. Within a few weeks, James ended this relationship. He reported feeling relieved.

James returned for a consultation 1 year later. He had been dating a new woman, and in the last month the episodic ED had returned. His health had remained good, there were no prominent medical factors, and James was still able to achieve firm, long-lasting erections on awakening and with masturbation. The variability of erectile function suggested a strong psychogenic component.

He began by stating: "Please don't tell me again that my penis is still smarter than I am." I asked if there was anything in the new relationship that made him uncomfortable. He spoke of his discomfort with the girlfriend's maintaining a friendship with her previous boyfriend. While she insisted that the relationship was "platonic," he was suspicious and increasingly uncomfortable. I focused the therapy on helping James talk to the girlfriend about his discomfort about this relationship. She became angry with James and broke off the relationship. He was hurt but realized that his sexual function served as a sensitive barometer of his psychological concerns, even before he became conscious of them.

Myths and Cognitive Distortions Associated With ED

Rosen, Leiblum, and Spector (1994) articulate eight forms of cognitive distortion that may interfere with erectile function:

1. All or nothing thinking: "I am a complete failure because my erection was not 100% rigid."
2. Overgeneralization: "If I had trouble getting an erection last night, I won't have one this morning."
3. Disqualifying the positive: "My partner says I have a good erection because she doesn't want to hurt my feelings."
4. Mind reading: "I don't need to ask. I know how she felt about last night."
5. Fortune-telling: "I am sure things will go badly tonight."
6. Emotional reasoning: "Because a man feels something is true, it must be."
7. Categorical imperatives: "shoulds," "ought tos," and "musts" dominate the man's cognitive processes.
8. Catastrophizing: "If I fail tonight, my girlfriend will dump me."

The myths most often held by partners of impotent men are that the failure to achieve erection indicates:

1. A diminution of affection for them
2. Their loss of personal attractiveness
3. The man's involvement with another woman

Sexual Confidence

Recent work on sexual confidence suggests that it may be the most important psychological variable in men with ED (Althof et al., 2006). Sexual confidence appears related to the concept of self-efficacy, the sense that one can control the outcome in his or her sexual life. Several randomized placebo-controlled studies of PDE5s in men with ED demonstrate that at baseline men with ED have low sexual confidence. Treatment with placebo yields little in the way of improvement, while treatment with PDE5 significantly improves sexual confidence. Given these research findings, we believe that psychological interventions in men with ED should focus on helping men to improve their sexual self-confidence or self-efficacy.

Confidence is restored by quickly demonstrating to the patient that he is able to achieve and maintain a good-quality erection. In these times, this is usually accomplished by careful instructions on how to use a PDE5. The drug is an "insurance policy" that "he will work." Prior to the PDE5s, we used to help regain confidence by asking those with primary psychogenic ED to make love without trying to have intercourse. When he followed our instructions and his potency returned, his confidence was restored. This did not work with men with significant organic factors. Thankfully, Viagra did in most cases. Clinicians offer them hope that they can get better. We direct them to focus on sensation and pleasure and to interrupt their negativistic thinking. Over time, success breeds success and improved confidence.

CONCLUSION

We hope that you have found this chapter helpful in understanding the problem of ED, the need for combined therapy, and in knowing what to focus on with men and couples with this problem. We want to assure you that helping men and women to regain sexual intimacy and satisfaction is highly rewarding. It is not always easy or always successful, but as you gain more experience, you will also gain more efficiency and facility for helping. It then gets easier.

We also hope that we have made you eager to begin work with these patients. As you prepare for your first encounters, we want to reiterate four ideas:

1. Combined therapy is more helpful than either psychotherapy or pharmacotherapy alone.
2. The essence of the psychological intervention is to help patients overcome obstacles that interfere with their making effortless use of a medical intervention.
3. You, the mental health professional, are the one professional who can provide the sometimes necessary, more intense thoughtful integration of behavioral, couple, psychodynamic interventions.
4. We know you will be pleased when you get to observe that your patient's sexual, emotional, and relational satisfaction have changed for the better.

Good luck.

REFERENCES

Abdo, C. H., Afif-Abdo, J., Otani, F., & Machado, A. C. (2008). Sexual satisfaction among patients with erectile dysfunction treated with counseling, sildenafil, or both. *Journal of Sexual Medicine, 5*, 1720–1726. This is one of several articles demonstrating the advantages of combination therapy for ED.

Althof, S. (2002). When an erection alone is not enough: Biopsychosocial obstacles to lovemaking. *International Journal of Impotence Research, 14*(Supplement 1), S99–S104. This article describes the psychosocial obstacles interfering with successfully using PDE5 therapy.

Althof, S. (2003). Therapeutic weaving: The integration of treatment techniques. In S. Levine, C. Risen, & S. Althof (Eds.), *Handbook of clinical sexuality for mental health professionals* (pp. 359–376). New York: Bruner-Routledge.

Althof, S. (2006). Sex therapy in the age of pharmacotherapy. *Annual Review of Sex Research, 17,* 116–132. This is expanded information on combination therapy and ways of delivering care for sexual problems.

Althof, S., Leiblum, S., Chevret-Measson, M., Hartmann, U., Levine, S., McCabe, M., et al. (2005). Psychological and interpersonal dimensions of sexual function and dysfunction. In T. Lue, R. Basson, R. Rosen, F. Giuliano, S. Khory, & M. Montorsi (Eds.), *Sexual dysfunctions in men and women* (pp. 73–115). Paris: Editions 21. This is a comprehensive review of the psychological and interpersonal dimensions of male and female sexual function and dysfunction.

Althof, S., O'Leary, M., Cappelleri, J., Crowley, A. R., Tseng, L., & Collins, S. (2006). Impact of erectile dysfunction on confidence, self-esteem and relationship satisfaction after 9 months of sildenafil citrate treatment. *Journal of Urology, 176,* 2132–2137.

Althof, S., & Seftel, A. (1999). The evaluation and treatment of erectile dysfunction. *Annual Review of Psychiatry, 19*(5), 55–87.

Althof, S., & Wieder, M. (2004). Psychotherapy for erectile dysfunction: Now more relevant than ever. *Endocrine, 23,* 131–134.

Annon, J. (1976). *The behavioral treatment of sexual problems: Brief therapy.* New York: Harper and Row.

Bach, A., Barlow, D., & Wincze, J. (2004). The enhancing effects of manualized treatment for erectile dysfunction among men using sildenafil: A preliminary investigation. *Behavior Therapy, 35,* 55–73.

Banner, L. L., & Anderson, R. U. (2007). Integrated sildenafil and cognitive-behavior sex therapy for psychogenic erectile dysfunction: A pilot study. *Journal of Sexual Medicine, 4,* 1117–1125.

Burnett, A. L. (1995). The role of nitric oxide in the physiology of erection. *Biology of Reproduction, 52,* 485–489. This is a classic article delineating the cascade of biological events resulting from PDE5 use.

Hartmann, U., & Langer, D. (1993). Combination of psychosexual therapy and intra-penile injections in the treatment of erectile dysfunctions: Rationale and predictors of outcome. *Journal of Sex Education and Therapy, 19,* 1–12.

Hawton, K., & Catalan, J. (1986). Prognostic factors in sex therapy. *Behavior, Research and Therapy, 24,* 377–385.

Keller, M. B., McCullough, J. P., Klein, D. N., Arnow, B., Dunner, D. L., Gelenberg, A. J., et al. (2000). A comparison of nefazodone, the cognitive behavioral-analysis system of psychotherapy, and their combination for the treatment of chronic depression. *New England Journal of Medicine, 342*(20), 1462–1470.

Laumann, E., West, S., Glasser, D., Carson, C., Rosen, R., & Kang, J. H. (2007). Prevalence and correlates of erectile dysfunction by race and ethnicity among men aged 40 or older in the United States: From the male attitudes regarding sexual health survey. *Journal of Sexual Medicine, 4*(1), 57–65. This excellent epidemiological article is on men over 40 and ED.

Lewis, R., Fugl-Meyer, K., Bosch, R., Fugl-Meyer, A., Laumann, E., Lizza, E., et al. (2005). Definitions, classification and epidemiology of sexual dysfunction. In T. Lue, R. Basson, R. Rosen, R. Giuliano, S. Khory, & F. Montorsi (Eds.), *Sexual medicine: Sexual dysfunctions in men and women* (pp. 37–72). Paris: Editions 21.

McCarthy, B., & Fucito, L. (2005). Integrating medication, realistic expectations, and therapeutic interventions in the treatment of male sexual dysfunction. *Journal of Sex and Marital Therapy, 31*(4), 319–328.

Melnick, T., Soares, B., & Nasello, A. (2008). The effectiveness of psychological interventions for the treatment of erectile dysfunction: Systematic review and meta-analysis, including comparisons to sildenafil treatment, intracavernosal injections and vacuum devices. *Journal of Sexual Medicine,* epub. *5,* 2562–2574.

NIH Consensus Conference. (1993). Impotence. NIH Consensus Development Panel on Impotence. *Journal of the American Medical Association, 270,* 83–90.

Perelman, M. (2005). Psychosocial evaluation and combination treatment of men with erectile dysfunction. *Urologic Clinics of North America, 32,* 431–435. More on combination therapy for men with erectile dysfunction is provided.

Phelps, J. S., Jain, A., & Monga, M. (2004). The PsychoedPlusMed approach to erectile dysfunction treatment: The impact of combining a psychoeducational intervention with sildenafil. *Journal of Sex and Marital Therapy, 30,* 305–314.

Rajfer, J., Aronson, W. J., Bush, P. A., Dorey, F. J., & Ignarro, L. J. (1992). Nitric oxide as a mediator of relaxation of the corpus cavernosum in response to nonadrenergic, noncholinergic neurotransmission. *New England Journal of Medicine, 326,* 90–94.

Rosen, R., & Leiblum, S. (1995). Treatment of sexual disorders in the 1990s: An integrated approach. *Journal of Consulting and Clinical Psychology, 63,* 877–890.

Rosen, R. C., Jackson, G., & Kostis, J. B. (2006). Erectile dysfunction and cardiac disease: Recommendations of the Second Princeton Conference. *Current Urological Reports, 7*(6), 490–496. This is a summary of the recommendations stemming from the Second Princeton Conference on ED and cardiac disease.

Rosen, R. C., Leiblum, S. R., & Spector, I. P. (1994). Psychologically based treatment for male erectile disorder: A cognitive–interpersonal model. *Journal of Sex and Marital Therapy, 20*(2), 67–85. This delineates the authors' cognitive–interpersonal–behavioral model for treating ED.

Thompson, I., Tangem, C., Goodman, P., Probstfield, J., Moinpour, C., & Coltman, C. (2005). Erectile dysfunction and subsequent heart disease. *Journal of the American Medical Association, 294,* 2996–3002. This important article describes the link between cardiovascular disease and ED.

Titta, M., Tavolini, I. M., Moro, F. D., Cisternino, A., & Bassi, P. (2006). Sexual counseling improved erectile rehabilitation after non-nerve-sparing radical retropubic prostatectomy or cystectomy—results of a randomized prospective study. *Journal of Sexual Medicine, 3,* 267–273.

Walkup, J. T., Albano, A. M., Piacentini, J., Birmaher, B., Compton, S. N., Sherrill, J. T., et al. (2008). Cognitive behavioral therapy, sertraline, or a combination in childhood anxiety. *New England Journal of Medicine, 359,* 2753–2766.

Wylie, K. R., Jones, R. H., & Walters, S. (2003). The potential benefit of vacuum devices augmenting psychosexual therapy for erectile dysfunction: A randomized controlled trial. *Journal of Sex and Marital Therapy, 29*, 227–236.

Zilbergeld, B. (1999). *The new male sexuality*. New York: Bantam.

Sixteen

Premature Ejaculation and Delayed Ejaculation

MARCEL D. WALDINGER, MD, PHD

INTRODUCTION

In 1992, a 30-year-old man visited me at my outpatient office and asked me to treat him for premature ejaculation. After taking his medical and sexual history, I told him about the usual treatment for premature or rapid ejaculation. This therapy consisted of the squeeze technique, a behavioral treatment in which a man learns how to delay his ejaculation using manual stimulation exercises in cooperation with a female partner. The patient became extremely upset by this requirement. He was sure that his girlfriend never would agree to it. During the 6 months that he had known her, he thought she was the woman of his life. The relationship was threatened because of her anger that she had no chance to get sexually aroused. She warned him that she would leave him if he did not seek help. He refused the behavioral therapy and insisted that I look for medication to treat him. I had heard that some depressed patients were experiencing a delayed or even an absence of ejaculation after being treated with the new antidepressant paroxetine. I told this despairing man that I felt it was worth trying this antidepressant to see whether it could delay his ejaculation. He agreed. He came back to see me in 3 weeks and was cheerful, happy, and grateful to me for prescribing this drug. To his and to my amazement, his ejaculations became retarded. His girlfriend was also satisfied with the change that had come about within only a few weeks. Six months later, they invited me to their wedding.

That was the start of my interest in premature ejaculation. At that time, I did not understand why paroxetine delayed ejaculation. It was generally thought in those days that only drugs that impaired certain peripheral nerves to the genitals (i.e., with sympatholytic side effects) were able to delay ejaculation. But, paroxetine had only a minimum of sympatholytic actions. How were we able to explain this clinical effect? It was only after I looked closely into animal research literature that I gradually began to understand what was probably happening. Since 1992, I have undertaken a large number of psychopharmacological and other types of studies on men suffering this problem. I have also studied the sexual behavior of male rats. Now, my colleagues and I have the largest outpatient clinic in Europe for the treatment of and research into premature ejaculation. In this chapter, I tell more about the subject of premature ejaculation, its history, its treatment, and the processes of clinical science.

Although far less is known about the relative inability to ejaculate, I also more briefly discuss this intriguing ejaculation pattern.

WHAT IS PREMATURE EJACULATION?

The phenomenon of too rapid ejaculation is likely to have existed throughout the history of humankind. But, has it always been a problem? That is a question we cannot answer. In our time, the capability for delaying ejaculation and for prolonging intercourse provides man with the means to make love in a more intimate and satisfactory way. Therefore, men like to control ejaculation until the male and his female partner feel that the right moment has come for him to ejaculate. We may speculate that this has always been the case, but the fact of the matter is that it was not until 1889 that the first report of rapid ejaculation appeared in medical literature. About 30 years later, Karl Abraham (1917), at that time a well-known psychoanalyst, wrote that rapid ejaculation is a manifestation of a man's unsolved unconscious conflicts. This rapidity, in his view and that of other psychoanalysts, meant that a man unconsciously wanted to punish a woman by giving her no chance to reach orgasm. Abraham termed rapid ejaculation *ejaculatio praecox*. Soon, this was translated as *premature ejaculation* and a difficult debate was born.

The question was, Premature for whom? Was it premature for the man or for his partner? Possibly, it was not for the man but only for his partner? This issue led to much unfruitful discussion among physicians and prevented finding a clinically satisfying definition of *premature ejaculation*. In the first half of the 20th century, psychoanalysts accepted Abraham's idea that premature ejaculation was a symptom of a neurosis. Accordingly, they argued, it had to be treated by classical psychoanalysis. And, that is exactly what happened, but with poor results. Patients probably gained insight into their unconscious conflicts through psychoanalysis, but there was no evidence that they achieved a delay of ejaculation.

In 1943, Bernhard Schapiro, a german endocrinologist, who had worked at the Institut fur Sexual Wissenschaft in Berlin, wrote an important article about his extensive dealings with men presenting with premature ejaculation. He argued that premature ejaculation was not a neurosis but a psychosomatic disturbance. In accordance with the accepted ideas of his time, he was of the opinion that men with premature ejaculation had an emotional problem that was translated into a physical genital symptom because they possessed weak genital mechanisms to ejaculate. Schapiro was the first to try to reconcile psychological and somatic factors in the pathogenesis of premature ejaculation. But, his publication was also important because he described two types of premature ejaculation. Men with type B premature ejaculation have always suffered from being rapid, from their first intercourse. Men with type A developed premature ejaculation later in life and often also experienced erectile dysfunction. Many years later, the field accepted his observations but changed the terms to primary (lifelong) and secondary (acquired) forms of premature ejaculation, respectively (Godpodinoff, 1989).

Schapiro (1943) also noticed that men with premature ejaculation had family members who experienced the same complaint. Having seen so many men with premature ejaculation myself, I asked my patients whether they knew if any other members of their family had premature ejaculation. It will probably not come as a surprise to you when I say that the majority of my patients did not have any such knowledge of their family members as the rapidity of making love is not something that people—and even less so members of a family—are likely to discuss. It is one of the most strongly taboo topics in sexual discussion. But, some men spontaneously did tell me that they already knew this about some family members or would be willing to ask male relatives whether they were sexually rapid. It then emerged that a relatively high percentage of male family members also suffered from premature ejaculation. In 1998, we published the results of that first study on a possible genetic influence on lifelong premature ejaculation (Waldinger, Rietschel, Nothen, Hengeveld, & Olivier, 1998). A decade later, in 2009, we were proud to have been the first in having found and published regarding a gene polymorphism of men with lifelong premature ejaculation that determines part of the rapidity of their ejaculation (Janssen et al., 2009).

PSYCHOLOGICAL TREATMENT

Let us now return to the psychological approach. Little has been published on this subject for decades. In 1956, there was a small article by an American urologist (Semans, 1956). He described a method of learning how to control the penis from being rapid; this is known as the *stop-start method*. It includes manual stimulation of the penis by the female partner until just prior to ejaculation, at which point the man feels preejaculatory sensations and removes his partner's hand. When the preejaculatory sensations cease, the woman begins with manual stimulation again. After practicing this procedure, men are instructed to lubricate the penis during stimulation because ejaculation occurs more rapidly when the penis is wet. Semans's publication did not attract much attention.

It was not until 1970 that this behavioral approach gained any notice, when two well-known American sexologists, Masters and Johnson, reported using his method. They added a small variation and renamed the method the *squeeze technique*. Today, this technique is practiced all over the world. Masters and Johnson claimed that the method was more effective if the man tells his partner about the sensations experienced preejaculatory, and she then squeezes the coronal ridge of the penis between her thumb and first two fingers for about 4 seconds. This then leads to a loss of the premonitory sensations and partial reduction in the erection. After waiting for a further 30 seconds or so, manual stimulation begins again. The couple is told not to have intercourse during this period until there is progress in the man's ability to delay ejaculation. Gradually, vaginal containment of the penis is allowed but without pelvic thrusting. Later, pelvic thrusting and other coital positions may be attempted.

Masters and Johnson (1970) argued that premature ejaculation arose out of anxiety and was a learned activity. For example, it could be associated with hurried contact in nonprivate places, such as the backseat of cars. Treatment should thus be a matter of training the man to lose his performance anxiety.

In addition to the squeeze technique, all sorts of psychotherapies have been suggested, ranging from Gestalt therapy, to transactional analysis, group therapy, and bibliotherapy. The effectiveness of these therapies has only been alluded to in case reports; effectiveness has never been investigated in well-designed controlled studies. For example, the assumption of initial hurried sexual contacts mentioned by Masters and Johnson (1970) has never been demonstrated by evidenced-based data (Waldinger, 2002).

The squeeze method is the only psychological treatment known to produce even any short-term effectiveness. Two studies in addition to Masters and Johnson (1970) original sample of 196 couples confirmed initial effectiveness of this method. Unlike Masters and Johnson's optimistic findings of no return of premature ejaculation over 5 years, these studies showed that the initially attained ejaculatory control had virtually been lost after a 3-year follow-up (DeAmicis, Goldberg, LoPiccolo, Friedman, & Davies, 1985; Hawton, Catalan, Martin, & Fagg, 1988).

PHARMACOLOGICAL TREATMENT

Historical Pharmacological Approaches

For much of the 20th century, urologists considered premature ejaculation to be caused by hypersensitivity of the glans penis, too short a frenulum of the foreskin, or urethral abnormalities. Their treatments included anesthetizing ointments, incision of the frenulum, or operations on the urethra, respectively. Since the 1940s, case reports occasionally appeared concerning drugs other than topical anesthetics that delayed ejaculation. These included sympatholytic drugs to inhibit the sympathetic nerves to the genitals; neuroleptics, which are usually prescribed to psychotic patients; and monoamine oxidase inhibitors (MAOIs), which are used for severe depression. Most men with premature ejaculation are in excellent physical and mental health and were not keen on using drugs that have quite disturbing and rare dangerous side effects.

But in 1973, Eaton published the first report on clomipramine, a classical antidepressant, describing it as an effective treatment for premature ejaculation. Later case reports and double-blind, placebo-controlled studies repeatedly demonstrated that low daily doses delay ejaculation. In 1993, the American psychiatrist Taylor Segraves published a double-blind, placebo-controlled study demonstrating that clomipramine in doses of 25–50 mg, taken approximately 6 hours prior to coitus, is effective in delaying ejaculation. The on-demand treatment was replicated in later studies (Segraves, Saran, Segraves, & Maguire, 1993).

The Selective Serotonin Reuptake Inhibitors

In the mid-1980s, a new class of antidepressant drugs, the selective serotonin reuptake inhibitors (SSRIs), was introduced. The introduction of SSRIs led to a revolutionary change in the understanding and treatment of depression, anxiety, and obsessive–compulsive disorder. Recall that I introduced this chapter by recounting my coincidental discovery of the ejaculation-delaying effects of paroxetine, one of the six SSRIs that are currently on the market. In 1994, our group published the first placebo-controlled study demonstrating the effectiveness of 40 mg/day of paroxetine. The efficacy of paroxetine in daily doses of 20–40 mg has been replicated in studies for both daily and on-demand dosing. The efficacy of other SSRIs, such as sertraline in a daily dose of 50–200 mg and fluoxetine in a daily dose of 20 mg, has also been demonstrated (Waldinger, Hengeveld, Zwinderman, & Olivier, 1998a). All of these studies used evidence-based methodology and were designed and conducted by clinicians without the control of pharmaceutical companies.

Pharmaceutical companies have been interested in this arena since 2000. Currently, there are two drugs that may become officially registered (e.g., approved by the government agencies for use) for the on-demand treatment of premature ejaculation: dapoxetine and TEMPE (topical eutectic mixture for premature *ejaculation*). Dapoxetine is an SSRI with a short half-life. It is rapidly degraded after oral intake (Pryor et al., 2006). TEMPE, which is an anesthetizing topical spray containing lidocaine and prilocaine, rather immediately penetrates the skin of the glans penis. TEMPE quickly leads to diminished sensation of the glans penis (Dinsmore et al., 2007). If registrated, future research should compare the advantages and disadvantages of these new drugs to the SSRIs, which are widely used off-label drugs for premature ejaculation.

DEFINITIONS

The debate about the nature of premature ejaculation and its etiology seriously delayed the exact definition of the disorder. Masters and Johnson (1970) and Kaplan (1974) used qualitative descriptions for definitions. Masters and Johnson defined *premature ejaculation* as the man's inability to inhibit ejaculation long enough for his partner to reach orgasm 50% of the time. Their definition implies that any male partner of a female having difficulty in reaching orgasm could be labeled with the disorder. It also implies that females *should* reach orgasm in 50% of occasions of intercourse. Kaplan thought the essence of the problem was the inability to choose the moment of ejaculation. In a semiquantitative fashion, others suggested that premature ejaculation should be defined by ejaculatory latency or the number of thrusts prior to ejaculation (e.g., between 1 and 7 minutes after vaginal intromission or 8 to 15 thrusts).

Can we seriously accept that men who maintain thrusting for 5 to 7 minutes are rapid? It is important to consider how these writers achieved these figures. Did they measure with a stopwatch? Certainly, they did not. The cutoff points of 1 to 7 minutes were not derived from objective measurements; they were subjectively chosen by the authors.

The *DSM-IV-TR* (*Diagnostic and Statistical Manual of Mental Disorders, Fourth Edition, Text Revision;* American Psychiatric Association [APA], 2000) defined *premature ejaculation* as "persistent or recurrent ejaculation with minimal sexual stimulation before, upon, or shortly after penetration and before the person wishes it." Is this a satisfying definition? In my view and that of others, it is not because it does not clarify the meanings of "persistent," "recurrent," "minimal," and "shortly after" (Waldinger, Hengeveld, Zwinderman, & Olivier, 1998b). How long precisely is "shortly after"? Is it 1 or 2 minutes?

The Stopwatch

For our psychopharmacological treatment studies, it was imperative to have an empirically derived definition of premature ejaculation. We had to be sure that the men we wanted to treat did indeed suffer from true premature ejaculation. The solution arrived in the form of a simple instrument: the stopwatch.

In 1973, the psychoanalyst Tanner used a stopwatch to measure the ejaculation time. While this was a splendid methodological advance, in the next 20 years there were only two publications about the use of a stopwatch. Al Cooper and Ralph Magnus from the University of Western Ontario in Canada

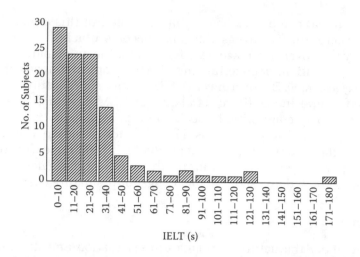

Figure 16.1 Intravaginal ejaculation latency time (IELT) measured with a stopwatch in 110 men with life-long histories of rapid ejaculation. Of men, 90% ejaculate within 1 minute after vaginal penetration, with 80% actually ejaculating within 30 seconds. (From Waldinger et al., *Int J Psych Clin Pract* 1998 (2), 287–293 With permission.)

used it in 1984. In 1995, the American psychologist Stanley Althof and psychiatrist Stephen Levine used the stopwatch in a clomipramine study (Althof, Levine, Corty, Risen, & Stern, 1995).

Our group in the Netherlands used the stopwatch to empirically derive a definition in a study of 110 consecutively enrolled Dutch men with lifelong premature ejaculation (Waldinger, Hengeveld, Zwinderman, & Olivier, 1998b). I instructed their female partners to use a stopwatch at home during each coitus for a period of 4 weeks. The study demonstrated that 90% of these men ejaculated within 1 minute of intromission, with 80% ejaculating within 30 seconds (Figure 16.1). Thus, the stopwatch revealed that lifelong premature ejaculation is a matter of seconds and not of minutes. We replicated these results in another study (Janssen et al., 2009). We also demonstrated that the self-perceived—thus not measured with a stopwatch—intravaginal ejaculation latency time (IELT) of 90% of men with lifelong premature ejaculation was also within 60 seconds (Waldinger et al., 2007).

A number of other stopwatch studies have been conducted in various countries (Patrick et al., 2005). However, they have differed in methodology and design. For example, these studies contained a mixture of men with lifelong and acquired premature ejaculation. Moreover, they defined premature ejaculation according to complaints of diminished control and satisfaction with intercourse. Consequently, these studies are less suitable for the investigation of the key characteristics of lifelong premature ejaculation. Still, these studies done in different countries provide useful information to suggest that they are not that different from Dutch men with lifelong premature ejaculation.

NEW DEFINITION OF LIFELONG PREMATURE EJACULATION

A few years after the millennium, readers of the literature on sexual medicine witnessed a fierce debate on an appropriate definition of premature ejaculation. On the one hand, there were some clinicians—I was one of them—who stated that the current *DSM-IV-TR* (APA, 2000) definition is inadequate and had to be changed in the next edition. On the other hand, others wrote that the *DSM-IV-TR* definition should not be changed. Fortunately, it was agreed that the *DSM-IV-TR* definition was not evidence based. In the midst of the debate, in 2007, the International Society of Sexual Medicine (ISSM) organized an international panel to convene in Amsterdam to find consensus on a new definition of premature ejaculation. The ISSM panel concluded that there was insufficient data for an evidence-based definition of acquired premature ejaculation. However, it succeeded in formulating a fully evidence-based new definition of lifelong premature ejaculation (McMahon et al., 2008): *Lifelong premature ejaculation* is characterized by

1. Ejaculation that always or nearly always occurs prior to or within about 1 minute of vaginal penetration
2. Inability to delay ejaculation on all or nearly all vaginal penetrations
3. Negative personal consequences, such as distress, bother, frustration, or the avoidance of sexual intimacy

THE NEUROBIOLOGICAL AND GENETIC APPROACH

It is only since 1995 that more insight into the background of premature ejaculation has been gained. I can imagine that older psychotherapists do not like to hear this, but although various psychological and psychotherapeutic hypotheses have been postulated, there is a serious lack of well-designed psychological studies that have tested the validity of the hypotheses. Indeed, most of the psychological hypotheses have never even been investigated or been proved in a scientific way. Still, many therapists insist on using psychotherapy. Personally, I believe this is the critical moment to undertake such psychotherapeutic studies. We may even be in a now-or-never situation because if these studies are not undertaken, it will become more and more difficult to maintain the assumption that premature ejaculation, particularly lifelong premature ejaculation, is in general related to psychological disturbances.

Currently, evidence-based medicine is the key feature of a scientific medical approach. There is a reasonable amount of neurobiological evidence of how the central nervous system is involved in eliciting premature ejaculation (Waldinger, 2002).

Animal Studies

Neuroscientists were already investigating the role of serotonin and dopamine in ejaculation in the 1970s. Serotonin and dopamine are compounds in the brain that are involved in transferring messages from one nerve or neuron to another. They are called *neurotransmitters*, and the process of sending messages from one nerve to the other is called *neurotransmission*.

Around 1990, the important neurobiological data known to neuroscientists were hardly known to the clinicians who saw male patients with premature ejaculation. So, the paradox existed that although clinicians were employing behavioral therapy, neuroscientists had completely different information about the ejaculation process. This has changed since 1995. Basic neurobiological knowledge has become integrated with clinical practice. What we have learned so far from animal studies is that serotonin (also called 5-hydroxytryptamine, abbreviated 5-HT) is probably the most important neurotransmitter that is involved in the ejaculatory process. Of the 17 or so serotonin subtype receptors, it is the 5-HT_{1A} and the 5-HT_{2C} receptors that are crucial for ejaculation. In male rats, activation of the 5-HT_{2C} receptor delays ejaculation, whereas activation of the 5-HT_{1A} receptor results in a shorter ejaculation latency.

Based on 5-HT_{2C} and 5-HT_{1A} receptor data in animals, I formulated the hypothesis that in lifelong premature ejaculation there is diminished 5-HT neurotransmission or either a hyposensitivity of the 5-HT_{2C} or a hypersensitivy of the 5-HT_{1A} receptor (Waldinger et al., 1998; Waldinger & Olivier, 2000). I found evidence for this hypothesis by performing various stopwatch studies. Investigation of five different SSRIs, which all activate the 5-HT_{2C} receptor, showed that all SSRIs—albeit with different intensity—delay ejaculation, while nefazodone and mirtazapine, two antidepressants that impair the 5-HT_{2C} subtype receptor, do not delay ejaculation (Waldinger, Zwinderman, & Olivier, 2001). Hard evidence that diminished 5-HT neurotransmission is associated with a shorter IELT came from our study on the DNA of men with lifelong premature ejaculation (Janssen et al., 2009). We showed that men with the LL genotype of the 5-HTTLPR polymorphism have 100% faster ejaculations than men with SS and SL genotypes (Janssen et al., 2009).

Neuroanatomy

Neuroscientists have gained much knowledge of the areas in the brain that are specifically involved in ejaculation. This knowledge came from male rat studies. For an in-depth understanding, one has to distinguish among brain, brain stem, and spinal cord regions that become activated before and following ejaculation (Figure 16.2). When discussing neuroanatomy, we cannot avoid using technical terms.

The medial preoptic area (MPOA) in the hypothalamus and the nucleus paragigantocellularis (nPGi) in the medulla are important players in the process leading toward ejaculation. Electrical stimulation of the MPOA promotes ejaculation. In addition, serotonergic receptors have been found to be present in the nPGi. The discovery of serotonergic neurons in the nPGi and the well-known ejaculation delay induced by serotonergic antidepressants suggests that SSRIs delay ejaculation by actions on the nPGi. However, the precise location where SSRIs inhibit ejaculation has not yet been demonstrated.

Around 1995, Veening and Coolen (1998), Dutch neurobiologists, made some interesting discoveries. They found that after ejaculation occurred, specific areas in the brain become activated. Let us talk about the posteromedial part of the bed nucleus of the stria terminalis (BNSTpm), a lateral subarea in the posterodorsal part of the medial amygdala (MEApd), the MPOA), and the medial part of the parvicellular subparafascicular nucleus (SPFps) of the thalamus. These areas become activated to inform the brain that an ejaculation has occurred. During their activation, the brain has to pause a moment before it can stimulate the genitals for another ejaculation. Men and women may not like this pause, but it is inevitable from a neurobiological perspective.

By the way, did you know that male rats start to sing after ejaculation? They do. It is a low-frequency postejaculatory song. And, as long a male rat is singing, his female partner rat stays silent and immobile. She only gets lively again when he stops singing and then shows she is willing to copulate with him again.

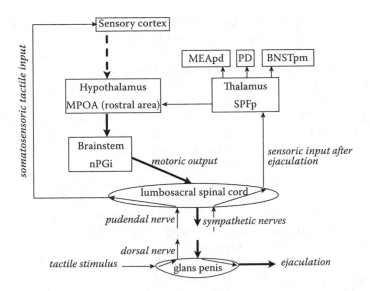

Figure 16.2   Areas in the central nervous system that are involved prior to, during, and after ejaculation. Somatosensory fibers reach the sensory cortex. Efferent pathways run from the hypothalamus down to the sacral spinal cord and genitals. After ejaculation, information transmits back from the genitals to various areas in the cerebrum. For full names of abbreviations, see text. (From Waldinger et al., *Int J Psych Clin Pract* 1998 (2), 287–293. With permission.)

How about human studies? It will not come as any surprise that no neuroanatomical studies on men with premature ejaculation have been done. The only way in which we can look into the brains of men with premature ejaculation is by performing brain imaging studies. Thus, by performing a positron emission tomographic (PET) scan study, we are able to investigate the brain areas that are active during a specific human function. PET scan studies of premature ejaculating men may in the future contribute to better understanding of the circuitry that is disturbed among lifelong premature ejaculators.

Biological Variation of the Ejaculation Latency Time

In performing animal studies, my colleague and neuropharmacologist Berend Olivier and I noticed that during each experiment with a specific number of male rats, there is always a certain number in the group for which there is very rapid sexual behavior and in the remainder a number for which it is very slow. About 70–80% of the rats perform copulation in the same period of time. That phenomenon led us to postulate that possibly there might also exist such a biological variation of the IELT with men. We defined *IELT* as the time between the start of vaginal penetration and the start of intravaginal ejaculation (Waldinger, Hengeveld, & Zwinderman, 1994). We postulated that in each random sample of men there is a range among men in the duration of their IELTs. The range extends from those who ejaculate rapidly, to those who do so at an average speed, to those who ejaculate slowly, to those who do not at all. Considered in this way, it is just bad luck for a man who is born with a rapid rate of ejaculation.

But, what is the evidence for our bad luck hypothesis? For a long time, it was unknown how the IELT was distributed in the general male population. With the financial support of Pfizer International, we performed the first stopwatch study of the IELT in an unselected cohort of men in the general male population. The study, performed in 491 men of five countries (Netherlands, United Kingdom, Spain, Turkey, and the United States), showed that the IELT has a skewed distribution. The median IELT is 5.4 minutes, ranging from 0.55 to 44.1 minutes (Waldinger, Quinn, et al., 2005; Waldinger, Zwinderman, Olivier, & Schweitzer, 2005). As postulated, there is, indeed, an impressive variability of the IELT in the general male population. We were able to calculate the normal and abnormal ranges of the IELT. By applying the statistical rule that every value beneath either the 0.5 or the 2.5 percentile is abnormal in a skewed distribution, the study showed that IELT values of less than 1 minute are statistically regarded as abnormal. It is therefore no coincidence that 90% of men with lifelong premature ejaculation who seek medical treatment have IELTs of less than 1 minute. We replicated this study—again with the financial support from Pfizer International—a few years later in the same countries but with new volunteers (Waldinger, McIntosh, & Schweitzer, 2009). However, in this second study, we handed the participants a blinded timer device instead of a stopwatch. The couples were unable to see the time that was measured during intercourse. The median IELT was 6.0 minutes (range 0.1 to 52.1 minutes), which is rather the same median IELT as in our first study. Because of this outcome, we concluded that real-time measurement with a stopwatch is an accurate, reliable, and valid way to measure the IELT.

The assumption of a population-based variability of the ejaculation time implies that lifelong premature ejaculation should be considered a biological phenomenon rather than a psychological–behavioral abnormality. This biological phenomenon likely carries different connotations, according to individuals, populations, and cultures. There are men and women who cope very well with lifelong premature ejaculation and do not find it a major problem. But, for others premature ejaculation may become a psychological or emotional problem. This problem may become so severe that psychotherapeutic intervention may be useful. The psychology of lifelong premature ejaculation is therefore a secondary problem rather than the primary cause.

Ejaculation Threshold Hypothesis

To understand the suggested biological variation of the IELT in relation to the serotonergic system, delaying effects of SSRIs, and suggested genetics, we have proposed the existence of a central nervous system threshold of the IELT.

In the case of a low set point of the threshold, men can sustain only a low sexual arousal prior to ejaculation. Whatever these men do or fantasize about during intercourse, any control of ejaculation remains marginal, and these men ejaculate easily even when they are not fully aroused. I have postulated that the low threshold is probably associated with a low 5-HT neurotransmission and a hypofunction of the 5-HT_{2C} receptor (Waldinger, 2002).

When men have a higher set point, they will experience more control over their ejaculation time. They can sustain more sexual arousal before ejaculating. In these men, 5-HT neurotransmission varies around a normal or average level. We might say that the 5-HT_{2C} receptor functions normally.

When men have a high or very high set point, they may experience difficulty in ejaculating or are unable to ejaculate at all, even when fully sexually aroused. At a high set point, 5-HT neurotransmission is supposed to be increased, and it is suggested that the 5-HT_{2C} receptor sensitivity is enhanced, or both of these occur.

It is still unknown which neural mechanisms or pathways finally determine the set point. Men with premature ejaculation or those on serotonergic antidepressants activate and desensitize 5-HT_{2C} receptors and 5-HT_{1A} receptors. Desensitization of these postsynaptic 5-HT receptors can therefore switch the set point to a higher level, leading to a delay in ejaculation. The effects of SSRIs on the set point appear to be individually determined; some men respond with an intense delay, whereas others experience only a small delay with a given dose of the drug. Moreover, cessation of treatment results in a uniform reset of the set point within 3–5 days to the lower individually determined reference level, that is, at the level that is, according to my opinion, genetically determined.

I presume that the threshold is mediated by serotonin neurotransmission and 5-HT receptors in the brain stem or spinal cord. These may be terminal points of nuclei that mediate somatosensory (e.g., tactile) information from the genitals. It is suggested that SSRIs enhance the inhibitory effects of these serotonergic neurons. However, the cerebral cortex may also mediate inhibitory impulses, but this has not yet been demonstrated. The SSRIs might also delay ejaculation by interfering with spinal cord motoneurons of peripheral neurons that inhibit the internal genitals. Further studies are needed to unravel this important and intriguing question.

Course of Rapidity Over the Life Cycle

It is generally believed that aging delays ejaculation. This assumption might be true for men with a normal or average ejaculation time but has never been investigated in men with lifelong premature ejaculation. Men with lifelong premature ejaculation told me that they were often reassured by their general physicians that the problem would become better as they became older. As there was no evidence on which this reassurance was based, I started a study to investigate the tendency in the history of rapidity. The study informed us with new important data. Of 110 consecutively enrolled men (aged 18 to 65 years) with lifelong premature ejaculation, 76% reported that throughout their lives, their speed of ejaculation had remained as rapid as at the first sexual contacts in puberty and adolescence; 23% reported that it had even gradually increased in speed with aging. Only 1% reported that it had become slower.

These data lend support for my view that in lifelong premature ejaculation there is a fixed rate of rapidity across a life span and even a paradoxical shortening of the ejaculation latency time. This fixed and paradoxical pattern while getting older should be recognized as a part of the pathogenetic process of premature ejaculation. Taken together with our hypothesis of a biological variation of the IELT, I believe that the phenomenon of lifelong premature ejaculation is an inevitable consequence of a normally occurring biological variation of the ejaculation time in men. However, I consider its fixed and even paradoxical course through life as pathological. In other words, when a man occasionally suffers from rapid ejaculation, this does not have to be considered pathological. It can be explained as the result of too much arousal or due to some psychological mechanisms. However, when a man is premature with each intercourse on a continuing basis, then premature ejaculation has to be considered as a symptom of the clinical syndrome of primary (lifelong) premature ejaculation. As yet, there is no real cure for lifelong premature ejaculation, although serotonergic drugs may alleviate the symptoms, but only as long as they are taken.

PREMATURE EJACULATION AND ERECTILE DYSFUNCTION

It is important to know that some men with premature ejaculation may express their complaint as an erectile disorder. In that case, they do not mention the rapidity of ejaculation but focus on the immediate detumescence of the penis after ejaculation. It is therefore always important to ask about premature ejaculation in men complaining of erectile disturbances. On the other hand, a true erectile dysfunction may be superimposed on the existence of a lifelong pattern of premature ejaculation, either because of the efforts of these men to minimize their sexual excitement or due to general causes of erectile dysfunction. One may wonder whether premature ejaculation itself is associated with an increased neurobiological risk to develop erectile dysfunction. As yet, there is no evidence for such an associated risk. To study whether there is such a risk, longitudinal prospective studies in men with premature ejaculation and matched controls are necessary but not yet undertaken.

The majority of men with a lifelong history of premature ejaculation do not suffer from concomitant erectile difficulties, and most of these men do not seek help for being rapid. However, there are some men who look for help only when they also begin to suffer from erectile difficulties. This may bias the population of men with premature ejaculation that presents at an urological clinic.

When we recruited men with premature ejaculation through advertising, we learned that 75% had never sought help for premature ejaculation, mostly out of embarrassment, and 95% did not suffer from erectile difficulties (Waldinger et al., 2001). Many of these men reported having an erection very quickly. In 1943, Schapiro called this phenomenon *erectio praecox.* Although this term has never been referred to in literature, I would like to introduce and use it again as I have heard over and over again, both from men with lifelong premature ejaculation and from their partners, that erection occurs very quickly. However, obviously we need controlled studies before we can state that erectio praecox is a true concomitant symptom of lifelong ejaculatio praecox.

The proven effectiveness of SSRIs in serotonergic-related disorders, like depression, anxiety disorders, obsessive–compulsive disorder, and impulsivity, may pose the question whether men with premature ejaculation are at risk because of these disorders. Our studies using a clinical interview and the Symptom Check List with 90 items (SCL-90) have repeatedly and clearly demonstrated that men with lifelong premature ejaculation are in general mentally and physically healthy individuals and as healthy as the average for the age controls of the general (nonpsychiatric) male population.

PROPOSAL FOR A NEW CLASSIFICATION

I proposed a new classification of premature ejaculation for the *DSM-V* and *ICD-11* (*International Statistical Classification of Diseases and Related Health Problems, 11th Revision*) (Waldinger, 2006; Waldinger & Schweitzer, 2006). I proposed that premature ejaculation should be classified according to a "syndromal" approach and suggested to add to premature ejaculation's two well-known forms, lifelong and acquired, two additional categories "natural variable premature ejaculation" and "premature-like ejaculatory dysfunction" (Waldinger, 2006). In natural variable premature ejaculation, men only occasionally suffer from early ejaculations. This should be regarded as part of the normal variability of ejaculatory performance in men and not a symptom of underlying psychopathology. In premature-like ejaculatory dysfunction, men experience or utter complaints of premature ejaculation while having objectively long durations of the IELT of 4–20 minutes.

In the new proposal, the four premature ejaculation syndromes are defined according to the symptomatology discussed next.

Lifelong Premature Ejaculation

Lifelong premature ejaculation is a syndrome characterized by the cluster of the following core symptoms (Waldinger, 2007b):

1. Ejaculation occurs too early at nearly every intercourse.
2. Ejaculation occurs with (nearly) every woman.
3. Ejaculation occurs from about the first sexual encounters onward.
4. Ejaculation occurs in the majority of cases (80–90%) within 30–60 seconds or between 1 and 2 minutes (10%).
5. Ejaculation remains rapid during life (70%) or can even aggravate during aging (30%).

Some men ejaculate during foreplay, before penetration (*ejaculatio ante portas*), or as soon as their penis touches the vagina (*ejaculatio intra portas*). It should be noted that there is no hard evidence that lifelong premature ejaculation can be cured—that is, disappear forever—by medication or psychotherapy. Lifelong premature ejaculation is a chronic ejaculatory dysfunction but during drug treatment with SSRIs ejaculation in these men has a high chance of getting postponed.

Acquired Premature Ejaculation

The complaints of men with acquired premature ejaculation differ in relation to the underlying somatic or psychological problem.

1. Premature ejaculation occurs at some point in a man's life after he had normal ejaculatory experiences.
2. There is either a sudden or gradual onset.
3. The dysfunction may be due to
   - urological dysfunctions (e.g., erectile dysfunction or prostatitis; Screponi et al., 2001), although there is still debate about the evidence that prostatitis actually leads to premature ejaculation
   - thyroid dysfunction (Carani et al., 2005)
   - psychological or relationship problems (Althof, 2005; Hartmann, Schedlowski, & Kruger, 2005)

The acquired form of premature ejaculation can be cured by medical or psychological treatment of the underlying cause.

Natural Variable Premature Ejaculation

Men with natural variable premature ejaculation only coincidentally and situationally experience early ejaculations. This type of premature ejaculation should not be regarded as a symptom or manifestation of underlying psychopathology but of normal variation in sexual performance. This subtype is characterized by the following symptoms:

1. Early ejaculations are inconsistent and occur irregularly.
2. The ability to delay ejaculation (i.e., to withhold ejaculation at the moment of imminent ejaculation) may be diminished or lacking.
3. Experiences of diminished control of ejaculation go along with either a short or normal ejaculation time (i.e., an ejaculation of less or more than 1.5 minutes).

Treatment of these men should consist of reassurance and education that this form of premature ejaculation is just a normal phenomenon and does not need drug treatment or psychotherapy.

Premature-like Ejaculatory Dysfunction

Men with premature-like ejaculatory dysfunction experience or complain of premature ejaculation while the ejaculation time is in the normal range (i.e., around 2–6 minutes) and may even be of very long duration (i.e., between 5 and 25 minutes) (Waldinger, 2008). This type of premature ejaculation should not be regarded as a symptom or manifestation of medical or neurobiological pathology. Psychological or relationship problems may underlie the complaints. The syndrome is characterized by the following symptoms:

1. Subjective perception of consistent or inconsistent early ejaculation during intercourse
2. Preoccupation with an imagined early ejaculation or lack of control of ejaculation
3. An actual IELT in the normal range or maybe longer duration (i.e., an ejaculation that occurs between 3 and 25 minutes)
4. Ability to delay ejaculation (i.e., to withhold ejaculation at the moment of imminent ejaculation) may be diminished or lacking

As the duration of the ejaculation time in this form of premature ejaculation is normal, we may conclude that there is nothing medically or neurobiologically disturbed in these men. On the contrary, there is either a misperception of the actual ejaculation time—and there is a multitude of psychological and cultural reasons for such a misperception—or the ejaculation time is really too short for the female partner to attain an orgasm. My personal feeling is that we should explore their complaints to alleviate the complaints by the various sorts of psychotherapy that are available. However, I fear that in the near future when drugs against premature ejaculation are registrated, physicians will find it easier to immediately prescribe such drugs to these men. When we realize that approximately 25% of men who have a normal ejaculation time are discontented with it (Waldinger et al., 2009), and therefore probably have this subtype of premature ejaculation, one may speculate that pharmaceutical companies may wish to stimulate this particular group of men to use their drugs. This, however, should not be regarded as a medical treatment. It is just an example of the use of lifestyle drugs.

A CLINICAL TRAP

Do you remember that I described how lifelong premature ejaculation may become worse some time in later life? That is the trap if you are not aware of this phenomenon. Some men who have this pattern may hardly ever or not at all have realized or been confronted by others that they were at the margins of being very rapid. Only when the rapidity becomes worse during aging do they seek help. If the patient focuses on telling you that it is premature now when it was not before, and if the clinician does not explicitly focus on the ejaculation latency time before the man noted his current ejaculation time, then the clinician may mistakenly conclude that this particular man suffers from acquired premature ejaculation. Such an incorrect diagnosis usually means an inappropriate treatment.

Ejaculation Time Measurement

By comparing open-ended questions, answers on questionnaires, and stopwatch measurements, I have noticed that most men and women are unable to judge time properly. Try it yourself; try to estimate with a random task, for example, walking three times from your house to a particular street corner, how precisely you can judge that time. First estimate or guess it and write the time on a bit of paper; then repeat this task, but this time check it using a clock or stopwatch. Now, try a second task—I mean, you should really try to do this—if you are a male reader, estimate the time that you take to have an ejaculation after vaginal penetration of your partner. If you are a female reader, estimate this time as well for your male partner or for yourself until you have an orgasm. Then, check it with a stopwatch.

By performing this task yourself, you will better realize how subjective a patient's answer on time estimation is. So, what to do? It is obvious that a clinician cannot provide a stopwatch for each patient who has complaints of premature ejaculation. But, the clinician also cannot rely on just a guess about the ejaculation time. I have found the following method to be more accurate to get an estimation of the ejaculation latency time: First, I ask the patient to estimate or guess the duration of the time that he gets an ejaculation after vaginal penetration of his female partner. The answer is written. Then, I take a stopwatch from my desk and explain the following test to him. I ask the patient to imagine having foreplay with this partner. I tell him that at a certain moment, I will say "now," and that this means that foreplay is over, and vaginal penetration starts. He then has to imagine that he penetrates and thrusts with his penis and has to say "yes" when he thinks or feels that he would have an ejaculation at home. I press the start button of the stopwatch at the moment I say "now" and the stop button when the patient says "yes". In the majority of men, I have found that there is a clinically important difference from his first spontaneous answer. Then, I tell him the time—for example, 15 seconds—that was measured by the stopwatch and then the time that he had told me earlier (e.g., 1 minute). In addition, I say to him, "Now let's check the time that you first mentioned. You told me 1 minute." I start the stopwatch, and after 1 minute, I say "One minute." I then suggest, "Try to find out whether this is the time that you can manage to keep up your ejaculation at home." Very often, the answer I get is, "No, I think I overestimated the time." This imaginative time assessment procedure, checked by stopwatch, is helpful in achieving better knowledge of the ejaculation time and is helpful for the man in realizing the subjectivity of his time assessment. But, of course, this method is also not exact. It is nevertheless better than just a wild guess by the patient. Be aware that this test may be embarrassing as it confronts the man with the likely reality that he is even more rapid than he thought.

I also use this method for men's partners to get an impression of a man's ejaculation time. After an initial talk, I usually ask one of the partners to leave the room so that I can talk to the other individually. I perform, with each of them separately, this "imagined time with a stopwatch test." As tests must have a name, let us call it the ITS test. The ITS test is also helpful to get an impression of the validity of each person's estimate. After I have seen each of them individually, I then bring them back together in my room and explain my diagnosis and choices of treatment.

DELAYED EJACULATION

Ejaculation and orgasm usually occur simultaneously in men even though they are separate phenomena. Ejaculation occurs in the genital organs, whereas orgasmic sensation is mainly a cerebral event that involves the whole body. The syndrome of anesthetic ejaculation demonstrates how orgasm and ejaculation may exist independently. Men with anesthetic ejaculation ejaculate without orgasmic sensation (Williams, 1985). Both ejaculation and orgasm are influenced by psychological processes.

It is unfortunate that a clear distinction between orgasm and ejaculation has not been made in the *DSM-IV-TR* (APA, 2000), in which ejaculation disorders are categorized under orgasmic disorders. Delayed ejaculation has been called "male orgasmic disorder," analogous to "female orgasmic disorder," whereas premature ejaculation has not been called "premature orgasm" (Waldinger & Schweitzer, 2005). *DSM-IV-TR* is not in line with current neurobiological understanding that orgasm and ejaculation have different neurobiological pathways and utilize different neurotransmitters (Waldinger & Schweitzer, 2005). We have suggested that the next edition should use the term *delayed ejaculation* instead of male orgasmic disorder.

Complaints of Delayed Ejaculation

Not every complaint of having had a delayed ejaculation is the result of an ejaculatory "disorder." For example, a woman may believe her partner to have a delayed ejaculation even though from an objective point of view he is ejaculating within a normal ejaculation time. This example contrasts with men who are never able to get an ejaculation by masturbation or intercourse. Such men suffer from the disorder delayed ejaculation.

Lifelong and Acquired Delayed Ejaculation

Clinicians distinguish lifelong (primary) delayed ejaculation from acquired (secondary) delayed ejaculation. If delayed ejaculation has been present from early adulthood, the disorder is termed *lifelong*. In the acquired form, delayed ejaculation becomes apparent some time in life after prior normal ejaculatory functioning. Unfortunately, there is a paucity of well-designed studies on lifelong delayed ejaculation. This may be due to its rather low prevalence. Also contributing, however, is the frequent clinical misjudgment that delayed ejaculation helps a man to satisfy his sexual partner to have one or multiple orgasms. However, lifelong delayed ejaculation is involuntarily and may induce many emotional and practical problems for both sexual partners. Apart from reproduction difficulties, many men become frustrated by the lack of ejaculations and orgasms. Female sexual partners can also become victim as they imagine that they are unattractive to their partner in facilitating ejaculation, and they even might think that perhaps another woman is needed. Intense prolonged thrusting may become painful for either partner. It is the failure to conceive, however, that often is the main reason for couples to seek help.

Symptoms of Delayed Ejaculation

Delayed ejaculation means that a man finds it difficult or impossible to ejaculate despite the presence of adequate sexual stimulation, erection, and conscious desire to achieve orgasm. Some struggle to ejaculate to the point of complete physical exhaustion of both sexual partners. Delayed ejaculation may occur in coitus, masturbation (either by the patient or by the partner), as well as during oral intercourse.

If ejaculation is delayed in all situations, in all sexual activities, and with all partners, then the disorder is *generalized*. The disorder is classified as *situational* if the delayed ejaculation is limited to certain situations or with certain partners. Situational delayed ejaculation may therefore give rise to different clinical presentations: A man is unable to ejaculate intravaginally but can do so by masturbation, a man is able to ejaculate during sex with a man but not with a woman, a man is able to ejaculate with one particular woman but not with another, a man is able to ejaculate with the same woman on one occasion but not on the next, or a man can only ejaculate when the sexual act is accompanied by specific stimulation or a specific fantasy.

Prevalence of Delayed Ejaculation

Lifelong delayed ejaculation is a relatively uncommon condition. In many studies analyzing the distribution of sexual dysfunctions in clinics, delayed ejaculation always is the least frequent sexual complaint. However, the prevalence of delayed ejaculation in the general population differs. For example, in a general U.S. male population it was 8% (Laumann, Paik, & Rosen, 1999), but in a study in Iceland, the prevalence was less than 1% in men aged 55 to 57 years (Lindal & Stefansson, 1993). And in France, the prevalence of delayed ejaculation was 4% (Spira, Bajos, Giami, & Michaels, 1998), whereas in a Swedish study among men aged 18–74 years, it was 2% (Fugl-Meyer & Sjogren Fugl-Meyer, 1999). In the last study, the prevalence was higher at older age. One should always realize that these prevalence data may be biased by lack of accurate measurement tools.

LIFELONG DELAYED EJACULATION

Psychological Theories

According to the classical psychological view, lifelong delayed ejaculation is attributed to fear, anxiety, hostility, and relationship difficulties (Kaplan, 1974; Munjack & Kanno, 1979; Shull & Sprenkle, 1980). Many different manifestations of anxiety and fear have been hypothesized, some of which are difficult to understand if one is not acquainted with psychodynamic theory. For example, what should be thought of fears of death and castration, fear of loss of self resulting from loss of semen, fear of castration by the female genitals, fear that ejaculation would hurt the female, and fear of being hurt by the female? More easy to understand are performance anxiety, unwillingness to give of oneself as an expression of love, fear of impregnating the female, and guilt secondary to a strict religious upbringing. I do not reject any of these hypotheses because in individual cases unresolved unconscious conflicts may contribute to delayed ejaculation. Moreover, there is no psychological theory available that adequately explains delayed ejaculation in men. In scientific terms, some of these psychological explanations have face validity in some individual cases, but it should be noted that there are no well-controlled studies available that support a generalization of any of the hypotheses. Still, there are many anecdotal data of successful behavioral treatment, illustrating that psychological and environmental factors contribute to lifelong delayed ejaculation.

Assessment

A complete medical and sexual history is crucial in each patient with delayed ejaculation. One should clarify whether delayed ejaculation is generalized or situational (location, sexual activity, specific partner); whether the complaint existed from the first sexual encounters (lifelong) or occurred later in life (acquired); whether ejaculation or orgasm are lacking; and one should inform about the frequency of delayed ejaculations and the duration of the ejaculation time.

Treatment

Various treatments have been used to treat men with delayed ejaculation. Vibratory and electrical stimulation, sexual exercises, and a range of psychotherapeutic techniques have been used separately or in combination (Apfelbaum, 1989; Delmonte, 1984; Delmonte & Braidwood, 1980; Gagliardi, 1976). Successful ejaculation in delayed ejaculation by vibration of the penis has been previously published, but data on long-term improvements are lacking (Beckerman, Becher, & Lankhorst, 1993). Transrectal electrical stimulation of the internal genitals (electroejaculation) is mainly used to obtain semen in paraplegic men (Dekker, 1993). This intervention, however, is extremely painful if used in neurologically healthy men and is not an option to treat lifelong delayed ejaculation. Masturbation exercises have been extensively described as a way to treat delayed ejaculation (Kaplan, 1974). Apart from masturbation exercises, individual psychodynamic psychotherapy, marital therapy, rational emotive therapy, and social skills training have been previously published. The overall impression is that with each technique, variable results can be achieved, but definite answers need controlled clinical trials. Due to scientific uncertainties, no firm conclusions or recommendations about treatment can be given (Dekker, 1993).

Neurobiological Research

In an animal experiment in the 1940s, it was demonstrated that rats reared in isolation are either not capable to achieve ejaculation or remain sexually inactive after repeated exposure to a receptive female (Beach, 1942). In contrast, rats who grew up in groups with either same-sex or heterosex cage mates did not show these clear deficits in copulatory behavior. Importantly, in most but not all of the isolation-reared males sexual performance gradually improved with experience. These early findings suggest not only that early traumatic experiences may induce delayed ejaculation but also that experience and learning play a role in rat copulatory performance.

As I discussed in the premature ejaculation portion of this chapter, central serotonergic neurotransmission, including the amount of serotonin turnover and involvement of serotonergic receptors, is involved in the ejaculatory functioning in animals and men (Waldinger, Berendsen et al., 1998; Olivier, van Oorschot, & Waldinger, 1998). In studies in laboratory rats, it was attempted to create hyposexual behaviour, mimicking delayed ejaculation, by manipulating the level of sexual experience (Mos, Olivier, Bloetjes, & Poth, 1990). For example, in sexually "naïve" male Wistar rats (e.g., rats with no previous encounter with a female rat) who were exposed to female receptive rats (in estrus) for the first time during tests of 15 minutes each, 8.3% of the study sample showed no sexual activity at all. From all rats, 82% displayed sexual activity but failed to ejaculate during the test. However, sexual performance of these sexually naïve male rats improved after treatment with 5-HT$_{1A}$ receptor agonists. In particular, two selective 5-HT$_{1A}$ receptor agonists (i.e., 8-OH-DPAT and flesinoxan) enhanced sexual behavior almost to sexually experienced levels. Sexual performance was also facilitated after partial 5-HT$_{1A}$ receptor agonists (i.e., buspirone and ipsapirone), although sedation became enhanced after buspirone in higher doses. Furthermore, α_2-adrenoceptor antagonists like yohimbine and idazoxan also appear effective in shortening ejaculation time of sexually naïve rats (Mos et al., 1990; Mos, Van Logten, Bloetjes, & Olivier, 1991). These findings indicate that naïve male rats are able to perform sexual activities reminiscent of sexually "experienced" rats in a very short time.

Mos et al. (1990) also showed that males treated with 5-HT$_{1A}$ receptor agonists (flesinoxan, gepirone) were more attractive to receptive females in comparison with placebo-treated males. In animals, it has also been shown that hyposexual behavior in sexually inactive rats can be reversed by the opioid receptor antagonist naloxone (Gessa et al., 1979). Following these findings, several other studies have shown that also other pharmacological compounds and certain neuropeptides can act beneficially toward copulatory behavior in sexually inactive rats. For example, the 5-HT$_{1A}$ receptor agonist 8-OH-DPAT clearly increased sexual activity in rats that were sexually inactive (Haensel, Mos, Olivier, & Slob, 1991). Similarly, the erectogenic drug sildenafil (Ottani, Giuliani, & Ferrari, 2002) and low doses of the hormone melatonin (Drago & Busa, 2000) did also show reversibility of hyposexual behavior of sexually inactive rats.

These pharmacological studies strongly suggest that specific neurobiological mechanisms should be held responsible for hyposexual behavior in the sexually inactive rat. Indeed, in recent years neurobiological differences have been found between rats that are sexually inactive and rats that display normal sexual behavior. Despite the fact that more animal studies are needed, it seems to be attractive to study these substrates in men with delayed ejaculation and anejaculation. However, until today these studies have hardly been conducted in a scientifically appropriate way.

Brain Imaging

Nothing is known about the brain regions involved in delayed ejaculation and anejaculation. However, a very interesting PET scan study on anejaculation was performed by Georgiadis and Holstege (2004). In 11 healthy male volunteers who tried to achieve ejaculation in the PET scan, only half of the attempts were successful. Successful ejaculation resulted in very marked increases of regional cerebral blood flow (rCBF) in the mesodiencephalic transition zone and the cerebellum (Holstege et al., 2003).

The scans of the unsuccessful attempts showed activations in the right orbitofrontal cortex, the left dorsal prefrontal cortex, and bilaterally in the anterior insula. Comparison with the scans of successful attempts of ejaculation showed that nonejaculatory performance involves more cortical activity than ejaculation, especially in the left temporal pole and most anterior amygdala, structures that are important for vigilance and fear behavior. It was concluded that higher levels of activity in the anterior temporal lobe may lead to anejaculation (Georgiadis & Holstege, 2004). Although the volunteers were not patients with persistent anejaculation, this study provides interesting information because the unsuccessful attempts may mimic the real-life situation of anejaculation in men who have no urogenital abnormalities.

ACQUIRED DELAYED EJACULATION

Psychological Causes

There are no specific characteristics of psychologically induced acquired delayed ejaculation. Obviously, the ejaculation disturbance has not existed previously. In addition, the onset may occur suddenly with a situational or intermittent delay. One should always look for provocative psychological trauma (e.g., the discovery of the partner's infidelity) or lack of sexual and psychological stimulation (inadequate technique or lack of attention to sexual stimuli).

Somatic Causes

A moderate but acceptable delay of ejaculation occurs during aging. Androgen deficiency, traumatic or surgical spinal injuries with damage of lumbar sympathetic ganglia and the connecting nerves, abdominoperineal surgery, lumbar sympathectomy, and neurodegenerative disorders (e.g., multiple sclerosis or diabetic neuropathy) may lead to delay or failure of ejaculation. A wide range of drugs (SSRIs, tricyclic antidepressants, antipsychotics, α-sympatholytics) and alcohol (either directly during acute consumption or chronically) can impair ejaculation through central and peripheral mechanisms.

Treatment

Physicians need to be alert with patients taking ejaculation delaying drugs. With regard to antidepressant-induced ejaculation delay, there are theoretically five treatment strategies (Waldinger, 1996):

1. Waiting until the side effects spontaneously disappear
2. Reduction of dosage
3. Stopping the drug a few days before intercourse (drug holidays)
4. Switching to another antidepressant
5. Use of an antidote

However, there is a remarkable lack of placebo-controlled studies investigating these strategies and even fewer well-controlled studies comparing these strategies. In general, the best strategy is to switch to another antidepressant that is known to have fewer ejaculation-delaying side effects. Vascular or neuropathic damage is usually irreversible, and the patient should be counseled to look for alternative methods to satisfy sexual wishes of both sexual partners. Androgen deficiency requires appropriate testosterone replacement therapy. General instructions vary from advice to enjoy more time together, to minimize alcohol consumption, to make love when not tired, and to practice pelvic floor training.

Currently, the best way to treat men with lifelong delayed ejaculation is to inform them about existing factors that can delay their ejaculation and to instruct them through counseling. Beneficial effects through psychotherapy depend on the severity of delayed ejaculation and the individual receptiveness to go along with counseling. Most successful appears to be a combination of masturbation exercises and general therapeutic interventions. Effective drug treatment is not yet available.

Future Drug Research

It is of utmost importance to further unravel the neurobiology of ejaculation and its interaction with psychological factors. A major requirement for well-controlled clinical research remains the clinically objective investigation of the IELT, the masturbation ejaculation latency time (MELT), and the oral ejaculation latency time (OELT) by use of a stopwatch (Waldinger, 2007a). Psychopharmacological animal research remains pivotal. As the prevalence of lifelong retarded ejaculation is presumably rather low and the development of drugs is extremely expensive, there is little chance that a pharmaceutical company will agree to develop a specific drug for this indication in the next few years. Therefore, currently a better option to find drugs against lifelong or acquired retarded ejaculation is to seek for the secondary medical use of existing drugs on the basis of animal research information.

CONCLUSION

I hope that you have noticed that premature ejaculation and delayed ejaculation are serious problems. Reassurance and diminishing the severity of it by superficial remarks by physicians, as I have heard too often from my patients, is not at all helpful. They simply contribute to the hopelessness and isolation of the man or his partner. Since 1992, I have found conducting research into the subject of premature ejaculation satisfying and rewarding, knowing the remarkable effects on and enthusiastic response of couples using the medication. I hear their expressions of gratitude toward me for taking a serious interest in this problem. Many of these couples were willing to cooperate in scientific studies that use a stopwatch, for which I am very grateful. In case you, your partner, or one of your patients suffers from premature ejaculation, I hope that you will use, advise, or prescribe a drug as it can make such a difference in your or your patients' lives. And, with the increasing knowledge of the pharmacology and genetics of ejaculation, I do hope that in the next decade we will find better options to effectively treat delayed ejaculation.

REFERENCES

Abraham, K. (1917). Ueber ejaculatio praecox. *Zeitschrift fur Aerztliche Psychoanalyse, 4*, 171.

Althof, S. E. (2005). Psychological treatment strategies for rapid ejaculation: Rationale, practical aspects, and outcome. *World Journal of Urology, 23*, 89–92.

Althof, S. E., Levine, S. B., Corty, E. W., Risen, C. B., & Stern, E. B. (1995). A double-blind crossover trial of clomipramine for rapid ejaculation in 15 couples. *Journal of Clinical Psychiatry, 56,* 402.

American Psychiatric Association. (2000). *Diagnostic and statistical manual of mental disorders* (4th ed., text rev.). Washington, DC: Author.

Apfelbaum, B. (1989). Retarded ejaculation: A much-misunderstood syndrome. In S. R. Leiblum & R. C. Rosen (Eds.), *Principles and practice of sex therapy. Update for the 1990s* (2nd ed., pp. 168–206). New York: Guilford Press.

Beach, F. A. (1942). Comparison of copulatory behaviour of male rats raised in isolation, cohabition, and segregation. *Journal of Genetic Psychology, 60,* 3–13.

Beckerman, H., Becher, J., & Lankhorst, G. J. (1993). The effectiveness of vibratory stimulation in an retarded ejaculatory man with spinal cord injury. *Paraplegia, 31,* 689–699.

Carani, C., Isidori, A. M., Granata, A., Carosa, E., Maggi, M., Lenzi, A., et al. (2005). Multicenter study on the prevalence of sexual symptoms in male hypo- and hyperthyroid patients. *Journal of Clinical Endocrinology and Metabolism, 90,* 6472–6479.

Cooper, A. J., & Magnus, R. V. (1984). A clinical trial of the beta blocker propranolol in premature ejaculation. *Journal of Psychosomatic Research, 28,* 331.

DeAmicis, L. A., Goldberg, D. C., LoPiccolo, J., Friedman, J., & Davies, L. (1985). Clinical follow-up of couples treated for sexual dysfunction. *Archives of Sexual Behavior, 14,* 467.

Dekker, J. (1993). Inhibited male orgasm. In W. O'Donohue & J. H. Geer (Eds.), *Handbook of sexual dysfunctions* (pp. 279–301). New York: Simon and Schuster.

Delmonte, M. M. (1984). Case reports on the use of meditative relaxation as an intervention strategy with retarded ejaculation. *Biofeedback and Self-regulation, 9,* 209–214.

Delmonte, M., & Braidwood, M. (1980). Treatment of retarded ejaculation with psychotherapy and meditative relaxation: A case report. *Psychological Reports, 47,* 8–10.

Dinsmore, W. W., Hackett, G., Goldmeier, D., Waldinger, M., Dean, J., Wright, P., et al. (2007). Topical eutectic mixture for premature ejaculation (TEMPE): A novel aerosol-delivery form of lidocaine-prilocaine for treating premature ejaculation. *BJU International, 99,* 369–375.

Drago, F., & Busa, L. (2000). Acute low doses of melatonin restore full sexual activity in impotent male rats. *Brain Research, 878,* 98–104.

Eaton, H. (1973). Clomipramine in the treatment of premature ejaculation. *Journal of International Medical Research, 1,* 432.

Fugl-Meyer, A. R., & Sjogren Fugl-Meyer, K. (1999). Sexual disabilities, problems and satisfaction in 18–74 year old Swedes. *Scandinavian Journal of Sexology, 2,* 79–105.

Gagliardi, F. A. (1976). Ejaculatio retardata; conventional psychotherapy and sex therapy in a severe obsessive-compulsive disorder. *American Journal of Psychotherapy, 30,* 85–94.

Georgiadis, J. R., & Holstege, G. (2004). Ejaculation or no ejaculation: The left anterior temporal lobe decides [abstract]? *Program No. 214.18.2004 Abstract. Viewer/Itinerary Planner.* Washington, DC: Society for Neuroscience.

Gessa, G. L., & Paglietti, E., & Pellegrini-Quarantotti, B. (1979). Induction of copulatory behaviour in sexual inactive rats by naloxone. *Science, 204,* 203–205.

Godpodinoff, M. L. (1989). Premature ejaculation: Clinical subgroups and etiology. *Journal of Sex and Marital Therapy, 15,* 130.

Haensel, S. M., Mos, J., Olivier, B., & Slob, A. K. (1991). Sex behavior of male and female Wistar rats affected by the serotonin agonist 8-OH-DPAT. *Pharmacology, Biochemistry, and Behavior, 40,* 221–228.

Hartmann, U., Schedlowski, M., & Kruger, T. H. C. (2005). Cognitive and partner-related factors in rapid ejaculation: Differences between dysfunctional and functional men. *World Journal of Urology, 23,* 93–101.

Hawton, K., Catalan, J., Martin, P., & Fagg, J. (1988). Prognostic factors in sex therapy. *Behaviour Research and Therapy, 24,* 377.

Holstege, G., Georgiadis, J. R., Paans, A. M., Meiners, L. C., van der Graaf, F. H., & Reinders, A. A. (2003). Brain activation during human male ejaculation. *Journal of Neuroscience, 23,* 9185–9193.

Janssen, P. K. C., Bakker, S. C., Rethelyi, J., Zwinderman, A. H., Touw, D. J., Olivier, B., & Waldinger, M. D. (2009). Serotonin transporter promoter region (5-HTTLPR) polymorphism is associated with the intravaginal ejaculation latency time in Dutch men with lifelong premature ejaculation. *The Journal of Sexual Medicine, 6,* 276–284.

Kaplan, H. S. (1974). *The new sex therapy.* New York: Brunner-Mazel.

Laumann, E. O., Paik, A., & Rosen, R. C. (1999). Sexual dysfunction in the United States: Prevalence and predictors. *Journal of the American Medical Association, 281,* 537–544.

Lindal, E., & Stefansson, J. G. (1993). The lifetime prevalence of psychosexual dysfunction among 55- to 57-year-olds in Iceland. *Social Psychiatry and Psychiatric Epidemiology, 28,* 91–95.

Masters, W. H., & Johnson, V. E. (1970). *Human sexual inadequacy*. Boston: Little, Brown.

McMahon, C. G., Althof, S., Waldinger, M. D., Porst, H., Dean, J., Sharlip, I., et al. (2008). An evidence-based definition of lifelong premature ejaculation: Report of the International Society for Sexual Medicine (ISSM) Ad Hoc Committee for the Definition of Premature Ejaculation. *The Journal of Sexual Medicine, 5*, 1590–1606.

Mos, J., Olivier, B., Bloetjes, K., & Poth, M, (1990). Drug-induced facilitation of sexual behaviour in the male rat: Behavioural and pharmacological aspects. In A. K. Slob & M. J. Baum (Eds.), *Psychoneuroendocrinology of growth and development* (pp. 221–232). Rotterdam: Medicom.

Mos, J., Van Logten, J., Bloetjes, K., & Olivier, B. (1991). The effects of idazoxan and 8-OH-DPAT on sexual behaviour and associated ultrasonic vocalizations in the rat. *Neuroscience and Biobehavioral Review, 15*, 505–515.

Munjack, D. J., & Kanno, P. H. (1979). Retarded ejaculation: A review. *Archives of Sexual Behavior, 8*, 139–150.

Olivier, B., van Oorschot, R., & Waldinger, M. D. (1998). Serotonin, serotonergic receptors, selective serotonin reuptake inhibitors and sexual behaviour. *International Clinical Psychopharmacology, 13* (Supplement 6), S9–S14.

Ottani, A., Giuliani, D., & Ferrari, F. (2002). Modulatory activity of sildenafil on copulatory behaviour of both intact and castrated male rats. *Pharmacology, Biochemistry, and Behavior, 72*, 717–722.

Patrick, D. L., Althof, S. E., Pryor, J. L., Rosen, R., Rowland, D. L., Ho, K. F., et al. (2005). Premature ejaculation: An observational study of men and their partners. *The Journal of Sexual Medicine, 2*, 358–367.

Pryor, J. L., Althof, S. E., Steidle, C., Rosen, R. C., Hellstrom, W. J., Shabsigh, R., et al. (2006). Efficacy and tolerability of dapoxetine in the treatment of premature ejaculation: Integrated analysis of two randomized, double-blind, placebo-controlled trials. *Lancet, 368*, 929–937.

Schapiro, B. (1943). Premature ejaculation: A review of 1130 cases. *Journal of Urology, 50*, 374.

Screponi, E., Carosa, E., Stasi, S. M., Pepe, M., Carruba, G., & Jannini, E. A. (2001). Prevalence of chronic prostatitis in men with premature ejaculation. *Urology, 58*, 198–202.

Segraves, R. T., Saran, A., Segraves, K., & Maguire, E. (1993). Clomipramine versus placebo in the treatment of premature ejaculation: A pilot study. *Journal of Sex and Marital Therapy, 19*, 198.

Semans, J. H. (1956). Premature ejaculation: A new approach. *Southern Medical Journal, 49*, 353.

Shull, G. R., & Sprenkle, D. H. (1980). Retarded ejaculation reconceptualization and implications for treatment. *Journal of Sex and Marital Therapy, 60*, 234–246.

Spira, A., Bajos, N., Giami, A., & Michaels, S. (1998). Cross-national comparisons of sexual behaviour surveys—methodological difficulties and lessons for prevention. *American Journal of Public Health, 88*, 730–731.

Tanner, B. A. (1973). Two case reports on the modification of the ejaculatory response with the squeeze technique. *Psychotherapy Theory Research Practice, 10*, 297.

Veening, J. G., & Coolen, L. M. (1998). Neural activation following sexual behavior in the male and female rat brain. *Behavioural Brain Research, 92*, 181.

Waldinger, M. D. (1996). Use of psychoactive agents in the treatment of sexual dysfunction. *CNS Drugs, 6*, 204–216.

Waldinger, M. D. (2002). The neurobiological approach to premature ejaculation [review article]. *Journal of Urology, 168*, 2359.

Waldinger, M. D. (2006). The need for a revival of psychoanalytic investigations into premature ejaculation. *Journal of Men's Health and Gender, 3*, 390–396.

Waldinger, M. D. (2007a). Four measures of investigating ejaculatory performance. *The Journal of Sexual Medicine, 4*, 520.

Waldinger, MD. (2007b). Premature ejaculation: State of the art. *Urologic Clinics of North America, 34*, 591–599.

Waldinger, M. D., Berendsen, H. H. G., Blok, B. F. M., Olivier, B., & Holstege, G. (1998). Premature ejaculation and serotonergic antidepressants-induced delayed ejaculation: The involvement of the serotonergic system. *Behavioural Brain Research, 92*, 111–118.

Waldinger, M. D., Hengeveld, M. W., & Zwinderman, A. H. (1994). Paroxetine treatment of premature ejaculation: A double-blind, randomised, placebo-controlled study. *American Journal of Psychiatry, 151*, 1377.

Waldinger, M. D., Hengeveld, M. W., Zwinderman, A. H., & Olivier, B. (1998a). Effect of SSRI antidepressants on ejaculation: A double-blind, randomized, placebo-controlled study with fluoxetine, fluvoxamine, paroxetine and sertraline. *Journal of Clinical Psychopharmacology, 18*, 274.

Waldinger, M. D., Hengeveld, M. W., Zwinderman, A. H., & Olivier, B. (1998b). An empirical operationalization study of *DSM-IV* diagnostic criteria for premature ejaculation. *International Journal of Psychiatry in Clinical Practice, 2*, 287.

Waldinger, M. D., McIntosh, J., & Schweitzer, D. H. (2009). A five-nation survey to assess the distribution of the intravaginal ejaculatory latency time among the general male population. *Journal of Sexual Medicine, 6*, 2888–2895.

Waldinger, M. D., & Olivier, B. (2000). Selective serotonin reuptake inhibitors (SSRIs) and sexual side effects: Differences in delaying ejaculation. *Excerpta Medica, 1*, 117–130.

Waldinger, M. D., Quinn, P., Dilleen, M., Mundayat, R., Schweitzer, D. H., & Boolell, M. (2005). A multi-national population survey of intravaginal ejaculation latency time. *The Journal of Sexual Medicine, 2*, 492–497.

Waldinger, M. D., Rietschel, M., Nothen, M. M., Hengeveld, M. W., & Olivier, B. (1998). Familial occurrence of primary premature ejaculation. *Psychiatric Genetics, 8*, 37, 1998.

Waldinger, M. D., & Schweitzer, D. H. (2005). Retarded ejaculation in men: An overview of psychological and neurobiological insights. *World Journal of Urology, 23*, 76–81.

Waldinger, M. D., & Schweitzer, D. H. (2006). Changing paradigms from an historical *DSM-III* and *DSM-IV* view towards an evidence based definition of premature ejaculation. Part II: Proposals for *DSM-V* and *ICD-11*. *The Journal of Sexual Medicine, 3*, 693–705.

Waldinger, M. D., Zwinderman, A. H., & Olivier, B. (2001). Antidepressants and ejaculation: A double-blind, randomized, placebo-controlled, fixed-dose study with paroxetine, sertraline, and nefazodone. *Journal of Clinical Psychopharmacology, 21*, 293.

Waldinger, M. D., Zwinderman, A. H., Olivier, B., & Schweitzer, D. H. (2005). Proposal for a definition of lifelong premature ejaculation based on epidemiological stopwatch data. *The Journal of Sexual Medicine, 2,* 498–507.

Waldinger, M. D., Zwinderman, A. H., Olivier, B., & Schweitzer, D. H. (2007). The majority of men with lifelong premature ejaculation prefer daily drug treatment: An observational study in a consecutive group of Dutch men. *The Journal of Sexual Medicine, 4,* 1028–1037.

Williams, W. (1985). Anaesthetic ejaculation. *Journal of Sex and Marital Therapy, 11,* 19–29, 1985.

V

ADDITIONAL VITAL TOPICS

Seventeen

Confronting Sexual Trauma and Enhancing Adult Sexuality

BARRY W. MCCARTHY, PHD, AND ALISA BREETZ, MA

THE AUTHORS AND THEIR MODEL

Barry W. McCarthy: I am a clinical psychologist who specializes in sex therapy, sexual trauma, and couple therapy. I entered the sexuality field in the early 1970s as a college professor teaching a human sexual behavior class and providing therapy for individuals and couples with sexual problems. My involvement in the sexual trauma field began in the 1980s as I tried to understand the pendulum swing from denial of sexual trauma to the opposite extreme of sexual trauma being the defining life experience (McCarthy, 1992). In my clinical work with adults who have a history of sexual abuse and trauma, I try to help them make meaning of their sexual history so they can process, accept, and honor the trauma but not allow it to control their sexual self-esteem.

My clinical work in the sexual trauma field has been heavily influenced by the writings of Wendy Maltz (2001), who advocates for couple sex therapy as the optimal approach for couples when one or both partners have a trauma history. Maltz's guideline is to confront the extremes of being a "shameful victim" who does not share or process the trauma and the "angry victim" who feels controlled by the trauma history. The basic tenet is to make meaning of the trauma so the person genuinely feels and acts like a "proud survivor." Emotionally and sexually, the individual and couple embrace the cognition "living well is the best revenge." While respecting individual differences and the complexity of trauma history and relationship dynamics, I have found this approach empowering for my individual and couple clients. I am enthusiastic about sharing these therapeutic strategies and techniques with you.

Alisa Breetz is a graduate student in the clinical psychology doctoral program at American University. We have collaborated on texts on human sexuality, couple sex therapy, and sexual dysfunction and share a theoretical framework in our approach to the treatment of sexual trauma. Her clinical work in the sexual trauma field has focused primarily on asylum seekers and refugees who experienced trauma and torture (sexual, physical, and emotional) in their home countries. Her experiences remind all of us of the importance of cultural and value factors in response to sexual trauma. She and I stress the multidimensionality of human sexuality. We both strive to help clients make unique meaning of their trauma rather than falling to either extreme of denial or self-definition.

The field of sexual trauma is one of the most controversial and conflictual in mental health. For most of the previous century, sexual abuse was viewed as a shameful secret by clinicians and the public. Now, many believe that childhood sexual trauma, especially repressed memories of sexual abuse and incest, is often associated with severe adult psychopathology (Bass & Davis, 1988) as well as other detrimental effects, including sexual dysfunction and distress (Beitchman, Zucker, Hood, & DaCosta, 1992). Our model therefore becomes very important when we realize the widespread prevalence of negative sexual experiences and sexual trauma as well as the potential depth of their impact. Such negative consequences are not universal or necessarily inevitable (Collishaw et al., 2007; Rind, Tromovitch, & Bauserman, 1998). Many people who have experienced sexual trauma continue to live full and successful lives, incorporating their past into their self-view while not allowing it to become the defining factor.

While our model is intended most specifically for those with a history of sexual trauma, it may also be applicable for addressing other negative sexual experiences. We view negative sexual experiences, sexual abuse, and sexual trauma as existing on a continuum of severity. To define terminology, negative sexual experiences during childhood, adolescence, young adulthood, or adulthood include sexual humiliation; sexual harassment; sexual rejection; an unwanted pregnancy; a sexually transmitted infection; victimization by exhibitionism, voyeurism, or frotteurism; shame concerning masturbation or sexual fantasies; stigma about sexual dysfunction; or a label by a partner as a "sexual loser." Unfortunately, one or more of these experiences is probably nearly universal. The essence of trauma is the subversion of the person's assumptions of emotional and bodily safety and integrity. Sexual trauma can involve objective factors such as physical violence (a stranger rape with a weapon) and breaking emotional trust bonds (father–daughter incest). These objective factors may be associated with an increase in specific negative outcomes (such as a link between violence during abuse and later suicidality). Three other factors seem to be equally important to the outcome of these experiences: how the trauma was dealt with at the time; whether the person views the experiences as a shameful secret; and whether the person angrily believes the experience controls general and sexual self-esteem. In this way, experiences that might fall in the category of negative sexual experiences for one individual may be sexual trauma for another. Our hope is that this model will help you to deal with a variety of abusive and traumatic life experiences as well as less-severe negative sexual experiences.

FREQUENCY OF SEXUAL TRAUMA

The prevalence of sexual trauma is ultimately uncertain because many individuals do not report its occurrence, and researchers use varying definitions of trauma. The common estimate of child sexual abuse (before age 12) is approximately one in three girls and one in seven boys (Finkelhor, Hotaling, Lewis, & Smith, 1990). While the most common forms of incest involve cousins, stepbrothers, and uncles, clinical writing tends to focus on father–daughter and stepfather incest. These forms of incest are presumed to have the most enduring impact on the child through a violation of the trust bond (Barrett & Trepper, 2004). Across all ages, acquaintance rape is far more common than stranger rape. Rape occurrence estimates vary from 15 to 70% of adolescent and adult women.

OUR THEORETICAL ORIENTATION

We are social learning theorists. Our interventions focus on integrative cognitive–behavioral therapy techniques. The goal is to help clients to see themselves as proud survivors rather than as passive, shameful victims. We want them to learn how to avoid being angry or anxious victims whose lives and sexuality are controlled by sexual trauma.

We recognize that the sexual trauma field lacks well-validated assessment, intervention, and effectiveness data. In part, this is because powerful emotional, political, and value issues are generated by sexual trauma (Rind et al., 1998). So many factors seem to affect how the individual and the couple deal with sexual trauma that we clinicians need to be modest in generalizing about the applicability and effectiveness of interventions. One model, including ours, does *not* fit all clients.

THE STRUCTURE OF THERAPY

In the first therapy session, couples often ask whether the best treatment approach is individual, couple, or group therapy. They wonder whether the focus should be on their current sexual relationship or on the sexual trauma per se. The answers to these important questions are still matters of disagreement and controversy among professionals who specialize in this area (Wieksma, 2003).

The model discussed here emphasizes couple sex therapy for adult clients (who may have experienced trauma as a child, adult, or both). It is based on the following concepts:

- Ongoing distress from sexual abuse, incest, or rape is created both by the trauma inherent in the experience and by other negative influences stemming from how the incidents were processed and dealt with at the time and how they were incorporated into the person's sexual self-esteem.
- Sexual trauma can result in a range of adolescent and adult sexual symptoms.
- Effective treatment requires careful consideration of the values and culture of both individuals and the couple.

THERAPEUTIC PROCESSING OF SEXUAL TRAUMA

Typically, clients who ask for assistance for sexual trauma do not view their trauma as the primary problem. In the past, most people minimized or denied the presence, extent, or impact of the abuse. In part because of the increased services, awareness, and attention paid to childhood sexual abuse since the 1980s, more clients volunteer that sexual trauma has been a causal factor in their psychological, relationship, or sexual problems.

Once abuse issues are raised, our focus is to help the client to identify the attitudes, behaviors, and emotions that are likely to be subverting their psychological, relational, or sexual function. We are committed to honestly deal with the trauma in an empathic, respectful manner and to honor its impact. We work to enable the client's comfort in sharing and clarifying experiences, perceptions, and feelings. We believe that processing these experiences is vital to the therapy. We intend to reduce the client's guilt, shame, and sense of deficiency. We speak of resolving the trauma. We employ the adage "living well is the best revenge" as we talk about the trauma.

INCORPORATING A TRAUMA HISTORY INTO SEXUAL SELF-ESTEEM

We focus on three levels of victimization: (1) the abuse incident itself, (2) how the abuse was dealt with at the time, and (3) how the abuse was incorporated into adult self-esteem. We believe that the second and third levels are often more damaging than the abuse per se (McCarthy, 1997). Because many subcultures viewed sexual abuse as a shameful secret, many people experiencing abuse never told anyone of those experiences. The holding of the secret usually meant that the person did not fully process the experience, and the result was that it was not integrated into his or her life. Anxiety, depression, alcohol or drug abuse, disordered eating, or sexual dysfunction became the consequence.

Cultural changes in America over the last generation have resulted in an increased number of children (as well as adults, particularly those experiencing acquaintance rape) disclosing their trauma. It is important to understand that reporting sexual abuse may not be helpful or therapeutic—the impact depends on how the revelation is handled. Sadly, often a multitude of individuals with disparate perspectives get involved when minors disclose. These include social workers, ministers, guidance counselors, police, trauma specialists, and prosecutors. The child or adolescent is barraged by a panoply of questions, suggestions about what happened, advice about what to do, and interpretations of what it means to be abused. Police and attorney involvement is inherently adversarial and often further stigmatizes the victim. Many people, including family and friends, discuss the incidents in ways that add to subversion of the person's needs for privacy and support. The abuse then can become the defining event of the year or of childhood.

A POSITIVE APPROACH TO DEALING WITH SEXUAL ABUSE

Our view is that the ideal response to a child's disclosure of sexual abuse consists of disclosing it to a trusted, empathic adult who listens for the child's needs. These usually include (1) stopping the abuse; (2) helping the child to understand what happened without feeling blamed or guilty; (3) having the perpetrator take responsibility; and (4) seeing to it that the perpetrator apologizes to the child (Saywitz, Mannarino, Berliner, & Cohen, 2000). Clearly, there are times, particularly in instances of stranger abuse, when steps 3 and 4 cannot occur. Even in the absence of these last steps, the goal remains to help the child to develop a new positive understanding of sexuality so that adult love, intimacy, touching, and sexuality are conceptually differentiated from sexual abuse. These approaches protect the person (whether child or adult) from feeling only like a sexual victim. It reinforces the message of being a proud survivor. Positive adult sexual experiences become evidence of their personal resilience.

DEALING WITH A RANGE OF SEXUAL TRAUMA HISTORIES

There is a broad range of sexually traumatic experiences that present differently in therapy (Haugaard, 2000). It is thought that the most traumatizing factor is physical violence, with the fear of injury or death during rape creating the most intense symptoms. For many middle-class adolescents and young women, rape is their first experience with physical violence. The combination of violence and sex often overwhelms a person's coping capacities.

Most child sexual abuse and incest does not involve physical force. Most incidents of sexual abuse are perpetrated by a person who the child knows. The closer the relationship—brother, minister, counselor, brother-in-law, teacher, or grandfather—the more impact it will have because it violates the child's assumption of being protected emotionally by family members or adult authority figures. Father–daughter incest is a monumental violation of trust.

Ongoing abuse, especially when it is intermittent and unpredictable, has more impact than a single incident. Predictable abuse, however painful, allows the child to go along passively knowing what to expect. In unpredictable, intermittent varieties, the child is unsure of what is happening and is more likely to blame him- or herself, feeling that he or she could control the abuse if he or she did something or had not done something else. The girl or boy is self-punishing and believes that he or she had the power to stop it. Of course, the responsibility for abuse is always the adult's, not the child's.

Male children feel embarrassed about and deny abuse. Most of the cultural focus emphasizes abuse of girls. Sexual abuse is not supposed to happen to males, so male victims feel more stigmatized and shameful about their abuse. They deny it to themselves longer and are fearful that it means they are homosexual or that abuse will make them homosexual.

THREE CASES

We want to share several cases that were treated (by Dr. McCarthy) employing our clinical strategies and techniques. As we tell each story, we also provide commentary that aims to generalize these techniques for wider application. We use these cases to address relapse prevention and legal redress. We hope this approach will give you a road map and some confidence as you try to help the first few individuals and couples who are coping poorly with a background of childhood, adolescent, or adult sexual abuse. Remember, we are stressing that there is not one "right" approach; we must, however, carefully listen to the needs, feelings, and preferences of the individual and couple.

Case 17.1: Christine and Steven

When Christine and Steven presented for therapy, they were a deeply ambivalent and demoralized couple. For the past 8 months, Christine had been attending an incest survivors self-help group. She had been sexually abused by a brother and was not sure whether she had also been abused by her father, uncles, or other males. Steven had initially been supportive but was now frustrated by Christine's anxiety and depression and blamed her for the nonsexual state of their 4-year marriage. Steven felt that Christine was only marginally involved in parenting their 18-month-old son, largely because she was so obsessed with exploring past abuse that she had no energy left for the marriage or for parenting. Christine felt that Steven was her worst critic. She felt emotionally alienated from him and reported severe inhibited sexual desire.

Two years earlier, Christine and Steven had consulted their minister and attended a couples' retreat. Afterward, they consulted a marriage therapist for five sessions but felt that there was no clear direction or therapeutic focus. Although they were committed to the marriage, their marital bond was badly stressed. They were stuck in a cycle of blame and counterblame, with growing frustration and alienation on both sides. Christine alternated between self-blame and blaming Steven. Steven was disappointed in Christine, the marriage, and the absence of sex.

At the first meeting, I (Dr. McCarthy) proposed a four-session assessment contract (initial couple interview, an individual history-taking session for each client separately, and a couple feedback session). I told Christine and Steven that we would be evaluating individual, relational, medical, situational, and sexual topics to develop a therapeutic plan (McCarthy & Thestrup, 2008). They accepted the approach and became hopeful that treatment would provide guidance and facilitate change.

In the initial couple session, I taught that sexuality is a couple issue. My work was not going to be based on a biomedical model because that approach views the problem as an individual issue and strives to ensure the proper diagnosis so that the right medication can be prescribed. A comprehensive, integrative, psychobiosocial sex therapy model combines personal responsibility for sexuality (including dealing with past sexual trauma) and being an intimate team (including being partners in healing).

The conjoint session focused on Christine and Steven's views of the sexual problem and on Christine's trauma history. Their marital commitment, motivation for change, and attitude toward therapy were explored. Each signed release of information forms to discuss past treatment with the marital therapist. Christine signed a release to contact her incest survivors group sponsor to obtain the sponsor's perceptions of Christine's progress in the program.

I then saw each person separately once. I began each of their sessions by saying, "I want you to be as frank and honest as possible about your sexual development and experiences, both positive and negative, including before you met and in this relationship. At the end, I'll ask if you want to flag any sensitive or secret material you do not want shared with your spouse. I will respect that and will not share anything without your permission, but I need to know as much as possible in order to help you resolve the emotional and sexual problems."

Typically, I structure such inquiries chronologically and move from questions that provoke less to those that can be expected to create more anxiety. "How did you learn about sexuality?" was the first question. This allows for exploration of family, religious, educational, peer, and cultural influences.

I then say that it is important to know about your experiences with child sexual abuse, incest, rape, and other negative sexual experiences. I ask about such things as unwanted pregnancy; sexually transmitted infections; being caught masturbating; guilt about sexual thoughts or fantasies; sexual rejection or humiliation; unsuccessful or painful first intercourse; being exhibited to, peeped on, or rubbed against; receiving obscene phone calls; or sexual harassment. When a person acknowledges one or more of these experiences, I ask about their thoughts and feelings at the time of the incident. I specifically inquire about how it was dealt with and ask how the experience was incorporated into the person's sexual self-esteem. One way to get at such material is to ask how old the client was when he or she left home, then, "As you think back on your childhood and adolescence, what was the most negative, confusing, guilt-inducing, or traumatic experience that occurred?"

> For Christine, this process was very different from what occurred in the self-help group. The developmental focus allowed her to more fully and objectively assess sexual learnings, including abusive incidents. Her incest survivors group was highly emotional as it confronted denial, shame, and pathology. Christine realized that the most stressful experience of childhood was not the sexual behavior but how the situation degenerated when her father and uncles became drunk, with threats of violence and chaos. She remembered clinging to her two older brothers for comfort. The oldest brother would leave, making Christine more dependent on the brother who was 3 years older. It was with this brother that the sexual abuse incidents occurred. Although the sexual touching was confusing and negative, it was not physically forced. The brother orally stimulated Christine's genitals, and then she manually stimulated him to orgasm. This scenario occurred two to three times a month over a 4-year period beginning when Christine was 7. The sexual abuse ended after that brother was beaten up by the father and two uncles in a separate conflict. The brother was then removed from the home by social service authorities. In our session, Christine realized for the first time that her fear about her father, uncles, and their friends revolved primarily around alcohol and violence, not sexuality. A second individual session with Christine completed her sexual history, solidified the developmental insights, and focused on her adult sexual strengths and vulnerabilities.
>
> Steven's sexual history revealed that he had felt humiliated by male relatives' jokes about his masturbation. Steven felt sensitized to rejection in dating situations, which generalized to feelings of rejection with Christine. He felt that he was a sexually inadequate, unattractive man.

In the young adult and marriage phases of the sexual history, the clinician can explore positive and negative experiences with dating, how the couple met and began their sexual relationship, their best and worst sexual experiences, what each values most about the marriage, and what changes the person wants from the spouse and marriage. Sensitive issues such as masturbation, affairs, dysfunctional sex, compulsive sexuality, and sexual trauma are carefully explored. Toward the end of the sexual history, the therapist asks, "As you review your entire life, what is the most confusing, negative, traumatic, or guilt-inducing sexual experience you had?" About one in four people, especially males, then disclose an additional sensitive or traumatic experience.

In my experience, when I ask clients if there is any material that should not be shared with their spouse, 75 to 85% of people specify something. After a brief discussion of the motivations for keeping it secret, the majority of clients agree to share the material during the couple feedback session. I encourage sharing past traumatic sexual experiences (McCarthy, 2002) because I have found that most spouses are empathic, supportive, and willing to be "partners in healing" (Maltz, 2001). When it is the male who has been sexually traumatized, the wife is usually eager to be an intimate, supportive partner. The clinician and the couple need to be aware that too much caring and sympathy can inadvertently result in antierotic feelings.

When the client does not want a secret shared, the therapist should not break a promise or coerce the person. You can help the person carefully consider the costs and benefits of keeping sensitive material secret. It is usually easier to share secrets such as guilt over compulsive masturbation or shame about having been sexually abused. While the fear is that the spouse will be harsh or rejecting, the usual outcome is that the spouse's empathy and support increase. In this way, the client comes to understand the potential benefits as well as the psychological and sexual costs of keeping the secret.

The Couple Feedback Session

The couple feedback session is usually scheduled for 90 minutes. The feedback session provides three vital elements to the couple: a new narrative for each individual about intimacy and sexuality, a therapeutic plan, and the assignment of the first homework exercise.

> The feedback session had quite an impact on Christine and Steven. Steven had only a vague sense of Christine's past sexual trauma. He felt shut out when Christine was involved with the 12-step program. Rather than being a partner in healing, Steven felt that as a male he was seen as part of the problem and perhaps as a perpetrator.
>
> Christine was able to discuss traumatic childhood experiences and feelings in a way that Steven could experience empathy and understanding. Christine felt that being in the incest survivors group had increased her consciousness of sexual victimization and supported her in giving voice to her concerns. However, she had outgrown the usefulness of the group. The pressure from Christine's sponsor and from the group spokeswoman to search out other repressed memories was confusing and stressful. She felt that the 12-step approach was too focused on past pathology. Christine believed that she needed to focus on psychological and sexual healing, which was best done in couple sex therapy.

The Role of Sex Therapy in Couple Work

A core component of couple sex therapy is a series of psychosexual skill exercises designed to reduce anxiety and restore a sense of pleasure and control during a sexual interaction. This involves monitoring attitudes, behavior, and emotions and individualizing the sexual experiences in response to couple feedback. This is especially significant for people with a history of sexual trauma who experience high levels of anxiety and no control over what happened to them and how their body responded to it (Messman-Moore & Resnick, 2002). The clinician's role is to individualize the exercises to fit the client's needs, address inhibitions and resistance that arise as the couple tries out new sexual scenarios and techniques, and keep the couple focused and motivated to move through the therapeutic process to a successful resolution.

Progress is seldom linear. A major function of the psychosexual skill exercises is diagnostic—to identify anxieties, inhibitions, and skill deficits. What constitutes success varies from couple to couple. We strive to help the couple experience the sexual interaction as voluntary, intimate, and pleasure oriented. When the person experiences desire, arousal, orgasm, and satisfaction, he or she is no longer controlled by the trauma history. The couple task is to develop a unique sexual style that is comfortable and functional for both partners (McCarthy & McCarthy, 2009).

Christine learned to view Steven as a "partner in healing." This process nurtured and energized their marital bond. Christine needed to know that she could veto a sex experience she found too anxiety provoking or antierotic and that Steven would honor her veto. It is very difficult to say "yes" to pleasure-oriented sexuality unless you can say "no" to aversive sexuality. However, rather than have the "no" end the sexual interaction, thus reinforcing avoidance and failure, I instructed Christine to request a comfortable, sexual way to remain connected to Steven. They developed a scenario she felt good about—lying in Steven's arms with her head on his chest, listening to his heartbeat. This became their "trust position," which they could utilize when Christine felt anxious.

They later reported a poignant example when Christine was feeling responsive to Steven's manual genital stimulation and impulsively said "go down on me." When he did, she experienced a flashback to an experience with the brother, "froze up," and began to shake. Steven stopped and asked how he could help. Christine requested the trust position, which reestablished their connection and allowed them to resume manual stimulation and kissing but refrain from oral stimulation. This experience reinforced their sense of a secure attachment (Johnson, 2002).

Relapse Prevention Strategies and Techniques

The techniques of relapse prevention are an integral component of comprehensive couple sex therapy, especially for those who have been sexually traumatized. Relapse prevention has five components (McCarthy, 1999). The first is dealing with thoughts, feelings, and experiences regarding past trauma. The second is maintaining a comfortable, functional couple sexual style. For Christine, this meant being able to recall and process the sexual trauma with both Steven and her minister in a manner that honored the reality of the experiences and their attendant feelings.

Christine felt that she had dealt with the trauma, accepted the experiences, and took pride in being a survivor. As Christine explained, "It was a sad, painful chapter in my life, but it does not control my life. I appreciate the present chapter so much more." Now when Christine has flashbacks, thoughts, or feelings about child sexual abuse, she accepts these without panicking, avoiding, or feeling out of control. She has mastered the skill of emotional acceptance and regulation.

When Christine processes traumatic material with Steven, it is outside the context of their sexual relationship. Although it has not happened in months, Christine knows that if she feels uncomfortable, she can veto an activity, and Steven will honor her veto and switch to their trust position. Christine realizes that she will never feel totally comfortable with her trauma history but is confident that it no longer controls her or their marital sexuality.

A third element in relapse prevention is to maintain positive, realistic sexual expectations. This begins with the clinician's expectations for the couple, especially for intimate sexuality. A healthy expectation is that 40 to 50% of sexual encounters will be positive for both spouses, 20 to 25% will be quite good for one and okay for the other, 20 to 25% will be okay but unremarkable, and 5 to 15% of sexual encounters will be unsatisfying or dysfunctional (Frank, Anderson, & Rubenstein, 1978). It is particularly important that the partners not overreact to their occasional unsatisfying or dysfunctional experiences.

Christine and Steven now can joke about a disappointing experience and reconnect in the next 1–3 days when both are receptive and responsive.

The fourth key to relapse prevention is not to take marital sexuality for granted or to treat it with benign neglect but to devote the time and psychological energy to keeping it vital and satisfying.

> Christine and Steven planned a sensual or playful date every 2 months, with the understanding that it would not result in intercourse. They planned a couple weekend away twice a year and would discuss special intimate and erotic times. They built bridges to sexual desire instead of settling into a mechanical sexual routine (McCarthy & McCarthy, 2003). Christine very much appreciated Steven's acknowledging how much he values the marriage and her psychological and sexual growth.

The fifth and final element is follow-up at 6-month intervals, ideally for 2 years. This helps to ensure that the couple implement and maintain therapeutic gains and allows for a new goal for the next 6 months. Therapists should reiterate that the process of personal and couple growth is a continual one.

Case 17.2: Tim

We now present a case of male incest treated by Dr. McCarthy. Incest is significantly higher in stepfamilies, cohabiting families, and families in which there is alcohol or drug abuse (Finkelhor et al., 1990). Boys are less likely to disclose abuse than girls and are more likely to deny or minimize its impact.

Tim was 7 when his mother remarried, 8 when sexual abuse began, 10 when anal intercourse began, and 14 when the marriage ended. Tim never told anyone about his stepfather's abuse. He was dragged in by his girlfriend of 4 months for therapy when he was 24. The complaint was ejaculatory inhibition (EI). She was the first sexual partner to inform Tim that he had a sexual dysfunction. Tim used to brag about how he was a stud who pleased women because he could "go all night." Male friends envied Tim's intercourse prowess. Tim had no difficulty ejaculating during masturbation using pornographic videos, Internet stories, or fantasies with dominance and submission themes. Never orgasmic with a partner, he liked to fantasize spanking the woman until she bled.

The girlfriend delivered Tim to therapy and then broke up with him to return to a boyfriend. Tim felt duped and angry. I focused on his feelings of being betrayed rather than on sexuality issues. I had him write a letter to the ex-girlfriend (which he did not send) to express his hurt and anger. This allowed Tim to represent himself well and to realize that he deserved to be treated better. Tim came to tell me that he felt powerful and in control of the sexual performance scenario, even though he knew he was cheating himself from sexual pleasure.

After five sessions, Tim felt ready to participate in a comprehensive sexual history assessment. He only disclosed the incest in response to the question, "What was the most confusing, negative, traumatic, or guilt-inducing experience you had in childhood or adolescence?" After providing the information, Tim said that he would not have volunteered this information without the help of this question.

Tim had not known how to process these incidents at the time and still could not. While it was hard for him to admit that he had been sexually abused, it was even more difficult to admit that he had a sexual dysfunction that was in part caused by the abuse. He initially preferred explanations that focused on a compulsive masturbation pattern and the use of pornography with a single fantasy theme. I helped him to see that he focused on performing for the woman rather than seeking intimate, interactive sexuality. I told him that to deal with the self-defeating pattern of EI, he would need to be emotionally open and to see the woman as an intimate and erotic ally. This was a challenge for him.

Tim was deeply embarrassed by the fact that he regularly attained orgasm when as a boy he was anally receptive. He asked, "If I was orgasmic how could it be abuse?" "Does this mean I am gay?" "Why can't I ejaculate with a woman?"

To answer these questions in way that was reasonable to him, I had to help him process a broad range of feelings. I prescribed writing exercises between sessions to facilitate this. I first ask him to write the positives and negatives of the sexual abuse.

He was surprised by the length of his list of negatives, including many self-defeating beliefs regarding trust and sexuality. He listed only one positive—his commitment to never again be sexually victimized. I called his commitment a strength. Tim had several empowering insights: "I want to maintain a dominant role with women so as not to be vulnerable to being hurt." "My pornography allowed me to identify with the macho extreme perpetrator rather than the victim." He cried as he said that this was not him, adding, "I don't want to hurt anyone, sexually or otherwise," and "The abuse cycle will stop with me."

Tim read two male victim self-help books but did not find them helpful. He attended two male victimization self-help groups and found he did not respect or identify with these men. Some men, however, find both of these approaches useful. Many initially enthusiastic responses fade in a short time. Still others find group experiences harmful.

Tim agreed to throw out and delete all the pornography with domination–submission and spanking themes. He began to use a variety of erotic fantasies with themes that were transferable to couple sexuality. He began masturbating only when he felt sexual desire. He stopped masturbating out of habit, as a tension reducer, or as a mood regulator. He began to focus on "orgasm triggers" that could be utilized in partner sex.

In an ideal outcome scenario, Tim would have found a new partner he was comfortable with, attracted to, and trusted. He would share the abuse history and work with her to overcome the EI. Unfortunately, a healthy relationship did not develop. Tim came to see me four times for follow-up over 2 years and occasionally called for a booster session.

Tim called 5 months after the follow-up session to invite me to his wedding. He was marrying a conservative Christian woman with two children. He reported that the EI was gone, and they were pregnant. Eleven months later, he saw me in distress over his recent separation. His wife had demanded that he relinquish legal rights for their child; she refused to come to see me with Tim. She preferred to see a Christian pastoral counselor. Six weeks later, panicky, depressed, confused, and devastated, Tim returned. He felt blamed by his wife and the pastoral counselor for the impending divorce. I said that he sounded like he had been victimized by them. He then decided to follow his attorney's recommendation to have a paternity test. It demonstrated that Tim was not the father. Tim and I came to realize that his wife's enthusiasm for sex with him was a ploy to deal with her pregnancy.

Tim continued seeing me. We focused on his sad reality, staying motivated to proceed to divorce, and annulling the marriage in his church. Tim realized that he learned how to overcome EI in this relationship and was now clear that he no longer wanted anything to do with his ex-wife. I was pleased to see that he did not experience shame or blame himself for this traumatic relational experience. He asked for a referral to a female psychodynamic clinician to explore his emotional, relational, and sexual vulnerabilities. I was pleased that Tim managed to maintain his pride in being a survivor who aspired to and deserved a healthy marital and sexual relationship.

Legal Redress of Childhood Sexual Trauma

The issue of sexual trauma, especially those based on recovered memories, is still highly controversial (Knapp & Van de Creek, 2000). Courtois and Ford (2009) suggested using professionally validated guidelines for assessment and treatment to minimize political and litigious aspects of the problem. They pointed out that anger stimulated by the adversarial legal system often victimizes the person anew. Even a monetary settlement does not yield the hoped-for validation and closure. Clinicians step on dangerous ground when they become legal advocates because such advocacy is antithetical to building a self-concept as a survivor who retakes control of his or her life and sexuality. Winning a legal process requires emphasizing one's victimhood, and the process itself tends to create an angry, bitter victim (Bartoi & Kinder, 1998).

We therapists need to confront the labeling of sexual victimization as the main event of childhood. We do not want self-esteem to be defined by "I grew up in an incest family," "My sexuality was stolen by the rapist," or "Sexual harassment caused me to change my career." Such concepts reinforce passivity and give the trauma unnecessary control of the person's life. McCarthy (1986) emphasized four points that remain useful years later:

1. Careful exploration of past and present attitudes, behavior, and emotions about the sexual victimization
2. Realization that since responsibility for the abuse lies with the perpetrator, guilt and shame are inappropriate and self-punitive
3. Self-acceptance of the incident and its repercussions supported by the notion that one has coped and survived in the best way one could given the resources available at the time
4. The need to commit to a life as a proud survivor and to aspire to enjoy a psychologically, relationally, and sexually healthy life

Here is a final example of how these four concepts can be used in therapy:

Case 17.3: Karen

Karen was a 26-year-old college graduate who presented for psychotherapy complaining of anxiety, depression, career dissatisfaction, and low self-esteem. In the second session, she revealed that a year and a half earlier she experienced an acquaintance rape. Karen said that this caused a great deal of stress at the time, but she had dealt with it. I (Dr. McCarthy) asked her open-ended questions about her sex education and what she had learned about sexual assault (rape). Like many young women, Karen erroneously believed that the most common type of rape was by a stranger using a weapon. I told her that her experience was the norm—her rapist was a man she knew through work friends; they had both been drinking, which impaired perception and judgment; neither a weapon nor physical force was used; and the initial touching had been consensual. When Karen tried to end the encounter, she was overpowered, and nonconsenting intercourse ensued. He denied that there was anything wrong, much less that this had been an acquaintance rape.

Karen did not seek medical treatment. She was taking the birth control pill. Although she was concerned about a sexually transmitted infection, she did not seek testing. Karen did talk with siblings and other friends about the sexual incident but had not discussed it with work friends. She avoided any contact with the man, and when his name came up, she would leave the room.

Karen had a number of psychological concerns; healing from the rape was not a stated concern. I encouraged Karen to have an HIV test and sexually transmitted infection screening. When the results came back negative, Karen was visibly relieved.

My approach emphasized the need for her to increase her self-efficacy. I stressed that she should be an active problem solver in terms of her career, living situation, and physical health. Karen joined an exercise group, which improved her mood and eventually resulted in moderate sustained weight loss. This theme, enhancing self-efficacy, was the context in which sexuality and the rape was explored. Karen was now tired of the dating scene with its sexual games. Her goal was to marry and have children, but she felt demoralized about finding a life partner. She interpreted the rape as meaning that she did not deserve a successful relationship or a sexual life. The rape was a shadow over Karen's self-esteem and self-efficacy. She felt that she had led the man on by being drunk. She wanted to keep the incident from coworkers because she feared being stigmatized and judged. The incident lowered her sense of attractiveness and increased her cynicism about men and sexual relationships. Paradoxically, she felt guilty that it had not affected her sexual responsiveness.

I felt that Karen was self-punitive and had failed to learn anything positive or develop any empowering motivation from the rape/trauma. I employed one of my favorite adages, "living well is the best revenge."

I asked Karen what she thought would make her less vulnerable in the future. I urged her not to pile on negative judgments of herself but rather acknowledge that he was responsible for the sexual assault. I supported that she retained her capacity for desire, arousal, and orgasm after the rape. "Sexual responsivity is a sign of psychological strength and resiliency." I spoke of her as a person who took back control of her body from the rapist.

Karen declined the invitation for a 6-month follow-up session. Two months later, she called for a referral to a career counselor, saying she wanted to change careers before 30. A year later, she called for a couple consultation. She wanted help with the question of whether she was in a relationship that could/should lead to marriage.

Brad was a 38-year-old, never-married, accomplished entrepreneur who had a high level of interest in Karen emotionally and sexually and total optimism about her past trauma history. He readily agreed to an individual assessment, during which he was forthcoming and disclosed several important issues that he had not discussed with Karen. He had been diagnosed with bipolar disorder 5 years earlier and had been unreliable in taking his medication. He reported binge drinking associated with sexual activity. He had no desire to marry; 3 years ago he had a vasectomy. Surprisingly, Brad agreed to share this material in the couple feedback session.

Two days before the couple session, Karen called me to say that Brad told her these things, and she felt destabilized. She was unsure whether they should keep the appointment. I urged her to do so; we could discuss how to make a "wise" decision regarding the relationship. I focused on establishing clarity about personal information and perceptions about them as a dating couple and as a potential marital couple. While it was clear that they were a validating, fun, and sexual couple, Karen had not identified the connection between drinking and their sexual activity. Karen questioned whether they could be a serious, marital couple and family. Brad said he was absolutely not going to have children and would not consider a marriage discussion until he had been with a woman for at least 5 years. Karen thanked him for being blunt and for his willingness to engage in this assessment.

Karen was ebullient in the follow-up individual session. Although we had previously discussed the difference between a sexual friendship and a serious, committed relationship, she felt that "this time I got it." She decided that she would continue the relationship with Brad for another few months until she left town to attend business school.

The intervention with the most impact that I used with Karen was a cognitive exercise to learn a process for choosing an intimate partner. She listed the positive characteristics she needed in a man and the "poisons" or fatal flaws that would subvert a relationship. By engaging in this exercise, Karen became aware of how the rape experience exacerbated her tendency to see herself as undeserving and to settle for men she did not respect or trust. Karen decided to set a "higher screen" for dating and not waste her time on "second-class" partners. She shared her newly structured story of the acquaintance rape with her minister. She received reassurance of being in God's good graces. Karen decided she would share the acquaintance rape experience with a new partner but not until she was seriously involved. She would not be apologetic or defensive but would make him aware of specific sensitivities and of her need to feel safe, especially of her need for his willingness to honor a "no" from her. Karen felt she now had the skills to make a wise choice of a partner in the future. She was committed to establishing a satisfying and stable relationship in which sexuality would play a positive, energizing role.

THERAPIST ISSUES IN DEALING WITH SEXUAL TRAUMA

Sexual trauma work is personally challenging and stressful for the therapist. Some clinicians are not interested in the topic, some feel unequipped to deal with the trauma, and others experience personal anxieties based on their own sexual history. It is an unrealistic demand that a therapist be skilled and comfortable with all kinds of therapy, all types of issues, and all types of clients (Meichenbaum, 1994). Most clinicians gradually gain the knowledge and skills and can successfully monitor their anxieties. Helping clients with these problems can be professionally quite satisfying and can help us to better understand ourselves.

A prime challenge is to maintain an empathic, respectful stance when dealing with these emotionally charged issues. Here are some common therapist mistakes:

1. Providing sympathy rather than empathy and respect
2. Making the patient feel that he or she is deficient and needs to be taken care of
3. Failing to emphasize how to think about the trauma and lead their lives as survivors
4. Placing too much emphasis on exploring the feelings of victimization and not enough emphasis on assuming responsibility for the self in the present
5. Considering the exploration of the trauma as too painful

CONCLUDING REMARKS

Sexual trauma is too common and clinical work with it too important to leave to subspecialists. We believe that effective work with sexual trauma requires that the clinician be comfortable with individual therapy and couple therapy and talking about sex. The clinician has to be willing to explore attitudes, experiences, and feelings about the sexual trauma as it is an important part of the person's developmental history. We hope we have increased your motivation to take on these challenges. Good luck.

REFERENCES

Barrett, M., & Trepper, T. (2004, January/February). Intrafamilial childhood sexual abuse. *Family Therapy Magazine*, pp. 34–39.

Bartoi, M., & Kinder, B. (1998). The effects of child and adult sexual abuse on adult sexuality. *Journal of Sex and Marital Therapy, 24*, 75–90. This describes a well-controlled, empirical study that demonstrated the quite variable effects of sexual abuse on adult sexual attitudes and functioning. This study challenged the popular and professional misconception that severe effects of sexual abuse are universal and inevitable.

Bass, E., & Davis, L. (1988). *The courage to heal.* New York: Harper and Row.

Beitchman, J., Zucker, K., Hood, J., & DaCosta, G. (1992). A review of the long-term effects of child sexual abuse. *Child Abuse and Neglect, 16*, 101–118.

Collishaw, S., Pickles, A., Messer, J., Rutter, M., Shearer, C., & Maughan, B. (2007). Resilience to adult psychopathology following childhood maltreatment: Evidence from a community sample. *Child Abuse and Neglect, 31*, 211–229.

Courtois, C., & Ford, J. (2009). *Treating complex traumatic stress disorders.* New York: Guilford.

Finkelhor, D., Hotaling, G., Lewis, L., & Smith, C. (1990). Sexual abuse in a national sample of adult men and women. *Child Abuse and Neglect, 14*, 19–28.

Frank, E., Anderson, A., & Rubenstein, D. (1978). Frequency of sexual dysfunction in "normal" couples. *New England Journal of Medicine, 229*(3), 111–115.

Haugaard, J. (2000). The challenges of defining child sexual abuse. *American Psychologist, 55*, 1036–1039. This article spells out many misconceptions and overgeneralizations about child sexual abuse. Haugaard proposes a more specific, operational, and multidimensional approach to defining and measuring types of sexual abuse.

Johnson, S. (2002). *Emotionally focused couple therapy with trauma survivors.* New York: Guilford. Johnson utilizes a challenging, alternative therapeutic approach to couple therapy with trauma survivors. She employs emotionally focused therapy and, via case vignettes, vividly illustrates the multicausal, multidimensional aspects of trauma on the person and the couple.

Knapp, S., & Van de Creek, L. (2000). Recovered memories of childhood abuse. *Professional Psychology, 31*, 365–371. The issue of recovered memories of childhood sexual abuse is one of the most political, value-laden, and emotionally charged in mental health. This thoughtful article attempts to treat the issues with the complexity they deserve and proposes a professional consensus on understanding and treating trauma in a therapeutic manner.

Maltz, W. (2001). *The sexual healing journey.* New York: Harper-Collins. The writings of Wendy Maltz about individuals and couples dealing with the aftermath of sexual abuse and trauma are the most empathic and humane in the entire field. She suggests a healing approach that is applicable to both individuals and couples. Her concept of the spouse as a "partner in healing" is particularly valuable.

McCarthy, B. (1986). A cognitive–behavioral approach to understanding and treating sexual trauma. *Journal of Sex and Marital Therapy, 12*, 15–19.

McCarthy, B. (1992). Sexual trauma. *Journal of Sex Education and Therapy, 18,* 1–10.

McCarthy, B. (1997). Therapeutic and iatrogenic interventions with adults who were sexually abused as children. *Journal of Sex and Marital Therapy, 23,* 118–125. It is crucial to realize that well-intended therapeutic concepts and interventions can cause iatrogenic damage to the individual and the couple. Therapeutic guidelines are proposed to differentiate helpful and potentially harmful interventions. Case examples are used to illustrate the adult sexual healing process.

McCarthy, B. (1999). Relapse prevention strategies for inhibited sexual desire. *Journal of Sex and Marital Therapy, 25,* 297–303.

McCarthy, B. (2002). Sexual secrets, trauma, and dysfunction. *Journal of Sex and Marital Therapy, 28,* 353–359.

McCarthy, B., & McCarthy, E. (2003) *Rekindling desire.* New York: Routledge.

McCarthy, B., & McCarthy, E. (2009). *Discovering your couple sexual style.* New York: Routledge.

McCarthy, B., & Thestrup, M. (2008). Couple therapy and the treatment of sexual dysfunction. In A. Gurman (Ed.), *Clinical handbook of couple therapy* (4th ed., pp. 591–617). New York: Guilford.

Meichenbaum, D. (1994). *A clinical handbook/practical therapist manual for assessing and treating adults with post-traumatic stress disorder (PTSD).* Waterloo, Canada: Institute Press.

Messman-Moore, T., & Resick, P. (2002). Brief treatment of complicated PTSD and peritraumatic responses in a client with repeated sexual victimization. *Cognitive and Behavioral Practice, 9,* 89–99.

Rind, B., Tromovitch, P., & Bauserman, R. (1998). A meta-analytic examination of assumed properties of child sexual abuse using college samples. *Psychological Bulletin, 124,* 22–53. This is arguably the most politically controversial study ever published in a scientific journal, at least in mental health. It is a meta-analysis of college student samples and reactions to sexual abuse. The authors suggested that some adult–adolescent sexual experiences were consensual and nonharmful, which led to the creation of a congressional resolution attacking the study and the American Psychological Association.

Saywitz, K., Mannarino, A., Berliner, L., & Cohen, J. (2000). Treatment for sexually abused children and adolescents. *American Psychologist, 55,* 1040–1049. This is a thoughtful review of treatment strategies and techniques for treating children and adolescents. Good treatment at the time reduces the likelihood of adult psychological and sexual symptoms.

Wieksma, N. (2003). Partner awareness regarding the adult sequelae of childhood sexual abuse for primary and secondary survivors. *Journal of Marital and Family Therapy, 29,* 151–164.

Eighteen

Recognizing and Reversing Sexual Side Effects of Medications

R. TAYLOR SEGRAVES, MD, PHD, AND RICHARD BALON, MD

Taylor Segraves: I became aware of treatment noncompliance because of drug-induced sexual side effects while working in a psychopharmacology clinic in a Veteran's Administration hospital over 20 years ago. I noted that a large number of my patients were discontinuing psychiatric drugs prematurely and were being rehospitalized because of illness relapses. I discovered that one of the reasons for their discontinuing medications against my advice was that the drugs I had prescribed were causing sexual problems. Until that time, it had never dawned on me to inquire if my prescriptions brought sexual side effects. These side effects were not discussed in psychopharmacology texts. In the early 1980s, there was minimal published information on this issue. I became fascinated with the topic and have continued to study it in my clinical practice and in clinical trials.

 Richard Balon: I became interested in this area almost 20 years ago when a colleague discussed an innovative research project with me. Later, when he asked me to take over the study of sexual dysfunction associated with antidepressants, I was hooked. After we published the results, I started to get invited to talk about sexual dysfunction associated with medications. The topic of medication-associated sexual dysfunction proved to be of considerable interest to clinicians. As there was a dearth of knowledgeable people, I was perceived as an "expert" without really being one. I realized, however, how little I, and others, knew. I started to study the literature, ask my patients about their experiences, and ultimately write about the problem. I became a colleague and later friend of Taylor Segraves through my writing. He has taught me a lot and still does. By now, I hope I have grown into my reputation as an expert.

INTRODUCTION

We are both pleased to have this opportunity to share one of our professional life's major interests with you. We hope this chapter will be useful for both the physician and the psychotherapist. We start with two brief patient stories.

Mrs. D, a 35-year-old vice president of a medium-size community bank, had consulted a psychotherapist because of fatigue, insomnia, appetite loss, indecisiveness, and hopelessness. The managed-care company referred the patient to a psychiatrist for evaluation for pharmacotherapy of depression and approved six sessions of psychotherapy with a counselor. The psychiatrist began the patient on fluoxetine (Prozac). In psychotherapy sessions, she discussed her difficulties balancing the time demands of being a wife, a mother, and a successful businesswoman. She felt guilt that she might be sacrificing her family for her career. Her mood gradually improved, she became more efficient at work, and she began to enjoy her free time with her family. The managed-care company did not approve further psychotherapy sessions. A few months later, the husband called the psychiatrist saying that his wife needed to be seen immediately as she had mentioned thoughts of suicide. The psychiatrist asked if she was still on fluoxetine. Her husband replied that his wife had discontinued fluoxetine after about 3 months as she was feeling much better and was having trouble reaching orgasm. The patient had not mentioned this problem to her counselor or her psychiatrist.

A psychotherapist followed Mr. T, a 42-year-old man, who lived in a supervised psychiatric group home. A primary care physician monitored his medications, while his psychotherapist focused on social skills training and problems of living. He was stabilized on haloperidol (Haldol) but would occasionally become noncompliant and have to be rehospitalized. The reason for his medication noncompliance was initially unclear. One day, he asked his psychotherapist about sildenafil (Viagra). The therapist inquired about the reason for his interest and discovered that the patient had experienced erectile problems since starting haloperidol. The therapist suspected that the man's partner was a prostitute and informed the patient about the importance of safe sex. The therapist then called the primary care physician, explained the situation, and asked if a sildenafil prescription should be considered. The primary care physician said, "Insurance will never pay for it, but I have samples." In the next session, the patient stated that the primary care doctor agreed to save sildenafil samples for him. He was happy about that. The patient did not seem to want to discuss the matter further and then added, "It's nice to feel normal. I know that normal people don't hear voices, but they do have sex!" The therapist noted that the patient was more self-confident than usual. The patient has remained treatment compliant and has not been rehospitalized since being given sildenafil samples.

PERSONAL DIGNITY AND SEXUAL DYSFUNCTION

We present these two case vignettes to illustrate several points. Regardless of their social strata, patients may prefer to become medication noncompliant rather than brave the social discomfort of volunteering to discuss their sexual activities with a therapist or physician. Our clinical impression is reinforced by the fact that studies in the United States, Great Britain, and Spain have shown that only one third of patients experiencing sexual side effects on drugs volunteer this information to their physicians without being asked directly. During an acute illness episode, sexual function may become relatively unimportant. However, on recovery, sexual function may assume a greater importance. The sexual dysfunction may be an unspoken cause of medication noncompliance. We cannot assume that sexual function is unimportant to a patient with a psychotic disorder. We should never underestimate the desire to feel normal among patients with severe psychiatric disorders.

This chapter has four sections:

1. A review of the major classes of psychiatric drugs associated with sexual side effects and their medical management
2. Management of sexual problems associated with widely used medications
3. The sexual problems associated by substances of abuse

4. Our views about medication treatment of hypoactive sexual desire disorder in each sex

DIAGNOSIS OF DRUG-INDUCED SEXUAL DYSFUNCTION

Straightforward Situations

The diagnosis of drug-induced sexual dysfunction is based on a careful sexual history after good clinician–patient rapport has been established. Baseline evaluation of sexual functioning is a very important part of diagnosing medication-induced sexual dysfunction. Relying on a patient's memory or retrospective reports of sexual functioning is not a reliable way of evaluating the patient's premorbid sexual functioning. Evaluation of sexual functioning should be part of every comprehensive initial evaluation and should be repeated prior to starting any medication.

In a healthy male or female patient with good premorbid sexual function, the recognition of drug-induced sexual dysfunction can be relatively easy. Typically, drug-induced sexual dysfunction begins within days to weeks of drug initiation or a dose increase. The difficulty is also usually present in all sexual situations: Problems with erection, ejaculation, and orgasm occur in masturbatory as well as partner-related activities. A decrease in libido includes a decrease in sexual fantasies and thoughts. The diagnosis is confirmed when a trial off medication restores pretreatment sexual function.

Four Complicated Situations

Diagnosis is complicated if the disease being treated is also associated with sexual dysfunction. Psychiatric diseases associated with sexual dysfunction include bipolar disease, depression, anxiety disorders, anorexia, some personality disorders (e.g., borderline personality disorder), and schizophrenia. Physical diseases associated with sexual problems include hyperlipidemia, diabetes mellitus, hypertension, other cardiovascular diseases, multiple sclerosis, epilepsy, and renal failure. The diagnosis can be difficult to discern as well when the sexual side effect occurs gradually during long-term therapy. Both digoxin (Lanoxin) and carbamezapine (Tegretol) may require several months of treatment prior to the development of sexual side effects. Evaluation is complex when less-than-normal function preceded treatment of the psychiatric or medical disorder. For example, some individuals prior to becoming depressed have sexual dysfunction. Their depression diminishes their libido. Their treatment may further impair their sexual function.

Psychiatric Drugs Associated With Sexual Dysfunction

A large number of drugs have been associated with sexual dysfunction. Probably most evidence concerning sexual side effects of drug usage concerns psychiatric drugs. It is ironic that a reason for the existence of this knowledge base in psychiatry is that several pharmaceutical companies have used the relative absence of sexual side effects of their product to competitively market their agents. Their efforts to find a competitive advantage have educated physicians about drug-induced sexual side effects. Sexual side effects appear to be common with most classes of psychiatric drugs.

The magnitude of the effect of antidepressant drugs on sexual function was not appreciated until these drugs had been in active clinical usage for a number of years. The previous source of information about the incidence of sexual side effects, the *Physicians Desk Reference* (2008), was inaccurate because its data were based on clinical trials in which direct inquiry was not used—only patient spontaneous reporting was.

In reviewing drug side effects on sexual function, we assessed different levels of evidence to determine our level of confidence in stating that a given side effect was indeed present with each drug. The highest level of evidence was multiple placebo-controlled clinical trials using proper methodology and direct assessment of sexual function before and after drug initiation compared to the same in a placebo control group. The next level of evidence concerned controlled comparisons in which a placebo condition was not utilized or in which the evaluator was not "blind" regarding the condition investigated. After that, we considered reviewed large clinical case series. The last level of evidence was individual case reports. Rarely, we considered consensus expert clinical opinion when no other evidence was available.

Detecting Drug-Induced Sexual Dysfunction

Differentiation of drug-induced sexual dysfunction from other causes of sexual difficulties in psychiatric patients can be difficult. The etiology of difficulties with libido can be especially difficult to determine as disturbances of libido can be part of major depressive disorder, anorexia nervosa, and some anxiety disorders. Similarly, the emotional problems that prompted the prescription of psychiatric drugs may have by themselves put additional strain on interpersonal relationships. These resultant interpersonal problems may in turn cause sexual difficulties. Ultimately, a careful history will provide clues regarding the etiology of the sexual difficulty. Most drug-induced sexual difficulties occur at the initiation of drug therapy or with dose increases. In addition, the problems will manifest themselves in all situations, not just in partner-related activity. Ultimately, return of function with a trial off the drug, successful use of an antidote, or switching to an alternative agent with resultant normal function will provide presumptive evidence that the problem was drug induced.

When treatment is split between a psychotherapist and a physician, the therapist is often better able to detect drug-induced sexual dysfunction because of better rapport with the patient. Some psychiatrists may feel threatened when a nonphysician detects a drug side effect that they overlooked. Here is a suggestion for a nonthreatening way to transmit the information to the physician: Send an e-mail or call the doctor and say that the patient discussed a new-onset sexual problem with you because he or she was embarrassed to discuss this directly with the psychiatrist. Ask the psychiatrist if he or she thinks whether the difficulty could be drug induced.

Antidepressants

Serotonergic antidepressants, especially the selective serotonin reuptake inhibitors (SSRIs), are associated with orgasm or ejaculatory delay and decreased libido. Some studies suggest that a small subgroup of men on some SSRIs experience erectile failure. Most, but not all, studies have found that the frequency of sexual side effects is higher in men than in women. It is unclear whether this is a true sex difference or an artifact of how the data were collected. A partial list of serotonergic antidepressants associated with sexual

Table 18.1   Serotonergic and Dual-Action Antidepressants
Associated With Orgasmic Dysfunction

Citalopram (Celexa)
Clomipramine (Anafranil)
Desvenlafaxine (Pristiq)
Duloxetine (Cymbalta)
Escitalopram (Lexapro)
Fluvoxamine (Luvox)
Fluoxetine (Prozac)
Paroxetine (Paxil)
Sertraline (Zoloft)
Venlafaxine (Effexor)

dysfunction (orgasm delay or anorgasmia) is listed in Table 18.1. Monoamine oxidase inhibitors and tricyclic antidepressants are also associated with orgasm delay.

Selective Serotonin Reuptake Inhibitors

The most common sexual side effect of the SSRIs is ejaculatory and orgasmic delay. Among the SSRIs, this is most common with paroxetine (Paxil), fluoxetine (Prozac), and sertraline (Zoloft). In fact, this side effect has been used by some clinicians to treat premature ejaculation. Approximately 30–40% of patients on SSRIs experience some orgasmic delay with these agents. Citalopram (Celexa) and fluvoxamine (Luvox) seem have a lower incidence of orgasmic dysfunction than fluoxetine, paroxetine, and sertraline. Around 20% of patients treated with the SSRIs may report decreased libido. However, the exact incidence of sexual dysfunction associated with SSRIs varies from study to study and may depend a little on the funding source of the study.

Other Antidepressants

Controlled evidence suggests that clomipramine (Anafranil), a tricyclic antidepressant with strong serotonergic activity, creates the most ejaculatory delay of any of the tricyclic antidepressants. Venlafaxine (Effexor), which acts as a serotonin reuptake inhibitor at low dosages but is a dual-action (serotonin and norepinephrine) medication in higher doses, appears to have an intermediate effect on orgasm. Pristiq (desvenlafaxine), a recently introduced medication, is structurally related to venlafaxine. It, like another dual-action antidepressant duloxetine (Cymbalta), seems to have a slightly lower incidence of associated sexual dysfunction than some SSRIs. The incidence of sexual dysfunction associated with these antidepressants has not been well studied. Mirtazapine (Remeron) may have a lower incidence of sexual dysfunction than other antidepressants have, but this has not been confirmed in controlled studies. Bupropion (Wellbutrin) and nefazodone (Serzone; the brand name of this medication was discontinued due to associated liver problems, but the generic formulation is still available) clearly have extremely low rates of causing sexual dysfunction. Table 18.2 lists the antidepressants with minimal sexual side effects.

We actively monitor and treat antidepressant-induced sexual side effects to encourage treatment compliance in depressive disorder, a possibly lethal and

Table 18.2   Antidepressants With Lower Incidence of
Sexual Dysfunction

Minimal or no sexual side effects
  Bupropion (Wellbutrin)
  Nefazodone (Serzone)
SSRIs with the fewest sexual side effects
  Citalopram (Celexa)
  Fluvoxamine (Luvox)
Antidepressants suspected to have lower incidence of sexual dysfunction
  Duloxetine (Cymbalta)
  Mirtazapine (Remeron)

often recurrent disorder. Some evidence suggests that insufficient treatment
may increase the likelihood of recurrence. Depression severely distresses
relationships. This is a critical issue because the social support of an intimate sexual relationship may facilitate recovery. One clearly wishes to restore
sexual intimacy as soon as possible to a relationship that is already stressed
by nonsexual factors.

MANAGEMENT OF DRUG-INDUCED SEXUAL DYSFUNCTION

Antidepressants

A variety of strategies have been employed to manage antidepressant-induced
sexual dysfunction. Occasionally, dose reduction can alleviate sexual side
effects without causing a return of depressive symptoms. Some clinicians
have advocated "drug holidays" (e.g., taking several days off medication for
sexual activity, then a resumption of taking the antidepressant). This strategy
has three important drawbacks:

1. Timing of sexual activity on a limited scheduled basis creates a sense
   of artificiality that many couples find unpleasant.
2. Suggesting drug holidays might inadvertently encourage treatment
   noncompliance. The patient may conclude that if skipping the drug
   for sex is safe then he or she no longer needs to take the drug on a continuous basis.
3. Some agents, such as venlafaxine, paroxetine, and sertraline, can be
   associated with unpleasant withdrawal effects that may be misdiag-
   nosed as the "flu." Drug holidays should not be used with these agents.

Drug substitution can be employed to manage antidepressant-induced sexual dysfunction. We usually substitute bupropion, nefazodone, or mirtazapine
in place of the agent that caused sexual dysfunction. If an SSRI is required,
citalopram, escitalopram (Lexapro), or fluvoxamine may be substituted for fluoxetine, paroxetine, or sertraline. Citalopram and fluvoxamine seem to have a
lower incidence of sexual dysfunction than the other SSRIs. Drug substitution
is limited by the fact that all antidepressants do not have the same efficacy
in all patients, and different drugs may vary in their side-effect profile and
ability to treat comorbid conditions. For example, we would not substitute
bupropion for fluoxetine in a patient with major depressive disorder and panic

Table 18.3   Management of SSRI-Induced Sexual
Dysfunction

Selection of an antidepressant with lower incidence of sexual dysfunction
Dose reduction
Drug holidays (rarely)
Drug substitution
Antidotes

Table 18.4   Antidotes of Proven Efficacy

Buspirone (Buspar)
Bupropion (Wellbutrin)
Sildenafil (Viagra) and probably other phosphodiesterase-5 inhibitors
(tadalafil [Cialis], vardenafil [Levitra])

disorder as bupropion is not effective in panic disorder. We would use caution in switching from sertraline to fluvoxamine or nefazodone in a patient on
multiple pharmacological agents as fluvoxamine and nefazodone have different drug–drug interactions than sertraline does.

Management strategies for SSRI-induced sexual dysfunction are listed in
Table 18.3.

Use of Antidotes

A number of antidotes to antidepressant-induced sexual dysfunction have
been reported in the literature. We first emphasize the antidotes that have
proved effective in double-blind studies and then discuss antidotes that are
used in clinical practice but have not been established by double-blind studies. Controlled studies have demonstrated that 50–100 mg of sildenafil are
effective in reversing erectile and ejaculatory problems that are caused by
SSRIs. One such study suggested that sildenafil might reduce the orgasmic
delay associated with antidepressant therapy. The clinical significance of this
approach remains unclear. Another controlled study demonstrated that 60 mg
of buspirone (Buspar) for 2 weeks will reverse SSRI-induced sexual dysfunction in 60% of patients of both sexes.

Some of the most commonly prescribed antidotes, however, are less scientifically proven. These include bupropion, yohimbine (Yocon), and cyprohep-
tadine (Periactin). Case reports, which are less powerful scientifically than
placebo-controlled studies, suggest that the addition of low doses of nefazodone or mirtazapine may reverse SSRI-induced sexual dysfunction.

The adverse effects of SSRIs on sexual function are hypothesized to be mediated by the serotonin 5-HT$_{2a}$ (5-hydroxytryptamine 2a) receptor. Nefazodone
and mirtazapine block this receptor. These drugs would be expected to be
effective on theoretical grounds. However, few compounds have been tested
in controlled studies. Antidotes of proven efficacy for SSRI-induced sexual
dysfunction are listed in Table 18.4.

Tranquilizers/Anxiolytics

Most of the minor tranquilizers, such as alprazolam (Xanax), clonazepam
(Klonopin), chlordiazepoxide (Librium), chlorazepate (Tranxene), diazepam

(Valium), and lorazepam (Ativan), have been reported to cause sexual problems, especially ejaculatory and orgasmic delay. The effect of diazepam on orgasm delay has been demonstrated in a controlled, double-blind laboratory study in women. Lorazepam has been reported to be useful in the treatment of premature ejaculation. It is not clear whether certain benzodiazepines are worse than others in producing adverse sexual effects. Switching to another benzodiazepine or buspirone may be a successful strategy to manage sexual dysfunction associated with anxiolytics.

Antipsychotic Drugs

Antipsychotic drugs have also been implicated in causing sexual dysfunction. Patients taking antipsychotic drugs are reluctant to volunteer the presence of drug-induced sexual side effects to their physicians. The extent to which antipsychotic drug-induced sexual dysfunction contributes to treatment noncompliance is unknown. Several investigators have postulated that antipsychotic drugs that cause prolactin elevation are more likely to cause decreased libido and erectile dysfunction than the prolactin-sparing antipsychotics are. Most of the aliphatic, piperidine, and piperazine phenothiazines have been reported to cause ejaculatory and erectile problems. The few studies that included females found that female patients report anorgasmia on these agents. Examples of these agents include chlorpromazine (Thorazine), thioridazine (Mellaril), mesoridazine (Serentil), trifluoperazine (Stelazine), fluphenazine (Prolixin), perphenazine (Trilafon), perchlorperazine (Compazine), chlorprothixine (Taractan), and thiothixine (Navane). The exact frequency of these side effects is unclear. However, one study with thioridazine found that approximately 40% of patients experienced both erectile and ejaculatory problems. Other traditional antipsychotics, such as haloperidol, pimozide (Orap), loxapine (Loxitane), and molindone (Moban), have been associated with erectile difficulties. The newer antipsychotics appear to have lower incidences of sexual dysfunction, with the possible exception of risperidone (Risperidal). Aripiprazole (Abilify), olanzapine (Zyprexa), quetiapine (Seroquel), and ziprazodone (Geodon) appear to have a very low incidence of sexual dysfunction.

Case reports and clinical series suggest that drug substitution or the addition of sildenafil is usually sufficient to reverse antipsychotic drug-induced sexual dysfunction. Some clinicians have advocated the use of dopaminergic agents such as bromocriptine and amantadine (Symmetrel). But, psychiatrists need to be careful because these agents may trigger psychotic symptoms. Cabegoline (Dostinex) has also been reported to reverse sexual side effects caused by antipsychotic drugs that elevate prolactin. Antipsychotic drugs with minimal sexual side effects are listed in Table 18.5. The commonly used

Table 18.5 Antipsychotics That Cause Minimal Sexual Problems

Aripiprazole (Abilify)
Olanzapine (Zyprexa)
Quetiapine (Seroquel)
Ziprasidone (Geodon)

Table 18.6 Antidotes for Antipsychotic-Induced
Sexual Dysfunction

Amantadine (Symmetrel)
Bromocriptine
Cabergoline (Dostinex)
Sildenafil (Viagra) and possibly other phosphodiesterase-5 inhibitors

antidotes for antipsychotic drug-induced sexual dysfunction are listed in Table 18.6.

Priapism

Many of the antipsychotic drugs have been associated with priapism, a prolonged erection that can be painful and can result in permanent damage to the corporal cavernosal tissues and erectile dysfunction. If a patient reports erections that persist for several hours after ejaculation without additional stimulation, it would be prudent to consider switching to a different agent. Priapism that lasts 4 hours is a medical emergency that should be treated immediately. Clitoral priapism can also occur and can be quite painful. It does not appear to cause permanent damage. Drugs reported to be associated with priapism are listed in Table 18.7.

Mood Stabilizers

Evidence regarding the incidence of sexual problems in those on lithium carbonate and other mood stabilizers is unclear. Mania is associated with increased libido, so it is difficult to ascertain whether decreased libido on mood stabilizers is due to treatment of mania or a drug-induced difficulty. The available evidence suggests that lithium may have adverse effects on libido and erectile function in some patients. Some reports suggest that

Table 18.7 Psychiatric Drugs Thought/Reported
to Cause Priapism

Aripiprazole (Abilify)
Bupropion (Wellbutrin)
Buspirone (Buspar)
Chlorpromazine (Thorazine)
Clozapine (Clozaril)
Fluphenazine (Prolixin)
Haloperidol (Haldol)
Mesoridazine (Serentil)
Molindone (Moban)
Olanzapine (Zyprexa)
Perphenazine (Trilafon)
Quetiapine (Seroquel)
Risperidone (Risperdal)
Thiothixene (Navane)
Thioridazine (Mellaril)
Trazodone (Desyrel)
Ziprasidone (Geodon)

Table 18.8   Other, Nonpsychotropic Drugs That Cause Sexual Dysfunction

Amiodarone (Cordarone)
Cimetidine (Tagament)
Clofibrate (Atromid-S)
Disopyramide (Norpace)
Gemfinrozil (Lopid)
Ketoconazole (Nizoral)
Lovastatin (Mevacor)
Metoclopromide (Reglan)
Propranolol (Inderal)
Propafenone (Rythmol)
Pravastatin (Pravachol)
Sotalol (Betapace)
Simvastatin (Zocor)

lithium plus benzodiazepines may have unusually frequent adverse effects on sexual function. Among anticonvulsants frequently used in psychiatric practice, gabapentin (Neurontin) has been reported to be associated with ejaculatory delay. Whether other anticonvulsants are associated with sexual problems is unclear.

Nonpsychotropic Drugs

Most of the antihypertensive agents have been reported to cause erectile problems. There has been minimal study of the effects of such agents in women. Sildenafil appears capable of reversing these side effects in most patients. Case reports suggest that a large variety of other drugs, such the gastrointestinal drugs metoclopromide (Reglan) and cimetidine (Tagamet), the antifungal agent ketoconazole (Nizoral), and antiarrthymic agents such as disopyramide (Norpace), propafenone (Rythmol), amiodarone (Cordarone), and sotalol (Betapace), may be associated with erectile dysfunction. Other drugs reported to be associated with erectile dysfunction include digoxin and many of the hypolipidemic drugs, such as clofibramate (Atromid-S), gemfibrozil (Lopid), lovastatin (Mevacor), pravastatin (Pravachol), and simvastatin (Zocor). As cardiovascular disease and hyperlipidemia are associated with erectile dysfunction, it is unclear whether the relationship between cardiovascular drugs and sexual problems is causal. Isolated reports suggest that sildenafil will reverse most forms of drug-induced erectile problems. Whether sildenafil will reverse drug-induced female sexual dysfunction is unclear. A partial list of other drugs possibly causing sexual dysfunction is listed in Table 18.8. It should be emphasized that the evidence concerning these relationships is mainly from case reports and may prove false.

Cancer Treatment

Both chemotherapy and radiation therapy of cancer are associated with problems with libido, erection, and lubrication. The precise agents responsible are difficult to identify as most cancer chemotherapy regimes contain numerous agents. Many of these are neurotoxins or induce menopause. An increased frequency of sexual problems is found in survivors of most types of cancer.

The most widely studied group of cancer patients is those with breast cancer. Many young women experience early menopause and suffer severe dyspareunia because of fragility of the vaginal epithelium and decreased capacity to lubricate when sexually aroused.

Whether estrogen replacement is safe in this population is unknown. Some clinicians feel that the suspected risk of estrogen therapy is more than offset by the real improvement in quality of life that estrogen replacement provides. We find it important to remember that loss of libido in patients with breast cancer is not necessarily the result of altered body image but may be the result of the toxicity of chemotherapy itself.

DRUGS OF ABUSE

Various drugs of abuse have been associated with sexual dysfunction. Many substances of abuse are touted as *aphrodisiacs*, drugs that enhance sexual functioning. In all fairness, some of them may have a positive effect on sexual functioning, frequently during the initial phase of use. However, their positive effect on sexual functioning is usually a myth, and many drugs of abuse that are considered to enhance sexual functioning actually exert deleterious effect on sexual functioning.

Alcohol and Tobacco: Legal Substances of Abuse

Alcohol is a case in point of a substance used to enhance sexual encounters yet is deleterious to it. This "social lubricant" has been touted as a substance that enhances sexual functioning forever. However, both acute and chronic intake of alcohol frequently have a negative impact on sexual functioning. The acute intake may interfere with arousal in both men and women and with orgasm. Chronic alcohol intake may lead to feminization in men due to testicular atrophy and inhibition of testosterone and sperm production. It seems that hypoactive sexual desire disorder is more common in women who abuse alcohol.

The negative impact of smoking on the ability to achieve firm erection is well known. Nicotine is a potent vasoconstrictor, and smoking contributes to the development of atherosclerosis. There is not much known about the impact of smoking on female sexual functioning.

Patients should be counseled about the negative impact of these two substances on sexual functioning and helped to stop using them.

Illegal Substances of Abuse

Cannabis (marijuana) has been reported to increase sexual pleasure and satisfaction and quality of orgasm. On the other hand, chronic marijuana users report decreased libido frequently. The acute use of cocaine leads frequently to increased sexual desire and even increased arousal (cases of priapism have been reported), probably through its potent dopaminergic effect. However, chronic cocaine users frequently suffer from impotence or even decreased ability to reach orgasm. Amphetamines (including methamphetamine) have a similar pattern of impact on sexual functioning: Acute use increases desire and facilitates sexual behavior and may intensify orgasm and prolong coitus, while chronic abuse lead to a host of sexual problems, including erectile dysfunction and prolonged orgasm.

Opioids (e.g., codeine, heroin, hydromorphone, methadone, oxycodone) are usually associated with sexual dysfunctions such as decreased desire and impaired orgasm.

Ecstasy (MDMA, 3,4-methylenedioxymethamphetamine) has a mostly positive effect on sexual functioning. The sexual experience is enhanced; users describe being more sensual, empathic, and close to others and more sexually satisfied. Arousal could be either enhanced (more in women?) or impaired (erection). Orgasm is usually prolonged and described as more intense.

DRUG TREATMENT OF LOW LIBIDO

Treatment of low libido varies according to etiology. Low libido due to psychological and interpersonal problems should be treated by psychotherapy. Drug-induced libido difficulties should be managed by drug substitution or the use of antidotes. Next, we share with you our thoughts about the problem of low libido of unknown etiology or low libido from hormonal difficulties.

Men

A number of drug treatments for men with low libido have been proposed. Androgen replacement in hypogonadal men is a well-established intervention. Current evidence indicates that a certain minimal level of androgen, perhaps between 200 and 450 ng/ml, is sufficient to restore normal sexual activity. Supraphysiological doses above that level are without much benefit. In most cases of hypogonadism, the clinician first needs to establish if the problem is primary gonadal failure or is due to a lesion of the hypothalamic–pituitary system. The usual laboratory screening tests include serum testosterone, serum hormone-binding globulin, luteinizing hormone (LH), follicle-stimulating hormone (FSH), and prolactin. If low free testosterone is found with high LH and FSH, one can usually safely conclude that the problem is primary gonadal failure, which can be treated with hormone replacement. Low testosterone in the presence of low LH and low FSH indicates that further evaluation of the pituitary–hypothalamic system is necessary. For example, it is possible that a pituitary tumor is responsible for gonadal failure in such cases.

Hormone replacement can be administered via transdermal systems, a gel applied to the skin, oral methyltestosterone, or testosterone enanthate injection. With all methods, it is necessary to obtain a baseline serum-free testosterone level. This should be repeated after treatment to establish the proper dosage. Most clinicians prefer either testosterone gel (Androgel) or transdermal system (as opposite to injections). Hepatic toxicity has been reported with oral methyltestosterone. Testosterone enanthate produces a supraphysiological level that falls to nearly hypogonadal levels prior to the next injection. The transdermal system and testosterone gels produce levels that approximate normal testosterone production. The starting dose of the transdermal system is usually the 5-mg system. The starting dose of testosterone gel is either the 25- or the 50-mg system. If one treats a patient with testosterone, routine monitoring of serum lipids, hematocrit, and prostate-specific antigen is necessary as testosterone may alter blood lipids adversely, increase erythropoesis, and possibly worsen the prognosis with prostate carcinoma.

Women

A large number of clinicians in many different countries are using androgen supplementation in females with complaints of low libido. The indications for this treatment, its long-term effects, and the normal levels of androgen in females are not well established. A number of studies have indicated that supraphysiological levels of testosterone in females increase libido. There is minimal evidence that variations of testosterone within normal limits have a clinically meaningful effect on libido. Some studies have found that increases of testosterone within normal limits have the same effect on libido as placebo. However, in postmenopausal women not receiving estrogen therapy, treatment with a testosterone patch (300 µg/day) resulted in a modest but meaningful improvement in sexual function in a recent study of 814 women with hypoactive sexual desire disorder. The long-term effects of testosterone, including the answer to the question whether it will increase the incidence of breast cancer, were not assessed in this study. As female testosterone is approximately 1/10 the value of testosterone in the male, some clinicians recommend diluting testosterone gel from 25 to 0.25 mg. It should be emphasized that neither the efficacy nor the safety of this approach has been proved. A testosterone patch is available in Europe; however, its use in low libido in the United States is off label.

There have been a number of studies of the effects of peripheral vasodilators (e.g., sildenafil) on female arousal and libido complaints. In general, these studies have demonstrated that peripheral vasodilators increase lubrication without having a beneficial effect on sexual pleasure or desire. Some women report unpleasant increased sensation with sildenafil use. A number of case reports suggested that some antidepressants may increase libido. One controlled single-blind study of nondepressed women in good relationships found that a bupropion sustained-release formulation increased various signs of libido. This effect was attributed to bupropion's effect on dopamine reuptake. The dosage used was 300 mg per day. A history of seizures or serious head injury is a contraindication to the use of this compound. This effect of bupropion is now being investigated in a double-blind, multicenter study.

New substances, such as bremelanotide and flibanserin, are being studied in hypoactive sexual desire disorder and other indications.

CONCLUSION

We have been fortunate to be involved in the study of human sexual functioning for almost two decades. We have been delighted to watch the knowledge in this previously neglected area expand rapidly. We now know that a number of psychiatric and other drugs widely used in medicine cause sexual side effects, and these side effects contribute to treatment noncompliance. In most situations, we can use alternative agents or antidotes to reverse drug-induced sexual dysfunction. The study of drug treatment of low libido is still in its infancy, however. We expect knowledge to expand rapidly in the next decade.

We think that the future challenges will be to determine when and how to use pharmacological agents for sexual problems and when to combine them with psychotherapies. We both have had the good fortune to work in academic centers and to see practice patterns change. It is rewarding to see the psychiatrists of tomorrow now inquire about sexual side effects and to seek ways to minimize these problems. We are heartened by our observations that mental health professionals who are not physicians also are increasingly aware of this issue, and that together all of us can maximize patient compliance with the psychotropic medications that have been of significant help to them.

REFERENCES

Aizenberg, D., Zemishlany, Z., Dorfman-Etrog, P., & Weizman, A. (1995). Sexual dysfunction in male schizophrenic patients. *Journal of Clinical Psychiatry, 56*, 137–141. The authors systematically investigated the presence of sex dysfunction in 20 drug-free patients with schizophrenia, 51 schizophrenic patients receiving treatment, and 51 normals. Comparing the treated to the nontreated group, the authors hypothesize that treatment may impair sexual function. They also suggest that schizophrenia may be associated with diminished libido.

Clayton, A., Kornstein, S., Prakash, A., Mallinckrodt, C., Wohlreich, M. (2007). Changes in sexual functioning associated with duloxetine, escitalopram, and placebo in the treatment of patients with major depressive disorder. *Journal of Sexual Medicine, 4*(4 Part 1), 917–929. Short-term treatment (8 weeks or less) demonstrated a higher incidence of treatment-emergent sexual dysfunction with escitalopram compared to treatment with duloxetine and placebo. Interestingly, after 12 weeks of treatment, no significant differences were observed between active drugs, and discontinuation rates for sexual adverse effects were not significantly different ($p = 0.07$). After 8 months, the incidence of sexual dysfunction was 33.3% with duloxetine, 43.6% with escitalopram, and 25% with placebo.

Davis, A. R. (2000). Recent advances in female sexual dysfunction. *Current Psychiatry Reports, 2*, 211–214. Science trails hope.

Davis, S. R., Moreau, M., Kroll, R., Bouchard, C., Panay, N., Gass, M., et al. for the APHRODITE Study team. (2008). Testosterone for low libido in postmenopausal women not taking estrogen. *New England Journal of Medicine, 359*, 2005–2017. This study demonstrated the modest but meaningful efficacy of testosterone in postmenopausal women with hypoactive sexual desire disorder.

Ferguson, J. M. (2001). The effects of antidepressants on sexual functioning in depressed outpatients: A review. *Journal of Clinical Psychiatry, 62*(Supplement 3), 22–34. The author reviews the published double-blind studies and clinical series concerning the effects of antidepressants on sexual function. The data are consistent in finding that mirtazapine and bupropion have the lowest rates of sexual dysfunction.

Gelenberg, A. J., Delgado, P., & Nurnberg, G. (2000). Sexual side-effects of antidepressant drugs. *Current Psychiatry Reports, 2*, 223–227. This article is another demonstration of the SSRI problem.

Guay, A. T. (2001). Advances in the management of androgen deficiency in women. *Medical Aspects of Human Sexuality, 1*, 32–38. This article is a urological approach to hypoactive sexual desire.

Gutierrez, M., & Stimmel, G. (1999). Management and counseling for psychotropic drug-induced sexual dysfunction. *Pharmacotherapy, 19,* 823–832. This article summarizes strategies to treat antipsychotic-induced sexual dysfunction and discusses possible mechanisms by which antipsychotic drugs might adversely affect sexual function. They recommend dose reduction, drug holidays, and antidotes such as amantadine, cypropheptadine, and sildenafil.

Hummer, M., Kemmler, G., Kurz, M., Kurzthaler, I., Oberbauer, H., & Fleischbach, W. W. (1999). Sexual disturbances during clozapine and haloperidol treatment for schizophrenia. *American Journal of Psychiatry, 156,* 631–634. This is the report of a prospective study of the development of sexual dysfunction in patients with schizophrenia treated with either haloperidal or clozapine. Both drugs initially had a high incidence of sexual side effects that remitted over 2–3 months.

Isenberg, D., Sigler, M., Zemishlany, Z., & Weizman, A. (1996). Lithium and male sexual function in affective disorder. *Clinical Neuropharmacology, 19,* 515–519. This is one of several clinical series finding suggestive evidence that lithium carbonate may induce sexual problems. Thirty-five men with bipolar disease, who were on lithium and euthymic, were questioned regarding their sexual activity. Approximately 20% reported decreased sexual thoughts and difficulty with erectile function while on lithium.

Jensen, J., & Lendorf, A. (1999). The prevalence and etiology of impotence in 101 male hypertensives. *American Journal of Hypertension, 12,* 271–275. Erectile dysfunction is a high-prevalence problem among hypertensives.

Keene, L., & Davies, P. (1999). Drug related erectile impotence. *Adverse Drug Reactions Toxicology Review, 18,* 5–24. This article is a comprehensive review of the data associating erectile dysfunction with various medications.

Kennedy, S., Dickens, S. E., Eisfeld, B. S., & Bagby, R. M. (1999). Sexual dysfunction after antidepressant therapy in major depression. *Journal of Affective Diseases, 56,* 201–208. Sexual dysfunction adds to the already high sexual burden of depression.

Kotin, J., Wilbert, D. E., Verburg, D., & Soldinger, S. (1976). Thioridazine and sexual dysfunction. *American Journal of Psychiatry, 133,* 82–85. This is a classic article: 60% of patients taking thioridazine had sexual dysfunction.

Landen, M., Eriksson, E., Agen, H., & Fahlen, T. (1999). Effect of buspirone on sexual dysfunction in depressed outpatients treated with selective serotonin reuptake inhibitors. *Journal of Clinical Psychopharmacology, 19,* 268–271. The authors reanalyze data on the efficacy of buspirone in augmenting the antidepressant effect of citalopram and paroxetine. They find that the addition of 20 to 60 mg of buspirone is effective in reversing SSRI-induced sexual dysfunction in 60% of patients. The effect is usually noted by the end of the first week of antidote therapy.

Montego, A. L., Llorca, G., Izquierdo, J. A., & Rico-Villademoros, F. (2001). Incidence of sexual dysfunction associated with antidepressant agents: A prospective multicenter study of 1,022 outpatients. Spanish Working Group for the Study of Psychotropic-Related Sexual Dysfunction. *Journal of Clinical Psychiatry, 62*(Supplement 3), 10–21. This study is important because of the number of patients involved, the fact that standardized assessment was utilized in multiple centers, and the fact that the ratings took place in normal clinical practice. Over 1,000 patients were studied. Both sexes were represented in the study. The serotonin reuptake inhibitors were found to be associated with some form of sexual dysfunction in about 50% of the patients studied. Mirtazapine and nefazodone had very low rates of sexual dysfunction.

Mortimer, J. E., Boucher, L., Knapp, D., Ryan, E., & Rowland, J. (1999). Effect of tamoxifen on sexual function in patients with breast cancer. *Journal of Clinical Oncology, 17,* 1488–1492. Sexual life often deteriorated during and following treatment of breast cancer.

Nurnberg, H. G., Hensley, P. L., Heiman, J. R., Croft, H. A., Debattista, C., & Paine, S. (2008). Sildenafil treatment of women with antidepressant-associated sexual dysfunction: A randomized controlled trial. *Journal of American Medical Association, 300,* 395–404. Contrary to the studies done by the maker of sildenafil, the results of this study suggest that sildenafil may be useful in some women with antidepressant-associated sexual dysfunction.

Nurnberg, H. G., Hensley, P. L., Lauriello, J., & Bogenschutz, M. P. (2001). Sildenafil treatment of antidepressant-associated sexual dysfunction: A 12 case treatment replication in a naturalistic setting. *Primary Psychiatry, 8,* 69–78. This article involves a dissertation that was the stimulus for a double-blind placebo-controlled trial.

Palha, A. P., & Esteves, M. (2008). Drugs of abuse and sexual functioning. *Advances in Psychosomatic Medicine, 29,* 131–149. This is a thorough review of the impact of various substances of abuse and their impact on sexual functioning, with a good discussion of literature and possible etiology.

Physicians Desk Reference. (2008). Published by Thomson Reuters, Montvale, New Jersey, and updated annually, the *PDR* is a compilation of manufacturers' prescribing information.

Rothschild, A. J. (2000). Sexual side effects of antidepressants. *Journal of Clinical Psychiatry, 61*(Supplement 2), 28–36. The author reviews the data concerning antidepressant-induced sexual dysfunction and the medical management of this condition: dosage reduction, drug holidays, changes in time of dosing, and the use of antidotes.

Salerian, A. J. (2000). Psychotropic-induced sexual dysfunction in 31 women and 61 men. *Journal of Sex and Marital Therapy, 26,* 133–140. In this large clinical series, the author found that 50–100 mg of sildenafil was effective in reversing sexual dysfunction induced by antipsychotics, lithium, benzodiazepines, and antidepressants.

Segraves, R. T., Croft, H., Kavoussi, R., Ascher, J., Batey, S., Foster, V., et al. (2001). Bupropion sustained release (SR) for the treatment of hypoactive sexual desire disorder (HSDD) in nondepressed women. *Journal of Sex and Marital Therapy, 27,* 306–316. In this multisite single-blind study, women with idiopathic acquired HSDD were treated with 300 mg bupropion for 8 weeks. Interview ratings of desire for sexual activity, sexual thoughts, and sexual arousal all doubled during bupropion treatment.

Segraves, R. T., Kavoussi, R, Hughes, A. R, Batey, S. R., Johnston, J. A., Donahie, R., et al. (2000). Evaluation of sexual functioning in depressed outpatients: A double-blind comparison of sustained-release bupropion and sertraline treatment. *Journal of Clinical Psychopharmacology, 20,* 122–128. In a randomized, double-blind multicenter trial, the effects of bupropion and sertraline on sexual function were studied using standardized clinical interviews. As early as the end of the first week, there was a significant difference between the two drugs. Sertraline was associated with more sexual dysfunction than bupropion was. The major effect of sertraline was on orgasm and ejaculatory function. It also had adverse effects on libido, erections, and vaginal lubrication.

Than, P. V., Hamilton, S. H., Kuntz, A., Potvin, J., Andersen, S., Beasley, C., et al. (1997). Double-blind comparison of olanzapine versus risperidone in the treatment of schizophrenia and other psychotic disorders. *Journal of Clinical Psychopharmacology, 17,* 407–418. This article involves an international multicenter, double-blind, parallel-group comparison of olanzapine and risperidone was conducted. The incidence of sexual dysfunction was much lower on olanzapine than on risperidone. The major sexual dysfunction caused by risperidone was ejaculatory delay. Risperidone also caused more elevation of prolactin.

Tostes, R. S., Carneiro, F. S., Lee, A. J., Giachini, F. R. C., Leite, R., Osawa, Y., et al. (2008). Cigarette smoking and erectile dysfunction: Focus on NO bioavailability and ROS generation. *Journal of Sexual Medicine, 5,* 1284–1295. This is a thorough discussion of the impact of smoking on erection and the etiology of this problem.

Waldinger, M. D. (1998). Effect of SSRI antidepressants on ejaculation: A double-blind placebo-controlled study with fluoxetine, fluvoxamine, paroxetine and sertraline. *Journal of Clinical Psychiatry, 18,* 274–281. The effects of various serotonin reuptake inhibitors on ejaculation were studied in men with rapid ejaculation. Efficacy was monitored by the partner using a stopwatch during coitus. Paroxetine had the greatest effect in delaying orgasm.

Nineteen

Sexual Consequences of Cancer Survivorship

LORI A. BROTTO, PHD, AND SHERYL A. KINGSBERG, PHD

Lori Brotto: Although I had a long interest in the intersection of chronic medical illness and sexuality, my experience with it was largely from a research perspective. However, when I joined the faculty in the Division of Gynaecologic Oncology at the University of British Columbia in Vancouver, Canada, I was able to gain valuable clinical experience with cancer survivors. I quickly made two observations: Cancer survivors, regardless of their stage and prognosis of cancer, expected that sexuality should continue to be a vital part of their lives. There was a shocking lack of dialogue about sexual function between cancer patients and their care specialists. I hope to help you understand two large ideas in this chapter: The first is that for cancer patients, just like others, sexuality is a testament to their vitality—a reminder that they are not only still alive but also living; the second is that we clinicians must confront our prejudices about what constitutes a sexually competent individual to assist cancer patients.

Sheryl A. Kingsberg: My first exposure to the sexual concerns of cancer patients was as a clinician. I am one of only two psychologists in a large obstetrics and gynecology department with four gynecologic oncologists. I have been the recipient of numerous referrals from these oncologists as well as from the Ireland Cancer Center at University Hospitals of Cleveland. A large percentage of my caseload is this work. My interactions with cancer patients confirmed for me how fundamental their sexual identity is to their self-concept as something other than a body with cancer. I have seen how patients feel entitled to and capable of sensual pleasure. But, it also became clear to me that most cancer physicians actively avoided addressing their patients' sexual concerns. Thus, my experiences have exactly paralleled Dr. Brotto's. In this chapter, we introduce clinicians who have not had much professional familiarity with the psychology of having cancer to this topic to increase their comfort in addressing the sexual concerns. I present the case involving prostate cancer. Dr. Brotto provides a case of breast cancer.

INTRODUCTION

As a result of more cancer patients becoming "survivors" and having their lives extended, treatment has expanded from addressing the disease to include maintaining or restoring quality of life (QoL). However, sexuality is one domain of QoL that is frequently ignored by cancer specialists. It is apparent to even the most casual spectator that cancer and cancer treatments often greatly impair sexual function (Ofman, Kingsberg, & Nelson, 2008), and that their effects may persist long after cancer has been cured.

The range and frequency of sexual concerns after cancer treatment have been the object of empirical study since the early 1980s. In the 1990s, research on the prevalence of cancer-related sexual dysfunction began to link sexual difficulties with the pathophysiology of cancer and its surgery, radiation, chemotherapy, hormonal manipulation, and cytostatic medications. Current research focuses on the development of interventions to ameliorate the sexual side effects of cancer treatment. These interventions include medications, physical aids, and psychosocial treatments.

The context and the content of cancer make sex therapy with cancer patients different from traditional sex therapy. It basically doubles the work of the clinician by asking us to provide both education and sex therapy. We have to educate health care providers as well as patients. While your first experiences are likely to be only with patients, you also may eventually educate cancer care providers about the psychological and sexual consequences of cancer and treatments.

Quickly, we discover that the patients' partners also have concerns about their sexuality. They will ask questions such as, "Can my partner transmit their cancer to me through sex?" "Will sex aggravate or cause cancer to recur?" and "Will radiation be spread to my body if we have intercourse?" Thus, there are many matters that might arise.

Because the physiological, psychological, and social aspects of cancer are intertwined, a biopsychosocial model for assessing and treating cancer-associated sexual difficulties is necessary. This model of illness recognizes the intricate reciprocal interplay of biological, psychological, and social influences on the onset, course, and treatment of disease (Stanton & Burns, 1999). These interactions take place within diverse cultural foundations, which contain different attitudes and beliefs about sexuality and cancer. Some cultures believe, for example, that cancer is a matter of fate, and that praying is the only effective form of treatment. The biopsychosocial model ideally functions when there is collaboration and ongoing dialogue between an interdisciplinary team.

Barriers to Addressing Sexuality in the Cancer Setting

Cancer specialists believe that sexuality is much less important than their sole focus on the direct elimination of the cancer. Patients often initially share this one-dimensional, "survival-focused at all cost" view. In a highly representative study, nearly all women with cancer were found to want to discuss sexuality, but they were reluctant to do so for fear of rejection by their cancer care provider (Casey, 1996). In a study of gynecologic cancer patients, fewer than half of cancer specialists took a sexual history in new patients. Eighty percent of them felt that there was not sufficient time to devote to exploring sexual issues (Wiggins, Wood, Granai, & Dizon, 2007). Lack of professional education and training around the topic leads to personal discomfort, fear of embarrassment, and anxiety about what to do if a patient affirms the presence of sexual dysfunction. Despite the fact that only 21% of oncologists in another recent study broached the topic of sexuality, 100% of them and 100%

of their patients believed that it was a topic that should have been discussed before and throughout cancer treatment (Stead, Brown, Fallowfield, & Selby, 2003). The creation of an environment that ensures safety, confidentiality, and importance of sexuality as a QoL issue still is a distant goal in most cancer centers.

Psychological Mechanisms That Impair Sexuality

While new chemotherapies, nerve-sparing surgeries, and conformal radiation have greatly improved survival, their sexual implications remain somewhat unclear. Even if cancer treatments could steer clear of impairing sexual physiology, patients would remain at high risk for sexual problems from the psychological damage of receiving a cancer diagnosis and the impact of treatment on body image, self-confidence, and relationship equilibrium. The resumption of pretreatment sexual patterns is the natural goal of prosexual interventions, but this is often quite unrealistic. For example, at one year following the completion of cervical cancer treatment, when one might expect to resume prediagnosis sexual life, patients have more lubrication and desire problems as well as more worries about their sex life than they had one month after treatment (Jensen et al., 2003). This deterioration can be devastating for individuals who believe that they *should* be "back to normal" in all domains of their life. Cancer treatments are often painful, frightening, and intrusive. They may physiologically or anatomically interfere with sexual capacity. They often indirectly cause sexual problems by inducing menopause, profound fatigue, or disfigurement through scarring, ostomies, and weight changes.

Memories of the illness and treatment experience often disrupt sexual health. These psychological aftereffects may continue indefinitely and are often stirred up by routine follow-up medical care (Ofman et al., 2008). Impairments of self-image are not limited to physical appearance or identity as a "cancer patient." They may bleed into vocational concerns, such as, "Can I still work full time?" "Can I maintain my role as primary breadwinner?" or worries about leisure, such as "Will I still be able to go bowling?" "Can I keep my average bowling score up?" Altered self-image may impair sexual self-esteem and become another avenue of sexual impairment.

Effective treatment interventions begin with an appreciation of these identity alterations. We challenge these new negative cognitive self-perceptions and diligently work to restore positive self-esteem. Andersen, Woods, and Copeland's (1997) finding that sexual self-schemas play a key role in causing cancer-associated sexual dysfunction supports our view that treatments that target how the patients now view themselves are crucial to improving sexual function.

Partners of cancer patients are not immune to the effects of cancer and its treatment. The partners' new caretaker roles often diminish their view of the partner as a sexual person. Partners, of course, have considerable anxiety about recurrence, a future bout of caretaking, or the death of their partner. This leads to a diminished sense of control just as it does in the cancer patient. These worries can interfere seriously with the resumption of a sexual life (Cella & Tros, 1986). When caregiving spouses are considerably younger than the partner is, spouses have significantly more fear of recurrence than if the partners are of similar age (Mellon, Kershaw, Northouse, & Freeman-Gibb, 2007).

CASE PRESENTATIONS

We now illustrate these concepts by considering two cases.

> Jan, aged 55, presented with hypoactive sexual desire disorder 3 years after her 60-year-old partner, John, was treated for colon cancer. On first glance, it appeared that her loss of drive coincided with her menopausal transition 4 years prior because she reported a gradual decline in desire over the last few years. However, on closer examination of the timeline, it appeared that her low desire began shortly after John's diagnosis of cancer. When I inquired about the components of desire, I learned that Jan still had frequent sexual urges from "out of the blue" (sexual drive), but she no longer felt any sexual interest toward John (lack of motivation):
>
>> After taking care of him through the long ordeal from surgery, coping with his colostomy, and then nursing him through his miserable side effects from chemotherapy, it is hard to look at him as a sexual partner. Now he manages his colostomy without my help, and he is potent—he is almost back to his old self. But, I just can't seem to get turned on around him the way I used to. I have too many memories of being his nurse and cheerleader.
>
> Jan and John represent the classic example of the transformation of roles of wife and husband to nurse and patient, respectively. Jan's image of John's ravaged body is difficult for her to forget. Jan suffers from memories in a manner that is analogous to some men's loss of sexual interest in a wife on observing her giving birth vaginally. The sight of the baby's head crowning or the placenta being delivered may burn an image in his memory that returns for a while when making love. Compounding Jan's day in and day out role change during their long ordeal was the extensive breakdown in their communication. Jan stopped confiding her worries and anxieties to John because he was unloading his on her. Story and Bradbury (2004) point out that protecting a partner from emotional distress may damage the caregiver's well-being and harm the couple's relationship.

In this case, the sex therapist should have little difficulty in conducting a thorough assessment and formulating the diagnosis and treatment plan. Jan has a situational form of hypoactive sexual desire disorder. The therapist can help her to appreciate what she has experienced. The therapist might employ cognitive-behavioral therapy to alter Jan's perception of John as *her* patient and to modify the couple's behavior in and out of the bedroom. Personalized sensate focus exercises and gradual reintroduction of sexual behaviors might be necessary to rekindle their sexual activity, but rebalancing the relationship outside the bedroom might, by itself, improve their sexual intimacy and help Jan to see John again as an equal partner.

Therapy should enable them to communicate about the cancer again. The therapist should actively encourage and personally facilitate talking about the cancer experience and its impact on both of them. The couple can then feel like they are an intimate team; once again, it is "us against the world." During their ordeal, they each hunkered down into their private and closed-off foxholes. Schover et al. (2002) demonstrate that good sexual function in the female partner is a robust predictor of better sexual function in a male partner following prostate cancer treatment. Although Jan could easily be construed as the designated sex therapy patient and treated alone, Schover et al.'s work suggests that it might be wise to consider the couple as the patient.

Laura, a 32-year-old married mother of two, was treated for early-stage cervical cancer 1 year ago. She presented for treatment complaining of a complete loss of genital
response and pain with intercourse. Prior to cancer, Laura experienced high levels of
sexual arousal and pleasure and was multiply orgasmic. She and her husband enjoyed
their sexual life very much. Laura received rather aggressive treatment, including a
radical hysterectomy and radiation therapy. She elected to have her ovaries removed
because her mother, sister, and aunt had breast or ovarian cancers. Laura and Frank
ceased all sexual contact during the 3 months of treatment. When they attempted
intercourse for the first time, Laura experienced significant discomfort with deeper
penetration. She also reported a complete lack of physical pleasure and likened the
feeling of having her genitals stimulated to "having my elbows touched." She was
devastated by her perception that her capacity for experiencing pleasure had been
taken away.

The interaction between biological and psychosocial aspects of Laura's cancer and the impact on her sexual functioning are apparent. Because of the
aggressiveness of her treatment, Laura may not have predicted the impact of
radiation therapy, hysterectomy, and oophorectomies on her sexual health at
the outset of these treatments. Her oncological surgeon is likely not to have
discussed this topic if she did not raise the issue. Radical hysterectomy is
associated with more impairment in genital blood flow than surgery that
leaves the upper vagina intact (Maas et al., 2002). Thus, part of the impairment in genital sensitivity and deep pain may be a direct result of the surgery.
Pelvic radiation is associated with genital dryness and pain, may cause skin
thickening and contractures, and leads to visible changes in genital anatomy.
In addition to changes in vaginal vault length and elasticity, there may also be
loss of sensitivity to vulvar and clitoral areas. Compared to surgery alone, pelvic radiation therapy is associated with vaginal shortening and narrowing in
75%, compared to 1% in women receiving surgery alone (Abitbol & Davenport,
1974). Because of prophylactic removal of both ovaries, Laura experienced an
abrupt surgical menopause.

At age 32, she may experience hot flashes, vaginal dryness, and loss of sensitivity. Laura is likely to view herself as "menopausal before her time." For
a young woman with a vibrant precancer sex life, this physiological transformation can be psychologically devastating. Women who had a high level
of sexual response prior to cancer may experience their changes in sexual
functioning more dramatically than those whose precancer sexual adaptation was less intense or even impaired. When these couples try to resume sex
and encounter these problems, both partners should be expected to be deeply
disappointed and worried about whether they can ever get back sexually to
where they were before their ordeal began.

An appropriate treatment plan for Laura would address many layers of her
experience, ranging from information on sexual technique and use of dilators
to promote vaginal rehabilitation; addressing myths that may be problematic,
such as "unless I am highly in the mood, I cannot be sexual," or "if my genital
response is not as strong as it was before, I am broken." Hormonal treatment of
vaginal dryness may be considered in this case also. It would be imperative to
address Laura's sense of sexual esteem, her communication with Frank, and
her view of her body in any treatment plan.

THE IMPORTANCE OF THE PRECANCER SEXUAL ADAPTATION

The therapist must have an accurate understanding of a patient or couple's sexual life prior to cancer and treatment. We often get caught up in our own goal of maximizing sexual functioning without paying attention to a couple's premorbid functioning or their motivations for resuming sexual activity. This is a mistake. Education is the necessary first step; we share information about the known sequelae of cancer and its treatment with cancer survivors. In doing so, we carefully note their reactions to this information. We can teach them that sexual health prior to cancer is a major predictor of changes in sexuality following cancer. Because we know that those with preexisting difficulties are at much greater risk of having sexual dysfunction with cancer, we want to know what their sexual experience patterns have been.

HOW CANCER MAY IMPROVE THE SEXUAL RELATIONSHIP

Cancer may enhance some couples' sexual relationship. They are forced to consider alternative or new ways of sexual interaction that minimize pain and maximize pleasure. If ongoing fatigue accompanies their cancer treatment, planning sexual activity for times when they are feeling alert may be a necessary and positive change. Awareness of the precariousness of life or recognition of the potential loss can serve as a wake-up call and renewed appreciation for one's partner. In addition, forced changes in sexual repertoire due to treatment effects may reinvigorate a stale sexual pattern and enable the couple to communicate in ways formerly dispensed. Sometimes accepting that intercourse may no longer be possible (due to ongoing pain, fatigue, persisting erectile problems) can be a major goal in treatment.

THE RANGE OF CANCER IMPAIRMENTS

There is a range of impairments caused by cancer. These are listed by disease site in Table 19.1.

THE IMPORTANCE OF TIME SINCE TREATMENT

In assessing a person who has had cancer, pay attention to the time since treatment. The patient has a belief about the "normal" time to recover from his erectile dysfunction (ED), her loss of genital sensitivity, and so on after treatment. Within that self-defined window, patients will not be as "bothered" by the symptoms since they may have been expected. Thereafter, however, the level of bother increases. There is usually a discrepancy about the interval that physicians assume and the normal interval assumed by the patient. A survey (Chartier-Kastler et al., 2008) conducted by the French Urological Association reported that, of 2,644 radical prostatectomy patient responders, by 1–2 months after surgery 73% were frustrated by their ED, whereas 10% of urologists thought that ED was important to their patients at this time.

Table 19.1 Common Sexual Consequences by Disease Site

Disease	Women	Men
Anal cancer	Decreased desire Possible decreased clitoral sensitivity Dyspareunia Decreased lubrication due to radiation	Decreased desire Erectile dysfunction
Bladder cancer	Incontinence Dyspareunia Altered body image due to ostomy Decreased arousal Orgasmic difficulties	Incontinence Erectile dysfunction Orgasmic impairment Altered body image due to ostomy
Breast cancer	Altered body image, hair loss Menopausal symptoms following chemotherapy, hormone therapy, or aromatase inhibitors Loss of sexual desire	Altered body image
Colorectal cancer	Altered body image due to colostomy Dyspareunia Diarrhea inhibits sexual behavior	Altered body image due to colostomy Erectile dysfunction Diarrhea inhibits sexual behavior
Gynecologic cancers	Altered body image, hair loss Lack of lubrication Dyspareunia Chronic pelvic pain Difficulty with arousal Anorgasmia Decreased desire Loss of clitoral sensitivity	
Prostate cancer		Erectile dysfunction Reduced sensation during orgasm Incontinence Bowel dysfunction Altered body image due to feminization if on hormone treatment Altered body image
Testicular cancer		Altered body image Altered sensation during orgasm
Other cancers	Decreased desire due to chemotherapy side effects	Decreased desire due to chemotherapy side effects

Source: Table adapted from Ofman, Kingsberg, and Nelson (2008).

AN ASSESSMENT OF A COUPLE WITH PROSTATE CANCER

Ethan, a retired fireman, is 52, and his wife Diane, a bookkeeper, is 57. They have been married for 20 years. Each has two children from a previous marriage. After their divorces, they had one child together. Ethan is self-employed as a landscaper. Ethan, diagnosed with stage I ("early-stage") prostate cancer 2 years ago, underwent a laparoscopic radical prostatectomy (removal of prostate gland and some surrounding tissue). His prostate-specific antigen (PSA) level has remained at 0. No treatment was recommended despite the moderate-to-severe ED since his surgery. The urologist warned him that he might experience some "temporary" difficulties with erections and some incontinence. But now, 2 years postsurgery, he is worried that his ED may not be temporary.

> With encouragement from Diane, he told his urologist of his concerns. His urologist prescribed a PDE5 (phosphodiesterase type 5 inhibitor) and referred Ethan and Diane to a psychologist for assessment and psychotherapy as an adjunct to or instead of the PDE5. Urologists are generally aware that PDE5s alone do not successfully restore erections in men following radical prostatectomy. Further, the urologist had enough experience to know that there was a strong likelihood of a psychological source to Ethan's ED.

Prostate cancer is the second most common type of cancer and leading cause of cancer death in American men (American Cancer Society, 2007). About one in six men will be diagnosed with it. In contrast to these frightening statistics, the survival rates for prostate cancer continue to improve. The relative 5-year survival rate is 100% and for 10 years is 91% (American Cancer Society, 2009). While the survival statistics are great news, the high prevalence of sexual dysfunction following prostate cancer treatments (29 to 85%) is bad news (Schover et al., 2002). Furthermore, the incidence of ED following radical prostatectomy, the most common treatment for prostate cancer, is even higher. Dubbelman, Dohle, and Schroder (2006) estimate that the ED rate for this population is 81%. The cavernous nerves that are responsible for erectile function run bilaterally along the prostate. ED develops if these nerves are removed or stretched during surgery. "Nerve-sparing" surgical techniques have been developed to avoid this outcome, but their success in preventing ED is not to be assumed.

Publications have noted a range of ED of 31–86% with bilateral nerve-sparing and 13–56% with unilateral nerve-sparing procedures. It must be understood, however, that recovery may not begin to occur until 18–24 months postsurgery. Since the seminal vesicles are often removed along with the prostate, the volume of ejaculate is significantly reduced; the ejaculate contains primarily sperm without the suspending seminal fluid. While many men report no decrease in their ability to enjoy orgasm, many state that initially it feels "a little strange." Further inhibiting sex is the occasional experience of incontinence during foreplay.

A study found that only 38% of men with prostate cancer said that they would accept life-lengthening prostate surgery if it would lead to impaired sexual function. The majority of men stated that they would not accept surgery had they known unless it would have dramatically increased their survival time (Helgason, 1996). The high survival rates juxtaposed with the high prevalence of sexual side effects of all prostate cancer treatments present every patient with an uncomfortable choice that should be discussed prior to treatment,

Ethan's prognosis for survival is great. Yet, his QoL has greatly diminished. Can the sex therapist help him?

Goals of Treatment

The first step in treating Ethan will be to define his goals and what "success" means to him. Althof (2002) taught us that men have a narrow definition of success and tend to focus on only the mechanics of erectile function. Treatment of ED in men who have had any kind of cancer seeks to restore the ability to obtain and sustain an erection to the optimal ability given physical health and relationship status. However, research on specific interventions techniques is scarce.

The next step in Ethan's case is to take a thorough history and determine whether the etiology of his ED is largely organic due to the surgery or likely more psychogenic due to the changes in his role, his affective experiences, or shifts in his relationship with Diane.

> I interviewed both partners individually and learned that prior to Ethan's diagnosis, he and Diane had a satisfying sexual life. Both of them had noticed a gradual decline in their desire and subsequent sexual frequency. In the two years before Ethan's diagnosis, they would have sex about three times per month. Ten years ago, their frequency was at least once per week. However, despite this decline, both were satisfied with the frequency and their sexual response. Both were reliably able to maintain arousal and reach orgasm; intercourse was a favored activity. They were quite satisfied with their intimate relationship outside the bedroom as well.
>
> Ethan reported that his drive (spontaneous sexual interest) has returned to his baseline level of wanting sex about once per week. Nevertheless, he remains unable to obtain an erection sufficient for penetration. He does not awaken with a firm erection and has not been able to become erect with masturbation. He complains of decreased penile sensitivity and has had difficulty adjusting to "dry orgasms." Ethan and Diane first attempted to resume their sexual activity approximately six months after surgery. The urologist had warned them that it might take "several months, if ever" for his erectile capacity to return. Ethan was quite worried about his ability to "perform."

I concluded that Ethan's ED and orgasmic dysfunction are very likely the direct result of his cancer treatment. It was far more difficult to assess the extent of the contributions from performance anxiety and his lack of confidence that stemmed from his physician's warnings and from what Ethan read on the Internet and in patient information pamphlets. Fortunately, it was not essential to know the precise answer at the beginning of treatment. I simply assumed that even when the etiology of ED is organic, by the time a man reaches my office, performance anxiety will be present. Althof's (2002) prediction that the use of a medical intervention (such as a PDE5) plus psychotherapy would be the rule rather than the exception when treating men with ED seems particularly apt when treating men with prostate cancer.

This is precisely the case for Ethan. It is possible that Ethan's erections can be improved with the addition of a PDE5 (e.g., sildenafil, tadalafil, vardenafil). However, their success may well depend on my ability to effectively communicate four ideas to Ethan and Diane:

1. It may take up to six attempts at using a PDE5 before his penis and his brain respond. The relatively high rate of discontinuation of PDE5s is thought by urologists to be due to the patients' incorrect assumption that the first use of a PDE5 should result in a rock-hard erection. Many urologists now prescribe PDE5s to be used immediately and daily as a form of erectile rehabilitation/ED prevention. Ethan's urologist did not.
2. Desire and subjective arousal must be present before an erection can be expected. These drugs do not cause arousal. They only enable the vasocongestion of the penis to remain in the penis after the man's arousal causes blood to flow there in the first place.
3. What will be normal after surgery is not what was normal before prostate cancer treatment; for example, now dry orgasms are the reality.

4. A vicious cycle naturally occurs in which the man begins to be anxious whenever sex is in the offing. This anxiety can cause premature ejaculation in an effort to quickly complete the sexual act before he loses his erection, or it can lead to the man to focus his attention on nonerotic stimuli. Premature ejaculation, performance anxiety, and ED can cause depression, which then diminishes sexual drive and motivation.

When any therapist explains this cycle, most individuals and couples immediately recognize the parts of it that apply to them. They feel better knowing that they are not alone. They assume that the therapist may have some suggestions for overcoming the cycle of anxiety and fear and embarrassment or shame. Embarrassment and shame may be particularly intense among younger men with testicular cancer because of their new infertility.

As you can see, although Ethan is the identified "cancer patient" who carries the symptom of ED, treatment is geared toward the couple. The few psychological and sexual health support services that do exist tend to ignore the needs of partners. Chambers et al. (2008) proposed a couple-based sexuality treatment protocol following radical prostatectomy. They suggest that a couple approach is particularly effective because partners are often negatively affected sexually and psychologically, and the better adjusted the female partner is, the better is the prognosis for the patient with prostate cancer.

AN ASSESSMENT OF A WOMAN WITH BREAST CANCER

Lenna was a 59-year-old housewife whose stage 2 breast cancer was treated 3 years ago. She presented for treatment of loss of desire and arousal. Her husband of 41 years died 1 year after she completed her treatment. In the early years of their relationship, Lenna experienced sexual desire and arousal and was orgasmic with intercourse. Her transition through menopause at the age of 55 was difficult; she experienced debilitating hot flashes and night sweats. Her sleep never normalized to premenopause levels. Lenna's husband died just as she was finishing her radiation therapy. He had been ill with a debilitating chronic neurological condition. She was shocked by his death, and she experienced a significant reactive depression. She lost motivation for many of her regular activities, and she ceased her regular masturbation. For the next 2 years, grief and depression kept her relatively housebound. Her physician told her on the 2-year anniversary of her final cancer treatment that there were no signs of recurrence, and that she would no longer require regular surveillance. Lenna's friend insisted that she join her at a work social event to celebrate. Reluctantly, she attended and met John, who was also a cancer survivor. They ended up having a great conversation, followed by a few dates. For the first time in years, Lenna found herself imagining what it would be like to have sex again. However, she also convinced herself that her body was no longer capable of functioning given the menopause, mastectomy, and the effects of chemotherapy and radiation. When she concluded that she was no longer a sexual woman, she stopped all communication with John.

Breast cancer challenges a woman's sexual identity and sense of attractiveness—that is, it can directly change a woman's sense of her femininity and sexual self. In a sexual health program at a major American cancer treatment center, the most frequent group of cancer survivors who sought sex therapy was women with breast cancer. Their most common sexual complaints were pain with intercourse and vaginal dryness (Amsterdam, Carter, & Krychman,

2006). Despite the fact that breast cancer rates across all ages of women are decreasing in most countries, breast cancer remains the most common cancer among women. One in 9 women will develop breast cancer in her lifetime, and 1 in 28 will die from it (American Cancer Society, 2007). Sexual complaints in women treated by mastectomy, chemotherapy, or radiation are common. However, because of methodological differences across studies, precise prevalence rates are unknown. Here are some estimates: With modified radical mastectomy, there is a 25% chance of sexual dysfunction (Schover, 1991). Schover et al. (1995) compared 72 women who had partial mastectomy (lumpectomy) with 146 women who had mastectomy with immediate breast reconstruction. The women with partial mastectomy had better pleasure and frequency of breast caressing than those who underwent reconstruction. Chemotherapy produced significantly more sexual dysfunction, poorer body image, and more psychological distress.

An Italian study of 50 women with breast cancer who had received either a mastectomy or quadrantectomy followed by radiation therapy showed a high frequency of sexual dysfunctions that negatively impacted quality of sex life (Barni & Mondin, 1997). Forty-eight percent experienced a complete absence of sexual desire, and 32% had anorgasmia, while 38% had dyspareunia, and 42% had lubrication problems. However, in 12% of cases, the quality of sexual activity was considered to have improved.

In Lenna's case, certainly the loss of her breast contributed to a decreased sense of femininity and sexual self, but there was also the contribution of her chemo-radiation therapy and its ensuing effects on her physical sexual responsiveness. Combined with the reactive depression to losing her husband, Lenna experienced the effects of a complex interaction of cancer-associated as well as partner-associated influences on her sexual function.

From a large longitudinal study of sexual health in women after breast cancer, Ganz, Desmond, Belin, Meyerowitz, and Rowland (1999) developed a model of factors that influence sexual health. For sexually active breast cancer survivors in a partnered relationship, among the most important and consistent predictors of sexual health were the presence or absence of vaginal dryness, emotional well-being, body image, quality of the partnered relationship, and whether the woman's partner had sexual problems. The psychosocial variables were more powerful than any biological factor. In particular, the influence of partner-related factors was noteworthy. For Lenna, the loss of her husband and the associated depression that followed plus the anticipatory anxiety of beginning a new sexual relationship and having to convey her sexual limitations to John led her to choose avoidance over taking a risk of personal and partner disappointment.

In Fobair et al.'s (2006) longitudinal study of sexual functioning in 549 women aged 22–50 with breast cancer who were assessed shortly following surgery, 67% of partnered women were sexually active in the past 4 weeks. The most common reason cited for being sexually inactive was lack of sexual interest (50%). Among the 360 sexually active women, 52% reported having problems in two or more areas of sexual functioning or a definite or serious problem in at least one area. Greater sexual problems were associated with having vaginal dryness, poorer mental health, being married, partner's difficulty understanding her feelings, and more body image problems (Fobair et al., 2006).

Lenna did not receive treatment for her cancer with a selective estrogen receptor modulator (e.g., tamoxifen) or an aromatase inhibitor, despite the fact that these are commonly used in the treatment of breast cancer because of their inhibition of estrogen action and availability. (This is especially relevant for estrogen-sensitive breast tumors.) These medications can trigger iatrogenic menopause. A comparison of tamoxifen with aromatase inhibitors found the former to have significantly worse effects on vaginal dryness and low desire and the latter to have more deleterious effects on dyspareunia (Morales et al., 2004). In a woman who has lost fertility potential because of iatrogenic meno-pause, this can be a major insult to her sense of self-esteem.

Lenna's low sexual desire and arousal began prior to the cancer diagnosis. This fact became apparent during our careful history taking during her assess-ment. Such an observation is important to make to patients who believe that all of their sexual problems are exclusively due to the effects of cancer and its treatment. Because the occurrence of cancer cannot be reversed, they believe that neither can sexual sequelae of cancer. By helping patients to open their eyes to their precancer sexual patterns, we position them to develop a greater sense of control over the things they are capable of changing. For Lenna, the chronic stress of caretaking for her husband may have influenced her sense of postcancer sexual hopelessness. Her severe chronic sleep disruption may be a major contributor to her loss of desire. Fatigue has been found in numerous studies to predict sexual dysfunction after cancer. The literature suggests that in women without a history of cancer there is a strong association between sleep problems and sexual difficulties. Lenna's history of depression is an important factor in her sexual dysfunction as well. Depression is consistently found to be a major predictor of all components of the sexual response (in men and women) as it is characterized by loss of interest in many aspects of a person's life and former activities. The loss of her husband must also be con-sidered in light of the fact that relationship variables are more predictive of sexual response and satisfaction than nearly every other variable considered—including the influence of estrogen with menopause, as shown in longitudi-nal data from the Melbourne Women's Midlife Health Project (Dennerstein, Lehert, & Burger, 2005).

Lenna convinced herself that her body was incapable of experiencing plea-sure, and this may have acted as a self-fulfilling prophecy. Because she was now avoidant of sexual activity, despite having some desire to engage in sexual activity, her belief that her body was "broken after cancer" remained unchal-lenged and therefore strengthened.

Lenna's sexual dysfunction does not appear to have a predominant organic etiology. Our first aim in treatment was to provide Lenna with education on known rates of sexual dysfunction associated with breast cancer, followed by encouragement of her to consider for herself the many predictors of her current sexual complaints beyond cancer. I encourage these patients to fold a piece of paper in half and use the left side of the page to brainstorm all of the predisposing, precipitating, and now perpetuating factors contributing to their sexual complaints. On the right side of the page, I encourage the cancer survivor to document each of the protective factors operating at each level of predisposing, precipitating, and perpetuating factors. Lenna previously enjoyed self-stimulation; however, with the onset of her depression and the death of her husband, she ceased this once-enjoyable activity. In treatment,

I encouraged her to reintroduce self-stimulation as a means of experiencing that her body indeed is still alive and responsive. Combined with cognitive therapy to directly challenge irrational beliefs such as "my body is now broken," masturbation was encouraged as a healthy form of sexual expression.

Testosterone for Lenna's loss of sexual desire would be unlikely to be considered. In part, this is due to the fear of exacerbating breast cancer in estrogen-sensitive tumors given the aromatization of testosterone to estrogen. Another reason is that a study of a testosterone patch for estrogen-depleted cancer survivors, most of whom had a history of breast cancer, failed to find any significant beneficial effect of testosterone above placebo (Barton et al., 2007). Third, given that Lenna's loss of desire is more related to her altered sense of herself as a sexual woman, her loss of interest in many activities, her fear of being sexual again, and her fatigue, it is unlikely that testosterone would be helpful.

Perhaps the failure of drug treatments to receive approval for women's sexual dysfunction stems from the fact that merely improving genital blood flow does not tap into women's experiences and expressions of sexuality. In the woman with cancer, this point is particularly pertinent. Interventions need to target the psychological, social, and partner-related aspects of the woman's current life.

Psychoeducational treatments, which integrate education about physiological changes with cancer treatment with psychological and sexological techniques, are especially suitable for the cancer survivor with sexual dysfunction. However, the literature on this particular topic is extremely sparse. A three-session psychoeducational intervention combining mindfulness with cognitive–behavioral techniques for women with gynecologic cancer and sexual arousal disorder found significant benefits on some aspects of sexual response, including sexual desire and arousal, sexual distress, and mood (Brotto et al., 2008) in an uncontrolled trial.

Women were encouraged to practice mindfulness meditation in their non-sexual lives on a daily basis and then were given specific exercises for how to incorporate mindfulness while being sexual. Cognitive challenging of myths about cancer and sexuality was also an important component of the treatment as many women had false information about their own sexuality. Lenna might respond well to such an approach given her cognitions about her "dysfunctional" status and her fear about being sexual. The mindfulness exercises have a role in anxiety reduction as well and allow the patient to tune into existing sexual response and, possibly, enhance it.

The intervention I just described was administered by me, a mental health professional (Brotto et al., 2008); however, the literature on psychological interventions for cancer-associated sexual dysfunction suggests that trained peer facilitators or other health professionals might be equally effective. For example, Ganz et al. (2000) tested a nurse-led comprehensive menopausal assessment (CMA) to relieve menopausal symptoms, including hot flashes, vaginal dryness, and urinary incontinence—symptoms that are common following breast cancer treatment but which cannot be treated with conventional estrogen due to the known link with breast cancer. The intervention combined education, counseling, and specific pharmacologic and behavioral techniques. Sexual response, including sexual attractiveness for self and partner, sexual desire, sex frequency, arousal, lubrication, and orgasm and menopausal symptoms significantly improved in the CMA group compared to control. In another study of nurse-administered psychological intervention, Maughan and Clarke (2001) found that sexual intercourse resumed more quickly for women in the counseled group.

In a study of African American women with breast cancer, peer counseling with the aid of a detailed workbook focused on reproductive issues and sexual health found significant benefits on knowledge about reproductive health after breast cancer, psychological distress, sexual function/satisfaction, and menopausal symptoms (Schover et al., 2006). Kalaitzi et al. (2007) explored a brief psychosexual intervention following mastectomy. The first of six sessions occurred when women were still in the hospital and focused on discussing appearance and body image issues with the woman and her partner. Their reactions to seeing the surgical wound were explored. The following sessions focused on sensate focus, body imagery, and communication. Compared to a control group, the treatment significantly alleviated symptoms of depression and anxiety and increased orgasm frequency, sex initiation frequency, satisfaction with body image, and marital satisfaction.

Taken together, these studies suggest that psychosocial interventions for women cancer survivors are helpful for various aspects of sexual functioning and mood. They can be effective when administered by non-mental health professionals and need not be overly burdensome. Sexual clinicians and researchers might work toward preparing treatment manuals based on their psychosexual interventions and making such resources available directly at the cancer care centers where paraprofessionals might be trained.

We often suggest that cancer survivors read one of the few available books on the topic of sex and cancer. These are *Sexuality and Fertility After Cancer* (Schover, 1997), *Intimacy After Cancer* (Kydd & Rowett, 2006), and *Breaking the Silence on Cancer and Sexuality: A Handbook for Healthcare Providers* (Katz, 2007). For men, *Intimacy With Impotence: The Couple's Guide to Better Sex After Prostate Disease* (Alterowitz & Alterowitz, 2004) is excellent.

TREATING THOSE WITH TERMINAL CANCER

Sometimes, the therapist is called on to treat patients whose cancer is terminal. Although there is no way to accurately predict length of survival, it is necessary to consider how much time of relative health remains. Some of your patients will want to enjoy what remaining physical capacities they have for as long as they hold out, while others may already be defending themselves against loss (their own death or their partner's) by pulling back emotionally or sexually.

Cancer survivorship is not only about those with curative cancer. The National Cancer Institute defines a *survivor* as a person from the time of diagnosis through to the rest of their life, regardless of whether the cancer was successfully treated. Thus, our consideration of sexuality in the cancer survivor must also address those living with advanced disease—even if the range of sexual activities is limited due to pain, fatigue, nausea, palliation, or other issues relevant only to advanced disease. Here, myths abound as it is common for staff to assume that the individual with late-stage cancer is neither interested nor actively engaging in sexual activity. One colleague of ours tells the story of being paged in the middle of the night to write an order in the medical chart of a woman with stage 4 metastatic breast cancer allowing her husband to be in bed with her. There has been limited data exploring sexuality among cancer patients with advanced-stage disease. Among those with ovarian cancer, which is typically detected at a later stage and results in more aggressive interventions, there is more impairment in sexual response. Carmack Taylor, Basen-Engquist, Shinn, and Bodurka (2004) found that approximately 80% of women with advanced ovarian cancer reported significant disruption in sexual function.

The rich qualitative data on this topic illustrate that the meaning of sexuality is much broader than a narrow focus on sexual intercourse. Sexual behavior changes form over time to focus more on emotional aspects of sexual connection. The continuing experience of sexual behaviors reinforces a sense of validation that one is still alive.

LONG-TERM OUTCOMES

What happens to sexual functioning in the cancer survivor many years after cancer? Do sexual problems eventually remit if cancer has been cured? On this topic, there are very few available data. In a survey of 160 long-term survivors of vaginal and cervical cancer who were studied a mean of 25 years after cancer, sexual problems were significantly more prevalent among survivors than in the population-based comparison group (Lindau, Gavrilova, & Anderson, 2007). This was despite the fact that rates of intercourse frequency were comparable between the two groups. The prevalence of difficulty lubricating and dyspareunia were nearly three and seven times higher, respectively, among survivors. Almost half were affected by feeling unattractive because of physical appearance, and slightly less than half continued to have problems reaching orgasm. One third of the survivor sample continued to no longer find sex pleasurable. Survivors were also significantly more likely than those in the population-based sample to exhibit many and complex sexual dysfunctions even in the long term.

In contrast, another long-term follow-up study of cervical cancer survivors found that the majority (81.1%) were sexually active, experienced sexual desire (81.4%), and enjoyed sexual activity (90.9%) when assessed 6–29 years postdiagnosis (Greenwald & McCorkle, 2008).

The results of a meta-analysis of 54 studies of prostate cancer treatments in which the pretreatment functioning of subjects was known suggests that long-term maintenance of erectile function varies widely. This variability may be due to the type of treatments, which typically are brachytherapy, external beam radiation, brachytherapy plus external beam radiation, nerve-sparing radical prostatectomy, or non-nerve-sparing prostatectomy. While most men will reach their maximal recovery of erectile function by 24–36 months after surgery, some men may not develop erectile problems until a year after treatment has ended (Katz, 2005).

What these conflicting studies highlight is the fact that cancer survivors are likely a heterogeneous group in terms of long-term outcomes. In the long-term, the focus of clinical care must be on acceptance of where one is at as opposed to an exclusive focus on restoring premorbid sexual functioning. Our clinical experience suggests that those cancer survivors who first accept that cancer may have changed them in a permanent way are more likely to be motivated to find a "new normal" in terms of their sexual response and repertoire. Accepting as a clinician that sexual rehabilitation may not be an achievable (or even ideal) goal is a sobering experience for a sex therapist but one that encourages the clinician to expand his or her range of what entails healthy sexuality.

FINAL THOUGHTS

If you are fortunate enough to have the opportunity to treat men or women who have experienced cancer and its treatments, we hope that you will feel as honored and enlightened by the invitation to work with them as we have. Sexuality is vital to one's sense of self and to one's perceived QoL. Nowhere is this felt more intensely than in the midst of, or after, fighting for one's survival. It is an extraordinary opportunity to be asked to help improve the sexual health of an individual or couple who has faced such a life-altering medical crisis. Some of the satisfaction in working with this population is not so much that we can dramatically improve their sexual function; in many cases, the improvements made, sexually, are minimal. It comes more from having helped them to appreciate what they have been through; how they are altered anatomically, physiologically, and psychologically; and how love, support, and other physical pleasures, including giving pleasure, are what is possible and what is important. It is about helping them to explore their new normal. In this way, having the courage to work in this otherwise-frightening area rewards the clinician with a better sense of reality and enhances personal and professional maturation.

REFERENCES

Abitbol, M. M., & Davenport, J. H. (1974). Sexual dysfunction after therapy for cervical carcinoma. *American Journal of Obstetrics and Gynecology, 119*, 181–189.

Alterowitz, R., & Alterowitz, B. (2004). *Intimacy with impotence: The couple's guide to better sex after prostate disease.* Cambridge, MA: DaCapo Lifelong Books. This is a self-help book that clinicians may find useful to suggest as bibliotherapy for male cancer survivors and their partners.

Alterowitz, R., & Alterowitz, B. (2007). Sexual rehabilitation after cancer. In M. S. Tepper & A. F. Owens (Eds.), *Sexual health, volume 4: State-of-the-art treatments and research* (pp. 269–313). Westport, CT: Praeger. This chapter provides a primer specifically directed at sex therapists interested in learning these authors' specific cognitive–behavioral approach toward sexual rehabilitation of the person or couple after cancer.

Althof, S. E. (2002).When an erection alone is not enough: Biopsychosocial obstacles to lovemaking. *International Journal of Impotence Research, 14*(Supplement 1), S99–S104.

American Cancer Society. (2007). *Cancer facts and figures.* Atlanta, GA: Author.

American Cancer Society. 2009. *Cancer reference information.* Retrieved January 17, 2009, from http://www.cancer.org/docroot/CRI/content/CRI_

Amsterdam, A., Carter, J., & Krychman, M. (2006). Prevalence of psychiatric illness in women in an oncology sexual health population: A retrospective pilot study. *Journal of Sexual Medicine, 3,* 292–295.

Andersen, B. L., Woods, X. A., & Copeland, L. J. (1997). Sexual self-schema and sexual morbidity among gynecologic cancer survivors. *Journal of Consulting and Clinical Psychology, 65,* 221–229.

Barton, D. L., Wender, D. B., Sloan, J. A., Dalton, R. J., Balcueva, E. P., Atherton, P. J., et al. (2007). Randomized controlled trial to evaluate transdermal testosterone in female cancer survivors with decreased libido; North Central Cancer Treatment Group Protocol N02C3. *Journal of the National Cancer Institute, 99,* 672–679.

Barni, S., & Mondin, R. (1997). Sexual dysfunction in treated breast cancer patients. *Annals of Oncology, 8,* 1–5.

Brotto, L. A., Heiman, J. R., Goff, B., Greer, B., Lentz, G., Swisher, E., et al. (2008). A psychoeducational intervention for sexual dysfunction in women with gynecological cancer. *Archives of Sexual Behavior, 37,* 317–329.

Carmack Taylor, C. L., Basen-Engquist, K., Shinn, E. H., & Bodurka, D. C. (2004). Predictors of sexual functioning in OC patients. *Journal of Clinical Oncology, 22,* 881–889.

Casey, C. (1996). Psychosexual morbidity following gynaecological malignancy. *Irish Medical Journal, 89,* 200–202.

Cella, D. F., & Tros, S. (1986). Psychological adjustment to survival from Hodgkins disease. *Journal of Consulting and Clinical Psychology, 54,* 616–622.

Chambers, S. K., Schover, L., Halford, K., Clutton, S., Ferguson, M., Gordon, L., et al. (2008). ProsCan for couples: Randomised controlled trial of a couples-based sexuality intervention for men with localized prostate cancer who receive radical prostatectomy. *BMC Cancer, 8,* 226. This article describes the design of a three-arm randomized controlled trial to evaluate the efficacy of two couple-based sexuality interventions and may show the effectiveness of peer-based support for these couples. It is one of the few randomized controlled trials of a psychological intervention for the sexual sequelae of cancer.

Chartier-Kastler, E., Amar, E., Chevallier, D., Montaigne, O., Coulange, C., Joubert, J.-M., et al. (2008). Does management of erectile dysfunction after radical prostatectomy meet patients' expectations? Results of a national survey (REPAIR) by the French Urological Association. *Journal of Sexual Medicine, 5,* 693–704.

Dennerstein, L., Lehert, P., & Burger, H. (2005). The relative effects of hormones and relationship factors on sexual function of women through the natural menopausal transition. *Fertility & Sterility, 84,* 174–180.

Dubbelman, Y. D., Dohle, G. R., & Schroder, F. H. (2006). Sexual function before and after radical retropubic prostatectomy: A systemic review of prognostic indicators for a successful outcome. *European Urology, 50,* 711–720.

Fobair, P., Stewart, S. L., Chang, S., D'Onofrio, C., Banks, P. J., & Bloom, J. R. (2006). Body image and sexual problems in young women with breast cancer. *Psychooncology, 15,* 579–594.

Ganz, P. A., Desmond, K. A., Belin, T. R., Meyerowitz, B. E., & Rowland, J. H. (1999). Predictors of sexual health in women after a breast cancer diagnosis. *Journal of Clinical Oncology, 17,* 2371–2380.

Ganz, P. A., Greendale, G. A., Petersen, L., Zibecchi, L., Kahn, B., & Belin, T. R. (2000). Managing menopausal symptoms in breast cancer survivors: Results of a randomized controlled trial. *Journal of the National Cancer Institute, 92,* 1054–1064.

Greenwald, H. P., & McCorkle, R. (2008). Sexuality and sexual function in long-term survivors of cervical cancer. *Journal of Women's Health, 17,* 955–963.

Helgason, A. R., Adolfsson, J., Dickman, P., Fredrikson, M., Arver, S., & Steineck, G. (1996). Waning sexual function—the most important disease-specific distress for patients with prostate cancer. *British Journal of Cancer, 73,* 1417–1421.

Jensen, P. T., Mogens, G., Klee, M. C., Thranov, I., Petersen, M. A., & Machine, D. (2003). Longitudinal study of sexual function and vaginal changes after radiotherapy for cervical cancer. *International Journal of Radiation Oncology and Biological Physics, 56,* 937–949.

Kalaitzi, C., Papadopoulos, V. P., Michas, K., Vlasis, K., Skandalakis, P., & Filippou, D. (2007). Combined brief psychosexual intervention after mastectomy: Effects on sexuality, body image, and psychological well-being. *Journal of Surgical Oncology, 96,* 235–240.

Katz, A. (2005). What happened? Sexual consequences of prostate cancer and its treatment. *Canadian Family Physician, 51,* 977–982.

Katz, A. (2007). *Breaking the silence on cancer and sexuality: A handbook for healthcare providers.* Pittsburgh, PA: Oncology Nursing Society. This handbook is a practical guide for all cancer health care providers and takes a clinical approach to the topic. It provides education on human sexual functioning, offers tools for providers (especially nurses) on sexual health assessment and communicating with patients about sex, and discusses how cancer affects the family and the individual.

Kydd, S., & Rowett, D. (2006). *Intimacy after cancer: A woman's guide.* Redmond, WA: Big Think Media. The book is written with the female cancer survivor in mind. Dr. Kydd, the lead author, is a clinical psychologist and a survivor of breast cancer. Her book was inspired by her experience of sexual dysfunction following tamoxifen treatment and the gentle and caring guidance from one of her physicians on this sensitive topic. The first several chapters of the book focus on body image difficulties—a complaint plaguing many women even without a cancer history. There is also an excellent section on cross-cultural issues in cancer and sexuality; the authors outline some common cultural beliefs about the reasons for cancer. The book is well stocked with practical and useful information, ranging from how to select a lubricant, the many varieties of vibrators, and directions to reputable Web sites that provide lingerie and other sexual aids suitable for women with prostheses or ostomy bags.

Lindau, S. T., Gavrilova, N., & Anderson, D. (2007). Sexual morbidity in very long term survivors of vaginal and cervical cancer: A comparison to national norms. *Gynecological Oncology, 106,* 413–418.

Maas, C. P., ter Kuile, M., Tuynman, C., Laan, E., Weyenborg, P., Trimbos, J. B., et al. (2002). Disturbance of sexual response after radical hysterectomy: A psychophysiologic study. *International Journal of Gynecological Cancer, 12,* 613–614.

Maughan, K., & Clarke, C. (2001). The effect of a clinical nurse specialist in gynaecological oncology on quality of life and sexuality. *Journal of Clinical Nursing, 10,* 221–229.

Mellon, S., Kershaw, T. S., Northouse, L. L., & Freeman-Gibb, L. (2007). A family-based model to predict fear of recurrence for cancer survivors and their caregivers. *Psycho-Oncology, 16*, 214–223.

Morales, L., Neven, P., Timmerman, D., Christiaens, M. R., Vergote, I., Van Limbergen, E., et al. (2004). Acute effects of tamoxifen and third-generation aromatase inhibitors on menopausal symptoms of breast cancer patients. *Anti-Cancer Drugs, 15*, 753–760.

Ofman, U., Kingsberg, S. A., & Nelson, C. J. (2008). Sexual problems and cancer. In V. T. DeVita, S. Hellman, & S. A. Rosenberg (Eds.), *Cancer: Principles and practice of oncology* (pp. 2804–2815). New York: Lippincott Williams and Wilkins. This chapter provides an overview of the sexual consequences of all types of cancer and cancer treatments in both men and women. It is directed toward oncologists but is a useful overview for the mental health professional.

Schover, L. R. (1991). The impact of breast cancer on sexuality, body image, and intimate relationships. *CA: A Cancer Journal for Clinicians, 41*(2), 112–120.

Schover, L. R. (1997). *Sexuality and fertility after cancer.* New York: Wiley. Although more than a decade old, this book represents an excellent resource for information regarding sexual health following cancer for patients and health care providers. It is full of specific tips to enhance postcancer sexual adjustment.

Schover, L. R., Fouladi, R. T., Warneke, C. L., Neese, L., Klein, E. A., Zippe, C., et al. (2002). Defining sexual outcomes after treatment for localized prostate cancer. *Cancer, 95*, 1773–1785.

Schover, L. R., Jenkins, R., Sui, D., Adams, J. H., Marion, M. S., & Jackson, K. E. (2006). Randomized trial of peer counseling on reproductive health in African American breast cancer survivors. *Journal of Clinical Oncology, 24*, 1620–1626.

Schover, L. R., Yetman, R. J., Tuason, L. J., Meisler, E., Esselstyn, C. B., Hermann, R. E., et al. (1995). Partial mastectomy and breast reconstruction. A comparison of their effects on psychosocial adjustment, body image, and sexuality. *Cancer, 75*, 54–64.

Stanton, A., & Burns, L. H. (1999). Behavioral medicine approaches to infertility counseling. In L. H. Burns & S. N. Covington (Eds.), *Infertility counseling: A handbook for clinicians* (pp. 129–148). New York: Parthenon.

Stead, M. L., Brown, J. M., Fallowfield, L., & Selby, P. (2003). Lack of communication between healthcare professionals and women with ovarian cancer about sexual issues. *British Journal of Cancer, 88*, 666–671.

Story, L. B., & Bradbury, T. N. (2004). Understanding marriage and stress: Essential questions and challenges. *Clinical Psychology Review, 23*, 1139–1162.

Wiggins, D. L., Wood, R., Granai, C. O., & Dizon, D. S. (2007). Sex, intimacy, and the gynecologic oncologist: Survey results of the New England Association of Gynecologic Oncologists (NEAGO). *Journal of Psychosocial Oncology, 25*, 61–70.

VI

SEXUAL IDENTITY STRUGGLES

Twenty

Understanding Gay
and Lesbian Life

DAVID L. SCOTT, MD, AND STEPHEN B. LEVINE, MD

David Scott: I began working with sexual minority youth during my adolescent medicine fellowship. We worked with outreach organizations and the Los Angeles Free Clinic to serve homeless youth living in Hollywood. Our standard history included questions about sexual behavior and identity. We asked each patient regardless of gender about sex with "males, females, or both." I continued this aspect of my history taking during a long career at a suburban teenage and young adult practice. I learned early on that if I did not ask, the patients would not tell. So, I did ask, and the patients did tell. The volume of same-sex behaviors and self-identified gay and lesbian youth I was seeing initially surprised me. I found that frequently I was the first person a young person came out to, and I always felt privileged to have had that role. I also helped many families to access PFLAG (Parents and Friends of Lesbians and Gays).

After a career in teenage and young adult medicine, a large part of which is dedicated to reproductive health, I decided to retrain in psychiatry. During my residency, I continued to find satisfaction working with sexual minorities. I look forward to a psychiatry practice focused on sexual minority issues. I hope to continue to be an educator, advocate, and practitioner helping gay, lesbian, bisexual, and transgender (GLBT) individuals reach their full potential. This chapter shares some of what I have learned along the way from my patients.

Stephen Levine: I am an adult psychiatrist who has specialized in sexual life since 1973. In the course of providing care for individuals and couples with all types of sexual identities during my career, I came to understand how little I knew about the lives of sexual minority patients at the end of my residency. I think I would have been much more helpful to lesbian, gay, and bisexual patients along the way if I knew a fraction of the concepts that Dr. Scott and I have put together for your consideration.

INTRODUCTION

Homosexuality Is Not a Disease

It took years of scientific and political work to be able to confidently assert the idea that homosexuality is not a disease. Beginning with the psychometric research of Evelyn Hooker in the 1950s followed by 16 years of concentrated

351

political focus by the gay rights movement, homosexuality was removed as a mental illness from the *Diagnostic and Statistical Manual of Mental Disorders* (*DSM*) in two stages between 1973 and 1976 (American Psychiatric Association, 1968). Hooker demonstrated that carefully matched heterosexual and homosexual males were indistinguishable from one another when examined for psychopathology using projective testing (1993). Armed with this scientific fact, the gay rights movement eventually convinced the American Psychiatric Association (APA) to end the promulgation of the idea that homosexuals were "sick."

Why Discuss This Topic?

The majority of the chapters in this handbook focus on treatment of the forms of sexual suffering, sexual limitations, or sexual psychopathology that are included in the *DSM-IV-TR* (*Diagnostic and Statistical Manual of Mental Disorders, Fourth Edition, Text Revision*; APA, 2000). Our chapter joins the list of others, such as those on infidelity, cancer survivorship, and being single again, that discuss background forces that may lead to a diagnosable sexual problem. While homosexuality per se is not a mental disease, it does cause a significant amount of *dis*-ease in gay, lesbian, and bisexual patients; in their families; in people who are not under psychiatric care; and in mental health professionals (MHPs) who provide care for them. A homosexual issue, poorly managed, can lead to a variety of significant problems. Without sufficient knowledge of relevant topics, both MHPs and patients may approach the subject of homosexual or bisexual orientation with wariness and discomfort. The ultimate goal of this chapter is to decrease the anxiety associated with caring for homosexual patients and thereby to make the experience more comfortable and useful for all involved.

We realize that this chapter alone may fail to help every reader gain the understanding, comfort, and eagerness to be of assistance to members of the homosexual community. When we do fail, however, we hope that we will have stimulated greater awareness of what it means to be a gay or lesbian person in a world that assumes an inherent superiority of all things heterosexual (heterosexism). The current euphemism for a heterosexual therapist who can work calmly, competently, and helpfully with homosexual men and women is a "culturally sensitive clinician." We hope to help you obtain this status.

THE PROBLEM OF HISTORIC PREJUDICE

Same-sex behavior and same-sex relationships have always existed. Cultural attitudes, laws, and tolerance have dramatically changed over the centuries, although not necessarily in one particular direction. In ancient Greece, young men could engage in same-sex relationships without disapproval. For example, Alexander the Great (born in 356 BC) and Hephaistion were a well-known pair. Each was married and had children while maintaining their relationship. In AD 130, the Roman emperor Hadrian mourned the death of his male lover, Antinous. Lesbian love was also well known during this era.

In the first half of the 20th century, Gertrude Stein and Alice B. Toklas lived openly as a couple in Paris, entertaining and socializing with the artists and thinkers of the time. However, at the same time, many cultural institutions, ranging from psychiatry to various religions to laws in diverse countries, came to describe homosexuality with terms such as mental illness, perversion, sin, crime, and abomination. Men were imprisoned for homosexual behavior at the turn of the 20th century in England. Countries differ dramatically in their attitudes and laws concerning homosexual expression. In some countries today, homosexuality is punishable by death.

Despite the dramatic liberalization of attitudes in the United States among the educated, prejudice and discrimination are still prevalent. Sometimes, social forces coalesce to generate psychological abuse, violence, and murder. *Homophobia*, the fear of homosexuals and prejudice toward them, not infrequently still manifests in job and housing discrimination, adoption and child custody discrimination, avoidance of health care service delivery, end-of-life management of health information, and survivorship asset distribution discrimination. Marriage between same-sex individuals is currently under debate in several states.

DEFINITIONS

In this section, we begin with an uncommon degree of precision in terminology to capture the nuances of orientation. We use the word *erotic* to refer to what occurs within a person's subjectivity and the word *sexual* to refer to partner sexual behaviors. *Orientation* is a mental complexity that combines elements of private subjective erotic experiences and actual sexual behaviors with others. A problem arises, however, because when individuals experience and discuss their own orientation, they use different words than clinicians, epidemiologists, or scientists employ. We discuss both perspectives.

When erotic and sexual orientation are congruent, there is a simplicity and clarity to the concept of orientation. For example, a college student who has had exclusively homoerotic fantasies since age 13 and is now having sexual experiences with same-sex partners would be called *homosexual*. The erotic and the behavioral, however, are not always congruent. This is the reason for introducing you to the meanings of the suffixes *erotic* and *sexual*.

What Is Erotic Orientation?

The phrase *erotic orientation* refers to the functional organization of the mind based only on the fantasies, desires, dream imagery, and attractions for others. A person might be described as homoerotic, heteroerotic, bierotic, having undetermined eroticism, or anerotic based on the partners he or she imagines. Developmentally, erotic orientation usually makes its appearance before sexual behavior with others. Erotic orientation is often clarified for an individual by self-observation of the imagery that consistently accompanies masturbation. Recurrent erotic imagery often provides sufficient experience for a person to recognize him- or herself as gay or lesbian. When this occurs, the person considers him or herself to have a gay or lesbian sexual orientation. Obviously, the person does not employ our clinical terminology of the concept of erotic orientation.

What Is Sexual Orientation?

As partner sexual behaviors begin to occur, another dimension to orientation appears. A person experiences sexual behavior with another and decides based on the ease of arousal and naturalness of the experience that he or she belongs to one of five categories of orientation: homosexual, bisexual, heterosexual, or, rarely, indeterminate or asexual. When clinicians consider a patient's orientation, we take into account both the patient's erotic and partner sexual patterns. *Sexual orientation* to us, although not necessarily to the individual, includes both erotic and behavioral experiences. In males, sexual orientation is usually, but not always, clarified by late adolescence.

What Is a Homosexual?

A *homosexual* is an individual whose sexual orientation is toward members of his or her own sex as reflected in eroticism and behavior.

What Is Sexual Preference?

Preference implies a choice. Sexual orientation, itself, is not a preference because one does not choose his or her erotic orientation. Within any orientation, however, individuals make choices about how, when, and with whom they choose to express their sexual behaviors, which are their *sexual preferences*.

What Is Sexual Identity?

Sexual identity is a collection of self-definitions along three dimensions: gender identity, orientation, and intention. Most individuals have a subtle mosaic of masculine and feminine gender identifications, heteroerotic and homoerotic attractions, and peaceably mutual and paraphilic erotic intentions. This ordinary three-dimensional subjective complexity is generally not readily revealed to others. Many people summarize their identity as gay or straight and leave out references to their gender identities and intentions. MHPs, however, are expected to have the more comprehensive view of the mosaicism of sexual identity components. We are expected to be able to calmly and knowledgeably inquire and discuss the subjective and behavioral interplay between these three dimensions within heterosexual, homosexual, and bisexual persons.

What Do Gay and Lesbian Mean?

Self-identification as *gay* generally means, "I accept my orientation and my identity as a homosexual person." In this sentence, *gay* encompasses gay men and lesbian women. In most sentences, however, *gay* delineates a male. Similarly, self-identification as a *lesbian* implies that, "I accept the presence of same-sex desires and behaviors as an integral part of my sexual identity." *Gay* and *lesbian* are also important because the terms introduce us to the fact that some individuals have homosexual desires, attractions, and behaviors but do not incorporate these patterns into their sexual identity. They feel they are heterosexual, in transition, or bisexual. *Gay* and *lesbian* usually delineate self-acceptance. *Gay* also is used to refer to a community of interests, such as the gay rights movement, a gay section of town, or a gay cultural event.

What Is a Bisexual?

The two components of orientation—the subjective erotic one and the behavioral sexual one—combine in various forms in the population to produce many variations of bisexuality. Many more women than men spend part of their lives in heterosexual and part in homosexual pairings and experience their orientation as a mixture of heterosexual and homosexual elements. This is what is referred to when it is said that women's sexual orientation is more fluid than men's.

A person's current sexual behavior with partners may or may not correspond with the dominant pattern of their internal eroticism. Many women who are part of the lesbian community think of themselves as bisexual despite their recent exclusive sexual behavior with women.

Can Homosexual Behavior Not Reflect a Person's Orientation?

Yes, there are diverse situations in which men and women have homosexual sex but do not see their behavior as a reflection of their innate desire, private orientation, or sexual identity. This is partially reflected by the research term *men who have sex with men* (MSM). The designation *MSM* was created to acknowledge that in tracking HIV transmission patterns many of the homosexually active subjects did not self-identify as gay. Within some African American communities, the phrase "living on the down low" refers to men who identify as heterosexual but have sex with men. Heterosexual prisoners, males and females, are known to engage in same-sex behavior while in prison only to return to heterosexual behaviors when released.

THE IMPORTANCE TO CLINICIANS OF MYTHS ABOUT HOMOSEXUALITY

Homosexual men and women are a heterogeneous population. The gay and lesbian population is largely an invisible sexual minority. They come from all economic strata, religions, regions, and ethnicities. They gravitate toward all vocations. Their stories, their capacities, and their incapacities are each unique. They demonstrate all the variations that heterosexual human beings evidence, including the vital differences in how life is lived by males and females. In our clinical work, we prefer to understand homosexual phenomena by following this sequence: First, we understand their ordinary humanity, then their issues related to their gender, and finally what is unique about them because they are gay, lesbian, or bisexual. Of course, we have had the benefit of years of thinking about this topic. Many others approach the subject of homosexuality quite differently. They think of gays in stereotypic ways: Gay men work as hairdressers or florists; lesbians play softball and drive trucks. They think that homosexual couples divide life tasks, including sexual patterns, into male and female roles. We refer to such ideas as myths. Here are 10 of them:

1. Being gay or lesbian is a choice.
2. Being homosexual is an illness.
3. Being homosexual is a sin.
4. All gay men are effeminate; all lesbian women are masculine (butch).
5. Homosexuals would prefer to be the opposite sex.
6. Homosexuals are out to recruit young people to become homosexual.
7. Homosexuals are pedophiles.
8. Homosexuality is caused by domineering mothers and passive or absent fathers.

9. All bisexuals are really homosexuals who are not yet willing to admit to being homosexuals.
10. All gay men are only concerned with sex and are unable to sustain long-term relationships.

Such concepts are not based on reality. All of these preconceptions interfere with helping gay and lesbian patients. The more one learns about homosexuality, the less hold these ideas have on one's mind. The responsibilities of caring for homosexual patients requires the clinician, regardless of personal orientation, to be able to listen to the story of the person's life without the influence of these unexamined concepts. No therapist, not even gay and lesbian ones, knows "everything" about homosexual life possibilities. Please do not be embarrassed to ask your patient about something that you do not understand. There is no disgrace in asking, but it is dangerous to pretend to understand.

COMING OUT

Understanding the process called *coming out* is central to being a culturally sensitive clinician. Coming out is a developmental process that usually occurs in stages. In a subtle sense, it is a lifelong endeavor. *Coming out* refers to accepting one's homosexual orientation and sharing it with others. It is frequently a painful process; many suffer to accomplish it. Coming out essentially ends hiding one's orientation from others. Initially, individuals may have to break through their own denial and to overcome their own internalized homophobia and self-hatred to achieve its first steps. One first comes out to oneself, then to others. Some go through these steps quickly and completely, some slowly and partially, yet others at every conceivable point between these extremes. Completely coming out means the sharing of one's orientation and identity as a gay or lesbian with family, friends, coworkers, neighbors, and the community.

When coming out, a person risks ridicule, abuse, and loss of relationships. Parents may reject their child. Siblings may choose to completely avoid their brother or sister and keep them from their nieces and nephews. Teens may drop out of school when they are bullied there. Employers and landlords may abruptly terminate a job or a housing arrangement on the basis of "not wanting a homosexual person around." Some states today lack protections against such discrimination. It is reasonable to be wary of these dangers. When fear of these dangers leads to avoidance or marked delay in revealing one's orientation and identity, it is commonly said that the person is still "in the closet."

Clinical Caveats

The choice to come out or not rests with the individual. A MHP should not have an agenda to force the patient to come out more completely or to come out in a therapist-prescribed timetable or fashion. A prudent approach is to learn about the person's place in this process and to understand the reasons for that position. We call this *supportive*. This also applies when treating gay and lesbian couples who may evidence disparate degrees of being out. This disparity often causes relationship difficulties and is a fruitful topic for discussion.

When dealing with minors, as with any other personal information, the MHP should not disclose the patient's orientation to school officials, probation officers, and parents. Such "outings" may cause internal and external

psychosocial problems and conflicts. It likely will end the professional relationship because the patient will feel betrayed. We recognize that many MHPs
believe that patients are better off if they come out to others, and that might
be correct, but the superimposition of the therapist's agenda on the patient
violates the ethical principle of respect for patient autonomy.

The first person that an individual comes out to is often remembered for a
lifetime. When that person is the MHP, the MHP should recognize the courage
required on the part of the patient to reveal him- or herself, the trust implicit
in the occasion, and the honor the patient has bestowed on the MHP.

The Dawning of Awareness of Homosexuality

Most homosexual adults can recall feeling "different" as a child. Before they
had words to describe it, they were aware that something about them was not
like their age mates. This can be purely a subjective experience, but it is often
associated with some degree of atypical gender expressions or behaviors. They
may have been teased or taunted about these differences. By the time they
are aged 10, the average age that erotic attractions appear, they quickly realize from family, schoolmates, and society that being homosexual is not "normal." They begin to notice innuendos and hear jokes about gays. They note the
whispered tones about homosexual relatives, neighbors, and celebrities. They
hear hurtful language such as "that's so gay" referring to any unwelcome or
negative thing. They also witness their peers play "smear the queer," a game
in which the goal is to attack the identified "queer." They naturally hide their
growing awareness that they may be gay. The situation may manifest clinically as ostracism and rejection, bullying and peer harassment, poor psychosocial fit with family and peers, the sense of being stigmatized or shamed, and
low self-esteem. These phenomena are generally more intense for boys than
girls. If the individual is also a member of another ethnic, racial, or religious
minority the sense of "otherness" is even more onerous.

The Origins of Internalized Homophobia

These negative messages during childhood are internalized, applied to the
self, and give rise to some degree of worry, self-hatred, and low self-esteem.
This is referred to as *internalized homophobia*. It complicates the process
of coming out, making it more difficult to select when, where, and to whom
homosexuals disclose aspects of themselves.

A study by Wallien and Cohen-Kettenis (2008) of gender-atypical grade
school-aged children found that 80% had outgrown their gender identity
disorder by age 16 and had developed a homosexual or bisexual orientation.
Previous estimates based on the recollections of adult gay men suggested that
as many as two thirds recalled some childhood gender atypicality. Similarly,
many but not all adult lesbians recalled a tomboyish childhood. In childhood,
gender atypicality is stigmatized in boys more than girls. In adolescence and
adulthood, the issues are no longer about gender; they are about being gay
or lesbian. And, being gay or lesbian is treated in the dominant culture with
prejudice. It makes adaptive self-protective sense that adolescents who know
that they have a homosexual orientation do not completely come out to their
family and schoolmates. When and if children realize that they are homosexual varies among individuals within each gender. Males tend to be certain
of their orientation several years before females become certain.

Some heterosexual youth experiment with homosexual behavior. In large urban centers, it is trendy to be bisexual. In the 1940s, Kinsey found that 37% of his adult male sample reported a homosexual sexual experience to orgasm after age 18 (1948). Most individuals keep their occasional homosexual behavior a carefully guarded secret. Often, it is a therapist, after many sessions of psychotherapy, that first is told about same-sex behaviors. Clarifying one's orientation is a process that takes years for some adolescent males and females. This is one of the reasons that estimates of prevalence of "homosexuality" are wide ranging. Not only are accurate, methodologically sound scientific data difficult to obtain, but also many people do not really know what constitutes being a homosexual person.

Negative Impact on Some Adolescents

Hiding one's homosexuality has an impact on the successful completion of adolescent developmental tasks for many teenagers. The gay or lesbian adolescent may not learn to socialize and to date, for example. Fear of disclosure and abuse may contribute to poor grades, school avoidance, quitting school, substance abuse, and indiscriminate sexual behavior. Numerous studies have documented higher rates of substance abuse, depression, anxiety, and suicidal ideation among homosexual teens. A disproportionate number of teen runaways, throwaways (teens whose parents throw them out of the house), and homeless youth are gay and lesbian.

All teens, including gay and lesbian teens, largely are socialized to become heterosexual adults. Without identifiable role models, gay and lesbian teens are at a disadvantage in acquiring those skills necessary to function in the adult world as a homosexual person. Individualization and autonomy are often more difficult to achieve.

Informing Parents

When some teens tell their parents that they are gay, the parents respond with, "We have long known about this possibility; we love you, how can we help?" It is a joy to hear of such experiences because most of the situations in which we intervene represent a departure from this scenario. MHPs working with teens considering coming out to parents should make sure that they have a safe family environment that will be supportive of them.

When we see tension and conflict in the family after a teen comes out to them, we aspire to help this to be a temporary reaction rather than a prelude to extruding or abusing the teen. When an adolescent comes out to parents, the teen has usually thought about the issue for a long time. The teen may be taken aback by parental reactions. We should be quick to remind the adolescent that the parents are surprised and require a reasonable amount of time to process their feelings about the implications of having a gay child. Parents may try to reassure their child that it is just a phase, which, of course, invalidates the teen's experience and self-awareness. Parents may have to grieve the loss of their concept of their child's heterosexuality and the loss of the sequence of courtship of the opposite sex, marriage, and grandchildren. Parents often feel guilt, blame themselves, and worry about the safety of their child. Clinicians can help parents with their self-blame when parents inquire what the therapist knows about the cause of homosexuality. Some highly religious parents worry about the spiritual future of their child in God's eyes.

While clinicians can be enormously helpful to parents, PFLAG, an organization found in many urban areas, can often provide ongoing assistance to parents as they negotiate this issue. Clinicians often see parents briefly. PFLAG helps them over an extended period of time and puts them into social contact with other parents of homosexuals; many of these parents are role models of loving their gay child and integrating their child's partner into their family's life. Clinicians and support groups can also be helpful when the coming out process occurs in adulthood.

Suicide

Suicide is currently the third leading cause of death in youth 15–24 years old. For every completed suicide by youth, it is estimated that 100–200 attempts are made. GLBT youth are four times more likely to attempt suicide than their heterosexual peers. GLBT youth who come from rejecting families are nine times more likely to attempt suicide (Suicide Prevention Resource Center, 2008). It is estimated that as many as 26% of gay youth are forced to leave home because of conflicts over their sexual identity (Remafedi, 1987). One study found that 28% of GLBT youth were forced to drop out of school because of harassment resulting from their identity (Hershberger, 1995). A 2001 survey by the Gay, Lesbian, and Straight Education Network (GLSEN) showed that 68.8% of gay, lesbian, and bisexual students felt unsafe at school. In the same survey, 83.2% of GLBT students reported being verbally harassed because of their sexual orientation. Remafedi et al. found that 28.1% of gay or bisexual males in grades 7–12 had attempted suicide at least once compared to only 4.2% of heterosexual males; 20.5% of gay or bisexual females made attempts compared to 14.5% of heterosexual females (Remafedi, French, Story, Resnick, & Blum, 1998).

Factors that increase the risk of suicide for GLBT youth include the lack of protective factors available to non-GLBT youth; lack of important family support and safe schools; high rates of depression and substance abuse; coming out at an earlier age; stigma, discrimination, marginalization of GLBT youth; and isolation, family rejection, and lack of access to culturally competent care. The GLBT youth who are at highest risk for suicide are homeless, runaways, and throwaways; youth in foster care; and youth in the juvenile justice system.

The MHPs need to ask gay, lesbian, and bisexual youth about suicide. The Trevor Foundation runs the only 24-hour nationwide crisis and suicide prevention helpline for GLBT youth (1-866-4-U-TREVOR). Their goal is to promote acceptance of GLBT youth and to ensure that there is always a safe place for them to turn. In 2007, the Trevor Helpline received 12,000 calls from youth in crisis. GLSEN and gay/straight alliances in high schools are other resources available to homosexual teens. There are a few high schools dedicated to GLBT youth. The Harvey Milk High School in the Hetrick-Martin Institute in New York City provides educational and support opportunities for GLBT youth aged 12–21. The Point Foundation provides college scholarships for GLBT youth.

Embracing the Community

Typically, as an individual comes out there is a shift from a place of isolation to community involvement. The teenager or adult learns the language, style, and codes of the gay and lesbian community. Those new to the community quickly learn the norms of dating and social interaction. They become aware that there are many people in similar circumstances. They learn the history of the gay rights movement and the pivotal historical and social events, such as the Stonewall riots, the March on Washington, Proposition 8, and pride celebrations. Many learn about gay authors, celebrities, and politicians. Many also learn about the organizations that advocate for gay and lesbian rights: the National Gay and Lesbian Task Force (NGLTF); Human Rights Campaign (HRC); Gay, Lesbian Alliance Against Defamation (GLAAD). They come to know about the books and magazines, art, and galleries geared toward gays and lesbians. Some choose to move from more rural areas to larger cities to increase opportunities to mix with other gays and lesbians. The Internet has increased opportunities to meet other gays and lesbians for support, dating, or just sex. The most important lesson learned by embracing the community is that one is no longer alone.

The MHP should keep in mind that embracing the community is an evolutionary process. As gays and lesbians become more comfortable with their orientation, it gradually becomes just another part of who they are. As they integrate their sexual orientation into other parts of their lives, they feel more congruent and whole. They may then perceive that the options available to them seem to expand. They may choose to live in a gay ghetto or to live openly in the larger heterosexual community. They may find an affirming or accepting faith community. They may open a business that caters to the gay and lesbian community or chose to support these businesses with their patronage. They may join GLBT professional organizations in their fields or may join GLBT alumnae associations. Gay and lesbian patients may report that their lives seem more well rounded. Such a complete integration may take 5 years or more to achieve. The MHP can support this maturational growth by reassuring their patients that they can build a satisfying future for themselves.

Family of Choice

Since an individual's family of origin may have negative reactions to their gay or lesbian family member, gays and lesbians may surround themselves with accepting, empowering friends who feel like the family they wish they could have. This family of choice becomes the backbone of support and community for them. Often, holidays and typical family celebrations include the family of choice, which may or may not include members of the family of origin.

Living as a Gay Person After a Heterosexual Marriage With Children

Homoerotic men and women may marry, have children, and come out to themselves and to their spouse and others when they are middle aged (rarely older these days). They may make the transition to the gay community as a result of a new psychologically satisfying love relationship. They then bear all of the problems of divorce, including the spouse's sense of abandonment and betrayal, along with the special ones of coming out to an unhappy spouse, telling the children about their orientation and the sex of their lover, preserving their parental rights as they negotiate for custody arrangements, and coping with contagion of gossip about the reason for the divorce. The children gay people raise can be from their marriage, from their partner's marriage, from adoption, or from placement from a foster agency. There are many stories to be heard about how well some couples handle the transition to gay life after a marriage, but there are others that are quite sad.

VIOLENCE

Unfortunately, violence and abuse exists in the lives of many gay and lesbian individuals. Almost every middle-aged person knows someone who was beaten, shot, or killed because they were gay or lesbian. Violence for many homosexuals begins in their families. Often, abuse occurs at the workplace and in the neighborhoods where homosexuals live. Those who frequent bars are often targeted by youth from outside the gay neighborhoods because they are easy targets, the victims often do not report the crime, and the penalties are rarely strong enough to be deterrents to others. Another area of abuse is domestic violence between same-sex partners. This dark aspect of gay and lesbian life has long been hidden and avoided by community members and helping professionals. MHPs need to ask about symptoms of current or remote abuse or violence and look for signs of post-traumatic stress disorder (PTSD).

COURTSHIP AND RELATIONSHIP CONCERNS

Therapists will spend much time listening to the dating or relationship concerns of their patients. Finding love and dealing with hurt and breakups, personal cheating, and being the victim of infidelity are ordinary human concerns, as are the issues of when and if to have sex, who initiates and who says no, where to have sex, and monogamy. In conjoint therapy, gay and lesbian couples have ordinary concerns such as the loss of psychological intimacy, disagreements about money, coping with children living with another spouse, illness in the family of origin, and so on.

Heterosexual therapists commonly see patients with homosexual issues. Their challenges are to contain the residues of past stereotypical thinking and remain respectful and supportive of the patients' aspirations for greater mental ease. We suspect that MHPs who are gay or lesbian have a higher percentage of patients who belong to a sexual minority than therapists who are presumed to be heterosexual. Gay MHPs may have challenges about maintaining boundaries, running into their patients at gay cultural activities, and making decisions about revealing their orientation and coming out processes to their patients.

Generalizations About Differences Between Gay Men and Lesbians

Generalizations about members of this community pale in comparison to the uniqueness of every person and each couple. The differences between gay and lesbian relationships derive from their genders. We need to remember that we are comparing men with women.

Both gay men and lesbians have to sift through the limited dating pool of other gay and lesbian individuals to determine who will be friends and who will be lovers. Gay men tend to emphasize physical appearance when meeting each other. Their friendships often evolve from earlier sexual relationships, and these friendships may continue long after they no longer are having sex together. When two gay men become a couple, they may be missing the skill sets of nurturing and compromising, the absence of which makes early relationships difficult. This may lead to poor communication until they acquire these skills. Men have to overcome their tendency to be competitive with one another in order to be supportive of each other.

Lesbians place less emphasis on sex. They fall in love with their best friends, sex follows falling in love, and conversation is often foreplay. Lesbians' female skills of nurturing and compromise contribute to longevity in their relationships, but they may have to learn how to increase their independence while remaining supportively connected. The term *lesbian bed death* refers to partners who stop having sex. It is not a universal phenomenon, but when it occurs it is usually after 10 or more years together and frequently occurs in women who are too nurturing. Essentially, the partners become more like sisters than lovers. Lesbians also tend to continue to be involved with their ex-partners. Often, a lesbian couple's family of choice includes both partners' former partners and their new partners.

Gaydar

The term *gaydar* refers to an instinct that a gay individual has about a member of their same sex being gay or not. It usually involves the depth and length of eye contact between the two individuals as well as whether the other person exhibits any gender nonconformity. It can be highly inaccurate, but some gays and lesbians swear by their gaydar capacities.

Long-Term Relationships

Gay men and lesbians form long-term relationships, buy houses, start businesses, have children, raise children, provide care for each other when ill, and help their family of origin (when needed and accepted). Many aspire to get married and have all of the same privileges and responsibilities of marriage. Even without the legal right to marry, there are numerous long-term couples in these communities.

Homosexual couples share worries about getting older, losing one's partner, and entering a nursing home that may not support a homosexual life. Hospital visitation, access to health information, ability to make end-of-life decisions, and inheritance are issues facing older gay and lesbian partners. In the gay community, stories about estranged families of a deceased partner swooping in and taking the couple's possessions abound.

Many gay and lesbian couples without their own children seek ways of being parents. In many states, adoption and foster care agencies are quietly supportive of gay couples raising children. The Academy of Pediatrics has a position paper that confirms that there are no negative effects on children raised by gay and lesbian parents (2002).

Sexual Concerns

The good news about homosexual sex is that sex partners have an intuitive knowledge about their partners' bodies and how to effectively stimulate them. For some pairings, however, tension can arise over who is more dominant and who is more submissive. The more submissive male may feel less of a man. One partner may want sexual behaviors such as anal penetration that are not a choice of the other. There are differences in risk for infectious diseases depending on the role a partner plays. Safer-sex negotiations can complicate sexual relations. Some partnered gay men may have open relationships, which may or may not involve their partner. The partners may decide that outside partners are acceptable as long as the sex is not at their home or that the liaisons are discreet and do not interfere with the couple's time together. Lesbians and heterosexual couples do not seem to have this type of open relationship arrangement.

It is often surprising to heterosexual therapists how satisfying sex can be within lesbian and gay pairings. The details of sexual behaviors are a common curiosity of therapists. One can learn by asking, listening, or reading.

HIV

HIV and AIDS have had a huge impact on the gay and lesbian community. In the early 1980s, the gay and lesbian community organized to combat AIDS. Gay men's health centers and gay and lesbian community centers focused effectively on AIDS prevention and treatment. The community felt abandoned by their government and the medical profession. The community began to raise its own funds. Lesbian women stepped up to the challenge of caring for their dying gay male friends. An entire generation of gay men lost their lives before the improved treatments became available in the late 1990s. This has given rise to survivor guilt in those who are still living. A generation of gay men and lesbians faced the serious illness, dying, and death of their cohort of friends at significantly earlier ages then in previous generations.

Mental health professionals need to recognize the anger, guilt, shame, fear, loss, and grief that exist in the gay community related to HIV and AIDS. Gay and lesbian patients may present with other concerns and unless asked do not bring up these issues. Many adult homosexuals have lost partners and close friends to AIDS. Those infected with HIV carry the same crushing stress and anxiety as any patient with a potentially fatal illness. This worry has an impact on both partners in many small and large ways.

Ironically, the prevention efforts and superior treatments have given rise to prevention burnout and an increase in risky sexual practices. Barebacking, which is anal sex without protection, is increasing, especially among young gay males. This increase is attributed to improved treatments giving rise to the notion that AIDS is treatable and now, like diabetes, is a chronic medical condition. Some gay men have adopted a fatalistic attitude that it is just a matter of time before they get HIV, so "I might as well get it over with." Substance abuse, especially of crystal meth, has led to an increase in unsafe sexual practices.

HIV status discordance has an impact on same-sex relationships. Sometimes, an individual will lose interest in sex or develop erectile or other dysfunction from fear about acquiring HIV. Sometimes, individuals will serosort (i.e., seek partners of the same HIV status).

TWO OTHER ISSUES

Should the Therapist Disclose His or Her Sexual Orientation?

Heterosexual therapists typically do not worry about whether they should disclose their sexual orientation. A wedding ring, a picture in the office, or an offhand comment or response may subtly signal to the patient that the therapist is heterosexual. But, the absence of such clues may lead the patient to wonder about the therapist's orientation. This is not a topic that most patients will quickly discuss, but sometimes a patient will directly ask what your orientation is.

Whether or not you chose to answer the question, we would like to suggest that you first explore the reasons behind his or her question. If the patient cannot productively respond to your question in this regard, you can help the patient with a series of related questions, such as, "Why is this important to you now?" "What do you think the answer is?" "What led you to think that?" "What do you anticipate that you will feel and think if I tell you the answer?"

In responding this way, you have made use of the patient's question to explore the patient's mental processes and his or her sexual identity mosaic. We want to handle this question by asking ourselves whether the answer will be useful to the patient. If you chose to disclose, you have to be prepared to answer additional questions. A gay or lesbian therapist may wish to be a positive gay role model. A heterosexual therapist may wish to be seen as an affirming ally for the patient. While the gay or lesbian patient may be asking because he or she is having personal concerns about his or her own sexual identity mosaic, this is not always the case.

If the therapist decides not to answer the question, he or she might consider saying, "I don't like to answer such questions because I believe that it will cut off your imagination about me, which I always want to be able to explore."

We cannot say that a therapist should or should not reveal their orientation; that is your professional judgment. We can say not to treat the subject casually. Often, when you explore in detail the patient's reasons for asking the question, the patient no longer thinks the answer is that important.

Reparative Therapy

While church-sponsored organizational efforts to cure homosexual males still exist in major denominations, there is no scientific evidence that these efforts to convert a homosexual orientation to a heterosexual orientation work. They remain below community standards of appropriate care by MHPs, not only because they are ineffective but also because they have a potential to damage patients by increasing their identity conflicts and self-hatred. The American Psychological Association adopted a resolution stating that MHPs should avoid telling clients that they can change their sexual orientation through therapy or other treatments (APA Task Force, 2009).

OTHER SUPPORTS

There are many books and Web sites devoted to gay and lesbian concerns. There are many organizations that offer support and assistance to gay and lesbian individuals and their families. There are ample opportunities for MHPs to learn about gay life. In looking into gay life, the MHP will learn that there is no "gay agenda," and gay culture does not promote a "gay lifestyle." People are encouraged to walk their own path. As a result of the AIDS crisis, there seems to be a new inclusiveness among gay men and lesbian women, bisexual individuals, and the community's straight allies. There is also a sense of inclusiveness with transgendered individuals.

CONCLUSIONS

In this chapter, we presented concepts that we felt would be useful to therapists beginning their work with people who have issues relating to their lesbian, gay, or bisexual orientations. The idea of human first, gender second, and orientation third we believe is a wonderful way of thinking about the unique issues of sexual minorities because it forces us not to stereotype, not to alienate them in our thinking from others, and not to diminish their struggles to find a place in society that honors themselves, their history, and their aspirations to find happiness in love, sex, vocation, family life, and community. Although we have emphasized the uniqueness of all patients in this chapter, we ultimately return to the humanness of gay men and women as they live out their gendered lives. Like all patients, those who have homosexual or bisexual orientations have much to teach us.

REFERENCES

Aaron, D. J., Markovic, N., Danielson, M. E., Honnold, J. A., Janosky, J. E., & Schmidt, N. J. (2001). Behavioral risk factors for disease and preventive health practices among lesbians. *American Journal of Public Health*, *91*, 972–975.

American Academy of Pediatrics. (2002). Policy statement, Committee on Psychosocial Aspects of Child and Family. Coparent or second-parent adoption by same-sex parents. *Pediatrics, 109*(2), 339–340.

American Psychiatric Association. (2000). *Diagnostic and statistical manual of mental disorders* (4th ed., text rev.). Washington, DC: Author.

American Psychiatric Association. (1968). Committee on Nomenclature and Statistics. *Diagnostic and statistical manual of disorders,* 2nd edition. Washington, DC: Author.

APA Task Force on Appropriate Therapeutic Responses to Sexual Orientation. (2009). "Report to the Task Force on Appropriate Therapeutic Responses to Sexual Orientation." Washington, DC: American Psychological Association.

Berzon, B. (1988). *Permanent partners: Building gay and lesbian relationships that last.* New York: Dutton Adult.

Berzon, B. (1996). *The intimacy dance: A guide to long-term success in gay and lesbian relationships.* New York: Dutton Adult.

Bieschke, K. J., Perez, R. M., & DeBord, K. A. (2006). *Handbook of counseling and psychotherapy with lesbian, gay and bisexual clients.* Washington, DC: American Psychological Association.

Coleman, E., & Remafedi, G. (1989). Gay, lesbian, and bisexual adolescents: A critical challenge to counselors. *Journal of Counseling and Development, 68*, 36–40.

Division 44/Committee on Lesbian, Gay, Bisexual Concerns Joint Task Force. (2000). *Guidelines for psychotherapy with lesbian, gay, and bisexual clients.* Washington, DC: American Psychological Association.

Eichberg, R. (1990). *Coming out: An act of love.* New York: Plume.

Gilman, S. E., Cochran, S. D., Mays, V. M., Hughes, M., Ostrow, D., & Kessler, R. C. (2001). Risk of psychiatric disorders among individuals reporting same-sex sexual partners in the National Comorbidity Survey. *American Journal of Public Health*, *91*, 933–939.

Greenan, D., & Tunnell, G. (2002). *Couple therapy with gay men.* New York: Guilford Press.

Hayes, J. A., & Erkis, A. J. (2000). Therapist homophobia, client sexual orientation, and source of client HIV infection as predictors of therapist reactions to clients with HIV. *Journal of Counseling Psychology, 47,* 71–78.

Healthy People 2010: Companion Document for Lesbian, Gay, Bisexual, and Transgender (LGBT) Health. (2001). San Francisco, CA: Gay and Lesbian Medical Association.

Hershberger, S. L., & D'Angelli, A. R. (1995). The impact of victimization on the mental health and suicidality of lesbian, gay, and bisexual youths. *Developmental Psychology, 31*(1), 65–74.

Hooker, E. (1993). Reflections of a 40-year exploration: A scientific view on homosexuality. *American Psychologist, 48,* 450–453.

Jones, B. E., & Hill, M. J. (2002). *Mental health issues in lesbian, gay, bisexual and transgender communities* (Review of Psychiatry Series, Vol. 21, No. 4). Washington DC: American Psychiatric.

Kertzner, R. M. (2004). Psychotherapy with lesbian and gay clients from an adult life course perspective. *Journal of Gay and Lesbian Social Services, 16,* 105–111.

Kinsey, A. C., Pomeroy, W. B., & Martin, C. E. (1948). *Sexual behavior in the human male,* Oxford, UK: Saunders.

McNaught, B. (1988). *On being gay: Thoughts on family, faith, and love.* New York: St. Martins Press.

Mills, T. C., Stall, R., Pollack, L., Paul, J. P., Binson, D., Canchola, J., et al. (2001). Health-related characteristics of men who have sex with men: A comparison of those living in "gay ghettos" with those living elsewhere. *American Journal of Public Health, 91,* 980–983.

Remafedi, G. (1987). Adolescent homosexuality: Psychosocial and medical implications. *Pediatrics, 79*(3), 331–337.

Remafedi, G., French, S., Story, M., Resnick, M. D., & Blum, R. (1998). The relationship between suicide risk and sexual orientation: Results of a population-based study. *American Journal of Public Health, 88,* 57–60.

Russell, S. T., Franz, B. T., & Driscoll, A. K. (2001). Same-sex romantic attraction and experiences of violence in adolescence. *American Journal of Public Health, 91,* 903–906.

Suicide Prevention Resource Center. (2008). *Suicide risk and prevention for lesbian, gay, bisexual, and transgender youth.* Newton, MA: Education Development Center.

Wallien, M. S. C., & Cohen-Kettenis, P. T. (2008). Psychosexual outcome of gender-dysphoric children. *Journal of the American Academy of Child and Adolescent Psychiatry, 47,* 1413–1423.

Wetchler, J. L., & Bigner, J. (2004). *Relationship therapy with same-sex couples.* New York: Routledge.

Whitman, J. S., & Boyd, C. J. (2003). *The therapist's notebook for lesbian, gay, and bisexual clients: Homework, handouts and activities for use in psychotherapy (Haworth practical practice in mental health).* New York: Routledge.

SELECTED GLBT RESOURCES

AIDS Education Global Information System, www.aegis.org. The mission of AEGIS is to facilitate access to current patient and clinician information specific to AIDS/HIV. It is the largest virtual AIDS library, consisting of more than 1.3 million articles.

Association for Lesbian, Gay, Bisexual, and Transgender Issues in Counseling, www.algbtic.org. This organization provides resources about counseling of GLBT patients including a list of therapists.

Gay and Lesbian Alliance Against Defamation, www.GLAAD.org. Their mission is to promote and ensure fair and accurate representation of gays and lesbians in the media as a means to eliminate homophobia and discrimination.

Gay and Lesbian Medical Association, www.glma.org. This professional organization offers references and resources for physicians and patients.

Gay and Straight Education Network, www.GLSEN.org. Their mission strives to ensure that each member of every school community is valued and respected regardless of sexual orientation or gender identity/expression. They offer tools to establish gay–straight alliances in schools.

Human Rights Campaign, www.HRC.org. This civil rights organization works for equal rights for LGBT individuals. HRC envisions an America where LGBT people are ensured of their basic equal rights and can be open, honest, and safe at home, at work, and in the community.

Lambda Legal, www.lambdalegal.org. Lambda Legal pursues high-impact litigation, public education, and advocacy on behalf of equality and civil rights for lesbians, gay men, bisexuals, transgender people, and people with HIV.

National Coalition for Lesbian, Gay, Bisexual, and Transgender Health, www. LGBTHealth.net. This coalition works to improve the health of LGBT individuals through public education, coalition building, and advocacy.

National Gay and Lesbian Task Force, www.NGLTF.org. The mission of NGLTF is to build the grassroots power of the LGBT community by training activists and equipping state and local organizations with the skills needed to organize broad-based campaigns to defeat anti-LGBT referenda and advance pro-LGBT legislation.

National Youth Advocacy Coalition, www.nyacyouth.org. This national organization works to improve the lives of LGBT and questioning youth through advocacy, education, and information.

Parents, Families, and Friends of Lesbians and Gays, www.pflag.org. This national organization assists the families and friends of LGBT individuals through support, education, and advocacy.

Point Foundation, www.pointfoundation.org. This organization provides scholarships, mentoring, and leadership training to LGBT students.

The Trevor Project, www.thetrevorproject.org. The Trevor Helpline (1-866-4-U-Trevor) is the only national 24-hour suicide crisis and prevention helpline for LGBT youth. The project also does outreach, education, and advocacy.

SELECTED GENERAL LGBT READING

Duberman, M. (1993). *Stonewall.* New York: Dutton.

Heron, A. (1995). *Two teenagers in 20: Writings by gay and lesbian youth.* Boston: Alyson Books.

Kushner, T. (2003). *Angels in America: A gay fantasia on national themes: Part one: Millennium approaches, Part two: Perestroika.* New York: Theatre Communications Group.

Marcus, E. (1992). *Making history. The struggle for gay and lesbian equal rights 1945–1990.* New York: Harper Collins.

Nava, M., & Dawidoff, R. (1994). *Created equal: Why gay rights matter to America.* New York: St. Martins Press.

Perry, T., & Swicegood, T. (1991), *Profiles in gay and lesbian courage.* New York: St. Martins Press.

Shilts, R. (1987). *And the band played on: Politics, people and the AIDS epidemic.* New York: St. Martins Press.

Vaid, U. (1995). *Virtual equality: The mainstreaming of gay and lesbian liberation.* New York: Doubleday Anchor Books.

Twenty-One

Male and Female Homosexuality in Heterosexual Life

RICHARD C. FRIEDMAN, MD, AND JENNIFER I. DOWNEY, MD

INTRODUCTION

We are psychiatrist-psychoanalysts who have collaborated in teaching and scholarship for more than a decade. Before becoming a team, each carried out research on the biological and behavioral aspects of human sexuality. Dr. Friedman's book, *Male Homosexuality: A Contemporary Psychoanalytic Perspective* (1988), helped revise traditional psychoanalytic paradigms of sexual orientation. While working on a National Institute of Mental Health (NIMH) Career Investigator Grant, Dr. Downey was the first to demonstrate that the hormonal profiles of lesbians and heterosexual women did not differ.

We realized through our research, teaching, and clinical experience that the topic of human sexuality provokes anxiety in many clinicians, psychotherapists, and medical/surgical physicians and nurses as well (Friedman & Downey, 1994). We discovered that teaching together enabled us to more effectively overcome our students' tendencies to avoid sexual topics in their clinical work. We currently teach a course in human sexuality for psychiatric residents at the College of Physicians and Surgeons, Columbia University, New York State Psychiatric Institute, in New York City and cochair the Human Sexuality Committee of the Group for Advancement of Psychiatry (GAP). We also teach a seminar in sexual psychodynamics for advanced psychoanalytic candidates at the Columbia Psychoanalytic Center.

In 1997, *The Journal of the American Psychoanalytic Association* awarded a prize to our article on female homosexuality (Downey & Friedman, 1988) as the best submission of that year. In our most recent book, *Sexual Orientation and Psychodynamic Psychotherapy: Sexual Science and Clinical Practice* (Friedman & Downey, 2008b) and in this chapter, the author of the case material is of the same gender as the patient. The rest of this chapter, including discussion of the case vignettes, was written collaboratively.

HOMOSEXUAL PHENOMENA IN HETEROSEXUAL PATIENTS

Sara: A Political Lesbian

Sara came for consultation because she was bewildered about her sexual orientation. A 20-year-old student at a woman's college, she had decided to "renounce" men during her sophomore year of college. Majoring in women's studies, she concluded that women were discriminated against by men throughout the world, and that most societies were organized around "patriarchal" values. An ardent and outspoken feminist, Sara joined a group of feminist/lesbian political activists. They believed that "penetrative sex" placed the woman in an inferior power relationship with her lover and was inherently humiliating. Men used this type of sexual interaction to dominate and exploit women. Only women themselves could provide truly equal mutually supportive sexual partnerships with other women.

During her precollege life, Sara had experienced developmental milestones typical of girls on a heterosexual track. She had crushes on boys and men, never girls. When she began masturbating, in her late teens, the objects of her erotic fantasies were always men. Her only sexual partner prior to beginning college was a boyfriend. They became sexually active during the latter part of her senior year, and after an initial period of awkwardness, she became orgasmic during sexual activity, including sexual intercourse, which she found pleasurable. She and he were not in love, however, and broke off their relationship when they went to different colleges.

Coincident with adopting a role as feminist/lesbian, Sara began having sexual relations with women. She was fully sexually responsive, and during a 1-year period participated in sexual activity with two female partners, neither of whom she fell in love with, however. One evening, she found herself engaged in a political discussion with a male graduate student, and to her surprise, when he proposed that they become lovers a few days later, she accepted. She was drawn to him despite intellectual reservations about heterosexuality. Sara felt guilty about this relationship, believing that she had betrayed her political convictions. During the next few months, they became deeply involved, and their erotic life was profoundly satisfying to both. Even so, Sara found herself objecting to many of her lover's traits, which she attributed to "innate masculinity." He seemed more action oriented than emotionally communicative, was not particularly nurturant, and was deeply competitive with other men, at both sports and intellectual activities. Sara decided again that she preferred the company of women to men, yet, "almost against my will, my emotions drew me to him." For reasons of which she was unaware, the quality of sex with him was more satisfying than with female lovers, despite the fact that she condemned it for political reasons. The conflict between what she experienced sexually and what she believed she *should* experience led her to therapy.

Psychotherapeutic exploration uncovered many of the unconscious factors contributing to Sara's complex sexual adaptation. Importantly, I did not express an opinion about whether Sara was "really" homosexual or heterosexual, and I did not disagree with or affirm Sara's political beliefs. Sometimes, Sara would seek direct feedback, "Am I a true lesbian or what?" and I would reply, "Our job here is to help you understand yourself—let's see what comes to mind." I did not reveal whether I was married or my sexual orientation. Sara ultimately fell in love with a man who she married. I saw her again briefly after the birth of their second child years later. Sara had anxiety symptoms as a result of some (minor) congenital abnormalities of the baby. These symptoms improved after only a few sessions. With respect to her sexual orientation, Sara enjoyed a loving heterosexual relationship and saw herself as heterosexual. Looking back at her college years, she felt that her sexual experiences with women were authentic, as was her sense of lesbian identity during that phase of her life. She was comfortable with the awareness, however, that she had "moved to a different place" subsequently.

Discussion

We discuss this vignette with the goal of reviewing the questions of general clinical relevance that it raises.

Psychiatric Diagnosis

No matter what a patient's chief complaint, it is important to establish whether significant psychopathology is present. The meanings underlying the patient's request for therapy differ across different psychiatric diagnoses. Often, the patient attributes the cause of difficulties to factors that are different from those that the therapist might. In Sara's case, her psychopathology was not severe. For example, she did not have any Axis I disorders according to the *DSM-IV* (*Diagnostic and Statistical Manual of Mental Disorders, Fourth Edition*; American Psychiatric Association, 1994). She also was not borderline, either by *DSM-VIV* standards (borderline personality disorder) or using a more global psychodynamic referent (borderline level of personality organization; Kernberg, 1975); she did not meet criteria for other types of personality disorder.

Sara needed psychotherapy because important motivational issues influencing her sexuality were unconscious, but not because her sexual conflicts led to severe psychiatric symptoms. Thus, the problem that perplexed her at the outset of her treatment—"Am I homosexual or heterosexual?"—did not appear to disguise deep difficulties with identity consolidation, self-representation, or affect regulation. The therapist decided that was what she appeared to be: a young adult whose political value system was not fully integrated with her erotic responsivity. Her self-representation had not yet been fully fashioned in a way that seemed authentic to her.

Feminist Lesbianism

Feminist lesbianism is common and certainly not inherently psychopathological. Feminist/lesbian patients sometimes seek psychotherapeutic assistance, however, as did Sara. Sara happened to be the kind of person who left lesbianism behind and continued through life on a heterosexual pathway. Her course is best understood as being the product of her particular and idiosyncratic motivations. Someone with her "profile" might just as easily have continued through life on a lesbian track. As is true in many other areas of female psychology, there is great diversity with respect to the different types of women who become feminists/lesbians (Downey & Friedman, 1998; Friedman & Downey, 2008b). Sara saw herself as heterosexual until she left home to attend college. There she became a feminist, and she decided that it was better to interact sexually with women than men for political reasons. Sara's erotic fantasies and activities also became directed at women, however, a point not to be minimized. This type of psychosexual profile, in which a political value system seems to influence erotic responsivity, is much less common among men. Gay men, for example, tend to experience sexual attraction toward males from childhood. Their sexual desire profile tends, as a general rule, to remain in place for life (Friedman & Downey, 2008b). Although some also experience some degree of sexual desire for women and participate in heterosexual activity, there is no real counterpart of feminist lesbianism among men. Men do not tend to change sexual orientations for political reasons during young adulthood. This is but one example of difference between men and women in sexual plasticity, the degree to which erotic responsivity is fixed and rigid or may be modified in keeping with changing social and emotional context.

The Therapist's Stance

The therapist (J.I.D.) helped Sara understand different unconscious psychological conflicts that appeared to influence her sexual experience. She did this by being accepting, nonjudgmental, and relativistic. Thus, the therapist's personal sexual value system was not expressed. She was bounded, yet empathic. In considering this, it is important to stress the distinction between the *therapeutic process* and the specific features of the patient's sexual adaptation (e.g., the way in which her sexual orientation is experienced). Sara's psychotherapeutic experience reached termination because Sara accomplished her fundamental goal: to establish a sense of self-authenticity that included integration of her philosophical beliefs and sexual experience. A different patient working with the same therapist might well have become as productively engaged in therapy as Sara and accomplished similar *process* goals, with a different *outcome* with respect to sexual orientation. Psychotherapeutic exploration may have discovered that the patient's erotic desires for men masked underlying unconscious conflicts that, when explored, resulted in diminution of her heterosexual motives. Such a patient may have discovered that her sexual life with women was more profoundly satisfying and meaningful than with men.

The solution to sexual orientation difficulties of the type experienced by Sara is frequently not possible to predict at the outset of psychotherapeutic treatment. Thus, the search for identity might lead to lesbianism or to heterosexuality (or to some type of bisexuality) without the specific outcome considered innately healthy or pathological by the therapist. A sense of identity coherence and ego integration, however, should ideally be achieved no matter what type of sexual orientation outcome results. Although Sara's course is not "typical" (no course is), it is common enough and illustrates important general issues about sexuality. A key ingredient in the psychotherapeutic treatment of patients like Sara is the therapist's capacity to tolerate the patient's anxiety about "being" homosexual or heterosexual. Without directly saying so, the therapist ideally should convey acceptance of the patient as a *person* whose struggle for self-authenticity requires joint exploration that, if all goes well, leads to a sense of self-authenticity and security.

A Middle-Aged Heterosexual Woman Falls in Love With Another Woman

We have elsewhere described a marital relationship in which a heterosexual woman became passionately involved with another woman in a sexual–love relationship. We reproduce our description of the relationship here; the wife's pattern of sexuality illustrates homosexual responsiveness in someone who had considered herself heterosexual. Her sexual desire for another woman occurred later in life than the young woman described in the preceding discussion and for reasons that were deeply personal, not political.

> Consider the psychology of each partner in a marriage in which each experiences a loss of passionate vitality. The 50-year-old wife is struggling to cope with feelings of "emptiness" that have become insistent and persistent in recent years. At work, she

experiences loss of ambition and energy, a tendency to withdraw from social interactions and irritability. Although her appearance has not outwardly changed, she feels unattractive. Her efforts to obtain solace and support from her mate are frustrated by his attitude toward her. She experiences him as emotionally unavailable, and she feels lonely in his presence. She complains that his idea of being together is to participate in activities at the same time, such as watching television or socializing with friends. He offers her little sense of emotional connection or empathic understanding.

The husband experiences his wife as increasingly clinging, dependent, and self-preoccupied. He feels bewildered by her criticism that he is emotionally not present when he is physically in her company. His attempts to hug and hold her are angrily rebuffed when he becomes sexually aroused. She interprets his initiating physical intimacy as manipulative. "All you want is sex," she tells him. She begins to find intercourse invasive and intrinsically devaluing. He interprets her sexual withdrawal as infantile and frustrating. He complains that she wants him to relate to her as if she were a child.

The husband spends more and more time at work, where he is perceived as energetic and effective. It seems to his wife that the more she complains about her loneliness, the more he withdraws. Soon, he begins a sexual affair with one of his women colleagues. At this point, his wife begins to have lengthy conversations with a widow who lives nearby. The women meet each other frequently and commiserate about sex differences in behavior. Each feels that the other is warm, supportive, understanding, empathic, expressive, and caring. The friendship deepens, and the women discover sexual feelings for each other. Their emergence is a surprise to both. Each is heterosexist in attitude, has not experienced homosexual desire before, and has never engaged in homosexual activity. After a period of shock, turmoil, and mutual revelation, they realize that they have fallen in love and allow themselves to express their feelings sexually. Although their love relationship becomes fully sexual and deeply satisfying to each, neither considers herself a lesbian. In fact, neither feels it necessary to label their same-sex passionate relationship in terms of a particular sexual orientation/social role.

In this instance, intense intimacy kindled sexual desire in two women. Once this occurred, each felt attractive and desirable. The depression experienced by the first remitted. This type of "kindling" rarely occurs in men except in special situations. "A lifelong heterosexual man may develop intensely close friendships during middle or later life, but these are not likely to alter the sex of the object of his fantasies" (Downey & Friedman, 1998).

In women, much more frequently than men, sexual feelings emerge in the context of trusting, empathic, intimate relationships. This is compatible with differences between the sexes in the *onset* of erotic feelings during childhood and adolescence. In females, erotic feelings tend to emerge early in life in the context of meaningful relationships; in males, they tend to be triggered by visual stimuli and do not necessarily emerge in a relational context (Friedman & Downey, 2008b, 148).

Male Sexual Fantasy

In males, feelings of sexual desire usually emerge during mid- and late childhood. Boys are usually aware of feelings of sexually lustful desire prior to puberty, and the imagery associated with such stimuli is summoned during masturbation. Sexual fantasies, experienced during masturbation and at other times as well, consist of visual imagery of females, males, or both (in different men) and a rudimentary storyline. These fantasies motivate boys to be interested in pornography depicting their fantasies and to participate in sexual activity. The images and storyline tend to act as a limit, that is, stimuli that are outside the pattern and are not experienced as being sexual. Exclusively heterosexual men will not be aroused by homosexual stimuli, and exclusively homosexual men will not be aroused by heterosexual stimuli. Epidemiological studies indicated that a majority of men are heterosexual, a minority exclusively homosexual, and a somewhat larger minority bisexual (Billy, Tanfer, Grady, & Klepinger, 1993; Laumann, Gagnon, Michael, & Michaels, 1994). Thus, the most common timeline of psychosexual male development is that a boy is erotically attracted to girls and women from midchildhood. By puberty he masturbates to fantasies of nude women and is interested in heterosexual pornography. During adolescence, he participates in interpersonal sexual activity with young women, and he then maintains his heterosexual fantasy profile during the rest of his life. Gay men tend to follow a similar timeline except that the sexual object is male and not female.

HOMOSEXUAL EXPERIMENTATION AMONG HETEROSEXUALS

The importance of sexual fantasy in relationship to interpersonal sexual experience is illustrated by sexual experiences of identical twin men that occurred during early adolescence. The sexual histories of these boys were studied as part of a research project carried out by R.C.F. (Friedman, 1988).

The sexual incident in question concerned the conduct of a group of boys in an automobile. As many boys stuffed themselves into a small car as the car would contain. Heterosexual pornographic magazines were distributed, and the boys masturbated themselves and each other—while looking at depictions of nude women. One twin was exclusively heterosexual. Even though he achieved orgasm by being masturbated by a friend, the experience for him was heterosexual. The magazine imagery that conformed to his inner fantasy life was of the opposite sex. He imagined himself sexually involved with the model. The other twin was gay, however, and for him the experience in the automobile was deeply homoerotic. He paid no attention to the pornographic imagery, but rather attended to his inner fantasies, which were brought to life by the sexual activity enacted in the car.

The story of the twins illustrates that erotic fantasy programming shapes the way in which males interpret sexual context. It is also an example of sexual activity carried on between heterosexual boys. Such activity is common but tends to be interpreted according to preexisting sexual fantasy profiles. Thus (contrary to myths about homosexuality), adolescent boys who experiment with mutual masturbation do not tend to be "drawn into" homosexual orientation later in life.

Men and women develop similarly in many ways but differently in others. An important difference is that men are more likely to value homosexual phenomena negatively than women are. Clarification of the psychology of homophobia in heterosexual men helps place this phenomenon in perspective. It is important to emphasize that our entire discussion in this chapter is culture bound. Our experience has primarily been with American patients, and our observations about development are based on studies largely carried out in northern America or western Europe. This point bears particular salience in our consideration of the negative value attributed by many men toward phenomena they perceive to be homosexual or feminine, in others and in themselves. Attitudes toward homosexuality differ between societies and across historical epochs. In ancient Greece, for example, homosexual activity was not condemned. In fact, a specific type of relationship between an adolescent boy and older man was considered the ideal embodiment of passionate love (Dover, 1989).

HOMOPHOBIA IN HETEROSEXUAL MEN

Albert, a 45-year-old executive, requested help because of anxiety and depression associated with separation from his wife of 10 years. The couple had lost a sense of intimate connection with each other as each had become more and more professionally successful. During the year prior to the separation, each had become involved with other sexual partners. To his surprise, Albert, who prided himself on not being "possessive," found that he was jealous. He realized that it was "irrational" to object that his wife, a 40-year-old lawyer, was not monogamous as he himself was not. He felt that his "feelings and thoughts were not on the same page." Intellectually he believed that the same rules should govern the sexual behavior of both partners in a marriage, but his emotions responded as if this were not the case.

To his consternation and for the first time in his life, Albert was unable to perform sexually with extramarital partners. Typically, he experienced loss of sexual desire and of his erection just as the couple was about to have intercourse. He then felt deeply ashamed and puzzled. He decided that the reason for his difficulty might be "physical," but he was embarrassed to discuss sex with his family physician.

Albert discussed these symptoms and difficulties during his first consultation visit. Not until the second session, however, and only upon tactful probing by the therapist, did he reveal that something else was troubling him as well. More or less coincident with the other difficulties, he began to ruminate that he might be gay. Ego alien thoughts of being homosexual produced distress and occurred despite the fact that Albert's history of erotic fantasy and activity was entirely heterosexual.

Albert had 10 female sexual partners prior to his marriage. He had first engaged in sexual intercourse at age 17 with a high school girlfriend. Of his 10 partners, Albert had been in love with 1 and involved in intimate monogamous relationships with 4 others. The remaining encounters were casual. Albert dated the onset of his sexual desires/fantasies to about age 6 or 7. The object of his erotic desires had always been female. He began masturbating at age 12, and masturbatory fantasies were always of women, usually classmates and movie stars. During the year prior to his consultation, the very time when he worried that he might be homosexual, he continued to masturbate regularly, and his fantasized object was always female. From young adulthood, Albert had been interested in pornography to some degree, always heterosexual. Given that Albert's sexual history had always been exclusively heterosexual, he was understandably confused that he was concerned about being homosexual for no apparent reason.

Albert was treated with supportive psychotherapy, and he and his wife responded positively to marital therapy. They reconciled and resumed satisfying sexual activity. Albert, who had never experienced sexual symptoms with his wife, gave up extramarital sexual activity. His worries about being homosexual faded away.

DISCUSSION

Albert had grown up in a sexist, blue-collar environment. The values of his adulthood and childhood were quite different. Having enjoyed an excellent university education and traveled widely, Albert prided himself on being humanistic and cosmopolitan. However, at an unconscious level, he tended to endorse the sex/role stereotypes with which he had been raised. Despite the fact that he did not consider himself homophobic, imagining himself as homosexual was unacceptable. In fact, Albert considered the imagery and meaning of male homosexuality as representing masculine inadequacy. To Albert, "I am homosexual" symbolically meant "I am a weak, unmasculine man." Albert had (unconsciously) concluded that his wife had rejected him because he was not sexually adequate. He suffered a sense of competitive defeat because of his (unconscious) conviction that his wife's lovers were better men than he was. His dread that he was not "a real man" seemed to be confirmed by his difficulty performing sexually with other women. Albert represented his feeling of poor masculine self-esteem with a thought, "I am homosexual." The thought took the form of an obsessional worry: an ego alien, repetitive, irrational idea.

It was not necessary during Albert's treatment to make his unconscious irrational ideas conscious. What was crucial, however, was for the therapist to understand that Albert was deeply insecure about his masculinity, and that his homosexual thoughts symbolically represented this insecurity. In Albert's case, couple therapy and individual supportive therapy led to marital reconciliation and symptom improvement. Other patients with this type of symptom often require additional forms of treatment. For example, in some cases an obsessional worry such as Albert's may be part of a more pervasive obsessional personality disorder. These patients might experience diverse nonsexual obsessions and compulsions, and their treatment generally involves pharmacological treatment with serotonin selective reuptake-inhibiting drugs in addition to psychotherapy. Still other patients require exploratory psychotherapy. In these instances, the unconscious connections between the patient's irrational fears and conscious experience are explored as part of the therapeutic process.

Although guidelines for the different types of therapeutic strategies that help different types of patients are not possible in this chapter, a good rule of thumb is for the therapist to attempt to provide the intervention that will produce the greatest therapeutic effect with the least cost—personal and financial—to the patient. For example, in Albert's case, the fact that his symptom remitted with supportive interventions led to the therapeutic decision that prolonged insight-oriented therapy was not indicated, at least at this time.

PSEUDOHOMOSEXUAL ANXIETY: A PSYCHOANALYTIC CONCEPT PROPOSED IN THE 1950S

The psychoanalyst Lionel Ovesey (1969) was the first to clarify the reasons that men whose erotic programming is heterosexual nonetheless may experience thoughts, sometimes in the form of worries, that they might be homosexual. Ovesey, who studied the dreams, associations, and symptoms of his patients, suggested that some men symbolically represented conflicts about power and dependency in the form of homosexual imagery. Feelings of competitive defeat in struggles with other men were often depicted as homosexual imagery in the man's fantasy life and dreams. For example, Ovesey reported the dream of a man who felt intimidated by his boss:

> I tore into his office madder than hell. He was sitting behind his desk. This time I was really going to tell him. He looked up and said, "What in hell do you want?" I just stood there and couldn't say anything. Then I turned around, but instead of walking away, I crawled away on my hands and feet with my ass up in the air. (p. 40)

Ovesey (1969) collected a number of examples of such cases and suggested mechanisms by which some men represented competitive failure in the unconscious part of their minds: "I am a failure = I am not a man = I am castrated = I am a woman = I am a homosexual" (p. 57). Thus, in the clinically disturbed group of patients he discussed, three different types of ideas were condensed in the minds of the patients: (1) ideas about masculine adequacy in terms of competitive success or failure, (2) ideas about gender identity/gender role, and (3) ideas about sexual orientation.

Homophobia in Heterosexual Men

Ovesey (1969) discussed his patients many years ago. Today, these men would be considered homophobic. In fact, unconscious homophobia is sometimes expressed by heterosexual men even when these men do not consider themselves homophobic at a conscious level. At the time Ovesey discussed the phenomena he termed "pseudohomosexual," homosexuality itself was considered pathological. Most therapists considered it to be the end result of developmental derailment. Today, we know that these ideas were invalid. It is important therefore to distinguish homosexual worries and fears of heterosexual men from the motivations of those who are gay. Because of social conflict surrounding all aspects of discussion about homosexuality, this point bears particular emphasis. In gay men, homosexual motivation is not based on a sense of defect or inadequacy.

Representations of the self as unacceptably unmasculine or feminine are not uncommon among clinical populations of heterosexual men, although there are no epidemiological studies that suggest how frequently this occurs. This being the case, we have no way of knowing whether the frequency of such phenomena has decreased following the depathologization of homosexuality and associated with generally diminished sexism over the years.

The question arises of why men who are not gay sometimes represent themselves as homosexual when they are anxious or depressed. A developmental perspective sheds light on this. We have observed that the developmental roots of male homophobia are in mid- and late childhood (Friedman & Downey, 2000b). During this phase of life, children tend to move out of the social world of their families and into that of peers. Peer play is a crucially important mode of social interaction of older children. Studies of children in many societies indicated that mid- and late childhood peer play tends to be sex segregated. Boys tend to play with boys and girls with girls (Friedman & Downey, 2008; Maccoby, 1998). Although there are many exceptions to this general tendency, studies of children throughout the world indicated that in all societies in which free play during late childhood has been investigated, sex-segregated play is the rule. Juvenile play is a core building block of late childhood peer culture.

The developmental psychologist Eleanor Maccoby has observed that the peer cultures that are formed by boys and girls are quite different.

Understanding this difference is important for understanding the origins of homophobia in boys.

Boys' groups tend to be more aggressive, competitive, xenophobic, and hierarchically structured than girls' groups are. Juvenile-aged boys tend to be intolerant of cross-gender behavior, and those that are perceived as feminine are often abused or ostracized. From the perspective of juvenile-aged boys, traits that are viewed as feminine are valued negatively, whether they occur in others or oneself. To be considered girl-like is to be devalued in juvenile male peer culture. The difference between the sexes in value assigned to cross-gender behavior at this age is illustrated in the meanings that are commonly assigned to terms denoting such behavior. "Sissy" has a negative connotation, whereas "tomboy" does not.

The sex stereotyping that commonly occurs during late childhood is not an invariant phenomenon. Many boys are tolerant and accepting. Extreme reactions are much more common than most adults would like to believe, however. Some men leave homophobic attitudes and values behind as they grow older. Others, however, who belong to specific pathological subgroups, are likely to activate the childhood roots of their masculine insecurity under stress. Their negative self-images, expressed in symbolic terms, may best be understood as an adult manifestation of internalized homophobia that has persisted since late childhood. This phenomenon remains to be adequately studied, and it is possible that the pathological subgroups alluded to are heavily weighted toward boys who come from home environments of abuse, neglect, or extreme psychopathology of the caretakers.

DEVELOPMENTAL DIFFERENCES BETWEEN THE GENDERS

In this chapter, we have discussed commonly occurring homosexual phenomena in heterosexual people. During childhood, girls and boys often participate in sexual play and exploration with members of the same sex. Sometimes, such activity involves mutual masturbation, sometimes masturbation in groups, as occurred in the twins that we discussed. There is no evidence that such activity influences children to become gay or lesbian later in life; in fact, most grow up to become heterosexual.

Understanding psychosexual developmental differences between boys and girls, men and women, provides a useful context for placing homosexual phenomena in heterosexual patients in a therapeutically useful framework. Boys tend to be more uniform with respect to psychodevelopmental milestones than girls and women are. In boys, sexual fantasies are experienced during a range from 4 to 12 years old. Boys begin to masturbate during mid- and late childhood and early adolescence. Interpersonal sexual activity tends to occur during adolescence and early adulthood. During their entire lives, the sexual activity in which men engage tends to be in keeping with fantasies experienced during childhood. Most men are sexually attracted exclusively to women, a small minority (1–2%) exclusively to men, and an additional 5% more or less to both sexes (Friedman & Downey, 1994, 2000a). Since American society has no bisexual social niche, some men in the last group label themselves heterosexual and some gay. (Some privately consider themselves bisexual, of course.) There is no relationship between the objects of a person's sexual desires (men, women, or both) and psychopathology. Thus, we believe no health value should be assigned to being heterosexual, gay/lesbian, or bisexual, no matter how these terms are defined.

Subgroups of girls appear to follow different timelines with respect to the earliest occurrence of sexual fantasies, masturbation, interpersonal sexual activity, and self-labeling as heterosexual or lesbian. In many girls, the time-table sequences are similar to those of boys. In others, however, including those discussed in this chapter, they are not. One reason for this concerns sex differences with respect to plasticity of the erotic object. In most men, sexual fantasies are inclusionary and exclusionary. Stimuli outside a person's sexual profile are experienced as neutral. Men who are exclusively heterosexual, for example, are not sexually interested in imagery that arouses gay men and vice versa. Heterosexual women, much more frequently than men, appear to have the capacity for homoerotic desire to emerge during adulthood in certain conducive situations, such as a deep intimate relationship, or as a function of intense political convictions. We suspect that this occurs partly because plasticity with respect to erotic imagery is part of the "hardwiring" of the brains of women (for reasons that are outside the scope of this article).

Another difference between the sexes concerns the value attributed to feminine versus masculine traits. Women and girls appear to be more tolerant of cross-gender behavior in themselves and others. Boys and men are often intolerant of perceived unmasculine or feminine behavior in themselves as well as other boys. This may take the forms of symptoms of *internalized homophobia* in heterosexual men. When this occurs, the man labels himself "homosexual" in a symbolic and devaluing way—to connote a sense of masculine inadequacy. The psychotherapeutic treatment of such men requires empathic exploration of the underlying causes of their gender/role insecurity.

Even though gay men and lesbians are different in many respects, they are similar in others. For example, many have been or are married. Many a clinician has been surprised to discover that a person who is stably married, organized around traditional "family values," is also actively involved in sexual/love relationships with a partner of the same sex. Sometimes, these relationships are secret—the person is in the closet. Sometimes, however, the person may be "out" (e.g., out of the closet) to greater or lesser degree and carrying out personal lives in different sexual/romantic spheres successfully. The most important guideline we offer therapists to be helpful to patients in this situation is to be nonjudgmental. Sexual value systems of therapists vary widely, but include many who endorse monogamy or "honestly" conforming to one's perceived sexual orientation. Thus, people whose lovers are of the same gender "should be" gay; people whose lovers are of the opposite gender "should be" heterosexual. Therapists who attempt to impose their personal value systems on patients are likely to be unhelpful and may even be harmful. People take many different pathways toward finding fulfillment in love and passion during their lives, and therapists must respect these differences no matter how anxiety provoking this may be.

CONCLUSION

Exposure to homosexual experiences and activities among heterosexual people can provoke considerable anxiety in clinicians. Our own experience has been instructive in that regard. We have found it helpful to have regular discussions with each other in which we review our clinical work. We have found that an honest and detailed discussion of clinical processes with a trusted colleague diminishes countertransference responses, including those provoked by homosexual phenomena in heterosexual patients. Although our personal peer review experience has involved a dialogue between therapists of different genders, we believe that many different structures for peer discussion may be helpful.

The material that we have presented in this chapter was selected for many reasons. Two of the most important are that the clinical situations we have discussed are common, and that we have found that they often stimulate defensive responses in therapists. We are pleased that since the first publication of this volume, great strides have been made in overcoming antihomosexual prejudice in society. Serious problems remain, however, and the clinical issues that we discuss here still regularly occur. This chapter was written in the hope that awareness of homosexual phenomena in heterosexual patients will diminish countertransference responses and facilitate therapeutic work.

REFERENCES

American Psychiatric Association. (1994). *Diagnostic and statistical manual of mental disorders* (4th ed.). Washington, DC: Author.

Billy, J. O. G., Tanfer, K., Grady, W. R., & Klepinger, D. H. (1993). The sexual behavior of men in the United States. *Family Planning Perspectives, 25,* 52–60.

Dover, K. J. (1989). *Greek homosexuality.* Cambridge, MA: Harvard University Press.

Downey, J. I. (in press). Sexual psychodynamics: Pedagogical issues. *The Journal of the American Academy of Psychoanalysis and Dynamic Psychiatry.* This article was delivered as the Keynote Lecture at the combined meeting of the American College of Psychoanalysts and the American Academy of Psychoanalysis and Dynamic Psychiatry in San Francisco in 2009. It discusses the way a psychodynamically informed approach to sexuality can be helpful in the education of mental health professionals.

Downey, J. I., & Friedman, R. C. (1998). Female homosexuality: Classical psychoanalytic theory reconsidered. *Journal of the American Psychoanalytic Association, 46,* 471–506.

Downey, J. I., & Friedman, R. C. (2008). Homosexuality: Psychotherapeutic issues. *British Journal of Psychotherapy, 24*(4), 429–468. In this article, we discussed modern psychodynamically informed approaches to the assessment and psychotherapeutic treatment of nonheterosexual women and men.

Friedman, R. C. (1988). *Male homosexuality: A contemporary psychoanalytic perspective.* New Haven, CT: Yale University Press. This book integrated sexual science with psychoanalytic developmental theory. It reviewed the psychoanalytic literature in detail and demonstrated that a commonly accepted paradigm that homosexuality is inherently pathological was supported by neither scientific sexology nor the psychoanalytic literature itself. The book extensively discussed bisexuality. It provided clinicians with a way of conceptualizing the psychodynamics of gay, hetero-, and bisexual men who had Axis I and Axis II psychiatric disorders.

Friedman R. C. (2006). The issue of homosexuality in psychoanalysis. In P. Fonagy, R. Krause, & M. Leuzinger-Bohleber (Eds.), *Identity, gender and sexuality 150 years after Freud* (pp. 79–102). Madison, CT: IUP Press. Dr. Friedman's 2006 Sandler Lecture to the International Psychoanalytic Association is published here. He discussed the pathological model of homosexuality once generally accepted and now repudiated as an example of historic and systemic bias in psychoanalysis.

Friedman, R. C., & Downey, J. (1994). Medical progress: Homosexuality. *New England Journal of Medicine, 331,* 923–930. In this special article, we discussed the epidemiology, endocrinology, genetics, and psychological aspects of homosexuality.

Friedman, R. C., & Downey, J. I. (2000a). Psychoanalysis and sexual fantasies. *Archives of Sexual Behavior, 29,* 567–586. This article and the following article (Friedman & Downey, 2000b) on sexual fantasy, development, and gender role psychology are reproduced and elaborated on in our book.

Friedman, R. C., & Downey, J. I. (2000b). The psychobiology of late childhood: Significance for psychoanalytic developmental theory and clinical practice. *Journal of the American Academy of Psychoanalysis, 28,* 431–448.

Friedman, R. C., & Downey, J. I. (2008a). Sexual differentiation of behavior: The foundation of a developmental model of psychosexuality. *Journal of the American Psychoanalytic Association, 56,* 147–175. In this article, we explain why knowledge of sexual differentiation of the brain and behavior must be the foundation of an appropriately modern psychodynamically informed paradigm of psychosexual development.

Friedman, R. C., & Downey, J. I. (2008b). *Sexual orientation and psychodynamic psychotherapy: Sexual science and clinical practice.* New York: Columbia University Press. In this book, we discussed sexual orientation in men and women and concentrated on research and clinical material presented during the prior decade. Little of the material we considered was discussed in Friedman's earlier book (1988) on male homosexuality. The first half of the book is developmental, and we explained the basis for conceptualizing female sexual orientation as part of the psychology of women and male sexual orientation as a dimension of the psychology of men. We also discussed the origins of male homophobia in late childhood. The clinical section "Sexual Orientation and Psychoanalysis" is devoted to understanding and treating homophobia and internalized homophobia. Although the scientific and clinical sections of our book are integrated, each part stands on its own. Clinicians interested in the psychodynamic aspects of homophobia, for example, can read this part of the book separately.

Kernberg, O. (1975). *Borderline conditions and pathological narcissism.* New York: Aronson.

Laumann, E. O., Gagnon, J. H., Michael R. T., & Michaels, S. (1994). *The social organization of sexuality: Sexual practices in the United States.* Chicago: University of Chicago Press.

Maccoby, E. E. (1998). *The two sexes: growing up apart, coming together.* Cambridge, MA: Harvard University Press.

Ovesey, L. (1969). *Homosexuality and pseudohomosexuality.* New York: Science House.

Twenty-Two

Men Who Are Not in Control of Their Sexual Behavior

I. DAVID MARCUS, PHD

INTRODUCTION

Years ago, while wandering through the vast career possibilities that the field of psychology offers, I happened on the late Al Cooper. Dr. Cooper had become a leading voice in the field of sexual compulsivity. Working with him, I found the nexus of psychological struggles: people—mostly men—who verbalize strong values and display kind, thoughtful behavior in many areas of life yet harm themselves and those they love with their sexual behavior. They certainly did not want to ruin their lives, but through relationship and sometimes legal troubles as well as filling themselves with shame and guilt, they did. Treating them in an effective and sustaining manner was extremely difficult. I entered work rolling up my sleeves and doing battle beside them against what often felt like life-or-death situations. And, the more I looked and read, the more I saw: more and more cases, more and more ruined families and lives. I decided that this is where I could make a difference; I felt like a psychological surgeon trying to extract malignant behavior.

As others have, I view sexual compulsivity as a disorder related to the inability to tolerate psychological intimacy (Adams & Robinson, 2001; Schwartz & Masters, 1994). Sexual compulsivity is rarely about the sex; it is more often about control and the fear of vulnerability. The word *intimacy* means seeing through another person. Many men long to feel close to another person but fear being seen, like a starving person being scared of food. It is estimated that "as many as 95% of sexual addicts are unable to form close attachments" (Leedes, 2001, p. 218). So, I seek to provide an authentic and nurturing relationship as the basic vehicle for change. I know that the healthy relationship that I aspire to create in psychotherapy is often a critical first step to increasing the client's tolerance of psychological intimacy. It alone does not cure him. The ultimate cure rests on understanding that the man's sense of danger in interpersonal connection drives much of his compulsive sexual behavior (CSB). If he learns to tolerate emotions in my office, I believe that he will increase his capacity to engage in healthier relationships outside my office and not rely on the pseudointimacy—the rush without the vulnerability—that comes from CSB.

I discuss in detail a treatment program that involves a careful evaluation, a subsequent treatment process in which the core issues coalesce, and an

383

ending process that helps the client consolidate his gains and grasp what he will face in the future. I hope to help you avoid some of the errors that I made when I was starting to work with sexually compulsive men.

WHAT IS SEXUAL COMPULSIVITY?

Sexually compulsive behaviors include serial affairs, masturbating so much it has an impact on other areas of life, viewing pornography, using a fetish, cybersex (sexual chatting or viewing porn on the Internet), phone sex, seeing prostitutes, getting sensual massages, and attending strip clubs. Such behaviors can involve paraphilic (e.g., socially deviant) or nonparaphilic activities. Men who struggle with CSB also struggle with shame, which in turn makes them want to hide, so you have to ask specific questions about their behavior. Even if you know about one or two behaviors, be exhaustive in your inquiry to know the full extent of the problem.

While sexual compulsivity is not yet a diagnosis according to the *Diagnostic and Statistical Manual of Mental Disorders, Fourth Edition* (*DSM-IV*; American Psychiatric Association [APA], 1994) diagnosis, it is commonly employed by clinicians when most of the following criteria are met: The sexual behavior interferes with social, recreational, or occupational responsibilities; repeated efforts to stop or decrease the behaviors have been unsuccessful; the time and money spent on these activities are excessive or increasing; more of the activity is required to reach previous levels of arousal; and the behaviors are kept secret from his partner.

I prefer the term *sexual compulsivity* for these patterns, but other writers synonymously employ the terms *sexual addiction*, *hypersexuality*, and *sexual dependency*. I often use the term *sexual acting out* as well. There is not a lot of precision to be found in our informal nosology. I try to use the least-stigmatizing language.

ONLINE SEXUAL ACTIVITY

Often, CSB occurs solely on the Internet, and the majority of people who act out in other ways still use the Internet as part of their repertoire (Cooper, 2000). Delmonico and Carnes (1999) reported that 65% of subjects who scored high on the Sexual Addiction Screening Test (SAST) reported problems with their Internet sexual activity. Often powered by the Internet's triple A engine of access, affordability, and anonymity (Cooper, 1998), fantasies are enacted that would otherwise never find expression. Those who might have casually looked at a *Playboy* magazine in the past now enter an online world of behaviors that they cannot easily exit. Even some people who never even opened a magazine find pornography online and gradually become ensnared in a slowly closing trap.

Online sexual activities include looking at erotic pictures or videos, reading sexual material, engaging in sexual chat, exchanging explicit sexual e-mails or pictures, sharing sexual fantasies while masturbating, and searching for people who are willing to meet to have sex. Again, you must be thorough in your questions. When a man says he looks at Web sites, ask what kind. In terms of treatment, there will be a difference between clients who seek variety versus those who have one specific type of image they seek.

COMORBIDITY AND ETIOLOGY

Clinicians who are experienced with CSB now recognize that four categories of significant comorbidities are frequently present among these patients: substance abuse disorders, affect disorders, anxiety disorders, and attention deficit disorder. We no longer dismiss the acting out to a mere but complex symptom of one of these *DSM–IV-TR* (*Diagnostic and Statistical Manual of Mental Disorders, Fourth Edition, Text Revision*; APA, 2000) diagnoses. Treating these underlying conditions is typically necessary but not sufficient for eliminating acting out. It is at the end of a long fruitful therapy that we are best able to judge the relationship between the client's various problematic patterns.

Compulsive sexual behavior has been linked to a history of childhood trauma—often involving a parental attachment. Many of these men seem to have a deep sense of emotional abandonment. Many of them began crossing normative sexual boundaries relatively early in childhood through sexual abuse by an adult, hearing about or seeing a parent's sexual exploits, or having access to pornography before puberty. Many have not experienced either parent as a source of soothing. Because of this, they cannot internally soothe themselves and instead seek external means, such as sex, to modulate their emotions.

SEXUAL MINORITIES

Working with gay, bisexual, polyamorous, and transgendered males helps us to see that all people can struggle with sex. The line between healthier and less-healthy sexual behavior is blurrier when there is a cultural bias toward promiscuity. Refraining from sexual partners outside a committed relationship—monogamy—is not as strongly publicly endorsed in gay communities as it is in the dominant culture. Thus, the threshold for what is viewed as sexually acting out may be higher for gay clients as well as gay clinicians. In discussing life before AIDS, Baum and Fishman (1994) note that, "Recreational sex—including anonymous sex, sometimes with multiple partners—was an accepted and, in fact, a celebrated badge of belonging" (p. 256). I have seen gay couples in which one partner has his foot firmly planted in a promiscuous way of being while the other deeply values and requires monogamy. As with many heterosexuals, clients who belong to sexual minorities many not acknowledge or realize that there is a problem. Establishing this is often the first step in treatment (Prochaska, Norcross, & DiClemente, 1994).

TREATMENT OPTIONS

I endorse Kafka's (2000) view that effective treatment of nonparaphilic hypersexuality involves a multimodal approach, utilizing behavioral, psychodynamic, group, psychoeducational, and pharmacological treatments. I run groups for sexually acting out men and find that it is a critical aspect of effective change (Line & Cooper, 2002). I believe that treatment has the best chance of success when it is part of an integrated program offered by those with at least some specialized training in this area (Freeman-Longo & Blanchard, 1998). A comprehensive program also requires couple therapy if the client is in a committed relationship. Medications can address comorbid conditions, reduce the amount and urgency of sexual thoughts, or ameliorate sexual disinhibition (Kafka, 2000). When wealthy clients' CSBs are dangerous to themselves or others, are experienced as out of control, or are refractory to outpatient treatment, inpatient residential programs can be considered (see http://www.sash.net/ for a list of programs).

There are many cognitive-behavioral approaches—including the 12-step program Sex Addicts Anonymous—that focus more on the problematic behavior and less on the underlying psychological developmental issues. In my experience, these programs are more effective in catalyzing initial change and less so in ensuring enduring change. However, sexual behaviors are very powerful, ingrained, and sometimes tenacious; all treatment approaches struggle with maintaining lasting change, especially if the client does not have a committed relationship in which to engage.

TREATMENT

I offer psychodynamic treatment to my clients and subscribe to Goodman's (2001) concept that, "The primary goals of psychodynamic psychotherapy in the treatment of addictive disorders are to enhance individuals' self-regulation and to foster their capacity for meaningful interpersonal connections" (p. 208). I roughly divide my treatment into the evaluation process that merges into the beginning treatment, treatment, and the end phase, which deals with termination or transition into a different type of treatment. My work is greatly influenced by the principles of intensive short-term psychodynamic psychotherapy (Coughlin Della Selva & Malan, 1996; Neborsky, McCullough, Shapiro, Malan, & Solomon, 2001). This work has taught me to help clients to precisely and fully experience their emotions.

In terms of nuts and bolts, my work focuses on the "three R's of therapy": relationship, resistance, and reality.

Relationship

Since I view sexual compulsivity as a relationship disorder, it seems natural to me to assume that the correct path to change begins by my forming an authentic relationship with the client. My relationship, my "alliance" with him, is a real-time, although subtle, example of how he relates to others. As psychotherapy usually produces emotional turmoil for the client, our alliance is the glue that allows him to stick to treatment when his impulses say, "Get out." My relationship with the client teaches me how he attempts to distance people in his life. His descriptions of his day-to-day relationships warn me of the potential traps that I will face with him.

The gender of the therapist is an important early consideration, particularly for the client. Clients often want the therapist with whom they feel more comfortable, but it is more helpful if they choose the gender with which they experience less comfort. My experience is that the gender of the therapist will ultimately dissolve as psychological intimacy is achieved. But, from the therapist's perspective, taking on these men may initially be easier for male therapists. More frequently than male therapists, women therapists have to be prepared to be the object of CSB in the room, such as clients describing their behavior in excessive sexual detail (B. Line, personal communication, 2004).

Men who sexually act out typically enact erotic scripts that are based on views of the nature of men and women. Changing these scripts indirectly through the new authentic relationship with the therapist is a catalyst to change. This is why it is important to ask the client how he feels about working with a man or woman. You and the client can repeatedly return to the idea that he is used to how he was treated by his parents, but that life can be and is, in fact, different now. It is a powerful experience for the client to realize that he can be emotionally safe experiencing intense feelings with his male therapist. Similarly, he can realize that he does not have to maintain a facade with his female therapist. He simply can share his real feelings. Women therapists worry that their heterosexual clients will sexually act out in the room through fantasy, sexualized language, or body language in the same way that male therapists may worry that their homosexual clients will act out in therapy. While we can voice these concerns in supervision or with peers, as long as we therapists stay present and focused on the client's mental processes, even this can be a golden opportunity to illustrate to him how he uses CSB to avoid sharing his nonsexual feelings.

Resistance

Resistance is inevitable in therapy. Despite the client's request for assistance, he will make unconscious attempts to maintain his pattern. Part of him wants to maintain the behavior. Freud suggested that a symptom is an unconscious compromise between a force toward health and an opposing one (Freud, 1912). Apprehension about coming into treatment is explained, in part, by the client's terror at the prospect of changing his behavior as well as by the fear that he might not be able to do so. The difficulties of being in treatment seem immediate, while the advantages appear uncertain.

To assess the client's motivation, I ask him why he has come to seek treatment. Usually, another person (e.g., his partner, employer, legal system) has demanded that the client enter treatment. However, this is not enough. Resistance is a force, and a more powerful force must be accessed to counteract it. The client must see how his CSB has harmed him by producing or exacerbating shame and guilt, by making him bear a secret life, by separating him from those he loves and, essentially, creating a false life for his partner. The client must feel regret about his behavior and dedicate himself to change. This is often the most difficult part of treatment. Prochaska et al.'s 1994 book is instructive in this area.

Resistance diminishes the value of therapy. It is critical to focus on the client's initial concerns about therapy. We should never act as though their ambivalence surprises us. Men who sexually act out are adept at keeping relationships superficial. Our plan for deeper conversations is threatening. It is fine to discuss this threat and to predict that he may be searching for justifications for leaving treatment.

To learn how an individual's resistance may manifest, I ask about other relationships. I ask what did and did not work in any prior therapy relationships. I ask about how well family relationships did or did not meet his needs. And, of course, I ask about his romantic and sexual relationships. I ask if he leaves, or does he push the other person away so he is left? Is there a final contact, an explosive scene, or does he just disappear?

I am constantly looking for parallels. Missed appointments may be our version of missed trysts. Attempts to keep the therapy brief will be our one-night stand. If he reports that he frequently feels disappointed and betrayed, he is likely to find what I say to be simplistic, off the mark, or otherwise disappointing. If he has found his relations to be not exciting or fulfilling enough, he is also likely to find the therapy to be insufficient or not stimulating enough. These clients might "cheat" on us, getting a bit more on the side, by seeing another therapist when they find our therapy "not satisfying enough." I talk about parallels early and often, and while I think of them as resistances, I do not necessarily label them with this technical term.

Reality

Many men believe that sexually acting out is a victimless crime. They compartmentalize by keeping their behavior and their husband and father roles apart. Reality involves understanding the impact that CSB has on his life and the lives of others. The fact is that CSB fills most men with shame and guilt. The fact is that if he is in a relationship, his partner is now living a lie. If he is not in a relationship, the acting out intensifies *the belief* that he is unworthy to be in one. Sexually compulsive men are masters at maintaining an image, but they do not realize the harm their behavior causes.

Finally, reality involves the client's history. Often, he has denied or minimized the difficulties he endured in childhood, and his CSB has been a way to maintain this denial. In this regard, I often wait several sessions to get historical information because initially the main priority is for the client to have an emotional experience around his current state of affairs. At times, I struggle with the fine line of getting details and hearing the client's compelling stories and the competing goal of slowing the session and helping the client feel the emotions associated with his current state or his past tragedies.

Let us walk through some sessions, working toward our goals while paying attention to the 3 R's: relationship, resistance, and reality.

Evaluation/Early Treatment

My evaluation typically lasts one to two sessions. I have four goals: to allow the client to experience my style to see if it works for him, to establish a treatment contract, to ascertain what the client wants (not what his partner wants), and to help the client experience the sadness of how his CSB has and continues to harm him. In this way, evaluation and treatment converge.

> In the waiting room, Kevin has his head riveted down as he reads a magazine. Sitting upright and stiff, he does not move when I call his name. As I walk back to the office, I notice that he has not followed, as if he will only come in on his terms. Just when I am about to go back, he ambles in and sits in a chair instead of on the couch. He immediately addresses me by my first name and says, "I have a few questions to ask." I answer the questions that seem pertinent to treatment, including the fact that he will control with whom I can and cannot share information. I emphasize that he owns the information in the room except for several exceptions that I review.

Kevin's relationship themes start from the moment of first contact. He already seeks to gain control. First, he does not come back immediately, which seems to say, "We will do this on my terms." He then tries to erode boundaries by using my first name and asking questions first. I typically do not directly address these issues immediately but make note of them. My concerns are that his resistance is high and that he will bolt. So, I want to put him somewhat at ease. I will answer all the questions I think are reasonable. He is terrified to know that we will take a deep look at him. So, he must feel safe.

Establishing trust is one of the first challenges. Typically, the sexually acting out man trusts no one, so why should he trust me? There is often a sense that I will hurt him through judgment, humiliation, or abandonment. He assumes that the pathologic view he has of himself must be my view as well. I want him to know that I will not disappear. He needs to know that I will not shame him. I bring out my best confidentiality speech, emphasizing its importance and making clear any limitations. Sexually compulsive men look for chinks in the trust, and a little lapse or contradiction is not soon forgotten. I am very conscious of what I say and the words I use. I am constantly scanning myself for negative reactions to what he says so I can stay honest. If there is an unexpected change in the client's behavior, I take note of it and usually comment because waiting may result in not seeing him again.

It is also extremely helpful to have collateral information (e.g., get releases to talk to other providers), as well as to keep a keen eye on "frame issues," including payments, scheduling, and boundary violations. How the client handles such issues can be like a personality fingerprint and will likely show up in his CSB as well.

Kevin states that his wife is considering leaving him unless he seeks help. He states that he had a brief affair with a woman he met on an airplane. He has stopped that "thing" but his wife is still upset because she also found that he had been accessing "porn sites" on his computer. When asked about whether he has had prior affairs, Kevin asks, "What do you mean by affairs?" When I clarify, he says "no" but acknowledges that he often goes to strip clubs with a group of friends and loves the challenge of arranging sexual liaisons with the strippers for money or, even more exciting, not for money. He says that he does not consider them affairs because it is only sex, not love. I ask if he acts out in any other way. "Isn't that enough?" he asks.

As the saying goes, wherever you go there you are. Here, Kevin tells what seems like very difficult information as if he were reporting the weather. Where is the emotion? I could address the content of what he says all year but not make any progress because he is not emotionally engaged with himself or me. This points to a high level of resistance. I assume that Kevin will only change when he engages his own emotional experience instead of intellectually dissecting his life.

I do not want to get seduced by what Kevin says. While he has given me important information, I must allow for the fact that he may also be concealing important information. Clients lie, especially through omission, and being able to tolerate and respond to lies in a productive manner is important. I do this by pointing out how withholding information harms him and point to what is essentially a masochistic side. He is spending his time and money while preventing benefit through lying.

When asked what part of sex he enjoys the most, Kevin looks confused and, for a fleeting moment, vulnerable. He pauses as though gathering his response and finally says, "It's funny … but I don't enjoy sex that much." When I ask what part of being with sexual partners he does enjoy, he says, "The yes. I love it when they indicate we've got something going."

Clients often mistakenly believe that CSB is simply the result of a strong sex drive. I hope you see now that this is not the case. There is often an emotional lynchpin that maintains the sexually acting out behaviors. When evaluating the client, I attend to the aspects of the sexual relationship (e.g., the chase, the courtship, the infatuation, the climax) that turn him on. I seek to define the gravitational pulls to acting out again and again. The dysthymic client who chronically feels empty may be pulled by the intensity of sexual activity, while the one who feels shame may gravitate to the partner's acceptance ("If she has sex with me, I must be okay"). Some want to be controlled. Some want to control. Others are drawn to the conquest. Some men need to know that they can make another person happy. Break it down: What are the critical components? But, allow people to be complex; often, their behavior is multidetermined.

Kevin describes being drawn to the moment of acceptance. This enables me to begin to lay out the blueprint of treatment. His goal is to "get something going" with himself and not rely on strangers. After he discovers the basis for his negative self-evaluations, he will learn what it means to care for and ultimately accept himself. When he can accept himself, despite what others cast at him or how his parents may have harmed him, he will have a fuller life and control his CSB.

> Kevin details his family's multigenerational promiscuity. He recalls how his single mother had numerous men coming over to the house at all times and how his grandmother not only talked often about sex and wore skimpy clothing, but also encouraged Kevin to walk naked around the house. His father died before his second birthday, so the men his mother had over were his most common masculine contacts. When I ask how he feels talking about his father's death, he says, "Well, of course I'm not happy about it." When I invite him to pay closer attention to himself, he says, "I'm tired of wallowing in that." I point out that in this moment he avoids sadness that he clearly has in him, and if he truly chooses to stop his acting out, he must fully experience his sadness, although he does not seem ready to take that step now. At the end of the session, Kevin smiles and comments on the fact that I work late, and that I must be very dedicated.

In this session, some of the emotional "traumas" that Kevin experienced become clear. His mother's love went primarily toward numerous other men (not him), and his father abandoned him. The perceived costs of emotional intimacy become clear. Why would he get close to any woman when the one who should have given him unconditional love gave that love to others? Why would he make himself vulnerable to people when they can leave at any moment? How does he know that I will care enough for him, especially when I see other clients? How does he know that I will not die? It is essential to know what is at stake for your clients when you implicitly ask them to change. If change were easy, it would not be a problem.

Part of Kevin's reality lies in multigenerational sexual compulsivity. He competed with many men, and what he had to offer his mother was not good enough. Even the relationship with his grandmother, a traditional source of comfort, confused him and made it appear that his value was in his sexuality. I glimpsed his reality when he responded to what part of sex he enjoyed most.

In the second session with Kevin, he tells me how he seduced a stripper the day after our meeting and did not have to pay for her. And, when I ask him about how he feels telling me about his latest acting out, he smiles but says, "Ashamed." When I point out his smile, he says, "I'm not aware of it," and returns to the details of what happened. I challenge by asking what he wants right now, and he says, "To not be so alone all the time." I reply, "Do you see how your acting out creates distance, this time between you and me? You fill yourself with shame and talk about details to separate you from me. This leaves you alone." As Kevin acknowledges this, his smile disappears and sadness appears in his eyes. I ask him, "What is the hardest part of this right now." Kevin's tears intensify, and he says, "I feel so out of control." I acknowledge this, then say, "Here we are together, and you are sad. Do you feel this relief?" He nods, and I say, "You may act out again, but it is the acting out that harms you and is out of control. At this minute, you are gaining control."

At this stage, experiencing emotions makes Kevin feel more out of control than acting out does. The theme of control that became evident in our first session appears again. By acting out shortly after our session, he creates the perception of being back in the driver's seat that he apparently experienced as being pushed out. Having a sense of Kevin's struggles, I try to pivot him so he goes against his CSB. It is essential for him to turn his will against it, to see that what may have been protective behavior in the past harms him now. Also, I test his alliance with me. When he stops smiling and starts feeling, he becomes vulnerable with me. Here, Kevin engages in courageous behavior by risking being vulnerable. Years of behavior will not be extinguished immediately. As CSB has effectively soothed anxiety, anger, and other strong feelings for many years, it is not easily given up. It has seemed to him that the benefits of acting out have outweighed its risks. The client will have urges and slips, and by predicting these I am trying to disarm the shame he will feel when they occur. If he does feel shame, that might become a trigger for further acting out. Thus, the typical reactions of others often send these men scurrying back to their acting out, creating a vicious cycle.

In this work, it is easy to bring our own biases to how the client should behave. We are not the arbiters of what is acceptable behavior. Every person must experience for himself what is healthy behavior. The main issue about people who are constantly focused on sex is that they do not take an inward focus on the self. Their sexual behavior is a barrier toward such a focus.

The client clearly benefits from learning how to feel—what I call "self as a second language"—then reexperiencing his life while feeling (not intellectualizing). Often in this process, the client feels a profound sense of sadness or regret. He sees that by being focused on sex he has planted the seeds of isolation. While his CSB may have been considered selfish by himself or others, it is actually neglectful because through it he has ignored himself. His sexual behavior has been a form of abandoning himself. This approach helps the client commit to how he wants to proceed with his life. Such a commitment is tremendously valuable when difficulties arise in the therapy process since it can be evoked again and again as a promise that he has made to himself.

The other choice I make in this session is that I focus more on his feelings and less on the acting out per se. There is an important choice. Some focus on the acting out is required to understand the behavior, but by examining the feelings he experiences beneath the acting out, I teach him to take an inward focus and learn what dynamically, affectively, perpetuates his behaviors.

If the client believes my goal is simply to eliminate his behavior, he will keep himself emotionally distant. Similarly, if there is a sense of zero tolerance, then the client may feel defeated when the inevitable "slip" occurs and will find therapy to be another situation in which he has no control and will fail. He needs to experience that I can hear about the behaviors that he finds repulsive and still care about him. He needs to hear from me why his acting out "makes sense"—how once upon a time it was an adaptive response to difficult circumstances, but now it is our common enemy. I will tell him that his behavior is a symptom, and that the reasons why he acts out need to be a focus of treatment. What was once protective is now destructive.

At the end of the evaluation, I ask the client how the evaluation felt to him and how it was to work with me. I suggest that you also should probe for negative feedback and doubt from your clients since they will generally avoid these. Based on what Kevin says, I make treatment recommendations regarding who to see (am I the best choice?), what kind of therapy (a combination of individual, group, and couple therapy) is most appropriate, and what kind of challenges he is likely to face. If he will see me, I establish a specific treatment contract that includes the frequency of the treatment and the *minimum* number of sessions. I usually ask the client to commit to at least 10 sessions, after which I ask him and myself whether we are on the right track and determine what, if any, modifications are needed. Agreeing on a specific number of sessions is important because it gives the client a sense of control, it helps him understand that he will not be in therapy forever, and it helps keep him in treatment when he wants to leave. Together, we set a reasonable treatment goal. Maybe, as a first step, the initial goal is calling someone or going for a walk before acting out to develop some control.

Midtreatment

The relationship themes elucidated during the evaluation unfold during midtreatment, which is the sessions between the evaluation and termination. During midtreatment, clients often vacillate between feeling very close to and distant from me. I find that three interdependent themes predominate during this period: the client seeking immediate relief while I try to strengthen the alliance, keeping the client in treatment, and dealing with shame. Let us look at these one by one.

Establishing an Alliance/Establishing Immediate Relief

During session 11, Kevin tells me that psychotherapy is a "soft science," and that there are no clear indications that it works. "Either way," he says, "You get your money." I ask him how he feels telling me this. He pauses and says, "I don't mean to hurt your feelings, but you want me to be honest, and that's honest." Again, I ask him how he feels telling me this. "Scared," he replies. He responds to my quizzical expression by saying, "I know you have helped me, but I keep getting the sense that this could all just end." After a pause, I say, "Just like your dad" and watch his eyes water. When I point out that it is okay to feel sad, that it will bring us closer not push us farther apart, Kevin looks stunned and says, "What a foreign concept."

I hope you can now see how I approach treatment as a relationship that ultimately invokes the dynamics of the client's world of other relationships. When the therapeutic alliance is strong, therapy is a safe forum for the client to play out his issues. He sees his interpersonal behavior more clearly and practices making different choices. Here, Kevin risks expressing anger to me via hostility. Many children become angry with their parents but when the presence of the parents seems tenuous, the anger will not be expressed. There is a fear that the parents can be destroyed. This becomes a template for all relationships, and the unexpressed anger fuels acting out. He needs to learn that feeling emotions such as anger will enrich his life, not damage it.

Keeping the Client in Treatment

> Kevin misses session 14 without a call, then returns the next week only to say that he has decided to end therapy because he "has nothing else to talk about and feels better." I recall that during the last session, for the first time, I had discussed his father in depth.

In most cases, the relationship that I forge with the client will be the most honest, intimate, revealing relationship he has ever had. Often, the client will work hard to keep the exchanges intellectual since he is frightened of the vulnerability that being "seen" evokes. As his relationship deepens with me, he feels the emotions against which he so diligently defended. Fears emerge regarding how deep or bottomless the emotions may be. The client often feels that his painful emotions will go on forever. A hint of sadness or anger portends a terrifying loss of control.

To help the client have enough confidence in his ability to not be overwhelmed by his emotional experiences, it is important to be aware of his pace. Before going into dark places, ask "headlight" questions such as, "What would it be like to talk about that?" "What might happen in here if you cry?" "What is your concern about how I might judge you when you reveal that?" and "What is the most frightening part of telling me about this?" These questions prepare the client to discuss difficult issues and provide him with that needed sense of control.

Working Through Shame

> Kevin looks different as he presents for session 16. Instead of sitting back confidently on the couch with his legs casually crossed, he perches at the edge. As opposed to his usual unflinching gaze, his eye contact is fleeting, and he looks like a scared little boy. During the session, he talks about the pain of hurting his wife, and how he increasingly feels that he is not a real man as he "let down a good woman." At the end of the session, as he stands up, Kevin blurts out, "I want you to know that as a teenager I had sex with another boy."

No matter how defended, there is always some element of shame in sexually compulsive men. Shame can be understood as condemning the person, while guilt condemns the behavior. While it is important for the client to feel healthy guilt, which serves as a curb against harmful behaviors, shame often triggers further acting out. Like Adams and Robinson (2001), who note that shame is the "primary feeling the addict is trying to medicate, rework and compensate for" (p. 26), I find that sexually compulsive men *subject themselves* to intense shame. In this way, shame can be both a product of CSB and a trigger for it.

Expressions of shame tend to emerge later in the therapy because they both require and elicit deep vulnerability. The client must trust me with previously unmentioned memories. Often, he has told no one about these memories. Shame can change the very way the client interacts with me. In the evaluation phase, the interactions may feel like sparring as themes of control and power predominate. There is a palpable difference when the client becomes more vulnerable. I expect longer pauses and increased sensitivity to my nonverbal responses as he tries to discern my judgments. Often, I ask him what response he anticipates and wonder whether he expects me to judge him as he judges himself.

To complicate matters, men have learned that they should not express certain emotions, so the very feelings dislodged by the therapy can intensify the shame. Sadness, especially if it involves crying, is a usual suspect, although fear and in some cases unexpected anger can also produce shame. In this way, many men who have lost control of their sexual behavior experience shame as a meta-emotion, an emotional response to other feelings. They are adept at judging and have strong beliefs about what feelings are tolerable. As one of our clients stated, "I'm afraid of the emotions. Fear is the doubt that anyone will like the real person behind the façade. The difficulty comes from accepting myself, warts and all."

It is not unusual for the client to again lose control of his sexual behavior during this period, although often it is not as severe (e.g., the person is able to limit his behavior to online sexual activities). While initial gains are commonly made during the beginning of treatment, the shame generated by uncovering feelings and their attendant memories produces the exact type of affective responses warded off by the sexual behavior. Remember that the client engaged in his sexual behavior for a reason, and in many respects, the behavior worked all too well. By predicting this type of situation during the evaluation, you can now tell the client, "You just had a slip. If we can understand it, it will be an isolated event—a lapse not a relapse." This is a time when I might recommend that the client increase the number of people he tells about his issues and garner more support. Alternatively, he might consider increasing the frequency of his therapy or adding other adjunctive supportive activities that might not already be in place, such as group or couple therapy.

The End Game/Transition

> Kevin discusses the day his mother died. She was on a trip abroad and died unexpectedly after, he believes, not receiving adequate medical care. Kevin has told me this story before but always with anger. Today, he looks sad. I comment on the sadness, and he cries. In nearly a year of treatment, this is the first time he has fully cried. I ask what it is like to cry in front of me, and he says, "I'm scared to death. I'm scared you'll be angry or tell me to stop it." I sit quietly as Kevin recounts the phone call informing him of his mother's death, having to go through her clothes, never being able to say goodbye, and his new recognition of how alone he was during that time. When I observe that he stayed sad throughout the story, that he kept going, he exhales and says, "That stuff has been in there a long time. It feels good to tell you about it."

When to end treatment is perhaps the most difficult decision to make. Like many of these men, Kevin has a history of being emotionally abandoned.

However, he learns that by experiencing his feelings he is soothing and not abandoning himself. He can tolerate situations that he previously perceived as overwhelming. He will need to have some control in how we move toward the end. It is often the case that therapy is gradually decreased with the understanding that it can be increased as needed. This is also when groups can be extremely helpful as the client generalizes the relationship he has established with me.

At this point, the therapy also changes qualitatively. Sessions move from more problem-oriented content—in which treatment is a necessary condition for change—to self-growth in which treatment is an optional condition for change. For termination to be indicated, the client must display significantly greater comfort in his feelings and in the dynamics of relationships. He must take an inward focus and acknowledge what he feels. He will look *less* to others for approval. When the question of ending treatment arises, he applies his new ability to slow down and look at his feelings. My task is to respect his growing ability to make healthy autonomous decisions and allow him to leave without having to destroy the relationship. Stopping treatment too early and too late both run risks. The former can lead to quick relapse, and the latter can foster dependence. I believe that consultation with a colleague about when and how to end is helpful. Here are the criteria that I use about ending a treatment:

- Can the client use relationships to bolster his own self-soothing?
- Can the client feel his emotions and be more present in his life?
- Does he seem to have a realistic idea of the course ahead?

Soothing Not Using

The first termination criterion is whether the client seems to have learned that relationships can be soothing, that being with another person actually makes him feel better. I echo Leedes's (2001) assertion that, "As comfort towards interpersonal relationships increases, the power of objectified fantasies is diminished" (p. 223). Sexually compulsive men tend to view interpersonal relationships as a means to an end, as a tool to fix their needs. The other person is little more than a prop to be used. In his former relationship model, there was little risk because there was little investment. His relationships were designed to keep feelings limited in intensity and scope.

The therapeutic relationship, in contrast, involves vulnerability and feeling intensely. It provides a safe place to be emotional. Having stayed in the room and engaged the process, the client has experienced feelings previously avoided. He has learned how it feels to be emotionally connected to another person—to me—and how sharing feelings is profoundly soothing, an experience that was previously unimaginable. As Levine (1992) explained, "psychological intimacy soothes the soul. ... Both people feel an inner peace" (p. 45). Once the client has experienced the benefits of relating to another person, relationships outside the room feel different. Suddenly, he notices what it feels like to be distant from his partner. He is aware of when there is and is not an emotional connection. He does not have to rely on scraping by on extremely limited, sex-focused interactions. He is no longer satisfied with "just sex."

Feeling the Feelings

Think of a time you have been very angry or sad. Remember how you experienced the emotion: the force in your body, the intensity. When a client is ready to leave therapy, he will want to fully experience his emotions as he discusses situations in his life. He will be able to tell you when he is angry, sad, guilty, happy or anxious and correctly label the emotion (e.g., not "angry" when he tears up or sad when he is anxious). As discussed above, CSB blocks the full experience of emotions, so if the client is still uncomfortable with them or misreads *himself* he is very vulnerable to relapse. It is critical to remember that CSB is typically not about the sex. It is about blocking intimacy. If the behavior has stopped but the client still veers away from feeling his emotions in the room with you, then it is unlikely that he will stay in remission. Conversely, if the client can look you in the eye and accurately tell you what he is feeling, then he can likely tolerate the storms and stresses of life and the emotions that accompany them without resorting to CSB to block his experience.

The Course Ahead

If termination is indicated, I try to help the client realistically appraise the course ahead—the likely challenges to be faced, the potentials for relapse, and the red flags pointing to a need to resume treatment. It is also important to predict and explore the many difficult feelings that are inherent in returning to therapy. Sometimes, in those least likely to ask for help, scheduling "check-in" sessions far in advance helps them to feel the therapist's presence more constantly even prior to the visit. When the client is determined to leave without as much progress as is optimal, I need to keep in mind that it is better to lose the battle than the war. Even if a bit premature, an ending that is planned and discussed rather than impulsive greatly increases the likelihood that the client will return.

Relapse is a key hazard on the road ahead. The client will have urges to act out again. If he becomes self-punitive over a slip, he is much more vulnerable to relapse. However, if he notices the urges and wonders, "Why now?" they may not throw him into a tailspin. The goal is to understand. Part of relapse prevention is learning to accept mistakes. Of course, the exact nature of the slip is critical, and while therapeutically I may understand it, the client's partner may not. Here, a few sessions of couple therapy may help them both decide the severity of the episode and whether they can get back on track.

SUMMARY

From the time I began to write this chapter and the time you read it, I have become better at the process I just explained. I now understand better what I do and why I do it. In this sense, I am grateful to you for enabling me to grow professionally. I know that just like my clients will never be perfect people, I will never be a perfect therapist or truly finished in my quest to understand the sources and the effective therapy techniques for sexually acting out. I also must learn to value the journey as much as the outcome.

Accompanying these men in therapy is not easy. I have to listen to my head and heart amidst raw, primitive emotions. As you immerse yourself in this important arena, try not to be overly concerned with mistakes. I make many of them, as will you. If the client feels let down, he feels let down. I accept his feelings and try to understand the parallels to other relationships in his present or past. If the difficulties can be tolerated in the therapy between us, he will have experienced an important model for tolerating other difficulties in his current or future family.

Whether it is a steady or an interrupted course of treatment, the client's relationship with me is real. By maintaining a caring relationship through both easy and difficult disclosures, I indirectly ameliorate his fears of being seen and his need to stay hidden. He learns to experience a wider range of deeper emotions and to be in control of, instead of being controlled by, them. Paradoxically, the client may find that what he has so assiduously avoided is what he needs the most. He replaces despair with hope. Both client and therapist must be willing to experience the risks and rewards of being intimately involved with another person for there to be a real relationship. When this happens, the client is changed forever. This is quite a weighty responsibility. I hope I never forget, however, that therapy is not a one-way street. I, a fellow human, am also changed by my relationship with him. This, of course, is the private joy of being a psychotherapist. I hope that you will soon find a similar contentment as you take care of men who long to be freed from their sexually acting out behaviors.

REFERENCES

Adams, M. A., & Robinson, W. R. (2001). Shame reduction, affect regulation, and sexual boundary development: Essential building blocks of sexual addiction treatment. *Sexual Addiction and Compulsivity, 8*, 45–78. This is an excellent article, especially regarding how attachment affects the capacity to tolerate affect, a skill so critical to sexually compulsive men.

American Psychiatric Association. (1994). *Diagnostic and statistical manual of mental disorders* (4th ed.). Washington, DC: Author.

American Psychiatric Association. (2000). *Diagnostic and statistical manual of mental disorders* (4th ed., text rev.). Washington, DC: Author.

Baum, M. D., & Fishman, J. M. (1994). AIDS, sexual compulsivity and gay men: A group treatment approach. In S. A. Cadwell, R. Burnham, & M. Forstein (Eds.), *Therapists on the front line: Psychotherapy with gay men in the age of AIDS.* Arlington, VA: American Psychiatric Press.

Cooper, A. (1998). Sexually compulsive behavior. *Contemporary Sexuality, 32*(4), 1–3. This is a brief summary of sexual compulsivity. The late Dr. Cooper paved the road for many practitioners in this field and provided critically valuable services to many patients. He was coauthor of the original version of this chapter.

Cooper, A. (Ed.). (2000). *Cybersex and sexual compulsivity: The dark side of the force.* New York: Taylor and Francis.

Coughlin Della Selva, P., & Malan, D. (1996). *Intensive short-term dynamic psychotherapy: Theory and technique synopsis.* London: Karnac.

Delmonico, D. L., & Carnes, P. J. 1999. Virtual sex addiction: Why cybersex becomes the drug of choice. *Cyberpsychology and Behavior, 2*, 457–464.

Freeman-Longo, R. E., & Blanchard, G. T. (1998). *Sexual abuse in America: Epidemic of the 21st century*. Brandon, VT: Safe Society Press. This excellent book explores factors contributing to sexual abuse and sexual offenders. It also offers suggestions for treatment; both on an individual and a societal level.

Freud, S. (1954). The dynamics of transference. In J. Strachey (Ed. & Trans.), *The standard edition of the complete psychological works of Sigmund Freud* (Vol. 12, pp. 97–108). London: Hogarth Press. (Original work published 1912)

Goodman, A. (2001). What's in a name? Terminology for designating a syndrome of driven sexual behavior. *Sexual Addiction and Compulsivity, 8*, 191–213. This article does a very good job of outlining the pros and cons of the various terms, such as sexual addiction, sexual compulsion, and so on, and the treatment ramifications.

Kafka, M. P. (2000). The paraphilia-related disorders: Nonparaphilic hypersexuality and sexual compulsivity/addiction. In S. R. Leiblum & R. C. Rosen (Eds.), *Principles and practices of sex therapy* (3rd ed.). Kafka is another leader of the field who also offers valuable issues to be considered in the assessment and treatment of sexual compulsivity. Kafka's work is a "must read" for clinicians who want to be grounded in the literature.

Leedes, R. (2001). The three most important criteria in diagnosing sexual addictions: Obsession, obsession, and obsession. *Sexual Addiction and Compulsivity, 8*, 215–226. This is helpful to read in conjunction with the Goodman (2001) article to get a different perspective.

Levine, S. B. (1992). *Sexual life: A clinician's guide*. New York: Plenum Press. This is a well-written, comprehensive book on sexuality and outlines several of the most common issues faced by those working in this field.

Line, B., & Cooper, A. (2002). Group therapy: Essential component for success with sexually acting out problems among men. *Sexual Addiction and Compulsivity: Journal of Treatment and Prevention, 9*, 15–32. This article provides a detailed description of a successful group program for men with CSB. It is valuable to those who are interested in starting a group.

Neborsky, R. J., McCullough, L., Shapiro, F., Malan, D., & Solomon, M. F. (2001). *Short-term therapy for long-term change*. New York: Norton.

Prochaska, J. O., Norcross, J., & DiClemente, C. (1994). *Changing for good: A revolutionary six-step program for overcoming bad habits and moving your life forward*. New York. Avon Books. Buy this, read it, and be happy to have it on your bookshelf. You will use it often.

Schwartz, M. F., & Masters, W. H. (1994). Integration of trauma-based, cognitive, behavioral, systemic, and addiction approaches for treatment of hypersexual pair-bonding disorder. *Sexual Addiction and Compulsivity, 1*, 57–76.

SUGGESTED READING

Amparano, J. (1998, September 25). Sex addicts get help. *The Arizona Republic*, p. 1.

Byrne, D., & Osland, J. A. (2000). Sexual fantasy and erotica/pornography: Internal and external imagery. In L. T. Szuchman & F. Muscarella (Eds.), *Psychological perspectives on human sexuality* (pp. 283–305). New York: Wiley.

Carnes, P. (1989). *Contrary to love: Helping the sexual addict.* New York: Bantam. Carnes is one of the leaders of the field, and this is one of the core books on these issues.

Cooper, A., Boies, S., Maheu, M., & Greenfield, D. (1999). Sexuality and the Internet: The next sexual revolution. In F. Muscarella & L. Szuchman (Eds.), *The psychological science of sexuality: A research based approach* (pp. 519–545). New York: Wiley.

Cooper, A., Delmonico, D., & Burg, R. (2000). Cybersex users and abusers: New findings and their implications. *Sexual Addiction and Compulsivity: Journal of Treatment and Prevention, 7,* 5–29. This is a research article with findings on online sexual compulsivity.

Cooper, A., Griffin-Shelley, E., Delmonico, D., & Mathy, R. (2001). Online sexual problems: Assessment and predictive variables. *Sexual Addiction and Compulsivity: Journal of Treatment and Prevention, 8,* 267–285. This article provides clinicians with several factors found to be correlated with online sexual problems.

Cooper, A., McLoughlin, I., & Campbell, K. (2000). Sexuality in cyberspace: Update for the 21st century. *Cyberpsychology and Behavior, 3,* 521–536. This is a helpful review of online sexuality.

Cooper, A., Putnam, D., Planchon, L., & Boies, S. (1999). Online sexual compulsivity: Getting tangled in the net. *Sexual Addiction and Compulsivity: Journal of Treatment and Prevention, 6*(2), 79–104. This article received an award for excellence from the journal.

Cooper, A., Scherer, C., Boies, S., & Gordon, B. (1999). Sexuality and the Internet: From sexual exploration to pathological expression. *Professional Psychology, 30*(2), 154–164. This research article details findings of the first large-scale study of Internet sexuality. It also has some interesting suggestions on implications for public policy.

Cooper, A., Scherer, C., & Marcus, D. (2002). Harnessing the power of the Internet to improve sexual relationships. In A. Cooper (Ed.), *Sex and the Internet: A guidebook for clinicians.* New York: Brunner-Routledge. This chapter provides a look at some ways the Internet can be used to facilitate therapy and enhance sexuality.

Herring, B. (2001). Ethical guidelines in the treatment of compulsive sexual behavior. *Sexual Addiction and Compulsivity, 8,* 13–22.

Kafka, M. P. (1997). A monoamine hypothesis for the pathophysiology of paraphilic disorders. *Archives of Sexual Behavior, 26,* 505–526.

Strupp, H. H., & Binder, J. L. (1984). *Psychotherapy in a new key: A guide to time-limited dynamic psychotherapy.* New York: Basic Books. This book does a wonderful job of discussing how the relationship plays out in dynamic psychotherapy. It explains how an individual's history, presenting complaint, and the experience of the therapy relationship combine to provide a powerful tool for change.

Twenty-Three

Paraphilic Worlds

J. PAUL FEDOROFF, MD

INTRODUCTION

Of psychiatric disorders, none evoke such an immediate emotionally negative visceral reaction as the paraphilias. This is a shame since having a paraphilia is *not* synonymous with being a sex offender and since having been a sex offender is *not* synonymous with being a future sex offender, especially if treated with modern techniques. About a decade ago, I coauthored an article in which I listed a series of myths and misconceptions about sex offenders (Fedoroff & Moran, 1997). On the basis of the empirical evidence available at the time, I recommended either dismissing or revising the following nine statements about sex offenders:

1. Sex offenders are all socially deprived men.
2. Sex offenders are the result of childhood abuse.
3. Sex offenders should not masturbate.
4. Sex offenders have too much testosterone.
5. Sex offenders cannot be cured.
6. Sex offenders always lie to stay out of treatment.
7. Sex offenders are sex maniacs.
8. Public notification of sex offender release protects the community.
9. Sex offenders are all the same.

A lot has happened since I wrote that article, but the myths have persisted. In this chapter, my aim is to provide some suggestions for nonspecialists about how to care for men and women with paraphilias. Since my recommendations are based on both my review of the literature and my clinical experience, let me first tell you a bit about myself.

I began university study as a philosophy student fascinated with Descartes' "mind–body" problem. In the process of exploring how thoughts can influence physiology and vice versa, I switched to psychology, then medicine, then (after a brief stint as a family physician), to psychiatry, then neuropsychiatry, and finally to forensic psychiatry, in which I now specialize in problems that involve the ultimate mind–body interactions: the paraphilias.

I am currently director of one of the world's most well-known clinics for the treatment of problematic sexual behaviors, the Sexual Behaviors Clinic (SBC) of the Royal Ottawa Health Care Group. I take no credit for the SBC's fame since it was world renowned before I got here. The SBC is academic, provides teaching and education, conducts research, is fully affiliated with the University of Ottawa, and receives referrals from eastern Ontario, including some of the most "high-risk" sex offenders in Canada. The SBC is multidisciplinary and (in no particular order of importance) includes nurses, social workers, psychologists, occupational therapists, and psychiatrists. Our staff has been consulted by programs around the world for advice about how to organize their practices.

The SBC conducts both assessments and treatment, often simultaneously. This sometimes comes as a surprise to visitors, who have been indoctrinated into thinking that sex offenders cannot be treated until they have been sentenced or fully confessed all their crimes. In fact, there is no evidence to support those beliefs. I have found that, for the most part, men accused of sex crimes become enthusiastic participants in therapy once they understand that the aim of therapy is to help them as opposed to being some form of punishment or clever way to extract information from them.

Although the SBC does pretrial and presentence assessments on men in custody, and although it has a special treatment unit within the provincial correctional system, the SBC is primarily an outpatient clinic. This is because paraphilic disorders per se do not require inpatient treatment unless accompanied by other serious diseases. The SBC has arguably been successful (e.g., no known new hands-on sexual reoffenses for outpatients entered into the full SBC treatment program in the past 8 years).

All case vignettes in this chapter, while clinically accurate, are fictitious.

About 25 years ago, I was a psychiatry resident at Johns Hopkins Hospital (Baltimore, MD) on a general psychiatry ward. A woman was admitted with severe depression. Her depression resolved quickly, but she was increasingly perplexed. Something was wrong, so I delayed her discharge. In a private interview with me, she responded by disclosing that she had initially sought treatment because she had erotic thoughts about her pastor, who was a woman. She had kept a voluminous diary that would have shocked the Marquis de Sade himself. It documented sadistic fantasies involving her pastor's torture and dismemberment. I asked her why she had kept this to herself. Her answer: "I think I might be lesbian, and I am so ashamed."

I described what I had learned to my attending physician and was advised to consult one of the most renowned experts in paraphilias: Dr. John Money. Fortunately, his office was nearby in the research section of the hospital. I told him about the "case." I gave him a copy of the diary (with the patient's permission). Dr. Money asked me what I thought about the case. I recall saying something about how surprised I was that the patient seemed more upset about being lesbian than about being a sadist. Dr. Money was kind enough to invite me to attend his weekly invitation-only, bring-your-own-lunch seminars in his museum-like office. The meetings were a forum for sexology experts to discuss what they were working on, what they were thinking about, and why. "You might learn something," Dr. Money had said. It turned out, I received 5 years of mentorship, and in the process I did learn a thing or two.

GENDER VERSUS ORIENTATION VERSUS SEXUAL INTEREST

Both patients and professionals often confuse three different concepts: gender, sexual orientation, and sexual interest. *Gender identity* describes how "male" or "female" you feel. *Gender role* is the sexual role (or stereotypes) you present to the public. *Sexual orientation* describes the gender role to which you feel romantically attracted. Epidemiologists who distinguish between "gay men" and "men who have sex with men" recognize the fact that orientation reflects romantic attachment rather than simple sexual activity. This means that gender identity and sexual orientation are on independent orthogonal dimensions to *sexual interests*, including the paraphilias.

Unfortunately, until recently, researchers and clinicians have confused the immutability of gender identity and sexual orientation with the transformability of sexual interest. This has led to the misconception that paraphilias cannot be treated with sufficient effectiveness to eliminate evidence of the disease. Dr. Money may have contributed to the confusion when he coined the term *lovemaps* to describe the individualized set of idealized conditions each person develops that are maximally interesting in terms of forming an erotic and romantic bond (Money, 1986). Dr. Money believed that paraphilias represented "vandalized" lovemaps resulting from some disorder of development, with onset around age 8. It is notable that he referred to lovemaps and not sex maps. This is because Dr. Money was thinking of "pair bonding" when he described lovemaps. As a result, at the time I started to learn about paraphilias, I was taught that they were incurable disorders, and that the best that could be hoped for was management of a condition that with luck would not deteriorate. Things have changed to the point at which I now routinely tell new patients their prognosis is excellent, and that they can expect to have no evidence of disease in less than a year.

BEGINNING THEORIES

The etiology of paraphilic sexual disorders is unknown. Given their diverse and variable presentation, it is unlikely that a single cause will ever be found. Instead of clinging to a single explanation, I recommend considering every case from four complementary perspectives. The disease perspective is based on the premise that there is a broken part due to a pathophysiologic event (e.g., a brain lesion). The behavioral perspective is based on the premise that problems can arise from faulty learned associations (e.g., a fetish resulting from association of a specific odor with orgasm). The dimensional perspective is used to explain pathologic variations as simply the extreme variation of normal distribution (e.g., sadism may be an extreme expression of dominance). The life story perspective acknowledges that people by nature assign meaning in an attempt to understand (e.g., a person with masochism may decide that their sexual preference was determined by being spanked as a child). These perspectives and their historical importance in thinking about the paraphilias are discussed in more detail elsewhere (Fedoroff, 2009). The important point is that all four perspectives have strengths and weaknesses and are best used in combination (McHugh & Slavney, 1983).

John Money argued that humans are genetically programmed to develop both before and after birth but with "critical periods" during which time changes somehow became "hardwired." For example, every human child who undergoes normal embryologic development is born with the potential to speak any of the world's 6,700 existent spoken languages. The language the child eventually speaks is determined within the first few years of life by the child's environment—typically the language of the child's caretakers. Once the language is learned, it becomes the child's "mother tongue." From that moment, the mother tongue determines how the child thinks, what words the child can understand, and with whom and in what manner the child interacts.

Similarly, when children are born, they have the potential to develop a wide range of sexual interests, including paraphilic ones. Until recently, it was thought that once sexual interest is determined, it is hardwired just like the child's mother tongue. John Money argued that paraphilias are as unchangeable as language, gender, or sexual orientation.

Let us think about that. Language can be modified by learning new words, new phrases, and when and where to say different things. Entire new languages can be acquired. Although gender identity and sexual orientation are resistant to change, these personality characteristics are fundamentally different from sexual interest, which can change but does so with regularity. In the last 5 years, there has been a paradigm shift from conceptualizing the paraphilias as disorders characterized by unchangeable deviant sexual interests to disorders in which consensual sexual interests have failed to develop (Marshall, Marshall, Serran, & Fernandez, 2006). This has changed the way I approach paraphilic disorders, and in this chapter I provide some tips on how to successfully treat them.

What Are We Talking About?

In the *DSM-IV-TR* (*Diagnostic and Statistical Manual of Mental Disorders, Fourth Edition, Text Revision*; American Psychiatric Association [APA], 2000), the paraphilias represent a subcategory of psychiatric disorders that fall under the umbrella term of "sexual disorders." There are four categories of sexual disorders: sexual dysfunctions, gender identity disorders, sexual disorders NOS (not otherwise specified; such as distress about sexual orientation), and the paraphilias. According to the *DSM-IV-TR,* the essential feature of paraphilic disorders is the presence of recurrent, intense sexually arousing fantasies, sexual urges, or behaviors generally involving nonhuman objects; the actual suffering or humiliation of oneself or one's partner, children, or other nonconsenting persons; or any combination of these. It should be noted that the editor of the *DSM-IV-TR* (APA, 2000) has admitted that the published criteria contain a mistake since it was never intended that the diagnosis could be made "solely on the basis of history of repeated acts of sexual violence" (First & Frances, 2008).

The latest version of the American Psychiatric Association catalogue of psychiatric disorders lists only eight paraphilias (with an additional NOS category). In the *DSM-IV-TR* (APA, 2000), paraphilic disorders that may involve criminal acts (exhibitionism, frotteurism, pedophilia, sexual sadism, and voyeurism) all have a category B criterion that states: "The person has acted on these sexual urges, or the sexual urges or fantasies caused marked distress or interpersonal difficulty" (p. 569). In contrast, the paraphilias that are less likely to be associated with criminal acts (fetishism, sexual masochism, and transvestic fetishism) have a category B criteria that states: "The fantasies, sexual urges, or behaviors cause clinically significant distress or impairment in social, occupational, or other important areas of functioning" (p. 570).

The *DSM-IV-TR* (APA, 2000) definitions may seem cumbersome but can be simplified by noting that paraphilic disorders generally involve sex that precludes the possibility of a consensual, mutually reciprocal relationship. A more comprehensive list of paraphilias, including *International Statistical Classification of Diseases and Related Health Problems, 10th Revision* (*ICD-10*, 1992) paraphilic disorders, is provided in Table 23.1. Many of these

Table 23.1   Paraphilias

Paraphilia	DSM-IV-TR	ICD-10	Essential feature: Persistent sexual arousal toward	Comments
Abasiophilia	302.9	F65.9	Disability	
Acoustophilia	302.9	F65.9	Sounds	
Acrophilia	302.9	F65.9	Heights	
Acrotomophilia	302.9	F65.9	Amputees	
Agorophobia	302.9	F65.9	Fighting	Typically observing
Agrexophilia	302.9	F65.9	Being heard having sex	
Algolagnia (philia)	302.9	F65.9	Pain	Typically genital pain
Amaurophilia	302.9	F65.9	Blindness	
Anasteemaphilia	302.9	F65.9	Height difference	
Andromimetophilia	302.9	F65.9	Woman with male features	*See also* Gynemetophilia
Anthropophagy	302.9	F65.9	Eating human flesh	
Apotemnophilia	302.9	F65.9	Being an amputee	Also known as body integrity identity disorder or amputee identity disorder
Arachnephilia	302.9	F65.9	Spiders	
Asphyxiophilia	302.9	F65.9	Being asphyxiated	Also known as autoerotic (self-) asphyxia
Autoagonistophilia	302.9	F65.9	Being on display	
Autoassassinophilia	302.9	F65.9	Being hunted	Also known as phygephilia
Autoabasiophilia	302.9	F65.9	Being crippled/ handicapped	
Autophagy	302.9	F65.9	Self-ingestion/cannibalism	
Autonepiophilia	302.9	F65.9	Diapers	
Biastophilia	302.9	F65.9	Nonconsensual adult intercourse	Also known as paraphilic rapism or raptophilia
Candaulism	302.9	F65.9	Spouse with another partner	
Catheterophilia	302.9	F65.9	Catheterization	
Chrematistiophilia	302.9	F65.9	Sex for money	
Chronophilia	302.9	F65.9	Age discrepancy	
Claustrophilia	302.9	F65.9	Being confined	
Coprophilia	302.9	F65.9	Feces	
Dacryphilia	302.9	F65.9	Emotional distress	
Dendrophillia	302.9	F65.9	Trees or foliage	
Dermatophilia	302.9	F65.9	Skin	Typically leather or animal skin/fur
Dippoldism	302.9	F65.9	Spanking children	Sometimes refers to sadism by proxy
Doraphilia	302.9	F65.9	Smell or feel of animal skin/fur	*See also* Dermatophilia
Ecouteurism	302.9	F65.9	Overhearing sex	
Emetophilia	302.9	F65.9	Vomiting	
Ephebophilia			Youth	

Continued

Table 23.1   Paraphilias (*Continued*)

Paraphilia	DSM-IV-TR	ICD-10	Essential feature: Persistent sexual arousal toward	Comments
Erotophonophilia	302.9	F65.9	Murder	
Exhibitionism	302.4	F65.2	Exposure to strangers	
Fetishism	302.81	F65.0	Inanimate objects	Excludes "sex toys"
Formicophilia	302.9	F65.9	Insects	Technically ants; entomophilia refers to insects
Frotteurism	302.89	F65.8	Rubbing groin against others without consent	*ICD* has no specific listing
Gerontophilia	302.9	F65.9	Elderly	
Gonyphilia	302.9	F65.9	Knees	Typically female knees
Gynemimetophilia	302.9	F65.9	Males with breasts	
Harpaxophilia	302.9	F65.9	Being robbed or burglarized	
Hebephilia			Young adults	Also known as nymphophilia
Hierophilia	302.9	F65.9	Religious object	
Hodophilia	302.9	F65.9	Travel to foreign places	
Homeovestism	302.9	F65.9	Same sex clothing	
Homilophilia	302.9	F65.9	Religious speeches/ sermons	
Hoplophilia	302.9	F65.9	Guns	
Hybristophiia	302.9	F65.9	Criminals	
Hygrophilia	302.9	F65.9	Body fluids	
Hyphephilia	302.9	F65.9	Fabrics	
Iatronudia	302.9	F65.9	Medical doctors	
Infantalism			Wearing diapers/being treated as an infant	Also known as autonepiophilia
Infantaphilia	302.2	F65.4	Infants	Also known as nepiophilia
Katoptronophia	302.9	F65.9	Mirrors	
Kleptophilia	302.9	F65.9	Stealing	
Klismaphilia	302.9	F65.9	Receiving enemas	
Lactaphilia	302.9	F65.9	Lactation	
Maieusiophilia	302.9	F65.9	Pregnancy	
Mask fetishism	302.9	F65.9	Masks or mask removal	
Melissophilia	302.9	F65.9	Bee stings	
Morphophilia	302.9	F65.9	Discrepancy in size of sex partner(s)	Also known as dysmorphophilia
Mysophilia	302.9	F65.9	"Filth"	Typically involving "soiled" (worn) panties
Nanophilia	302.9	F65.9	Short partner	
Narratophilia	302.9	F65.9	Erotic talk	
Necrobestialism	302.9	F65.9	Dead animals	
Necrophilia	302.9	F65.9	Corpses	
Nosophilia	302.9	F65.9	Terminal illness	
Odaxelagnia	302.9	F65.9	Biting	
Olphactophilia	302.9	F65.9	Odors	

Table 23.1 Paraphilias (*Continued*)

Paraphilia	DSM-IV-TR	ICD-10	Essential feature: Persistent sexual arousal toward	Comments
Omorashi	302.9	F65.9	Full bladder	Also known as bladder desperation
Partialism			A single body part	
Pecattiphilia	302.9	F65.9	Sin	
Pedophilia				
Attraction				
Males				
Females				
Both				
Exclusivity				
Incest only				
Exclusive				
Nonexclusive	302.2	F65.4		*ICD* does not differentiate
Phobophilia	302.9	F65.9	Fear	
Picquerism	302.9	F65.9	Stabbing	Also "piquerism"
Pictophilia	302.9	F65.9	Photographs	
Pseudozoophilia	302.9	F65.9	Partner pretending to be an animal	Also describes act of pretending to be an animal for sexual arousal
Psychrocism	302.9	F65.9	Being cold or freezing	
Public masturbation			Masturbation in public	No wish to be seen/also known as agoraphilia (sex in public)
Pygmalionism	302.9	F65.9	Statues	Also known as statuephilia/ agalmatophilia
Pyrophilia	302.9	F65.9	Fire	
Rhabdophilia	302.9	F65.9	Being flagellated	
Saliromania	302.9	F65.9	Physical degradation of appearance	
Salirophilia	302.9	F65.9	Perspiration	
Scoptic syndrome	302.9	F65.9	Being castrated	
Scoptophilia	302.9	F65.9	Consensual viewing	
Sexual masochism	302.83	F65.5	Loss of control	*ICD* combines into sadomasochism
Sexual sadism	302.84	F65.5	Nonconsensual control	
Somnophilia	302.9	F65.9	Sleeping sexual partner	
Stethnolagnia	302.9	F65.9	Female body building	
Stigmatophilia	302.9	F65.9	Piercings/tattoos/uniforms	
Stitophilia	302.9	F65.9	Food	
Symphorohilia	302.9	F65.9	Disasters	
Taphophilia	302.9	F65.9	Being buried alive	Also sexual excitement from cemeteries
Telephone scatalogia	302.9	F65.9	Obscene phone calls	

Continued

Table 23.1   Paraphilias (*Continued*)

Paraphilia	DSM-IV-TR	ICD-10	Essential feature: Persistent sexual arousal toward	Comments
Teratophilia	302.9	F65.9	Deformity	
Thesauromania	302.9	F65.9	Collecting belongings of women	
Timophilia	302.9	F65.9	Wealth or social status	
Toucherism			Nonconsensual groping	*See also* Frotteurism
Transvestic fetishism	302.3	F65.1	Wearing clothes of the opposite sex	±Gender dysphoria; *ICD* does not subclassify
Trichophilia	302.9	F65.1	Hair	
Urophilia	302.9	F65.9	Urine	Also known as urolagnia or undinism
Voyeurism	302.82	F65.3	Spying	
Vampirism			Blood	Also known as hematophilia
Vorarephilia	302.9	F65.9	To physically consume or be consumed	
Xenophilia	302.9	F65.9	Strangers	
Zelophilia	302.9	F65.9	Feeling jealous	
Zoophilia	302.9	F65.9	Animals	
Zoosadism	302.9	F65.9	Harm to animals	
Paraphilia NOS	302.9	F65.9		*ICD*: Disorder of sexual preference unspecified
Other disorders of sexual preference		F65.8		

paraphilics are briefly described elsewhere (Love, 1999). An even more extensive list consisting of 547 entries has been published, although it also includes combination paraphilias (e.g., necropedophilia) and nonparaphilic behaviors (e.g., "zwishenstufe"—"arousal from a person of the same sex") (Aggrawal, 2009).

You will notice in this chapter that I avoid discussion of prevalence of paraphilic disorders. In my opinion, the question is unanswerable since any survey must deal with the fact that people are highly reluctant to disclose unconventional sexual interests, especially to surveyors. Most authors who do venture to propose prevalence rates suggest 1% of the population. Usually, they actually mean 1% of the adult male population. I suspect paraphilic disorders are far more prevalent than 1%, but I also think the prevalence fluctuates; more importantly, we are now able to offer treatment that can change the rate of paraphilic disorders.

ASSESSMENT AND TREATMENT GUIDELINES

I want to outline my suggestions for approaching these complex sexual developmental problems so that you will feel more comfortable in dealing with your initial encounters with these interesting but sometimes concerning problems.

Be Explicit With the Patient/Client About Who Has Retained You

Sadly, people rarely seek help for sexual problems until they think they have no choice. It is very important at the beginning of any assessment to establish why the patient has sought help from you at this time. Besides asking the person this question, ask yourself, "Who is paying for this assessment?" and "To whom will I be reporting the results of this assessment?" If a third party has retained you (e.g., lawyer, children's aid society), you should make sure that the person you are assessing knows this fact.

I receive a written referral from a lawyer whose client is a police officer charged with indecent exposure. According to SBC protocol, I request a referral from his family doctor as well. The reason is that exhibitionists should receive treatment immediately since without treatment the risk of reoffense increases prior to trial (I once saw a man who had been charged subsequently expose himself to a group of women on the courthouse steps following his bail hearing). In addition, I tell the lawyer to send me a copy of the police synopsis or summary of the allegations, a copy of her client's criminal record (including both convictions and charges), and any other information anyone involved in the case thinks may be relevant. I also request a formal retainer letter from the lawyer agreeing to be responsible for my quoted fee schedule.

A few minutes later, I received a faxed summary of the case marked "Highly Confidential." Detective Urskin (all names are fictitious) is age 50, married for a second time, with one daughter from his first marriage (age 20) and two children from his second marriage, a son age 10 and a daughter age 3. He also has two stepdaughters, aged 10 and 13, from his second marriage. He lives with his wife, his stepchildren, and children from his second marriage. He works in an elite homicide investigation unit of the police force and has been decorated for his past accomplishments. On the day in question, Detective Urskin attended a tanning salon during the noon hour on a Sunday when the salon was typically not busy. Following his tanning session, the attendant alleged Detective Urskin walked out of the tanning booth completely naked, approached her, and asked her for a towel. She alleges he had an erection and smiled at her as she fearfully handed him a towel. She said she would not have called the police aside from the fact that her 5-year-old daughter had been with her, and she was frightened for her daughter's safety.

Be Honest About the Limits of Confidentiality

Every province and state in North America has laws requiring professionals to disclose known abuse of children who are identifiable. Although the specifics of the requirements vary between jurisdictions, the principle that professionals must act if a child is at risk is universal. It is important to be honest about your moral, professional, and legal obligations.

I meet the detective the next day and begin the session by telling him that his lawyer has retained me to produce an expert report that will be sent to her. I explain, "If she does not like the report, no one besides her will ever read it. However, if she decides to use the report, then she will send a copy to the prosecution, who will have the right to cross-examine me about anything on which I base my opinions." I also explain, "I have accepted the retainer on the understanding that my opinions may not be helpful to your case, and that I am obliged to be honest about my professional opinion." Following a discussion about disclosure issues, he has the opportunity to read and sign a consent form allowing me to send a report to his lawyer. I tell him that he is welcome to consult with his lawyer at any time in private. He can also discontinue the interview whenever he likes or decline to answer any questions, although I will need to record that fact. Next, I ask him whether he would like me to send a consultation report to his referring physician. I explain that most doctors like to know the results of consultations, but that he may request me simply to send a brief note requesting signed consent before I send a consultation note.

In my clinic, new patients or clients are scheduled to arrive 1 hour before I see them. They are given an extensive questionnaire to complete. On the cover is a caution that advises them that they are not obliged to answer any questions on the form. It also indicates that the SBC complies with provincial laws requiring that I inform the Childrens' Aid Society (CAS) if I am concerned that anyone who is still a child is or may be in danger of emotional, physical, or sexual assault.

The next 45 minutes are spent reviewing the results of the questionnaire to ensure that Detective Urskin understood the questions and that I understand his answers. Included in the information I obtain are the following items: family history (including history of psychiatric disorders, substance abuse, medical and criminal history); birth and early development history (including evidence of genetic conditions, fetal alcohol syndrome, and developmental delay syndromes and childhood conduct disordered behaviors); school and work history (including failures, suspensions, expulsions, firings, and military history, including court martials and dishonorable discharges); marital history and children (including previous encounters with CAS and current degree of contact with children); substance abuse history (including prescribed drugs currently and at the time of the events in question); criminal history (including crimes associated with paraphilic activities, such as "trespass by night" (voyeurism) or "public urination" (exhibitionism); medical history (including history of head trauma, seizures, endocrine disorders, and medications [current and past]); and psychiatric history. There is also a detailed section reviewing sexual issues: how the patient learned about sex, the patient's self-perceived sexual orientation on the Kinsey scale, masturbation and intercourse history, signs and symptoms of sexual dysfunctions (impairments in ability to engage physically in sexual intercourse), signs and symptoms of gender identity disorders, concerns about sexual orientation, and signs and symptoms of paraphilic sexual disorders.

The question of whether the patient was abused as a child is assessed in several ways. Questions about physical, emotional, and sexual abuse are embedded in the body of the questionnaire separate from the sex questions. Separate questions ask about how sex was learned, when the individual first had sexual relations, how old the first sexual partner was, and whether the event was mutually consensual. It is not uncommon for someone not only to report that he or she was never sexually abused but also to indicate that they first had sexual intercourse at age 8 with a 16-year-old babysitter.

After reviewing the intake materials, I always conduct a full mental status exam to assess the person's current mental state and to screen for psychiatric disorders such as major depression, bipolar disorder, schizophrenia, anxiety disorders, or disorders associated with cognitive impairment. Detective Urskin is neatly groomed, looks fit, and is clearly fully alert, if not hypervigilant. I cannot help thinking that anyone who saw him stride into my office would never guess the charges he faces.

Do Not Try to Be a Police Detective

Your job is to assess and treat people who seek your help for specific problems. Although it is important to be thorough and to critically evaluate all the information you can obtain, you are not a detective or a judge. Do not pretend that you are: This will lead to therapeutic mistakes. Some therapists believe it is essential that people with paraphilias (particularly, criminal paraphilias) fully disclose every offense they have ever committed or have thought of committing. This is a waste of time. Exhibitionists may have thousands of victims.

Confessing each one is impossible. Instead, focus on what is happening in the present. There is rarely a lack of material, and it represents issues about which something can be done.

Detective Urskin has taken the full hour to complete the intake questionnaire. On the basis of clinical experience, I know that (after accounting for intellectual disability and dyslexia) the longer people take to complete the intake forms, the more likely it is that they will deny guilt. I think this is because admitters have less to remember and do not have to second-guess the implications of answers. In contrast, deniers (especially those who in fact are guilty) must check to make sure their current story is consistent. This takes time and energy. I ask Detective Urskin my standard question: "Are you guilty?" I am partly right, "Well, what she says is true, but I was not exposing," he says. Together, we review the police synopsis. He agrees that the attendant saw him naked, but insists that she had followed him into the tanning booth and pulled off his towel. He did not recall if he had an erection. He never realized a child had been there.

From a clinical perspective, the detective's assertions seem hard to believe. Rather than challenge them directly, I explain my role to the detective as follows:

You are clearly in a very uncomfortable position, and I know you are accustomed to being on the other side of the desk. I want to remind you that I am neither judge nor jury. I have no idea whose version of what happened is correct or if either is. Fortunately, as far as I am concerned, it does not matter. That is because on the basis of the information available, there are three possibilities. The first is that you have had the misfortune of encountering a woman who engaged (or thinks she engaged) in inappropriate acts with you and then reported you to the police. If that is what happened, you need a lawyer and not a psychiatrist.

The second is that you have personality vulnerabilities that led you to think that the attendant would welcome seeing your unexpected nakedness. You would not be the first I have seen with this problem. You may be surprised to know that people with this problem often have jobs in which they are "in charge," such as police, military, judges, business executives, or physicians. In psychiatric terminology, these people are known as "malignant narcissists" or "psychopaths." If this is the case, then I can help you, but there is no urgency because this is a long-standing problem, and I bet you have dealt with these problems in the past, maybe by switching jobs, cities, or relationships.

The third possibility is that you have exhibitionism, which is a psychiatric condition in which there is sexual arousal from exposing your penis to a nonconsenting person. If that is what you have, then I strongly recommend immediate treatment because most untreated exhibitionists reoffend.

I continue:

As I said, I have no way of knowing which of the three problems you are facing. There are some aspects that make exhibitionism less likely, the most important being that you are alleged to have exposed to someone who had your name on file, making it unlikely that you could escape. Also, most exhibitionists have multiple previous offenses by the time they reach middle age. However, whatever your actual diagnosis is, you have a bigger problem, and that is the fact that you are alleged to have exposed to a child.

Get as Much Information as Possible

Sex is complicated. It usually involves more than one person. The more you know, the better. If there are legal documents (e.g., disclosure of the alleged activities) or previous assessments, ask for them. Many professionals are sometimes confused about their ethical obligations in this area. Although the rules of confidentiality forbid disclosure of information unless a child is at risk, nothing forbids a professional from listening to information provided by others. If your patient's wife calls you because there is something she thinks you should know, listen to her. You may not tell her anything about her husband without permission, but there is no reason why you cannot collect information from her. Whenever a person has a legal sexual partner, it is worthwhile, with permission, to interview the partner in person.

> At this point, I explain to Detective Urskin what the options are, beginning with a more elaborate investigation. I ask him for permission to speak with others who know him well. He tells me that he would prefer I not speak with his wife since he has not told her about the charges. I make a note of this since as a general rule, the more secrets there are, the more likely there will be surprises. I explain to the detective that he is in charge, but if my opinions are based only on what he tells me, the prosecution is certain to notice. I next explain the standard SBC assessment protocol, which consists of four parts.

SBC Assessment Battery

The first part of the SBC assessment protocol is a standard psychiatric interview that allows for the development of a differential diagnosis. Detective Urskin is happy when I tell him that we have already completed that part of the assessment. The second part involves a battery of blood and urine tests to provide a screen for medical conditions. Of particular interest are the following screening tests for endocrine disorders: fasting blood glucose, thyroid-stimulating hormone (TSH), follicle-stimulating hormone (FSH), luteinizing hormone (LH), and free testosterone. Urine tests for illegal substances are not routinely ordered since this conveys the impression that the SBC is in the business of catching liars. The third part involves administration of a battery of standardized self-administered psychological tests. The purpose of asking for the same information in different ways is not to trick anyone but rather to acknowledge that the assessment of problems, explanations, and solutions is a collaborative process. For example, some people may say they have no alcohol-related problems but indicate on a second questionnaire that they have been arrested for driving while impaired.

The fourth investigative tool is penile plethysmography (PPG). This method is based on the observation that penile tumescence is associated (although not perfectly) with sexual arousal. During this procedure, the man being assessed is presented with a variety of stimuli in the form of pictures, videos, or audiotapes while a recording device electronically measures the degree of change in the circumference or volume of the man's penis. To account for the variability in penile responsivity between men, responses across different stimulus sets for each man are compared to produce ratios or differences between maximal response to normal sexual stimuli and responses to abnormal stimuli (typically children or coercive and nonconsensual sexual scenarios). Details of the uses and limitations of PPG testing have been published (Blanchard, Klassen,

Dickey, Kuban, & Blak, 2001; Bourget & Bradford, 2008; Fedoroff, Kuban, & Bradford, 2009).

> I present Detective Urskin with the SBC consent form for the proposed tests. He says that he does not want to do the PPG testing because pornography upsets him. He becomes tearful and whispers that he was the victim of sexual abuse when he was placed in a training school after his parents died. He tells me he has never told anyone about this before. "Why didn't you tell me about this earlier?" I ask. He answers, "I did not trust you." Of course, I am happy that he is speaking in the past tense since by implication his degree of trust has changed. This is common during assessments, and I attribute much of the process to the fact that I avoid confrontation and frequently remind people who seek my assistance that my job is to help them. A routine of asking for consent before proceeding is also helpful. However, in my opinion the most important factor is the fact that I tell people the truth about what I am thinking. "What did you think would happen if you told me you had been sexually abused as a child?" I ask Detective Urskin. He tells me that he was worried that would make me think he was guilty. His comment does not surprise me. The myth that being sexually abused causes abuse victims to become sex offenders is so prevalent that even offenders believe it. In one study, sex offenders who denied guilt for their offenses were significantly more likely also to deny having been sexually abused (Fedoroff & Pinkus, 1996). I explain to him that PPG testing is not designed to determine guilt or innocence. In my practice, I use PPG testing to establish baseline patterns of sexual interest on the day of testing in our lab under clearly artificial circumstances. Sometimes, the results are extremely helpful. For example, in planning treatment it is useful to know that a man with pedophilia is secondarily most attracted to adult men as opposed to adult women. Detective Urskin insists that viewing pornographic materials will be upsetting to him. I commiserate but explain that many (if not most) medical investigations are unpleasant. "If I were a cardiologist and you came to me with chest pain, I would want to check your blood pressure and conduct an electrocardiogram (an EKG). What do you suppose would happen if you told your cardiologist that you decline the EKG because it is unpleasant, and you think you just have indigestion?" Detective Urskin thought about it a minute and laughed, "I expect that he would tell me to get the hell out of his office."

Do Not Refer Someone for the Purpose of Fulfilling Your Duty to Report

If you discover that an adult is molesting an identifiable child, you must report the fact to the CAS without delay. Referring the person to an "expert in sex abuse" does not discharge your duty. In addition, the fact that you did not file a report promptly can convey the false impression that child abuse is not an emergency or that reporting is only an optional activity.

Detective Urskin has reported that he was abused in a training school when he was a child. This disclosure is not reportable since laws in most jurisdictions leave the option of whether to report a past sex crime up to the adult. Presumably, the reasoning is that the victim should have the option of whether to proceed with legal prosecution. This approach ignores the fact that many untreated sex offenders against children reoffend and is opposite the approach taken by the state in serious crimes such as spouse assault. However, it is a widely accepted principle of jurisprudence in North America.

It is important to be aware of the precise legislation concerning reporting of child abuse in your jurisdiction. For example, the definition of "child" differs from place to place. Having said this, most legislation is common in its intent, which is (1) to ensure that children who are being abused or who are in danger of abuse receive immediate help and (2) to ensure that no professional who reports concerns in good faith (i.e., without malicious intent) can be held liable for breach of confidentiality. It is not uncommon for the SBC to receive referrals from professionals in the community who become aware that someone they are treating is abusing a child. On these occasions, I always tell the referring agent to call the CAS immediately since that agency can do the appropriate investigations and immediate necessary interventions.

In my own practice, new patients are informed of reporting laws and sign a consent form acknowledging they are aware of them before they meet me. If they disclose reportable information, I take this to mean they want the information reported. I always give patients the option of reporting the information themselves. With their permission, I call the CAS in their presence and provide a brief explanation to the operator, then hand the phone to the patient. Typically, the process of disclosing to the CAS in this context is therapeutic since it becomes a process of taking responsibility. After hanging up, most patients thank me for helping them and their victims. In this context, breach of confidentiality issues never arise.

Do Not Accidentally Condone Illegal Activity

If patients disclose that they are engaging in illegal sex acts (e.g., exposing), tell them they must stop immediately. Do not accept the excuse that they are "out of control and can't help it." One man in treatment for exhibitionism was certainly persistent. He exposed himself on the courthouse steps after having just come from an arraignment. He said he could not resist exposing himself. I pointed out that he had somehow managed to avoid exposing himself while he was before the judge. I also told him that he managed to arrive for treatment, get past the office staff, and sit through an hour-long session without succumbing to the "irresistible" urge to expose himself. He agreed. I started him on medication for the purpose of lessening his discomfort at not exposing. It was not to "make him stop" exposing. This is his responsibility. Inexperienced clinicians can overlook the fact that claiming the condition is untreatable or sure to get worse are sending the message that it is expected they will offend. This is a self-fulfilling prophecy. It is a major mistake since there is no evidence that people with paraphilias have higher (or more irresistible) sex drives than anyone else. Engaging in therapy for problematic paraphilic behaviors while condoning the paraphilic activities (either explicitly or implicitly) is equivalent to providing marital therapy to a couple while one or both of your patients are having affairs.

Most people who seek treatment for paraphilic sexual disorders are more than happy to discontinue their paraphilic activities, especially if they understand that it is part of the treatment and not a punishment or test. I tell my patients that we need to find out what they get from their paraphilic activities, and the quickest way to find out is for them to stop the problematic acts and see what happens. The type of treatment we select will be influenced by whether discontinuation of the paraphilic act results in depression, anxiety, anger, loneliness, or escalation in substance abuse.

A special case involves treatment of psychopaths with or without paraphilic interests. "Psychopathy" is not a *DSM*-recognized diagnosis but is now a well-recognized psychological construct that is useful in the consideration of individuals (usually men) who enjoy taking advantage of others in a "cold-blooded" manner. Given their personality vulnerabilities, it is not surprising that they often engage in a wide range of criminal activities without consideration of the consequences for themselves or others. Telling a psychopath to "just say no" is about as useful as asking an adolescent to sign a "pledge of virginity" (Tanne, 2008). In the case of adolescents, in a matched group study comparing adolescents who signed a "pledge" promising to wait until marriage before having sex with a similar group who did not sign the pledge, the only difference was that those in the pledge group were more likely to have sex without a condom. In the case of psychopaths, simply requiring them to sign a pledge not to commit crimes does little more than give them an excuse to drop out of therapy.

Let us suppose that Detective Urskin is in fact a psychopath. Of course, most detectives and police officers are not psychopaths. However, there is evidence to indicate that many psychopaths are attracted to the lifestyles they imagine detectives live. They like the idea of being "first on the scene" at grizzly situations that involve people suffering. They like the idea of "being in charge" and of knowing secrets. Detectives are aware of this, which is why they have learned to pay attention to people who volunteer to search crime scenes or go on "ride-along" programs or to people who return to the scenes of crimes.

Supposing Detective Urskin is a psychopath, here is how an early treatment session might enfold:

Dr. F.: Hello again. I see you ended up being convicted of the offenses I saw you for a couple of years ago. Your probation officer has sent you to me for treatment. From the look on your face, I am guessing you would rather be somewhere else. Am I right?

Det. U.: You got that right, Doc. I am innocent, and as far as I am concerned, the system is gonna pay.

Dr. F: I can see why you would feel that way if you are innocent. As you may recall, I told you when I first met you that it is not my job to figure out whether or not you are guilty. Given the nature of the allegations, the only people who know for sure are you and the tanning salon attendant (and maybe her daughter).

Det. U.: Got that right.

Dr. F.: Thanks. Here is how I see it. For some reason, the judge found you guilty. Like it or not, you now have a sex crime on your criminal record. Being an ex-detective, you know what cops are going to think when they see that on your rap sheet when you get pulled over for speeding in a reduced speed zone (like in front of a school). Am I right?

Det. U: Damn right. I have been there. You do not even need a conviction. Where there is smoke there is fire.

Dr. F.: So it looks like one thing we can work on is making sure that no cops get the wrong idea about you. That means helping to be sure no one can make any accusations about you like the one that got you sent to me in the first place. I think I can help you with that. Before we get into that, can I tell you a secret?

(Note, psychopaths love secrets. In my practice, whenever I want to make a clinical point to a psychopath, I make it a secret. If it is something I really want to make stick, I whisper.)

Det. U.: Your secret is safe with me, Doc.

Dr. F.: Thanks. Here is the thing. The way I see it, your probation officer wants you to come see me for therapy for 2 years. I have accepted you as my patient. As you know, I only treat voluntary patients, meaning that if you want to fire me, that is your right. However, if you decide to keep coming to see me, that means we are more or less stuck with each other. Now, here is the secret: You may not believe this at first, but the fact is, I get paid whether you tell me the truth or not.

(Pause)

Det. U.: Can you say that again?

Dr. F: Sure. Like I have told you, my job is different from what yours used to be. As a detective, you needed to get to the truth. It made a big difference if people lied to you. You were on the side of good, and everyone else was a suspect. In my office, the only people are my students, my patients, their guests, and I. The aim is to help my patients by ending their need to engage in harmful sexual activities and to be sure that they are never accused of committing sex crimes again. The interesting thing is that I get paid either way. Some guys decide to "shoot the bull"; we talk about the weather, and they usually get rearrested. Others decide to get their money's worth. We talk about what is going on in their lives. I give them advice. They try it out. Usually, I am right. Sometimes, I am wrong. When that happens, we learn from the mistake and try something new until they are happy. The choice is yours: weather or work?

Det. U.: So, what you are saying is that you are going to help me and not judge me, and that I call the shots except if I am harming a child or committing crimes and using the fact that I am in therapy as an excuse. Can my wife also come to these sessions?

Do Not Tell Someone You Just Met That He or She Is Incurable

Most people with paraphilic disorders who receive modern treatment get better. Even the most severely disturbed sex offenders, as a group, do extremely well. The average published rate of relapse for sex offenders is below 14%, making the success rate for the treatment of paraphilias in general better than almost any other psychiatric condition (e.g., Hanson & Morton-Bourgon, 2008). It is also important to remember that meta-analyses combine different treatments. Some treatments fit some offenders better than others (Marshall, Fernandez, Hudson, & Ward, 1998).

There are several reasons for the widespread myth that paraphilias have a dismal prognosis. Probably the most important one is the fact that people who get better never tell anyone. Those who recidivate are often reported in the media and are rarely forgotten. By analogy, bacterial pneumonia is a curable disease. However, in every major city, every day, people die from pneumonia. They die because they have comorbid conditions or because they did not receive adequate treatment. Medical students are not taught that pneumonia is incurable. They are not trained to tell people they cannot be cured, just before sending them to specialists. If the media ran headlines every time someone died from pneumonia, it is likely that the public would start to believe the disease was incurable, especially if people never reported when patients got better.

After consulting with his lawyer, Detective Urskin elected to complete the full SBC assessment. The results of the assessment were reviewed with him the same day. They were essentially normal with the exception of an elevation on his "heterosexual pedophile index" computed by dividing his penile response to audiotapes describing a sexual interaction between a man and a female child by his penile response to an audio-taped description of a consensual sexual interaction between an adult man and woman. Detective Urskin again denied any sexual interest in children, an idea he said he found disgusting, but admitted that treatment together with other men who had similar test results would make sense. He of course was upset with the test result and asked if he could "retake" the test. I explained that a new test would not undo the first test results, especially since some experts believe that the only valid PPG test is the first PPG test. Detective Urskin asked if he could take the Abel screen, which is a test based on visual reaction time. This test has become popular in the United States, likely because it uses test stimuli that depict only clothed models. It is based on the observation that people tend to look at pictures of people they are sexually attracted to longer than ones for which they have no sexual interest. I explained that the fact he knew enough about the Abel screen to ask for it made it invalid since it is easy to manipulate the results once the mechanism is known.

We discuss treatment options. I begin by emphasizing that accepting treatment is in no way an admission of guilt. I promise to testify to this fact if needed. I explain that accepting treatment is simply the action that any reasonable man would make in response to being accused of the crimes he is facing. The SBC is a multidisciplinary program with participation from social work, nursing, and psychology. A psychiatrist sees each patient individually. In addition, couple therapy is offered to everyone who is in a stable legal romantic relationship. Separate therapy is offered to spouses or long-term partners of sex offenders due to the observation that this group is often more stigmatized by the offenders themselves. While the decision about whether the spouse stays in the relationship is of course left to the spouse, only spouses who have not decided to leave the relationship are included in the group therapy. Some sex offenders report having been sexually abused themselves; some have symptoms of depression, mania, schizophrenia, substance abuse, anxiety disorders, or diseases characterized by cognitive impairments or various types. These patients are triaged to the appropriate specialist clinics for full assessments or, in some cases, assumption of care.

Psychotherapy Options

In terms of group therapy, the SBC offers three treatment groups. The first is a group designed specifically for forensic patients with major mental illness (primarily schizophrenia) that focuses on principles of occupational therapy, including healthy recreation and preparation for occupation pursuits. The second is a "sex education and social skills" group. This group is designed to assist patients not only to pursue healthy recreation and occupational endeavors but also to establish healthy social supports, including friendships and romantic and sexual relationships. This group is open to anyone assessed in the SBC who accepts treatment. While sexual issues are discussed routinely, discussion of the participant's personal sexual history is discouraged. As a result, transvestites, exhibitionists, pedophiles, sadists, and zoophiles can be treated together without incident. The third major group offered by the SBC is designed specifically for men in whom concerns have arisen about their sexual interest in children. Included are men who have never been charged and those pretrial, presentence, and postrelease. Deniers are welcomed as are admitted serial murderers who have been released to the community (provided that they have at least some current or past sexual interest in children). Intellectual ability is not an issue as long as the person is able to attend on their own, and we have found that those with mental retardation are adept at asking the questions that keep psychopaths on their toes. The groups are open-ended, and people attend as long as they feel they are getting some benefit. Typically, 50 offenders a week are seen in the groups.

In addition, sex offenders who are released from the federal program (a minimum in-custody sentence of 2 years) are encouraged to affiliate with a Circle of Support and Accountability (COSA). This consists of a group of community volunteers who assist the offender with reintegration into the community. They assist with such seemingly prosaic issues as finding accommodation, getting a bed, opening a bank account, and finding my office. Preliminary studies indicate that affiliation with a COSA group significantly reduces the risk of reoffense (Bates, Saunders, & Wilson, 2007).

I ask Detective Urskin what he thinks of the therapy options described so far. "What else have you got?" he says. "Glad you asked," I respond.

Pharmacotherapy Options

We now have a variety of pharmacological options. Several good reviews of the pharmacological options are available (e.g., Bradford & Greenberg, 1996). Ten to 20 years ago most patients elected to start with a selective serotonin reuptake inhibitor (SSRI) (Fedoroff, 1995). There is no evidence that one is better than another, but some patients who fail to respond to one SSRI do very well on another. Choice of a specific SSRI should therefore be on the basis of side effects. One important side effect to ask about is inhibited orgasm. Often, patients with paraphilias will report a normalization of their paraphilic interests until they begin to experience inhibited orgasm. The onset of this disorder is often accompanied by a return to paraphilic fantasies and behaviors, which defeats the purpose of treatment. Because the side effect of inhibited orgasm caused by SSRI medications is dose dependent, reducing the dosage of the SSRI is often more effective than increasing it.

Some patients require pharmacological inhibition of all sexual interest (normal and paraphilic), at least temporarily. Generally, patients will choose antiandrogen medications for this purpose. Physicians in the United States are currently limited to medroxyprogesterone acetate, which can be given either orally or by weekly injection. In Canada, cyproterone acetate is also available in oral or intramuscular formulations. Both of these medications decrease serum testosterone levels, and patients often report an accompanying decrease in their sexual interest. A third approach involves gonadotropin-releasing hormone (GnRH) analogues such as leuprolide, gosserelin, or tryptolerin. These medications are available only in intramuscular injection formulations. They act centrally on the pituitary–hypothalamic axis to decrease the production of gonadotrophic hormones. Treatment with these medications results in a dramatic diminution in testosterone blood levels and appears to decrease sexual desire of all types. The primary problematic side effects caused by all medications that decrease testosterone are osteoporosis and hot flashes. The other important difficulty in using GnRH analogues is the high cost associated with these medications.

When I first started to treat sex offenders, I found that few selected antiandrogen medications (Fedoroff, 1995). This is no longer the case, and in fact antiandrogens, especially GnRH analogues, are now the preferred medication. I think there are two reasons for this dramatic turn of events. The first is due to a profound change in the way I now think about the paraphilias. When I was a student I was taught that gender = orientation = lovemap. Since gender and orientation were either unchangeable or not needy of change, it followed that lovemaps should also be viewed in the same light. I no longer believe this. In fact, sexual interest is naturally modifiable. This is what I told Detective Urskin:

> "Detective, as I keep telling you, I have no idea whether or not your sexual interests are normal. The allegations against you and our test results suggest you may have a problem. Fortunately, we have a lot of ways to fix things. I have explained the groups we offer, and I am happy that you want to try them out. Let me know what you think. I have described three classes of medication to you: SSRIs, antiandrogrens, and GnRH analogues. Which, if any, is your favorite?" I look at the floor to avoid accidentally signalling any specific recommendation. The answer comes as it almost always does: "GnRH please." "You realize that GnRH meds are extremely powerful and will reduce your testosterone levels to below what they were before you went through puberty?" He answers, "I know, that is the last time I was happy." We discuss the choice. Like so many before him, without admitting guilt, Detective Urskin says that sex has not brought any pleasure to his life. I ask him whether his wife agrees with the idea of him going on a GnRH medication. He tells me she supports it fully. "To tell you the truth Doc, we have not had sex for years unless I was drunk. What made up her mind was one thing you said, 'the effects are reversible.' Once I learn how to have a normal intimate relationship, I can stop the medication and go through puberty again, but this time with someone I love and who loves me."
>
> "That sounds pretty convincing," I say. "Was there anything else that convinced you?" Detective Urskin squints at me and smiles. "The truth? Okay, you know the guy who sits by the door during the evening group? There was one night when he talked about how his life changed from wanting to kill himself to living in his own apartment with a good job, a car, and looking forward to holidays with his family. At the coffee break, I asked him what happened. He told me he went on a GnRH. He said it was like for the first time in his life he went on vacation."

WHY BE OPTIMISTIC ABOUT PARAPHILIA TREATMENT?

In spite of an absence of any sign of liberalization of attitudes toward sex offenders, the rate of reported sex offenses has decreased around the world. For example, in Canada in 1996, the population was 28,816,761. That year 27,026 sex offenses were reported to police. In 2006, the population of Canada had increased to 33,390,141, but the number of reported sex offenses fell to 22,136. This represents a 20% decrease in absolute numbers of reported sex offenses and a 30% decrease in the per capita incidence of sex offenses (Juristat, 2008) According to the U.S. Department of Justice (2008), in the United States, the incidence of rape fell from 2.5 per 1,000 over age 12 to 0.5 per 1,000 over age 12, representing a 50% drop in absolute numbers.

Recidivism of convicted sex offenders has also dropped. For example, one study of 534 sex offenders assessed as medium-to-high risk reported an expected 5-year sexual reoffense rate of 16.8% based on one standardized actuarial risk assessment scale, the Static-99 (Hudson & Thornton, 1999). The observed reoffense rate was 3.2% after a mean time in the community of 5.42 years (Marshall et al., 2006). More recent research involving analysis of new data sets of sex offender recidivism indicates that the Static-99 reoffense rate may have to be lowered, especially for offenders in the higher-risk categories (L. Helmus, 2008, personal communication).

Of even greater importance has been the revolutionary discovery that human brains retain neuroplasticity throughout life (Doidge, 2007). This finding lends support to the proposition that lovemaps, far from being static, are continuously modifiable. This explains how a couple can remain sexually attracted to each other from the time they first meet as youths to the time they become great-grandparents. It also provides hope to people with criminal or debilitating paraphilic disorders. One new treatment approach derived from this idea is to begin treatment with a GnRH analogue with the aim of suppressing sex hormones to prepubertal levels. Typically, this results in a dramatic decrease in sexual interest. With sexual issues out of the way, patients are assisted in establishing healthy relationships with age appropriate partners. If the relationship flourishes and both parties voluntarily decide to add sexuality to the relationship, the GnRH medication is cautiously decreased, resulting in the reemergence of sexual feelings within the context of a nonparaphilic relationship.

SUMMARY AND CONCLUSIONS

Many people wonder how I manage to tolerate treating men and women with paraphilic disorders. The answer is simple: The problems with which they present are significant, scientifically fascinating, and extremely satisfying to treat since the prognosis is excellent, and thank you letters come not only from patients but also from spouses, former victims, law enforcement, and the public. Terms like (negative) "countertransference" become invalid since treatment typically is short term and does not involve psychoanalysis and because individuals in treatment inspire admiration for the positive changes they make on a daily basis. It is important to remember that men and women with paraphilic disorders who seek treatment have crossed an important hurdle. As a professional care provider, your first task is to convey the message that you understand how hard it is to seek treatment for a condition that is publicly reviled and condemned. Your second task is to convince the man or woman before you that treatment will be efficient, effective, and result in an improved sex life that is happy, healthy, and more fulfilling than they have previously experienced.

Since 2004, the following events have occurred:

1. Sex crime rates have continued to decline.
2. Modern treatment facilities are now reporting long-term reoffense rates below 5%.
3. Neuroscience has confirmed clinical impressions that so-called hard-wired characteristics such as sexual interest are changeable.
4. There has been a paradigm shift from equating sexual interest with gender or sexual orientation.
5. A new class of medications, the GnRH analogues, has become standard first-line treatment for sex offenders.
6. Men and women are now presenting for treatment before committing hands-on sex offenses.

Further details about these dramatic steps forward have been published (Fedoroff, 2008; Fedoroff, 2009).

We now have a wide variety of effective treatment options. What works for one patient may be utterly ineffective for the next. This is not the fault of the treatment, the therapist, or the patient. No two people are the same. The first step is to conduct a thorough assessment. This should include obtaining as much collateral information as possible. The aim of the assessment should be not only to diagnose any paraphilic disorders correctly but also to rule out disorders that can masquerade as paraphilic disorders (e.g., organic syndromes, obsessive–compulsive disorders, personality disorders) and to identify comorbid disorders (e.g., substance abuse). The next step is to review the findings with the individual seeking treatment. Next, treatment options should be reviewed and agreed on. The specific form of treatment should be individualized so that the treatment is seen as helpful rather than simply punitive. Formats for psychotherapy include individual, group, and couple therapy. One therapy format does not preclude the use of others simultaneously or sequentially. The risks and benefits of accepting or declining psychotherapy or pharmacotherapy should be reviewed. The aim of therapy should always be not only to eliminate evidence of disease (all signs and symptoms of the presenting paraphilia) but also to promote the emergence of healthy sexual interests and behaviors.

Do not set your goals too low. Patients will not be enthusiastic about treatment that aims to end their sex life, end their "denial," or prove that they belong in jail.

The aim for everyone should be the establishment of a lawful, happy, fulfilling sex life within the context of a meaningful and balanced lifestyle. For some people, celibacy is their preferred option. For others, a nonmonogamous lifestyle is ideal. What is important is that lifestyle choices be voluntary, healthy, and fulfilling. This should be the aim of every psychotherapeutic intervention. Do not keep this a secret from the patient. Patients will work hard if the goal is worthwhile.

The only common feature among people with paraphilias is that they have problems due to unconventional sexual interests. Not all paraphilic interests are criminal, and even among people with criminal sexual interests, not all act on their criminal interests. Treatment of paraphilic disorders is usually successful and rewarding. Patients, their spouses, and even their victims are grateful. It is hard for me to imagine a more intellectually interesting or professionally rewarding endeavor. In this chapter, I have briefly described how the field I work in has changed. I would be remiss if I did not mention that the future looks even more promising. This is because word is now getting out that effective treatments are available. In addition, the Internet has allowed people with paraphilias to learn that they are not alone. Increasingly, men and women are seeking help before committing crimes. As a rule, the earlier people receive treatment the better the prognosis. If the trend continues, clinicians who provide treatment for people with paraphilic disorders will become the first group of mental health providers to move from offering primarily tertiary care to offering secondary and even primary prevention.

I hope I have inspired some of you to eagerly look forward to your clinical encounters with paraphilic individuals. They may feel and your teachers may feel that their sexual patterns are unchangeable, but I want to give the last word to 70-year-old masochistic grandfather who I treated many years ago:

> All my life, I was an outsider. I had an interest that I knew was a disease, but I couldn't tell anyone. I couldn't get any help. It separated me from my friends, my family, my wife. If I had known I was not alone and that there was treatment, I would have lived a different life. Now I am free of the disease. I may be old now, but I know the rest of my life will be better than the first 70 years. I just can't help thinking how many other people there are like me out there. Please tell your doctor friends to keep asking their patients about their sex problems. You will save a lot of lives if you do.

REFERENCES

Aggrawal, A. (2009). *Forensic and medico-legal aspects of sexual crimes and unusual sexual practices*. Boca Raton, FL: CRC Press.

American Psychiatric Association. (1994). *Diagnostic and statistical manual of mental disorders* (4th ed.). Washington, DC: Author.

American Psychiatric Association. (2000). *Diagnostic and statistical manual of mental disorders* (4th ed., text rev.). Washington, DC: Author. This is the "bible" for psychiatric classification of psychiatric disorders in North America. Although the *ICD-10* probably retains preeminent international acceptance, the *DSM-IV* is fully compatible. The "text revision" form of the *DSM-IV* retains identical diagnostic criteria to that of the *DSM-IV* but has added minor text revisions in the accompanying diagnostic preamble.

Bates, A., Saunders, R., & Wilson, C. (2007). Doing something about it: A follow-up study of sex offenders participating in Thames Valley Circles of Support and Accountability. *British Journal of Community Justice, 5,* 29–38. This important article describes another study supporting the hypothesis that so-called high-risk sex offenders can be safely managed in the community by paying attention to restorative justice principles.

Blanchard, R., Klassen, P., Dickey, R, Kuban, M. E., & Blak, T. (2001). Sensitivity and specificity of the phallometric test for pedophilia in nonadmitting sex offenders. *Psychological Assessments, 13,* 118–126. This is one of the best published assessments of the usefulness of a very specialized test instrument.

Bourget, D., & Bradford, J. M. W. (2008). Evidential basis for the assessment and treatment of sex offenders. *Brief Treatment and Crisis Intervention, 8,* 130–146.

Bradford, J. M. W., & Greenberg, D. M. (1996). Pharmacologic treatment of deviant sexual behavior. *Annual Review of Sex Research, 7,* 283–306. This is one of the best (and most comprehensive) reviews of the developing field of pharmacological treatments of paraphilic disorders.

Doidge, N. (2007). Acquiring tastes and loves: What neuroplasticity teaches us about sexual attraction and love. *The brain that changes itself* (pp. 93–131). New York: Viking.

Fedoroff, J. P. (1995). Antiandrogrens versus serotonergic medications in the treatment of sex offenders: A preliminary compliance study. *The Canadian Journal of Human Sexuality, 4,* 111–122. This comparison of compliance and acceptance of serotonergic and antiandrogen medications shows that serotonergic medications are much more frequently selected by sex offenders. This trend may now be changing, with patients selecting GnRH medications as first-line treatments.

Fedoroff, J. P. (2008a) Sadism, sadomasochism, sex and violence. *The Canadian Journal of Psychiatry, 53,* 637–646.

Fedoroff, J. P. (2008b). Treatment of paraphilic sexual disorders. In D. Rowland & L. Incrocci (Eds.), *The handbook of sexual and gender identity disorders* (Chapter 18).

Fedoroff, J. P. (2009). The paraphilias. In M. G. Gelder, J. J. Lopez-Ibor, & N. Andreasen (Eds.), *The new Oxford textbook of psychiatry* (Vol. 1). New York: Oxford University Press.

Fedoroff, J. P., Kuban, M., & Bradford, J. M. W. (2009). Laboratory measurement of penile response in the assessment of sexual interests. In F. M. Saleh, A. J. Grudzinskas Jr., J. M. Bradford, & D. J. Brodsky (Eds.), *Sex offenders: identification, risk assessment, treatment, and legal issues.* New York: Oxford University Press.

Fedoroff, J. P., & Marshall, W. (2009). Apparent problems in CBT treatment of paraphilic sexual disorders. In J. Abramowitz, S. Taylor, & D. McKay (Eds.), *Treatment refractory cases in CBT.* Washington, DC: American Psychological Association.

Fedoroff, J. P., & Moran, B. (1997). Myths and misconceptions about sex offenders. *The Canadian Journal of Human Sexuality, 6,* 263–276.

Fedoroff, J. P., & Pinkus, S. (1996). The genesis of pedophilia: Testing the abuse to abuser hypothesis. *Journal of Offender Rehabilitation, 23,* 85–101.

First, M. B., & Frances, A. (2008). Issues for *DSM-V:* Unintended consequences of small changes: The case of paraphilias. *American Journal of Psychiatry, 165,* 1240–1241.

Hanson, R. K., & Morton-Bourgon, K. (2008). Public Safety and Emergency Preparedness Canada. *Predictors of sexual recidivism: An updated meta-analysis 2004-02.* Retrieved November 30, 2008, from http://ww2.psepc-sppcc.gc.ca/publications/corrections/pdf/200402_e.pdf. At the time of writing, this was the most comprehensive meta-analysis of sex offender recidivism studies.

Hanson, R. K., & Thornton, D. (1999). *Static-99: Improving actuarial risk assessments for sex offenders.* User Report 99-02. Ottawa: Department of the Solicitor General of Canada. www.sgc.gc.ca

Juristat, Canadian Centre for Justice Statistics. (2008). Retrieved December 31, 2008, from http://www.statcan.gc.ca

Love, B. (1999). *Encyclopedia of unusual sex practices.* London: Greenwich Editions. This wide-ranging compendium of unconventional sexual practices includes brief descriptions of many of the paraphilias listed in this chapter.

Marshall, W. L., Fernandez, Y. M., Hudson, S. M., & Ward, T. (Eds.). (1998). *Sourcebook of treatment programs for sex offenders.* New York: Plenum. This is another encyclopedia of resources. This text reviews a wide variety of treatment programs. Details about treatment methodology and results, accompanied by extensive contact information, make this text indispensable.

Marshall, W. L., Marshall, L. E., Serran, G. A., & Fernandez, Y. M. (2006). *Treating sexual offenders: An integrated approach.* New York: Routledge. This book describes how the psychotherapeutic approach to sex offenders has evolved from one in which the focus is on "relapse prevention" to one in which the focus is on the establishment of a "good life."

McHugh, P. R., & Slavney, P. R. (1983). *The perspectives of psychiatry* (2nd ed.). Baltimore: Johns Hopkins University Press.

Money, J. (1986). *Lovemaps.* New York: Irvington. *Lovemaps* is arguably the masterpiece work by a scholar who wrote on virtually every aspect of human sexual behavior. *Lovemaps* fully describes an explanatory and descriptive theory of paraphilias.

Tanne, J. H. (2008). Virginity pledge ineffective against teen sex despite government funding, U.S. study finds. *British Medical Journal, 337,* a3168.

U.S. Department of Justice. (2008). Retrieved November 30, 2008 from http://www.ojp.usdoj.gov/bjs/glance/tables/viortrdtab.htm

World Health Organization. (1992). ICD-10: The ICD-10 classification of mental and behavioral disorders: Clinical descriptions and diagnostic guidelines.

SUGGESTED READING

Fedoroff, J. P. (1998). The sex offender (volumes I & II), edited by B. K. Schwartz & H. R. Cellini. Book review in the *Journal of Sex and Marital Therapy.*

Schwartz, B. K., & Cellini, H. R. (Eds.). (1995). *The sex offender: Corrections, Treatment and legal practice.* Kingston, NJ: Civic Research Institute. This is one of a series of edited texts that thoroughly summarize the field. For a full review of these two volumes, see Fedoroff (1998).

Seto, M. (2009). *Pedophilia and sexual offending against children: Theory, assessment and intervention.* Washington, DC: American Psychological Association. I highly recommend this book for a thorough up-to-date review of current thinking concerning sex offenders against children, published by the newest member of the SBC .

Seto, M., & Eke, A. (2005). The criminal histories and later offending of child pornography offenders. *Sexual Abuse: A Journal of Research and Treatment, 17,* 201–210. For more on the characteristics of sexual internet offenders, I recommend this publication.

Von Krafft-Ebing, R. (1965). *Psychopathia sexualis.* New York: Putnam. (Original work published 1886) This is one of the most comprehensive attempts to catalogue the range of (criminal) sexual behaviors. It was originally published in 1886 in Latin. The cited edition is the first fully translated English edition. It is worth reading to appreciate the fact that most of the sex crimes reported in the media as "crimes of the century" were equaled by those of criminals of previous centuries.

Ward, T. W., Polaschek, D. L., & Beech, A. R. (2006). *Theories of sexual offending.* Chichester, U.K.

Twenty-Four

Understanding Transgendered Phenomena

FRIEDEMANN PFÄFFLIN, MD

INTRODUCTION

When asked to update the chapter I had written for the first edition of this handbook, I thought it would be an easy job. I had given a very personal report of my first encounter with a patient presenting in the office of a famous German forensic psychiatrist and sexologist asking for a sex change operation. This was in 1972, when such a request was rare and usually was rejected. Transsexualism was not then an established diagnosis. There was no word "transgender." Health insurance did not pay for the treatment. There were almost no facilities in Germany that offered sex reassignment surgery (SRS) to patients. If someone wanted SRS, he (or she) usually went to Morocco. After having returned, she could not change her name or legal status as a man. She could not marry a man if she so wished. Sexual interactions between adult men were still felonies in my country until the 1960s. Quite a few people with transsexualism ended up in prison or locked up in psychiatric facilities. The early work with transsexuals was a missionary job. We interested psychotherapists, psychiatrists, endocrinologists, surgeons, lawyers, and politicians in taking care of these individuals and supporting their plea and fight for acceptance.

My goal for the first edition of the handbook was to counter the public and professional neglect of the suffering, desires, and needs of those who felt themselves to be strangers in their own bodies. I wanted to increase the number of sympathetic listeners for these patients. This included the patients, their families, their employers and insurance companies, judges deciding about legal name change and change of sexual status, and of course, my psychiatric colleagues. The tone or the melody of that chapter was decidedly positive, sympathetic, and encouraging.

Since the first edition of this handbook, there have been tremendous changes in the public discussion of transgender issues. There is now a strong demand for free choice of personal sex/gender status as a civil right independent of lifestyle, gender role behavior, stereotypical sex characteristics, and any medical treatment. Transgender phenomena now are recognized as having implications far beyond the narrow world of medicine.

In their monograph, "The Transgender Phenomenon," Ekins and King (2006) describe this development from a sociological point of view. In 2004, the United Kingdom passed the Gender Recognition Act, allowing legal sex change independent of previous treatment. Presently, the United Kingdom has one of the most progressive legislation in the world regarding gender change. Some consumer groups advocate the deletion of gender identity disorders from the fifth edition of the *Diagnostic and Statistical Manual of Mental Disorders* (*DSM*). They see this as a step to liberating transgendered people from psychiatric stigmatization. Groups that advocate for those with intersex conditions also strongly support this movement. Gender issues are discussed in practically all fields of society. They are delicate issues that are not always discussed delicately.

All these changes challenge clinical practice. They have changed the melody of this chapter. Patients are now much better informed than in previous decades. Most of them have already had contact with consumer groups, are in transgender chat rooms in the Internet, and are often informed about treatment options before they contact a mental health professional. When planning for this chapter, my goal was to assist clinicians with their early cases of gender identity disorders. I am not making political or sociological arguments.

Identity, whether gender, religious, political, ethnic, and so on, refers to the sense of sameness in oneself over the course of time despite the many changes that invariably occur. Our professional identity and understanding of our role with the transgendered has subtly changed over time. Throughout this discussion, I stress how our professional thinking has evolved during my career.

MY FIRST ENCOUNTER

As a medical student, I appreciated the opportunity to regularly assist a famous psychiatrist, Eberhard Schorsch, at the Institute of Sex Research at Hamburg University, Hamburg, Germany. At that time, Dr. Schorsch was almost exclusively active in forensic psychiatry. He saw the most extraordinary people who had committed serious crimes to prepare psychiatric expert evaluations for courts. During his examinations of criminals, for example, who had committed sexual murders, he enabled his patients to talk by being reserved, treading softly, and listening attentively. The patients themselves, their lawyers, the courts, and the public often became aware of the motives for and circumstances of the patients' horrible deeds, and the psychiatrist was admired for his capacity to create such insight.

However, in the case of the first patient with transsexual symptoms whom I saw with him, Dr. Schorsch's typical engaging reserve gave way to total passivity. The patient talked almost unendingly—without appearing to need a stimulus. Dr. Schorsch never interrupted him even when it was apparent that my mentor did not get a single answer to any of his questions. It was as if the patient was allowed to talk into empty space. The patient did not appear at the next session. When this same pattern of psychiatric passivity repeated itself with the second and third transsexual patient, I asked Dr. Schorsch about the reasons for his different behavior with these patients. I recognized that I had strongly identified with the patients and what I perceived to be their feeling of being at a total loss because of the doctor's lack of response.

He told me that he could only minimally relate to the patients' wish for "sex change" and "not much could be done anyway." "Certainly, it is true that only in Casablanca, Morocco, where most European transsexuals go, is sex reassignment surgery frequently performed. The chances of success are not great, and the University Clinic of Hamburg does not have sufficient personnel to tackle this difficult problem. This is in contrast to the United States, where the situation is more advanced, with a number of large gender identity clinics." The psychiatrist suggested that if I was interested, I could do a clinical attachment there.

I spent several weeks at the Johns Hopkins University Gender Identity Clinic in Baltimore, Maryland, which since 1965 was the first American university clinic to carry out "sex changes." Along with members of the staff, I was able to talk to a large number of patients who sought assessments, therapy, or follow-up. I was amazed to observe how openly patients with transsexual symptoms were received. I was also fascinated by the patients themselves and developed a great interest in sex and gender issues. Later, back in Germany, I became Dr. Schorsch's assistant. Since then, I have dedicated most of my professional life to transsexuals, transgenderists, and related issues.

DIFFERENT RESPONSES BY MENTAL HEALTH PROFESSIONALS

Dr. Schorsch and my responses to the person wishing to change sex mark two extremes of possible reactions: total detachment on his side, overinvolvement on my side. Obviously, there is something very irritating about such a wish. It seems hard to remain neutral, to listen, to watch, and to develop empathy before taking refuge in activism. This is true for friends, partners, and relatives and for professionals. I provide three more first encounters to illustrate the diversity of reactions to such irritation.

A Dramatic Encounter

A famous sexologist described his first encounter with a transsexual patient. It occurred during a time when public reports on transsexualism and transgenderism were not yet available, and most physicians had never heard of such a phenomenon. According to the information he had received from his receptionist, he was expecting to see a man and was thunderstruck when a beautiful lady entered his office, pulled a gun out of her handbag, aimed at him, and said: "If you don't issue a referral to the surgeon for sex reassignment surgery immediately, I will shoot you."

It is hard to conceive of a more dramatic first encounter between a patient and a doctor. What did the doctor experience? Fear? Anxiety? Horror? What would you have done? Would you have knocked the gun out of her hand without hesitation because you are trained in self-defense? Would you have cried for help? Would you have tried to escape? Or, would you politely have offered her a seat?

To calm you: The doctor is in good health. I was shocked to discover that he made up the story. I have wondered why he published this account. What was his purpose? I have no doubts that he was horrified when confronted with the transsexual desire. In addition, it seems remarkable that he exclusively blames the patient for causing this horror. But, what was it that frightened him so much that he published a fictitious account? He published his fantasy. Might it be possible that he was, due to personal unresolved conflicts, deeply afraid of women so that he could conceive of a woman only as an aggressive phallic being, as a *pistolièra*?

An Administrative Solution

A family doctor saw a male patient with the same request. The only difference was that her patient pleadingly uttered his request in a very low voice, not demandingly. The doctor was so touched by this, the patient's depressive state and suffering, that she felt incited to immediately take action. She sent him to me with a letter: "Dear colleague, the patient wants a sex reassignment. Please let me know if health insurance will pay for the operation and if I will be liable when recommending such a treatment. I also need information on how much estrogen material [sic] has to be injected."

The doctor thus tried to solve by administrative steps the private crisis that she experienced when confronted with the patient's desire. That the man had come and said, "I cannot be a man, please help me, I cannot stand it any longer, I cannot live like that," seemed to have moved her so much that she threatened to become depressed herself. She responded by resorting to an administrative solution. She took his wish at face value, without exploring it in more depth and even without asking me to do this. Her irritation and her doubts were expressed only indirectly in her seemingly neutral question of whether she might be liable.

Taking Time and Reflecting on One's Irritation

The third example I owe to a psychotherapist who is strongly opposed to sex reassignment and who hoped to get out of the affair by telling his patient after the first encounter that he did not want to refer the patient to a surgeon but would be willing to find another doctor or institution with more experience in handling transgender problems that might help. Between the intake and the second interview, he busily inquired about alternative treatment centers, discussed the case with many colleagues, and during that discussion, became increasingly uncertain regarding why he wanted to get rid of this patient so quickly. He realized that he was both uneasy and fascinated by the patient.

He opened the second interview explaining that he had used the time to ponder the first one, and that he had decided that *he* would not help the patient find a surgeon. Instead, he would like to offer the patient the opportunity to discuss his wish for SRS and any doubts he might have about such a treatment. The patient's expression froze. To prevent the patient from leaving angrily, the therapist continued talking by referring to a remark of the patient's during the first interview: "You said that you made up your mind that you needed sex reassignment surgery to 99.5%. I want to know how large the remaining half percent is."

Hesitantly, the patient nodded, thus indicating at least partial agreement. The therapist explained that he thought he was able to help the patient best in his search for certainty by keeping a neutral stance and not taking the side of encouraging or discouraging his wish for surgery. Instead, the psychotherapist wanted to support the patient in finding certainty for himself. With this empathic intervention, he respected his own limits but at the same time opened a wide space that allowed the patient to explore his wishes in great detail and to engage in very fruitful psychotherapy in which he resolved a deep depression underlying his transsexual symptoms.

TRANSGENDERISM: A CHALLENGE TO THOSE WHO ARE NOT TRANSGENDERED

The wish to change one's sex is a challenge to most people, not only to mental health professionals. Most people feel and experience themselves as either male or female, and never in their lives would they waste a thought on a life in the cross-gender role. Women are proud of their femaleness, especially of those body parts and functions that constitute this femaleness. The same holds true for men. They are usually proud of their male genitals, their deep voice, and their ability to grow a beard even if they may not actually like to grow a beard. People see themselves as males or females, and they want to be mirrored in the eyes of others in their respective sex and gender. The sex of a person is not just a bodily attribute, but it usually constitutes the person as a whole. In addition, it is a signal to others and contributes to a large extent to the kind and quality of interactions, attachments, and relationships that people may establish during their lives.

Being confronted with somebody who does not share this pride in his or her own bodily form is experienced by most people as an attack against their own identity. Automatically, they try, as is usually the case in conversations, to identify with the other person's wish, and they rapidly come to the conclusion: "That, I would never want to do. For me, it would be the worst thing I can think of." For transgendered people, such a reaction may be a source of great distress. They also want to be acknowledged and mirrored in the eyes of their beholders in the same way that they see themselves.

The Transgendered Phenomenon: What Is It?

During the 1980s, *transgenderism* slowly became an umbrella term for a variety of transitional lifestyles between the traditional dichotomous extremes of being either male or female. The word *lifestyle* may not exactly be the proper term for all the subjective phenomena involved, but it has some utility.

The term *transgenderism* was coined in an attempt to leave the limitations of a clinical and medical interpretation behind and to promote a broader understanding of people in transitional or in-between states. It allows such individuals to have pride about themselves. Some of these states might best be understood and helped clinically. Others unfold in individual or social activities beyond clinics and treatment centers. A description of the full spectrum is found in Ekins and King's (2006) monograph.

The term *lifestyle* connotes free choice for many people. Some *transgenderists* have chosen to live permanently either in the opposite gender role or somewhere in-between the extremes of stereotypical maleness and femaleness, and they are happy with it. It is a civil right to them.

Others have the feeling of being trapped in the wrong body (e.g., a male body), but that they really are female or vice versa. They suffer from the discrepancy of their gender identity and their cross-sexual bodily form. They cannot help feeling different. They do not experience a free choice but instead an irresistible urge to change, or they have changed their bodies with the help of medication and surgery so that their bodies may fit their gender identities. Traditionally, this phenomenon is called *transsexualism*.

Again, others switch clothes and gender roles temporarily. Some of them are sexually excited when doing so; others are not. Sometimes, cross-dressing is sexually exciting, and the fascination for cross-dressing vanishes rapidly after the person has had an orgasm. Then, the individual feels ashamed and does not want to have anything to do with it any longer, but the desire and urge for it return, and the story starts all over again. Traditionally, this phenomenon is called *transvestism*. In many biographies of transgendered people, sexual excitement in the context of cross-dressing initially played an important role only to fade over time.

There are transitions between all three phenomena. Somebody may start as a transvestite and end up as a transgenderist or a transsexual. Nobody can really foretell which route and which developmental path an individual may eventually take.

Ethnological Parallels

Transgenderism was observed in many cultures, although it had other labels and often a different significance. Ethnologists of the 18th and 19th century described transgenderists in native American cultures as *berdache,* an inappropriate name that in fact was derived from Arabian and French words for male prostitutes in the old Arabian world. In some of the more than 130 North American Indian cultures, berdaches were believed to have spiritual powers and thus had an outstandingly honored social position and sometimes the function of a witch doctor. But, this was not true for all Indian cultures. Today, the term has been replaced by reference to *two-spirit* people (Lang, 1998), although some of these same cultures know of more than two genders.[1]

Similar, yet different, phenomena such as transgenderism in the Western world were found in other parts of the world, for example, the *hijras* in India, the *kahtoey* in Thailand, the *mak nyahs* in Malaysia, and the *kushra* in Pakistan. Western individualism may explain the differences between these phenomena in various parts of the world. Forerunners of the phenomenon have been found in old mythology and in the 17th and 19th centuries in the Netherlands and France.

Why All Those Names and Categories?

One might wonder why we cannot do with just one name for a variety of similar phenomena. When a new term is coined, it is usually due to the awareness that interests of special subgroups need to be addressed. In 1910, the sexologist Magnus Hirschfeld (1910/1991), a protagonist of the gay liberation movement, coined the term *transvestism* when the gay liberation movement was at risk of failing. Some noblemen with close connections to Kaiser Wilhelm II were convicted of homosexual acts, then still a felony in Germany. One faction, oriented toward an idealized Greek type of socially well-adjusted lifestyle, therefore feared the failure of its attempts to abolish criminal sanctions against gay men if homosexualism included so-called effeminate styles, drag queens, fags, and so forth. Hirschfeld reacted by presenting a two-volume monograph with the title *Die Transvestiten* (*The Transvestites*), thus separating it from homosexuality. Today, many of the case histories in the book would be characterized as having forms of transgenderism.

Transvestite remained the leading term for cross-dressing men, less frequently for women, until the 1960s, regardless of whether these persons changed their roles only temporarily, wanted to live permanently in the opposite sex and gender role, or wished for hormonal and surgical treatment. Hirschfeld first mentioned the term *transsexualism* in 1923 in passing.

That transsexualism became a category of its own was mainly due to the availability of hormonal and surgical sex reassignment. More or less silently, such operations had been rarely performed in Europe since 1912. The general public learned about such interventions only in 1951, when news of the former American soldier Christine Jorgensen's sex change spread like wildfire around the globe. By 1965, when Johns Hopkins Hospital established its Gender Identity Clinic, surgical interventions gradually become more accepted.

To justify medical treatments, you first need a proper medical diagnosis. The term *transvestism* was not suitable for this purpose because it implied such a wide range of behaviors, some of which were even criminalized in some states of the United States. Focusing on cases of severe suffering, Harry Benjamin (1966), in *The Transsexual Phenomenon*, argued that transsexualism was a medical problem that had to be tackled. His work was the source of the diagnosis of transsexualism. This term was first included in the *DSM* in 1980 (American Psychiatric Association [APA], 1980). In 1991, the *International Classification of Diseases* (ICD-10), edited by the World Health Organization, adopted it and closely connected the diagnosis with hormonal and surgical treatment, as if the diagnosis automatically implied one specific form of treatment.

Gender identity clinics and other treatment centers developed admission criteria for SRS. To be on the safe side, they selected patients for whom they expected the best prognosis and the least amount of trouble. In some clinics, the admission rate was much lower than 10% of applicants. All applicants had to undergo diagnostic psychiatric procedures. Many did not want to comply with these. They defined their problem as a mistaken body, not a sick mind. They did not want to be labeled psychiatric patients. "Why should I engage in psychotherapy when I know I want hormones and SRS?" That was what they wanted in order to live freely and proudly. They resented having to submit to any psychiatric and medical preconditions (Levine & Solomon, 2009). That was the background for the birth of the term and the movement of *transgenderism*. We now recognize that most transgender phenomena escape clinical awareness and are studied instead by anthropologists and sociologists.

The *Diagnostic and Statistical Manual of Mental Disorders* of the APA dropped the term *transsexualism* from its fourth edition (1994). The *DSM-IV-TR* (*DSM, Fourth Edition, Text Revision*; APA, 2000) employs the diagnosis gender identity disorders and leaves open what kind of treatment might be appropriate. Presently, it is uncertain whether the fifth edition will maintain a diagnosis or what it will be called.

CLINICAL PRESENTATIONS

There remain, however, a large number of persons who seek psychological and medical support. The way in which they present their distress to clinicians varies widely. There are clients who avoid mentioning their main complaint and instead present totally inconspicuous wishes. For instance, they just regularly come to the doctor's office to pick up the prescription for their spouses for hormonal contraception. The doctor has no suspicion whatsoever that they take the pills themselves. Others come with minor cosmetic complaints. They may ask for a hair transplant because they are going bald at their temples. Or, they may ask for a cartilage shaving of a prominent Adam's apple or nose surgery, presenting these complaints as isolated aesthetic problems and independent of any gender identity conflict. I have seen patients who have had up to 10 minor surgical interventions who had not spoken a single word about their gender problem before they came to my office. Others may come depressed or have suicidal ideation, not revealing the true cause of their distress. With patients who survived a severe suicide attempt, the mental health professional should always consider that a gender identity problem might be an underlying conflict. Mental health professionals should not be surprised to discover that one of their patients treated for another problem one day surfaces as having a long-standing gender problem.

In recent years, most patients are much more straightforward. Well informed—and sometimes also misinformed—by self-help organizations or by Internet contacts, they immediately voice what they want. They may or may not be willing to discuss the services they request. Frequently, they are much better informed than are providers. Mental health professionals should respect what the patient knows; a lot may be learned from the patient. Listening closely to what the patient complains about, reports, and requests usually gives enough clues regarding how to proceed. Immediate referral to a specialist may be an all-too-hasty decision. In time you also will become more expert simply by listening and learning from patients. I often hear from patients about previous providers who were unwilling to listen or reacted to them with prejudice. Some of the professional literature on transgender phenomena only focuses on severe pathology, points to major deficits, and neglects the resources and creative forces of patients. This literature does not contain the whole story. Some providers appear to their patients to underestimate the patient's competence. It is fine to be inexperienced with the problem and to lack an in-depth understanding. When you do not know an answer to a patient's question, please admit that and explore with the patient where an adequate answer may be found. You will quickly learn.

Forms in Males and Females

Although males and females usually have the common aim of changing their sex, they clearly differ in their ideas of what this might mean.

Males

Some males would already be satisfied if something could be done about their deep voices and their beards. The greatest desire for others is to grow breasts, and they may not be interested in getting rid of genitals that they still frequently use for pleasure from masturbation or partner sex. Still others clearly want to have a vagina, and some even would like to get a transplant of a uterus and of ovaries to be able to become pregnant and give birth to a child. In ongoing professional relationships, the therapist may recognize that specific wishes surface step by step, with the patient first checking whether the mental health professional has an open ear for them. On other occasions, the full scope is demanded from the very beginning.

Among transgendered males who contact a mental health professional, the variety of their desires and behaviors is much greater than among females. Often, they contact a mental health professional after they have already taken many steps by themselves, for example, adoption of a female first name, dressing in public and at work as a woman, and taking hormones obtained surreptitiously. They want to demonstrate how sure they are. They want to safeguard themselves against critical and doubtful questions. Others are very shy and full of doubts, have not yet thought about a new first name, and fear very much being ridiculed by family members, friends, and colleagues. They may need a lot of time and encouragement to deal with their doubts.

Comorbidity may be absent, or it may catch the eye from the onset of the first contact. Once a working alliance is established, the patient and the mental health professional may want or even have to discuss priorities of the treatment. I think that suicidal ideation and behavior should be dealt with first to establish a safe base for future work. Antisocial acting out should also be addressed as soon as it occurs so that a secure frame for the treatment is guaranteed. Psychotic disorders must—like any other comorbidity—also be taken seriously and addressed. It is essential to address all important aspects of the patients' lives so that they can find relief from their distress as soon as possible, no matter what their goals may be in the long run. Dealing with problems at hand will strengthen the working alliance and allow the patient to consider all of the available options over time.

Adult patients present at all ages, some very young, others as husbands and as fathers, and some even after retirement. The follow-up literature suggests that late onset has a poorer prognosis for passing in the new gender role. Although this may be statistically valid, there are exceptions. I have seen a number of men in their 50s and 60s who waited until their children had their own families before they dared to consult a mental health professional about their long-standing distress. Despite having had a hard time, they had not wanted to burden beloved family members. Usually, these patients did extremely well after sex reassignment. The same is true for the rare cases of women who had given birth to a child and waited until their 40s before seeking treatment.

When I started to work with transsexuals, our clinic would not accept a married person for sex reassignment. I regularly met the wives and learned that quite a few loved their partners and wanted to stay with them even if they socially or physically transitioned to being women. Apart from financial disadvantages of divorce, there was no real rationale for demanding a couple get a divorce. The first couple that I met in 1974, parents of three small girls, are still together. I receive a Christmas card every year from them. Now close to 80 years old, they are happy to witness their grandchildren founding their own families. About one fifth of the more than 1,300 transgendered patients whom I have accompanied, mostly for longer periods, were still or had been married (some several times) and had fathered—and a very few mothered (or borne)—children. It was not infrequent that spouses supported their husbands and stayed together with them.

The admission rules in specific treatment centers contribute to the clinical variety of patients who are seen there. When The Johns Hopkins University Clinic started its gender identity program, sexually active patients were excluded. The administration, as well as the staff of the program, feared public opposition to the treatment if patients were promiscuous or paraphilic.

At the beginning of Australian treatment programs for transsexuals, the staff also adhered to this rule and did not see sexually active transsexuals. This concept of the relatively asexual person shaped the conceptualization of transsexualism for quite a while. Whoever did not fulfill this admission criterion was labeled a nontranssexual or a secondary transsexual, not a true transsexual. Now that we are aware that this concept was an artifact, we are beginning to realize that transgendered persons range from the shyly chaste to the extremely sexually active.

Sometimes, transgender issues gain importance during a couple's separation conflict. It may be the wife who complains about the man's increasing preference for cross-dressing. But, such an increase may also be a man's reaction to his wife's tendencies to act more independently or even to separate from him. I usually offer couple sessions in such situations to resolve the partner conflict first. The status of the transgender issue that caused the patient or the couple, respectively, to ask for a consultation is often better understood when the more urgent issue of staying together or separation has been discussed.

Females

The group of females with transgenderism and transsexualism seems to be more homogeneous than the male group. On an average, they come about 5 to 7 years earlier in life for their first consultation, often before marriage. Few marry, and fewer give birth to a child. Their aversion to sexual intercourse causes them to reject such opportunities. Some get pregnant through rape, which strengthens the aversion. Their tomboyish and masculine behaviors are recognized early by family members, peers, and teachers, but their desire to live as a male is met with resistance by their families.

Even though this group seems more homogeneous, their goals of treatment differ widely. Most state that they first want to get rid of their breasts. Those who have breasts that can easily be hidden under their clothes find it much more important to grow a beard or to deepen their voice. Some are most preoccupied with ridding themselves of menstruation. Others are fixated on getting a penis to urinate in a standing position, to perform intercourse, or both. As in males, their wishes are not always presented from the beginning, or they change when they learn about the realities of plastic surgery. But, you might also find that even though the patient initially only talked about mastectomies, a little later, despite knowing about the risks of a phalloplasty from those who have been disappointed by the operation, the patient begins to insist on getting the operation.

When, in 2008, the press reported about an American citizen who had only had breast surgery but kept his uterus and ovaries and had given birth to a child, a big TV company offered a large sum to one of my patients with the same bodily conditions to undergo insemination and give birth to a child. The patient experienced this as an indecent suggestion and rejected it. One can easily become skeptical about the media's need for a hot story.

Severe comorbidity is less frequently perceived among females than males, but it occurs in all variations, including suicidal behavior, anorexia, psychosis, severe sexual trauma, and so forth. When not accepted as males, that is, in the way they see themselves, some resort to drug and alcohol addiction. We are happy when the staff of an addiction center where they end up first explores the real background for their addiction and supports them in living their desired lives.

I have experienced many a dramatic situation with transgendered people. Sometimes, I felt as desperate as my patients did. I remember a young girl who had just finished high school and came for a sex change. Her parents knew about her visit—she needed their insurance card for admission to the outpatient clinic where I worked. The parents sent me a registered letter prohibiting my treating her. Threateningly, they scheduled their own visit with me and then cancelled it for trivial reasons. The patient herself would not convey much of her inner world. She was angry with me for insisting on regular visits for at least 1 year before making a decision for hormone treatment. At that time, this was the rule in the clinic. She came once a month, which was the maximum amount of closeness she could bear. But, she appreciated that I intervened at the national admissions office for medical students and attested to her being a special hardship case. She was enrolled as a medical student. She had very poor marks in college, and twice she failed the preliminary exams for medical students. In medical school, when she experienced an insurmountable disgust and uneasiness during anatomy, I again intervened.

She eventually had mastectomies with poor results. The surgeon illegally experimented on her, clipping the sutures on the right breast and sewing them on the left one to find out which side would give better results. Eventually, she had a legal SRS.

From then, this new male was a fairly good student. He became active in the student's organization and in various subcommittees. He passed his final exams, married a colleague, and worked in a number of clinics without anybody knowing his natal gender. He was able to give plausible explanations for his scars at his job physical examinations.

He eventually became an effective and respected forensic psychiatrist and a psychotherapist. Fifteen years after our first encounter, he contacted me again and asked for psychotherapy as he was now prepared to look into his history. We worked for 3 years, and he had to travel a whole day for the appointments. I came to learn a lot about his family background and the severe traumas of his youth, including nearly being killed for his gender presentation.

The patient reflected that had it been possible to reveal all of this 15 years earlier and to work it through, SRS possibly could have been circumvented. He knew, however, that it was impossible for him to talk about his traumatic development 15 years ago. A lot of mourning was necessary to say goodbye to lost alternatives and to parents who were both loved and hated. Today, he seems content.

WHAT SHOULD BE OFFERED AT THE INTAKE INTERVIEW?

When I was a student, one of my professors gave me this advice: "If you want to become a researcher, don't try to understand and explain schizophrenia or some topic as large as that. Restrict yourself to describing what you can observe and investigate more specific questions with small groups of patients." When I started to work with self-defined transsexuals, their requests seemed comprehensible to me; they only wanted hormone treatment and SRS. As I came to understand that they also wanted to be understood and accepted and wanted to understand and accept themselves, my task became more complex.

When talking to a patient, I never want to understand transsexualism or transgenderism. Rather, I want to understand the person I am talking with now. Some clinicians think that when they have seen one transsexual, they have seen all of them. They suggest it is always the same story. What may be true about such an observation is that there are certain patterns and slogans, for example, "Since I can remember, I have wanted to be a boy (girl)," that reoccur. But, it is always a different story and an individual person. Similarly, one might say that falling in love regularly follows the same patterns, yet every lover would rightfully protest and characterize his or her specific condition as singular.

Some patients do not present as persons but as types, calling themselves just "transsexual," "transgender," or "trans." By employing such a name, they think everything should be clear to you. I get mail from all over the world from authors who write, "I am trans. Please give me an appointment for an operation." I am not a surgeon, but even if I were, I would probably become as depressed as I do as a psychotherapist when reading such mail. When somebody reduces his or her whole life, his or her whole person, and his or her whole individuality to such a label, I think this is depressing. At the same time, I feel that I am being reduced to a slot machine, where you insert the trans coin and pull out some genitals. The richness of the human being and of existential interaction is thus lost, and it is my feeling that it has to be regained first, no matter what the practical treatment consequences might be. Usually, a space for reflecting is opened when the mental health professional does not present him- or herself as a gatekeeper to sex change but as a person interested in how patients get relief from distress and gain more competence in getting along with their everyday lives. Then, all those issues come to the fore that you encounter in other therapies. You and your patients might come to realize that the topic of sex change or gender identity does not even get touched on during some sessions. No one was avoiding it; it was just that other issues, such as getting along with the partner and the children, were more relevant.

If it is not obvious at first glance whether I am talking to a man or a woman, as judged from outer appearance, I usually ask the person how he or she wants to be addressed, and I comply with those wishes. Only on very rare occasions did I experience such a deep discrepancy between the appearance of the patient and his or her wish to be addressed with the cross-gender pronoun that it seemed necessary to dedicate some time to clarify the unease stemming from the discrepancy. As in all other clinical interviews, it is essential that the patient, as well as the therapist, feel at ease when talking with the other person. There are patients who sometimes show up as males and sometimes as females. Usually, I would then ask them how they want to be addressed on the specific occasion.

When you see your first few transgendered persons, see yourself as a discoverer who has just found a treasure. Paradoxically, keep in mind King Solomon's saying that there is nothing new below the sun. This paradox between the treasure of your experience and its lack of novelty will keep you enthusiastically engaged and modest. You will not rush out to publish a single case study and take pride in explaining the whole transgendered world. Many other authors have erred in this fashion, usually at the expense of the patient. Such activities have resulted in some major brouhahas (Dreger, 2008).

There are many theories about the causes and nature of transsexualism and transgenderism. Most of these offend the patient.

WHAT SHOULD BE OFFERED?

From my point of view, the most important thing a mental health professional can and should offer is the invitational stance. Listening closely, being interested in how the patient lives, how he or she copes with intra- and interactional conflicts, what he or she suffers from, what hopes he or she cherishes, and what resources he or she has. I am well aware that this is a very general, perhaps even formal, statement and only describes a stance. To illustrate this, I would need to transcribe hours of tape-recorded sessions, which, of course, would put everyone to sleep. Here is one piece of specific advice, however: If a patient asks for information about specific aspects of treatment, risks, and perspectives, about contacts to consumer groups, outcomes of treatment, and so forth, this information should be generously given.

WHAT SHOULD NOT BE OFFERED?

Do not put yourself under pressure to offer the patient so-called deep interpretations in the first session by explaining the logic of his transgender development from inborn conditions, unconscious early childhood experience, and family structure. Apart from the fact that the patient in all likelihood has pondered these issues many times without finding satisfactory explanations, such effort usually is in vain and produces at best rationalizations without explanatory power. They may satisfy the clinician but usually not the patient.

Similarly, it is of little use to confront the patient with the fact that after a sex change, he will not be able to have children or he or she might be exposed to social discrimination. Again, others have told the individual such things long ago, the patient has often thought about it or even experienced it, and it causes the individual great distress. That is why the patient is consulting you. The famous late director of the gender identity program at Charring Cross Hospital in London wrote in a survey about his work that a person with transsexualism will never become a full member of the opposite sex, and that a former man, after a sex change operation, will be but a castrated man (Randell, 1969, p. 375). Such crude utterances had long-lasting repercussions in the legislation of the United Kingdom, which until 2002 did not allow a postoperative person with transsexualism to get married in the new gender role. It was the European Court of Human Rights that finally forced the United Kingdom to change the law. In 2004, the United Kingdom passed the Gender Recognition Act dissolving the link between bodily status and legal sex/gender.

STANDARDS OF CARE

When sex reassignment was still a controversial issue, doctors were afraid to offend generally accepted customs and to go against laws protecting the integrity of a healthy person, for example, laws prohibiting castration. Naturally, they wanted to be on the safe side, and they wanted their patients to be on the safe side. They did not want to be seen as quacks, especially as there is a lot of quackery around for rare conditions that are unknown to many health professionals.

Against this background, it was essential to formulate standards of care for the treatment of people with transsexualism. Unlike people with transvestism, who usually do not need psychological or medical advice on how to cross-dress, those contemplating sex change need our assistance.

Such standards were first formulated in 1979. In reverence to Harry Benjamin (1966), the author of the first monograph on transsexualism, they were later called the *Harry Benjamin International Gender Dysphoria Association's: The Standards of Care for Gender Identity Disorders* (*SOC*). The first edition of the *SOC* had focused almost exclusively on suggestions how to regulate the access to SRS for transsexuals. The *SOC* was regularly updated. The two most recent versions are freely accessible on the Internet.[2] The seventh version is in preparation and will likely contain many changes. If one carefully reads each version, one can see the shifts of emphasis and how they become new standards. The clinical scientific community is not a monolithic rock. Many aspects of the SOC were, and some still are, highly controversial, starting with the use of a diagnosis according to the *DSM*. The controversies have become much more extensive during the last decade due to political developments. One can predict that these controversies will further intensify. Do not forget: Standards are guidelines, and they should be used neither as laws nor as cookbooks that do not allow any latitude. As cookbooks, they give a good orientation for the beginner. The art of cooking allows for variations and refinements. And, many transgendered persons want to determine their own route. Only some of these routes lead to SRS. As a cotraveler, the mental health professional may get to know fascinating parts of inner and outer worlds yet unknown to the professional when he or she is open to individual route planning as long as it is not hazardous. As a responsible person, the mental health professional will take care of him- or herself as well as of the patient.

As guidelines, the *SOC* found international recognition and distribution, although in some other countries, various medical and psychological committees issued their own standards, and in other countries even the legislative, the administrative bodies, or the courts regulate the access to sex change. But, as mentioned, there are various groups who altogether call the need for this kind of standards of care into question.

OUTCOME OF TREATMENT: SURPRISES

Provided proper treatment is offered, the outcome is usually favorable. One should talk of outcome in plural, however, as there are a number of different possible outcomes. Some patients will, with or without ongoing counseling or psychotherapy, reconcile with their primary bodily condition and the appropriate gender role. For others, this is impossible, and they will move on. They might stop at any stage in between the two extremes, or they might progress to full sex change.

Mental health professionals should not kid themselves about knowing the long-term outcome when meeting a transgendered person for the first time or about knowing what would be best for this person. I remember a number of first encounters when I thought, why not prescribe cross-sex hormones? Or even, why not send this patient immediately to the surgeon if he so wishes?

The respective patients were so overwhelmingly convincing in their appearance in the desired gender role and their histories seemed so coherent and typical that it did not seem to make sense to further explore the conditions of their everyday lives and to encourage them to expose themselves to what the standards of care call the real-life experience.

On the other hand, I saw persons I could not conceive ever passing successfully in the desired gender role because their stature, their large hands and feet, their prominent chin, their dark beard, and their deep voice contributed to such a striking appearance that they would always attract undue attention.

In both instances, I repeatedly witnessed surprising developments. Some of the initially perfect people with transsexualism gave up their wish to live as females and, in the long run, settled as males. On the other hand, some of the seemingly unsuited candidates finally found peace in the new gender role and got along quite well. Transgenderism and transsexualism are first and foremost inner conditions, and these inner conditions are decisive for what might be best for the patient. To judge patients according to stereotypes of how a woman should look does not do them justice.

Outcome of Treatment: Statistics

During the economic recession of the 1980s, it suddenly became an issue in my country whether health insurance companies were obliged to pay for sex reassignment. They had paid earlier with little ado as there were not so many cases, and most of the patients had gone abroad for surgery—mainly to Morocco—and had paid for it out of their own pockets. In 1980, a new law was passed in Germany allowing change of first name and of legal sex. It was discussed widely, and the public feared that a large number of persons would now want to have SRS. Insurance companies feared the costs and suddenly started to refuse reimbursement. Quite a few patients went to court. Expert witnesses were called, among them a famous forensic psychiatrist, who regularly wrote that the outcome of sex reassignment was extremely poor, and that there were many regrets.

When I was also called as an expert to promote some of my patients' claims, I started to study the evidence. A colleague, Astrid Junge, and I evaluated more than 75 reviews and individual follow-up studies after SRS from the international scientific literature published between 1961 and 1991 covering more than 2,000 persons after SRS (Pfäfflin & Junge, 1992). The results were encouraging and proved that this treatment had been scientifically evaluated more thoroughly than were quite a number of other treatments generally accepted in various fields of medicine. This holds true even though a number of follow-up studies included in this survey hardly met scientific research criteria.

We identified seven factors associated with effectiveness: (1) the patient's continuous contact with a treatment center, (2) cross-gender living or real-life experience, (3) cross-hormone treatment, (4) counseling and psychotherapy, (5) surgery, (6) quality of surgery, and (7) legal acknowledgment of sex change.

On an average, about two thirds of the individual samples had improved on most measures applied in the different studies; close to one third had not impressively changed, neither for the worse nor for the better; and only a few had worsened. The last is, of course, an appalling outcome, as is the 1 to 2% of patients who regretted sex reassignment in the long run.

Presently, together with a coworker, I am preparing a similar survey of the follow-up studies published since 1991. In general, their scientific quality has not much improved, and many have limitations. There are no randomized controlled studies. Documented criteria and follow-up times vary. Most studies are retrospective. This is no surprise as the samples in many treatment centers are rather small, most research grants have short time limits, and most of the staff also have only limited contracts. When collecting the evidence of many studies, however insufficient the individual study may be, it is still possible to find sound results. Evidence-based medicine requires randomized controlled trials. The model is very good to test drugs. For such complex constellations as a gender conflict, and for the many options for treatment that may result from it, such standards do not fit.

Apart from the lack of adequate control groups, it has often been deplored that there are no follow-up studies of patients who do not end up with SRS. Some of them finish psychotherapy and come to terms with their primary bodily condition. This subgroup could be followed. Most psychotherapists work in private practice, however, and they have only small samples of patients with the same diagnosis, not enough to conduct a follow-up study that can be published, at most a single case study. Sometimes, psychotherapists might also be reluctant to contact the patients again after some years, fearing that the results of the treatment may not have lasted.

> I know of a colleague whom I had seen as a medical student more than 25 years ago. As he lived far away, I recommended that he contact the university department for psychotherapy. He had inpatient treatment there for 9 months and, after release, additional psychodynamic psychotherapy for some years. His analyst wrote an impressive article about the success of the treatment, and there is no doubt that the patient profited greatly from it. Three years ago, nevertheless, this patient, had sex reassignment. Depending on when this patient might have been assessed in follow-up, different conclusions could have been drawn. Some might assume that the psychotherapy was a success at one point, a failure at another. But, we can also see that the psychotherapy might have been highly useful to the patient even though it did not permanently eradicate the wish to live as a woman.

Without having calculated the numbers exactly, it seems to me that a considerable number of patients who primarily had contacted me with the desire for sex change neither fully settle with their primary bodily condition nor put much energy in achieving their goal. In a way, the topic of "sex change" seems to be a kind of entrance ticket to a form of treatment that does not push them to achieve a certain goal. Instead, it is a place to reflect on one's life with constant companionship of the therapist. After a higher initial frequency, these visits regularly occur at greater intervals. It is an open-ended journey that contributes much to the stability of the patient. To invite such a patient to a follow-up study (for patients with transgenderism who formerly had wanted SRS and who have given up this wish during the treatment with a mental health professional) would seem to me like an intrusion. That there are no publications describing samples of such patients does not mean that no one knows what their fates have been.

Regrets

It is tragic when people find out only after SRS that the route they have taken was misleading. It is tragic for the patient as well as for those mental health professionals who were involved in their treatment. I know for sure of four of my patients with whom this occurred, and we are still having regular contact. Three of them clearly emphasize that at the time when they made the decision for the operation, they believed that they had no alternative. I cannot but agree with them, although I am aware of shortcomings of the treatment, be it poor surgical results or neglect of the fact that one of these patients skipped many appointments in psychotherapy, always having "good reasons," but without us reflecting what may have been concealed behind such good reasons.

I got to know some postoperative patients who had been treated elsewhere only many years after they had returned to their former gender role and were now asking for my advice on whether they should go for surgical restitution, usually a rather futile undertaking. Their suffering affected me very much, and at first glance I thought it would last forever. But even then, exploring their histories and their former striving to have surgery usually revealed bio-graphical constellations and inner worlds that allowed one to understand that what they had done had been necessary for them at the time they did it. In all but one case, lasting reconciliation was achieved.

ETIOLOGY: LOOKING BACK, LOOKING IN THE PRESENT, LOOKING INTO THE FUTURE?

The reader might be astonished to find a paragraph on etiology so late in the chapter. When therapists are interviewed by journalists or asked by spouses, parents, and other relatives of transgendered persons, the first questions asked are the following: "Where does it come from?" "What are the causes?" and "How do you explain the trans phenomenon?"

First, would it make a difference for your present contact with your patient if you knew the answers? There are many phenomena for which we do not know the causes. And, even if we knew them, nobody can change the past. Patients sit in front of you and want to be relieved from their distress. They do not want an academic discussion of causes, elaborated as these may be. They want to have their problems solved now.

Second, if your argument is that you want to know the causes for the sake of prevention, do you really want to prevent people from becoming transgen-dered? The same etiological discussion was expanded endlessly with homo-sexuality. What argument should we use to prevent men from wanting to be gay and women to be lesbian?

When voiced by family members, especially parents, the causal questions, even if formulated in the same words as the journalists', have a different underlying melody: "Who is responsible, and who can be blamed?" Under such circumstances, I regularly say: "It is certainly not your fault. Your son (or daughter) is not here to blame you but to solve his (or her) own problem."

Third, science gives some answers to the etiological questions and sums them in one sentence: "There are many factors that may contribute to a trans-gender development, for example, genetics and environment." This seems to be a convenient and comprehensive answer, yet it does not explain anything. Of course, this summary may be fanned out into more detail. Let us take environment: Is it the intrauterine hormonal environment or medication that the pregnant mother might have taken? Is it trauma at birth? Having been an unwanted child? Early life parental attachment problems? The position in the sibling order? Conscious or unconscious wishes of the parents to have a child of the opposite sex? Having been teased as a toddler for certain play and toy preferences? The list could be continued endlessly. The same is true for the genetic perspective: Is there a chromosomal deficiency, a mutation, and a cell count difference in certain regions of the brain, a hormonal imbalance?

The Gender Identity Research and Education Society (GIRES) is collecting all evidence that can be found on causal or supposedly causal factors for atypical gender development. It is a long list, and there is a long list of signatories under the GIRES report. Many of the data reported by GIRES (2006) yet are but hints.

Interesting as each of these hypotheses may be, it is rather unlikely that you will ever be able to adequately solve them for your individual patients. Discussing their lives with them, in great detail, however, you might get a hint regarding where to put greater emphasis in the individual cases if the patients are interested in finding an answer. Most answers will stay hypothetical, though, as long as you have the patient in treatment.

I was frequently impressed by patients who had read much of the literature and were convinced that one specific hypothesis offered the very explanation why they had "caught" transgenderism. Others knew of a hypothesis from hearsay and were convinced that it applied to them. It is, of course, interesting and often enlightening to investigate why it is exactly this hypothesis that the patient favors. And, from a scientific point of view, it is no doubt interesting to find out the cause or—much more likely—a number of causes or constellations that might contribute to atypical gender development. Before I would adopt any of these causes, I would wish that they had survived for at least 10 years and been confirmed by independent research teams. In my short professional life, I have already witnessed too many 9-day wonders.

Instead of looking back and asking the source of the present condition, you and the patient may use your time more efficiently by asking where it leads or, more precisely, where the patient wants to go. Together, you may explore patients' anxieties that stop them from doing what they allegedly want to achieve so urgently, as well as explore their fears and doubts; provide information on what realistic perspectives there are; and support them in their resources. I have often observed that patients' first challenge is to allow themselves to be supported by the mental health professional. It is only after this trust has occurred that they feel safe enough to explore such luxuries. Remember that it took 15 years for one of my patients to be ready to think about the precursors of his condition. The search for causes, constellations, forerunners, and factors of influence can become a most interesting expedition when both partners in treatment can trust each other enough to tolerate extreme states of mind and not just chat about generally accepted hypotheses without any link to their biographical data.

IS PSYCHOTHERAPY A PREREQUISITE?

In the beginning of SRS, the psychotherapy intervention was justified as a last resort, after all other—at that time, often drastic—psychiatric treatments (e.g., electroshock, lobotomy, long-term hospitalization in closed wards) had failed. In the 1970s and 1980s, when SRS became available in many parts of the world and could not be denied as a helpful form of treatment any longer, some renowned psychotherapists in North America and in Europe started a campaign against such "mutilating interventions," as they preferred to call sex reassignment. After they had lost the battle between the alternatives of either psychotherapy or hormones with surgery, they finally had to give in. Some of them then argued that somatic treatment should be offered only when the failure of a psychotherapeutic attempt had been demonstrated. This line of argumentation is a kind of hara-kiri. As long as patients know they will get what they want only by letting the therapist fail, one can predict the outcome. And, a psychotherapist whose explicit intentions are counter those of the patient has no chance and even deprives the patient of considering alternative routes.

Psychotherapy is one of the factors of effectiveness in regard to a good outcome for SRS, granted it is started and pursued open-mindedly. The more that I, as a therapist, want patients to give up their wish for sex reassignment, the less I give patients a chance to arrive at the decision. In contrast, when I am open for all options, including surgery, patients have a chance to find the route appropriate for themselves.

ARE TRANSGENDER PHENOMENA MENTAL HEALTH ISSUES?

There is a twofold answer to the question of whether transgender phenomena are mental health issues. They are not, considering the varieties of lifestyles throughout space and time. When an employer asks me, and when the patient has given written informed consent for my response, I will explain that, usually, a transgender phenomenon does not interfere with job performance and effectiveness.

The second half of the answer is, yes, they are. When an individual is distressed by a transgender issue, it is legitimate and reasonable to consult a mental health professional and have counseling or psychotherapy. If it should turn out during such work that this individual needs hormone treatment and SRS, then there is a medical indication, and the treatment should be covered by health insurance.

CHILDREN, YOUTH, AND ADOLESCENTS

Not all, but many, transgendered persons report having felt differently from very early or for as long as they can remember. When in the 1960s clinical reports appeared about very young cross-dressing children, clinicians and scientists thought they had found transsexuals *in statu nascendi*. These children seemed to confirm the adult transsexuals' retrospective reports. Evidently, more research was needed, and two clinical scientists, Green and Stoller, started a prospective study following up these children for nearly 20 years (Green, 1974).[3] Most of these children turned out to become homo- or heterosexual, not transgendered.

Most of the children of this sample had behaved so extremely that they were identified as clinical cases and brought by their parents for diagnostics and therapy. It is, however, not uncommon that children, for certain periods of time, may prefer cross-gender typical toys and plays, wear mothers' or siblings' clothes, and take cross-gender roles in role-plays, such as father, mother, and child. Mostly, these are transient phenomena in which the children explore their gender roles without yet being fixed to either gender role. Most parents do not take it all too seriously but enjoy the playfulness and exploratory behavior of their children.

In some children, such behavior persists; in others, it comes to the fore only around puberty. Many a time it is acted out only secretly, and when detected by parents, often a critical event, it results in punishment of and shame for the child. In some families, such an event is then denied and is never again openly discussed, but its dynamics remain powerful under the cloak of superficial harmony and silence.

The problem is rarely unveiled to the mental health professional, but if it is, it happens in two typical ways. There are parents who want you to "cure the child from his deviant behavior," at the same time denying all possible conflicts within the family. Alternatively, parents bring their child of 7 or 12 years to demonstrate how cute the child is in the cross-gender role and ask you to start hormone treatment.

Both alternatives are challenging. I am not a child and adolescent psychiatrist but was repeatedly contacted by such parents and their children as there is a great lack of specialists in the field. I felt great pity for these children, posing like dolls in the hands of their parents and sometimes like weapons between conflicting parental parties. Almost automatically, I found myself on the side of the child and felt impulses to rescue the child from these parents. Parents will sense such a partiality immediately and may withhold the child from further contact. It is therefore essential to find a balance, both reflecting the parents' needs and respecting their defense mechanisms. It is a delicate situation, usually easier to handle when working in a team with family therapists. As those are not readily available everywhere, the focus should lie in establishing and fostering contact to be able to further explore the family situation and possibly to refer these families to more experienced specialists or, at least, to establish such a cooperation for supervision of one's own work.

Since the 1990s, some centers have specialized in treating children, youth, and adolescents with gender identity disorders (e.g., in Toronto, Canada; London; Utrecht as well as Amsterdam, the Netherlands; Hamburg and Frankfurt, Germany). There are now reports showing that cross-gender identity may actually be fixed in some adolescents long before they reach legal maturity. These kids and their parents should be encouraged to have the child enroll in school in the desired gender role. For some adolescents, it may even be indicated to give medication to cause pubertal delay. The rationale for this is that they, as adults with transsexualism, will otherwise have to undergo costly and painful electrolysis of their facial hair, long vocal training if their voice has already broken, and other interventions that will not be necessary if they do not develop the full somatic characteristics of their primary sex.

For the handling of these problems, the Royal College of Psychiatrists in London first issued guidelines in 1998, which later were incorporated into the *SOC*. A recent follow-up study of a large Dutch sample of children having first been presented with gender dysphoria at a mean age of 8.4 years (age range 5–12 years) and followed up after 10.4 ± 3.4 years showed that most children with gender dysphoria will not remain gender dysphoric after puberty and finally will have a homosexual or bisexual orientation. In those, however, with more severe gender dysphoria in childhood, the final route will lead in the direction of gender identity disorder (Wallien & Cohen-Kettenis, 2008).

CONCLUSION

Patient and *patience* have, as words, the same root. As psychologists and medical doctors, we are trained to work quickly and effectively and to provide solutions for many seemingly and not infrequently really unsolvable problems. Efficiency is the magic word in modern medicine, although in the long run, we are not as efficient as we claim to be. All our patients, as well as ourselves, will eventually be hauled in by death. Many patients and many mental health professionals prefer fast solutions and often would profit more from patience, allowing conflicts to develop and opening new spaces for never-thought-of solutions. My more than 30 years of continuous work with transgendered persons have not resulted in fatigue. For me, it is as fascinating as on the first day. Every person is a new challenge, and taking up this challenge is usually rewarding. To embark on a new encounter is like embarking on a journey to new shores, with new riddles to be solved and new treasures to be found.

NOTES

1. In the Amarete culture in the Andes mountains in Bolivia, for instance, a gender proliferation is found, with up to 10 different gender roles, some of which are permanent, whereas others are dependent on the land one owns, on the office one holds, or what one does. They are not combined with transvestism; see Rösing (2001).
2. The Harry Benjamin International Gender Dysphoria Association (HBIGDA) has been renamed World Professional Association for Transgender Health (WPATH). Old issues of the *International Journal of Transgenderism,* including the most recent version, the sixth, in Volume 5, number 1, 2001; the previous version, the fifth, in Volume 2, number 2, 1998, are now located on the WPATH Web site (www.wpath.org).
3. Meanwhile, a number of new studies of children and adolescents with gender identity conflicts have been published (e.g., Di Ceglie & Freedman, 1998; Cohen-Kettenis & Pfäfflin, 2003).

REFERENCES

American Psychiatric Association. (1980). *Diagnostic and statistical manual of mental disorders* (3rd ed.). Washington, DC: Author.

American Psychiatric Association. (1994). *Diagnostic and statistical manual of mental disorders* (4th ed.). Washington, DC: Author.

American Psychiatric Association. (2000). *Diagnostic and statistical manual of mental disorders* (4th ed., text rev.). Washington, DC: Author.

Benjamin, H. (1966). *The transsexual phenomenon. A scientific report on transsexualism and sex conversion in the human male and female.* New York: Julian Press. For information on an electronic version of this out-of-sale book contact the World Professional Association for Transgender Health (www.wpath.org).

Cohen-Kettenis, P., & Pfäfflin, F. (2003). *Transgenderism and intersexuality in childhood and adolescence. Making choices.* Thousand Oaks, CA: Sage.

Di Ceglie, D., & Freedman, D. (1998). *A stranger in my own body: Atypical gender identity development and mental health.* London: Karnak Books.

Dreger, A. (2008). The controversy surrounding *The Man Who Would be Queen*: A case history of the politics of science, identity, and sex in the Internet age. *Archives of Sexual Behavior, 37,* 366–421. See the comments on this article by Adler, Bancroft, Barres, Bettcher, Blanchard, Caretto, Clarkson, Gagnon, Gladue, Green, Lane, Lawrence, Mathy, McCloskey, Meana, Moser, Nichols, Rind, Roberts, Rosenmann and Safir, Serano, Windsor, Wyndzen, and finally the reply by Dreger in the same issue of *Archives of Sexual Behavior* on pages 422–510.

Ekins, R., & King, D. (2006). *The transgender phenomenon.* London: Sage. This excellent book is recommended to all clinicians who want to look beyond their daily routines. Similarly stimulating is Phillips (2006).

Gender Identity Research and Education Society (GIRES). (2006). Atypical gender development—a review. *International Journal of Transgenderism, 9,* 29–44. There were several researchers invited to sign the review who decided not to do so. Their arguments can be found in the same issue of the *International Journal of Transgenderism,* pages 45–59, and the response to these arguments by GIRES is on pages 61–74.

Green, R. (1974). *Sexual identity conflict in children and adults.* London: Duckworth.

Hirschfeld, M. (1991). *Transvestites: The erotic drive to cross-dress.* Buffalo, NY: Prometheus Books. (Original work published 1910 in German: *Die Transvestiten. Eine Untersuchung über den erotischen Verkleidungstrieb mit umfangreichem casuistischem und historischem Material.* Berlin: Pulvermacher)

Lang, S. (1998). *Men as women, women as men: Changing gender in Native American cultures.* Austin: University of Texas Press. Lang gives a survey of the history and various interpretations of transgender phenomena in Native American cultures.

Levine, S., & Solomon, A. (2009). Meaning and political implications of "psychopathology" in a gender identity clinic: Report of ten cases. *Journal of Sex and Marital Therapy, 35,* 40–57.

Pfäfflin, F., & Junge, A. (1992). Nachuntersuchungen nach Geschlechtsumwandlung. Eine kommentierte Literaturübersicht 1961–1991. In F. Pfäfflin & A. Junge (Eds.), *Geschlechtsumwandlung. Abhandlungen zur Transsexualität* (pp. 149–457). Stuttgart, Germany: Schattauer. An English translation of this chapter is found in the book section of the *International Journal of Transgenderism,* accessible free of charge on the Internet: Pfäfflin, F., & Junge, A. Sex reassignment. Thirty years of international follow-up studies: A comprehensive review, 1961–1991. For information contact the World Professional Association for Transgender Health (www.wpath.org).

Phillips, J. (2006). *Transgender on screen.* New York: Palgrave Macmillan.

Randell, J. (1969). Preoperative and postoperative status of male and female transsexuals. In R. Green & J. Money (Eds.), *Transsexuals and sex reassignment* (pp. 355–381). Baltimore: Johns Hopkins Press.

Rösing, I. (2001). *Religion, ritual und alltag in den Anden. Die zehn Geschlechter von Amarete, Bolivien* [Religion, ritual and every day life in the Andes Mountains in Bolivia]. Berlin: Dietrich Reimer Verlag.

Wallien, M. S. C., & Cohen-Kettenis, P. T. (2008). Psychosocial outcome of gender-dysphoric children. *Journal of the American Academy of Child and Adolescent Psychiatry, 47*, 1413–1423.

VII

THE FORGOTTEN

Twenty-Five

Sexual Disorders and Intellectual Disabilities

J. PAUL FEDOROFF, MD, AND DEBORAH A. RICHARDS, BA, CHMH

Individuals with physical, cognitive, or emotional disabilities have a right to education about sexuality, sexual health care, and opportunities for socializing and sexual expression.

Sexuality Information and Education Counsel of the United States

INTRODUCTION

People with intellectual disabilities and problematic sexual behaviors are a therapist's dream. They present with fascinating and unique problems. They are diagnostically interesting since they have a higher incidence of genetic and medical conditions. They are typically highly self-disclosing. They usually have a support staff that provides objective verification of therapeutic progress. They almost all improve, and most improve dramatically. And, in the end, everyone is grateful: the patient, the patient's family, the patient's staff, and, very often, the patient's victims.

We make this optimistic statement after running a sexual consultation clinic for adults with developmental challenges for the past 15 years. The clinic began when Dr. Fedoroff noticed that Ms. Richard's staff was overwhelmed by their weekly 2-hour drives (each way) to Dr. Fedoroff's clinic in Toronto. Typically, two staff would arrive with one or two patients. One staff drove while the other person supervised the patients. When Dr. Fedoroff suggested that it would be more efficient if he came to the agency instead, a new service was born. This excellent idea freed staff, decreased transportation costs, increased the number of patients seen, improved the quality of care, and supported research and education programs.

When the monthly clinic began, the initial focus was only on sex crimes and paraphilias, but as we gained more experience, we realized that many of our patients had concerns relating to sexual function, orientation, and gender identity. We know the problems of the developmentally challenged are not unique to our region in southern Ontario, Canada. We plan to explain what we do in great detail so that you can deal effectively with similar patients in your community.

Most of the developmentally challenged patients whom we see have one or more of the following disorders: intellectual disability; pervasive developmental disorder, including autistic disorder; and Asperger's disorder;

Down syndrome; fragile X syndrome; fetal alcohol spectrum disorder; and Klinefelter's syndrome. Other developmental challenges exist, but many of them, such as Rett's disorder and childhood disintegrative disorder, are so severe that they preclude a standard consultation about sexual matters.

While the term *mental retardation* (MR) exists in the *Diagnostic and Statistical Manual of Mental Disorders, Fourth Edition, Text Revision (DSM-IV-TR,* American Psychiatric Association, 2000), this term has gradually become a derogatory label. In January 2007, The American Association on Mental Retardation (AAMR) officially changed its name to American Association on Intellectual and Developmental Disabilities (AAIDD). AAIDD is world renowned for advocating for those who have intellectual developmental disabilities. AAIDD's president commented that "intellectual disability" was a more modern and accurate term. In this chapter, we employ *intellectual disability* for MR as well as for the autistic and Asperger's forms of pervasive developmental disorder.

SYSTEM ISSUES

For people with intellectual disabilities, sex and sex-related problems are systemic. When we employ the term *systemic*, we are invoking several concepts. The first is that sexual behavior of one person requires the coordinated functioning of physiologic and psychologic systems. When we think of sex between two persons, we know that each of their physiologic–psychologic individual systems have to interact in a reciprocal fashion. This coordination of two individuals constitutes another system. Others have referred to this ordinary complexity of systems as the couple's sexual equilibrium. People with intellectual disabilities are more intensely influenced by the rules and conventions of the community in which they live than other people. The relationship between these individuals or these couples and their community constitutes another system. We clinicians recognize that sexual problems can arise from malfunction of any physiologic, psychologic, community, or cultural system (Griffiths, 1999, 2007, 2008; Richards, Miodrag, Watson, Feldman, Aunos, & Cox-Lindenbaum, 2008). In different cases, we target our interventions to specific systems.

Family doctors, often at the request of agency workers, are the source of most referrals to our clinic. Most of the patients' doctors have little idea about the sex-related problems of their patients. Our patients are more likely to disclose sexual concerns to the agency personnel who help them with other day-to-day problems, like buying groceries and choosing what clothes to wear when it rains. To facilitate respectful and confidential communication between professionals, we use a brief two-sided progress note (see the Appendix at the end of this chapter). At the end of the session, the patient signs the note. With his or her permission, one copy is given to the agency worker and one is hand delivered to the family doctor by the agency worker.

Standardized progress notes make it possible to intervene quickly while keeping everyone "in the loop." Agency workers say the process of hand delivering the note to the doctor immediately after the consultation is universally appreciated. Patients like the fact that their professionals are sharing their knowledge. They also like being asked to sign off on the notes, just like the doctor. The entire process reinforces the idea that they are the most important part of the team.

SEXUAL ORIENTATION

Sexual orientation is a description of an erotic and sexual bias typically toward one gender; it is not a disorder. However, it can be especially difficult for people with intellectual disabilities to establish comfort with being gay or lesbian, straight, bisexual, or asexual. For most people, awareness of romantic interests and sexual exploration happens in tandem with a gradual increase in independence from their families. In North America, learning to drive an automobile coincides in time with confident identification of sexual orientation. Many people with an intellectual disability never get a driver's license, never purchase cars, and do not leave their parent's home during adolescence. By the time they move into agency housing, they have missed opportunities for sex education and socialization. For those who are not prototypically heterosexual, there has usually been no access to discussion, gay affirmative opinions, or support for their nonheterosexual orientation. Agencies typically assume every patient to be heterosexual (Richards et al., 2008; Watson, Griffiths, Richards, & Dykstra, 2002).

The following is a clinical vignette. All case vignettes in this chapter, while clinically accurate, are fictitious.

John is an 18-year-old unemployed man with Down syndrome living with his parents. His 60-year-old mother called the agency in a state of alarm. While tidying his room, she discovered a cache of gay pornographic magazines. Her son looking at pornographic magazines was not the problem; the gay themes were. The mother wanted to know where he got the magazines since he only left the house with a family member or an agency worker. She wanted to know what the agency was going to do about it.

John was illiterate. He was frightened when he arrived at the clinic and spontaneously promised never to look at another magazine again. Workers said that the mother's call had prompted a new policy of forbidding purchase of pornography. It was also decided that only female workers could work with John.

At this point in the consultation, we excused the workers from the consultation. We explained confidentiality to John. We emphasized that our job was to help him. At first, John refused to speak. We joked with him about whether he read the magazines or looked at the pictures. He asked if he could get in trouble for stealing. With reassurance, he disclosed that he took the magazines from his next-oldest brother's closet when he moved out. He said that he knew that guys like magazines with naked people. Asked if he enjoyed looking at the magazines, he said he would prefer ones with women, but he did not know how to get those.

Further inquiry supported the view that John was heterosexual but that his older brother (unknown to his family) was gay. The agency requested phallometric testing. We explained that phallometric testing is not necessary to determine sexual orientation. We recommended that John be allowed to purchase legal magazines of his choice. To satisfy agency policies, it was agreed that John could buy any legal magazines using money saved by decreasing the amount he smoked. He could also buy the magazines without needing to disclose to staff what he bought. He was referred to a sex education group with men his own age and intellectual ability. We did not disclose the suspected orientation of John's brother. John's mother was advised to respect John's privacy when she helped him tidy his room. She was encouraged to support his independence and ability to socialize with both men and women. Some information about sexual orientation was also provided. To the best of our knowledge, John has never purchased a homosexual magazine. As an unexpected side effect of treatment, he quit smoking.

In John's case, secrecy and lack of independence led to misunderstandings. Sometimes, the opposite can happen.

Another agency asked for an emergency assessment of Sam after he had been discovered in a sexual interaction with a resident in the stairwell of his group home while a third resident watched. Sexual activity of any type, but especially homosexual activity, was not allowed by the agency. The sex acts in question, while not consented to by the agency, were fully consensual to the men. Our assessment focused on the agency.

1. What was the agency policy concerning privacy?
2. What about consensual sexual activities?
3. Did the agency have a sex education program for residents and their families?

Workers admitted that they had privately been concerned that the human rights of the people in their care to enjoy consenting and healthy sexuality were not fully respected. However, they indicated no one knew how to go about changing the policies. What will the residents' families say? What if the resident takes advantage of another resident?

Our interventions were directed to the agency. We explained that a policy simply forbidding sex is as ineffective for people with intellectual disabilities as it is for the general population. We referred them to materials on policy issues relating to the rights of people with intellectual disabilities to receive sex education appropriate to their intellectual abilities; privacy appropriate to their level of independence; and freedom from prejudices based on sexual orientation.

According to Owen, Griffiths, and Arbus-Nevestuk (2002), agency policies should support their clients' sexuality. They should not impose rules that further marginalize the individuals. It is important that there be a focus on training for parents, staff, and individuals that leads to patients' increased decision making and consent probability and promotes healthy sexuality.

In our experience, people with intellectual disabilities have a high frequency of same-sex and opposite-sex encounters that may not reflect their true sexual preferences. This can lead to ambiguous situations in which it may not be clear whether both participants in a sexual encounter are fully consenting. If a person has no access to opposite-sex partners, there is an increased likelihood of engaging in same-sex sexual activities. Sam was homosexual, but he did not disclose this until he was comfortable that there would be no retribution.

Variations of sexual orientation significantly affect attitudes of care providers. For example, the decision to assign only female staff to work with gay men makes as much sense as assigning only men to work with heterosexual men with intellectual disabilities. Aside from making the dubious assumption that no staff is lesbian or gay, it implies that sexual relations between staff and patients are acceptable. This not only is wrong but also sets up a paternalistic atmosphere in which the person with an intellectual disability is "protected" from living in a normalized community in which there are men and women of all ages, some of whom are potential or actual friends or lovers, some of whom are staff, some of whom are affiliated professionals or consultants, and so on.

GENDER IDENTITY DISORDERS

The pathognomonic feature of gender identity disorders (GIDs) is persistent cross-gender identification. This symptom requires the ability not only to identify with the opposite sex but also to be uncomfortable with the current (biological) sex. GIDs require a considerable degree of cortical ability, especially in terms of self-perceived empathy for opposite-sex roles. People with intellectual disabilities are less likely than others to explicitly voice concerns about gender identity or have familiarity with the available literature (Griffiths, Fedoroff, Richards, Cox-Lindenbaum, Langevin, & Lindsay, 2007a,b). As people with intellectual disabilities are more likely to have their clothes chosen by others, they have less chance to cross-dress in secret and therefore are more often brought to clinics due to concerns about cross-dressing.

John is a 42-year-old, proudly single man who stoically said that he knows he is "slow" but added that he is also tall and strong, all of which is true. He lives in a supervised group home with three other men. He was referred to us by a gender identity clinic at which he was diagnosed with GID, attracted to both males and females. They rejected him as a candidate for sex reassignment surgery (SRS) since he had MR. Intellectual disability is an exclusion criterion for SRS in most gender clinics. Being turned down for SRS had been explained to John by telling him that since he did not have a job he would never be able to afford the surgery. He was not told that the cost of SRS surgery is covered in Canada. John accepted the staff's explanation and abandoned his interest in pursuing SRS. However, he still longed to cross-dress in public. His group home staff had decided that it would be acceptable for John to cross-dress in his room but forbade him from doing so in the common rooms because it would upset his housemates. They told him that he could not leave the house cross-dressed because they were concerned about his safety.

John had no interest in interventions aimed at alleviating gender dysphoria aside from those that would allow him to "pass" as a woman in public. He was invited to join a "social skills" group consisting of men with a variety of problematic sexual behaviors or interests. The unique characteristics of the social skills group are summarized in Table 25.1 (discussed under the treatment section of this chapter).

John attended the group that evening and was surprised to discover he was welcomed, even when he disclosed his wish to cross-dress. Another group member commented, "We are all here because we want to work on social skills, and you have the guts to show us how to do it on your first night. Any time you want to cross-dress here, you have my respect."

A few days later, John's social worker faxed a note: "John met with the group home board of directors and told them he had GID. He told them his group had accepted his wish to cross-dress. The board agreed. John's housemates have been told that respect goes two ways. The board allowed John to cross-dress in his home and in public. John was so relieved that he agreed to his father's request that he "be his son" (by dressing in male attire) for Sunday dinners at his parent's home.

Table 25.1 Characteristics of Traditional and Sexual Behavior Clinic Groups

Characteristic	"Traditional" ID group	SBC group
Number of sessions	12 (closed)	Unlimited (open)
Length of sessions	1–2 hours	2 hours with break
Timing of sessions	Weekly	Weekly (okay to miss)
Number in group	8–12	Unlimited (average 20–30)
Homogeneous IQ	Yes	No
Homogeneous diagnosis	Yes	No
Homework	Sometimes	Rare
Theme	Relapse prevention	Good lives

In this case, "treatment" involved reframing the problem from concerns about a man wearing women's jeans to celebrating a man with disabilities asserting his self-identity.

SEXUAL DYSFUNCTIONS

Sadly, we rarely receive referrals concerning how to improve consensual sexual relations. This is not because men with intellectual disabilities have no problems with erections, ejaculations, or sexual interest or that the women are immune from dyspareunia, vaginismus, orgasmic disorder, or diminished arousal. We think it is because the system regards this population as children (Griffiths, 1999, 2007). It promulgates an "ask no questions" paradigm when it comes to interpersonal sexual behavior in this population. On consult requests/referrals, we often see under sexual dysfunction the "problem" listed as "has a girlfriend," "wants a family," or "asking about masterbation." In our view, these are not problems. We recognize that sex education is needed not only for many patients and their family but also for care providers and agency administrators (Watson, Griffiths, Richards, & Dykstra, 2002).

SOCIAL SKILLS GROUP

The social skills group meets weekly for 12 sessions. A schedule is made for each person to have his or her care provider present for at least one of the group sessions. Care providers are invited only on the condition that the patient consents. This policy demonstrates to the patients that they are in charge and respects their autonomy. It also gives us a chance to show how important consent is, especially concerning sexual issues. We have discovered that inviting support staff to attend the social skills group helps the staff learn the importance of the sexual health and fulfillment of the needs of the people they support and increases their comfort about dealing with patients' sexual concerns. This strategy also gives us first-hand information about the attitudes of the care providers and their ways of dealing with conflicts.

One group consisted of five men and three women with similar sexual knowledge based on the Social Sexual Knowledge and Attitudes Test–Revised (SSKAAT-R) (Griffiths & Lunsky, 2003). Although we run coed groups, we only include couples who have never been in an intimate (homosexual or heterosexual) relationship. Group sessions discuss anatomy, dating, relationships, social behavior, decision making, self-esteem, and information about safer sex practices. Sessions are tailored to take into consideration the learning styles of all the participants. One patient had difficulty with his vision, so larger pictures were provided during one exercise. Information is always repeated in multiple formats, including role-playing. We try to keep reading and writing to a minimum since literacy is an issue for many of our patients, and many will decline treatment rather than admit that they have problems with the written homework.

George is a 40-year-old male with a lifetime history of limited social and sexual relationships. He has a same-aged new woman friend, Linda. He asked his primary care provider if he could talk to someone about this new relationship. The care provider asked if it was about sex. George said that he thought so. He was referred to the "clinic" for consultation. We had him join the social skills group.

One session began with the topic of "What's on your mind today?" This prompted an earnest discussion about what an erection is; where, when, and how much to masturbate; and what ejaculations are. The women in the group were not too sure about this topic, but several of the men knew what ejaculation was and were quite excited to discuss this.

However, Sam looked at the therapist and said in confusion, "That has never happened to me. I never get that stuff coming out of my penis even when I try." Immediately after, George piped up and said, "It's okay Sam, me neither." George turned to the therapist and stated with confidence, "Teacher, I guess that only happens to some of us guys, right?" With that, Sam looked at George with relief and said that his penis seldom gets hard, even when he wants it to happen. George agreed with Sam and said that he has the same thing happen to him even when he is with his girlfriend. George went on to say that he had asked to come to the clinic because he thought that there was something wrong, and now he found out that there are other people just like him. He said he was happy that it was his friend, Sam. The session ended that day with several more questions than answers.

After the session, the therapist spoke individually to George and Sam. Both hoped that the therapist would tell Dr. Fedoroff about what they talked about in group. The therapist promised them she would and asked them if they would like to meet with Dr. Fedoroff so that they could tell him themselves. After the men had left, Kathy asked to speak with the therapist. She was trembling and tearful but had a lot to say. She had been quiet during the discussion because it reminded her of discussions in a foster home where she had been placed as a little girl. She said the older brothers talked about sex but not with her consent. They had "done things to her," and it made her hate sex. She had never told anyone about this before.

This vignette illustrates the way in which the creation of a safe environment in which these adults are treated like adults leads to new opportunities to be of help. People who are treated like responsible adults are more likely to act like responsible adults. George decided to invite Linda to his appointment with us. After meeting privately with George, and with his permission, Linda was asked to join us. We assured her that George was the patient, not her. But, we were very happy to hear from her since she was an expert on George. She confirmed that they had sex problems. She thought he did not find her attractive. We explained that George's problems most likely were due to his medication, and we could fix the problem by changing either the medication or its dosage. They were both happy with this news.

Sam's symptoms were lifelong. He had some physical symptoms suggestive of chronic low testosterone: a tall, slim build and gynecomastia. Serum free testosterone was low. Genetic testing revealed that he had 48 chromosomes and confirmed the diagnosis of Barr-Shaver-Carr syndrome (Barr, Shaver, & Carr, 1963). This is a variant of Klinefelter's syndrome, which is caused by an extra X chromosome (XXXY). While both disorders are associated with primary hypogonadism and low testosterone, men with Klinefelter's syndrome may have normal or above normal intelligence.

Sam accepted a referral to an endocrinologist for management of the medical complications of low testosterone, such as osteoporosis. He also agreed that it would be best to complete the social skills course and establish a circle of friends and professional supports before accepting treatment with exogenous testosterone. We have found that men with intellectual dysfunction and hypogonadism who suddenly have their low testosterone levels "corrected" may find the sudden surge of sexual (and more often aggressive) feelings problematic (Saleh, Fedoroff, Ahmed, & Pinals, 2008).

Kathy's problems are the most complex and, unfortunately, the most frequent. People with intellectual disabilities, especially women, have a higher-than-average history of sexual abuse (Sobsey & Doe, 1991; Sobsey & Mansell, 1993). The first step was to assure Kathy that nothing would happen without her explicit consent. We assured her that we understood it was difficult to come forward with information like this, and that we admired her courage. We of course did not blame her. What would she like? We told her we could help her if she wanted to take legal action. We told her that regardless of her decision about legal action, we wanted to make sure that her feelings about sex would change from fear to safety. She said she wanted to stay in the group, and she would think about whether she wanted to talk to the police. As she left the appointment, she stopped for a moment and smiled, "By the way, my boyfriend knows what masturbation is, too."

PARAPHILIC DISORDERS

Our clinic specializes in the assessment and treatment of men and women with intellectual disabilities and paraphilic sex problems. Word spreads. Referral sources have learned that when they are asked, "Does the person you care for have both a sex problem and intellectual disability?" that they should say, "Yes" because this response opens our doors immediately. We try to see new referrals quickly. If they are in driving distance of our clinic, that means within 7 days. If they are in southern Ontario, they receive intake documents the same week and are seen within 6 weeks, at the very latest. We think paraphilias deserve attention as soon as possible. Professionals and patients are often surprised because they believe the myth that nothing can be done. We disagree.

Shy Joe

Inappropriate touching; impulsive behavior; rude; controlling; invades personal space; obsessive; aggressive; has temper tantrums: These are some of the descriptors commonly included on consult requests for men and women with intellectual disability and paraphilic behaviors. Joe was seen 2 weeks after the consultation request, which was the soonest he could get to the clinic. He presented as a shy, 35-year-old man, visibly anxious, speaking quickly and fidgeting in his seat, and flapping his hands occasionally. Joe's face is elongated with prominent ears. When we meet men like Joe, we often ask the care provider: "Has Joe ever been diagnosed with fragile X syndrome?" The staff in this case answered, "No. But it's funny you would ask that question since a psychologist who assessed Joe asked the same question." Family history and florescent in situ hybridization (FISH) testing is diagnostic.

The chief complaint involved Joe being questioned by the police on three occasions. We asked why this had happened. Joe explained that he had been meeting at the park with a 10-year-old boy who lived in the neighborhood. When the boy's parents learned Joe had invited the boy to his apartment, they put a stop to the meetings. A few months later, Joe was caught contacting an 8-year-old girl from his apartment building. He called her several times a night. She told him to stop. When staff learned about these concerns, they sternly told him to stop or he would be arrested. Soon after, Joe was discovered by day program staff to be "luring lower-functioning" people into the men's washroom.

After several staff meetings, it was decided that Joe was "at risk of sexually assaulting someone, and in particular a child, and will therefore be supervised 24 hours per day." Joe was very unhappy about this as he no longer has any freedom. The agency required to fund 24-hour supervision is also concerned.

Joe's medical history consisted of a recent diagnosis of mitral valve prolapse. As a child, he was diagnosed with attention deficit/hyperactivity disorder (ADHD) and treated with methylphenidate. He had recurrent ear infections as a child, and it has been said that he may have a hearing deficit, but no tests have been done to confirm this deficit. Aside from an antipsychotic medication used on an as-needed basis for aggression, he is taking no medications.

On examination, Joe was very engaging and appears completely truthful and self-disclosing. He does not know why he does things that get him into trouble. He really would just like to be alone and sometimes free to go to the mall without having people have to supervise him. Joe also told us he wants a girlfriend but does not know how this could happen. He asked us to help him.

Joe represents a man referred due to concerns about his peculiar activities, which turn out to be typical of men with his genetic disorder, in this case, fragile X syndrome. The first point we want to make clear is that not all men with fragile X syndrome engage in problematic sexual behaviors.

However, specific genetic conditions like fragile X syndrome, Asperger's disorder, or environmentally induced congenital disorders like fetal alcohol spectrum disorder (FASD), increase the likelihood of being referred to a clinic dealing with sexuality issues (Goldstein & Reynolds, 2005; Attwood, 2007). We think this is because these disorders contribute to asocial behaviors. Intellectually intact sex offenders are more likely to exhibit antisocial behaviors.

Joe was referred for genetic testing. He was referred for phallometric (penile plethysmography) to determine his sexual preferences (Fedoroff, Kuban, & Bradford, 2009). He was referred to an audiologist to test his hearing. Test results confirmed the diagnosis of fragile X syndrome. Phallometric test results excluded pedophilia but confirmed that his primary sexual interest was toward adult men. His hearing was significantly impaired, and he was fitted with hearing aids that according to staff immediately and dramatically improved his "responsivity." He was referred to a social skills group. Although phallometry showed primary interest in adult men, for his own protection, he agreed to avoid any unsupervised contact with children. There have been no further police contacts. Joe is now taking dancing lessons and especially enjoys the tango.

ASSESSMENT AND TREATMENT

Each case is unique. By following the recommendations in this section, you will maximize the chances that every patient improves quickly and significantly. Specialist referrals will rarely be needed, not because nothing can be done, but because your patient has responded to treatment and is no longer symptomatic.

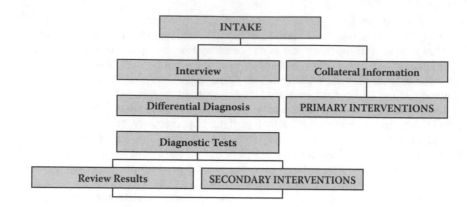

Figure 25.1   Assessment and Management Flowchart.

The First Step

Our assessment and treatment protocol is diagrammatically summarized in Figure 25.1. We place a lot of emphasis on getting background information (in Figure 25.1 as "collateral information"). We do this by sending new referrals an extensive intake questionnaire to complete before we meet with the patient. By collecting the information in advance, during the first meeting we can review it quickly to ensure that we have an accurate summary (McCreary, 2005). This allows us to focus on the referral problems more quickly.

We have five goals for the first meeting: (1) to help the patient; (2) to make sure the patient returns; (3) to obtain enough information to create a differential diagnosis about what the problem *might* be; (4) to create hope that things will improve; and (5) to establish trust and mutual respect. Typically, the support people have been led to believe that there is no hope for improvement, and that the only answer is indefinitely supervising the person more closely. Often, referrals occur in the context of an acute crisis. Our first interventions involve measures to ensure the safety of the patient, staff, agency, and community (in that order). While this is the reverse order of parole boards, our effective approach is based on the idea that people who feel safe, understood, and respected are people who will change their problematic behaviors (Saleh, Federoff, Ahmed, & Pinals, 2008).

Keeping the patient safe and informed is the single most important intervention that keeps the community safe (Fedoroff, Fedoroff, & Peever, 2002). However, safety of staff and the reputation of the agency are also paramount. Therefore, we do not hesitate to recommend increased levels of supervision and higher levels of security if necessary. Most patients accept these types of interventions once they understand that the changes are to protect them from offending and that the changes are temporary. We tell our patients we understand that no one likes to be charged for things they did not do. We tell them that we can help them avoid ever being accused again. All our patients like this idea, guilty or innocent.

At the end of the first session, we tell the patient and staff what we think are the explanations for the presenting problems. In presenting our differential diagnosis, we discuss diseases, behaviors, social factors, and system forces that may contribute to the problem. Our goal is not to stigmatize; it is to expand everyone's thoughts about the causes and cures.

The Second Step

The next step is to investigate the differential diagnosis by performing diagnostic tests and interventions designed to challenge the diagnostic hypotheses. Diagnostic self-report inventories that have not been standardized on populations with intellectual disabilities should not be used, especially if the patient is illiterate. From a psychometric perspective, there is a large difference between completing a self-report questionnaire in private and completing it with the assistance of a care provider who interacts with other housemates and who provides a monthly report to the patient's parents. We also caution against using actuarial risk assessment instruments that have been standardized primarily or exclusively on populations that do not include people with intellectual disabilities.

An instrument specifically developed for adults with intellectual disabilities is the Socio-Sexual Knowledge Attitudes Assessment Tool-Revised (SSKATT-R). Seven key areas are measured, including anatomy, women's and men's bodies, intimacy, pregnancy, birth control and sexually transmitted infections (STIs), and healthy boundaries and behaviors (Griffiths & Lunsky, 2003). Another is the Short Dynamic Risk Scale (Quinsey, 2004). This is an eight-item form completed by care providers that assists in forecasting the emergence of new problems. We use penile tumescence testing (PTT) to assist in evaluation of sexual preference. We always explain that PTT test results are not intended to establish guilt or innocence but rather to provide further data for discussion. At the end of the second step, we have established the working diagnosis.

The Third Step

We make a problem list (see the Appendix) and propose solutions in the third step.

Group Treatment

Many of our patients elect to join close-ended groups homogeneous in terms of level of intellectual ability. These groups are didactic; patients often refer to them as "class" and to the therapist as "teacher." Others elect to join mixed groups in which they are seen together with nonintellectually delayed patients with problematic sexual interests or behaviors. We are impressed by how well this works. Patients with intellectual disabilities often ask the questions that everyone is thinking (including us). In contrast, the nonintellectually delayed patients often come to see their own vulnerabilities played out by the intellectually disabled patients. They frequently become protective of them.

Medication Use

We employ a full range of psychotropic medications. Cautions in this population relate primarily to the fact that patients often arrive on medication cocktails. Therapeutic "breakthroughs" come as often from reducing or stopping medications as from starting new ones. This is especially true if the medications are inducing difficulty in reaching orgasm or erectile dysfunction, two of the main reasons for medication noncompliance. Patients with antiandrogens, especially the more effective gonadotrophin-releasing hormone (GnRH) analogues, should be screened for osteoporosis with bone densitometry at this step and yearly thereafter.

TOP 10 TIPS FOR SUCCESSFUL CLINICAL CONSULTATIONS

1. Make contact prior to the initial consultation appointment. Request that the care providers explain the processes of the consultation to the patient to inform and gain consent for the meeting. Have prior phone consultation with a coordinator. Our clinic uses a standardized questionnaire that assists the patient and care providers to collect important information. The questionnaire is sent to the new patient to complete and bring to the appointment. This makes the in-person interview less stressful and more productive. Patients may not fully understand the process of the consultation, but they should know that sensitive sexual issues will be discussed

2. Always informally introduce yourself and your staff to the patient. It is important for you and your team who will interact with the patient to identify yourselves. Always have the care providers explain their roles after you have had the patient identify him- or herself. We often remind the patient that he or she is the "boss." This never fails to change the dynamics of the meeting. We ask the patient who they would like to have in the room. We do these things to make the patient feel more comfortable in the unfamiliar setting, to build trust, and to increase the likelihood of future meetings. We repeat the process at the start of each subsequent contact. Patients are not the only ones who have difficulty remembering names.

3. Be flexible with the appointment time frame. Set aside 90 minutes for the initial appointment with the understanding that it may be shorter. Do not go beyond 90 minutes since dealing with sexual issues can be exhausting for the patient. It is unlikely that the problem will be completely solved on the first visit. Take your time. Patients need to be encouraged and empowered to speak for themselves. Talk to your patients in ways they understand. Four-letter words beat polysyllabic words every time. When the patient has impaired communication skills, use the methods they use. Your patients naturally want to look like they understood what you just said to them. They may repeat back what you said to assume a "cloak of competence." This does not necessarily mean that they have understood. People with intellectual disabilities may understand common words in unexpected ways (e.g., for many people, if you ask about their body, they may think of one particular area of their body). Each person communicates in unique ways.

4. Beware of the term *inappropriate* sexual behavior. People with intellectual disabilities, with or without communication problems, may have difficulty quickly telling what the real problem is. If the patient reports that the main problem is "inappropriate sexual behavior," you can be sure that they are using the term someone else gave them. Always ask the patient what they think the problem is (if any). Sometimes, it helps to excuse the care providers from the room.

5. Individuals with intellectual disabilities are not children. Adults with intellectual disabilities have adult bodies. Most are capable of falling in love and having their hearts broken. Most aspire to establish meaningful relationships and having children, and many will. Be careful not to infantilize them.

6. These individuals deserve a proper investigation and treatment. Do not accept concerns that a sexual history might be traumatizing or that more specialized investigations like phallometric testing will be too "exciting." Any concern about sexuality should be taken seriously. This may require invasive investigations. Consent is important for these procedures (Fedoroff, Fedoroff, & Peever, 2002).

7. Do not misjudge the significance of the problem. Sometimes, problems are overrated. A woman "caught" watching adult movies on living room cable TV in her group home likely only needs her own television. However, if the problem is neglected, it may lead to a range of more serious problems, including being labeled a "sex addict," vulnerability to sexual exploitation, ostracism, or eviction. In cases like this, we might offer social skills training with a condition that the care providers also attend. In contrast, during a routine review of systems, a person may describe current or past sexual abuse as casually as they may describe that day's breakfast. It is important to take comments like this seriously even if not accompanied by the affect expected.

8. Make the patient your primary source of information. People with intellectual disabilities often arrive with an entourage of attendants. These people are vitally important, but they are not the patient. Be sure that the patient knows this. Always attempt to speak to the patient first. Pay attention but also watch the support workers. Are they agreeing? Do they look shocked or surprised? Next, ask the patient if it would be okay to see what the support workers think. By following this routine, the patient learns that his or her statements are valued (he or she gets to speak first), and the patient is consulted about who speaks next. Similarly, while the support worker is speaking, pay attention but also watch the patient's body language and responses. If the person looks uneasy, simply ask further questions. Sometimes, a support worker will take over and answer questions. It is important to listen and then follow up with clarification from the patient. There may be other times when the person asks the support worker for help, and this is also okay. We recommend taking note of when this happens since it can indicate areas in which there is trust as well as areas in which there may be mistrust or disagreement.

9. Have the whole team that supports the person present. It is critical to gather as much information as possible to develop your treatment plan. The most effective way to do this is to have all of the supports present during a visit. Sometimes, it is good to get information from the individual's support system as well as the person with an intellectual disability. Support people can often retrieve times and dates and have greater access to medical information than you do. Often, they were on the scene when an event happened. There may be discrepancies in the information you get. Sex problems are almost all situational. It is good to hear all points of view.

10. Keep going. The addictions literature used to comment on the fact that many people with alcoholism would present initially with depression. This was a "gateway" chief complaint. For the intellectually disabled, sex problems may be gateway complaints. Always consider comorbid physical, psychological, psychiatric, and other systemic problems. Also, remember that sex problems tend to run together. It pays to explore widely.

Let the person know that your primary role is to make his or her life better. When the patient is in legal trouble because of personal behavior, let the patient know that you want to help them stay out of trouble in the future.

Use phrases such as the following to assure the person:
- I will let you know what I am thinking and tell you what I think needs to be done.
- You have the right to say no.
- It is important that you tell me what you are thinking so we can work together.
- We are all working together to help you.
- You are in control of these appointments.

SUMMARY AND CONCLUSIONS

According to the World Health Organization, sexuality is an integral part of the personality of people and a basic need and aspect of being human (1975). The hope that people with intellectual disabilities can live independent and meaningful lives, have sexual desires, fall in and out of love, and marry or become parents one day has notably been ignored, disregarded, and neglected (Richards, Miodrag, & Watson, 2007; Richards et al., 2008). These challenges are greater than they need be due to society's misunderstandings and responses to the sexuality of people with intellectual disabilities (Griffiths, 1999). There have always been myths about the sexuality of people with intellectual disabilities (Griffiths, 2007). This has led to neglect of their right to treatment. We have developed a treatment approach that starts with the patient and includes the care providers. We share our patients' goals for healthier sexual experiences and relationships. We think you can do the same in your community. Our clinic has been running for 15 years. So far, we are unaware of a single hands-on sexual reoffense committed by any of the people treated in our clinic. This may seem hard to believe but we have seen the power of our relatively modest interventions to affect the lives of disadvantaged, previously ignored and forgotten people. It motivates us to continue.

APPENDIX: SBC PROGRESS NOTE (TWO-SIDED)

Progress Note

This note is an official record of professional contact between [doctor's name] and the patient listed below. Unless otherwise indicated please hand-deliver a copy of this note to the patient's family physician. Please forward any comments/concerns to: [email addresses or phone numbers].

Date: _____

Clinic Location: City #1   ☐
                     Cith #2   ☐

Patient Name: _____

Time Seen: _____

Accompanied by: _____

****

Problem List:

(0 = Resolved 1 = Much Improved 2 = Improved 3 = No Change 4 = Worse 5 = Much Worse)

	Problem	Change (0–5)
A.		
B.		
C.		
D.		
E.		

Medications

	Name	Dose	Times	Changes	Reason(s)
1.					
2.					
3.					
4.					
5.					
6.					

(please turn over)

Observations:

_____
_____
_____
_____
_____
_____
_____
_____
_____
_____
_____
_____
_____

Recommendations (see also Meds on reverse side):

_____
_____
_____
_____
_____
_____
_____
_____
_____
_____
_____
_____
_____
_____

Follow-up Appointment: _____

_____   _____
[doctor's name, M.D.]   Patient signature

REFERENCES

American Association for Intellectual and Developmental Disabilities (AAIDD). (2007). *World's oldest organization on intellectual disability has a progressive new name.* Retrieved February 14, 2009, from http://www.aaidd.org/news/news_item.cfm?OID=1314

American Psychiatric Association. (1994). *Diagnostic and statistical manual of mental disorders* (4th ed.). Washington, DC: Author.

American Psychiatric Association. (2000). *Diagnostic and statistical manual of mental disorders* (4th ed., text rev.). Washington, DC: Author. This is the "bible" for psychiatric classification of psychiatric disorders in North America. Although the *International Statistical Classification of Diseases and Related Health Problems (ICD-10)* probably retains preeminent international acceptance, the *DSM-IV* is fully compatible. The "text revision" form of the *DSM-IV* retains identical diagnostic criteria to that of the *DSM-IV* but has added minor text revisions in the accompanying diagnostic preamble.

Attwood, T. (2007). *The complete guide to Asperger's syndrome.* London: Kingsley. This is one of a series of useful books focusing on pervasive developmental delay.

Barr, M. L., Shaver, E. L., & Carr, D. H. (1963). An unusual sex chromatin pattern in three mentally deficient subjects. *Journal of Mental Deficiency Research, 3,* 78–87.

Fedoroff, J. P., Fedoroff, B., & Peever, C. (2002). Consent to treatment issues in sex offenders with developmental delay. In D. M. Griffiths, D. Richards, J. P. Fedoroff, & S. L. Watson (Eds.), *Ethical dilemmas: Sexuality and developmental disability* (pp. 355–386). Kingston, NY: NADD Press.

Fedoroff, J. P., Kuban, M., & Bradford, J. M. (2009). Laboratory measurement of penile response in the assessment of sexual interests. In F. Saleh, A. Grudzinskas Jr., J. M. Bradford, & D. J. Brodsky (Eds.), *Sex offenders* (pp. 89–100). New York: Oxford University Press. This chapter provides an up-to-date review of the history, current status, and future of penile plethysmography.

Goldstein, S., & Reynolds, C. R. (Eds.). (2005). *Handbook of neurodevelopmental and genetic disorders in adults.* New York, Guilford Press. This book is highly recommended as a summary text for many of the comorbid disorders that accompany people with intellectual disability and sex-related problems.

Griffiths, D. (1999). Sexuality and people who have developmental disabilities: Myth conception and facts. In I. Brown and M. Percy (Eds.), *Developmental disabilities in Ontario* (pp. 443–451). Toronto, Ontario, Canada: Front Porch.

Griffiths, D. (2007). Sexuality and people who have intellectual disabilities. In I. Brown & M. Percy (Eds.), *A comprehensive guide to intellectual and developmental disabilities* (pp. 561–572). Baltimore: Brookes.

Griffiths, D., Fedoroff, J. P., Richards, D., Cox-Lindenbaum, D., Langevin, R., Lindsay, W. D., et al. (2007a). Sexual and gender identity disorders. In R. Fletcher, E. Loschen, C. Stavrakaki,* M. First (Eds.), *Diagnostic manual— intellectual disability (DM-ID): A textbook of diagnosis of mental disorders in persons with intellectual disability* (pp. 411–457). Kingston, NY: NADD Press. This is the definitive diagnostic manual for making *DSM* diagnoses in patients with intellectual disabilities.

Griffiths, D., Fedoroff, J. P., Richards, D., Cox-Lindenbaum, D., Langevin, R., Lindsay, W. D., et al. (2007b). Sexual and gender identity disorders. In R. Fletcher, E. Loschen, C. Stavrakaki, & M. First (Eds.), *Diagnostic manual— intellectual disability (DM-ID): A clinical guide for diagnosis of mental disorders in persons with intellectual disability* (pp. 249–275). Kingston, NY: NADD Press. This is a shorter version of the book listed in Griffiths et al. (2007a), complete with annotations.

Griffiths, D., & Lunsky, Y. (2003). *Sociosexual Knowledge and Attitudes Assessment Tool (SSKAAT-R).* Woodale, IL: Soelting.

Griffiths, D., Richards, D., Fedoroff, P., & Watson, S. (2002). Sexuality and mental health in persons with developmental disabilities. In D. Griffiths, C. Stavrakaki, & J. Summers (Eds.), *An introduction to the mental health needs of persons with developmental disabilities.* Mental Health Resource Network, Ontario, Canada.

McCreary, B. (2005). *Developmental disabilities and dual diagnosis: A guide for Canadian Psychiatrists.* Kingston, Ontario, Canada: Queens University. This is a concise but highly informative and informed manual for assessment and care of people with intellectual disability.

Owen, F., Griffiths, P. M., & Arbus-Nevestuk, K. (2002). Sexual policies in agencies supporting persons who have developmental disabilities: Ethical and organizational issues. In D. M. Griffiths, D. Richards, J. P. Fedoroff, & S. L. Watson (Eds.). *Ethical dilemmas: Sexuality and developmental disabilities* (pp. 53–76). Kingston, NY: NADD Press.

Quinsey, V. L. (2004). Risk assessment and management in community settings. In W. R. Lindsay, J. L. Taylor, & P. Sturney (Eds.), *Offenders with developmental disabilities* (pp. 131–142). Chichester, UK: Wiley.

Richards, D., Miodrag, N., & Watson, S. (2007). Sexuality and developmental disability: Obstacles to healthy sexuality throughout the lifespan. *Developmental Disabilities Bulletin, 206*(1/2).

Richards, D., Miodrag, N., Watson, S., Feldman, M., Aunos, M., Cox-Lindenbaum, D., & Griffiths, D. M. (2008). Sexuality and human rights of persons with intellectual disabilities. In F. Owen & D. Griffiths (Eds.), *Challenges to the human rights of people with intellectual disabilities* (pp. 318–381). London: Kingsley.

Saleh, F., Fedoroff, J. P., Ahmed, A. G., & Pinals, D.A. (2008). Treatment of violent behavior. In A. Tasman, J. Kay, J. A. Lieberman, M. B. First, & M. Maj (Eds.), *Psychiatry* (3rd ed., Chapter 127). London: Wiley.

Sobsey, D., & Doe, T. (1991). Patterns of sexual abuse and assault of people with developmental disabilities. *Sexuality & Disability, 9*(3), 243–259.

Sobsey, D., & Mansell, S. (1993). The prevention of sexual abuse of people with developmental disabilities. In M. Wagler (Ed.). *Perspectives on Disability* (pp. 283–292). Palo Alto, CA: Health Marketing Research.

Watson, S., Griffiths, D., Richards, D., & Dykstra, L. (2002). Sex education. In D. M. Griffiths, D. Richards, J. P. Fedoroff, & S. L. Watson (Eds.), *Ethical dilemmas: Sexuality and developmental disability* (pp. 175–224). Kingston, NY: NADD Press.

World Health Organization. (1975). *Education and treatment in human sexuality* (Technical Report Series No. 572). Geneva: Author.

Twenty-Six

Sex and Chronic and Severe Mental Illness

WILLIAM L. MAURICE, MD, FRCPC, AND MORAG YULE, BSC, BA

Isn't that the least of their problems?

A Health Care Colleague

Bill Maurice: While a resident in psychiatry four decades ago, I had the extraordinary experience of completing an elective in Masters and Johnson's Reproductive Biology Research Foundation. Since then, most of my career focus has been on the subspecialty of sexual medicine, which in turn has meant talking with individuals and couples about sexual matters (Maurice, 1999). The kinds of sexual problems experienced by my patients were mostly in the area of sexual dysfunctions (rather than paraphilias or gender identity disorders—the three major categories of sexual and gender problems listed in the *Diagnostic and Statistical Manual of Mental Disorders, Fourth Edition, Text Revision* [*DSM-IV-TR*]; American Psychiatric Association, 2002). Apart from their sexual dysfunctions, most patients were psychiatrically well. To be sure, many were unhappy to varying degrees about the connection between their sexual difficulties and their relationship with a partner or the link between their problems and associated physical disorders.

The development of the Sexual Medicine Team (SMT) took place later in my career and represented an effort to apply the knowledge and skills acquired in the general area of sexual medicine to patients with a chronic and severe form of mental illness. The context was a large outpatient mental health service that takes care of the needs of severely psychiatrically ill patients in the city of Vancouver, British Columbia, Canada: the Vancouver Community Mental Health Service (VCMHS). The service has a caseload of over 6,000 patients, is staffed by more than 200 health professionals, is well organized (eight teams), and has been highly praised (Torrey, Bigelow, & Sladen-Dew, 1993). As far as I know, the SMT is unique in the sense of being a dedicated sexual medicine clinic within a larger mental health service.

Morag Yule: I became interested in the topic of sexuality and mental illness while working as a researcher in a hospital setting. A few years ago, I was fortunate enough to become involved in sexuality research at the University of British Columbia as well as at the department of Obstetrics and Gynecology in a large Vancouver hospital. I came to understand the importance of providing excellent sexuality education and support for all people, regardless of their mental health status. I became fascinated with this area and hope to pursue this topic during my training in clinical psychology, both as a clinician and as a researcher.

If someone is acutely psychotic, common sense says that sexual matters are not at the top of the list of problems for patients[1] and their caregivers. But, after the acute phase of the illness has passed, the disorder is under control, and the patient has been discharged from the hospital, sex and intimacy do indeed loom large in the lives of the mentally ill (Bengtsson-Tops & Hansson, 1999).

With patients living in the community, opportunities for sexual events to occur are much more evident to health professionals compared to the "mental hospital" era. And yet, the topic of sexuality arises so *infrequently* in the assessment and care of these patients—especially puzzling in view of the fact that even those with a physical disorder would prefer to talk with their own primary care team about sexual matters rather than talk to a specialist (Schover, Evans, & Von-Echenbach, 1987).

One can only guess at the reasons why "sex" is not discussed since the explanations are usually not obvious. Rarely is a mental health professional (MHP) so uncomfortable with the subject that no discussion on this topic is ever possible. More often, there is a "conspiracy of silence" between the patient and the MHP. The patient will not volunteer information because of embarrassment. The MHP will not broach the subject for fear of being asked a question that he or she feels unable to answer. Sometimes, this fear is supported by the (mistaken) belief that the topic is irrelevant in patients who lack partners. All it really takes to open up this topic is for the MHP to ask a single question, like "Do you have any sexual concerns?" (Maurice, 1999). Patients generally do not lie when asked; however, most will not be spontaneous in talking about sexual issues without such an invitation.

Mental health professionals tend to underestimate their own sex history-taking and interviewing skills when faced with a patient's sex-related concern. Initially, MHPs could at the least use their personal developmental and adult life experience as a frame of reference in asking questions. With practice, sex history-taking and interviewing boundaries widen immensely as the MHP hears stories that go beyond his or her personal sexual thoughts, feelings, and experiences.

No one actually knows how common sexual problems are among the mentally ill. Factors such as the high frequency of sexual problems in the general population, rampant poverty in the mentally ill (and consequent poor diets), medication side effects, sexually transmitted infection (STI) vulnerability, and exposure to sexual assault all lead to the conclusion that the prevalence is likely substantial (Maurice, 2003).

The kinds of patient concerns we and others see especially include sexual desire problems in men and women, as well as ejaculation and erection problems in men and confusion around sexual orientation and gender identity in both sexes (Raja & Azzoni, 2003). To give you a flavor of stories we hear, we describe six patients who have been seen by sexual medicine specialists working at VCMHS. The sexual concerns of these patients are, of course, the "problem" but equally so is the "system," which does little to encourage the identification and treatment of these concerns.

While the patient's case manager is always included in visits (more is discussed on the rationale), we have no expectation that they will initially imitate us when meeting a patient—as a result either of reading this chapter or of watching the conduct of a consultation. We know that it takes some history-taking experience to get to the point at which one could talk with patients about sexual matters with the same neutrality that others have in talking about an injured arm, kidney disease, or an episode of depression. Nevertheless, many case managers have told us that they extract portions of what they see done and apply them in their clinical practice. Our goal in this chapter is to assist our readers in doing the same.

Patients 1 and 2 illustrate problems in both men and women, singles, and couples and show the range of sexual issues arising in those with a mental illness as well as the use of different treatment approaches.

PROBLEM 1: THE PATIENT (PATIENTS 1 AND 2)

Patient 1

Jim, a 47-year-old man with a 15-year history of schizophrenia, was referred because of "premature ejaculation" and "erections that were not firm." He had read a brochure concerning a "sex" clinic while in the waiting room of the mental health center and asked his case manager for referral. Jim provided only superficial information regarding his sexual concerns to his therapist. No details were available prior to the first visit. Jim lived with his family of origin, worked part time as a janitor, was maintained on risperidone (2 mg/day), had never used street drugs, only occasionally used alcohol in the past, smoked one package of cigarettes a day since his late teens, and had always been in good physical health. Jim's sole current sexual activity was masturbation, which occurred a few times each week. He had experienced intercourse three times in his life and only with prostitutes, the last being about 1 year prior. Jim's level of sexual desire had diminished in recent years. He reported sexual thoughts several times each week, whereas about 5 years ago these had been daily experiences. Erections with masturbation and in the morning had also lessened; they were now 5/10 (on a scale where 0 meant that his penis was entirely soft and 10 meant that it was full and firm).

The last time he experienced erections that he could rate as 9/10 or 10/10 was about 15 years prior. Ejaculation and orgasm (he had no concern about the latter) took place regularly about 2 minutes after he began stimulating himself. Ejaculation occurred more quickly than he thought was normal. He had considerable warning that ejaculation was imminent and made no attempt to delay it from happening. Jim was under the impression from watching sexually explicit videos that the process should take much longer.

Jim's principal sex-related diagnoses were (1) hypoactive sexual desire disorder; (2) erectile dysfunction (ED), acquired (vs. lifelong) and generalized (vs. situational); and (3) unrealistic expectations concerning the timing of ejaculation and orgasm. Recommendations concerning ED included a physical exam (his family doctor indicated that no abnormalities were apparent), a lab exam, and possible use of sildenafil. We attempted to reassure him (by way of educational intervention) concerning his experience with ejaculation and orgasm.

The only abnormal values on the lab exam were very high lipid levels. He was referred to the dietician associated with the mental health service in an attempt to institute a low-fat diet and was advised to return to his family doctor for continuing care of his elevated lipids. In addition, we answered Jim's many inquiries concerning male and female genital anatomy and physiology (using diagrams and rubber models), as well as his questions about "normal" sexual and emotional aspects of relationships.

Jim's ED was successfully treated with discussion and sildenafil, samples of the drug having been obtained from the drug company. Diminished sexual desire and premature ejaculation ceased to be concerns following continued treatment. He was pleased with the outcome of the consultation and agreed that a fourth visit was unnecessary.

Patient 2

Rosalyn, a 32-year-old married woman with an 11-year history of one depressive period and many manic episodes (but presently euthymic), was referred because of intrusive and disturbing sexual thoughts. She had discussed these thoughts in detail with her case manager, who suggested referral to the SMT. Rosalyn lived with her husband of 8 years in a one-bedroom apartment, did not work, was maintained on carbamazepine, had never used street drugs, used alcohol only occasionally, never smoked cigarettes, had never been pregnant (neither she nor her husband wanted to have children), and was in good physical health.

Rosalyn had no concerns about her own or her husband's sexual *function*, but this was not equally true about her view of their sexual *practices*. They experienced a variety of sexual activities, all of which many people would consider to be mainstream. Nevertheless, and unbeknownst to her husband, she ruminated about certain sexual acts that she found objectionable based on religious ideas as well as on statements made by family members when she was a child.

Most recently, her preoccupation was with what she thought to be her husband's desire for anal intercourse, which in fact had never taken place between the two of them. Past history revealed that she had been anally, orally, and vaginally raped in her teens on several occasions. Rosalyn's current sexual thoughts seemed to be related to her past history of sexual assault, family-of-origin issues, and the inability to be candid about sexual matters with her husband. After we explored the first two issues in several visits, her husband was included in the next session. He convincingly stated that he had much concern about his wife's history of sexual assault and had no inclination to force her into any form of sexual activity that she found unacceptable. Specifically, he stated that he was not at all interested in anal intercourse and attempted to reassure her generally that he found their sexual experiences enjoyable and sufficient. Her sexual concerns lessened considerably. Six months later, she returned in a similar state of mind, but this time her focus was on oral sexual activity. In telephone discussions, her primary psychiatrist (we were clearly secondary) considered the notion that she might be experiencing obsessive–compulsive symptoms that might benefit from a more specific form of drug treatment. In fact, she was given an antiobsessive medication and at follow-up 1 year later had no sexual obsessions. In addition, there was some initial effort at exploring her past sexual assaults.

PROBLEM 2: THE SYSTEM—SEXUALITY IN THE REHABILITATION OF PATIENTS WITH MENTAL ILLNESS

Given the acceptance of attending to sexual issues in the rehabilitation of patients with a chronic and severe *physical* disability (Szasz, 1989), one might wonder why this same focus has been so minimal in the care of those with a chronic and severe *mental* disability. Attitudes toward sexuality in the mentally ill seem similar to those that existed in the early days of attention to sexual issues in people with a physical illnesses (Anthony, Cohen, Farkas, & Gagne, 2002). In that era, health professionals seemed to assume that patients should be so grateful for the help that they were already receiving that they should not expect to have their sexual concerns addressed as well.

In fact, there *have* been two sex-related areas in which the mental health system *has* become more mindful, that is, medication side effects and STIs (especially HIV/AIDS). MHPs have been concerned about drug side effects because of their potential interference with compliance (see Chapter 18, this volume, "Recognizing and Reversing Sexual Side Effects of Medications"). Likewise, MHPs have been attentive to STIs because of the desire to protect those under care from the negative impact of chronic physical illnesses (Kelly et al., 1992). As important as these two areas are, the sex-related focus of the system has been selective and idiosyncratic in that it has not spread to other sexual topics. The system response to the issue of STI exposure has often been to place condoms in the washrooms of mental health centers. Although potentially helpful, condoms in the washrooms are not enough. Providing condoms may make MHPs feel better because we can think that we are actually *doing* something in the area of safer sex to help our patients. And, although condoms no doubt send an important message, they are no substitute for talk. Furthermore, such an approach might fairly be seen as the mental health equivalent of the avoidant medical doctor who only provides patients with a book to read when they (the patients) bring up a sexual problem.

Although the practical value of free condoms may be limited, they are symbolically connected in a positive way with the rehabilitation of patients with a serious and chronic mental disorder. Condoms convey the message that the "system" considers some aspects of sexuality important in patients' care. Furthermore, these free condoms transmit the notion that social and mental rehabilitation must take place in an environment that is safe, and that the concept of safety includes *sexual* safety.

When MHPs accept the idea that talking about preventing STIs and drug side effects is best accomplished within the context of talking about sexual matters in general, sexuality can join other issues (e.g., housing, transportation, and vocational rehabilitation) in the list of goals for the care of the mentally ill.

ONE WAY OF MELDING THE TWO PROBLEMS: THE SEXUAL MEDICINE TEAM

When accepted to one of the general psychiatric teams that comprise VCMHS, the patient is assigned both a psychiatrist and a "case manager." The former is in charge of biomedical aspects of treatment and, depending on needs, sees the patient occasionally, and the latter (usually a social worker or nurse) sees the patient much more frequently and handles psychosocial issues.

The SMT is permanently based at the location of two of the general psychiatry teams, although services are available to all of VCMHS; it operates on an ad hoc basis, and patients are seen by referral and only from within the service. Two preconditions exist for referrals: (1) the case manager accompanies the patient to *all* visits, and (2) the psychiatric disorder is under control.

Patient 3 illustrates what might occur when a psychiatric disorder is incompletely treated.

Patient 3

Carl, a 38-year-old man with schizophrenia since his late teens, was referred because of trouble with "sexual arousal." His case manager referred him, hoping that "sex" was one of the problems that could be solved and thinking that he should be sent since she was "not trained in this area."

Carl was on disability income, did not work, lived in a group home, did not use street drugs, had a past history of excessive alcohol use, smoked one package of cigarettes each day, and had not been on medications for many years but in recent weeks had been treated with olanzapine.

Carl had a profound thought disorder and frequently switched topics; there was extreme difficulty understanding his current sexual concerns and his past sexual history. Through the fog of Carl's story, it seemed as though he might have experienced sexual intercourse in recent years with many different partners. An HIV test was suggested both to him and to his family doctor. The result was negative.

The case manager, as usual, accompanied the patient to the consultation. She quickly came to understand the impossibility of proceeding with the consultation request at that time. The consultant explained to the case manager and psychiatrist that he would only be able to assist Carl in the future when Carl could be understood. Six months later, Carl was seen with his case manager, and his psychiatric status was sufficiently improved to the extent that he was able to relate his sexual concerns. One could then comprehend what he was describing. Four productive visits took place.

Referrals of patients with any type of sexual difficulty are accepted to the SMT. In practice, however, most are related to two problems: sexual dysfunctions and having unsettling sexual thoughts. Patient 4 is an example of the latter.

Patient 4

Don was 23 years old and had had schizophrenia for 4 years. His main sexual worry was that others thought that he was gay, and he wondered whether this was accurate. Don had mentioned his concern about being homosexual to his case manager on several occasions. Don was living in a group home with four other men, had a part-time janitorial job, was maintained on risperidone, had used alcohol and street drugs for several years in his teens but not recently, smoked one package of cigarettes a day, and was in good physical health. In talking with Don about sexual orientation, it became clear that his many past sexual experiences with partners had been solely with women, he had no sexual desire for men whatsoever, his sexual fantasies were entirely heterosexual, and he enjoyed viewing only heterosexual events when looking at sexually explicit images in magazines or on the Internet.

After asking many pertinent questions about his orientation, a categorical statement was made to him that he was heterosexual rather than gay or even bisexual. On the second visit, he said that he was pleased with the outcome of the first, and that he was thinking of this matter much less often. The case manager, patient, and psychiatrist agreed that more visits were unnecessary since he now felt more comfortable talking about the topic with his case manager. The eventual disappearance of concern about sexual orientation was confirmed when I spoke with his case manager 7 months later. (She was, of course, pleased with the outcome and spontaneously described herself as now much more able to raise sexual issues with her other patients.)

The Inclusion of the Case Manager

We initially worried that the presence of the case manager might hamper the process of gathering sex-related information from patients. It quickly became apparent that our misgivings turned out to be a nonissue. Having this familiar and trusted person present when talking to a health professional, who was nevertheless a stranger, about this most personal subject proved to be crucial to the patient. We were also unclear about what to do when the patient was a young man and the case manager a woman—a common occurrence—and the patient was reluctant to be explicit about sexual matters in her presence. Again, experience taught us that, with encouragement, the patient would accede to our request that she be present, and that the problem would quickly evaporate.

From our point of view, the presence of the case manager was advantageous for two additional reasons. First, watching us ask detailed sex-related questions as we explored concerns, completed an assessment, and established a treatment plan provided both a skill and knowledge-related continuing education experience for that health professional, the latter relating to the notion that sex and intimacy matters could and should be included in a patient's rehabilitation. Second, the presence of the case manager underlined the notion that he or she retained primary responsibility for the patient's continuing care.

Comments From Some Case Managers About Their Experience With SMT Referrals

What were the benefits to you of referring your patient to the SMT and participating in the assessment?

It opens up the dialogue between me and the client. ... It gives permission to the client to open the topic with me and vice versa. ... There is role modeling. ... I watch how you phrase questions and open up topic areas. ... It makes me ask questions more clearly. ... I ask questions about sex more often after a session with you.

Were there any "downsides" for you or the clients?

Clients have found the experience to be surprisingly easy, [whereas] I have less choice. ... I find that I'm fairly comfortable talking about sexuality with a friend or a partner, but in a professional setting it's like talking in public. ... so the way I talk makes a difference. The occasional client has said he didn't want me involved, but when you insisted, it didn't seem to be a problem for the person at the time or even afterward.

What did the clients think of the experience?

They normalized the experience quite quickly. ... They were interested in what was explained. ... Worries were dispelled. ... There was an improvement in sexual problems ... some hope for the future.

The Assessment Process

The procedure that we have followed is such that the first visit or two has consisted of detailed history taking, obtaining health-related information from the family doctor, and ordering relevant laboratory tests. In the assessment, emphasis has been given to the sexual concern rather than to the psychiatric disorder since the latter information had already been explored and documented by the principal psychiatrist and, in any case, was not the reason for the referral. We have always included a review of the patient's current medication regimen in the initial visit because of our experience that changes in drugs often take place in the interval between initiation of the referral and the first visit. As well, we appreciate the great impact that medications used in psychiatry often have on sexual function (see Chapter 18 in this book).

Patients have been seen by the SMT for as long as all parties see potential value in continuing the process. In practice, this typically has meant up to 6 visits. Fewer visits have been necessary if we were able to quickly determine that the referral was premature or that it was desirable for the patient to be referred to another sex specialist with different skills. Patient 5 is an example of the latter.

Patient 5

Kerrie, a 28-year-old woman with a history of episodes of depression since her midteens, was referred because of a long history of confused feelings about both her sexual orientation and her gender identity. She was on disability income, did not use alcohol or drugs, did not smoke cigarettes, and was in good physical health. She had been on various antidepressants in the past but was not on any medications at the time of evaluation. Kerrie had previously cut her hair in a traditionally masculine way and dressed in male clothing. More recently, she described allowing her hair to grow and was dressing in a more feminine manner. In contrast, she described feelings and fantasies in which she was more masculine. She felt "in drag" when out in public and wearing more traditionally feminine clothing. When asked to describe her fantasies, she categorized them as "male–female."

Over the course of two visits, much information was obtained about Kerrie's growth and development, her past sexual experiences with both men and women, and her objectives in wanting to talk with us, which was *not* to find a method for obtaining sex reassignment surgery but rather to help clarify her orientation and gender status. A referral was made to a well-established gender clinic in Vancouver. One year later, she was still in psychotherapy.

More visits are generally required when patients want to talk about a long-standing concern that pre-dated the onset of their psychiatric disorder. Patient 6 illustrates such an issue.

Patient 6

Mike was a 50-year-old man of Irish heritage who had had a bipolar disorder since age 32 for which he was currently taking valproic acid. He said that he had never had a close relationship with anyone in his life, and that he had never had "even a heartbeat" when it came to women. He was on disability income, did not drink alcohol or use drugs, and had smoked one package of cigarettes each day since his teens.

Mike described having had a great deal of concern in the past about being homosexual but having "come to terms with it now." He was still in anguish, however, over not having had a child and not having ever had a close relationship with another man because of the dual fears of rejection and of being infected with HIV.

Mike's elementary and high school experience had been at a private Catholic school. In the past (and the present), he felt considerable guilt about his homosexuality, sexual fantasies about men, and experience with masturbation and felt that it would all "lead to hell."

Over the course of five visits and in contrast to his past experience with MHPs, Mike was pleased about being able to discuss sexual issues openly. He was encouraged to be more candid about sexual matters with his (male) case manager. Such discussions had, in fact, taken place in the intervals between visits, and Mike came to the conclusion that visits to the SMT were redundant. Mike explained that he had overcome his hesitancy in talking with his case manager (and vice-versa).

Explanations for a change in sexual *function* have often been difficult to establish. Patients frequently attribute such problems to the use of medications, and that conclusion is sometimes accurate. But often, the story is more complex. Drug side effects may be a central determinant when, for example, orgasm is delayed or absent (in men or women), but they are more likely to be only one of several elements when trying to understand the reason for the problem of diminished sexual desire. For example, when erectile problems exist, the same factors that explain the high prevalence of this problem in the general population are also pertinent with mentally ill patients: high blood lipid levels, high blood pressure, cigarette smoking, diabetes, and abnormal levels of testosterone and prolactin. Impaired insight, which so often accompanies schizophrenia and bipolar illness, may not permit a patient to understand that the impairment in the capacity to experience psychologically intimate relationships may limit the treatment of a sexual function difficulty of any kind.

SEX AND INTIMACY

The words *sex* and *intimacy* are often confused with one another. Indeed, some years ago one would hear those words used as synonyms; they are even used that way now from time to time (Ditzen, Hoppmann, & Klumb, 2008). But, to many MHPs and when used by others in common parlance, these words are *not* equivalent, but the distinction, while important, may be difficult to define. As used here, *intimacy* refers to relationships that are more than transient and includes such issues as the individual's capacity to identify, understand, and exchange feelings with another person—feelings that may be sexual but that encompass the whole panoply of connections between two people. "The word intimacy conjures up notions of familiarity, understanding, affection, and privacy" (Levine, 1992, p. 37).

Sex and *sexuality,* on the other hand, are much more specific and relate to feelings, thoughts, and actions that are sexual and that may, or may not, involve another person. Sex can manifest in three ways: (1) sexual activity with a partner, (2) sexual activity with oneself through masturbation, and (3) sexual thoughts and feelings within an individual. MHPs who care for those with a chronic mental illness tend to focus on the first of these issues and to discount the second and third, when in fact sex for this group of patients is often in those last two areas since many do not have partners. (The thinking on the part of the MHP may be that "no partner" equates to "no sex," and therefore one does not have to talk to a patient about this subject.)

In humans, sex is a biological attribute that has psychosocial ramifications, whereas intimacy is a psychosocial attribute that may have biological ramifications. Patients with severe and chronic mental illness frequently have problems in both areas as part of their disorder. In the same way that sex and intimacy are different, so are sex problems and intimacy problems. MHPs are usually better equipped to deal with the latter, and such problems do not necessarily require referral to a health professional who specializes in sexual medicine.

The roots of intimacy difficulties are in the patient's past. In our zeal to deal with here-and-now issues, we are liable to forget the possible implications of such a past. This part of the patient's life needs to be thoroughly explored because it might well have included turmoil in the family of origin, as well as a dearth of love and nurturing connections that are so often a rehearsal for love relationships later in life. Likewise, the patient's past may not have included the experimental love and sexual relationships of adolescence in which so much learning takes place about oneself and others. For heterosexuals, one of the consequences of the absence of adolescent experiences is missed opportunities to learn about biopsychosocial aspects of sexuality in the opposite sex. As a result, knowledge of basic facets of opposite-sex anatomy and physiology are often lacking and therefore need to be part of any treatment intervention.

SEXUAL PROBLEMS AND ATTITUDES TO MEDICATIONS

Mental health professionals tend not to take the initiative in asking questions about medication side effects but rather respond when a patient raises the subject. Besides learning of that dynamic from patients many years ago, one of us (W.L.M.) had the opportunity to observe a group of psychiatry residents while they practiced interviewing patients in preparation for specialty oral exams. In 12 interviews watched, only one candidate ever asked anything about drug side effects (or, in fact, about *anything* related to sexual matters), and he had previously worked in the department's Sexual Medicine Clinic.

Could it be that MHPs avoid asking about medication sexual side effects because we do not want patients to connect sexual problems with their drugs and therefore stop using their medications? This notion might be similar to the discredited idea of not asking a patient about suicide because it might suggest that to the patient. In fact, the patient grapevine is such that patients are well versed in medication side effect information, including those drugs that affect sexual function, long before this might be discussed with a MHP. Contrary to what many expected, patients have often told us that they would prefer to use psychiatric drugs and bear the consequences of continuing sexual function disruption if the alternative meant the possibility of experiencing another episode of psychiatric illness.

THE SEXUALITY AGENDA IN THE CLINICAL PRACTICE OF GENERALIST MHPs

In our assessments, we attempt to cover eight sex-related areas. Screening questions about each of these areas could *easily* be asked by any MHP at appropriate points within the first few visits of a new patient.

1. Does the patient have *a sexual symptom of a psychiatric disorder* (depression and diminished sexual desire are common examples), or if there is a sexual concern, did it coincide with, or precede, the onset of the psychiatric illness?
2. Is there any sex-related facet of the patient's *personal and social history* (e.g., past sexual assault) that might help to explain current sexual concerns?
3. Are there *reproductive consequences* (especially to women) to the patient's illness? Examples include the effect of pregnancy on the patient's illness or the effect of the illness on the patient's pregnancy, the ability of the patient to manage child care, and the use of birth control (Dickerson et al., 2004).

4. Are the patient's *sexual practices* such that there are STI-related consequences to the person or their psychiatric disorder? (Recent literature has emphasized the vulnerability of mentally ill patients to STIs generally and the increased prevalence of HIV /AIDS in those with schizophrenia in particular; ACOG Committee Opinion, 2008; Gray, Brewin, Noak, Wyke-Joseph, & Sonik, 2002; Sohler, Colson, Meyer-Bahlburg, & Susser, 2000).

5. Are there any *major general physical health problems* that might have a sex-related impact on the patient? Examples include obesity, diabetes, high blood pressure, and heart disease (Leucht, Burkard, Henderson, Maj, & Sartorius, 2007).

6. Separately from the patient's psychiatric disorder and apart from the order of appearance, are there any *preexisting sex-related issues that require attention*? Examples include sexual dysfunctions (especially common), gender identity concerns, as well as offending and nonoffending paraphilic behavior (Drake & Pathe, 2004).

7. Is there any sex-related aspect of the patient's current *mental state* (such as thoughts of sexual aggression or violence)?

8. Is the patient receiving any *medications* that might interfere with sexual function?

SUMMARY

Our experience in the care of men and women with sexual concerns in the context of severe and chronic mental illness taught us that in such individuals

- *Sexual problems* in general occur at least as commonly as in the population at large.
- *Attitudes toward partner-related and solo sexual activity* among MHPs involved in their care are often such that, in the absence of a partner, discussion of sex-related issues is not felt to be a priority. The implication seems to be that solo sexual activity and sex-related thoughts and feelings (apart from acts) are not worthy of attention.
- *Knowledge of sexual anatomy and physiology, as well as of the intricacies of sexual relationships,* is often deficient—somewhat similar to what may be found in adults who have physical developmental problems beginning in childhood.
- *Absence of initiation of discussion of sexuality issues by the treatment team* results in an inability to fill patient knowledge deficits and repair sex-related damage.
- *Sexuality difficulties* (1) are extremely common because the disorder often impairs the patient's ability to establish and maintain intimate relationships and (2) may precede the onset of the psychiatric disorder.
- *MHPs infrequently ask* patients within the first few visits about sexual function difficulties and specifically women about their history of sexual assault in spite of the fact that many have major concerns in these areas.
- Specific *sexual function difficulties* (1) are most commonly (in both sexes) in the area of lack of sexual desire, (2) occur more than in the

general population partly because of the medications that are used to treat serious psychiatric disorders, and (3) in men manifest especially in ED, which is often impaired for similar reasons to those in the general population, one of the most salient of which is poverty, resulting in turn in poor diet and atherosclerosis.

- *Adult sexuality* is problematic, partly because the intimate family relationship rehearsals of childhood often did not occur or were distorted, and likewise, experimental love relationships that are a normal part of adolescence usually did not occur.
- *In the treatment of sexual difficulties,* a precondition is that the patient's psychiatric status must be in good control.
- *Reassurance about sexual concerns* can sometimes have a powerful impact.

EPILOGUE

In the days of the mental hospital, sexual issues were ignored until patients ended up in bed with one another. In the days of deinstitutionalization, HIV/AIDS, medications for ED, and the Internet, there is no way that MHPs could convincingly say that they are providing comprehensive care to patients without also addressing their sexuality in a manner that is explicit, skillful, regular, and accepting.

NOTE

1. The words *patients*, *clients*, and *consumers* are all used in mental health settings. We use *patients* here because of either having been medically trained (W.L.M.) or currently working in a medical environment (M.Y.).

REFERENCES

ACOG Committee Opinion No. 417: Addressing health risks of noncoital sexual activity. (2008). *Obstetrics and Gynecology, 112*, 735–737.

American Psychiatric Association. (2002). *Diagnostic and statistical manual of mental disorders* (4th ed., text rev.). Washington, DC: Author.

Anthony, W., Cohen, M., Farkas, M., & Gagne, C. (2002). *Psychiatric rehabilitation* (2nd ed.). Boston: Center for Psychiatric Rehabilitation. This is an excellent, comprehensive, up-to-date, and easy-to-read (sidebars and chapter summaries) outline of current concepts in psychiatric rehabilitation.

Bengtsson-Tops, A., & Hansson, L. (1999). Clinical and social needs of schizophrenic outpatients living in the community: The relationship between needs and subjective quality of life. *Social Psychiatry and Psychiatric Epidemiology, 34,* 513–518.

Dickerson, F. B., Brown, C. H., Kreyenbuhl, J., Goldberg, R. W., Fang, L. J., & Dixon, L. B. (2004). Sexual and reproductive behaviors among persons with mental illness. *Psychiatric Services, 55,* 1299–1301.

Ditzen, B., Hoppmann, C., & Klumb, P. (2008). Positive couple interactions and daily cortisol: On the stress-protecting role of intimacy. *Psychosomatic Medicine, 70,* 883–889.

Drake, C. R., & Pathe, M. (2004). Understanding sexual offending in schizophrenia. *Criminal Behavior and Mental Health, 14*, 108–120.

Gray, R., Brewin, E., Noak, J., Wyke-Joseph, J., & Sonik, B. (2002). A review of the literature on HIV infection and schizophrenia: Implications for research, policy and clinical practice. *Journal of Psychiatric and Mental Health Nursing, 9*, 405–409.

Kelly, J. A., Murphy, D. A., Bahr, G. R., Brasfield, T. L., Davis, D. R., Hauth, A. C., et al. (1992). AIDS/HIV risk behavior among the chronic mentally ill. *American Journal of Psychiatry, 149*, 886–889.

Levine, S. B. (1992). *Sexual life.* New York: Plenum.

Leucht, S., Burkard, T., Henderson, J., Maj, M., & Sartorius, N. (2007). Physical illness and schizophrenia: A review of the literature. *Acta Psychiatrica Scandinavica, 116*, 317–333.

Maurice, W. L. (1999). *Sexual medicine in primary care.* St. Louis, MO: Mosby. Retrieved January 20, 2009, from the Kinsey Institute Library and Special Collection, http://www.kinseyinstitute.org/resources/maurice.html. The first half of the book is entirely devoted to sex-related interviewing and history taking, the second half to reviews of sexual dysfunctions, and the appendices to, for example, sex-related drug side effects and reading suggestions for patients.

Maurice, W. L. (2003). Sexual medicine, mental illness, and mental health professionals. *Sexual and Relationship Therapy, 18*, 7–12.

Raja, M., & Azzoni, A. (2003). Sexual behavior and sexual problems among patients with severe chronic psychoses. *European Psychiatry, 18*, 70–76.

Schover, L. R., Evans, R. B., & Von-Echenbach, A. C. (1987). Sexual rehabilitation in a cancer center: Diagnosis and outcome in 384 consultations. *Archives of Sexual Behavior, 16*, 445–461.

Sohler, N., Colson, P. W., Meyer-Bahlbarg, F. L., & Susser, E. (2000). Reliability of self-reports about sexual risk behaviors for HIV among homeless men with severe mental illness. *Psychiatric Services, 51*, 814–816.

Szasz, G. (1989). Sexuality in persons with severe physical disability: A guide to the physician. *Canadian Family Physician, 35*, 345–351.

Torrey, E. F., Bigelow, D. A., & Sladen-Dew, N. (1993). Quality and cost of services for seriously mentally ill individuals in British Columbia and the United States. *Hospital and Community Psychiatry, 44*, 943–950.

Author Index

Note: Page numbers in italics indicate references.

A

Aaron, D.J., *365*
Abdo, C.H., 255, *263*
Abitbol, M.M., 333, *344*
Abraham, K., 268, *288*
Abramovici, H., 198, 200, *211*
ACOG Committee Opinion No. 417, 479, *480*
Adams, J.H., 342, *347*
Adams, M.A., 383, 393, *397*
Adams, M.S., 132, *137*
Adolfsson, J., 336, *346*
Afif-Abdo, J., 255, *263*
Agans, R.P., 164, *178*
Agen, H., *325*
Aggrawal, A., 408, *422*
Aguirre, O., 223, *224*
Ahmed, A.G., 458, 460, *468*
Aizenberg, D., *324*
Albano, A.M., 255, *265*
Alberoni, F., *54*
Alexander, J., 215, 223, *225, 226*
Alterowitz, B., 342, *344*
Alterowitz, R., 342, *344*
Althof, S.E., 252, 253, 254, 255, 256, 257, 259, 261, 262, *264*, 271, 272, 273, 279, *288, 290*, 336, 337, *344*
Amar, E., 334, *345*
American Academy of Pediatrics, 362, *365*
American Association for Intellectual and Developmental Disabilities, 452, *467*
American Cancer Society, 336, 339, *344*
American Psychiatric Association, 144, 145, 148, 149, 150, 151, 152, *157*, 173, 183, *191*, 194, 196, 197, *209*, *210*, 271, 273, 282, *288*, 352, *365*, 371, *380*, 384, 385, *397*, 404, *422*, 431, *445*, 452, *467*, 469, *480*
American Psychological Association, 28, *35*, 364, *365*
Amparano, J., *398*

Amsel, R., 194, 195, 196, 197, 198, 203, *212, 213*
Amsterdam, A., 338, *344*
Andersen, B.L., 331, *345*
Andersen, S., *327*
Anderson, A., 303, *309*
Anderson, D., 343, *346*
Anderson, E.R., 130, *137*
Anderson, J., 27, *36*
Anderson, R.U., 255, *264*
Anjani, C., *249*
Ankarberg, C., 221, *224*
Annon, J., 256, *264*
Anthony, W., 472, *480*
Anton, R.F., *101*
APA Task Force on Appropriate Therapeutic Responses to Sexual Orientation, 364, *365*
Apfelbaum, B., 284, *288*
Arbus-Nevestuk, K., 454, *468*
Archer, D., *177*
Arnold, L.D., 195, *210*
Arnow, B.A., 165, *175*, 255, *264*
Aronson, W.J., 254, *265*
Arver, S., 336, *346*
Ascher, J., *326*
Atherton, P.J., 341, *345*
Atkins, L., *55*
Attwood, T., 459, *467*
Aunos, M., 452, 453, 464, *468*
Avis, N.E., 163, *176*
Ayling, K., 195, *210*
Aziz, A., 167, *175*
Azzoni, A., 470, *481*

B

Bach, A., 255, *264*
Bachmann, G.A., 195, *210*
Bader, E., 135, *138*
Bagby, R.M., *325*
Bahr, G.R., 473, *481*
Bailey, J.M., 169, *176*
Bajos, N., 283, *290*
Bakker, S.C., 269, 271, 274, *289*
Balcueva, E.P., 341, *345*
Baldwin, S.A., 103, 111, *120*

Subject Index

Note: *f* indicates figures, *t* indicates tables, *n* indicates notes.

A

Abasiophilia, 405*t*
Abel screen, 417
Abilify, 318, 319*t*
Acceptance-based strategies, 111–112
Acoustophilia, 405*t*
Acquired immunodeficiency syndrome (AIDS), 133–134, 363, 479
Acquired sexual dysfunction
definition of, 17
delayed ejaculation, 283, 286–287
female orgasmic disorder, 184, 189–190
premature ejaculation, 279, 281
Acrophilia, 405*t*
Acrotomophilia, 405*t*
Acting out, 91; *see also* Infidelity
Addiction, *see* Alcohol use; Drugs of abuse; Sexual compulsivity
Adolescent(s); *see also* Adolescent males; Children
concerns of, 233
homosexuality and, 358–359
sexual development of, 75–76, 233
transgenderism of, 443–445, 445*n*3
Adolescent males, 231–247; *see also* Adolescent(s); Children
cases, 233–234, 235–237, 239–241, 242–244
delayed ejaculation of, 233, 238–240
developmental tasks of, 75–76, 231–234
homosexuality and, 240–242, 246, 358–359
male erectile dysfunction of, 234–237, 245–246
overview of, 231, 246–247
pornography and, 244
premature ejaculation of, 233, 237–238, 246
sexual abuse of, 233, 242–244
therapist assumptions and, 244–245
therapist experience with, 232

Adultery, *see* Infidelity
Affairs, *see* Infidelity
Age factors; *see also* Development; *specific age groups*
in dating, 123–125
in delayed ejaculation, 286
menopause factors vs., 217–219
optimal sexuality and, 59–61
premature ejaculation and, 277–278, 281–282
sexual desire and, 48, 49, 58, 166–167, 216–217
Agency in couples therapy, 114–115
Agorophobia, 405*t*
Agrexophilia, 405*t*
AIDS, 133–134, 363, 479
Alcohol use
arousal and, 321
infidelity and, 99
male erectile dysfunction and, 235–236
sexual desire and, 155–156
sexual trauma and, 301, 306–307
Algolagnia (philia), 405*t*
Amaurophilia, 405*t*
Ambition of love, 41–42
Ambivalence, 387
Amphetamines, 321
Anafranil, 238, 270, 315
Anal cancer, 335*t*
Anal sex, 363
Anasteemaphilia, 405*t*
Androgen-deficiency syndrome, 166
Androgens; *see also* Antiandrogen medications; Testosterone
menopause and, 221–222
sexual desire and, 166, 221, 322, 323
Andromimetophilia, 405*t*
Aneroticism, 12, 12*t*
Anesthetic ejaculation, 282
Anorgasmia, *see* Female orgasmic disorder
Anthropophagy, 405*t*
Antiandrogen medications, 418–419, 461–462
Antiarrthymic agents, 320
Anticonvulsants, 320

497